Actus reus and participation in European criminal law

School of Human Rights Research Series, Volume 60

The titles published in this series are listed at the end of this volume.

Actus reus and participation in European criminal law

Johannes Keiler

Cambridge – Antwerp – Portland

Intersentia Ltd
Trinity House | Cambridge Business Park | Cowley Road
Cambridge | CB4 0WZ | United Kingdom
Tel.: +44 1223 393 753 | mail@intersentia.co.uk

Johannes Keiler
Actus reus and participation in European criminal law

ISBN 978-1-78068-135-1
D/2013/7849/42
NUR 828

Cover image: Finsiel/Alinari Archives – Reproduced with the permission of Ministero per i Beni e le Attività Cultural, Italy.

British Library Cataloguing in Publication Data. A catalogue record for this book is available from the British Library.

ACKNOWLEDGEMENTS

During one of our first meetings in 2007 my supervisor warned me that "writing a PhD may jeopardise your health". At this point in time I thought he was joking; after all I had just landed my dream job. Five years later I am still convinced that doing legal research is my dream job, but I also came to realise after some sleepless nights pondering criminal liability, that there might be a kernel of truth in this statement. Corresponding to the current *zeitgeist* one should perhaps even consider printing this statement in bold letters on top of every PhD contract.

Writing this book has overall been an immensely enjoyable experience; one which would not have been possible without the help of many people, to whom I am very grateful. First and foremost, I would like to thank Gerard Mols, Michael Faure, Jacques Claessen and John Spencer for reading and approving the manuscript of this book. I would also like to thank everyone at Maastricht University and the department of criminal law for making this book possible and for creating a very enjoyable working atmosphere.

Moreover, thanks are due to my supervisor André Klip. Your clear and critical view of criminal law and legal research has helped and guided me throughout this research and has shaped and influenced my thinking on criminal law. Your passion regarding European criminal law has been truly inspiring. Thank you for your confidence in me and your ever–calm presence when I was on the verge of panic.

I wish to thank my co-supervisor, David Roef, for all our inspiring and challenging discussions about the foundations of criminal law and criminal liability (long may they continue!). Thank you also for all your invaluable feedback, advice and support during this project. You have greatly contributed to my growth as a scholar.

Part of this project also consisted of verifying the results of this comparative research with academics and practitioners from the investigated penal systems. In Germany Oberstaatsanwalt Lutz Bernklau and Richter Gerd Nohl helped to improve my knowledge of German criminal law and the German legal culture. In England I am indebted to Peter Alldridge, David Ormerod, William Wilson and Jeremy Horder. Thank you for welcoming me in London and giving me ample opportunity to discuss many issues of English criminal law. I am particularly indebted to William Wilson for closely reading and commenting on one of my early drafts on English criminal law.

At Oxford Andrew Ashworth diligently read and commented on my draft report on English criminal law. Thank you for warmly welcoming me at this beautiful University and for our valuable discussion on criminal law.

A factor which was very influential to this book was that I had the privilege to be part of the research team on European criminal law at Maastricht University, consisting furthermore of Jeroen Blomsma, Anne-Sophie Massa and Christina

Peristeridou-Rübenach. I have learned a lot from all of you and you have greatly contributed to my development as a researcher. Thank you. Our common visits of many conferences and trips abroad will always remain with me.

Jeroen, my partner in crime during the last five years: thank you for our invaluable countless discussions on criminal liability, this research project, etc. You have been my perfect counterpart in this project and you played a huge role in making me feel at home here in Maastricht.

Roland, thank you for making me feel at home here in Maastricht and for all our immensely interesting, stimulating as well as hilarious discussions in and outside the University. You have certainly helped to sharpen my view on the different shades of grey always to be found between the clear black and white poles of a matter.

I would also like to thank everyone in and outside the university for all their support and for all the great spare time activities. You know who you are!

Kati, thank you for being there and for your endless support, patience and understanding throughout the past five years. Thank you also for your very valuable feedback and comments on earlier drafts of this book. You were always willing to listen and help out wherever possible and you always knew when it was time for me to take a break. Without you this book would not have been possible.

Last but not least, I would like to thank my family and friends back home. Mum, Dad, Steffi, thank you for your support during my entire life. You shaped me and without you I would not stand where I stand now. Mats, Nielse, Leo, Mike and Much, thank you for warmly welcoming me every time I return to Austria, be it only for a few days. Your friendship means a lot to me and you are the living proof that the saying "out of sight out of mind" need not always be true.

Maastricht,

12 November 2012

Contents

Chapter III
Modes of liability – The multiple actor scenarios 153

List of Abbreviations

AC	Appeals Cases
AG	Advocate General
appl. no.	application number
Art	Article
All ER	All England Law Reports
BayObLG	Bayerisches Oberstes Landesgericht
BeckRS	Beck-Rechtsprechung
BGH	Bundesgerichtshof
BGHSt	Bundesgerichtshof's Official Gazette, criminal cases
BVerfG(E)	(Decision of the) Bundesverfassungsgericht
CLR	Commonwealth Law Reports
COM	Document originating from the EU Commission
Cox CC	Cox's Criminal Cases 1843–1945
CPS	Crown Prosecution Service
Cr App R	Criminal Appeal Reports
Crim LR	Criminal Law Review
DPC	Dutch Penal Code
DPP	Director of Public Prosecutions
EC	European Communities
ECHR	European Convention of Human Rights
ECtHR	European Court of Human Rights
ECJ	European Court of Justice
ECR	European Court Reports
EP	European Parliament
EPPO	European Public Prosecutor's Office
EU	European Union
EWCA	England & Wales Court of Appeal
EWCA Crim	England & Wales Court of Appeal (Criminal Division) Decisions
EWHC	England & Wales High Court
GA	Goltdammer's Archiv für Strafrecht
GDR	German Democratic Republic
GPC	German Penal Code
HMG	Hoog Militair Gerechtshof
HRRS	Online-Zeitschrift für Höchstrichterliche Rechtsprechung im Straftecht
HR	Hoge Raad
JA	Juristische Arbeitsblätter
JR	Juristische Rundschau
Jura	Juristische Ausbildung

JuS	Juristische Schulung
JZ	Juristenzeitung
KB	King's Bench
LJ(J)	Lord Justice(s) of Appeal
MDR	Monatsschrift für Deutsches Recht
MPC	Metropolitan Police Commissioner
NbSr	Nieuwsbrief Strafrecht
NJ	Nederlandse Jurisprudentie
NJB	Nederlands Juristenblad
(N)JW	(Neue) Juristische Wochenschrift
NJOZ	Neue Juristische Online Zeitschrift
NStZ(-RR)	Neue Zeitschrift für Strafrecht (-Rechtsprechungsreport)
OJ L	Official Journal of the EU – Legislation
OJ C	Official Journal of the EU- Information and notices
OLAF	European Anti-Fraud Office
OLG	Oberlandesgericht
OWiG	Ordnungswidrigkeitengesetz
QB(D)	Queen's Bench (Division)
R	Regina
Rb.	Rechtbank
Re	Regarding (ablative of *res*)
REV	Revised version of a EU document
RG	Reichsgericht
RGSt	Reichsgericht, criminal cases
s	Section
StV	Strafverteidiger
StGB	Strafgesetzbuch
TEU	Treaty on the European Union
TFEU	Treaty on the functioning of the European Union
UK	United Kingdom
UKHL	United Kingdom House of Lords
UKPC	United Kingdom Privy Council
US	United States (of America)
v	versus
WLR	Weekly Law Reports
ZRP	Zeitschrift für Rechtspolitik
ZStW	Zeitschrift für die gesamte Strafrechtswissenschaft

Chapter I
Introduction

1. European criminal law

Ever since the entering into force of the Maastricht treaty the European Union has gained more and more competences in regard to criminal law and accordingly has exerted more and more influence on national criminal law. This evolution has reached a level where one can now speak of a genuine European criminal law.[1] European criminal law can be described as a hybrid system, a multi-layered patchwork of legislation and case law in which the national and European legal order mutually influence and shape each other.[2]

The Treaty of Lisbon (TOL) significantly boosts the competences of the Union in regard to criminal law. Article 67 (1) of the Treaty on the functioning of the European Union (TFEU) provides that "the Union shall constitute an area of freedom, security and justice with respect for fundamental rights and the different legal systems and traditions of the Member States." To achieve that goal Article 83 (1) TFEU grants the Union the power to "establish minimum rules concerning the definition of criminal offences and sanctions in the areas of particularly serious crime with a cross-border dimension resulting from the nature or impact of such offences or from a special need to combat them on a common basis." This provision constitutes the latest step in the development of European Union law almost exclusively focused on economic integration to an emerging European Criminal Justice System.[3] Yet, the Union not only possesses the competences to legislate in the realm of criminal law but over the years an emergence of a variety of bodies such as Eurojust, Europol or the European Judicial Network have emerged which can be viewed as the first signs of an institutional framework of the emerging criminal justice system. The height of this institutional development so far would arguably be the establishment of the European Public Prosecutor's Office as foreseen in Article 86 TFEU.

The Union has over the past years legislated extensively on a variety of criminal law topics such as terrorism, trafficking in human beings, weapons or drugs, organised crime, money laundering, subsidy fraud, etc.[4] However, European criminal law has developed in an incoherent and fragmented manner. Most notably, European criminal law has thus far merely focused on specific offences and lacks explicit general principles dealing with criminal liability. This is in stark contrast to

---

1 See: Klip, 'European Criminal Law' (2012), p. 1.

2 Klip, 'European Criminal Law' (2012), pp. 1, 159.

3 Klip, 'European Criminal Law' (2012), pp. 165–169, 479–481.

4 For a good overview see the table of legislation in: Klip, 'European Criminal Law' (2012), pp. 531–545.

many national criminal justice systems where the criminal code is often divided into two parts. The so called "special part" generally contains the definition of offences while general principles of criminal liability are laid down in the "general part".[5] The two parts are frequently seen as interrelated and considered to influence each other. The one cannot be understood without reference to the other and most crucially the scope of criminal liability enshrined in the "special part" is determined by the rules and principles of the "general part".[6] Exactly which rules belong to the general and which to the special part however is contentious.[7] There is a continuing disagreement about how the general part should be defined. The best that can probably be said is that "the general part consists of doctrines, rules and definitions that are not tied to any specific offence or set of offences".[8] The general part in essence can be seen to consist of generalisations about the offences forming the special part of criminal law.[9]

The general part has as its object the description, analysis and study of concepts that are common to most offences and therefore warrant an assessment in isolation from the particular area of application.[10] If attempt is an issue in fraud, rape, homicide and theft cases alike then the contours of attempt are arguably better worked out in a general manner which allows the creation of a coherent theory encompassing the problems of each specific application. A special part, i.e. a (random) set of criminal offences arguably necessarily contains traces of the general part, as concepts such as causation, conduct, fault, etc. are constituent elements of most offences. If one were thus content with the mere creation of specific offences without developing general principles guiding the application of these offences this may seriously undermine legal consistency and legal certainty.

In any case, in many penal systems the general part contains *inter alia* the following doctrines. First, the basic building blocks of criminal liability, i.e. actus reus and mens rea, furthermore, generally applicable defences (i.e. justifications, excuses, etc.) as well as subsidiary forms of liability, expanding the scope of the law, such as for example, inchoate liability and participation. These doctrines generally determine and shape the scope of criminal liability within a penal system, apply across the board to all offences and also contain general maxims of criminal justice which warrants their analysis and discussion in isolation from the specific offences to which they apply.

A general part thus, amongst others, ideally increases consistency in law. Furthermore, it avoids the duplication of efforts in comparison to the situation when

---

5 Fletcher, 'Basic Concepts of Criminal Law' (1998), p. 3.

6 Ambos, 'Is the development of a common substantive criminal law for Europe possible? Some Preliminary Reflections' Maastricht Journal of European and Comparative Law (2005), p. 175.

7 See: Simester and Shute, 'On the General Part in Criminal Law', in Simester and Shute (eds), Criminal Law Theory: Doctrines of the General Part (2002), pp. 1–12.

8 Duff, 'Answering for Crime' (2007), p. 3.

9 Husak, 'Overcriminalization' (2008), p. 65.

10 Fletcher, 'Rethinking Criminal Law' (1978), p. 393.

these doctrines would need to be repeated every time a new offence is created.[11] The consistency provided by a general part can moreover foster and emphasis values flowing from fundamental legal principles such as legality as the predictability of the law is increased. If the notion of attempt denotes the same meaning in murder as well as in theft then it is arguably easier for the subjects of law to determine where the threshold of liability lies.[12] The absence of a "general part" on Union level can therefore be seen as problematic for a variety of reasons, to which this research now turns.

This chapter will be structured as follows. After having discussed the practical and theoretical relevance of this research (section 2), the central research question of this thesis (section 3) and the methodology applied (section 4) will be outlined. Subsequently the discussion turns to the central concept of this research, i.e. criminal liability. First, some preliminary issues pertinent to the topic will be discussed to set the scene (section 5) before commencing the comparative analysis in chapter II.

2. The need for a general part

2.1. Practical Relevance

As already mentioned, while the "special part" of criminal law generally contains a wide range of definitions of specific offences such as money laundering, murder, rape, fraud, etc. the "general part" contains rules, principles and doctrines that by and large apply to all these offences.[13] The rules of the "general part" thus *inter alia* strive to secure a transparent and equal application of criminal law.[14] In regard to European criminal law the requirement of a uniform application of the law is arguably of particular importance. It is settled case law that the need for a uniform application of Union law makes it necessary that a provision of Community law must normally be given an autonomous and uniform interpretation throughout the European Union.[15] The lack of a general part can however jeopardise the uniform application of European criminal law. An example may elucidate the matter further.

---

11 Simester and Shute, 'On the General Part in Criminal Law', in Simester and Shute (eds), Criminal Law Theory: Doctrines of the General Part (2002), p. 4.

12 Simester and Shute, 'On the General Part in Criminal Law', in Simester and Shute (eds), Criminal Law Theory: Doctrines of the General Part (2002), p. 4.

13 Duff, 'Answering for Crime' (2007), p. 2.

14 Gröning, 'A Criminal Justice System or a System Deficit? Notes on the System Structure of the EU Criminal Law' European Journal of Crime, Criminal Law and Criminal Justice (2010), p. 126.

15 See for instance: 17 July 2008, Case C-66/08, *proceedings concerning the execution of a European arrest warrant issued against Szymon Kozlowski* [2008] ECR I-06041, para 42, 16 November 2010, Case C-261/09, *proceedings concerning the execution of a European arrest warrant issued in respect of Gaetano Mantello* [2010] not yet reported, para 38.

Article 3 of the Directive on preventing and combating trafficking in human beings and protecting its victims obliges Member States to criminalise also attempts of an offence referred to in Article 2.[16] As will subsequently become evident, the scope of criminal attempts however varies widely among Member States. This may result in different scopes of criminal liability within the European Area of Freedom Security and Justice depending on the definition of attempt applied in a respective country. At the level of legislation this may lead to an asymmetrical application of Union law as Member States will implement the common rules enshrined in a legislative instrument in accordance with their rules on the general part. On the level of adjudication this can lead to the unwanted outcome that similar cases are decided differently due to diverging interpretations of common rules.[17] As a result there is thus the very real risk of an unequal treatment of those charged with EU Crimes as well as the risk of an unequal protection of European citizens against crime. The establishment of a general part would thus remedy these shortcomings and thereby facilitate and drive forward the ongoing integration process.

The establishment of a general part could furthermore provide guidance to the European Court of Justice (ECJ) as well as national courts when applying legal instruments in the field of criminal law. In addition it may assist the European legislator to improve the quality of its legislation by taking into account general principles and theories when drafting a new instrument. The concepts of the general part can arguably be of great importance in the legislative process. The efficiency of a criminal code may increase if recurrent themes are dealt with in a single and uniform manner.[18]

Moreover, Member States will profit from the establishment of a general part as well when implementing legislation as it provides them with further insights on the specific effects and goals which the European Union aims to achieve with a piece of legislation. Furthermore, guidance may also be provided to accession candidates when adapting their legal system to that of the European Union. It may provide future Member States with a model on how to adapt their penal systems to the requirements of European criminal law.

In addition, the creation of some common rules may also enhance and foster the cooperation in criminal matters. Cooperation in criminal matters is based on the principle of mutual recognition which presupposes a sufficient degree of mutual trust among the judiciaries and law enforcement agencies of the Member States. A set of common rules enshrined in a general part may arguably strengthen mutual

---

16 Directive 2011/36 of 5 April 2011 on preventing and combating trafficking in human beings and protecting its victims, and replacing Council Framework Decision 2002/629/JHA, OJ 2011, L 101/06.

17 Gröning, 'A Criminal Justice System or a System Deficit? Notes on the System Structure of the EU Criminal Law' European Journal of Crime, Criminal Law and Criminal Justice (2010), p. 130.

18 Fletcher, 'Rethinking Criminal Law' (1978), p. 394.

trust and thereby facilitate the mutual recognition of judicial measures among Member States.

Finally, the creation of a general part can be seen as a prerequisite for the establishment and smooth functioning of the direct enforcement of criminal rules as foreseen by the establishment of a European Public Prosecutor's Office pursuant to Article 86 TFEU. In order to determine when the European Public Prosecutor may initiate proceedings it will be necessary to determine when the office has jurisdiction, when one can speak of an attempt, or who qualifies as perpetrator or accomplice.[19]

To summarise, it can be stated that most notably European criminal law lacks a coherent general part. It developed in a fragmented and incoherent manner which, as has been attempted to demonstrate, can have detrimental effects. In order to construct such a general part the fragments of European criminal law should be merged with general principles of criminal law to be derived from the national penal systems of the Member States. This research aims to contribute to the construction of such a general part by establishing an essential part of these general principles.

2.2. Theoretical relevance

Apart from these practical considerations the creation of a general part of European criminal law is also of theoretical relevance. By investigating and discussing issues that cut across all or most offences of criminal law in a comparative manner, it is the aim of this thesis to unearth common structures and principles within criminal law in general. These common principles may contribute to better understand and further develop what has been called "the universal grammar of criminal law".[20]

Moreover, the comparative method applied in this thesis may highlight and explain similarities and differences between different penal systems, which in turn may foster mutual understanding among the different legal traditions in Europe. It may also put national solutions, which are often taken for granted into perspective and convince scholars to critically assess and perhaps rethink some national doctrines.

One assumption of this research is that the solutions provided in the criminal law among penal systems constitute societal responses to universal problems. If the problems are constant, a comparative approach may not only reveal that legal cultures may have more in common than they think, but it may also provide the reader with an inventory of potential resolutions on which further academic discussion can be based and from which legislators may draw inspiration. The doctrines discussed in this thesis are the result of long lasting theoretical and practical discussions within a respective penal system. A comparison of the

---

19 See also: Klip, 'European Criminal Law' (2012), pp. 460 et seq.

20 Fletcher, 'Basic Concepts of Criminal Law' (1998), p. 5.

different doctrinal solutions may therefore also assist theorists and reformers to further develop these doctrines, make them more comprehensible and consistent and adapt them to the needs of contemporary society.

As already mentioned, the establishment of general principles of European criminal law, to which this thesis hopes to contribute, may also increase coherency and consistency in the law and help to remedy some of the shortcomings created by the fragmented development of the subject thus far. A coherent structure will provide room for a systematic discussion of certain fundamental aspects which may improve the quality of the law and facilitate to assure that like cases are treated alike and different cases differently all over Europe.

3. Research questions

3.1. Introduction

It is the aim of this research to contribute to the development of a general part of criminal law for the European Union. Previous projects such as the Corpus Juris have paved the way for this endeavour but were more limited in focus. The Corpus Juris was for instance exclusively concerned with fraud against the budget of the European Union. The chosen research method relied on country reports and the overall focus of the project lay on codification.

This research is distinguishable from the former, as its scope is not limited to specific forms of crime. It is the goal of this thesis to provide an overall assessment of the general rules and principles of the general part to be found within a selection of European penal cultures without prima facie limiting the inquiry to particular forms of wrongdoing. It is hoped that this will lead to a coherent picture of how a general part of European criminal law could look like. In addition, as will be described in more detail below this research relies on a different methodology than the aforementioned Corpus Juris.

This thesis is part of the bigger project "Towards a General Part of Criminal Law for the European Union" which commenced in 2007 and consists of four related but independent projects aimed to cover the vast area of the general part. The main focus of this thesis will lie on the objective elements of criminal liability. This discussion will commence with the basic objective ingredients of criminal liability enshrined in the legal concept of actus reus and subsequently proceed to investigate the auxiliary part of criminal law such as the rules on participation, inchoate liability and finally, corporate liability. In short, the central aspect of this study is thus what one might call the objective modes of establishing criminal liability.

It is a general principle of law that the attribution of criminal liability requires an analysis of two aspects. Each crime can be split up into an actus reus, the material element of crime, and mens rea, the mental element of a crime.[21] In order to incur criminal liability, a perpetrator generally needs to fulfil the actus reus and mens rea of the respective crime. This legal fact is often expressed by the famous Latin phrase *actus non facit reum nisi mens sit rea*, which can roughly be translated as "an act does not make a man guilty unless his mind is (also) guilty".[22] This dichotomy stems from the distinction between the objective or tangible side of a person's conduct, which is susceptible to objective assessment and the intangible, subjective side of a person's conduct, i.e. his state of mind, which is not. In order to be held criminally liable the two concepts need to coincide, as a person cannot be held liable in a liberal society for conduct which he either did not intend or merely "contemplated about" (thoughts are free).

As already mentioned, it is a basic rule of criminal law that there should be no criminal liability without a (blameworthy) conduct. The underlying rationale is that the law should treat persons as subjects and not as objects and that no one should be punished for his thoughts alone.[23] Thus the notion of actus reus constitutes an important first threshold in the establishment of criminal liability, by, *inter alia*, excluding situations in which the person has not (yet) externalised his, as the case might be morally reprehensible thoughts.

As will be shown in more detail, the concept of actus reus can be seen as a collection of principles and doctrines concerned with the (objective) attribution of criminal liability. The term actus reus, or mens rea respectively, can best be seen as an analytical tool for theorists and practitioners which helps to guide and understand the discussion and application of these doctrines.

The distinction between actus reus and mens rea is however not a hard and fast one. The two concepts do not constitute a strict dichotomy but rather constitute interrelated concepts. The notions of actus reus and mens rea are perhaps best perceived as communicating vessels.[24] If the objective requirements of a criminal offence are stringent the subjective requirements may be lower. What is required is that an overall assessment of the two concepts warrants the conclusion that the defendant can justly be held liable for his deeds. In the converse situation where the objective threshold for liability is low, as is for instance the case in regard to criminal attempts and preparation, where the objectively perceivable conduct is often outright innocuous or at best ambiguous, a higher standard will generally be required by subjective requirements in order to ensure that the overall benchmark

---

21 However, the terminology applied varies among the different penal systems. While actus reus and mens rea are typical common law concepts, German scholars tend to distinguish between "objektiver und subjektiver Tatbestand" and Dutch scholars refer to the two components as: "objectieve en subjectieve zijde van het strafbaar feit". See also: Badar, 'Mens Rea – Mistake of Law & Mistake of Fact in German Criminal Law: A Survey for International Criminal Tribunals' International Criminal Law Review (2005), p. 204.

22 Simester and Sullivan, 'Criminal Law: Theory and Doctrine' (2007), p. 8.

23 Fletcher, 'Basic Concepts of Criminal Law' (1998), pp. 43–58.

24 Van der Wilt, 'Genocide, Complicity in Genocide and International v. Domestic Jurisdictions' Journal of International Criminal Justice (2006), p. 256.

for the imputation of liability does not fall below a certain threshold. The interrelatedness of the two concepts will particularly become apparent in the realm of causation where aspects of fault may facilitate, respectively hamper the establishment of a causal link. If the fault element is for instance reduced to a minimum, as is the case in regard to strict liability offences, the (objective) doctrine of causation can compensate this absence by requiring a strict causal connection between the defendant's conduct and the occurred result.

As already stated, the main focus of this research will lie on the actus reus or the objective side of the crime as well as on subsidiary forms of liability. However, as actus reus and mens rea are occasionally inextricably bound up and due to the aforementioned interrelatedness of the two concepts, the notion of mens rea will in regard to some topics be touched upon. One important reason for this investigation "outside the box" of the actus reus is that for instance an investigation of the scope of criminal liability for attempt and complicity is not possible without taking into account the scope of the mens rea provisions as well. As regards corporate criminal liability, the notion of mens rea will also be investigated, and together with an examination of the construction of corporate mens rea will facilitate a discussion on the scope of corporate liability in more precise detail.

The central question of this research can accordingly broadly be summarised as follows: What should the objective elements of attribution of a general part of European criminal law consist of? Or, put differently, how should the (objective) imposition of criminal liability in a general part of European Union law be evaluated and assessed?

3.2. Elaborated research questions and outline

The general research question, outlined above can in turn be divided in several sub questions. By doing so, the general structure of this book will also become apparent. After having outlined the general scope of the thesis in this chapter (Chapter I), the discussion will commence with the basic (objective) building blocks of criminal liability as identified in different European penal systems (Chapter II). Subsequently subsidiary forms of liability such as participatory (Chapter III) and inchoate liability (Chapter IV) will be discussed. The final chapter on substantive criminal law will be devoted to corporate criminal liability (Chapter V) before the result of this research will be briefly summarised (Chapter VI).

3.2.1. Perpetration

The person bringing about the actus reus and mens rea of a crime is usually called the perpetrator or principal. Criminal law traditionally departed from a strong individualistic conception of crime which is why the basic building blocks of criminal liability have been tailor made to apply to individual wrongdoing. Thus, the concept of the perpetrator can be seen as pivotal in the realm of criminal law.

Accordingly chapter II will start with an evaluation of the general rules regarding perpetration as they appear from the criminal justice systems of a representative selection of European Member States. Briefly stated, which rules states have conceived in order to hold a person criminally liable for harm will be investigated here. The questions to be dealt within this chapter are: (i) Which requirements do Member States impose in order to regard a particular behaviour as criminal? (ii) Is this assessment confined to human behaviour or are also legal entities considered to be able to act in a way relevant for the attribution of liability? This requirement is often referred to as the act requirement. Is the traditional approach in the national penal systems still based on the "willed bodily movement" concept or have other more mental forms of action been incorporated? The choices taken here at this very early stage of determining criminal liability will predetermine a systems approach to related concepts such as omissions, inchoate liability etc. and are therefore of utmost importance. (iii) Subsequently it will be investigated what the underlying concepts and rationales of these different approaches are and which baseline for the attribution of liability can be derived from them.

An issue inherently situated in the discussion about the act requirement is the issue of omissions. It is widely accepted that the perpetrator can not only bring about the actus reus of a crime by positive action but also by omitting to conduct acts which society expects him to carry out. In recent years the concept of omissions seemingly is invoked more frequently as our society arguably not only becomes more duty based, but also because the issue of crime prevention has become a central feature of our penal culture.

In regard to omission liability the concept of a duty of care is of pivotal importance and will therefore constitute the central aspect of the discussion. *Inter alia* the different requirements when an omission constitutes a crime will be discussed. Central research questions of this section will be: (i) Which duties of care are recognised in the different Member States and (ii) how are these duties created? (iii) Does the scope of the duties vary depending on the social position of the perpetrator? (iv) Which aspects and principles generally influence the establishment of a duty of care and (v) which aspects circumscribe them? By answering these questions one will gain insight into the scope of the archetypical form of criminal liability and one will furthermore gain a rough yardstick to determine how far and under which conditions criminal liability can flow from an omission to act.

Subsequently this chapter will dwell on the doctrine of causation. This doctrine is crucial for actions and omissions alike. As far as result crimes are concerned, questions of causation have to be discussed in order to establish the required link between action/omission and result. The criminal law endeavours to hold people only liable for harmful consequences which they have caused, i.e. are responsible for. It is not concerned with accidents, i.e. "acts of god" (*actus dei nemini facit injuriam*; The act of god prejudices no one). In this section the following questions will be dealt with: (i) Which doctrines are invoked in the Member States to establish a causal link between action and result? (ii) Which acts are deemed to break the chain of causation and therefore exculpate the perpetrator? (iii) Which theoretical conception of the doctrine is reflected in the rules on causation in the respective Member States? (iv) Finally this research will seek to assess whether and to which extent subjective elements influence the assessment of a causal link?

Having read this chapter, one should now be acquainted with the basic design of criminal liability in different Member States and in European Union law. The chapter attempts to provide insights into the basic tenets of criminal liability and will have unearthed the underlying concepts and doctrinal friction points.

3.2.2. Participating in crime – the multiple actor scenarios

Criminal justice systems have adopted different strategies to respond to cooperative criminal efforts. These different strategies frequently find expression in the law of complicity and the different stances adopted hinge to a considerable extent on the acceptance of a conglomerate of fundamental tenets pertinent to criminal responsibility in the respective legal system.[25] It is these different strategies and approaches that will form the centre of the discussion in chapter III.

Succinctly stated, "the function of the law on complicity is to determine the circumstances when one person (the accessory) by virtue of prior or simultaneous activity or association will be held criminally liable for the wrongful behaviours of another person (the perpetrator)."[26] It is thus of utmost importance to determine when and why accessories to a crime ought to be held liable and how much involvement will be necessary as a minimum threshold in order to trigger criminal liability of the participant.

The research questions to be discussed here are the following: (i) How have Member States regulated the law of complicity and what are the underlying concepts? (ii) Which modes of participation can be found in the different Member States? (iii) Which forms of assistance are prescribed and with which form of mens rea must they be carried out? (iv) Furthermore, it will be investigated if there is a hierarchy between the different forms of participation and (v) if the distinction between the different forms of participation is drawn already at the level of attribution, or "merely" at the sentencing stage (unitarian vs. differentiated system)?

3.2.3. Inchoate liability

Traditionally the focus of criminal law lay on the retrospective imposition of punishment for harmful conduct. In the course of time the 'searchlight' of criminal law has however widened and it is nowadays common ground that criminal law may also be invoked to reduce the mere risk of harm. The increasing criminalisation

25 Smith, 'A Modern Treatise on the Law of Criminal Complicity' (1991), Preface.

26 Smith, 'A Modern Treatise on the Law of Criminal Complicity' (1991), p. 1.

of preparatory conduct may serve as an example here. Penal systems have resorted to different methods to reduce the risk of harm in society, one being the introduction of inchoate liability. Yet, these different methods can cause frictions with certain fundamental principles of criminal law and if taken to extremes risk transforming criminal law from an instrument securing the peaceful development of society into a tool of state oppression.

The investigation will focus here on (i) the principles and rationales underlying the criminalisation of preparatory conduct and subsequently assess (ii) which methods have been used to reduce the risk of harm by penal systems. (iii) What are the advantages and disadvantages of a respective method and (iv) how can these methods be reconciled with the protective function of criminal law? (v) Finally this research will tentatively assess whether certain principles can be invoked to guide and circumscribe the introduction and application of these measures to establish the outer limits of criminal liability?

Another species of inchoate liability and adjacent to the realm of preparation is the law of attempt. The central research questions discussed here are: (i) Do Member States adopt a subjectivist or an objectivist approach towards attempts, i.e. do they regard the potential harm to the legally protected interest or the evil intention of the perpetrator as central? This distinction is crucial in order to distinguish the exact scope of the doctrine and will also reveal fundamental doctrinal currents of the penal system itself. (ii) A core question to be dealt with in this chapter is when an act will qualify as a criminal attempt. Which doctrines are in place to demarcate preparatory acts from criminal attempts? (iii) How are impossible attempts treated in the national penal system and how is the line between possible and impossible attempts established? (iv) Finally it will be investigated whether Member States recognise withdrawal from the criminal enterprise and if so under which conditions? The different approaches taken by the Member States will be compared here and the underlying rationales as well as the advantages and disadvantages of the respective approach discussed. (v) The notion of voluntary withdrawal is further linked to the question whether there is a distinction made between finished and unfinished attempts and how the notion of voluntariness is defined?

3.2.4. Corporate Criminal liability

Finally, the focus of this research will turn to corporations as perpetrators. Corporations have become important members of our society and just like any human member occasionally get entangled in wrongdoing which gives rise to harmful consequences. As regards legal entities as perpetrators of a criminal offence, the central research questions are the following: (i) How do penal systems attempt to regulate corporate wrongdoing? (ii) Do Member States adopt a nominalist or realist point of view in regard to corporate criminal liability? The choices taken here are of utmost importance as they will predetermine and shape the approach taken by the penal system regarding corporate liability. The advantages and disadvantages of a respective approach in this respect will subsequently be discussed. (iii) Furthermore it will be assessed whether Member States adopted an anthropomorphic point of view in regard to corporate liability and apply doctrines originally created for individual wrongdoing to corporations, or whether corporate specific tools have been created. (iv) To what extent are corporations deemed capable to act? (v) What is the role of duty of care provisions in this respect? (vi) Finally some attention will be devoted to which rules and concepts Member States have devised and apply to establish corporate mens rea?

By addressing these different questions in a comparative manner it is hoped that a set of common principles and values can be established, which may constitute a first step towards the creation of a general part of European criminal law. Before descending into *medias res*, it seems however pertinent to first outline the methodology with which this research was conducted.

4. Methodology

4.1. Introduction

The research has been carried out in three stages. In the first stage the rules regarding the objective attribution of liability and their application in the investigated penal systems have been studied and cast into preliminary country reports. The results of this stage have been discussed with various experts from these legal traditions during visits in order to assess the reliability of the gathered data. In the second stage the fragments pertinent to the topic of this thesis in European Union legislation, case law and scholarly writing have been gathered and analysed. From these instances it has been attempted to infer the relevant pieces of a general part from European Union law. Special heed has thereby *inter alia* been paid to European competition law. Articles 101 and 102 TFEU prohibit any restriction of competition within the internal market and effectively function similarly to criminal offences. In practice also the ECJ treats competition law as criminal law and considers all guarantees of the European Convention of Human Rights as also relevant to competition law.[27] It is however acknowledged that competition law constitutes an area of law with its own specific peculiarities which must be treated with care as the peculiarities and rationales underlying competition law may not be equally applicable to criminal law in general. Nevertheless can European competition law be seen as a useful source of inspiration for this discourse, as it constitutes a first micro criminal justice system at the European Union level.[28]

27 Klip, 'European Criminal Law' (2012), pp. 2–3.
28 Klip, 'European Criminal Law' (2012), p. 459.

In the third stage the results of stages one and two were merged and some of the preliminary results were presented and discussed at a conference in Maastricht in January 2011 in which legal scholars and experts from a variety of European Member States participated.

4.2. Comparative research

4.2.1. The investigated penal systems

It has been decided to limit this research to three different European penal systems representing different legal traditions in Europe; the penal systems of England and Wales, Germany and the Netherlands. To provide a backdrop for the following discussion on substantive criminal law and to explicate the selection of these systems, it seems pertinent to briefly introduce them and to highlight some crucial characteristics. This will further provide the reader with additional information in order to better place the doctrinal solutions discussed below in perspective.

England and Wales

In comparative law a distinction frequently drawn between legal traditions is the one between common and civil law traditions. The penal system of England and Wales belongs to the former and can even be described as "the mother of all common law traditions".[29] Common law traditionally denotes that the foundation of the legal system in question cannot be found in a criminal code, but that the primary legal principles of the system have been created and developed by judges from case to case. Thus, the law developed organically from jurisprudence rather than it was systematically created. "The common law is a historical development rather than a logical whole, and the fact that a particular doctrine does not logically accord with another or others is no ground for its rejection".[30] While this excellently depicts the vantage point of the English penal system, it should be emphasised that in the past decades strong opposite tendencies were discernible. Parliamentary law-making has gained a lot of ground which led to a significant increase of detailed and sometimes complex statutory law.

The casuistic approach of common law has in the past often provoked the objection that it lacks systematic coherence. This however appears to be a blatant oversimplification. For one, statutory law is of course drafted in a systematic fashion and displays a systematic order. Furthermore, consider for instance the English Law Commission which plays an important role in shaping the English common law. Its task is "to take and keep under review all the law [...] with a view

---

29 Darbyshire, 'Eddey & Darbyshire on the English Legal System' (2001), p. 10.
30 Lord Porter, in Best v Samuel Fox & Co. Ltd [1952] AC 716.

to its systematic development and reform".[31] By reviewing the law and publishing the results in reports often recommending far-reaching changes, the Law Commission significantly contributes to the academic discussion as well as to the systematic development of the law.[32]

The adversarial trial mode prevalent in England also significantly shapes doctrines and laws. The function and public conception of the trial as well as its effect on legal reasoning is, in comparison to civil law countries, arguably very different in the English common law systems. As the law had to be tailor-made for application by lay persons, such as the jury, judges were at pains to avoid any unnecessary doctrinal complexity and strived to stay as close as possible to common sense and experience.[33] Simply put, a criminal law doctrine is considered only as good as it can be transformed into a jury instruction in English law.[34] This fact may explain why English doctrines have in general not reached such a high level of abstraction as is the case for instance in the German penal system. The influence of scholars on criminal law can therefore be described as more indirect in England as is for instance the case in Germany.[35] This is however not to say that English courts do not refer to scholarly writing for guidance on certain aspects. On the contrary. Moreover, since the end of the twentieth century, English scholarly writing has increasingly focused on the philosophy of criminal law, a development which is nowadays also discernible in textbooks and at times in the work of the Law Commission.[36]

The prevalent judicial style in jurisprudence can be described as pragmatic and almost exclusively focused on the case at hand rather than on abstract principles. English law, generally speaking, seems to be more concerned with results rather than method, with function rather than shape and effectiveness rather than style. From a birds-eye view, the amount of statutory and common law offence seems impressive, which could be seen to indicate a broad scope of criminal liability. However this formally broad scope is in practice circumscribed by prosecutorial discretion flowing from the opportunity principle applied in the English penal system.

Germany

The German penal system can in many respects be viewed as the exact opposite of the English common law system. The German penal system is a strict code-based system and in regard to criminal law may be considered as one of the most

---

31 Law Commission Act 1965, c. 22.

32 Riesenhuber, 'English common law versus German Systemdenken? Internal versus external approaches' Utrecht Law Review (2011), pp. 117–130.

33 Bohlander, 'Principles of German Criminal Law' (2009), p. 7.

34 Dubber, 'The Promise of German Criminal Law: A Science of Crime and Punishment' German Law Journal (2005), p. 1059.

35 Ashworth, 'United Kingdom', in Heller and Dubber (eds), The Handbook of comparative criminal law (2011), p. 534.

36 Ashworth, 'United Kingdom', in Heller and Dubber (eds), The Handbook of comparative criminal law (2011), p. 534.

influential penal systems. The latter is for instance demonstrated by the fact that countries like Japan or Greece adapted their penal systems along the lines of Germany. Jurisprudence generally does play an important role in the development of the law especially if the judgments stem from the Supreme Court (BGH) but it is not of such fundamental importance as in the English penal system.

Common law lawyers are often flabbergasted when they hear that according to the German point of view criminal law is considered a science. Doctrines and principles are not developed but rather discovered by scholars who undertake a scientific inquiry into the ontology of crime.[37] Scholars have traditionally played a significant role in shaping and developing the law as well as influencing jurisprudence.[38] They consider themselves not so much as the servants of the judges but rather as the guiding light.[39] In the view of German academics, jurisprudence ought to follow abstract reasoning rather than a problem based case by case approach. This may also explain why the German penal system can be characterised as unparalleled in doctrinal sophistication and complexity.

German criminal law is strongly influenced by systemic thinking and much of criminal theory is devoted to classification which is sought to increase internal consistency and comprehensiveness. German law in contrast to common law is not fact, but concept-driven. As a result German law often tends towards a certain formalism. Certain differences in the substantive law as well as the high doctrinal complexity in comparison to the English penal system can also be linked to the inquisitorial trial mode applied in Germany.

First, the trial is not considered to constitute a contest between parties, but rather a judge-led inquiry into the material truth.[40] Although lay participation formally takes place in the German criminal process, the influence of lay judges is rather weak in practice. The professional judge with his expertise in criminal law doctrine dominates the trial especially as doctrinal writing is created by experts for experts and often is inaccessible and incomprehensible for the man on the street. Second, it should be noted that in the German penal system the Public Prosecutor is bound by the principle of legality and may only drop cases if permitted by law. This arguably increases the need for doctrinal consistency and complexity as intricate legal problems, even though they may be of low practical relevance, need to be solved in an effective (doctrinal) manner and cannot be pragmatically dispensed with.

Simply stated, the style of judicial reasoning in Germany can be described as deductive as it tries to find solutions to the case at hand by deriving them from the general rules and principles enshrined in the penal code. Conversely, the style of the

---

37 Dubber, 'The Promise of German Criminal Law: A Science of Crime and Punishment' German Law Journal (2005), p. 1049.

38 Dubber, 'The Promise of German Criminal Law: A Science of Crime and Punishment' German Law Journal (2005), p. 1049.

39 Bohlander, 'Principles of German Criminal Law' (2009), p. 9.

40 Bohlander, 'Principles of German Criminal Law' (2009), p. 10.

common law can be described as inductive as general principles are attempted to be derived from the solutions found in individual cases.

Finally, it can be observed that the judicial style of the courts in Germany is notably different to, the English courts for example. English judgments are in their style and wording so much more open and outspoken than German. English courts generally tend to state clearly what they think, whereas in Germany, considerations of penal policy are often cloaked under a smokescreen of systematic and deductive reasoning.[41]

The Netherlands

The Dutch penal system can be characterised as a variation of the civil law traditions. During the occupation of the country by Napoleon, the Code Penal was introduced and traces of the French judicial style are still discernible at the time being. It effectively takes a medium position between the English and the German penal system. Doctrinal writing is considered important and to some extent certainly influences the development of the law but this influence is arguably dwarfed by the influence taken by case law, particularly from the Supreme Court. Accordingly a great deal of academic work discusses, interprets and builds on jurisprudence. Traditionally the Dutch penal system had the reputation of being one of the most lenient in Europe. However, recent punitive tendencies have arguably changed that picture. By now the claim of a mild penal system may be nothing more than a stereotype, with the notable exception of the Dutch drug policy which still constitutes an exceptional approach among penal systems.[42] Just like the English system, also the Dutch penal system operates on the principle of opportunity, granting prosecutors discretion to drop cases considered trivial, etc.

The Dutch penal system is just like the German a code based system. It is however less dogmatically driven and less formalistic than its German counterpart. Often the guiding maxims are pragmatism and practicality which may explain why the doctrinal solutions discussed by scholars are generally less intricate and sophisticated than in Germany. A just and most important workable solution of the problem at stake is often considered more important than systematic coherency, while in Germany the situation often seems converse. The development of the law is influenced by scholarly work which often takes place via the Advocate Generals at the courts who, much like their counterparts at the ECJ, in a case give a thorough overview about the relevant legal principles and doctrines applicable to the case at hand to provide guidance to the courts.

41 Markesinis, 'Judicial style and reasoning in England and Germany' Cambridge Law Journal (2000), p. 398.

42 See: Klip, 'Slappe rechters' Delikt en Delinkwent (2010), pp. 1253–1263. See also: Tak, 'The Dutch criminal justice system', (2003) WODC report Nr 205, p. 12.

Lay participation is generally absent from the Dutch penal system. Judgments are rendered by professional judges either sitting alone or in chambers.[43] The system is generally underlined by a strong faith in the judiciary. This is *inter alia* demonstrated by the absence of specific minimum sentences for serious offences in the criminal code and the wide discretionary powers enjoyed by courts in sentencing.

As already mentioned, the overall judicial style can be described as practical and pragmatic. Dutch courts may be impressed by the length and thoroughness of the argument in German decisions, most notably in decisions of higher courts. "German legal style is much more differentiated, scholarly worded; the style of Dutch courts is pragmatic, trying to use language which might be understandable even to the parties involved".[44] To conclude, it can be stated that the Dutch penal system effectively takes a medium position between the highly systematic and complex German and the casuistic and result-orientated English system.

Following this brief description of the penal systems investigated in this thesis, is a discussion of the methodology with which it will be attempted to deduce principles of criminal liability for a general part of European criminal law.

4.2.2. Comparative methodology

In this research it has been decided to use a comparative methodology. This method is the selected tool for conducting this research, as it first and foremost highlights common difficulties that states experience in distributing criminal liability. It further forces the researcher and reader to critically appraise the concepts of his own criminal law system by putting them into a broader perspective. Moreover, it can also provide the researcher with potential new solutions for a problem which might not be discussed in one penal system. In other words, comparative research might pave the way for a fruitful cross-fertilisation of doctrines as penal systems may have arrived at different solutions to one and the same predicament.

The comparative method applied in this thesis will primarily be the functional method. It takes as starting point the premise that the different solutions adopted in penal systems constitute responses to common problems.[45] Different (national) solutions are considered to provide answers to similar problems that are doctrinally different. This approach will in turn facilitate the finding of common elements and principles. One reason for this is that in the course of the comparison the solutions found in the different penal systems must be liberated "from their conceptual context and stripped of their national doctrinal overtones so that they may be seen

43 Tak, 'The Dutch criminal justice system', (2003) WODC report Nr 205, p. 35.

44 Blankenburg, 'Patterns of legal culture: The Netherlands compared to neighboring Germany' The American Journal of Comparative Law (1998), p. 40.

45 Michaels, 'The functional method of comparative law', in Reimann and Zimmermann (eds), The Oxford Handbook of Comparative Law (2006), p. 346.

purely in the light of their function as an attempt to satisfy a particular legal need".[46]

The comparative research will not be confined to "the law in the books", but will also cover "the law in practice". Most Member States have only formulated at the most very vague texts on actus reus, participation etc., to give sufficient leeway to the judiciary and scholars to elaborate on these concepts. The functional approach of comparative law forces the researcher not only to look at legal rules (law in books) but also at the result of their application (law in action) as responses to societal needs. Various sources have therefore been utilised in this thesis, reaching from doctrinal writing and case law to a multitude of other official documents which lawyers in a particular system would use to solve a judicial problem.

In this research an integrated problem-based form of presentation will be used, where the different penal systems will be compared with each other in a comprehensive manner. This will preliminary be done when the solutions found in the different Member States are sufficiently similar. In case significant differences emerge from the different penal systems, a more horizontal form of presenting the results of the research will be applied where the different systems will be juxtaposed. The elements of the general part flowing from European Union law will, where possible be presented in a separate section following the comparison of national law. Subsequently the results will be merged and possible solutions indicated.

While the functional method is a valuable tool in conducting a comparison among different penal systems, it reaches its practical limits in regard to evaluating the different solutions and more crucially in merging the different solutions found into a general part of European criminal law. The focus on functions allows the researcher to master complexity in the law and discover communalities and differences, but it has little to contribute to the evaluation process. The functional equivalents identified are by definition of equal value and it seems impossible to deduce in this context an 'ought' from an 'is'.[47] The yardstick for merging and assessing must therefore be found in other criteria outside and different to the criteria of comparability. It is these criteria that will now be discussed.

4.3. Criteria for synthesis

4.3.1. External criteria for the synthesis

There are two sets of criteria which will be applied to merge the two pictures emerging from the comparison of national penal systems on the one hand and

46 Zweigert and Kötz, 'Introduction to comparative law' (1998), p. 44.

47 Michaels, 'The functional method of comparative law', in Reimann and Zimmermann (eds), The Oxford Handbook of Comparative Law (2006), p. 374.

European Union law on the other. First, a set of external criteria will be applied to establish general framework requirements for the synthesis. Second, a set of criteria internal to a liberal criminal law will be utilised to establish a normative framework for the merger.

At a more general level, the merger must respect the fundamental values as they result from the constitutional traditions of the Member States pursuant to Article 6 TEU. It should furthermore respect the constitutional traditions of the Member States as enshrined in Article 4 TEU. This requirement has been termed the principle of coherency.[48] This principle essentially holds that a European criminal law ought to as far as possible respect the basic values, customs and choices of a society expressed in its penal code, and therefore the Union legislator should when drafting more rules interfere as little as possible with the inner coherence of national criminal law.[49]

Furthermore, the principles developed must comply with the requirements under the European Convention of Human Rights (ECHR) as well with the Charter of Fundamental Rights of the European Union as stipulated by Article 6 TEU. "The Charter, being the compass of all EU policies, provides for a binding core of rules that protects citizens" and is therefore to be respected.[50] Of particular importance therefore may be the principle of legality as enshrined in Article 7 ECHR and Article 49 of the Charter.

From a systematic point of view the synthesis should strive for a system which is coherent and consistent.[51] Coherency and consistency in this respect refers to a systematic approach that will safeguard the principle of equality which according to settled European case law requires that comparable cases must not be treated differently and that different cases must not be treated in the same way unless such treatment is objectively justified.[52]

A further guiding principle for the synthesis arguably ought to be simplicity. A general part should not be overburdened with abstract and complex dogmatic

---

48 See: A Manifesto on European Criminal Policy, Zeitschrift für Internationale Strafrechtsdogmatik (2009), pp. 707–716. The need for coherency has also been acknowledged by the Commission and the European Parliament, see: Towards an EU Criminal Policy: Ensuring the effective implementation of EU policies through criminal law, 20.09.2011, COM (2011) 573 final; European Parliament Report on harmonization of criminal law in the EU, 24.04.2012, no. 2010/2310.

49 Asp, 'The importance of the principles of Subsidiarity and Coherence in the development of EU Criminal Law' European Criminal Law Review (2011), p. 44–55. See also: Articles 82 (3) and 83 (3) TFEU.

50 Towards an EU Criminal Policy: Ensuring the effective implementation of EU policies through criminal law, 20.09.2011, COM (2011) 573 final. See also: European Parliament Report on harmonization of criminal law in the EU, 24.04.2012, no. 2010/2310.

51 See: European Parliament Report on harmonization of criminal law in the EU, 24.04.2012, no. 2010/2310.

52 See: 3 May 2007, Case C-303/05, *Advocaten voor de Wereld VZW v Leden van de Ministerraad* [2007] ECR I-3633, para. 56, 6 October 2009, Case C-123/08, *criminal proceedings against Dominic Wolzenburg* [2009] ECR I-9621, para. 63.

constructions but should confine itself to the basic rules of attribution.[53] A general part should be "simple and easy to apply and at the same time conceptually rich enough to enable a judge to make all those distinctions that must play a role in the administration of criminal justice".[54]

These general principles will provide a first yardstick for the synthesis. Yet, there is a further set of criteria that will be of great significance when merging the results of the comparative research with Union law. These criteria are inherent in the subject of investigation, i.e. criminal law.

4.3.2. Internal criteria for the synthesis

One aspect which usually informs and shapes the national discussion on criminal law and its general part is criminal policy. As will subsequently become evident, a fully-fledged EU criminal policy still awaits creation. Nevertheless the existing and identifiable fragments may be taken into consideration in establishing general principles of European criminal law in this thesis. Besides this, other criteria can be identified which will play a role in this research. These criteria flow from fundamental principles of criminal law which are linked to its function and role in a liberal, democratic society. Before dwelling on these criteria this research will however first turn its attention to the issue of criminal policy.

European Criminal Policy

A general part of criminal law can be said to give expression to certain choices of criminal policy. Within the national setting these policy choices can in many instances be identified by analysing parliamentary debates surrounding the introduction of certain rules or codes, explanatory memoranda or statements of reason as well as other political documents. Furthermore, academic commentators may in the course of time have shed some light on policy considerations underlying a specific discussion. Matters are however a bit more complicated at the European level. Given the early stage of development of European criminal law a European criminal policy has yet to fully emerge. Explanatory memoranda are by and large alien to European law which leaves only the preamble of a respective legal instrument for deducing the intention of the drafters. This however only provides insights into the rationale of this particular instrument. A comprehensive and coherent European criminal policy has until the time being not yet been agreed upon. This complicates the establishment of general principles as an important general guiding factor for preferring one doctrinal solution over another is absent. There have however been some recent initiatives which constitute a first step toward

---

53 Ambos, 'Is the development of a common substantive criminal law for Europe possible? Some Preliminary Reflections' Maastricht Journal of European and Comparative Law (2005), p. 178.

54 Ambos, 'Is the development of a common substantive criminal law for Europe possible? Some Preliminary Reflections' Maastricht Journal of European and Comparative Law (2005), p. 178.

the creation of an European criminal policy and which may function as a yardstick for discussion.

The Commission recently announced that:

> An EU Criminal Policy should have as overall goal to foster citizens' confidence in the fact that they live in a Europe of freedom, security and justice, that EU law protecting their interests is fully implemented and enforced and that at the same time the EU will act in full respect of subsidiarity and proportionality and other basic Treaty principles.[55]

The protection of individual rights accordingly seems to play an important role. Similarly, the Council has laid down its view as to the application of European criminal law in draft guidelines and model provisions, thereby emphasising the importance of principles such as proportionality, *ultima ratio* and harm.[56] Likewise, the European Parliament stressed in its report on criminal law in the European Union the importance of principles such as proportionality, subsidiarity, *lex certa, nulla poena sine culpa* and *ultima ratio*.[57]

Further guidance for the development of general principles of European criminal law can arguably also be derived from the scope of the EU's competences. Article 83 (1) TFEU refers to serious forms of wrongdoing with a cross-border dimension. It mentions, terrorism, trafficking in human beings, sexual exploitation of women and children, illicit arms trafficking, money laundering, corruption, counterfeiting of means of payment, computer and organised crime. These crimes are not only of a particular serious nature but they are also most likely to be carried out by groups or in an organisational context which may have implications for the establishment of criminal liability.

Furthermore Article 83 (2) TFEU allows the European Parliament and the Council, following a proposal of the Commission to adopt minimum rules if this proves essential to ensure the effective implementation of a Union policy. Therefore one may think of primarily economic policy areas and of "measures to fight serious damaging practices and illegal profits in some economic sectors in order to protect activities of legitimate business and safeguard the interests of taxpayers".[58] The application of European criminal law therefore seems to be strongly related to and geared to protect certain economic and quasi-economic interests which may in turn also have an impact on the development of general principles.[59] The Union seems to

---

55 See: Towards an EU Criminal Policy: Ensuring the effective implementation of EU policies through criminal law, 20.09.2011, COM (2011) 573 final, p. 2.

56 Draft Council conclusions on model provisions, guiding the Council's criminal law deliberations, Brussels, 27 November 2009, 16542/2/09 REV 2.

57 European Parliament Report on harmonization of criminal law in the EU, 24.04.2012, no. 2010/2310.

58 Towards an EU Criminal Policy: Ensuring the effective implementation of EU policies through criminal law, 20.09.2011, COM (2011) 573 final, p. 10.

59 See also: Klip, 'European Criminal Law' (2012), pp. 218–220.

predominantly focus on financial crimes as well as other serious forms of wrongdoing which may have an impact on the functioning of the internal market or relate to policy areas of the Union such as drugs, the environment, road traffic, custom rules, etc.

This thesis aspires to contribute to the establishment of common substantive standards, rooted in common values, which will be necessary to create a full-fledged European Criminal Justice System and help to develop a European criminal policy. It will strive to highlight, where possible, pertinent policy choices and discuss their implications for European criminal law. A common understanding and safeguarding of these guiding standards is arguably a necessity to improve and drive forward the integration process in this area of the law.

The function and nature of criminal law

Criminal law as the harshest mechanism of the state to achieve social control has in the course of time developed a set of principles that circumscribe and guide the application of punitive measures. These principles emerge from the very function and nature of criminal law as well as from the constitutional traditions of the Member States. They form the identity of criminal law and are closely linked to the protection of fundamental rights and the rule of law. These principles generally constitute the hallmark of liberal, democratic societies and as the Union endorses the same values (such as human dignity, liberty, equality, etc.) they must also be respected at Union level.[60]

Criminal law is a body of rules, "by which the state participates in the ordering of its citizens lives".[61] Every society is based on a multitude of rules (i.e. social, legal, moral rules, etc.) which make the existence of this very society possible. By "joining" a society an individual submits to the rules of this society, thereby waiving part of his or her own freedoms in order to benefit from the rights and freedoms flowing from its membership.[62]

The most salient feature of criminal law arguably is that a violation of its rules, i.e. the establishment of criminal liability by a court, triggers the imposition of public censure and often severe punishment. It is the potential imposition of punishment which distinguishes criminal law from other fields of law and confers special social significance on it. However, it is evident that the imposition of criminal punishment is a severe encroachment on an individual's

60 Kaiafa-Gbandi, 'The importance of core principles of substantive criminal law for a European criminal policy respecting fundamental rights and the rule of law' European Criminal Law Review (2011), p. 8. See also: Article 2 TEU and the rights enshrined in the Charter of Fundamental rights of the European Union.

61 Simester and Sullivan, 'Criminal Law: Theory and Doctrine' (2007), p. 1.

62 Wilson, 'Central Issues in Criminal Theory' (2002), p. 17. See also: Rousseau, 'Gesellschaftsvertrag' (1998), pp. 5–153.

autonomy[63] which requires a clear social justification, because, in a modern liberal society, the state should support individual autonomy and freedom rather than restrict it.[64] This is at least the view of traditional criminal law, which emerged in the slipstream of the enlightenment held.

In any event, justifying the use of criminal law has received a lot of attention in scholarly writing.[65] One obvious ground for the usage of criminal law is the retribution of criminal harm that the perpetrator has brought about. However, while this might be one possible justification, it should in itself not be a sufficient reason for the application of criminal law. Therefore also utilitarian and preventive reasons are often additionally invoked by penal systems to justify the imposition of punishment. Thus, penal systems frequently rely on a mixture of rationales to justify the use of punitive measures. Criminal law is not merely an instrument of vengeance it is more importantly an instrument of social control, or put differently a tool of social engineering. It influences and regulates behaviour in a way we see fit in our society. Hence, in its broadest sense, its ambition is to impair certain socially detrimental behaviours and to promote socially desirable behaviour, thereby creating and maintaining the foundations of human society. This is done by limiting and creating freedoms at the same time. Criminal law creates freedom for human beings by protecting their interests e.g. property rights. On the other hand it limits freedoms by closely circumscribing their scope and boundaries. An example might elucidate the matter further. Criminal law protects property by prohibiting the unlawful appropriation of property, theft for instance, but also circumscribes the scope of the usage of this property by proscribing that no other human being ought to be harmed by it. Thus, the tool of criminal law is used in our society to promote law-conform behaviour and prevent criminal conduct from occurring, as well as to diminish the disturbance and strife caused by criminal wrongdoing. The latter is achieved *inter alia* by the imposition of criminal punishment and coercion and their monopolisation in the hands of the state.

In the light of the foregoing it becomes apparent that criminal law has two functions which require delicate balancing. On the one hand it is a tool to maintain public order and control deviant social behaviour; on the other hand its function is to canalise and circumscribe the application of coercive measures and punishment in legally determined channels. In other words, it lays down the rules under which the state can exercise its powers and thereby protects the citizen from arbitrary state measures. Thus, criminal law functions as a tool of the state against its citizens to control deviant behaviour and on the other hand as a tool of the citizens against

63 Note that not only the imposition of physical punishment encroaches on the freedoms of the individual but also in the investigative stage of a criminal trial the individual's freedoms are under attack.

64 Wilson, 'Central Issues in Criminal Theory' (2002), p. 18.

65 See for instance: Bosch, 'Beginsel van Strafrecht' (2008), p. 10–13, Claessen, 'Misdaad en straf' (2010), pp. 161–237, Clarkson and Keating, 'Criminal law: Text and Materials' (2003), pp. 1–82, Remmelink, 'Inleiding tot de studie van het Nederlandse Strafrecht' (1995), pp. 883–917.

repressive state powers, i.e. it has a safeguard and a crime control function in our society.[66]

At this point it should already be noted however that the balancing of these two functions will be achieved differently depending on the area of criminal law which will be examined. Accordingly it will become apparent that the control and prevention function of the law is often considered more important in regard to criminal law dealing with economic or environmental crimes, traffic offences or corporate crime. Conversely, the safeguard function of the law plays a much more significant role with respect to archetypical criminal law dealing with individual wrongdoing like murder, theft, rape, etc. However, it will also become evident that this generic pretension is in flux and that recent social developments have led to a doctrinal shift in the criminal law.

No legitimate approach to criminal law can arguably ignore the dual function of criminal law in society. Accordingly European criminal law must strive as well to carefully strike a balance between the safeguard and the crime control function of penal law.[67] This seems particularly important in the European Union, where historically the notion of security has played a central role. Not only in the realm of substantive law but also in the context of cooperation in criminal matters, the aim of Union policy was frequently to increase security within the Area of Freedom Security and Justice, neglecting the protection of fundamental rights and freedoms. However, the Union has lately acknowledged this lack of focus on the safeguard function of the law.[68] This underlines the necessity to strive for principles in this book which will allow the European Union to develop a balanced approach towards criminal law, respecting both its crime control and safeguard function.

The scope of criminal law – The harm principle a.k.a. the doctrine of protected legal interests

The foregoing discussion might have provided a scant insight into the functions and ambitions of (European) criminal law, but one is still left in the dark as to the question of why certain activities are prohibited by law, while others are not. This constitutes an important question regarding the issue of when the Union may employ criminal law. One central notion in determining whether a particular conduct should be criminalised is the concept of harm. Acknowledging the risk of protecting partisan instead of community interests, the harm principle in essence holds that the state may only criminalise conduct in order to prevent harm to others,

66 Bosch, 'Beginsel van Strafrecht' (2008), p. 13.

67 Kaiafa-Gbandi, 'The importance of core principles of substantive criminal law for a European criminal policy respecting fundamental rights and the rule of law' European Criminal Law Review (2011), pp. 7–12.

68 See: The Stockholm Programme – An open and secure Europe serving and protecting the citizens, European Council 17024/09; Towards an EU Criminal Policy: Ensuring the effective implementation of EU policies through criminal law, 20.09.2011, COM (2011) 573 final.

thereby ensuring that the state serves the interest of the polity and not its own.[69] The principle has its roots in the Enlightenment and accordingly served as a stronghold for individual liberties and as a limitation on the scope of government powers. This approach was eloquently outlined by John Stuart Mill in his essay *On Liberty*:

> [...] The principle is, that the sole end for which mankind are warranted, individually or collectively, in interfering with the liberty of action of any of their number is self-protection. That the only purpose for which power can be rightfully exercised over any member of a civilized community, against his will, is to prevent harm to others. His own good, either physical or moral is not a sufficient warrant.[70]

Thus, the state is authorised to protect a certain set of interests (individual or public) given their role in human welfare by forbidding and thus preventing conduct that threatens to cause substantial harm to those interests. On the other hand the state should keep the interference to a minimum in order to maximise individual liberty.[71]

Most continental European criminal theories take a similar starting point.[72] Dutch[73] and German[74] criminal theory for instance apply the so called *Rechtsgutlehre* (doctrine of protected legal interests) in order to determine which conduct ought to be criminalised. A *Rechtsgut* (legally protected interest) is a good which a community, governed by the rule of law recognises as being necessary for the social or individual welfare and therefore merits protection by the law against conduct that seriously threatens it.[75] Examples of legally protected interests are for instance property rights, life and limb, sexual integrity etc. In the context of a European criminal law, protected legal interests can arguably be derived from primary EU legislation as well as from the Charter of Fundamental Rights and from the constitutional traditions of the Member States. This could provide a useful restraint on the Union's legislative process as it would be obliged to make clear the purpose of each criminal provision it wants to adopt. However, it should be clear that the construct is a vague one and can only provide a first constraint on the punitive powers of the Union.[76]

---

69 Wilson, 'Central Issues in Criminal Theory' (2002), p. 19.

70 Cited in: Epstein, 'The harm principle and how it grew' University of Toronto Law Journal (1995), p. 372.

71 Wilson, 'Central Issues in Criminal Theory' (2002), p. 20.

72 Eser, 'The Principle of Harm in the Concept of Crime: A Comparative Analysis of the Criminally Protected Legal Interests' Duquesne University Law Review (1966), pp. 345–417.

73 De Hullu, 'Materieel Strafrecht' (2006), pp. 67–69, Remmelink, 'Inleiding tot de studie van het Nederlandse Strafrecht' (1995), pp. 16–17.

74 Bohlander, 'Principles of German Criminal Law' (2009), pp. 18–19, Jescheck and Weigend, 'Lehrbuch des Strafrechts: Allgemeiner Teil' (1996), pp. 7–8, 256–260.

75 Duff, 'Theories of Criminal Law' The Stanford Encyclopedia of Philosophy (2002), available at: http://plato.stanford.edu/archives/fall2008/entries/criminal-law/.

76 Böse, 'The principle of proportionality and the protection of legal interests' European Criminal Law Review (2011), pp. 35–43, Dubber, 'Theories of Crime and punishment in German criminal law' The American Journal of Comparative Law (2005), pp. 679–707.

In any case, generally speaking it can be said that the core of both doctrines is to protect certain interests from (potential) harm. The two doctrines can therefore be combined to increase and strengthen the protective function of criminal law and help to circumscribe the scope of liability more concretely.[77] Also the Council in its model provisions seems to have adopted such a view as it states that "criminal provisions should focus on conduct causing actual harm or seriously threatening the right or essential interest which is the object of protection"[...].[78]

The requirement of harm, as will be shown in due course, does however not only play a vital role in regard to the criminalisation of conduct, but also in the determination of criminal liability itself, as harm, by and large, constitutes the very essence of crime. Therefore the scope of the protected legal interest may be of particular importance. Take for instance the law of attempt. If one accepts that some form of endangerment of, or remote harm to the protected legal interest will be required for liability to arise, it becomes apparent that the scope of liability will vary depending on whether an individual (e.g. life and limb) or a collective legal interest (e.g. the environment, safety, etc.) is at stake. The broader the definition of a protected legal interest, the earlier and the greater number of forms of conduct may arguably be deemed to constitute an endangerment. The concept of harming a protected legal interest can thus be seen as a guiding principle of the general part.

Criminal liability should arguably not be imposed unless the occurred conduct can be considered (in some sense) wrongful.[79] The requirement that the conduct in question (wrongfully) caused harm to a protected legal interest is of importance in establishing objective rules of attribution. The conduct in question must have violated or (clearly) endangered a legal interest. The further conduct is removed from the occurrence of harm the more stringent the policy reasons as well as the general threshold of criminal liability should arguably become. Furthermore, the further the conduct in question is removed from harm the more salient and cogent the reasons put forward by the legislator should be to criminalise this behaviour despite the absence of harm. Arguably this should be supported by evaluation mechanisms that clearly establish that the statute under scrutiny unambiguously and directly advances the legislator's interest.

This aspect of the principle too has, however, come under considerable strain lately, by broadening the definition of the concept of harm or the legally protected interest respectively. While the principle used to constitute a bastion for the protection of individual liberties and interests, the principle nowadays is deemed to cover more and more collective, i.e. societal interests. Hence, a transformation has taken place from a bastion of liberty into an engine of social control that is said to

77 Generally see: Swoboda, 'Die Lehre vom Rechtsgut und ihre Alternativen' ZStW (2010), pp. 24–50.

78 Draft Council conclusions on model provisions, guiding the Council's criminal law deliberations, Brussels, 27 November 2009, 16542/2/09 REV 2.

79 Husak, 'Overcriminalization' (2008), pp. 72–77, 103–119.

justify more and more government intervention.[80] Metaphorically put, what was once a shield of individual liberty has over time been forged into a sword against it.[81]

David Garland in his influential book *The Culture of Control* has eloquently dwelled on this new phenomenon:

> Today, there is a new and urgent emphasis upon the need for security, the containment of danger, the identification and management of any kind of risk. Protecting the public has become the dominant theme of penal policy. [...] There is a relaxation of concern about the civil liberties of the suspect, and the rights of prisoners, and a new emphasis upon effective enforcement and control. The call for protection *from* the state has been increasingly displaced by the demand for the protection *by* the state.[82]

The principle of legality

The principle of legality generally contains a multitude of different aspects.[83] Most importantly for the purpose of this research is the requirement that an offence must be clearly defined in law. The principle also constitutes a cornerstone of Western penal traditions and is at the level of Union law enshrined in Article 49 (1) of the Charter of fundamental rights as well as Article 7 (1) ECHR. This requirement is according to settled case law satisfied if an individual can know from the wording of the provision in question which acts and omissions will make him criminally liable.[84] This means that it must be foreseeable for a citizen whether or not a certain conduct will give rise to criminal liability.

For the purpose of establishing general principles this arguably implies that vagueness and complexity should be kept to an utmost minimum. Doctrines should as far as possible increase foreseeablity for citizens and not obscure it. Citizens must be enabled to make their choices according to foreseeable and sufficiently precise rules.

One goal of the principle of legality is thus to increase legal certainty and "to provide effective safeguards against arbitrary prosecution, conviction and

---

80 Epstein, 'The harm principle and how it grew' University of Toronto Law Journal (1995), pp. 25–31, Eser, 'The Principle of Harm in the Concept of Crime: A Comparative Analysis of the Criminally Protected Legal Interests' Duquesne University Law Review (1966), pp. 345–417, Hassemer, 'Kennzeichen und Krisen des modernen Strafrechts' Zeitschrift für Rechtspolitik (1992), p. 380, Roef, 'Strafrechtelijke Verantwoordelijkheid in de Risicomaatschappij', in Vos and Calster (eds), Risico en voorzorg in de rechtsmaatschappij (2004), pp. 208–209.

81 Epstein, 'The harm principle and how it grew' University of Toronto Law Journal (1995), pp. 369–417.

82 Garland, 'The Culture of Control – Crime and Social Order in Contemporary Society' (2006), p. 12, (original italics).

83 For a general overview see: Peristeridou, PhD thesis, Maastricht University, forthcoming 2013.

84 See: *Cantoni v France*, appl. no. 17862/91, 11 November 1996.

punishment".[85] General principles of European criminal law arguably ought to contribute and improve foreseeablity for citizens and to minimise as far as possible at the same time the risk of an arbitrary establishment of criminal liability. In doing so the scope of foreseeability will arguably be influenced by (1) the content of the provision or doctrine at stake, (2) its envisaged scope of application, and (3) the number and status of those to whom it is addressed.[86] From this it can be deduced that in terms of foreseeability a distinction will have to be made between foreseeability for regular citizens and foreseeability for professionals in the business world. Regarding the requirements of foreseeability arguably more can be expected in regard to people carrying out professional activities as they are used to having to proceed with a high degree of caution when pursuing their activities. By the same token are they expected to be acquainted with prevalent standards of diligence, etc. applicable to their business sector.[87]

The principle of guilt

Another fundamental principle of criminal law which can be seen as the cornerstone of every Western penal system is the principle of guilt. In order to be held liable and be subjected to criminal punishment it generally ought to be established that a person's (objective) conduct resulted from a criminal intention. This is nicely expressed by the phrase, *actus non facti reum nisi mens sit rea* or *nulla poena sine culpa* – no punishment without guilt. Only under the condition that the person is blameworthy for the occurred conduct or result is the imposition of punishment thus warranted. The principle arguably has its roots in respect for human dignity as it gives citizens the possibility to control whether or not they become entangled in criminal wrongdoing.[88] A person can only be held liable for certain harm if he could have acted otherwise. If he was compelled to act as he did he can generally not be liable for the occurred harm for then he lacked effective control over his conduct. The principle fulfils an important safeguard function as it protects citizens from arbitrary state punishment by giving them the opportunity to conduct themselves according to a clear set of rules. Only if the citizen freely and deliberately chooses to violate these rules can he be considered guilty and subjected to punishment.[89] Such is the normative core of the principle of guilt.

At the European level the principle derives from Article 6 ECHR as well as from Article 48 of the Charter of Fundamental Rights. In essence both these provisions

---

85 See: *S.W. v United Kingdom*, appl. no. 20166/92, 22 November 1995. See also: *Kononov v Latvia*, appl. no. 36376/04, 17 May 2010.

86 See: *Kononov v Latvia*, appl. no. 36376/04, 17 May 2010.

87 See also: *Van Anraat v the Netherlands*, appl. no. 65389/09, 6 July 2010, para 81.

88 Van Dijk, 'Strafrechtelijke Aansprakelijkheid heroverwogen – Over opzet, schuld, schulduitsluitingsgronden en straf' (2008), p. 150.

89 Roef, 'Strafrechtelijke Verantwoordelijkheid in de Risicomaatschappij', in Vos and Calster (eds), Risico en voorzorg in de rechtsmaatschappij (2004), p. 215.

provide that "everyone charged with a criminal offence shall be presumed innocent until proven guilty according to law". This on first sight mainly procedural rule has also important implications for substantive criminal law. The European Court of Human Rights has for instance held:

> It is a fundamental rule of criminal law that criminal liability does not survive the person who has committed the criminal act. [...] In the court's opinion, such a rule is also required by the presumption of innocence enshrined in Article 6 §2 of the convention. Inheritance of guilt of the dead is not compatible with the standards of criminal justice in a society governed by the rule of law. [...][90]

In establishing general principles of European criminal law the principle of guilt must therefore be adhered to. With respect to participation in crime, this will for instance mean that every participant ought to be judged according to his own wrongdoing and culpability and that constructions facilitating the establishment of guilt by mere association should be avoided. Furthermore, the principle requires that the proscribed conduct in an offence must be sufficiently clear in order to give the citizen effective control whether or not he will come within the scope of criminal law. The last point shows that the principle has also close ties to the requirements flowing from the aforementioned principle of legality and that the two principles supplement each other.

After having outlined and discussed the criteria that will guide this quest for the establishment of general principles of European criminal law the discussion can now turn to the central theme of this thesis – i.e. criminal liability.

5. Criminal Liability

5.1. Definition

Criminal liability, the central aspect of this thesis, can roughly be defined as the final result of a legal evaluation process triggered by the violation of a penal norm by a legal subject. Criminal liability should conceptually be distinguished from responsibility, although the terms are often used interchangeably. Criminal responsibility constitutes a prerequisite for the attribution of liability. Responsibility is the broader concept and criminal liability is grounded in responsibility.[91] To be considered a responsible subject of criminal law a person must possess certain basic

---

90 *E.I., R.I. and J.O. –L. v Switzerland*, appl. no. 20919/92, 29 August 1997. See also: *Salabiaku v France*, appl. no. 10519/83, 7 October 1998.

91 Duff, 'Answering for Crime' (2007), p. 16. See also: Honoré, 'Responsibility and fault' (1999), p. 125.

capacities or characteristics so that (s)he can be (justly) held responsible for her deeds.[92]

One important concept in regard to responsibility as well as to the attribution of criminal liability arguably is control. People should only be held responsible for conduct or harm, the occurrence of which lay within their control.[93] Control is closely tied to agency. To view people as responsible subjects and to avoid the creation of objective, or risk liability will require that only conduct or harm that can be seen as an expression of agency can constitute the basis for imposing liability. Control is in part a matter of how far the world is responsive to agency, in how far agency can make a difference to the social and material world in which it is exercised.[94] Control constitutes an important baseline with respect to the attribution of criminal liability which resurfaces in several doctrines. There will be further discussion on the notion of control as concerns the conduct requirement, but control also plays a role in other fundamental elements of criminal liability such as the doctrine of causation and the principle of guilt.

The establishment of criminal liability generally requires the fulfilment of the offence definition of a crime. Every offence definition generally is composed of an actus reus and a corresponding mens rea, the fulfilment of which thus gives rise to liability.[95] To illustrate the matter consider for instance Article 2 (b) of Framework Decision 2004/68 which makes it a criminal offence to intentionally recruit a child into participating in pornographic performances.[96] The actus reus in this case, bluntly stated is the recruitment of children to participate in pornographic activities, which has to be carried out intentionally (mens rea). These two elements are frequently seen as the foundation of criminal liability. In combination they safeguard that liability is not imposed for thoughts nor for causing unavoidable or unforeseeable accidents.

Traditionally, criminal liability and the doctrines revolving around it, developed from the vantage point of individual wrongdoing. However, this vantage point, as will become apparent throughout this book has recently come under pressure. Crime in general has become more organised and often involves a variety of actors which causes frictions with traditional theories and doctrines. Furthermore, social developments have influenced and shaped the contemporary view on criminal liability. These developments and their implications for criminal law will be addressed in due course.

---

92 These basic capacities will be discussed in more detail in Chapter II. 2. See also: Honoré, 'Responsibility and fault' (1999), pp. 122 et seq.

93 Duff, 'Answering for Crime' (2007), p. 99.

94 Duff, 'Answering for Crime' (2007), pp. 57, 100.

95 A notable exception may be strict liability offences.

96 Framework Decision 2004/68 of 22 December 2003 on combating the sexual exploitation of children and child pornography, OJ 2004 L 13/44.

5.2. Harm versus Culpability and Objectivism versus subjectivism in the law

It has been shown that for analytical purposes the basic ingredients of criminal liability are frequently divided into subjective (mens rea) and objective (actus reus) parts. The objective subjective dichotomy however also plays an important role at a more fundamental level, namely in the interpretation of general principles, doctrines and concepts of criminal law. It can at times significantly shape and influence the scope of criminal liability. The dichotomy is arguably related to two different patterns of criminality pervading the law which adopt different views on what is paramount for criminal liability. The main dispute between these two patterns, briefly stated, revolves around the question whether harm or culpability should constitute the foundation of criminal liability.[97] This research will dwell more on these patterns in a subsequent chapter, for now suffices it to say that the two constitute extreme poles in regard to the application and interpretation of doctrines, principles, etc.[98] The effect of the two approaches is probably nowhere more salient as in the context of criminal attempts. The law of attempts and many other doctrines will differ in scope and guise, depending on whether one considers harm or culpability as the foundation of criminal liability. In regard to criminal attempts, it will become apparent that the bone of contention of the two approaches essentially is whether a certain conduct ought to be judged by its tendency under the known circumstances to cause harm, or rather by the actual intent with which it was carried out.

A related but nevertheless distinct subject in this context is how a particular doctrine should be interpreted; i.e. objectively or subjectively?[99] Are concepts such as mens rea or perpetration best conceived in an objective or a subjective manner? The objectivist approach departs from the premise that certain facts exist independently of the actor's mind and are objectively observable (such as for instance the fulfilment of the actus reus). Subjectivists reject the claim that there may be something like an "objective truth" and locate the seat of truth in the mind of the individual. In law, the subjectivist often queries "how did the defendant perceive the situation, his act? Did he according to his beliefs act, for instance, intentionally?" Thus, the clash between the subjective and the objective camp in regard to mens rea manifests itself in the question whether one should flesh out the notions of mens rea in a subjective or an objective manner.[100] Subjectivist frequently claim that the notions of mens rea ought to be constructed in terms of the defendant's own beliefs, capacities, intentions, etc. Objectivists on the other hand

97 See also: Ashworth, 'Defining criminal offences without harm', in Smith (ed), Criminal law – Essays in honour of J C Smith (1987), pp. 7–23.

98 See also: Chapter IV. 2.

99 See also: Chapter IV. 3.

100 See: Van Dijk, 'Strafrechtelijke Aansprakelijkheid heroverwogen – Over opzet, schuld, schulduitsluitingsgronden en straf' (2008), pp. 1–431. See also: Blomsma, 'Mens rea and defences in European criminal law' (2012).

claim that they should be construed according to the often invoked legal role-model i.e. the reasonable person, and should not be based on the actual state of mind of the defendant.[101]

Subjectivism certainly has its roots in the principle of individual autonomy on which the criminal law has traditionally been based.[102] However, it is increasingly recognised that individuals are also members of a community with mutual obligations, where common standards apply. Merely focusing on the individual thus neglects the social component and gives expression to a rather atomistic view of individual behaviour. Objectivism on the other hand, assesses individual behaviour in the social context according to objective (community) standards. Often rules of general experience, logic or other objective factors will play a role here, which however risk that certain individual factors and circumstances that bear on liability are not sufficiently taken into consideration in the case at hand. It should thus not come as a surprise that the objective/subjective distinction should not be seen as a strict dichotomy. To fully understand the doctrinal friction in criminal law one should be aware that objective and subjective views often interweave in the discussion and that both approaches are applied throughout the criminal law. A more realistic view on the matter would therefore be that "there are shades of subjectivism and objectivism along a spectrum".[103]

The distinction between a harm or culpability-centred criminal law as well as the objective/subjective distinction will serve as conceptual tools in this thesis in order to pigeon-hole different approaches regarding criminal liability and enhance our understanding of the respective approach by drawing attention to considerations underlying criminal liability. Where possible this research will highlight the doctrinal choices available for the legislator and practitioners and will attempt to discuss the effects of a given approach.

5.3. The framework of criminal liability

Criminal liability is often assessed according to a certain structure or framework. This framework constitutes another analytical tool in which criminal liability is assessed. It helps to structure and outline doctrines, concepts and principles in a systematic manner and provides practitioners with a logical scheme to assess the different elements.[104] English courts have traditionally followed a bipartite system simply distinguishing between objective (external) and subjective (internal) aspects of crime. Thus, criminal liability is deemed to require that a person commits the

---

101 Lacey, 'Responsibility and Modernity in Criminal Law' The Journal of Political Philosophy (2001), pp. 9–10, Simester and Sullivan, 'Criminal Law: Theory and Doctrine' (2007), p. 9.

102 Ashworth, 'Principles of criminal law' (2006), p. 244. See also: Norrie, 'Punishment, Responsibility and Justice' (2000), pp. 1–17.

103 Smith and Hogan, 'Criminal Law' (2008), p. 95.

104 See: Ambos, 'Toward a universal system of crime: Comments on George Fletcher's Grammar of Criminal Law' Cardozo Law Review (2007), pp. 2647–2673.

actus reus of an offence and possesses the corresponding mens rea.[105] This approach conflates mens rea, which can best be translated with fault element, with (moral) blameworthiness.[106] The two concepts however denote different things. A person could have fulfilled the objective elements of a criminal offence (i.e. the actus reus) with the corresponding fault element (i.e. mens rea) but still be able to escape liability due to the absence of blameworthiness. The latter is usually negated when an excusatory defence such as a mistake of law or duress is applicable. If Bart for instance provides false information to an authority, making him eligible for subsidies, not knowing that this constitutes a criminal offence (subsidy fraud) he will have committed the actus reus of the offence and has also acted intentionally with regard to the incorrectness of the information.[107] However, whether he can be blamed for his mistake is an entirely different question.

Actus reus and mens rea arguably constitute the first level in the evaluation scheme of criminal liability. Together they map out the definitional elements of a criminal offence. Besides this level one can also distinguish the levels of wrongfulness and blameworthiness. The former is generally negated by justificatory defences while the latter is negated by excusatory defences. In this way criminal liability is assessed in a tripartite evaluation scheme. When it can be proved that a person has committed the definition of an offence (actus reus and mens rea) the presence of wrongfulness and blameworthiness is generally assumed. Only if a justification can be invoked is wrongfulness negated or respectively blameworthiness in case of an excuse. These elements are traditionally not explicitly expressed in the offence definition in stark contrast to the requirements of actus reus and mens rea. This scheme does not only facilitate the proper classification of defences in justification and excuses but also has an important communicative function. If Ralph kills Simon under circumstances that amount to duress the law makes it explicit that Ralph's act was illegal and wrongful, but that for individual reasons he should not be blamed for the offence he committed.

The tripartite structure constitutes the prevalent approach in Germany and the Netherlands.[108] However, also in the English penal system the inadequacy of the mens rea/actus reus distinction is increasingly recognised.[109] In doctrinal writing

105 See for instance: Smith and Hogan, 'Criminal Law' (2008), p. 45.

106 See: Blomsma, 'Mens rea and defences in European criminal law' (2012).

107 Example taken from: Ambos, 'Is the development of a common substantive criminal law for Europe possible? Some Preliminary Reflections' Maastricht Journal of European and Comparative Law (2005), p. 179.

108 See: Bohlander, 'Principles of German Criminal Law' (2009), pp. 16 et seq, De Hullu, 'Materieel Strafrecht' (2009), pp. 149–212. For a critical evaluation of the tripartite structure see: Christopher, 'Tripartite structures of criminal law in Germany and other civil law jurisdictions' Cardozo Law Review (2007), pp. 2675–2695.

109 See: Robinson, 'Should the Criminal Law Abandon the Actus Reus – Mens Rea Distinction?', in Shute, et al. (eds), Action and Value in Criminal Law (1993), pp. 187–211.

the tripartite evaluation scheme seems by and large been accepted.[110] It seems therefore generally defensible that the tripartite evaluation structure of crime should also apply at the European level. It allows to better structure the evaluation of criminal liability and helps to distinguish the different doctrines and their effects on liability.

5.4. Criminal liability in the risk society

There has been a shift in the social and political framework of blame which has had a significant impact on contemporary conceptions of criminal liability. The social construction of events, their categorisation as accidents or crimes can be seen as one of the driving forces in every penal system.[111] The corollary flowing from this is that societal attitudes towards safety and risk will affect the propensity to blame as well as the target of this blame.[112] The importance of risk perception and risk assessment is increasingly recognised. One catchword which has been used to encapsulate these ongoing changes is "the risk society". This term, coined by the German sociologist Ulrich Beck, describes a society in which not the distribution of goods as in the traditional welfare state is central, but rather the distribution of "bads", i.e. the prevention and compensation of risks.[113] As Beck puts it, we are "living on the volcano of civilisation"[114], on a technological frontier which lies beyond our powers of conceptions and which creates an insecure future.[115] The risk society is one that creates "manufactured risks".[116] Science and technology not only make our lives safer, but at the same time they produce just as many risks and uncertainties.[117] Faced with these insecurities, the citizens of the risk society increasingly demand from their state, security, which has partially transformed the state into a risk management and prevention institution.

This also had an important impact on the law itself, as its institutions have become centres of risk management and of production of risk knowledge.[118] Accordingly, the law in general and criminal law in particular, is more and more concerned with the prevention of future harms than with the traditional

110 Fletcher, 'Rethinking Criminal Law' (1978), pp. 395–401, Fletcher, 'Basic Concepts of Criminal Law' (1998), pp. 82–85, Simester and Sullivan, 'Criminal Law: Theory and Doctrine' (2007), p. 666, Smith and Hogan, 'Criminal Law' (2005), p. 298.

111 Wells, 'Corporations and Criminal Responsibility' (2001), p. 40.

112 Wells, 'Corporations and Criminal Responsibility' (2001), p. 42.

113 Roef, 'Strafrechtelijke Verantwoordelijkheid in de Risicomaatschappij', in Vos and Calster (eds), Risico en voorzorg in de rechtsmaatschappij (2004), p. 203.

114 Beck, 'Risk Society – Towards a New Modernity' (1992), pp. 19–84.

115 Giddens, 'Risk and Responsibility' The Modern Law Review (1999), p. 4.

116 Giddens, 'Risk and Responsibility' The Modern Law Review (1999), p. 4.

117 Wells, 'Corporations and Criminal Responsibility' (2001), p. 42.

118 Wells, 'Corporations and Criminal Responsibility' (2001), p. 42.

retrospective punishment of manifested harm.[119] In addition, it has already been mentioned that the traditional focus of criminal law to protect individual interests has made way for the protection of collective interests like public health, security and socio-economic interests.[120] It has been recognised that the causes of risk are increasingly collective in nature. The causes of acid rain, particulate matter or the mad cow disease are highly complex and cannot easily be attributed to one or even several individuals.[121] It follows that the traditional concepts of individual liability are increasingly viewed as insufficient to deal with the ongoing complex processes in our society and are substituted by new forms of collective responsibility. As will tentatively be shown, criminal liability is more and more often based on the social role or position of a person or its membership to a certain group or category of citizens respectively. Consider for instance the position as a director, stakeholder, driver, entrepreneur, etc. which could be relevant to the attribution of liability.

The seeds of liability can thus nowadays already be discovered in the respective position or role as it is considered by society to entail responsibility for the risk that a certain crime will be committed. The paramount importance of the individual's conduct, i.e. his contribution to the manifestation of harm, traditionally the vantage point of criminal law has seemingly diminished.[122] Thus, the focus on risk prevention has arguably shifted the focus of the law away from the traditional offender to a new class of delinquents: those who create or control the opportunities for crime.[123] For instance, nowadays the primal focus in the assignment of blame is not on the employee who opens the valve to release oil into the ground water but rather on his supervisor or manager who created the opportunity by neglecting his duty of supervision or control. The importance of the aforementioned notion of control in the context of criminal liability should partially be evident here.

The corollary of these social developments is arguably an expansion of criminal liability. Criminal law is more and more invoked to address problems and conflicts in society, which is evidenced by the creation of many new penal offences. Furthermore, the focus on crime prevention, as already mentioned, has emphasised the instrumental crime control function of criminal law, at the expense of neglecting the law's safeguard function.[124]

---

119 Roef, 'Strafrechtelijke Verantwoordelijkheid in de Risicomaatschappij', in Vos and Calster (eds), Risico en voorzorg in de rechtsmaatschappij (2004), p. 209.

120 Roef, 'Strafrechtelijke Verantwoordelijkheid in de Risicomaatschappij', in Vos and Calster (eds), Risico en voorzorg in de rechtsmaatschappij (2004), p. 208.

121 Roef, 'Strafbare overheden – Een rechtsvergelijkende studie naar de strafrechtelijke aansprakelijkheid van overheden voor milieuverstoring' (2001), p. 32.

122 De Hullu, 'Zijn er grenzen aan de strafrechtelijke aansprakelijkheid?' (1993), pp. 30–39.

123 Shearing and Stenning, 'From the Panopticon to Disney World: The development of discipline', in Eugene McLaughlin, et al. (eds), Criminological Perspectives: Essential Readings (2003), p. 428.

124 See also: Ashworth, 'Conceptions of Overcriminalization' Ohio State Journal of Criminal Law (2008), pp. 407–425.

The law's struggle to effectively assign liability in an increasingly complex and high-risk society has moreover also led to an erosion or rethinking of traditional doctrines and differentiations which broadens the scope of liability.[125] If traditional boundaries and distinctions become blurred, inevitably more conduct will come under scrutiny.[126] This in turn can cause frictions with the principle of legality as legal concepts become vaguer. Vagueness however increases not only the potential scope of criminal law but also fosters flexibility which is a necessity for a criminal law that aims to provide citizens with security. To provide security from future risk, legal norms ought to be broad and flexible enough to address new and ever-changing societal problems.

These social changes have however not only impacted on the concept of liability but affected the entire criminal justice system which has triggered a change in the contemporary conception of crime. This has caused shifts in policing, sentencing, punishment, criminological theory, penal policy and so on. Overall, there seems to be a trend towards more punitiveness fostered by a new collective experience of insecurity within penal systems.[127] A new "culture of control" has emerged and spread among western penal systems by which we strive to come to terms with the risks and insecurities of the 21st century.[128] The described social developments are also of relevance for European criminal law. With the new and improved competences of the European Union in the realm of criminal law comes namely also a risk that, in the spirit of the culture of control, criminal sanctions will increasingly be used to enforce a big variety of European rules as well as for political and symbolic purposes, to provide citizens with the high level of security, as proclaimed by Article 67 TFEU. In order not to undermine the safeguard function of criminal law and due to the far-reaching implications of criminal law for individual rights and liberties such a development should certainly be avoided.[129]

These social trends and developments will form the background to the following discussion on criminal liability. Wherever possible this research will highlight the repercussions that the change in attitude towards crime has had on the interpretation and application of traditional criminal law doctrines. New tendencies in the context of criminal liability will be tentatively explained by reference to sociological and criminological literature. This will facilitate a critical appraisal of these

125 See: Roef, 'Strafrechtelijke Verantwoordelijkheid in de Risicomaatschappij', in Vos and Calster (eds), Risico en voorzorg in de rechtsmaatschappij (2004), pp. 201–226.

126 Hassemer, 'Kennzeichen und Krisen des modernen Strafrechts' Zeitschrift für Rechtspolitik (1992), p. 382.

127 Garland, 'The culture of high crime societies' British Journal of Criminology (2000), pp. 354–364.

128 See: Garland, 'The Culture of Control – Crime and Social Order in Contemporary Society' (2006), pp. 1–53.

129 See also: Klip, 'Criminal Law in the European Union' (2005), pp. 53–55, Klip, 'European Criminal Law' (2012), p. 26.

developments in the light of certain fundamental principles of criminal law as well as the identification of pitfalls and shortcomings.

Thus having set the scene for the analysis to come by discussing several preliminary issues and concepts, the quest may now commence towards the establishment of general principles of European criminal law.

Chapter II
Perpetration – The elements of crime

1. Introduction

This chapter begins by discussing the doctrine of conduct (including acts and omissions) and its underlying rationale. Secondly the doctrine of causation will be discussed before the focus will turn to the issue of participation in crime in Chapter III.

The discussion on criminal liability will commence from the paradigm case that one person brings about a prohibited criminal result. One can think here of incidents such as the killing of a human being, the stealing of a car, the trafficking in drugs, arms or human beings. These incidents can also be described in terms of the actus reus and mens rea of a particular criminal offence, which on the one hand mirror the age old Cartesian dualism of body and soul and on the other hand gives expression to the distinction between wrongdoing and culpability which pervades the criminal law and shapes its doctrines.

The concept of actus reus constitutes a basic building block of criminal liability. At a purely descriptive level the element of actus reus outlines the conduct made criminal by some statutory offence or other valid source of criminal law. It is prima facie fulfilled if a person has committed an instance of the type of conduct described in it. At a more normative level however, the core function of the notion "actus reus", besides being a conceptual tool, arguably is to establish a link between the person and the occurred criminal harm.[130] If such a connection can be established, criminal liability can be imposed and the person will be deemed to be the perpetrator of the occurred harm. Thus, the concept of actus reus translates an empirical event into a criminal one. The exact content of the actus reus depends of course on the particular underlying offence, and influences what elements the prosecution needs to prove. Depending on the constituent elements of the underlying offence, one can distinguish different categories of crimes. There are a myriad of grounds on which criminal liability can be imposed, and more may be developed in the future, but traditionally criminal liability rests on three pillars. The first is the conduct of the person held criminally liable, the second is the causal connection between the conduct and the harm, and the third is fault. Depending on which elements are enshrined in a particular offence definition one can distinguish different modes of crimes or criminal liability.[131]

---

130 Van Dijk, 'Strafrechtelijke Aansprakelijkheid heroverwogen – Over opzet, schuld, schulduitsluitingsgronden en straf' (2008), p. 7.

131 Hart and Honoré, 'Causation in the Law' (1985), p. xliv. The following brief evaluation can of course not claim to be exhaustive as there are other forms of lability conceivable such as risk liability, etc.

One of the most basic distinctions is the one between conduct and result crimes. Result crimes are offences for which the law requires a specific result to occur; the most prominent examples being murder, manslaughter, wounding, etc. Hence, the offence definition here requires conduct, causation and fault to be proven. Conduct crimes, like perjury, on the other hand do not require a specific result, but are consummated once the prohibited conduct has taken place. Thus, only conduct and fault need to be proven here; a causal connection is not required. In regard to conduct crimes the wrongdoing is constituted by the conduct itself, whereas result crimes prohibit a wide range of conduct if they lead to the prescribed harm. By contrast, in regard to another category of offences, i.e. inchoate crimes the subjective disposition of the offender seemingly constitutes the primary ground for responsibility.[132]

In any case, it is moreover also possible that only conduct and causation need to be proven, regardless of fault. These crimes are often referred to as strict liability offences. Strict liability offences constitute an exemption to the principle of guilt enshrined in the Latin phrase *nulla poena sine culpa* and can arguably only be justified on utilitarian reasons of effectiveness and efficiency. Strict liability offences are an integral part of the English and Dutch penal system and are often utilised in economic and regulatory offences. In Germany however, where the principle of guilt is interpreted rather strictly as it enjoys constitutional status and is also implied in §§15 and 18 of the German Criminal Code, strict liability is generally rejected. In the context of the European Union, strict liability seems to have been accepted by the ECJ in some circumstances. In regard to environmental law the ECJ held for instance that certain Articles in Directive 2004/35 […]

> must be interpreted as meaning that when deciding to impose remedial measures on operators whose activities fall within Annex III to the directive, the competent authority is not required to establish fault, negligence or intent on the part of operators whose activities are held to be responsible for the environmental damage.[133]

Finally, criminal liability can also arise from the violation of a duty of care in which case the notions of conduct, fault and causation can become fused together in a duty of care. Yet, leaving these different modes of liability aside and returning to the focal point of this discussion, an actus reus can also encompass certain further circumstances. These can for instance require certain qualities in the person who commits the crime or a further list of conditions which need to be fulfilled in order for criminal liability to arise.[134] Circumstances are thus facts which further specify

---

132 See also: Chapter IV.

133 9 March 2010, Case C-378/08, *Raffinerie Mediterranee (ERG) SpA, Polimeri Europa SpA and Syndial SpA v Ministero dello Sviluppo economico and Others*, [2010] ECR I-01919, para 65.

134 Note that the qualification of offences in Germany and partially also in the Netherlands is complex and overly dogmatic. See: De Hullu, 'Materieel Strafrecht' (2009), pp. 65–85, Roxin, 'Strafrecht Allgemeiner Teil, Band I Grundlagen: Der Aufbau der Verbrechenslehre' (2006), pp. 329–342. The Dutch and the German penal system also know the category of endangerment

the actus reus. Take for instance the offence of handling stolen property. The fact that the property in question is stolen, which the offender could have been aware of can be seen as a circumstantial element as it further specifies the actus reus of the offence. In Germany and the Netherlands circumstances are usually part and parcel of the actus reus and are therefore seldom explicitly distinguished. The distinction is however of importance in English law where the different elements of the actus reus can be subject to different mens rea standards. As will subsequently become apparent in the realm of attempt liability, English law often requires intention as to the consequence element of the actus reus while a lower degree of fault is often considered sufficient in regard to the circumstantial element.

What is however more important for the purpose of this research is that the actus reus or objective element of an offence generally is considered to include the doctrines of conduct (including omissions), causation as well as consequences and circumstances.[135] It already becomes evident from this enumeration that what is commonly referred to as the actus reus requirement is in fact a collection of entirely distinct doctrines with different functions.[136] Hence, it can be said that the actus reus is very much a heterogeneous concept.[137]

2. The doctrine of conduct or the conundrum of the baseline of criminal liability

2.1. Introduction

The doctrine of conduct plays an important role in regard to establishing and describing general preconditions for criminal liability. It constitutes a crucial yardstick in the quest of the courts to identify a criminally relevant conduct on which the imposition of criminal liability can be based. The conduct requirement is traditionally closely linked to the principle of individual autonomy as well as to the principle of legality. This is because on the one hand the conduct requirement is traditionally aimed to ensure that the law treats citizens as responsible beings capable of rational choice, and on the other gives them fair warning regarding the possible incident of criminal liability.

It is a fundamental question whether or not a conduct has occurred which warrants the application of criminal law and sanctions. Holding people liable

offences which do not require the occurrence of criminal harm, but are already consummated when a danger to a legally protected interest has been created. This category is alien to English law.

135 Bohlander, 'Principles of German Criminal Law' (2009), p. 29, De Hullu, 'Materieel Strafrecht' (2009), pp. 149–199, Roxin, 'Strafrecht Allgemeiner Teil, Band I Grundlagen: Der Aufbau der Verbrechenslehre' (2006), pp. 306–307, Smith and Hogan, 'Criminal Law' (2008), pp. 42–93.

136 Robinson, 'Should the Criminal Law Abandon the Actus Reus – Mens Rea Distinction?', in Shute, et al. (eds), Action and Value in Criminal Law (1993), pp. 187–211.

137 Ashworth, 'Principles of criminal law' (2006), p. 98.

despite doing nothing or because something happened to them would not only fail to respect citizens' autonomy but furthermore make the application of criminal law an arbitrary enterprise.

Regardless of the qualification of the offence, there is one common element without which no criminal liability can arise. All penal systems generally seem to agree that the imposition of criminal liability requires at the very least some form of conduct, controlled by the perpetrator. Generally put, some form of conduct constitutes the basic building block of an actus reus. This fundamental requirement is in legal theory often referred to as the "act requirement". However, the term act requirement is slightly misleading as it suggests that the imposition of criminal liability always requires an (voluntary) *act*. This is however a misconception as the criminal law also punishes people for offences of omissions, state of affairs and possessions, which can hardly be reconciled with the alleged requirement of an act. These offences suggest that there may be more to acts than mere voluntary *movements*.[138]

State of affair offences are problematic and controversial as they impose criminal liability for status rather than conduct and have therefore in some jurisdiction been declared unconstitutional.[139] They are to be treated with great caution as they impose liability for a state of affair which the law prohibits and with which the defendant is in some way connected.[140] Offences of this type are commonly associated with tyrannical regimes where for instance being an addict, being disabled or being a member of a particular political organisation, race or religion respectively is criminalised. Despite their controversial nature they remain however part of English law. Section 4 (2) of the Road Traffic Act 1988 criminalises for instance the state of affair of *being* in charge of a motor vehicle on a road or other public place while *being* unfit to drive through drink or drugs. Likewise, section 444 (1) of the Education Act 1996 holds the parent of a child of compulsory school age liable if the child fails to attend regularly at school.[141] These offences seem to impose liability in the absence of wrong*doing* but, as will subsequently become clear, are, if certain requirements are fulfilled not contrary to principle.[142] It should however be reiterated that status offences should be treated with great caution as they may stray too far from the paradigm

---

138 Wilson, 'Central Issues in Criminal Theory' (2002), p. 80.

139 See for example: Robinson v State of California, 370 US 660; Powell v State of Texas 392 US 514 (1968).

140 Glazebrook, 'Situational liability', in Glazebrook (ed), Reshaping the criminal law – Essays in honour of Glanville Williams (1978), pp. 108–119.

141 An instructive decision here is also the case of R v Larsonneur [1933] 24 Cr App R 74. Mrs Larsonneur, a French citizen was ordered to leave the UK. She went to the Irish Free State to avoid deportation but was detected and brought back to Liverpool by the police. She was convicted for being found in the UK as an alien to whom stay in the UK had been refused.

142 See: Chapter II. 2.2. In Germany and the Netherlands such situations would probably be tackled by imposing a duty of care on the driver, respectively the parent.

of criminal wrongdoing and may furthermore be used for highly objectionable purposes.[143]

Related to state of affair offences are possession offences. Possession offences are numerous in contemporary criminal law and also constitute on first sight a challenge to the claim that criminal liability is based on some sort of conduct.[144] However, possession is often defined in criminal law as an act of acquiring possession or an omission to rid oneself of possession, which in term puts the contradiction into perspective. Furthermore, it can be argued that in both situations the imposition of liability can be defended if the offender can be considered to have exerted control over the possession or state of affair. This minimum requirement may be satisfied if they resulted from prior conduct, or could have been averted by suitable conduct which could have reasonably been expected of the offender.[145]

In any case, it seems more appropriate to use the term *conduct* to refer to human actions, as it is broad enough to not only encompass bodily movements which will often constitute the standard form of criminal conduct but also the behaviour enshrined in the aforementioned offences of omission and possession. The view that criminal responsibility requires an act, as well as its methodological corollary that legal theory requires a theory of action has long held the criminal law hostage and has, as will become apparent below, led to the creation of a multitude of diverse theories of action.

In Germany the act requirement is central to the attribution of criminal liability; it is seen as its basic element. From a systematic point of view, the act requirement stands at the very beginning of the evaluation process into criminal liability. In England the act requirement is also seen as a fundamental principle of criminal law and forms part of the analysis of the actus reus.[146] It is most clearly visible in the defence of (sane) automatism which, if successful, denies the occurrence of the actus reus.[147] This goes to show that English criminal law generally departs from the presumption that the conduct was criminally relevant and only if the defendant can raise sufficient evidence to the contrary will the issue arise in courts.[148] To some extent the Dutch and German system proceed from the same presumption as the conduct requirement only rarely causes problems in practice. In the Dutch penal system the act requirement plays a central role in attributing criminal liability but is

143 Smith and Hogan, 'Criminal Law' (2008), pp. 58–60, Wilson, 'Central Issues in Criminal Theory' (2002), pp. 82–83.

144 For a general discussion of possession offences see: Chapter IV. 6.2.

145 See: Duff, 'Answering for Crime' (2007), pp. 105–107.

146 Simester and Sullivan, 'Criminal Law: Theory and Doctrine' (2007), pp. 103–104, Smith and Hogan, 'Criminal Law' (2008), pp. 51–58. See also: Bratty v A-G for Northern Ireland [1961] 3 All ER 523.

147 The defense of automatism is currently up for review in the English penal system. See: Insanity and automatism: a Scoping Paper (Law Commission 18 July 2012) and Insanity and automatism: Supplementary Material to the Scoping Paper (Law Commission 18 July 2012).

148 See: Bratty v A-G for Northern Ireland [1961] 3 All ER 523, Simester and Sullivan, 'Criminal Law: Theory and Doctrine' (2007), p. 118.

not regarded as *the* basic concept of criminal law as is the case in Germany.[149] It is generally recognised that human conduct bringing about a prohibited result will often consist of actions and omissions alike.[150]

The concept is thus, arguably best seen, as a legal one concerned with questions of criminal liability rather than with metaphysics. This more flexible approach is also apparent in Dutch legislation. Take for instance Art 307 DPC (negligent manslaughter) which reads as follows: "He to whom the death of another person is imputable is punished [...]". This wording bears witness to the fact that the emphasis does not exclusively lie on physical conduct. Furthermore in regard to economic crimes the conduct in a criminal provision is often defined not only in physical but often merely in causal terms (e.g. to export).

The focus on the criminal conduct also constitutes an answer to the question: what is punishment imposed for? When the focal point lies on the criminal conduct, one can speak of an act-based criminal law as opposed to an attitude or guilt-based criminal law, where punishment focuses on the guilt or subjective disposition of the offender regardless of any action.[151] An act based criminal law departs from the assumption that the act can be abstracted from the circumstances of its commission and from the offender himself.[152] Of course, also in an act-based criminal law it is necessary to prove the culpability of the offender, but this is subsidiary to the focal point, i.e. the act. In this line of thinking, Germany[153] and the Netherlands[154] can be classified as predominantly[155] act-based criminal laws. The English penal system seems to be more guilt based, but as already mentioned, also in this system an important role is played by the act requirement.[156] There the importance of subjective factors becomes particularly visible with respect to the demarcation of different concepts, notions and doctrines which is often sought along the lines of mens rea, rather than by invoking objective criteria. However, it should be added here that due to the fact that in all systems conduct is increasingly conceived in a more functional and abstract way and as omissions and duties of care become more and more important, the concept of an act-based criminal law becomes more diffuse. While the traditional criminal law of the enlightenment can be considered

---

149 See: Remmelink, 'Inleiding tot de studie van het Nederlandse Strafrecht' (1995), p. 171. See also: Walter Gropp, Strafrecht allgemeiner Teil, Springer 2005: Es gibt kein Strafrecht ohne Straftat und keine Straftat ohne Handlung.

150 De Hullu, 'Materieel Strafrecht' (2009), pp. 149–154, 171–173, Knigge, 'Doen en laten; enkele opmerkingen over daderschap' Delikt en Delinkwent (1992), pp. 128–154.

151 Fletcher, 'The Grammar of Criminal Law' (2007), pp. 28, 32–35. See also: Schönke and Schröder, 'Kommentar zum Strafgesetzbuch' (2006), Vorbem §13 Mn 3.

152 Fletcher, 'The Grammar of Criminal Law' (2007), p. 29.

153 Roxin, 'Strafrecht Allgemeiner Teil, Band I Grundlagen: Der Aufbau der Verbrechenslehre' (2006), p. 185.

154 De Hullu, 'Materieel Strafrecht' (2009), p. 149.

155 Predominately, because some recent developments in these systems clearly have guilt or actor-based connotations.

156 Ashworth, 'Grunderfordernisse des Allgemeinen Teils für ein europäisches Sanktionsrecht: Landesbericht England' ZStW (1998), pp. 462, 467.

as predominately act-based where an offender was judged according to his deed, it will be shown that in the criminal law of the culture of control the focus has shifted from the act to the actor.[157] Not the deed but rather the defendant's social role or position as well as his dangerousness become increasingly important.

2.2. The doctrine of conduct and the criminal law's image of man

The rules of criminal law constitute a scheme by which the imposition of criminal liability is guided. This scheme has as one of its goals the assurance that the imposition of criminal liability is fair and just in every individual case. Underlying this scheme is an image of man firmly rooted in the Enlightenment tradition.[158] In other words, at the core of criminal law lies the notion of the "average person" who is held responsible for his/her conduct (i.e. act or omission). As already mentioned, the image of man underlying the criminal law, is fundamental to the attribution of criminal liability in every contemporary penal justice system.[159] The issue also has close ties and is influenced by the contentious philosophical question of what is it that makes us responsible.

This underlying conception of man plays such a pivotal role in criminal law that "imagining a criminal law without it, would be like imaging a physics in which the speed of light through a vacuum is not constant".[160] This implies that first and foremost criminal law is concerned with the attribution of criminal liability and that the subject of criminal law must possess certain capacities in order to be rightfully held responsible.[161] It would be unreasonable to hold people criminally liable for conduct that is irreproachable. This constitutes a fundamental principle for the criminal law of a democratic society founded on the universal values of human dignity and the rule of law.[162]

The idea of a self-determining moral agent, bestowed with cognitive and volitional capacities of understanding and self control i.e. characteristics of the "average person" is deeply rooted in Western penal systems. Thus, criminal liability generally rests on a cognitive and a volitional pillar. The former refers to the person's intellectual capacities such as the ability to reason and distinguish right from wrong. The latter refers to the ability to control one's behaviour, to act goal-orientated and to decide whether to pursue or reject that goal. As already mentioned, the concept of

---

157 De Jong, 'Daad-Schuld' (2009), pp. 64, 68.

158 Lacey, 'Responsibility and Modernity in Criminal Law' The Journal of Political Philosophy (2001), p. 251.

159 Alldridge, 'Relocating Criminal Law' (2000), p. 69, Morse, 'Criminal Responsibility And The Disappearing Person' Cardozo Law Review (2007), p. 2545, Wilson, 'Central Issues in Criminal Theory' (2002), p. 104.

160 Alldridge, 'Relocating Criminal Law' (2000), p. 69.

161 Mooij, 'Handelingsvrijheid' Delikt en Delinkwent (1999), p. 840.

162 Also the European Union is based on these values. See: The Preamble to the Charter of Fundamental Rights of the European Union and Art 1, OJ 2007/C 303/01.

control takes an important baseline function in this respect and is closely linked to agency.[163] As responsible agents we possess the ability to control events in the outside world. By controlling our conduct we participate in, influence and change the social and material world around us. It is arguably only events over which we exerted some sort of control and which accordingly constitute an expression of agency for which we can be held responsible.[164] To hold otherwise would make people liable for events the occurrence of which lay outside their powers or were unavoidable. The law would then demand the impossible from its citizens.

Generally speaking, if a person lacking these characteristics causes harm to others, the criminal law should not attribute liability to him as he fell short of the average person standard and can therefore not be blamed for his conduct. Yet, the requirement of control (physical and rational or cognitive and volitional) only imposes minimum restraints on criminal law. This is due to the fact that the prima facie presumption that an agent cannot be held responsible for an event over which at the time of the commission he had no control can be rebutted by showing that at an earlier time he could have acted in a way that the event would not have occurred. Furthermore, it would also be mistaken to think that we can only be held responsible for effects over which we have complete control. The control humans exert over chain of events is often not complete and the occurrence or non-occurrence of a particular event is often to some degree a matter of luck, a fact which does not bar the imposition of criminal liability and will become clearer in the subsequent discussion on causation and attempt liability.

For the aforementioned problematic state of affair offences this means that they arguably ought to be condemned if they impose absolute liability, i.e. if they do not allow an accused to adjust his behaviour to remain within the boundaries of the law. However, they may constitute an acceptable basis for liability in some situations, given that the offence in question provides for a due diligence defence or requires proof that the punishable state of affairs was caused by the defendant or he failed to terminate it or failed to act in order to do so, when it was within his control and possible to do so.[165] Such an approach would ensure that liability only arises for state of affairs over which the defendant had some sort of control or where it would have been reasonable for him to have avoided getting caught up in the relevant state of affair or event.

2.2.1. The image of man in the Risk Society

This image of man has however come under pressure in the modern risk society.[166] Modern scientific insights have shed some doubt on the image of man underlying

---

163 See also: Chapter I. 5.1.

164 Duff, 'Answering for Crime' (2007), p. 58.

165 Smith and Hogan, 'Criminal Law' (2008), p. 60, Wilson, 'Central Issues in Criminal Theory' (2002), p. 83.

166 See: Morse, 'Criminal Responsibility And The Disappearing Person' Cardozo Law Review (2007), pp. 2545–2575.

and grounding the criminal law, but until now criminal law has by and large ignored the potentially far-reaching implications.[167] Modern science increasingly treats man as the mere product of his genes and environment. Humanity has to a certain extent been demystified by science. Due to this, human behaviour becomes more predictable and, more importantly, controllable. With the support of modern science and technology it has namely become easier to identify and label certain segments of society as risk groups and accordingly monitor and control their behaviour. Most crucially however, if we really are the product of our genes and environment, then our behaviour is determined by biological and environmental factors. This would deprive criminal law of its very basis as it imposes punishment for the free choices that we make.[168] Simply put, the view of criminal law cannot be reconciled with the image of man advocated by modern science. In criminal law we do not talk in terms of forces, genes, impulses and "firing neurons", but rather in terms of perceptions, intentions and objectives.[169] Central to the criminal law's image of man is the concept of a "human subject" as opposed to an object. Enlightenment thinkers emphasised that humans ought to be treated as subjects and not as a means to an end. The distinction between subject and object runs through the entire criminal law and provides useful insights into fundamental questions like who and what we are punishing for.

A subject is the origin of conduct and (self-) perception, as opposed to an object as something that is acted upon.[170] Yet, a subject possesses not only self – but also social – perception. The subject is focused on the world around him. His conduct is goal-orientated. Humans act because they strive to achieve something and by planning their action they can take into account the laws and probabilities of the world around them.[171]

The key feature of a subject is however the possibility of reflection. Humans' possess reason and (usually) the ability to distinguish right from wrong. Thus, it seems generally accepted that the conduct requirement is connected to a particular conception of criminal responsibility. This responsibility for crime is believed to be founded in a certain set of capacities.[172] It is our capacities for knowledge, awareness, reflection, deliberation and choice, which justify holding people responsible for their conduct.[173] Due to the fact that the law departs from the assumption that humans are free to choose their actions using their capacities, the

---

167 See: Mackor, 'Strafrecht en neurowetenschappen. Hoop, huiver of hype?' Rechtsfilosofie & Rechtstheorie (2010), pp. 3–8, Mooij, 'Toerekeningsvatbaarheid' (2004), pp. 14–37.

168 Mooij, 'Toerekeningsvatbaarheid' (2004), pp. 74–108, Vedder, 'Convergerende technologieën, verschuivende verantwoordelijkheden' Justitiele verkenningen (2008), pp. 54–66.

169 Mooij, 'Toerekeningsvatbaarheid' (2004), p. 17.

170 Mooij, 'Toerekeningsvatbaarheid' (2004), p. 17.

171 Mooij, 'Toerekeningsvatbaarheid' (2004), p. 17.

172 See for instance: Hart, 'Punishment and Responsibility' (2008), pp. 90–238, Mooij, 'Toerekeningsvatbaarheid' (2004), pp. 109–120.

173 Lacey, 'Responsibility and Modernity in Criminal Law' The Journal of Political Philosophy (2001), p. 255.

law holds us responsible for our choices. One could term these capacities "rational agent capacities". The responsible subject in the view of criminal law is an individual who possessed, or could have possessed the relevant knowledge of the context in which he acted or omitted to act and who had a fair opportunity to act otherwise.[174] The very baseline of criminal responsibility thus lies in the capacity to understand and control the (wrongful) conduct. We are not to be held responsible for who we are, or for our social status, but for the specific acts we do or refrain from doing.[175] However, new developments in crime control have also called this basic assumption into question.

What has fundamentally changed is our view of the delinquent. While offenders in the early sixties and seventies were perceived as citizens in need of support, they are now sometimes depicted as undeserving, dangerous individuals who need to be controlled by all means necessary.[176] Once the Rubicon into criminality has been crossed, the offender is no longer seen as a subject but rather as an abstract object, more or less deprived of citizenship status.[177] The German scholar Günther Jakobs has coined the term "criminal law for enemies" (*Feindstrafrecht*) which seeks to get rid of or at least to neutralise the offender.[178] While Jakobs describes the inevitability of a "criminal law for enemies" and claims that certain offenders ought to be treated as enemies, the term will be used here as an analytical tool and such a criminal law will be considered part of an undesirable development, which ought to be avoided.[179] Yet, arguably, tendencies of this kind are discernable in modern criminal law. It has already been mentioned that modern society has developed a "culture of control" in which crime prevention and management becomes the priority objective.[180] The most visible are those tendencies in regard to anti-terrorism legislation which can be found at national as well as at European level. Especially the dubious European practice of blacklisting alleged terrorist and freezing their assets can be named here. However there are other, less controversial tendencies discernible, which show that indeed criminal law gradually departs from the paradigm of an act-based criminal law and for the sake of crime prevention comes closer to an attitude based criminal law or a "criminal law for enemies". One can refer here to the increasing criminalisation of preparatory acts, the punishment of impossible attempts as well as the more and more common implementation of duties of care and endangerment

174 Lacey, 'Responsibility and Modernity in Criminal Law' The Journal of Political Philosophy (2001), p. 255.

175 Lacey, 'Responsibility and Modernity in Criminal Law' The Journal of Political Philosophy (2001), p. 255.

176 Garland, 'The Culture of Control – Crime and Social Order in Contemporary Society' (2006), p. 175.

177 Garland, 'The Culture of Control – Crime and Social Order in Contemporary Society' (2006), p. 181.

178 Jakobs, 'Bürgerstrafrecht und Feindstrafrecht' Ritsumeikan Law Review (2004), pp. 93–107.

179 Roxin, 'Strafrecht Allgemeiner Teil, Band I Grundlagen: Der Aufbau der Verbrechenslehre' (2006), pp. 55–56.

180 See: Chapter I. 5.4.

offences. In all these areas one can clearly see a shift away from wrongful conduct towards the (criminal) attitude and proclivities of the offender.[181] While these trends are clearly visible in all penal system and can be explained by the quest for crime prevention in modernity, it is submitted that one should not depart too far from the concept of an act-based criminal law as it would shift the focus to elusive concepts such as attitude. which do not warrant the application of the states most fearsome power, i.e. criminal punishment. Criminal liability ought to remain firmly based on the culpable commission of a wrongful conduct by a rational agent. Respect for human dignity in a liberal, democratic society arguably requires that people are treated as responsible subjects rather as objects of control. However, these developments and tendencies, outlined above, constitute a threat to criminal law as we know it. The objectified conception of human beings propelled by (neuro) science, and the focus on crime prevention as well as dangerousness arguably undermines the very foundation of criminal law. If conduct and more generally the subjects of law are stripped of their moral basis, the imposition of punishment seems no longer justifiable. What would remain is a pure instrument of behaviour control where no longer the fact that a person acted wrongfully will give rise to punishment but rather the fact that one poses a danger to the status quo will lead to negative reinforcement by means of sanctions. According to this point of view society would thus become a giant 'skinner-box'.

2.2.2. *Is criminal liability confined to human conduct?*

So far the discussion has focused exclusively on the hallmarks of human conduct and capacities, but it should not be overlooked that in some penal systems next to humans, legal entities as well can incur criminal liability. Legal entities, and especially large scale corporations, have secured a pivotal place in our everyday lives. They have arisen in the slip stream of the industrial revolution and have evolved to powerful entities wielding substantial financial, legal, political and social influence. But while some legal entities have proven to be a valuable asset to our society, not least by contributing to the national economy, some companies seem to repeatedly cause property damage, endanger the public, cause large scale financial losses or even cause serious physical injury and death. In other words, corporate crime has become a new species of wrongdoing in our modern, capitalist society.[182]

However, the concept of corporate criminal liability is a controversial one and the cardinal question which divides penal systems is whether or not corporations are fit subjects of criminal law. One reason why penal systems grapple with the concept of corporate criminal liability is that criminal law is a child of the

181 Heinrich, 'Die Grenzen des Strafrechts bei der Gefahrenprävention' ZStW (2009), pp. 94–130.

182 For an overview on the causes of corporate wrongdoing see: Friedrichs, 'ENRON et al.: Paradigmatic white collar crime cases for the new century' Critical Criminology (2004), pp. 113–132, Punch, 'Suit violence: Why managers murder and corporations kill' Crime, Law & Social Change (2000), pp. 243–280.

Enlightenment and the ideology of liberalism, which both emphasise the ultimate value of the individual person and individual responsibility.[183] As mentioned before, criminal liability is traditionally perceived to rest on individuals who we deem equipped with the natural capacity to rationalise their actions and to possess the autonomy to causally control them. This stern individualist focus can certainly be seen as a Western cultural bias, but with the increasing globalisation and interconnection of the world, as well as with the increasing importance of collective entities in our society we have also come to recognise that individualism is not the only prism through which we can view the organisation of life and attribution of responsibility.

Whereas in the Netherlands[184] and England[185] it is generally accepted that corporations can be subjects of criminal law, this position is rejected in Germany. Although the German penal system imposes administrative sanctions on legal entities in criminal law, the dogma of "*societas delinquere non potest*" is still prevalent. As the conduct of legal entities, so the argument goes, is not subjected to volitional control (in the sense of conduct controlled by will), they cannot act in a way relevant to the imposition of criminal liability.[186] Thus, German criminal law adheres to an individualistic stance where for the imposition of criminal liability only the acts of individuals can be relevant, even though the conduct in question constitutes a collective effort to bring about a certain result. This argument, based on the semantic of action however is hardly convincing.

It is submitted here that corporations can be subjects of criminal law. Corporations in our society have become influential actors, make deliberate, rational choices and thereby interact with society. They also exert control over their actions in ways not too different from humans. It is therefore argued that corporations possess "rational agent capacities" and that their conduct can therefore constitute the foundation for the attribution of criminal liability. They take rational

---

183 Wells, 'Corporations and Criminal Responsibility' (2001), p. 65.

184 Article 51of the Dutch Penal Code (DPC) reads as follows:
(1) Criminal acts can be committed by natural and legal persons.
(2) Where a criminal act is committed by a legal person, criminal proceedings may be initiated and such penalties and measures as are prescribed by law, where applicable, may be imposed:
  1. against the legal person, or
  2. against those who have ordered the commission of the act, and against those who have in fact supervised the unlawful behaviour, or,
  3. against the persons mentioned under 1 and 2. jointly.
(3) In the application of the preceding paragraphs, the following are deemed to be equivalent to a legal person: the unincorporated commercial association [vennootschap zonder rechtspersoonlijkheid], the partnership, the ship-owing firm and the special fund [doelvermogen].

185 See for instance the Corporate Manslaughter and Corporate Homicide Act 2007.

186 Roxin, 'Strafrecht Allgemeiner Teil, Band I Grundlagen: Der Aufbau der Verbrechenslehre' (2006), p. 239, Wessels and Beulke, 'Strafrecht Allgemeiner Teil, Die Straftat und ihr Aufbau' (2008), p. 33.

decisions on the market and possess the capacity for self-organisation and to adapt themselves to the ever-changing economic environment. Thus, corporations although lacking feelings and emotions nevertheless possess capacities for intelligent agency. The lack of emotions in this regard may accordingly foster rather than hamper rational choice.[187]

Admittedly, the conduct of corporations will be less tangible than human conduct and will often take the form of a violation of a duty of care. Furthermore, concepts like actus reus and mens rea are not readily applicable in the realm of corporate wrongdoing. These primarily "human concepts" cannot be applied easily to an inanimate fictional entity.[188] But this does not diminish the fact that corporations reportedly become engaged in criminal acts, and that we frequently in everyday life hold them responsible for their wrongdoing.[189] Thus, the prosecution of corporations within the orthodox model of criminal law creates difficulties; the modalities of overcoming such difficulties will be explored later. For the moment it is important to note that also the conduct of legal entities can constitute the basis for the attribution of criminal liability.

Such an approach would also be in line with the increasing efforts to tackle corporate wrongdoing flowing from the international or supranational plane. As corporations increasingly operate internationally, or even globally, it becomes more and more important for states to cooperate and bundle their efforts to counteract corporate crime. The European Union for instance in its second protocol to the Convention on the Protections of the European Communities Financial Interest requires Member States to impose criminal liability on legal entities for fraud, money-laundering and corruption.[190] Furthermore, the Joint Action on making it a criminal offence to participate in a criminal organisation in the Member States of the EU calls on Member States to hold legal entities criminally liable for offences set out in the legal instrument.[191] By the same token organisations like the OECD and the Council of Europe have increasingly targeted legal entities especially in regard to the ongoing fight against economic and environmental crime.[192]

If it is accepted that corporations are fit subjects of criminal law, one is subsequently faced with the question as to the nature of corporate personality. As when faced with the question of what constitutes the "average person" in the realm

---

187 Fisse and Braithwaite, 'The allocation of responsibility for corporate crime: Individualism, Collectivisim and Accountability' Sydney Law Review (1988), p. 487.

188 Gobert and Punch, 'Rethinking Corporate Crime' (2003), p. 10.

189 See: Punch, 'Suit violence: Why managers murder and corporations kill' Crime, Law & Social Change (2000), pp. 243–280.

190 Second Protocol of 19 July 1997 to the Convention on the protection of the European Communities' financial interests, OJ 1997, C 221.

191 Joint Action 98/733 of 21 December 1998 on making it a criminal offence to participate in a criminal organisation in the Member States of the European Union, OJ 1998, L 351.

192 For a general overview see: Huber, 'Corporate Criminal Liability: Requirements under International Conventions and Application in European Countries', in Cherif Bassiouni, et al. (eds), European Cooperation In Penal Matters: Issues and Perspectives (2008), pp. 295–313.

of criminal law it will now be necessary to address the question on what does it mean to be a corporate actor. By the same token as the answer above hinged on the underlying image of man, the answer to the nature of corporate personality depends partially on how corporations are perceived.

Regarding the nature of corporate personality, one can distinguish two diametrically opposed points of view. The atomic (or nominalist) view regards legal entities as nothing more than collectivities of individuals.[193] According to this line of thought, a corporation is simply a term for the collectivity of individuals, and the idea that the corporation itself can act and be at fault is merely a fiction.[194] On the other hand, the organic (or realist) view claims that an organisation has an existence independent of its individual members. According to this view, a legal entity is more than just the sum of its parts.[195] Accordingly, organisations are deemed to act and be at fault in different ways than the individuals constituting it.[196] Hence, the disagreement between the two views centres on the question, whether or not an organisation can be seen as a "living creature". In other words, the question is not so much whether a corporation can be seen as a person, especially if the organisation is viewed as a collectivity of human beings but rather whether that group can be seen as an individual, an indivisible one.[197]

Depending on the direction chosen at this early junction, different conceptions regarding criminal responsibility of legal entities will manifest in the respective penal justice system. If the criminal responsibility of legal entities is rooted in an atomic conception of corporate personality, corporate responsibility will necessarily be derivative.[198] The individual will remain at the focal point of the law, and the responsibility of the individual i.e. its criminal act and mind are imputed to the corporation.[199] By way of contrast, if the fundamental concept of corporate responsibility is based on the organic (or realist) view, the responsibility of the company is primary. This means that responsibility of a corporation will not depend on the responsibility of any individual. Thus, it becomes apparent that the challenging aspect of such an approach is to conceive a framework in which the conduct and mental state of the corporation can be analysed. In other words, the difficulties of this approach lie in devising a test of responsibility that is suitable for corporations.[200] These two different conceptions and their repercussion on the criminal law will be discussed in chapter V of this discourse. Yet, even if one accepts that corporations possess certain unique features which justifies regarding

193 Wells, 'Corporations and Criminal Responsibility' (2001), p. 75. Colvin, 'Corporate Personality and Criminal Liability' Criminal Law Forum (1995), pp. 1–2.

194 Colvin, 'Corporate Personality and Criminal Liability' Criminal Law Forum (1995), p. 2.

195 Colvin, 'Corporate Personality and Criminal Liability' Criminal Law Forum (1995), p. 2, Wells, 'Corporations and Criminal Responsibility' (2001), p. 75.

196 Colvin, 'Corporate Personality and Criminal Liability' Criminal Law Forum (1995), p. 2.

197 Wells, 'Corporations and Criminal Responsibility' (2001), p. 77.

198 Colvin, 'Corporate Personality and Criminal Liability' Criminal Law Forum (1995), p. 2.

199 Colvin, 'Corporate Personality and Criminal Liability' Criminal Law Forum (1995), p. 2.

200 Gobert and Punch, 'Rethinking Corporate Crime' (2003), p. 38.

them as persons, it could still be objected that they cannot be morally culpable, as they possess "no soul to damn, nor a body to kick".[201] It is however submitted that the question whether or not corporations can act morally is misleading. While the attribution of individual liability is frequently linked to moral blameworthiness, corporations are fundamentally different from human beings and they do not act or think according to models of blameworthiness on which criminal law has been premised. This does not mean that one should detach corporate personality (and responsibility) completely from moral blameworthiness, but rather that the paradigm of moral blameworthiness ought to be applied differently to corporations. Criminal responsibility requires certain capacities, like agency, rationality and autonomy, which one can also find in corporations.[202] To be sure, as tentatively demonstrated above, these capacities will acquire a different connotation in the realm of corporate as opposed to individual criminal responsibility. Nevertheless, legal entities in our society have become corporate agents and ought to bear responsibility for harm caused by their actions.

In any case, for the time being, suffice it to say that the nature of corporate personality given in a respective criminal justice system has far-reaching implications for the scope and nature of corporate responsibility. This research will for now leave the notion of corporate criminal liability aside and return to the different theories of conduct developed in criminal law. However, it is important to bear in mind that legal entities can be fit subjects of criminal law and accordingly a theory of conduct providing the basis for the attribution of criminal liability needs to be able to cater to this form of conduct as well.

2.3. Different theories of conduct

Over the years a myriad of different theories have emerged, trying to establish a unitary concept of action that can serve as a basis for the process of attributing criminal liability.[203] Actions, just like physical objects, are subject to different descriptions. As an in-depth analysis of all the different theories of action would go beyond the scope of this work, the discussion will be confined to some influential theories which have emerged in different penal systems over the years.

2.3.1. The causal theory of action – or the ghost in the machine

One theory of conduct, which has greatly influenced the criminal law's perception of conduct for many years and has shaped the contours of many criminal law systems is the "causal theory of action". In the 18th and 19th century it was the

201 Wells, 'Corporations and Criminal Responsibility' (2001), p. 78.

202 See also: Wells, 'Corporations and Criminal Responsibility' (2001), pp. 78–81.

203 It is however questionable, whether such a unitary concept of conduct covering all offences to be found in criminal law is achievable at all.

prevailing theory of conduct in all three investigated penal systems. According to this theory, a criminal act consists in a "willed muscular contraction" or a "willed bodily movement". This theory is based on a 19th century, dualistic concept of man as creatures of *animus* and *corpus*, which in itself can be disputed to say the least.[204] In other words, the *animus* i.e. the human will, was seen as the cause of physical action as willed bodily movements. Modern psychological insights have however shed some doubt on this vision. The division of *animus* and *corpus*, or the dogma of the ghost in the machine seems too simplistic to explain the multi-facets of human nature. The English legal philosopher H. L. A. Heart concluded already in 1968 that the belief in an internal, intangible motor was an "outdated fiction – a piece of eighteen-century psychology".[205] Despite this severe criticism the theory remained highly influential to criminal law thinkers and in the early 1990s the American legal philosopher Michael Moore returned to this view, which can also be found in §1.13 (2) of the Model Penal Code as the only sound "explanation" of human action.[206]

As already mentioned, the repercussions of this theory are still conceivable in contemporary theory and in some penal systems the theory is still by and large accepted. In its early days the causal theory of action was the prevalent theory in the German[207] and the Dutch[208] penal system, but both systems have by now discarded the theory due to its apparent shortcomings. In the English penal system the theory, by and large is still accepted.[209] However, also in England scholars have strongly criticised the traditional causal act requirement and have proposed different theories of conduct.[210] The causal act requirement, as will subsequently be shown, was heavily influenced by the naturalistic concept of causation and together with this doctrine formed and probably still forms the very backbone of many penal systems.

Despite its influential nature, it is submitted here that the causal act requirement from the early 19th century is not able anymore to capture the ever-expanding ramifications of modern criminal law. Criminal law should abandon this bifurcation

---

204 Nieboer, 'Schets materieel strafrecht' (1991), pp. 53–56.

205 Hart, 'Punishment and Responsibility' (2008), p. 101.

206 Moore, 'Act and Crime – The philosophy of action and its implications for Criminal law' (1993), pp. 28 et seq.

207 Roxin, 'Strafrecht Allgemeiner Teil, Band I Grundlagen: Der Aufbau der Verbrechenslehre' (2006), pp. 241–243, Wessels and Beulke, 'Strafrecht Allgemeiner Teil, Die Straftat und ihr Aufbau' (2008), pp. 30–33.

208 Gritter, 'Functioneel plegen door een natuurlijke persoon', in van der Leij (ed), Plegen en Deelnemen (2007), p. 6.

209 Smith and Hogan, 'Criminal Law' (2008), pp. 51–52, Williams, 'Criminal Law: The General Part' (1953), p. 15. For a different approach see: Wilson, 'Central Issues in Criminal Theory' (2002), p. 80.

210 Duff, 'Answering for Crime' (2007), pp. 95–121, Simester, 'On the so called Requirement for Voluntary Action' Buffalo Criminal Law Review (1998), pp. 403–430, Wilson, 'Central Issues in Criminal Theory' (2002), pp. 77–81. See also: Fletcher, 'On the moral irrelevance of Bodily movements' University of Pennsylvania Law Review (1994), pp. 1443–1453.

of the mental and the physical and accept the fact that the notions of mental and physical are all features of one world in which we live in.[211] 19th century theorists attempted to develop a "scientific" concept of crime. Accordingly they strived for an objective, scientifically, i.e. metaphysically grounded definition of offences, hence the definition of action as willed bodily movements. However, over time it became evident that a physical and mechanistic definition of conduct could not satisfactorily capture and explain the different manifestations of human behaviour. Even if in many cases criminal conduct will undoubtedly involve bodily movements, this is not always necessary, as modern human conduct, assisted by modern technologies has reached a level of sophistication that can no longer exclusively be defined in terms of willed bodily movements. This is *inter alia* the case because the results produced by the traditional act requirement contain a serious flaw, as action is investigated in a vacuum, disconnected from its social ramifications. This leads to a questionable outcome, as not nature alone determines what an act is but also the social context in which it occurs. The conduct requirement ought to explain our social world in the context of criminal law.[212] The shortcomings of this theory become particularly apparent in regard to omission liability.[213] If one conceives human action pursuant to the causal theory as willed bodily movements, it becomes clear that omissions do not readily fit this description of conduct. Moreover, conceiving for instance the act of libel as the vibration of the defendant's vocal cords caused by its will seems slightly out of touch with social reality and may ultimately be unconvincing. Furthermore, the doctrine due to its strict focus on human behaviour becomes largely unworkable in regard to an organic conception of corporate wrongdoing. However, an advantage of this theory might be its intuitive logic and simplicity which may explain its considerable impact on criminal theory, but this cannot counterbalance the aforementioned shortcomings.

2.3.2. The teleological theory of action – human conduct is "seeing", not blind

The shortcomings of the causal theory of action led the German scholar Hans Welzel to develop an entire school of criminal law based on the rejection of the theory. In his teleological theory of action he argued that human action was intrinsically purposive and not merely the external manifestation of an inner mechanism.[214] The causal and the teleological conduct requirement both depart from the assumption that human conduct constitutes the cornerstone of criminal liability and that its chief feature is the will. Likewise both can be classified as

211 Searle, 'The future of philosophy' The Royal Society (1999), p. 2074.

212 Jakobs, 'Der strafrechtliche Handlungsbegriff' (1992), p. 12, Wilson, 'Central Issues in Criminal Theory' (2002), p. 80.

213 Roxin, 'Strafrecht Allgemeiner Teil, Band I Grundlagen: Der Aufbau der Verbrechenslehre' (2006), p. 242.

214 Roxin, 'Strafrecht Allgemeiner Teil, Band I Grundlagen: Der Aufbau der Verbrechenslehre' (2006), pp. 243–248.

essentially metaphysical/ontological theories aiming to uncover certain basic tenets of human conduct. Moreover, the teleological, as well as the causal theory adopt a purely individualistic concept of conduct which places the emphasis on the actor, disregarding the effect of the conduct or the perception that other people have concerning the act. The crucial difference however is that the content of the will plays no role for the concept of action in the causal theory, while in the teleological theory the content of the will, i.e. the aim constitutes an element of the very concept of action. Thus, it escaped the flaws of the causal perspective by claiming that human conduct could only be understood by taking into account the agent's goals. It was argued that action was not blind, it was "seeing". As human action has an inherent teleological component, one cannot understand the nature and meaning of an action unless one also knows the actor's purpose. In regard to certain offences this insight is certainly correct. For instance, if someone is colour copying banknotes, it can be that his intention is to forge money or to carry out a practical joke on one of his friends. Here the notion of conduct (prohibited by law) cannot be sensibly applied without regard to the mental state of the accused. Likewise, with respect to certain preparatory offences it is necessary and even crucial to examine the mind of the accused, as the prohibition is entrenched in the purpose of otherwise innocuous behaviour.[215] It is for example an offence in England to carry an offensive weapon in a public place contrary to the Prevention of Crime Act 1953. However, whether an article is regarded as an offensive weapon hinges to a certain extent on the intention with which it is carried. Consider the case of a person walking down the street at dusk, carrying a hammer. It seems impossible to assess whether the person is in breach of the 1968 Theft Act, which criminalises the carrying of any instrument for use in a burglary without examining the person's mind. It is only by paying heed to the purposive element of the conduct that the actus reus can be understood in these situations.[216]

However, the teleological theory of conduct encounters insurmountable obstacles in regard to omission and negligence liability, as it is difficult to claim in these instances that the person acted goal-orientated and was accordingly rejected.[217] Yet, its basic tenet that acting and intending are bound together led to the adoption of the tripartite structure of crime in Germany.[218] As human conduct is intrinsically purposive, it also contains a mental element expressed in the wish, desire and knowledge that the act produces a certain result. By partially including intention in the actus reus, the concept of guilt became more normative and gained an independent place in the structure of crime which amongst others led to the integration of justification and excuses into the structure of crime. Accordingly, as

---

215 Lynch, 'The Mental Element in the actus reus' The Law Quarterly Review (1982), pp. 109 et seq.

216 Lynch, 'The Mental Element in the actus reus' The Law Quarterly Review (1982), p. 114.

217 See: Lampe, 'Willensfreiheit und strafrechtliche Unrechtslehre' ZStW (2006), pp. 11 et seq.

218 Roxin, 'Strafrecht Allgemeiner Teil, Band I Grundlagen: Der Aufbau der Verbrechenslehre' (2006), p. 247.

already discussed, the evaluative structure of crime in Germany today consists of (i) the offence definition (ii) wrongdoing and (iii) guilt.

2.3.3. The social theory of action – significance lies not in the act but in the context in which it is born

The social dimension of conduct is central to the so-called social theory of action. It stresses the social relevance of the conduct as a key concept. The doctrine in essence holds that a criminal conduct needs to be interpreted in the social context in which it occurred. Meaning is not fixed, it is socially negotiated, so it is argued. It conceives conduct as a social rather than a natural phenomenon. "Facts are made, they are the product of intellectual effort".[219] Conduct is regarded as a part of a social pattern which determines its relevance for the attribution of criminal liability.[220] Conduct is not conceived here as physiological phenomenon, seen from an objective scientific point of view, and neither purely psychologically, but rather as a socially constructed phenomenon. The movement of a hand can thus in one context be interpreted as a greeting and in another as a threat. Human conduct should not be understood as a pure ontological causal or teleological process. It simply cannot be separated from its context and the social reality in which the subject acts. Conduct acquires meaning in relation with a concrete society and as part of a particular social system or subsystem. It goes without saying that attributing meaning to conduct can never be value neutral, as social and legal norms will play a prominent role. Thus, the social theory of action is both descriptive and normative in nature combining ontological and normative criteria.[221]

The great advantage of this doctrine is that it is flexible enough to cover also omission liability, state of affairs and possession offences; which offences are hardly reconcilable with the causal act requirement, as they prima facie do not require any form of physical movement. The social theory of action makes it clear that physical conduct, which will often consist in deliberate movements like shooting, stabbing, stealing, robbing, is a sufficient, but not a necessary requirement for the imposition of criminal liability. The focus on the social context however, implies a casuistic approach which can lead to frictions with the principle of legality and to an unequal application of the law.[222] As one and the same conduct can acquire different meanings according to the social context in which it occurs, it becomes

---

219 Remmelink, 'Inleiding tot de studie van het Nederlandse Strafrecht' (1995), p. 161.

220 Gritter, 'Functioneel plegen door een natuurlijke persoon', in van der Leij (ed), Plegen en Deelnemen (2007), p. 14, Remmelink, 'Inleiding tot de studie van het Nederlandse Strafrecht' (1995), p. 161. See also: Roxin, 'Strafrecht Allgemeiner Teil, Band I Grundlagen: Der Aufbau der Verbrechenslehre' (2006), pp. 248–250, Wessels and Beulke, 'Strafrecht Allgemeiner Teil, Die Straftat und ihr Aufbau' (2008), p. 31.

221 Schönke and Schröder, 'Kommentar zum Strafgesetzbuch' (2006), Vorbem §13 Mn 33–34.

222 Vellinga, 'Eenheid in Daderschap?', in Harteveld, et al. (eds), Systeem in ontwikkeling: liber amicorum G. Knigge (2005), pp. 527–546.

more difficult to foresee in advance exactly which instances of conduct may lead to the fulfilment of the actus reus.

The emphasis on the social context of the conduct however also paves the way for the attribution of criminal liability without the involvement of physical movement, for instance to persons who have not physically committed a criminal offence but who are held responsible for the acts of another because they, due to a particular social rank had control over the conduct of the actual offender and were thus in a position to prevent the criminal harm from occurring. Likewise, the doctrine allows to perceive the conduct of corporations as relevant for the attribution of criminal liability. Corporations do engage in wrongful conduct and we frequently perceive the corporation as the author of a particular harm, as is well illustrated by the public outcry caused by the Enron affair and the oil spill in the gulf of Mexico after the collapse of a BP drill platform. In our society organisations and social networks take a prominent role which materialises in "new" concepts of criminal liability where the focus is no longer exclusively on the individual, physical perpetrator, but also on factual responsible perpetrators behind the scene.[223] This is excellently portrayed by the Dutch doctrine of functional perpetration and the German doctrine of hegemony over the act which will be discussed in due course. It is the social theory of conduct which nowadays is prevailing in the Dutch and the German penal system.[224] And while in the English system lip service is still formally paid to the causal theory of action, in scholarly writing the inclusion of the social context in the evaluation of the actus reus seems to gain more and more acceptance.[225]

By focusing on the social context and acceptance (i.e. interpretation) of conduct, some legal scholars have argued to abolish the requirement of physical conduct altogether and base criminal liability instead on the violation of a duty to care.[226] In other words, criminal liability in this view is not based on any form of physical conduct but is a legal consequence of a violation of a duty of care by the suspect. This approach could be termed "normative conduct (or act) requirement" and it constitutes a purely legal concept of conduct.

---

223 De Hullu, 'Materieel Strafrecht' (2006), pp. 146–147.

224 De Hullu, 'Materieel Strafrecht' (2006), p. 144, De Jong, 'Tussen schuld en gedraging: normativering', in Kempen, et al. (eds), De gedraging in beweging (2007), p. 66, Gritter, 'Functioneel plegen door een natuurlijke persoon', in van der Leij (ed), Plegen en Deelnemen (2007), p. 14, Remmelink, 'Inleiding tot de studie van het Nederlandse Strafrecht' (1995), p. 161. See also: Wessels and Beulke, 'Strafrecht Allgemeiner Teil, Die Straftat und ihr Aufbau' (2008), p. 32.

225 See: Duff, 'Criminal Attempts' (1996), p. 293 et seq, Duff, 'Answering for Crime' (2007), p. 98 et seq, Smith and Hogan, 'Criminal Law' (2008), pp. 51–52, Wilson, 'Central Issues in Criminal Theory' (2002), pp. 80–81.

226 Nieboer, 'Schets materieel strafrecht' (1991), pp. 113–143, Strijards, 'Hoofdstukken van materieel Strafrecht' (1992), pp. 60–64, Wedzinga, 'Grondslagen van strafrechtelijke aanspraakelijkheid' Delikt en Delinkwent (1999), pp. 868–877. See also for a discussion of the normative act requirement in the German penal system: Roxin, 'Strafrecht Allgemeiner Teil, Band I Grundlagen: Der Aufbau der Verbrechenslehre' (2006), pp. 250–255.

2.3.4. The normative act requirement – the legal normative view

This normative approach where the violation of a duty of care is at the heart of criminal liability fits well with recent social developments and needs, as well as with an increasingly popular conception of humankind in modern society. The liberal thinking where people were punished for their individual wrongdoing has become outdated. Society has become more multiform and complex and imposes higher demands on the individual due to an increasing mutual dependence which has altered the relationship between the individual and society strongly.[227]

The doctrine of normative conduct takes the legally protected interest underlying a respective criminal offence as a starting point. If one agrees to conceive criminal law as a normative system of rules designated to control human behaviour, it follows that legally protected interests lie in the backdrop of each rule which are regarded by society as worth protecting.[228] These particular interests are protected by rules which carry the threat of punishment. These rules again contain a duty imposed on the citizen by society, or the legislature respectively to avoid any behaviour that might impair the underlying protected interest of the rule. It goes without saying that the underlying protected interest varies for each offence, and that the pin-pointing of the precise interest might sometimes be difficult. However, these rules protecting the legal interest are addressed to every member of society, but the concrete duty that the general rule ought not to be violated is only directed at a particular group of people. The duty to avoid a violation of the particular rules lies only on those people who find themselves in a situation where the rule affects their behaviour, their available choices, i.e. their behaviour directed towards the realisation of particular goals. An example might shed some light on this rather abstract statement. Food and health regulations for instance are designed to protect the physical health of citizens and to maintain a certain food and hygiene standard. The duty not to impair those rules lie with the actors of the diverse food industry, which ranges from cooks, restaurant owners to multi-national companies. These actors however would like to lower those standards continuously in order to maximise their profits. Precisely because of the particular position they find themselves in, they are able to violate these rules. This is why they are under a duty not to violate the rules and impair the underlying legal interest. Thus, it follows that every criminal behaviour can be regarded as the violation of a legal duty and that these duties are strictly personal and determined by the particular situation and circumstances.[229]

Such an approach is compatible with certain areas of law such as economic or environmental offences, corporate liability and omission liability, and furthermore it corresponds to the changed perception of crime in the risk society. However, it is

227 Wedzinga, 'Grondslagen van strafrechtelijke aanspraakelijkheid' Delikt en Delinkwent (1999), pp. 868–877.

228 Strijards, 'Hoofdstukken van materieel Strafrecht' (1992), p. 60. See also: Chapter I. 4.3.2.

229 Strijards, 'Hoofdstukken van materieel Strafrecht' (1992), p. 63.

submitted that a general application of the doctrine might lead to an unwanted expansion of criminal liability. Although especially in economic and environmental offences the liberal attitude of the law i.e. allowed is everything that is not forbidden, has yielded to a more managerial approach, i.e. allowed is only what adheres to certain standards of diligence, it is argued here that in the realm of paradigm cases of wrongdoing such an approach would diminish the safeguard function of the causation doctrine as well as the doctrine of mens rea. If one were to conceive conduct exclusively in terms of omissions the distinction between conduct and blameworthiness will arguably become blurred. The violation of a broad (general) duty of care would then constitute the single basis for imposing criminal liability. It is however not only the basis of liability that is crucial, but criminal theory arguably also ought to outline the content and limits of liability.[230] It is submitted that it is the conduct and the corresponding intention in the respective offence definition as well as the causal linkage to the occurred harm that ought to be central to liability. For these provide better restraints to liability than duties of care. The concept of a duty of care, as will be discussed below, is a notoriously vague one which can be influenced by hindsight biases as well as considerations of expediency and efficacy which may be seen to militate against requirements flowing from the principle of legality.[231]

Having discussed some theories of conduct, it becomes apparent that it is questionable if a grand unified definition of conduct, applicable to all offences alike is feasible and desirable. One single theory of conduct seems to be incapable to account for all forms of human (and corporate) conduct which can give rise to criminal liability. This shows that it is difficult to speak of criminal conduct *in abstracto* as the wording of the underlying offence co-determines the respective conduct requirement.[232] Indeed it is submitted here that a uniform definition of conduct might not be as important as a uniform understanding of its function.[233] The core function of any theory of conduct is namely to filter out any conduct which cannot function as a foundation for the imposition of criminal liability.

2.4. The conduct requirement in practice

As intriguing and thought-provoking as the legal/philosophical discourse on the matter may be and no matter how fruitful it has proved to be for the development of criminal law, its practical importance nowadays, as mentioned before, remains

230 De Hullu, 'Zijn er grenzen aan de strafrechtelijke aansprakelijkheid?' (1993), p. 27.

231 See: Chapter II. 3.2.2.

232 De Hullu, 'Materieel Strafrecht' (2006), p. 147. See also: Bohlander, 'Principles of German Criminal Law' (2009), p. 37, Schönke and Schröder, 'Kommentar zum Strafgesetzbuch' (2006), Vorbem §13 Mn 37.

233 Loth, 'Zeven stellingen over de gedraging in het strafrecht', in Groenhuijsen, et al. (eds), De Schets nader bekeken (1992), pp. 25–35.

quite limited. For this reason a more pragmatic approach is now adopted here which will focus on what does not qualify as conduct in the investigated penal systems.

As discussed above, criminal law ought to treat people as subjects i.e. rational agents and therefore a criminally relevant conduct must reflect this agency. This is a fundamental requirement, because unless a person has the capacity and fair opportunity to adjust his behaviour to the law its penalties ought not to be applied to him.[234] "The movements of a person asleep, in a trance, suffering an epileptic seizure or responding reflexively are no more "actions" than the beating of one's heart or the motion of a falling tree".[235] It follows that conduct which cannot be seen as an expression of human agency cannot trigger criminal liability. Conduct can only be an expression of human agency if it is linked to human will, and consciousness i.e. control. As mentioned before, for the imposition of criminal liability it is not so much movement that matters, but rather conduct that lies within one's control and reflects the person as a rational agent.[236] If such a link is absent i.e. if the actor could not control his conduct, the imposition of criminal liability is unwarranted. We do not impose punishment in these situations for the same reasons, as we do not punish animals, minors or the insane.[237] One might think that a person lacking these "rational agent capacities" is incapable of forming the required mens rea of the alleged offence. However, these situations are not merely a denial of mens rea, but much more profound, namely the denial of a criminally relevant conduct. This distinction is of considerable practical importance as a denial of conduct can bar the imposition of criminal liability even in the case of strict liability offences, where no mental element needs to be proven.[238] What is missing in these cases is "a vital link between mind and body".[239] To treat people as subjects requires that criminal liability cannot be imposed unless the subject was responsible for the occurrence of the actus reus, i.e. unless its occurrence can be attributed to him. Thus, the core ingredients of a criminally relevant conduct are consciousness and control. This "deliberate control" over behaviour can be lost or impaired in two ways. First, the person's capacity to reason and control his behaviour can be disabled due to impaired consciousness. Second, the person's capacity to reason might be intact but due to some external events he may have lost the physical control over the movements of the body.[240] If this is the case, the occurred harm

234 Hart, 'Punishment and Responsibility' (2008), p. 181.

235 Finkelstein, 'Involuntary Crimes, Voluntarily Committed', in Shute and Simester (eds), Criminal Law Theory: Doctrines of the General Part (2002), p. 143.

236 See also: Duff, 'Answering for Crime' (2007), pp. 96–115.

237 Wilson, 'Central Issues in Criminal Theory' (2002), p. 104.

238 Chiao, 'Action and agency in the criminal law' Legal Theory (2009), p. 7, Smith and Hogan, 'Criminal Law' (2008), pp. 54–55.

239 Hart, 'Punishment and Responsibility' (2008), p. 107.

240 See also: Simester and Sullivan, 'Criminal Law: Theory and Doctrine' (2007), p. 104, Wilson, 'Violence, Sleepwalking and the Criminal Law: Part 2: The legal aspects' Criminal Law Review (2005), pp. 615–616.

cannot be described as springing from human agency but is rather conceived as an accident, i.e. a natural event.

2.4.1. Loss of physical control

All penal systems concur that conduct in which there is no voluntary involvement cannot qualify as criminally relevant conduct. This excludes conduct from the realm of criminal law in which a person is for instance used as an instrument or cannot control its actions due the absence of consciousness. Under this category fall for instance cases of *vis absoluta*. Suppose for instance that Rob is pushed by Peter from a diving platform and consequently lands on Carl who is severely injured. In this case Rob would not be held responsible for injuring Carl as he did not will the harmful conduct (*vis absoluta*).[241] Further actions which do not reflect a deliberate control over the conduct are reflexes e.g. Rob drops a glass after being stung by a bee, or kicks his doctor during an examination of his knee-jerk. Moreover, spasms do not qualify as criminally relevant conduct. The paralysed person who kicks his therapist due to spasms or the patient punching a nurse during an epileptic fit neither control nor will their actions and can accordingly not be held responsible for them. Finally the conduct of unconscious or sleeping persons cannot trigger criminal liability.

The current state of affairs in all three penal systems was nicely summarised by Lord Justice Denning in the English case of *Bratty v Attorney General for Northern Ireland*:

> No act is punishable if it is done involuntary: and an involuntary act in this context [...], means an act which is done by the muscles without any control by the mind such as spasm, a reflex action or a convulsion; or an act done by a person who is not conscious of what he is doing such as an act done whilst suffering from concussion or whilst sleepwalking.[242]

2.4.2. Impaired consciousness

The aforementioned cases all involve a complete loss of control over the movement of the body due to certain external or internal factors. However, a complete loss of

---

241 The criminal law would rather turn to Peter in this circumstances who used Rob as an "instrument". See also: De Hullu, 'Materieel Strafrecht' (2006), p. 152, Loth, 'Zeven stellingen over de gedraging in het strafrecht', in Groenhuijsen, et al. (eds), De Schets nader bekeken (1992), pp. 25–35, Remmelink, 'Inleiding tot de studie van het Nederlandse Strafrecht' (1995), pp. 162–163, Roxin, 'Strafrecht Allgemeiner Teil, Band I Grundlagen: Der Aufbau der Verbrechenslehre' (2006), pp. 266–271, Simester and Sullivan, 'Criminal Law: Theory and Doctrine' (2007), p. 104, Wessels and Beulke, 'Strafrecht Allgemeiner Teil, Die Straftat und ihr Aufbau' (2008), p. 34; See also: Schönke and Schröder, 'Kommentar zum Strafgesetzbuch' (2006), Vorbem §13 Mn 38–40.

242 [1961] 3 All ER 523.

control does not always seem necessary to bar criminal liability. Yet, to which degree consciousness/control ought to be impaired is open to debate and, as will become apparent, is often influenced by underlying policy reasons. Difficult in this respect are cases which involve automated conduct like driving a car. Conduct like shifting gears, breaking and accelerating takes place almost unconsciously, but also in these cases the person generally remains in control over his conduct and moreover also semi-skilled automated conduct arguably reflects the person as a rational agent. A pertinent example for such cases can be found in the German decision regarding a driver who lost control of his vehicle, crashing into another car, because a fly had flown into his eye. The court held that in such situations some form of willed control was involved in the conduct which therefore was deemed criminally relevant.[243] A comparable English case involving a form of impaired consciousness is *Attorney-General's Reference (No 2 of 1992)*, where it was held that the condition known as "driving without awareness", a trance like state caused by long journeys on straight, flat, featureless motorways, in which the focal point of forward vision gradually comes nearer and nearer until the driver is focusing just ahead of his windscreen, could not support a defence of automatism because the driver nevertheless retained some control.[244] Thus, a driver will only be able to escape liability if his actions at the relevant time were *wholly beyond his control,* the most obvious case being sudden unconsciousness.[245] If he however retains some, albeit imperfect control, and his driving judged objectively, was below the required standard, he remains liable. The threshold in law, led by policy considerations, to accept that no criminally relevant conduct occurred in driving cases is thus rather high.[246] It can accordingly be concluded that considerations of penal policy such as increasing road safety, protection of the public and reduction of road deaths, can influence the degree of deliberate control required for the conduct element of a particular offence.

Difficulties can also arise in cases of temporary impaired consciousness, as for instance, in regard to diabetics acting in a state of hypoglycaemia[247] or acts done by a person suffering from a mental illness short of insanity (e.g. stress psychosis).[248] These cases are difficult because the person in question may seem conscious and in control of his/her actions, but the control that those persons exert is in no way conscious control and therefore these actions will generally be regarded as not criminally relevant. However, much will depend on the exact circumstances of the

243 16 July 1974 OLG Hamm NJW 1975, 657.

244 [1993] 4 All ER 683.

245 [1993] 4 All ER 683.

246 In England courts have in regard to other offences sometimes adopted a less stringent approach. See for instance: R v Quick [1973] 2 All ER 347, where the defendant was allowed to raise the defence of automatism on a charge of assault which had been committed in an onset triggered by hypoglycaemia notwithstanding the fact that the defendants condition was one of "mere" semi-consciousness.

247 See for instance: R v Bailey [1983] 2 All ER 503.

248 See for instance: R v Bell [1984] 3 All ER 842.

case (e.g. was the impaired consciousness self-induced?) and on medical expert opinion. Finally one advances even further into the grey areas of the conduct requirement if one considers crimes committed while sleepwalking. Also in these cases the person does not exert conscious control over his conduct which is therefore not deemed criminally relevant.[249] Sleepwalking is also an interesting example, as it shows how closely related the conduct requirement is to general defences, as it can be disputed whether sleepwalking should be seen as criminally irrelevant conduct or rather as a form of insanity.[250]

Complex issues can arise in cases where the loss of deliberate control occurred due to the prior disregard of diligent standards or is self-induced. An instructive case here is the English decision of *R v Lipman*.[251] The defendant in this case had taken a considerable amount of LSD and believed he was fighting snakes and descending to the centre of the world, whereas he was actually suffocating his girlfriend. The court refused the application of the automatism defence on the ground that first and foremost the automatism was self-induced and moreover induced by the defendant's own fault. In Germany, it is a controversial question whether acts of senselessly intoxicated persons can qualify as criminally relevant conduct.[252] If the person's capacity was completely removed by the intoxication it is generally thought that no criminally relevant conduct occurred.[253] It should however be noted that German law provides for a specific offence for people who commit crimes while seriously intoxicated, for which they could otherwise not be punished.[254] Also in the Netherlands, the doctrine of *culpa in causa* is applied in such cases.[255] Thus, it is important to note that in these cases liability will not be barred completely. Courts will then frequently select an earlier conduct as the founding element for the imposition of criminal liability, applying a *culpa in causa*, or prior fault reasoning respectively. This approach has mainly, but not exclusively had a significant influence in various traffic offences. This is for instance the case where the driver of a vehicle falls asleep and then causes an accident, where liability is then often based on the driver's failure to stop when feeling drowsy.[256] Thus

---

249 Simester and Sullivan, 'Criminal Law: Theory and Doctrine' (2007), p.105, Wessels and Beulke, 'Strafrecht Allgemeiner Teil, Die Straftat und ihr Aufbau' (2008), p. 34.

250 Wessels and Beulke, 'Strafrecht Allgemeiner Teil, Die Straftat und ihr Aufbau' (2008), p. 34, Wilson, 'Violence, Sleepwalking and the Criminal Law: Part 2: The legal aspects' Criminal Law Review (2005), pp. 614–623. Mostly, due to the lack of conscious control, acts done while sleepwalking are deemed non-actions. See also: Rb. Zutphen 9 November 2007, *LJN* BB7529.

251 [1970] 1 QB 152.

252 Bohlander, 'Principles of German Criminal Law' (2009), p. 40.

253 Schönke and Schröder, 'Kommentar zum Strafgesetzbuch' (2006), Vorbem §13 Mn 39. See also: Fischer and Rehm, 'Alcohol consumption and the liability of offenders in the German criminal system' Contemporary Drug Problems (1996), pp. 707–729.

254 See: §323 a GPC.

255 De Hullu, 'Materieel Strafrecht' (2009), pp. 341–372.

256 See for instance the English Case of Kay v Butterworth [1945] 173 LT 191, where it was held that a driver could be held responsible for his antecedent failure to stop driving when he felt drowsy. For an almost identical ruling in Germany see: 18 November 1969 BGH NJW 1970, 520.

while the approach to the problem of self induced loss of deliberate control differs in the investigated countries, the results achieved are quite similar. On the one hand some deem the conduct involuntary and regard the offender's prior fault as sufficient in law to regard the subsequent involuntary conduct as blameworthy. On the other hand however others prefer to look back to an earlier act and impose liability on the basis of the actor's earlier conduct in culpably causing the loss of deliberate control. Examples for the latter approach would be to hold the mother who smothered her child while asleep responsible for the fact that she lay the baby next to her when going to bed or to hold the epileptic responsible for driving.

The former approach is based on the assumption that someone who intends to cause the conditions under which an offence is committed also necessarily intends to commit the offence.[257] The latter rejects this assumption, but causes frictions with the principle of concurrency, by linking the mens rea from earlier (not criminally relevant) conduct to the actus reus performed innocently at a later time.[258]

An important issue here is also to determine what will constitute a self-induced loss of deliberate control. A key aspect in determining this is whether the person was aware, i.e. could foresee the risk of suffering a loss of deliberate control when taking the substance in question or the risk of harm when commencing the conduct. This will for instance not be the case when the intoxicating substance was taken pursuant to medical advice and freak side-effects occur or when the susceptibility to the intoxicant is not known to the person, etc.[259]

2.5. The underlying rationale of the conduct requirement

First and foremost, the rationale underlying the conduct requirement is that mere thoughts, feelings and attitudes shall not be punishable. This principle enshrined in the Latin adage *Cogitationis poenam nemo patitur* can already be found in ancient Roman law and can also be found in Art 10 of the Charter of Fundamental rights of the European Union which holds that everyone should have the right to freedom of thought. It functions as a minimum threshold for criminal liability by generally requiring that the defendant's liability be based on some form of externalised conduct. Moreover, the principle also contains a normative dimension. As discussed

---

See also: 17 November 1994 BGH NJW 1995, 795 where an epileptic was found guilty of negligently causing bodily injury, as he drove despite being aware of his condition.

257 Robinson, 'Causing the conditions of one's own defence: A study in the limits of theory in criminal law doctrine' Virginia Law Review (1985), p. 27.

258 Finkelstein, 'Involuntary Crimes, Voluntarily Committed', in Shute and Simester (eds), Criminal Law Theory: Doctrines of the General Part (2002), p. 158. This seems to be the approach of the UK and Germany.

259 Robinson, 'Causing the conditions of one's own defence: A study in the limits of theory in criminal law doctrine' Virginia Law Review (1985), pp. 43–47. See also the Dutch decision in HR 16 November 1965, *NJ* 1966, 404, where it was held that a rare delay of the effects of sleeping pills was not foreseeable for the driver of a car.

above, it gives expression to the image of man underlying criminal law. It therefore ought to reflect humanity and sociality and thereby assure that citizens are treated as responsible agents under the rule of law rather than risk factors or enemies.

The conduct in question needs however not be physical, even if this will frequently be the case in paradigm cases. As will subsequently become apparent, recent developments have led to the adoption of less stringent and tangible, more mental definitions of conduct. The corollary of the shift to a broader understanding of the (criminal) conduct requirement is a broader concept of perpetration. The traditional (causal) conduct requirement of willed bodily movements, as applied in some penal systems, usually leads to a narrow concept of perpetration, as only the person who directly brings about the actus reus of an offence himself can be deemed a perpetrator. Other people involved in the manifestation of the criminal offence can only be held criminally liable as accessories.[260]

By the same token, it serves to exclude from the criminal law, incidents which cannot constitute the basis of criminal liability like conduct of animals, natural disasters, etc. Moreover, as pointed out above, the act requirement constitutes a first filter to avoid punishment for unexternalised thoughts by requiring a minimum objective manifestation of the perpetrator's intention in the outside world. In this sense the conduct requirement functions as a bearer of wrongdoing and therefore constitutes a prerequisite of criminal liability.[261] Thus can conduct function as the denomination of wrongdoing (e.g. theft, manslaughter).

Furthermore the act requirement is a useful tool to pinpoint the time and place of the occurrence of the offence. By identifying the temporal and spatial notions of an offence the act requirement helps to facilitate the application of notions like jurisdiction and statutes of limitation and establishes a nexus between the different concepts. Finally, it should not be overlooked that the requirement of an act mutely circumscribes the governmental powers in the creation of new offences. To be sure, the safeguard of this notion is only rudimentary, as can be easily demonstrated by reference to the aforementioned offences punishing possession and state of affairs. By the same token, the conduct requirement can be seen "as a buffer against overweening state powers".[262] It serves this function, as it claims to circumscribe the imposition of punishment to such matters that we deem fair to hold people responsible for.

Finally, also the underlying theories of punishment can influence the scope and shape of the conduct requirement. If we, for instance, see deterrence as an important reason for punishment, then logic dictates that conduct which is not consciously controlled should not warrant the imposition of punishment, as the law cannot deter unconscious actors like sleepwalkers.

---

260 See for instance the situation in England and Wales, Chapter III. 6.2.2.

261 Nieboer, 'Schets materieel strafrecht' (1991), pp. 84–85.

262 Fletcher, 'The Grammar of Criminal Law' (2007), p. 296.

2.6. Conclusion

The foregoing discussion has revealed that a strict demarcation of criminally relevant or irrelevant conduct respectively will not be always possible. Rather, grey areas will always remain, as the degree of consciousness or deliberate control can be gradually reduced, until one reaches a stage where the occurred conduct can no longer be seen as an expression of human agency. When however this will be the case will also co-depend on medical and scientific evaluations and insights. Often normative considerations might play a role here as well. However, leaving grey areas aside, the key ingredients of the conduct requirement seem to be consciousness and control, which make the occurred conduct a reflection of (human) agency. It should be kept in mind here that the requirement of conduct need not provide an answer to the traditional philosophical mind-body problem, but should rather constitute a first step in the attribution of liability. In other words, although the act requirement in criminal law has close ties to the philosophy of action it is nevertheless an autonomous concept which carries an important normative connotation. The very baseline of the conduct requirement is namely the fair and just attribution of criminal liability. Therefore, criminal law should also rid itself from traditional but obsolete categories of mind and body, matter and spirit, mental and physical.

To be sure, many offences will be committed in practice by classical physical conduct, so that as a starting point one can retain the paradigm of physical conduct for the imposition of criminal liability. But this need not necessarily be the case and in these instances one needs to evaluate conduct in the light of the underlying offence definition, the circumstances of the case at hand, etc. Thus, conduct ought to be evaluated within the social context in which it occurs. This approach can be termed the social conduct requirement and it is flexible enough to encompass also more mental forms of conduct where the emphasis of the criminal law has shifted to the control one person has over the commission of a criminal offence in which he is not physically involved himself, but nevertheless plays a crucial role. This theory thus gains an extra dimension once the focus shifts from the traditional individual direct perpetrator to the factual responsible perpetrators behind the screen or to legal entities.[263] On the other hand, for corporate conduct a more normative theory of action might be recommendable in order to capture the peculiarities of this form of wrongdoing. Thus, a mixed social/normative concept of action might correspond best to the needs of criminal law in modernity.

Broadly stated, all penal systems agree that conduct which cannot be seen as an expression of human agency can neither constitute the basis for imposing criminal liability. This excludes from liability conduct caused by spasms, reflex action or convulsion as well as conduct carried out while unconscious or induced by the irresistible force of natural events or a third person (*vis absoluta*). However, this

---

263 De Hullu, 'Materieel Strafrecht' (2009), p. 154.

basic rule can become watered-down by the influence of normative criteria such as duties of care, which becomes apparent in the realm of road traffic offences and self-induced loss of deliberate control. In the former cases the loss of control must be almost complete and in the latter cases concepts such as *culpa in causa* make the attribution of liability despite the loss of control possible.

At European level a definition or theory of conduct has not yet emerged.[264] At most it can be said that the concept of conduct in European Union law will encompass acts as well as omissions.[265] Thus, a theory of action catering to both manifestations of human conduct as proposed above would fit nicely into a framework of European criminal law.

Finally, it should be pointed out that in the penal systems of Germany and the Netherlands, a shift in the conception of conduct from a physical to a more functional/mental conception is conceivable. Suffice it here to refer the reader once more to the Dutch doctrine of functional perpetration and to the German concept of hegemony over the act, which will be discussed in more detail below.[266] These developments also strongly point to the direction of a social/normative concept of conduct and a move away from the orthodox causal act requirement. In the English system a broadening of the notion of conduct is less discernible. However, there the scope of liability has in some cases been broadened in order to bring new forms of wrongdoing into the realm of criminal law. This has for instance been done by extending the meaning of bodily harm enshrined in the 1861 Offences against the Person Act to include also psychological harm caused by silent phone calls and a campaign of harassment of women[267] as well as biological harm following an infection with the HIV virus through consensual sexual intercourse.[268]

3. Omissions: Criminal liability in absence of physical action?

3.1. Introduction

After having analysed the theory of action it is now possible to proceed to discuss the second manifestation of human conduct. At first sight it can seem odd to impose criminal liability on people for failures to act, as the number of things we omit doing every day, by far exceeds the amount of things we actively do. While reading a book, I for instance omit to help all the people sleeping rough in Amsterdam, Berlin or London. Or, do parents have a general duty to prevent their children from committing criminal offences? Must the host of a party prevent his guests from

264 Klip, 'European Criminal Law' (2012), pp. 201 et seq.

265 This can be deduced from Art 49 of the Charter of Fundamental Rights of the European Union which refers to acts and omissions. OJ 2007, C 303/01.

266 See: Chapter III. 7.2.1. and 7.2.2.

267 R v Ireland [1997] AC 147.

268 R v Dica [2004] QB 1257.

using drugs? These are the questions concerning the scope of omission liability that will be discussed in the subsequent chapter.

While the former examples might seem far-fetched and puzzling, the situation becomes already clearer if one considers the example of a gardener whose duty it is to water my precious flowers while I am on vacation. If he fails to do so and the plants die I might reasonably hold him responsible for the non-performance of his duty.[269] Thus, it is already evident that the key feature of omission liability can be found in the nebulous concept of duties of care. The discussion will commence by briefly focussing on some objections which have traditionally haunted the doctrine of criminal omissions. It will proceed with an investigation of how different penal systems have approached the topic and will subsequently attempt to highlight some differences and similarities as well as predicaments in regard to duties of care. From this this research will tentatively deduce a common framework of duties within the European Union.

While as discussed above, the archetype of criminal liability is the prohibition on the culpable doing of an (criminal) act, it is an ontological fact that human conduct can manifest itself not only in the form of action but also in the form of an omission. Consider for instance the famous textbook example of the bystander who intentionally omits to rescue a child from drowning. Accordingly all criminal law systems include offenses punishing the culpable omission of an act expected of the person by law. They differ however, in regard to the scope of liability for omissions recognised.

An omission can loosely be defined as a failure to perform a specific duty which has been imposed by law. At the heart of the concept of omission lies thus a value judgment that people can be punished for not fulfilling certain expectations, which society superimposed on the individual. One of the cardinal issues of omissions has therefore always been the scope of such expectations, i.e. duties, and legislators and courts in common law and civil law countries alike have been at pains to thoroughly outline the scope of these duties.

Regarding duties of care, two contrasting social currents, the "conventionalist view" and the "social responsibility view" can be identified.[270] The conventionalist view departs from an individualist conception of human life, advocating individual autonomy, and claiming that criminal law should be reluctant to punish failures to act, except in the most clear and severe cases.[271] The social responsibility view, on the other hand departs from a communitarian social philosophy, emphasising the co-operative elements in life and arguing that social solidarity makes it appropriate

269 Hart and Honoré, 'Causation in the Law' (1985), p. 38.

270 Ashworth, 'The scope of criminal liability for omissions' The Law Quarterly Review (1989), pp. 442–459.

271 Ashworth, 'The scope of criminal liability for omissions' The Law Quarterly Review (1989), pp. 442–459.

to impose a duty to act on citizens in certain situations.[272] The conventionalist view is rooted in a narrow 19th century doctrinal thinking which led to the general principle, to be found in all penal systems that omissions should only in exceptional cases lead to criminal liability.

These two currents are however not polar opposites, but they depart from different theoretical foundations which result in different scopes of omission liability. The subsequent discussion will reveal that both social currents had discernible impacts on the law of omissions in European penal systems. However, in recent years, the social responsibility view has gained more influence, resulting in an extension of omission liability. This change in emphasis can tentatively be explained by recent social developments, like the increasing division of labour and the growing interdependence of citizenry, which placed more emphasis on social co-operation. As will be discussed in more detail below, in the culture of control duties of care have become increasingly popular in criminal law.[273] To protect society from future risks, duties of care are a valuable tool as the diligent standard enshrined in them applies to a multitude of different instances and behaviour all of which could hardly be forged into an actus reus in terms of positive action.[274] Furthermore, duties of care are sought to increase the responsibility sentiments of the citizens towards the legally protected interest which incorporates citizens and private actors in the overall process of creating security. In other words, in order to provide its citizens with the desired security, the state imposes more and more duties on the polity in order to control their behaviour more effectively and to be able to intervene at a much earlier stage of the criminal event. This development seems also to be fostered by the trend to use criminal law for the protection of collective, rather than individual interests. In a society where collective interests gain more and more importance the idea of duties to act is arguably the corollary of an enhanced collective mindset.

Despite the increasing importance of omissions in the realm of criminal law, the concept remains highly debated in legal literature. There seems to be something untoward about imposing criminal liability for omissions, so that writers have raised a multitude of objections to imposing omission liability. This traditional retentiveness can amongst others be attributed to the fact that most of the general principles and doctrines of criminal law have evolved from the paradigm case involving cases of action. So, as will be shown below, the causality of an act for instance is of a different type than the causality of an omission, if one accepts that omissions can be causes at all. Likewise the mens rea of a person who shoots someone is different from a person who lets things run their course and omits to save his drowning enemy. The question whether a conduct was more than merely preparatory and will thus constitute a criminal attempt, is to be answered differently

272 Ashworth, 'The scope of criminal liability for omissions' The Law Quarterly Review (1989), pp. 442–459.

273 See also: Vogel, 'Norm und Pflicht bei den unechten Unterlassungsdelikten' (1993), p. 23.

274 Visser, 'Zorgplichtbepalingen in het Strafrecht' (2001), p. 21.

depending on whether one deals with a crime of action or inaction. Therefore, omission liability departs from the paradigm of criminal liability and is accordingly viewed with suspicion.

It will however be argued here that these objections are rooted in a traditional 19th century doctrinal thinking, which is no longer appropriate, as it distracts attention from more vital questions like the scope, origins and boundaries of the core concept of omissions, namely the duty of care. However, omissions liability and more particularly duties of care can cause frictions with the principle of legality. First, it can be argued that citizens are not accustomed to the concept of duties of care, in contrast to prohibitions, and may therefore incur criminal liability for conduct which they deemed to be in accordance with the law. The argument gains more force if one takes into consideration that duties of care are frequently created by jurisprudence *ex post*, i.e. after the conduct in question has taken place.[275] This casuistic approach, however, can make it difficult to foresee what conduct the law expects by a citizen in a particular situation. Furthermore, as will also become apparent in the following discussion, the scope and content of duties to act is a permanent bone of contention in all penal systems, which can make it unclear for the citizens in certain situations what the law requires in order to avoid criminal liability.[276] While these arguments might carry some weight in regard to duties of care directed to everyone, they are less convincing in regard to duties directed to people in a certain (social) position. The latter are namely expected by society, due to their expertise, education, etc., to know and adhere to the standard of diligence expected and required by a certain position.[277]

3.2. Omissions in criminal law

Criminal liability for omissions can usually arise in two forms. First a statute can explicitly impose liability for omitting to do something. These offences are defined in terms of a failure to act and impose a duty of care (such as the duty to report an accident to the police) on the citizens. Second, there are instances where offences, defined in terms of positive acts, like killing, burning, assaulting, can be committed by people who remain idle and let events run their course. Almost all European penal systems distinguish between these two manifestations of omissions. In England a distinction is made between offences of mere omission and offences of omission causing a result.[278] By the same token the Netherlands[279]

---

275 Jescheck and Weigend, 'Lehrbuch des Strafrechts: Allgemeiner Teil' (1996), pp. 608–609, Wilson, 'Central Issues in Criminal Theory' (2002), p. 98.

276 Wilson, 'Central Issues in Criminal Theory' (2002), p. 97.

277 Roef, 'Strafrechtelijke Verantwoordelijkheid in de Risicomaatschappij', in Vos and Calster (eds), Risico en voorzorg in de rechtsmaatschappij (2004), pp. 222–225.

278 Smith and Hogan, 'Criminal Law' (2008), pp. 61–62.

279 Eigenlijke and oneigenlijke omissiedelicte. See for instance: De Hullu, 'Materieel Strafrecht' (2006), p. 74.

and Germany[280] distinguish between proper and improper crimes of omission. This research will therefore also adhere to this dichotomy and distinguish between statutory duties of care and commission by omission.

3.2.1. Statutory duties of care

In situations where a statute requires an affirmative action, the legality objections, outlined above, have no thrust, as the statutes explicitly define the required conduct and circumscribe the scope of people under a duty of care. It is of course open to the legislator to cast duties of care into statutory provisions. It should however not be overlooked that the effectiveness and quality of these statutes strongly depend on the quality of the law-making.

The paradigm case of statutory duties of care in Germany and the Netherlands are probably so called "Good Samaritan" or "easy rescue statutes".[281] Art 450 of the Dutch Penal Code (DPC) imposes punishment for the failure to take steps, which one could take without danger to himself to save another from death.[282] The German counterpart, §323c of the German Penal Code (GPC), has a slightly broader scope, as it imposes liability for the failure to render assistance also in cases where no mortal danger for the victim is imminent.[283]

In England such an easy rescue provision is absent.[284] However, the desirability and feasibility of creating such a statute has been hotly debated. Critics in England have often argued that such an offence would be too general in nature and therefore unnecessary and unworkable. However, some have forcefully argued for the introduction of an easy rescue statute into the English legal system.[285]

Regarding statutory duties of care one will arguably have to distinguish between duties based on solidarity towards the weak (i.e. the victim) and what one might call

---

280 Echte and unechte Unterlassungsdelikte. See for instance: Jescheck and Weigend, 'Lehrbuch des Strafrechts: Allgemeiner Teil' (1996), pp. 605–608.

281 Note that usually these statutes do not refer to the result of the failure to render aid. The offender is held responsible for his failure to render aid and not for the result which he may have prevented. The Dutch statue, however constitutes an exception, as it refers to the death of the person in distress.

282 Article 450 reads as follows: A person who witnesses the immediate mortal danger of another person and who fails to render or procure such aid and assistance as he is capable of rendering or procuring where there is no reasonable expectation of danger to himself or others is liable to a term of detention of not more than three months or a fine of the second category, where the death of the person in distress ensues.

283 Section 323 c reads as follows: Whoever does not render assistance during accidents or common danger or need, although it is required and can be expected of him under the circumstances and, especially, is possible without substantial danger to himself and without violation of other important duties, shall be punished with imprisonment for not more than one year or a fine.

284 Smith and Hogan, 'Criminal Law' (2008), p. 74.

285 Ashworth, 'The scope of criminal liability for omissions' The Law Quarterly Review (1989), pp. 424–459, Ashworth and Steiner, 'Criminal omissions and public duties: the French experience' Legal Studies (1990), pp. 153–164.

administrative duties, i.e. duties aimed to ensure the smooth functioning of the criminal justice system.[286] Thus, the legal interest to be protected by the statutory duty of care seems to influence the acceptability of a given statute. While it has become apparent that duties based on solidarity towards the weak such as easy rescue statutes can be controversial due to their inherent moral dimension, administrative duties constitute an integral part of all investigated penal systems. Section 6 of the English 1988 Road Traffic Act for instance imposes liability on a motorist who fails to provide a specimen of breath to a police officer when so required. And section 170 (4) of the same Act imposes a duty on a driver in case of an accident to stop, report the accident and provide information or documents. In practice the most important statutory duties in English law are however to be found in sections 2, 3 and 4 of the Health and Safety at Work Act 1974. Section 2 contains duties placed upon employers to ensure the health, safety and welfare at work of all his employees. Section 3 places a general duty on employers and the self-employed to ensure their activities do not expose anybody to risks to health and safety. Section 4 on the other hand defines a duty of those in control of premises (e.g. commercial landlords, managers of serviced office accommodation and maintenance contractors) towards people who use the premises for work. Those premises, and the means of entry and exit must be, as far as reasonable practical, safe and without risk to health.

Statutory duties can also be found, although sporadically in common law offences. For example it is an offence to resist assisting a police officer in keeping up the Queens Peace. Moreover, the common law offence of misconduct in public office can be committed by omission in case that the office bearer (e.g. a police officer) was aware of the duty and reckless in its fulfilment.[287]

An example of a statutory duty of care based on solidarity towards the weak in the English penal system can be found in the Children and Young Person Act 1933, which requires legally dependent children under the age of 16 to be supplied with adequate food, health care, etc.[288] The Act applies not only to parents but to any persons legally liable to maintain a child such as, for instance, legal guardians.[289]

There are also a multitude of statutory duties to be found within the Dutch penal system. To name just a view within the traditional realm of criminal law, thereby leaving aside economic crimes etc. one could mention for instance Article 444[290],

---

286 An example of the latter at the European level can be found in Article 18 of Regulation 1/2003 of 16 December 2002 on the implementation of the rules on competition laid down in Articles 81 and 82 of the Treaties, OJ 2003 L 1/1, which obliges undertakings to provide the Commission with all necessary information during an investigation. See also: 7 January 2004, Joined Cases C-2004 P, C-205/00 P, C-213/00 P, C-217/00 P and C-219/00 P, *Aaborg Portland and others v Commission of the European Communities*, [2004] ECR I-00123, para 61 et seq.

287 See: Attorney-General's Reference (No 3 of 2003) [2004] EWCA Crim 868, where a drunken 37 year old died in a police custody suit.

288 Simester and Sullivan, 'Criminal Law: Theory and Doctrine' (2007), p. 67.

289 Section 2 (a).

290 Article 444 reads as follows: A person who has been duly summoned to appear as a witness, an expert or an interpreter and who is unlawfully absent is liable to a fine of the first category.

446[291] and 474[292] DPC.[293] Most proper crimes of omission within the Dutch penal system are misdemeanours, which accordingly carry only light sentences. This peculiarity shows that the Dutch legislator, embracing at the time a rather conventionalist view, conceived of crimes of omission as an exception to the rule and that probably in many instances they were incorporated in the penal code due to their exemplary function for the citizens.

Likewise, the German legislator has incorporated several statutory duties into the penal code. §138 GPC for example imposes a duty on citizens to report certain premeditated crimes which (s)he knows to the police.[294] Other cases in point are for instance §142 (2)[295], proscribing the unauthorised leaving of the scene of an accident, and §174, prohibiting the sexual abuse of wards.[296]

---

291 Article 446 reads as follows: A person who, in situations where the general safety of persons or property is at risk or upon the discovery of a serious offence in its commission, refuses to render the aid and assistance requested from him by the public authorities, and which he is capable without exposing himself to immediate danger, is liable to a fine of the first category.

292 Article 474 reads as follows: A master of a Netherlands vessel who fails to comply with the obligations specified in article 358a, section 2, or article 785 of the commercial Code, is liable to a term of detention of not more than three months or a fine of the second category.

293 For a general overview see: De Hullu, 'Materieel Strafrecht' (2006), p. 74.

294 §138 reads as follows:
(1) Whoever credibly learns of the planning or the execution of:
 1. a preparation of a war of aggression (Section 80)
 2. high treason in cases under Sections 81 to 83 subsection (1)
 3. treason or an endangerment of external security in cases under Sections 94 to 96, 97a or 100
 […]
 6. a murder, manslaughter or genocide (Sections 211, 21 or 220a)
 […]
 a robbery or robbery-like extortion (Sections 249 to 251 or 255)
 […]
 at a time when the execution or result can still be averted, and fails to make report in time to the public authorities or the person threatened, shall be punished with imprisonment for not more than five years or a fine. […].

295 §142 reads as follows:
(1) A participant in an accident who, after an accident in road traffic, leaves the scene of the accident before he:
 1. has made possible, on behalf of the other participants in the accident and the persons suffering damages, the determination of his identity, his vehicle and the nature of his participation through his presence and a statement that he participated in the accident; or
 2. has waited an appropriate period of time under the circumstances, during which no one was willing to make such determinations,
shall be punished with imprisonment for not more than three years or a fine
(2) A participant in an accident shall also be punished under subsection (1), if he:
 1. after expiry of the waiting period (subsection (1), number 2); or
 2. justifiably or excusably left the scene of the accident and subsequently does not promptly make the determinations possible.

296 For a general overview see: Jescheck and Weigend, 'Lehrbuch des Strafrechts: Allgemeiner Teil' (1996), p. 607.

By and large, statutory duties are in all three penal systems regarded as uncontroversial, as they penalise the noncompliance with a duty of care which is explicitly outlined in the offence, and furthermore in most cases explicitly outline the scope of people to which the duty is addressed. Thus, as already mentioned, they usually pose no problem of legality. The increasing amount of statutory duties in all penal systems dealt with here, however, shows that the national legislators are increasingly inclined to impose duties to act in modern welfare or regulatory offences. Especially in the industry, commerce and business context, general standards of diligence become more and more important, in order to circumscribe and prevent possible risks to the public. In many instances these diligence standards are nowadays enforced by means of statutory duties of care. While such an approach seems generally acceptable it should however be remembered that the acceptability of statutory duties also hinges to a considerable extent on the quality of the law making. If legislators choose to enact new statutory duties of care, they should do so with utmost care and diligence. Accordingly, the European Union as well should strive for the highest quality of legislation when enacting new statutory duties of care.

3.2.2. Commission by omission

Duties of care in the risk society

A duty of care can loosely be defined as a generally formulated obligation, which can be enforced by means of criminal law, to avoid certain acts or omission likely to cause harm to others.[297] Thus, duties of care usually oblige the citizens to observe a certain degree of diligence in regard to the interest protected by the respective law.[298] However, the duty of care concept is an elastic one, so that its scope and shape can be adapted to the individual case at hand. Due to their general nature, duties of care can be incorporated in a multitude of different crimes. To be sure, the paradigm case of duty of care provisions is the case of omission liability, but duties of care by definition are to be found in crimes of negligence and endangerment offences as well. In English law for instance duties of care are of particular importance in the realm of gross negligent manslaughter.

Recent developments show that duties of care have become increasingly popular tools in the context of criminal risk management.[299] The increasing importance of duties of care seems to be linked to the "risk society", which leads to the phenomenon that risks are more and more contained through an increasing responsibility for danger and accordingly manifested in an increasing amount and

---

297 Visser, 'Zorgplichtbepalingen in het Strafrecht' (2001), p. 4.

298 Visser, 'Zorgplichtbepalingen in het Strafrecht' (2001), p. 4.

299 Roef, 'Strafrechtelijke Verantwoordelijkheid in de Risicomaatschappij', in Vos and Calster (eds), Risico en voorzorg in de rechtsmaatschappij (2004), p. 222. See also: Vogel, 'Norm und Pflicht bei den unechten Unterlassungsdelikten' (1993), p. 23.

scope of duties. As already mentioned, these developments have also had an impact on the concept of duties of care. In the risk society, the concept is increasingly used to impose stringent codes of conduct on the citizens to align them to the common goal of crime prevention. In a world of omnipresent risks and dangers, the individual's possibility to act freely constitutes a risk in itself. As the consequences of human action can be drastic, the modern risk society allows individuals to act freely only if certain particular diligent standards are observed.

The increasing importance of duties in post-modern society is reflected by the fact that legislators increasingly introduce duty of care provisions and furthermore extend the scope of duties.[300] One reason for this development is that social reality has become too complex and changes too rapidly in order to be regulated by specific provisions.[301] Duties of care are flexible and vague enough to cover a great variety of detrimental conduct by imposing a certain standard of care on the citizens. Moreover, duties of care become more important in our society as the complexity and contingency of social relationships through the division of labour and modernisation increases.[302] Social relationships in our post modern society need to be reliable and predictable in order to assure a safe society and to provide a clearly defined social playing field. Therefore relationships need to be controlled and standardised, which can be achieved by introducing duties of care. These legislative trends reflect the desire of post modern society to make the future calculable and controlled; in other words, risk free and safe. Duties of care constitute a powerful weapon in the armoury of the legislator regarding behaviour control, but carry the inherent danger that the attribution of criminal liability will be guided by hindsight bias, expediency, and considerations of social engineering.

Our preoccupation with future risks may have, however, further altered our conception of solidarity, which lies at the heart of duties of care.[303] Solidarity can be said to depend on three intertwined conditions. Firstly, there has to be a large community of interest which, secondly will often be linked to bonds toward common objects and values. Thirdly, the level of solidarity will often depend on the degree to which parties share a common lot, i.e. their harm and welfare are collective and indivisible.[304] Yet, with the retreat of the welfare state and the emergence of neo-liberalism, the traditional webs of solidarity that are important in providing individuals with a sense of security have been undone.[305] The corollary

300 Ashworth, 'Is the Criminal Law a lost cause?' The Law Quarterly Review (2000), pp. 225–256, Roef, 'Strafrechtelijke Verantwoordelijkheid in de Risicomaatschappij', in Vos and Calster (eds), Risico en voorzorg in de rechtsmaatschappij (2004), pp. 228–229.

301 Roef, 'Strafrechtelijke Verantwoordelijkheid in de Risicomaatschappij', in Vos and Calster (eds), Risico en voorzorg in de rechtsmaatschappij (2004), p. 223.

302 Brammsen, 'Die Entstehungsvoraussetzungen der Garantenpflichten' (1986), p. 96.

303 Houtepen and Ter Meulen, 'New Types of Solidarity in the European Welfare State' Health Care Analysis (2000), pp. 329–340.

304 Feinberg, 'Doing & Deserving -Essays in the theory of responsibility' (1970), p. 234.

305 Garland, 'The Culture of Control – Crime and Social Order in Contemporary Society' (2006), p. 156.

of this development is the creation of a culture of fear, in which, fostered by the mass media and politicians, security becomes the all- determining interest and a grim portrayal of man emerges, where (fellow) citizens cannot be trusted and ought to be controlled.[306] Thus, a shift from positive solidarity has taken place i.e. the achievement of common welfare, to negative solidarity by common fear, which leads to social relationships created for the sole purpose of preventing, containing and managing risks.[307] Thus, while solidarity in general diminishes, a new form of solidarity has emerged which is based on an "us versus them" rationale in which peers are to be protected from members of dangerous, unruly groups which ought to be identified, managed and controlled.[308] This shift in solidarity and our preoccupation with future risks has also led to the return of the victim to the centre-stage of criminal policy.[309] Victimhood has become a common and collective experience which strengthens the position of the victim within the penal justice system. Publicised with the "it-could-be-you mantra" the concerns of the victim have been subsumed within the public interest that guides the prosecution and penal decisions of the state.[310]

While duties of care are increasingly applied as a means of crime control, it should not be overlooked that they can also fulfil a safeguard function, protecting the freedom of the citizen. Early authorities in all penal systems recognised that there were certain forms of omission which were properly regarded as criminal. However, it was equally clear that criminal law neither could nor should punish all forms of inaction. The tricky question was where to draw the line. The doctrinal solution to this predicament was to punish omissions only if the actor was under a legal duty of care. If the scope of people would not be circumscribed, in theory everyone aware of the situation but not acting could be held criminally liable for the harm occurred.[311] Thus, the need for a close circumscription of people being held responsible for an omission arises. The criminal law traditionally imposes negative duties (i.e. not to steal, or kill) on everyone, but enforces positive duties (i.e. to render assistance, prevent a particular harm) only in regard to people with a

---

306 Garland, 'The Culture of Control – Crime and Social Order in Contemporary Society' (2006), pp. 10, 122, 152–154.

307 Roef and Prakken, 'Strafbare Voorbereiding in Nederland: Juridische Overkill', in Verbruggen, et al. (eds), Voorbereidingshandelingen in het Strafrecht (2004), p. 226, Van Swaaningen, 'Justitie als verzekeringsmaatschapij – Actuarial justice in Nederland' Justitiele verkenningen (1996), pp. 82, 84.

308 Feely and Simon, 'The new penology: Notes on the emerging strategy of corrections and its implications' Criminology (1992), pp. 449–474.

309 Garland, 'The Culture of Control – Crime and Social Order in Contemporary Society' (2006), p. 11.

310 Garland, 'The Culture of Control – Crime and Social Order in Contemporary Society' (2006), p.11. See also: Schwitters, 'Risico's verzekerd, verantwoordelijkheden op drift' Justitiele verkenningen (1996), pp. 9–23.

311 Ashworth, 'The scope of criminal liability for omissions' The Law Quarterly Review (1989), p. 429.

special relationship to the victim, the source of danger, etc.[312] The notion of a duty of care assures that only people connected to the harm by such a relationship of responsibility will be subjected to criminal punishment for failure to act.[313] The duty of care requirement, thus, functions as a safeguard for individual freedom and autonomy, because were it not to exist, criminal law would severely encroach on our individual liberties by requiring us to prevent any harm known to us from occurring.[314]

It is generally recognised that the underlying relationship plays a pivotal role in regard to duties of care. However, what factors can form the basis for such a relationship of responsibility is a controversial subject in all penal systems.[315] In regard to positive actions, the criminal law imposes punishment because through his actions the perpetrator has set in motion a causal chain which led to the manifestation of the prohibited harm. Corresponding to this control over the chain of events is a certain dependence, susceptibility to the prescribed harm and defencelessness of the victim, in the realm of omissions. Thus, criminal liability for an omission seems only warranted in cases where the victim was dependent on the defendant's action to prevent the harm from occurring, because the victim could rely on the intervention of the defendant due to his/her social position. It is consequently necessary to closely evaluate the (social) relationship at hand to evaluate if a relationship of responsibility, i.e. dependence, can be established.

However, our social relationships are manifold and complex and consequently a multitude of relationships are conceivable to form the basis of a duty of care. For instance, blood, domestic as well as contractual relationships, etc., can all in theory be invoked to ground a duty of care. Which basis a particular penal system chooses is largely dependent on socio–political considerations prevalent in a particular society. In addition, duties can also flow from particular social roles. A social role can be defined as a social aggregate of conduct, expectations and obligations of people in relation to others.[316] A reason for the imposition of a duty of care flowing from particular social roles can be found in the high degree of specialisation in our society which creates a dependency on the knowledge of certain specialists and moreover requires people to conduct their every day business with a high degree of

312 Ashworth, 'The scope of criminal liability for omissions' The Law Quarterly Review (1989), p. 424.

313 Wilson, 'Central Issues in Criminal Theory' (2002), p. 90. Note that also the fault requirement, which must be present to make the omission blameworthy and the concept of "possibility to intervene" circumscribe the scope of omission liability.

314 Kugler, 'Two concepts of omission' Criminal Law Forum (2003), pp. 426–427. See also: Ashworth, 'The scope of criminal liability for omissions' The Law Quarterly Review (1989), p. 429.

315 Ashworth, 'The scope of criminal liability for omissions' The Law Quarterly Review (1989), pp. 424–459, Jescheck and Weigend, 'Lehrbuch des Strafrechts: Allgemeiner Teil' (1996), pp. 600–640, Wolswijk, 'Strafbaar nalaten: een zorgplicht minder', in Harteveld, et al. (eds), Systeem in Ontwikkeling. Liber amicorum G. Knigge (2005), pp. 547–565.

316 Tjong Tjin Tai, 'Zorgplichten en zorgethiek' (2006), p. 268.

diligence. For instance, in regard to medical treatment, representation in litigation, usage of pharmaceutical products, we all depend on the knowledge of specialists, for which high social standards and expectations exist.[317] Furthermore, for the provision of certain collective goods like health, welfare, justice, security, etc., we depend in a very real sense on certain persons. The high risks and responsibility involved in these activities demand a high degree of diligence and reliability, as the majority of the citizens is dependent on such persons to provide these goods.[318]

From the above, it flows that there may be stronger and weaker duties of care.[319] For instance, both the mother and the babysitter are equally responsible for the well-being of the child, but the duty of the mother seems stronger than that of the babysitter.[320] This can be explained on the one hand by the different degree of expectations imposed by society on the mother and the babysitter respectively. Furthermore the relationship of the babysitter to the child is of a very different nature and quality than the mother's relationship. These differences can affect the blameworthiness of an omission to act on the one hand and lead to different scopes of duties on the other.

As discussed above, the concept of duties of care itself has brought only little clarity to the conundrum of omissions, for it neither clarifies where the roots of a respective duty lie, nor does it delineate the boundaries of a duty of care. It has therefore been argued that the duty of care concept should be abolished and that the doctrine of causation should be applied in order to establish criminal liability for an omission.[321] It is however submitted here that the concept of a duty of care is both a useful and necessary tool in determining liability for omissions. It not only corresponds to our common parlance to speak of a person who is required to act as being under a duty to act but the concept of duties also provides the battleground for competing moral values in our society. As mentioned before, the conventionalist and social responsibility view arrive at different solutions in regard to the scope of omission liability. While most people would agree that it is morally desirable for a bystander to rescue a fellow citizen in danger, the law's conception of omissions need not necessarily arrive at the same result.[322] In other words, the values of individual autonomy conflict with the social responsibility view that citizens should show solidarity towards other citizens in need of help.[323] The duty concept functions as an umbrella term in this respect, allowing for different, nuanced solutions to the issue. It allows for socio-political compromises regarding criminal

---

317 Brammsen, 'Die Entstehungsvoraussetzungen der Garantenpflichten' (1986), pp. 120–124.

318 Tjong Tjin Tai, 'Zorgplichten en zorgethiek' (2006), p. 269.

319 Arzt, 'Zur Garantenstellung beim unechten Unterlassungsdelikt' JA (1980), p. 555.

320 Arzt, 'Zur Garantenstellung beim unechten Unterlassungsdelikt' JA (1980), p. 555.

321 Hogan, 'Omissions and the duty myth', in Smith (ed), Criminal law – Essays in Honour of J C Smith (1987), pp. 85–91, Leavens, 'A Causation Approach to Criminal Omissions' California Law Review (1988), pp. 547–591.

322 Norrie, 'Crime, Reason and History – A Critical Introduction to Criminal Law' (2001), p. 121.

323 Norrie, 'Crime, Reason and History – A Critical Introduction to Criminal Law' (2001), p. 121.

liability for failures to act around a particular social value judgment of what is expected of a citizen as a member of society.[324]

Finally, the controversies surrounding duties of care can also be explained by the fact that there is no single concept in the framework of criminal liability for positive action which bears the weight criminal law places on the concept of duties in cases of failure to prevent harm. The concept not only fulfils an attributive function as a breach of a duty is considered sufficient to attribute liability for the harm on the actor, but this very breach also provides the basis for assessing the culpability of the (non-) actor.

After having discussed the theoretical backdrop of the duty of care concept, it will now be examined how national penal systems have approached the topic.

Commission by omission in England, the Netherlands and Germany

This discussion will commence with a brief overview of the general approach adopted towards omission liability in England, the Netherlands and Germany and will subsequently investigate the different categories of duties of care recognised.

England

Due to the prevailing conventionalist view, common law courts and lawyers have long displayed some reluctance to impose criminal liability for omissions.[325] As early as in 1887 Stephen wrote in his digest of the criminal law: "A sees B drowning and is able to save him by holding out his hand. A abstains from doing so in order that B may be drowned, and B is drowned. A has committed no offence".[326] Thus English criminal law adheres to the general principle that individuals can be held criminally liable for their actions but not for their omissions.[327] However, it is nowadays generally accepted that omissions can trigger criminal liability in circumstances where a general legal duty of care exists which outweighs the interests of individual autonomy. English courts have devised the so-called continuing act doctrine in order to avoid problems posed by the doctrine of omission stemming on the one hand from the causal act requirement, and on the other hand from the sometimes cumbersome and elusive search for a duty of care, in which to ground criminal liability. This doctrine is generally applied when a defendant unintentionally brings about an actus reus and subsequently while the harmful consequences continue, intentionally omits to take reasonable steps to discontinue them. Accordingly liability will be imposed without the need to establish a legal duty. The continuing act doctrine is therefore sometimes regarded as an exception

324 Norrie, 'Crime, Reason and History – A Critical Introduction to Criminal Law' (2001), p. 121.

325 Smith, 'Liability for omissions in the criminal law' Legal Studies (1984), pp. 88–101.

326 Stephen, James Fitzjames, A Digest of the Criminal Law (Crimes and Punishments), 4th ed., London: Macmillan, 1887, Art 212, available at: www.lareau-law.ca/DigitalLibraryTwo.html.

327 Tadros, 'Criminal Responsibility' (2005), p. 183.

to the coincidence principle which holds that the actus reus and mens rea of an offence must coincide. The leading case on the matter is *Fagan v Metropolitan Police Commissioner.*[328] The defendant accidentally drove onto a police officer's foot but subsequently, when he became aware of the situation, refused to remove his car. He was convicted for assault. The Court reasoned that:

> his conduct could not be regarded as mere omission or inactivity and there was an act constituting a battery which at its inception was not criminal because there was no element of intention, but which became criminal from the moment the intention was formed to produce the apprehension which was flowing from the continuing act.[329]

It is important to distinguish this principle from duties of care, as its scope extends further than to offences that can be committed by omission. It gains particular importance where the formulation of the offence excludes liability for omission, as discussed below. However, it has also been argued that this principle should be avoided as it involves a legal fiction, undesirable for the criminal law.[330]

Another manifestation of this restrictive approach is the fact that English courts have in regard to commission by omission adopted an interpretive approach, in the sense that they try to reconcile an omission with the terminology found in criminal provisions.[331] Beyond that interpretive approach, English courts add the requirement of a special legal duty and capacity to act to the elements of the crime in question. The concept of a duty of care is however of particular importance in the English law of gross negligent manslaughter where in order for liability to arise it is required that (i) the defendant owed the victim a duty of care (ii) the defendant breached the duty of care (iii) the defendant's breach of duty caused the death and (iv) the breach of the duty was gross.[332] In this context, the question as to the exact scope and origin of duties of care thus re-surfaces in English criminal law, from which this research can also draw inspiration.[333]

In any case, due to the aforementioned interpretive approach adopted by the courts, some offences are regarded as non-susceptible to be fulfilled by omission, for as is argued, they specify a particular type of behaviour that is required.[334] Conversely the inference of omission is regarded as unproblematic for offences that encompass an unspecific behavioural element. This approach can sometimes lead to a fuzzy outcome. Courts have for instance long accepted that murder and manslaughter can be committed by omission. On the other hand, it has been held

---

328 [1968] 3 All ER 442.

329 [1968] 3 All ER 442.

330 Smith and Hogan, 'Criminal Law' (2005), p. 84.

331 Duttwiler, 'Liability for omission in International Criminal Law' International Criminal Law Review (2006), p. 30, Ashworth, 'Principles of criminal law' (2006), p. 110.

332 See: R v Adomako [1995] 1 AC. 171. See also R v Connolly [2007] EWCA Crim 790.

333 See: Herring and Palser, 'The duty of care in gross negligent manslaughter' Criminal Law Review (2007), pp. 24–40.

334 Simester and Sullivan, 'Criminal Law: Theory and Doctrine' (2007), p. 71.

that assault or battery cannot be perpetrated by omission. An assault, so the argument goes requires an act, consequently being entirely passive cannot constitute an assault.[335]

The Netherlands

In the Netherlands it is accepted that criminal liability can also arise from a failure to act. In order for liability for omission to arise, it is generally[336] required that the person in question had a general duty of care for the underlying legally protected interest and the capacity to do so.[337] The sources of these duties of care are, however diverse and the scope of the duties is not always clearly established.

First and foremost, if a particular criminal harm, for instance, pollution of the water, is brought about by an "instrument" such as a drain, it needs to be first established who had control over the drain. This person will in the eyes of the criminal law be deemed to have a duty to prevent the harm from occurring. Besides these straightforward cases, a multitude of legal duties are acknowledged in legal literature and jurisprudence.

In the Netherlands, the concept of omissions is well-established and not the cause of much controversy. This can *inter alia* be explained by the flexible act requirement applied in the Netherlands. The shift towards a more social concept of criminal conduct, has led to a better incorporation of omissions in the framework of criminal liability. Furthermore, the acknowledgment that human conduct often consists of an aggregate of actions and omissions has presumably contributed to the acceptance of criminal liability for omission in the Netherlands. In other words, in the Netherlands, where the notion of conduct despite having a crucial function is not regarded as *the* basic concept of criminal law, the concept of omission fits much easier in the framework of criminal liability. The origins and scope and boundaries

335 Simester and Sullivan, 'Criminal Law: Theory and Doctrine' (2007), pp. 71–73. However, there is some dispute as to whether assault can be committed by omission. It seems that liability for an assault by omission can ensue from the doctrine of supervening fault (Ingernez). See: Smith and Hogan, 'Criminal Law' (2008), pp. 64–65. See also: DPP v Santana Bermudez [2003] EWHC 2908 (Admin). In this case the defendant, who when later tested proved positive for HIV and Hepatitis C, allowed a police officer to carry out a body search knowing that there was a sharp needle in his pocket which stabbed the police officer. The Crown Court had acquitted the defendant on the basis that an omission could never amount to an assault. The High Court however, held: […] "where someone (by act or word or a combination of the two) creates a danger and thereby exposes another to a reasonably foreseeable risk of injury which materialises, there is an evidential basis for the actus reus of an assault occasioning bodily harm."[…].

336 Occasionally, however, the Dutch Supreme Court, imposes criminal liability for an omission without reference to a duty of care. For instance in HR 9 September 2003, *NJ* 2003, 637 a man was convicted for the sexual abuse (Article 247 DPC) of a minor (under the age of 16) by omission because he had not prevented the girl from touching his penis. The court reasoned that, given the goal of the provision, i.e. to protect the sexual integrity of the girl, he had breached the provision as he should have intervened and prevented the girl from touching his penis.

337 Remmelink, 'Inleiding tot de studie van het Nederlandse Strafrecht' (1995), p. 166.

of duties of care are not extensively discussed in legal literature and are to a certain extent opaque.[338] The discussion rather focuses on frictions caused by omissions within the doctrine of causality. Due to the repercussions of the causal theory of action it has for a long time been disputed that omissions can be causes. This extreme view, also due to the creation of a strictly normative, legal concept of causation, has however been discarded and it is now generally accepted that omissions can be the cause of criminal harm, just like positive actions. Nevertheless, the influence of this way of thinking is still conceivable, as the frictions caused by omissions in the Dutch Penal system are still the most visible in regard to issues of causation.[339]

Germany

To remedy some of the legality objections, discussed above, and contrary to the Netherlands and England, the German legislator has enshrined the concept of improper crimes of omission in §13 of the German Penal Code (GPC).[340] Before the introduction of §13 into the German Penal Code, the issue of omission was based on customary law and left to the courts for further interpretation. As already mentioned, the provision was mainly inserted due to considerations regarding the principle of legality, as the judicial development of the legal duties was in particular regarded contrary to Articles 103 (2) and (3) of the German Basic Law.[341]

The wording of §13 GPC makes it clear that just like in the Dutch and English legal system, criminal liability for an omission derives from a duty to act, which in Germany is, according to the prevalent view, subdivided again into the duty of care (*Garantenstellung*) and the scope of this duty (*Garantenpflicht*). In all three countries these duties are brought into existence by way of judicial decision.

§13 GPC further outlines two requirements which need to be fulfilled in order to regard an omission as equivalent to an act. (i) The person that fails to prevent a

338 See: Wolswijk, 'Strafbaar nalaten: een zorgplicht minder', in Harteveld, et al. (eds), Systeem in Ontwikkeling. Liber amicorum G. Knigge (2005), pp. 547–564.

339 See for instance the decision in the "Savanna" case, Rb. 's-Gravenhage, 11 November 2007, *LJN* BB8016, where the court acquitted a family guardian, because her omission was deemed not to be the cause of the child's death. See also: Strikwerda, 'Wie kan verantwoordelijkheid dragen voor de dood van Savanna?' Delikt en Delinkwent (2008), pp. 291 et seq.

340 §13 StGB reads as follows:
(1) Whoever fails to prevent a result which is an element of a criminal offense is punishable under this law only if he was under a legal duty to prevent the result, and the omission is equivalent to the realisation of the statutory elements of the crime through action.
(2) The punishment may be mitigated pursuant to §49 (1).

341 Art 103 German Basic Law reads as follows:
(1) In the courts every person shall be entitled to a hearing in accordance with law.
(2) An act may be punished only if it was defined by a law as a criminal offense before the act was committed.
(3) No person may be punished for the same act more than once under the general criminal laws.

particular harm must have been under a legal duty to prevent the result (*Handlungsäquivalenz*), and (ii) the omission must be equivalent to the realisation of the crime through action (*Modalitätenäquivalenz*). The latter requirement refers to crimes in which the definition of the offence specifies in which way the consequences set out in the actus reus must have been brought about. An illuminating case in point here is fraud. Pursuant to German criminal law, fraud requires a pecuniary loss by deception. Thus, in order for an omission to be equivalent to the realisation of the crime through action, the consequences must have occurred in the same way as outlined in the actus reus. In this example at hand it would mean that the omission must lead to a deception which subsequently causes the pecuniary loss.[342]

The former requirement raises the question under which circumstances an omission can be regarded as equivalent to an act. This is the case when the person was under a legal duty to act. To categorise the legal duties to act, German criminal law resorts to the notion of the guarantor (*Garant*). A person is generally regarded as a guarantor if he or she has a duty to safeguard any protected interests against dangers which are under his/her control (position of supervisor, *Sicherungsgarant*)[343], or in cases where due to a duty of care (*Obhutsverhältnis*) (s)he is obliged to protect a legally protected interest against harm (position of protector, *Obhutsgarant*).[344] In other words the supervisor is held responsible for a particular source of potential danger, while the protector has a duty of care for a particular legally protected interest. The duty to act, however, must be based on law.[345] A mere moral obligation is not sufficient. Furthermore, also in Germany the defendant must have had the capacity to act in order for omission liability to arise.

It needs to be pointed out here that all the categories of duties to be found in the particular Member States share several communalities. First, it is generally recognised that the imposition of omission liability requires the violation of a duty of care. Second, the different duties to act recognised in a penal system can generally not be neatly separated and frequently overlap.[346] Furthermore, the exact scope, origins and demarcation of these duties are usually subject to a fierce debate. The uncertainty in this area is so great that some have called it the darkest chapter

342 Rudolphi in Systematischer Kommentar zum Strafgesetzbuch (2000) §13 Mn 18.

343 The category of supervision can again be subdivided into duties to control potential dangers posed by third parties or by things.

344 Duttwiler, 'Liability for omission in International Criminal Law' International Criminal Law Review (2006), pp. 35 et seq, Wessels and Beulke, 'Strafrecht Allgemeiner Teil, Die Straftat und ihr Aufbau' (2008), p. 271.

345 This however is not confined to criminal law itself. It is recognised that the duties can stem from the whole domain of law.

346 See for instance the discussion around the English case of R v Stone and Dobinson [1977] QB 354, Smith and Hogan, 'Criminal Law' (2008), p. 67; and the infamous 'leather spray' decision in Germany, 6 July 1990 BGH NStZ 1990, 587 and the discussion in Roxin, 'Strafrecht Allgemeiner Teil, Band II: Besondere Erscheinungsformen der Straftat' (2003), pp. 778–784.

of the dogmatic discussion regarding the general part.[347] It is hotly debated here whether duties of care have their origin in one universal concept applicable to all, or if duties of care can emerge from different bases.[348] While some have argued that the principle of mutual trust can constitute the universal basis of duties of care,[349] it is submitted here that taking into account the great variety of duties to be found in society and the inherent vagueness in the notion of mutual trust, multiple bases for duties of care seem to be a more convincing solution. Accordingly, in all three countries, these categories of duties are first and foremost conceptual tools. In other words, with the help of these categories of duties it may become easier and clearer to establish when someone is under a duty to act, but one is still left in the dark as to the question why this person was under a duty to act. Despite the sometimes substantial differences regarding the theoretical foundation of duties of care to be found in the Member States, the similarities and concurrence in regard to the core aspects of omission liability is remarkable.

The duties to be found in England, Germany and the Netherlands are manifold and differ in terminology. Nevertheless they can, with regard to their content, be summarised in the following way.

Duties imposed on a person in a special relationship to the victim

There are a multitude of relationships conceivable which might give rise to a duty in the realm of criminal law. Those might range from family, domestic to business or economic relationships. The criminal law seems increasingly willing to protect a wide category of individuals on the basis of not only family but also economic ties. These relationships giving rise to a duty to act can be based on a continuum representing the (moral) strength of an obligation to act, reaching from parent–children and matrimonial relationships to the (business) relationship between the landlord and tenant. The roots of these duties can be diverse and to some extent reflect the attitude of a society towards particular, institutionalised relationships at a particular time. Thus, a duty of care may be seen to stem from family ties per se, mutual trust, dependence, reliance, voluntary undertaking, etc. The selected origin will, as will be shown below, have repercussions on the scope of the duty of care. Finally, it should be pointed out that the origins and scope of duties imposed on a person in a special relationship to the victim are reflecting social changes and developments. For instance, while family duties to act were in earlier days often seen to flow from blood/family ties per se, the demise of the traditional family pattern has led to a shift of the origins of this duty.

---

347 Roxin, 'Strafrecht Allgemeiner Teil, Band II: Besondere Erscheinungsformen der Straftat' (2003), p. 711.

348 Kühl, 'Die strafrechtliche Garantenstellung – Eine Einführung mit Hinweisen zur Vertiefung' JuS (2007), p. 500.

349 Otto, 'Grundkurs Strafrecht: Allgemeine Strafrechtslehre' (2004), pp. 159–186.

Parental duties

As already mentioned, the paradigm of this category of duties is probably the duty of parents to protect their children from harm. As parents play a vital role in the socialisation process of their children, society accordingly has high expectations of parents to safeguard this process and to integrate the child as a valuable member of society. These high expectations have been forged into a strong duty of care.

As stated above, in England, to some extent these duties are incorporated in the Children and Young Persons Act 1933, but common law duties may have a wider scope. So do parents for example owe a legal duty of rescue to their children[350] or are obliged to provide adequate medical aid.[351] In the English case of *Gibbins and Proctor*, for instance, the court established that parents owed a duty to their young child, which could, if the required fault element could be proven, result in a conviction for murder by omission.[352] In this case, Walter Gibbins had been left by his wife and had started a new relationship with Edith Proctor. She moved in with Gibbins to a house with their several children, one of whom was seven-year-old Nelly Gibbins. Gibbins earned good wages which he gave to Proctor to maintain the house and those in it. However, Nelly had fallen from grace with Proctor who hated and cursed the child. She was kept upstairs apart from the others and was insufficiently supplied with food. There was evidence that Gibbins knew of the condition of the child but did nothing to prevent her from starving to death. The court, rightly, regarded the duty of Gibbins and Proctor as established beyond doubt and convicted them of murder.[353]

A difficult question here is the scope of such a duty. For instance, does the parents' duty of care cease with the majority of the child, when the children move out, etc.? And is it also the parents' duty to prevent their children from committing crimes?[354]

---

350 R v Handley [1874] Cox CC 79 cited in Simester and Sullivan, 'Criminal Law: Theory and Doctrine' (2007), p. 67.

351 R v Sheppard and Another, [1981] AC 394.

352 R v Gibbins and Proctor [1919] 13 Cr App R 134.

353 The Court argued: "There is no case directly in point, but it would be a slur upon and a discredit to the administration of justice in this country if there were any doubt as to the legal principle, or as to the present case being within it. […]". See also: Ashworth, 'The scope of criminal liability for omissions' The Law Quarterly Review (1989), p. 441.

354 This raises difficult questions as the parents' liability effectively constitutes liability for the acts of another. Arguably, one ought to distinguish here between parental liability for conduct of children above and below the age of criminal responsibility. In the light of individual responsibility, children, as they develop, should bear increasing responsibility for their actions. Accordingly, the responsibility of the parents should gradually decline as the children approach adulthood. Other factors that might influence the establishment of such a duty are a child's known propensity to offend, the possibility of the parents to effectively influence the child's behaviour and due diligence considerations, i.e. whether the parents had fulfilled their parental responsibility to the best of their abilities. See for the German perspective on the matter: Brammsen, 'Die Entstehungsvoraussetzungen der Garantenpflichten' (1986), pp. 153–156; for

Be that as it may, the parental duty does cover situations, where one parent fails to prevent the abuse,[355] or death of the child by another.[356] In a pertinent Dutch case, a mother was convicted as being an accessory in the assault of her three-year-old daughter by the mother's boyfriend. The court ruled that because the woman had not taken appropriate measures to prevent the boyfriend abusing the child, nor intervened to stop the abuse, she could be held liable. The court held that the mother had a duty to care for the life, safety, health and well-being of her child which would have obliged her to take measures to prevent the abuse by her boyfriend.[357]

In Germany and the Netherlands, the parental duty of care for their children is frequently derived from civil law. Generally speaking, civil law duties can constitute a source of inspiration for criminal law and there certainly is some overlap between duties in these two areas of the law. In regard to gross negligent manslaughter in England it is even widely assumed that the notion 'duty of care' means the same as it does in tort law.[358] However due to the compensatory nature of tort law and the underlying equality of the parties involved, civil law duties can often be wider than criminal law duties. The very nature of tort law may accordingly require that different factors may be decisive in assessing a duty of care in comparison to criminal law. Criminal law fulfils a more distinct function in society than tort law and a conflation of the two areas should therefore be avoided. "Criminal proceedings are not about balancing the responsibility between the defendant and the victim, but in determining whether the activity engaged in by the defendant is sufficiently harmful and blameworthy in the eyes of the state to justify conviction".[359]

In any case, in Germany it is generally accepted that parents derive a duty of care to their children from several provisions of the civil code. Thus parents generally owe a legal duty to rescue their children, or are obliged to provide adequate medical help. That is as long as the child is dependent on the protection of its parents and/or has not reached majority yet. For example the BGH in the tragic case of *Dennis* which caused some turmoil in Germany without hesitation assumed a duty of care for the parents of the toddler who neglected the child over years and

---

the English perspective see: Hollingsworth, 'Responsibility and Rights: Children and their parents in the youth justice system' International Journal of Law, Policy and Family (2007), pp. 190–219. In the Netherlands, proposals were made to punish parents for negligent upbringing when their children commit criminal offences. See: Klip, 'Criminal Law in the European Union' (2005), p. 47.

355 See for instance: 20 December 1983 BGH NStZ 1984, 164, where a mother was convicted as an accessory to the sexual abuse of her two daughters by their step father, as she had omitted to report the abuse to the police.

356 Kühl, 'Die strafrechtliche Garantenstellung – Eine Einführung mit Hinweisen zur Vertiefung' JuS (2007), p. 501.

357 Hof 's-Gravenhage, 9 August 1988, *NJ* 1988, 979.

358 Herring and Palser, 'The duty of care in gross negligent manslaughter' Criminal Law Review (2007), p. 24.

359 Herring and Palser, 'The duty of care in gross negligent manslaughter' Criminal Law Review (2007), p. 36. See also: R v Wacker [2003] 1 Cr App R 22, para 33.

so eventually caused his death due to under-nourishment. This conclusion was reached despite the fact that the parents were backward (IQ of 55) and suffering from mental illness (borderline syndrome).[360]

Arguably, children owe a corresponding duty of care to their parents.[361] However, such a duty of children towards their parents can already prove controversial in practice. Accordingly, some have outright denied that (adult) children would owe such a duty to their parents,[362] while others have called for a cautious approach in such cases.[363]

Matrimonial duties

While the relationship of parents to their child might morally and legally be seen as the strongest case for the imposition of a duty of care, there are other relationships which can lead to the imposition of such a duty. Another, still rather strong and uncontroversial case might be the duty of spouses to care for one another. However, as will become apparent subsequently, controversy may arise as to the exact scope and cessation of such a duty. Furthermore, there is a myriad of other relationships conceivable which may or may not give rise to a duty of care.

Spouses in general owe a duty of care to each other in regard to dangers to life and limb.[364] A husband, who, omits to call for medical assistance for his ill partner in due time, or fails to rescue her from an imminent danger, might thus incur criminal liability. A pertinent example here is the English case of *R v Hood*.[365] In this case, a husband was convicted of manslaughter by gross negligence, as he only called for medical assistance a few weeks after his wife had been injured in a fall. The wife had earlier lost a leg as a result of heavy smoking, and she was additionally suffering from diabetes and osteoporosis. She suffered the fall in early March 2002, in which she broke several bones. However, it was not until April 2002 that the husband summoned medical help. The debilitated woman was brought to hospital where her condition deteriorated and, in May of that year, she died. The court had no difficulty in holding the husband, as the sole carer of his disabled wife, responsible for his spouse's death.

German courts frequently derive a duty to act from §1353 of the German Civil Code. Usually however, family ties as such are not deemed to give rise to a duty of

---

360 13 July 2007 BGH NStZ 2007, 402.

361 Smith and Hogan, 'Criminal Law' (2008), p. 66. See also: Brammsen, 'Die Entstehungsvoraussetzungen der Garantenpflichten' (1986), p. 156.

362 Simester and Sullivan, 'Criminal Law: Theory and Doctrine' (2007), p. 68.

363 Ashworth, 'The scope of criminal liability for omissions' The Law Quarterly Review (1989), pp. 441–443, arguing for a proximity requirement of living in the same household as a prerequisite for the imposition of a duty to act.

364 See: R v Hood [2003] EWCA Crim 2772; 24 July 2003 BGH NStZ 2004, 30; Rb. Breda, 27 November 2006, *LJN* AZ4427.

365 R v Hood [2003] EWCA Crim 2772.

care without further qualification.[366] Likewise, in the Netherlands a duty to act for spouses can be derived from the law. A court convicted for instance a husband for aggravated assault by omission, when he found his wife unconscious on the floor after she had fallen down the stairs. The husband omitted to call for medical assistance and merely poured some water over his wife's face. His wife did not react to the water, and so he cold-bloodedly left his wife on the floor and went to bed. Unbeknownst to him, his wife had suffered a fractured arm which caused internal bleeding causing her death. The court held that by law he would have owed a duty to care for his wife and convicted him of intentional physical assault causing death pursuant to Article 302 DPC.[367]

Whether or not the duty of care of married couples should also encompass other interests such as a duty to prevent criminal offences committed by the respected partner, or a duty to protect financial interests is a controversial matter. In regard to the question whether one should be under a duty to prevent crimes committed by another person from occurring, two rationales should be distinguished. On the one hand such a duty could be based on positive solidarity, where the interests of the victim outweigh considerations of individual autonomy. On the other hand a duty to prevent crimes could also be based on negative solidarity, where the general goal of crime prevention trumps individual freedoms. While duties based on the former rationale generally seem uncontroversial, duties based on the latter should only be accepted on an exceptional basis. In light of individual autonomy and equivalence, it is submitted that such a duty to prevent criminal offences for spouses would be too far reaching. Such a duty would make the marriage partners, guardians of each other's righteousness and would curtail the possible scope of behaviour in a marriage significantly.[368] Likewise, it is submitted that a duty to protect the financial interests of the partner should only arise if additional circumstances would warrant the imposition of such a duty.[369]

While a duty of care between spouses seems uncontroversial at first sight, problems can arise in the case of failure of marriage. Admittedly, one accepts that a duty of care exists between spouses, yet there are several ways conceivable in which such a duty may cease. If one opts for a formal approach and sees the marital status as the source of the duty of care it would seem logical to link the cessation of the duty to the legal divorce of the marriage. Considerations of legal certainty would advocate such a view, as it would be easy in practice to determine the end of the marriage and the duty of care. However, marriages can have failed long before a legal divorce is achieved and it would seem unduly onerous in such circumstances to assume a continuation of the spouses' duty of care. This is even more so, if one takes into consideration that in some cases one spouse might have an interest in

---

366 Bohlander, 'Principles of German Criminal Law' (2009), p. 43.

367 Rb. Breda, 27 November 2006, *LJN* AZ4427.

368 Otto, 'Die Grundlagen der Strafrechtlichen Haftung des Garanten wegen Unterlassens' Jura (1985), p. 542.

369 Such as an explicit mandate for instance.

delaying divorce proceedings for instance. This would speak in favour of setting the cessation of the spouses' duty before the time of the legal divorce. The difficulty thereby however is, to develop criteria which allow for a clear and precise line drawing regarding the cessation of the duty. When can it for instance be said that a marriage has failed? Is it when the spouses end the cohabitation or when a divorce is filed? Also a medium position, combining formal and material requirements, is defensible here, by requiring that the matrimonial community has ended and it cannot reasonably be expected that the spouses would revive the community.[370]

In regard to duties of care in criminal law it can generally be said that they ought to end when the condition(s) for their creation cease to exist.[371] The corollary of this is that the reasons for the cessation of a duty must correspond to the alleged origin of the duty.

Again, there are several origins for the spouses' duty of care conceivable. As already mentioned, one could see the marital status per se as the source. Furthermore, one could see the spouses' relationship of mutual trust as the cradle of the duty. Thus, the (detrimental) reliance on the other spouse is seen as a constituent element of the duty of care here. This view would accordingly entail that a duty of care would end with the disposal of the relationship of mutual trust. The difficulty therefore is to establish how this could effectively be proven in practice.

On the other hand, it is arguable that a husband/wife is under a duty of care for his wife/husband as (s)he may be in the best position to avert the harm. As the society ought to respect the domain of married couples, so the argument goes, people will expect and rely on the spouse to avert the harm.[372] Thus, according to this view, the duty of care flows *inter alia* from society's respect for the privacy of the marriage.[373] This view would accordingly require that it is overtly visible to society that the matrimonial relationship has ended. This would presumably entail a clear temporal and spatial separation of the spouses.

The demise of traditional family patterns and the ongoing social change in modernity have made a rethinking of the origins of this duty necessary. The duty should accordingly cease once these relationships have unambiguously (for the spouses and society) come to an end. The exact (temporal, etc.) requirements should, however, be carved out within a particular penal system, reflecting social values and expectations.

Other relationships giving rise to duty of care

The discussion will now turn to some other relationships which might give rise to a duty of care. Does for instance a duty of care exist between siblings, and how about

370 24 July 2003 BGH NStZ 2004, 30.
371 Ingelfinger, 'Zeitliche Grenzen ehelicher Garantenpflichten' NStZ (2004), p. 410.
372 Ingelfinger, 'Zeitliche Grenzen ehelicher Garantenpflichten' NStZ (2004), p. 411.
373 The central presumption of this view is that spouses will assist each other in case of need and that therefore society should not impose its assistance but rather remain coy.

marriage like relationships, friends and housemates, mountaineers or expedition members? These are difficult cases and they raise questions as to the possibility of drawing sensible lines between relationships that ought to be protected by the criminal law and those which should not. Arguably, marriage-like relationships should be put on an equal footing with marriages. It is also submitted here that core family members should owe each other a duty of care. Who belongs to the core family is, however, open to debate. Much will depend here on the quality of the underlying relationship. Generally a proximity requirement of living in the same household can function as a first yardstick for the imposition of a duty of care.[374] An example of such an approach can be found in the English Domestic Violence and Victims Act 2004 which *inter alia* prohibits causing or allowing the death of a child or vulnerable adult.[375] In *R v Khan* for instance a young Pakistani woman had died by the hand of her husband following a long line of domestic abuse. The husband was convicted of her murder and sentenced to life imprisonment. However, also three other defendants who were respectively sisters of and brother-in-law to the husband and had been members of the same household and were aware of the ongoing physical abuse, were convicted of allowing the death of the victim. The court concluded that the defendants had been aware of the risk of harm to the victim and failed to take protective steps which could have reasonably been expected.[376]

However, a proximity requirement in itself might not always be sufficient to warrant the imposition of a duty. Close attention will have to be paid to the quality of the underlying relationship and the intention with which the respective persons entered the relationship. Furthermore, also the amount of control regarding the manifestation of the criminal harm might be of influence here.[377] A case in point can be found in regard to fellow lodgers. People in a loose relationship, sharing an apartment for the sole reason of sharing the rent, should not be deemed to owe each

374 Ashworth, 'The scope of criminal liability for omissions' The Law Quarterly Review (1989), p. 442.

375 Section 5 (1) of the Act reads as follows:
A person ("D") is guilty of an offence if –
(a) a child or vulnerable adult ("V") dies as a result of the unlawful act of a person who –
  (i) was a member of the same household as V, and
  (ii) had frequent contact with him,
(b) D was such a person at the time of that act,
(c) at that time there was a significant risk of serious physical harm being caused to V by the unlawful act of such a person, and
(d) either D was the person whose act caused V's death or –
  (i) D was, or ought to have been, aware of the risk mentioned in paragraph (c),
  (ii) D failed to take such steps as he could reasonably have been expected to take to protect V from the risk, and
  (iii) the act occurred in circumstances of the kind that D foresaw or ought to have foreseen.

376 R v Khan and others [2009] 1 WLR 2036.

377 Rudolphi, 'Häusliche Gemeinschaft als Entstehungsgrund für Garantenstellungen?' NStZ (1984), p. 151.

other a duty of care. Only if it can be deduced from the actual form of cohabitation that they relied on each other in case of need, might a duty of care be assumed.[378]

It has been demonstrated that this category of duties of care encompasses a wide variety of relationships. The crucial question hereby is in which notions a duty of care should be rooted, as this choice already pre-determines the scope and stringency of the duty of care. It is generally submitted that, with the notable exception of parent-child relationships, a (blood) relationship should not be sufficient in itself to give rise to a duty of care. While one might be morally inclined to support such a duty of care, it is by no means clear that, in practice, a (blood) relationship establishes a strong enough connection between two persons to warrant the imposition of a duty. Couples can live apart while still legally married, siblings or parents and (adult) children can be at odds with each other. An additional, objective requirement would therefore be necessary to distinguish relationships worthy of protection from others. One solution would be to base these duties to act on concepts such as mutual trust, interdependence or actual reliance on the assistance of the other person. The cardinal question in all these concepts in particular is how to define and prove them in practice. For the sake of legal certainty, clear concepts should be established.

First, it is argued here that this category of duties should generally be confined to dangers to health and safety. Only when additional circumstances, such as entrustment with financial affairs, are present might a duty of care be warranted in these situations as well. Financial interests will also seem worthy of protection in regard to minors who the law deems incapable of contracting; but this circumstance would cease to exist once the age of majority is reached. Those above the age of majority should generally not owe a duty of care to their parents and neither should mature siblings owe each other such a duty. Only when additional circumstances, such as living in the same household, a voluntary undertaking to care, etc., can be established would such a duty seem warranted. Societal expectations in regard to these relationships have been diminished with the demise of traditional social patterns, such as the family as the nucleus of society, and accordingly the scope of these duties of care should not be stretched too far.

Undertaken duties

Under this category cases can be subsumed, where a person has voluntarily assumed a responsibility or has undertaken a duty, but not fulfilled his "obligation" which led to the occurrence of harm. One important decision in this context in English law is the case of *R v Stone and Dobinson*. In this case Mr Stone and his mistress, Ms Dobinson, both elderly and not very competent, allowed the sister of Mr Stone (the victim) to live with them and gave her the use of a room. The victim

[378] Rudolphi, 'Häusliche Gemeinschaft als Entstehungsgrund für Garantenstellungen?' NStZ (1984), p. 151.

was eccentric, suffered from anorexia nervosa and neglected herself. She avoided any contact with the other members of the household and spent days at a time confined to her room. She soon became immobilised and helplessly infirm. Both the man and the mistress were aware of the sister's deteriorating condition but failed to take any effective steps to summon help. The victim was eventually found dead in her bed from toxaemia caused by infected bed sores and prolonged immobilisation. The Court of Appeal upheld the conviction of Mr Stone and Ms Dobinson for reckless manslaughter by omission as they were found to have breached their duty of care towards the victim.[379] While Mr Stone's duty certainly partially arose from his family relationship to the victim, the court deemed Ms Dobinson's voluntary undertaking of responsibility for the victim significant for the establishment of a duty of care. The court stressed that Ms Dobinson had from time to time supplied the victim with food and tried to wash her on one occasion two weeks before her death with the help of a neighbour who had advised her to contact social services. Thus, the court arguably assumed here that Ms Dobinson had voluntarily undertaken a duty of care towards the victim.

In any case, one can however also think here of cases where the suspect has entered into a contract and a breach of this contract has caused harm to the victim.[380] In a pertinent English decision for instance, a self-employed builder and roofer (the defendant) had been hired by the victim to work on the chimney to deal with a damp problem. He had however carried out his work sloppily and taken a series of shortcuts which resulted in a large quantity of mortar falling down the chimney and blocking the boiler flue. As a result the victim had died due to carbon monoxide poisoning. The court held that the defendant had breached his duty of care towards the victim by *inter alia* failing to ensure that the chimney was clear and working properly upon completion of the work and handed down a prison sentence of two and a half years for gross negligent manslaughter.[381]

However, the situation becomes murkier if the harm did not affect one of the parties to the contract but a third party. Think for instance of situations where an employee, while carrying out his work causes harm to a third party. Thus, here the question resurfaces if one ought to have a general duty to prevent crime. It is submitted that in regard to employer-employee relationships such a duty should only cover crimes which fall under the normal business activities of the company and could accordingly have been prevented by a diligent exertion of the employer's authority to issue directives.[382]

---

379 R v Stone and Dobinson [1977] QB 354.

380 Ashworth, 'The scope of criminal liability for omissions' The Law Quarterly Review (1989), p. 443.

381 R v David Paul Johnson [2008] EWCA Crim 2976.

382 The discussion about the liability of the employer for the acts of his employee is particularly in Germany often seen as a form of omission liability. In England and the Netherlands such scenarios are often dealt with by the doctrine of vicarious liability or functional perpetration respectively. See also: 20 October 2011 BGH NStZ 2012, 142, where the German Supreme court

In some penal systems, a contract per se may function as a basis for a duty to act. This duty may also encompass third parties. Often cited here is the case of a railway gate-keeper who failed to close the gate and a cart subsequently passing through, was struck by a train.[383] Thus, a contract is deemed a sufficient basis for a duty, regardless to whom the contractual obligation is owed.[384]

In other penal systems, however, a contract in itself is not sufficiently strong to ground a duty to act as such. Only once responsibility has factually been assumed can criminal liability be imposed.[385] Yet, in the absence of a contract, factual assumption of responsibility can also be sufficient.[386] Such a factual assumption of responsibility could also occur in form of a transfer of a duty from another person.[387]

A controversial question here is how much weight one should give to the notion of a contract for the establishment of a duty of care and furthermore if one should confine the notion of contract to civil law obligations or if it ought to be given a broader reading. Surely, a swimming instructor ought not to be held criminally liable if he, for whatever reasons does not show up for a swimming lesson and his student subsequently drowns as he decided to practice on his own. Likewise, we would hold the swim instructor responsible if he fails to rescue his pupil, even when it turns out afterwards that the contract was void.[388] It is submitted that the notion of a contractual obligation is misleading here, as the criminal law usually does not protect contractual relationships. It is not the task of criminal law to enforce all breaches of a contractual duty; this ought to be first and foremost the function of tort law. It is rather the inherent risk of harm in certain activities which seems to warrant the imposition of a duty of care.[389] However, if the essence of these duties is the prevention of harm, one has to ask how it can be foreseeable for citizens in a specific situation that they are under a duty of care and by which standards this

held that an employer had no duty to prevent mobbing by employees, as this conduct would not fall under the normal business activites of the company.

383 R v Pittwood [1902] 19 TLR 37. Wolswijk, 'Strafbaar nalaten: een zorgplicht minder', in Harteveld, et al. (eds), Systeem in Ontwikkeling. Liber amicorum G. Knigge (2005), p. 550.

384 Ashworth, 'The scope of criminal liability for omissions' The Law Quarterly Review (1989), p. 444.

385 Duttwiler, 'Liability for omission in International Criminal Law' International Criminal Law Review (2006), p. 36. See also: 31 January 2002 BGH NStZ 2002, 421 at para 20 and 8 November 2000 BGH NJW 2001, 453, where the BGH held that in addition to a contractual relationship a strong relationship of mutual trust needs to be established for a duty of care to arise.

386 Bohlander, 'Principles of German Criminal Law' (2009), p. 43.

387 See the German case: 31 January 2002 BGH NStZ 2002, 421.

388 Roxin, 'Strafrecht Allgemeiner Teil, Band II: Besondere Erscheinungsformen der Straftat' (2003), p. 715.

389 Alexander, 'Criminal Liability for Omissions: An Inventory of Issues', in Shute and Simester (eds), Criminal Law Theory: Doctrines of the General Part (2002), p. 138. Also expressing doubts about contracts as a bases of criminal liability: Ashworth, 'The scope of criminal liability for omissions' The Law Quarterly Review (1989), pp. 443–445.

should be evaluated. As will be proposed, the scope of risk and potential harm involved in a certain activity should be a determining factor here.[390] Thus, one possibility would be to regard only undertakings related to welfare and safety as a basis for a duty of care.[391] This would diminish the importance of an existing contract and shift the attention to the question whether a responsibility for the health and safety of the victim has been assumed.[392] Accordingly, duties of care would be confined to cases where the harm occurred is severe and exclude cases of mere property damage, etc., which can easily be dealt with by tort law.

Be that as it may, it is proposed here that voluntary undertakings should constitute the basis for a duty of care in situations where they give rise to certain expectations on which the victim and society were entitled to rely. Voluntary undertakings create a connection of interests, a relationship of reliance, and therefore demand the safeguarding the interests of other persons.

The concept of undertaken duties is a broad one, which can be invoked in many situations. Its rationale is most likely the containment and management of (pre-existing or pre-programmed) risks in a rapidly changing society, where the increasing division of labour and specialisation demands a proper distribution of protective functions in different aspects of life. What is relevant to the assumption of a duty of care flowing from voluntary undertakings, seems therefore, to be the (detrimental) reliance of the victim on the actions of the duty bearer. This would confine duties to act to undertakings which, to a certain extent, induced the victim to act to his/her detriment.[393] The exact roots and scope of such a duty remain, nevertheless, open to debate.

Duty Based on specific qualities of the offender

Many people, whether at the workplace or otherwise, are subject to particular duties flowing from their social role/position.[394] Many of these duties will arise in regard to civil servants, who due to their social role are not only bestowed with certain powers but are also under a duty to fulfil their function diligently and properly. Consider for instance a policeman who lets a thief escape, because he is a friend. The omission to arrest the thief constitutes a violation of the respective duty of care.[395]

---

390 Ashworth, 'The scope of criminal liability for omissions' The Law Quarterly Review (1989), pp. 443–445.

391 Ashworth, 'The scope of criminal liability for omissions' The Law Quarterly Review (1989), p. 445.

392 Ashworth, 'The scope of criminal liability for omissions' The Law Quarterly Review (1989), p. 445.

393 Mead, 'Contracting into Crime: A Theory of Criminal Omissions' Oxford Journal of legal Studies (1991), pp. 153–155.

394 See for instance: 17 July 2009 BGH NStZ 2009, 686, 19 April 2000 BGH NStZ 2001, 188.

395 Bohlander, 'Principles of German Criminal Law' (2009), p. 44.

Furthermore, a particular occupation, which can also be categorised as the voluntary undertaking of a duty, can form the basis of a duty.[396] For instance different duties might apply to police officers, building contractors, foremen, managers or doctors. The standard of care required by this class of persons is usually considerably high. Taking into account their training and skill, they are deemed to react swiftly and diligently to prevent the occurrence of harm. Professional standards by which the conduct in question will be evaluated can therefore be of considerable importance. This becomes particularly evident in regard to patient–doctor relationships. This was outlined in the English case of *R v Adomako,* where an anaesthetist during an eye-surgery failed to detect the disconnection of a tube from the ventilator which caused the death of the patient.[397] It was held that "if a person holds himself out as possessing special skill and knowledge and he is consulted as possessing such skill and knowledge, […], he owes a duty to the patient to use due caution in undertaking the treatment."[398]

Such a standard of care seems to be applied to professional relationships in all penal systems. The conduct in question is thus to be judged by the standard of a reasonable competent person from the same profession. A good example of the difference in the standard of care required by professionals and other, less trained people can be found in the Dutch *Jomanda* cases. In 1999, a Dutch actress and comedian was diagnosed with breast cancer. Although she visited several regular doctors, she chose to forego regular treatment and consulted physicians who were trained conventional doctors but also applied alternative therapies. She also sought counsel from several paranormal and alternative healers, including the Dutch new age medium, Jomanda. Her condition steadily worsened and she died two years after the initial diagnosis. Jomanda and two doctors, who had, amongst others, applied alternative treatment to the actress were prosecuted for her death. The court in Amsterdam convicted the two physicians for the death of the actress, as they had violated their duty of care. The court argued that they had not applied the diligence which was reasonably expected by a doctor, by *inter alia* not properly informing her about the possibilities and impossibilities of the applied alternative treatment and had not insisted that the actress continued conventional treatment.[399]

The alternative healer, Jomanda, was however acquitted by the court. Although the court thought that Jomanda had violated a duty of care by corroborating the

---

396 See: 17 July 2009 BGH NStZ 2009, 686.

397 [1995] 1 AC 171.

398 See also the Dutch case: HR 14 June 2005, *LJN* AT1801, where a macrobiotic nutritionist was held responsible for the death of one of his patients who despite suffering from uterine cancer he had not advised to consult conventional medical assistance but had continued macrobiotic treatment. It was held that, on the nutritionist rested a duty of care which, according to the court, entailed that he should have shown less averseness to conventional medicine and had provided the victim with more information regarding the possibilities and impossibilities of macrobiotics. Especially as he was aware of the fact that no scientific evidence existed that macrobiotics could encapsulate, let alone cure cancer.

399 Rb. Amsterdam 12 June 2009, *LJN* BI7422; BI7370.

actresses' belief that she was not suffering from cancer, this violation was not the cause of the occurred medical malpractice.[400] The court clearly thought that the relationship between the medium and the actress was not sufficiently strong to warrant the attribution of criminal liability. Furthermore, as the knowledge and skill of the medium in regard to conventional medical treatment was not as advanced as the knowledge and skills of the two physicians, her role in the death of the actress was deemed only auxiliary.

An intriguing question is how the court would have decided here if only the medium Jomanda had been involved in the chain of events. The doctors strong social position now leads to a break in the chain of causation, but would that be different if only Jomanda was involved after the initial diagnosis? In that case, the conviction of the medium, arguably, seems more likely.

In conclusion it can be stated that duties based on specific qualities of the offender are strongly connected to his social role, education and skills, as well as to certain professional standards. A particular position or social role can thus give rise to a duty of care. The stringent amount of diligence required by these persons is warranted, given their special education and training, as well as the high amount of risk, mostly involved in the activities to be carried out by this category of persons. Furthermore, when entering a particular profession, people are expected to be familiar with or get acquainted with the standard of care required by a respective profession. Accordingly, this category of duties may play a crucial role in the economic sphere. People who in an economic environment are in control over the causal course of events and therefore possess the power to influence and control essential conditions for the (non-)occurrence of harm are often considered to have a duty to properly supervise and diligently carry out their tasks.

Duties based on ownership or responsibility for a source of danger

In regard to this subcategory the question arises whether a property owner, i.e. the owner of a car, house, etc., should have a corresponding duty to his property rights to prevent harm caused by his property. The paradigms of this sub-category can be found in the well-established duties of pet- and car- owners and of dangerous enterprises.[401]

Leaving paradigm cases aside, one possible route hereby is to convict the property owner as an accomplice to the crime committed by the perpetrator in his presence or on his property.[402] Criminal liability is imposed when a person had *a right to control* the actions of another and (s)he deliberately refrains from exercising it. In these circumstances, inactivity may be regarded as encouragement to another

400 Rb. Amsterdam 12 June 2009, *LJN*, BI7445.

401 27 July 1962 BGH NJW 1962, 2069, HR 17 March 1987, *NJ* 1987, 771, Dangerous Dog Act 1991.

402 Ashworth, 'The scope of criminal liability for omissions' The Law Quarterly Review (1989), p. 446.

to perform an illegal act, and, therefore as aiding and abetting.[403] In the English case of *Du Cros v Lambourne* it had been established that the defendant's car had been driven dangerously when he and another person were both in it.[404] It could however not be proven who was actually driving the vehicle. The defendant's conviction was upheld because, even if not the driver, he was a secondary party as he had the power to prevent P from driving or continuing to drive in a dangerous manner.[405]

The exact scope of this principle is far from clear. Does the concept expand to all property owners, or is it confined to certain dangerous activities like driving a car?[406] Is, for example, the host of a party obliged to intervene if he suspects that one guest is about to rape another guest in his house? Furthermore, should a duty of care only arise in regard to the welfare and health of others or should it encompass also other, for instance, financial interests? The discussion about the exact scope of the duty to act of property owners is ongoing. Should the possession of property give rise to a duty of care in general, or should such a duty only arise in cases where additional factors increase or contribute to the dangerousness of the situation?[407]

It is, for instance, possible to impose such a duty on the owner of a house only in the very narrow circumstances where either the property in itself constituted a source of danger or if a special relationship between the home owner and the victim existed.[408] Arguably, the responsibility for a source of danger can lead to the emergence of a duty of care. A home owner, occupant or landlord can thus be under a duty of care, if due to particular circumstances protected legal interests are endangered in the spatial sphere of the lodging. This would give rise to a duty of care for an occupant to prevent the impairment of legally protected interests if special circumstances, such as a special personal relationship to the victim or the perpetrator, for instance, would require an intervention.[409] In a pertinent Dutch case, a landlord had over years neglected the maintenance of the gas heating in one of his properties and had turned a blind eye to complaints from former occupants,

---

403 Smith and Hogan, 'Criminal Law' (2005), p. 117.

404 [1907] 1 KB 40.

405 See also: R v Webster [2006] EWCA Crim 415, where the defendant was convicted as a secondary party to causing death by dangerous driving. In the course of a journey the defendant had allowed A to drive his car, despite the fact that he knew that A had been drinking. A similar kind of reasoning can be found in R v JF Alford Transport LTD [1997] 2 Cr App R 326, where in the first instance a company was convicted for omitting to take steps to prevent its drivers from falsifying their tachograph records. See also the German decision: 7 August 1981 OLG Stuttgart NJW 1981, 2369.

406 See for instance: Otto, 'Grundkurs Strafrecht: Allgemeine Strafrechtslehre' (2004), p. 180 and 7 August 1981 OLG Stuttgart NJW 1981, 2369.

407 See also: R v Willoughby [2005] 1 Cr App R 29, where in the context of gross negligent manslaughter it was held that ownership in itself was insufficient to give rise to a duty of care, but that in connection with other factors (e.g. the dangerousness of the conduct etc.) such a duty to care could emerge.

408 Jescheck and Weigend, 'Lehrbuch des Strafrechts: Allgemeiner Teil' (1996), p. 627.

409 See for instance the German case: 25 April 2001 BGH BeckRs 2001, 30176446.

as a result of which one tenant died due to carbon monoxide poisoning. The Court of first instance convicted the defendant of intentional manslaughter (Article 287 DPC) as he had failed to properly maintain the heating system and accepted the risk of death by carbon monoxide.[410] Likewise, in a similar case an English court convicted a landlord who had wrongly installed a gas fire in one of his flats which caused the death of two young men for negligent manslaughter as he had violated his duty of care towards his tenants.[411] As will subsequently become evident, these cases could arguably also be dealt with under the category of duties based on the creation of a dangerous situation, indicating a possible overlap between these categories of duties of care.[412]

What furthermore becomes apparent from those aforementioned judgments that try to align private actors like property owners or shop keepers to crime control, is the struggle of all the criminal justice systems to reduce criminal opportunities, in order to provide citizens with the demanded feeling of safety and security. In the last decades, the idea of the sovereign state as the sole actor in crime control has given way to clear recognition that crime is a challenge to be tackled by society as a whole. Therefore, the states have started to relocate and redefine responsibilities, by imposing duties of care on private actors.[413]

The exact scope of these duties is however open to debate and centres around the question in how far property owners and similar persons should be held responsible for the acts of third parties. To return to the aforementioned example of the host of a party who suspects that one of his guests might rape another guest, much will depend on the exact circumstances of the case. A general duty of care based solely on the quality of a property owner, seems unwarranted. However, if the host knows of the plans of his guest and condones or approves of them, a duty of care seems more acceptable.

Furthermore, the question could be posed if one should for instance hold a property owner responsible for failing to remove an insulting graffiti from his wall? Or is the owner of a realty under a duty to remove potentially hazardous waste from his property which has been dumped there by a third party?[414] It is submitted here that the mere possession of economic control should be insufficient to ground a duty of care. Only in exceptional cases, where additional circumstances like the scope of the potential harm or mutual trust are present, does it seem to be warranted to limit the principle of individual autonomy by the imposition of a duty of care.

---

410 Rb. Arnhem, 13 May 2004, *LJN* AO9471.

411 R v Stanley John Rodgers [2004] EWCA Crim 3115.

412 See below.

413 Garland, 'The Culture of Control – Crime and Social Order in Contemporary Society' (2006), pp. 103–139.

414 See*:* Schmitz, '"Wilde" Müllablagerungen und strafrechtliche Garantenstellung des Grundstückseigentümers' Neue Juristische Wochenschrift (1993), pp. 1167–1171. These are essentially the facts of a Dutch case regarding the liability of legal entities, in which the Supreme Court gave an affirmative answer to the question. See*:* HR 21 October 2003, *LJN* AF7938.

This category of duties clearly stems predominantly from a social responsibility view.[415] The underlying rationale presumably is that with property comes certain responsibility. Nevertheless, these duties have something untoward to them. They impose a high burden on property owners and one could question whether such a high standard is justified. As a matter of principle, it is arguable that certain closely circumscribed duties of property owners might be beneficial for society as a whole but, on the other hand, a transformation of property owners into quasi-police officers should certainly be avoided.

Duties based on the creation of a dangerous situation

This source of duties to act is probably the best established source in all three investigated countries. It seems to be a generally accepted principle of law that one is under a duty to prevent harm caused by prior conduct which created a source of risk or danger. Presumably, a duty based on the creation of a dangerous situation flows from the general prohibition to cause harm to others (*neminem laede*). Who creates a risk of harm to another is under a duty to prevent the manifestation or, at least minimise the effects of that harm. However, the law does not proscribe any risky activity. On the contrary, it deems some activities, like driving a car, which imposes risks on others as permissible. In return, the law obliges us to take steps to prevent harm to others caused by our activities. These duties are clearly an acknowledgment of the fact that people can set in motion a chain of events which would result in the occurrence of harm if they were not interrupted by some positive action. Factors potentially influencing the emergence of a duty based on the creation of a dangerous situation are the amount of control over and the proximity to the source of danger. Thus, contrary to the aforementioned duties based on the responsibility for a source of danger, the law requires here that an endangered interest is "rescued" from the imminent danger rather than a general requirement imposing a duty to maintain safety.

As already mentioned, all penal systems recognise a duty of care based on the creation of a dangerous situation.[416] The main authority in English law on the matter (but also nicely reflecting the state of affairs in the Netherlands and Germany) can be found in *R v Miller* where a vagrant went to sleep with a lit

415 Ashworth, 'The scope of criminal liability for omissions' The Law Quarterly Review (1989), p. 447.

416 R v Miller [1983] 1 All ER 978. Wessels and Beulke, 'Strafrecht Allgemeiner Teil, Die Straftat und ihr Aufbau' (2008), p. 276, Bohlander, 'Principles of German Criminal Law' (2009), pp. 44–45. Remmelink, 'Inleiding tot de studie van het Nederlandse Strafrecht' (1995), pp. 166–168. HR 12 December 2000, *NJ* 2002, 516. Roxin, 'Strafrecht Allgemeiner Teil, Band II: Besondere Erscheinungsformen der Straftat' (2003), pp. 759–778, Sowada, 'Die Garantenstellung aus vorangegangenem Tun (Ingerenz)' Jura (2003), pp. 236–246. 19 December 1997 BGH NJW 1998, 1568, 18 August 2009 BGH NStZ-RR 2009, 366, 21 December 2011 BGH HRRS 2012, Nr 333.

cigarette in the house where he has been staying over a couple of weeks.[417] When he awoke he found that he had kindled his mattress. He did not take any steps to extinguish the fire, but simply went back to sleep in an adjoined room. The house caught fire and the vagrant was convicted of arson. Lord Diplock delivering the speech for the House of Lords stated:

> I see no rational ground for excluding from conduct capable to give rise to criminal liability conduct which consist of failing to take measures that lie within one's power to counteract a danger that one has oneself created, if at the time of such conduct one's state of mind is such as constitutes a necessary ingredient of the offence. I venture to think that the habit of lawyers to talk of actus reus, suggestive as it is of action rather than inaction is responsible for any erroneous notion that failure to act cannot give rise to criminal liability in England.

The Miller principle thus imposes a duty to counteract a danger that one has created. However, the failure to prevent the danger will not by itself be sufficient to trigger criminal liability. Furthermore, all the other elements of the offence, like mens rea, must be present. This qualification generally concentrates the main thrust of the principle on result crimes, requiring fault, where the preceding act was done without fault.[418]

Another instructive case can be found in the Dutch case of a housemate who was abused by his two other cohabitants. The victim was beaten by the two housemates on a regular basis *inter alia* with the help of a hand rail and to such an extent that he could barely walk. At one point the victim was beaten to such an extent that he remained whining in the bathroom of the house in a puddle of blood. Who had caused the injuries is not made entirely clear in the judgment but the first roommate (Peter S.) was aware of the situation and moreover annoyed by the whimpering and cries for help of the victim, so that he retreated to his room and set on the stereo. When the second roommate (Peter H.) returned home drunk he found the victim whimpering in the bathroom. Also annoyed by the whimpering of the victim he began to kick the victim which lead to his death. Roommate Peter S. was aware of what was going on in the bathroom but failed to intervene. The Court of Appeal had convicted both housemates as co-perpetrators for intentional manslaughter but the defence had argued Peter S. had no duty to protect the life, health or safety of the victim. The Supreme Court upheld the conviction and kept the findings of the Appeal court that the defendant had caused the defencelessness of the victim and had therefore a duty to protect the victim from the attacks of Peter H. intact. The court also emphasised that the victim was a housemate of the two perpetrators, but which weight this factor carried in assuming a duty of care is not apparent from the judgment.[419]

---

417 [1983] 1 All ER 978.

418 Smith and Hogan, 'Criminal Law' (2008), p. 69.

419 HR 12 December 2000, *NJ* 2002, 516.

What remains, however, unclear are the exact conditions regarding the nature and quality of the dangerous conduct. Should any prior conduct give rise to a duty of care, or should it also be required that the actor acted culpably in creating the dangerous situation? A more conventionalist approach would attempt to circumscribe the situations where prior conduct will give rise to a duty of care. Several limitations are conceivable. First and foremost, it could be argued that the prior conduct must have led to a disturbance of the social "public order" in order to exclude minor infringements from the realm of criminal law. In other words a danger for a legally protected interest needs to have been created.[420] A second limitation could be that the omitting person, according to the assessment of the legal order, has to be responsible for the respective state of risk due to his prior conduct. This will frequently be the case if the prior conduct was illegal. These requirements would circumscribe the duty based on prior conduct and make sure that the omitting person was obliged to prevent the emergence of the later unthwarted danger.[421]

Contrary to the aforementioned view, it is from a more social responsibility point of view, possible to give the duty based on prior conduct a much broader scope. A duty of care due to prior conduct can also arise through acts and omissions alike, regardless whether committed culpably or not and can be even further extended by holding that ethic damnability can be sufficient.[422] This latter view seems to be the approach adopted by common and civil law systems alike.[423]

Another disputed issue concerns the level of risk which the defendant is required to run in order to prevent the harm from occurring. Certainly, the law will not require a complete self-sacrifice by the actor to prevent the harm from occurring, but just how much is required from him is open to debate. Of course, this will highly depend on the nature and quality of the act creating the situation and also on the interest at stake in the case at hand. A threat to life and limb requires more far-reaching actions to prevent the harm than a danger to property. Be that as it may, the law in any case seems justified to impose a duty to act in these situations. The author's causal responsibility for the creation of the risk as well as his proximity to and knowledge of the danger warrant the imposition of a duty of care in these circumstances.[424]

In this context, frictions with the principle of individual autonomy can arise in certain situations. Consider a case where Arthur and Boris consume illegal drugs together. If Boris overdoses, should Arthur have a duty to call for medical

420 Rudolphi in Systematischer Kommentar zum Strafgesetzbuch (2000) §13 Mn 38.

421 Rudolphi in Systematischer Kommentar zum Strafgesetzbuch (2000) §13 Mn 40.

422 Arzt, 'Zur Garantenstellung beim unechten Unterlassungsdelikt' JA (1980), pp. 553–560, 647–654.

423 Bohlander, 'Principles of German Criminal Law' (2009), pp. 44–45, Remmelink, 'Inleiding tot de studie van het Nederlandse Strafrecht' (1995), pp. 166–168, Smith and Hogan, 'Criminal Law' (2008), p. 69.

424 Ashworth, 'The scope of criminal liability for omissions' The Law Quarterly Review (1989), pp. 440.

assistance? Such cases are problematic, as conventionalists would most likely argue, because it was Boris' free and deliberate choice to use drugs and, furthermore, if Arthur were under a duty to act, this would in essence most likely lead to his criminal liability for a drug offence. From a social responsibility point of view, it seems, nevertheless, advisable to encourage drug dealers and users to care for persons rather than to risk the death of a person simply to avoid detection and "save their own skin". Again, much depends here on the underlying relationship between the drug users. Relevant factors can be: who provided the drugs, which type of drug was involved and how experienced the persons involved in the incident were regarding drug use.[425] If the inactive person has ample knowledge about the potential dangers of drug use, the imposition of a duty of care seems more warranted than in the case of an inexperienced user. Amongst others, a further important question is at which exact point a duty of care arises. Arguably, to impose a duty of care for simply supplying the drugs, if death ensues, would be too far reaching. This would potentially open the floodgates to a finding that all drug dealers owe their customers a duty of care in drug homicide cases.[426] Such an approach would not only ride roughshod over the principle of individual autonomy but would also amount to a sort of risk liability for drug dealers.[427] It seems therefore more sensible to link the emergence of the duty of care to the occurrence of the dangerous situation, i.e. the medical emergency. This would mean that a duty of care would arise once the person shows clear, visible signs of drug poisoning, such as nausea, unconsciousness, etc. It is noteworthy here that the doctrinal predicament underlying these cases will resurface and become even more pressing in the context of legal activities where one will be faced with the question whether a gun seller or a business man dealing in dangerous substances, etc. ought to incur liability for crimes which his customers committed with the help of the legally supplied goods.[428]

In any event, in line with prevalent public opinion and driven by policy considerations, all penal systems impose a duty of care on those involved in drug abuse.[429] In accordance with the foregoing discussion, it seems that the duty of care in these cases is always linked to the manifestation of a danger for the life of the

---

425 Rb. 's-Gravenhage, 24 April 2007, *LJN* BA4036.

426 Williams, 'Gross negligence manslaughter and duty of care in "Drugs" Cases: R v Evans' Criminal Law Review (2009), p. 646.

427 See however a recent German decision where a dealer was convicted of negligent manslaughter, as he sold heroin to two customers, believing it to be adulterated cocaine. The court ruled that the dealer owed a duty to his customers to make sure that the substance sold actually constituted cocaine: 29 April 2009 BGH NStZ 2009, 504.

428 See: Chapter III. 9.5.

429 Rb. 's-Gravenhage, 24 April 2007, *LJN* BA4036, Rb. Groningen, 24 August 2006, *LJN* AY6882; 27 June 1984 BGH NStZ 1984, 452, 9 November 1984 BGH NStZ 1985, 319; R v Evans, [2009] 2 Cr App R 10.

drug user.[430] The general acceptance of this duty goes to show that in the culture of control penal systems increasingly try to address the risk of harm inherent in a socially discreditable enterprise, *inter alia* by imposing duties of care rather than addressing the wrongdoing of the conduct in question.[431]

Yet, the question remains as to whether considerations of public health and criminal policy can override or at least circumscribe individual autonomy, an issue which conventionalists would probably contest. However, the inherent dangers in drug abuse for society and considerations of social responsibility have tipped the scale here in favour of a duty of care. To conclude the discussion above, some guidelines which courts might use to ground the imposition of a duty of care will now be outlined.

3.3. Conclusion

Duties of care arguably have become an important element of criminal liability in modern criminal law. Legislators increasingly impose diligent standards on citizens to protect certain interests from the risk of harm. Diligent standards enshrined in duties of care apply to a variety of different forms of behaviour and can therefore easily be applied and adapted to any form of wrongdoing even if not initially foreseen by the legislator. In an ever complex and changing society general diligent standards laid down in duties of care help to guard a legal interest against unpredictable and unforeseeable future risks. Duties can however cause friction with the principle of legality, which emphasises the need for greater clarity and consistency in creating them.

After having discussed a variety of duties of care to be found in civil and common law countries, it has however become apparent that especially in the grey areas of these duties a lot of blind spots still remain. Although over the last years several theories concerning the emergence and binding character have merged, a convincing consensus is yet to be found. This is however understandable if one takes into consideration that duties of care can be established on a number of overlapping bases. The foregoing discussion has shown that duties can be based on the hegemony over the consequences for the omission, as well as on the general creation of a danger, (detrimental) reliance[432], mutual trust[433], contract[434], or

430 Note that the situation is not entirely clear (yet) in England. See: Williams, 'Gross negligence manslaughter and duty of care in "Drugs" Cases: R v Evans' Criminal Law Review (2009), pp. 631–647.

431 See also: Wilson, 'Dealing with drug induced homicide', in Clarkson and Cunningham (eds), Criminal liability for non-aggressive death (2008), pp. 177–199.

432 Alexander, 'Criminal Liability for Omissions: An Inventory of Issues', in Shute and Simester (eds), Criminal Law Theory: Doctrines of the General Part (2002), pp. 121–142.

433 Otto, 'Grundkurs Strafrecht: Allgemeine Strafrechtslehre' (2004), pp. 156–186.

434 Mead, 'Contracting into Crime: A Theory of Criminal Omissions' Oxford Journal of legal Studies (1991), pp. 147–173.

dependence.[435] It has moreover become clear that one and the same duty can have its roots in several of these bases.

Despite the fact that the duties to act to be found in the three investigated penal systems are manifold and are categorised in different ways, they can in substance be summarised to five categories of duties of care. It seems common ground that duties of care can flow from:

- a special relationship to the victim
- voluntary undertakings
- specific qualities of the offender
- ownership or responsibility for a source of danger, and
- the creation of a dangerous situation.

It has been shown that duties of care can have different, overlapping bases, which in turn influences the scope of the respective duty. This is not surprising, and maybe even a necessity, taking into account the constant variances and changes in our society. Considering these rapid changes in conjunction with the different moral currents, discussed above, it becomes apparent that a clear and final solution of the duty of care problematic would be neither desirable nor feasible.

While the creation of a uniform theory regarding the origin and scope of duties of care would go beyond the scope of this book, it is nevertheless possible to deduce some general guidelines for courts and legislators from the aforementioned case law. The foregoing discussion has shown that the solution to the conundrum of whether or not a duty of care exists in a particular situation adopted by the courts is often based on a 'factual matrix' and policy justifications.[436] Generally the underlying relationship between the people involved would seem of crucial importance. The relationship, in general terms, must be one of proximity between the party owing the duty and the party to whom it is owed. Proximity in this respect can take different forms. It can be based on physical proximity (in the sense of temporal or spatial closeness) between the person or property of the duty bearer and the victim, causal proximity (in the sense of creating a dangerous situation) or factual proximity based on the social role of the duty bearer (e.g. employer-employee, or a professional man and his client, etc.). Furthermore proximity can arguably be based on a special relationship of vulnerability or, on what may be of particular importance in economic relationships, control between the parties.[437]

It has become apparent that courts increasingly link duties of care to the respective social role of an actor. The position of each individual in our society, so

435 For a good overview: Otto, 'Die Grundlagen der Strafrechtlichen Haftung des Garanten wegen Unterlassens' Jura (1985), pp. 530–542, 592–602, 646–654.

436 For the approach in England regarding gross negligent manslaughter see: Herring and Palser, 'The duty of care in gross negligent manslaughter' Criminal Law Review (2007), pp. 24–40.

437 Herring and Palser, 'The duty of care in gross negligent manslaughter' Criminal Law Review (2007), pp. 31 et seq.

the argument goes, is defined by its social role. The social role one holds contains a set of conduct requirements (duties) which have to be obeyed for the common good. One can distinguish here two continuums of social roles which can give an indication of the existence and scope of a duty of care. On the continuum of solidarity the social ties potentially giving rise to a duty of care range from family ties over business relationships to strangers.[438] On first sight, family ties might give rise to the strongest and most far-reaching duties of care, business relationships would constitute a medium position, while the duties owed to strangers are often the most limited.

The other continuum of hierarchy, has at its poles "authority" and "equal" relationships.[439] If the person holds a social role, for instance a position with high responsibilities and the power to guide and control situations one might assume a strong and far reaching duty of care, while persons in a subordinate position might have a less far reaching duty of care. In regard to the social roles on this continuum, one should also keep in mind that a person in a certain industry sector is also expected by society to acquaint and conduct himself in accordance with the business and diligence standards prevalent in his field of work.

As appealing as this approach might seem at first sight, it suffers from one major deficiency; the concept of the social role is unable to prescribe exactly a duty to act in a particular situation. The emergence of a duty cannot be entirely explained by the notion of social roles but can only indicate the existence of such a duty.[440] In order to delimit and pinpoint the existence of a duty more precisely, it is submitted that the concept of social role ought to be supplemented by several other criteria. One of them is the concept of mutual expectations or reliance. As society expects the interference of an individual in certain situations, based on its social role, to prevent the occurrence of a proscribed harm, special heed needs to be paid to situations where society and the individual concerned rely and expect the interference of the person in question. In these situations a rebuttable presumption as to the existence of a duty of care may be assumed.

First and foremost, flowing from the principle of legality, the notion of foreseeability will play a crucial role in the establishment of duties of care. For the person involved it ought to be reasonably foreseeable that a certain conduct is expected of him by society. Foreseeability in this respect is probably best interpreted objectively, as duties of care express a general social value judgment. The law should therefore ask if, for a reasonable person in the position of the defendant it was foreseeable that a duty of care was owed.[441] Therefore a number of factors like

---

438 Haidt and Baron, 'Social roles and the moral judgment of acts and omissions' European Journal of Social Psychology (1996), pp. 202–203.

439 Haidt and Baron, 'Social roles and the moral judgment of acts and omissions' European Journal of Social Psychology (1996), pp. 202–203.

440 Otto, 'Die Grundlagen der Strafrechtlichen Haftung des Garanten wegen Unterlassens' Jura (1985), pp. 536–537, Otto, 'Grundkurs Strafrecht: Allgemeine Strafrechtslehre' (2004), p. 163.

441 Herring and Palser, 'The duty of care in gross negligent manslaughter' Criminal Law Review (2007), pp. 24–40.

his social role, individual capacities, the particular circumstances of the case at hand and prior conduct can play a role. The latter, is particularly relevant in situations where he bears some responsibility for the fact that the victim is dependent on his performance of certain acts, i.e. when the victim has been induced to act to his detriment.[442] Another important factor can arguably be found in the degree of dependency prevalent between the offender and the victim. Finally, the establishment of a duty of care should adhere to general requirements of criminal justice and therefore be fair, just and reasonable. This would also provide room for considerations of legal, social and public policy to enter the equation. Due to policy reasons the creation of a duty of care may for instance be considered unfair or unreasonable if it may lead citizens to give up socially beneficial activities or would force them to take unnecessary and costly safety precautions.

Based on this line of thought, it is argued that mutual (social) expectation or reliance ought to give rise to a duty to act if (i) the expectation is or should have been anticipated by the potential carrier of the duty in its respective social role, (ii) the expectation is conceived binding by society (iii) the carrier of the duty himself recognises or should have recognised that a particular action will be expected of him and (iv) the expectation is of such gravity that a disobedience of the duty to act would significantly shake the foundation of trust on which society is built.[443] Furthermore, it should be established that: (v) the required conduct could have reasonably been expected by the victim and (vi) the scope of harm warrants the imposition of a duty of care.

It is, thus, crucial to carefully balance the expectations of society, the perpetrator and the victim in order to ensure that criminal liability reflects the social expectations persisting in society. How this delicate balance can be achieved in practice is, however, another question. The weight given to the expectations of the victim might vary, depending on whether the victim acted responsibly, careless or absent-mindedly in regard to the occurred harm.[444] This is because in the modern risk society, crime prevention also becomes the responsibility of the victim.[445] The benefit of such an approach would be that a degree of flexibility to encompass social changes and corresponding changes in social expectations could be maintained. Duties of care in criminal law are an expression of a social value judgment, which should also include a form of risk assessment. This is in order to ensure that the potential harm flowing from a violation of a duty of care is significant enough to warrant the imposition of criminal liability. Especially the scope of a duty of care should be determined by reference to the gravity of the (potential) harm to the

---

442 See: Mead, 'Contracting into Crime: A Theory of Criminal Omissions' Oxford Journal of legal Studies (1991), p. 153.

443 Otto, 'Die Grundlagen der Strafrechtlichen Haftung des Garanten wegen Unterlassens' Jura (1985), p. 537.

444 Reichman, 'Managing Crime Risks: Toward an Insurance Based Model of Social Control' Research in Law, Deviance and Social Control (1986), pp. 158–160.

445 O'Malley, 'Risk, Power and Crime Prevention' Economy and Society (1992), p. 266.

legally protected interest. Criminal law should enforce duties of care only to protect interests related to the health and welfare of the victim and leave all other forms of harm to tort law, etc. Criminal law should censure people for and prevent serious wrongdoing in cases where other branches of law fail to provide a satisfactory remedy. Where an occurred harm can be remedied by other means, criminal law ought not to be applied.

Such an approach would also be in line with the case law of the European Court of Human Rights, in which it has been established that states have a positive obligation to ensure that rights flowing from the Convention are guaranteed and safeguarded. Especially the right to life enshrined in Art. 2 of the Convention entails a duty on the State to put in place "a legislative and administrative framework designed to provide effective deterrence against threats to the right to life".[446] This obligation applies in the particular context of dangerous activities, where "special emphasis must be placed on regulations geared to the special features of the activity in question, particularly with regard to the level of the potential risk to human lives".[447]

The European Union has not yet explicitly legislated on the concept of omissions, but it can be deduced from existing legal instruments that acts and omissions alike fall under the notion of conduct and can constitute the basis for imposing criminal liability. This follows *inter alia* from Article 49 of the Charter of fundamental human rights which refer to acts and omissions as well as for example from Directive 2008/99/EC on the protection of the environment through criminal law which in paragraph 6 of the preamble holds: "Failure to comply with a legal duty can have the same effect as active behaviour and should therefore also be subject to corresponding penalties".[448] Despite this lack of explicit European rules on omissions, it should not be overlooked that the wealth of European Union legislation regulating a particular work sector, product, environmental standards, etc., can give rise to or respectively determine the scope of duties of care. One might think here for instance about Regulations such as Regulation 561/2006[449] harmonising driving time, break and rest periods for drivers engaged in road transport, Regulation 396/2005[450], establishing maximum residue levels of

---

446 *Öneryildiz v Turkey,* appl. no. 48939/99, 30 November 2004, para 89. See also: *Osman v United Kingdom*, appl. no. 23452/94, 28 October 1998, para 115.

447 *Öneryildiz v Turkey,* appl. no. 48939/99, 30 November 2004, para. 90. See also: *Budayeva and others v Russia*, appl. nos. 15339/02, 21166/02, 11673/02 and 15343/02, 20 March 2008, in which the court reiterated its findings from the Öneryildiz case in the context of a natural disaster (a mudslide) where the authorities had failed to take proper precautions to safeguard human life, despite the fact of a foreseeable exposure of residents to mortal risks. (at para. 128–160).

448 Directive 2008/99 of 19 November 2008 on the protection of the environment through criminal law, OJ 2008 L 328/28.

449 Regulation 561/2006 of 15 March 2006 on the harmonisation of certain social legislation relating to road transport and amending Regulations 3821/85 and 2135/98 and repealing Regulation 3820/85, OJ 2006 L 102/1.

450 Regulation 396/2005 of 23 February 2005 on maximum residue levels of pesticides in or on food and feed of plant and animal origin and amending Council Directive 91/414/EEC, OJ 2005 L 70/1.

pesticides in or on food, or Regulation 466/2001[451], setting maximum levels for certain contaminants in foodstuffs. Thus, if for instance injuries are caused by a food product which exceeded the maximum level of contaminants or a lorry driver caused an accident as he exceeded the maximum driving time, there will be a prima facie violation of a duty of care. Accordingly in areas where the Union has outlined standards of care or has established permitted maximum levels, etc., duties of care can directly derive from Union legislation.

Furthermore, the Charter of fundamental human rights of the European Union could play a role in establishing duties of care. Amongst others, the right to life (Art. 2), integrity of the person (Art. 3) or respect for private and family life (Art. 7), might all play a role here. However, the Charter also contains a right to security in Article 6. This seems to point to an effective right of crime control for the Union citizen and gives the impression of a "consumer-like claim for safety", which might well result in an expansion of duties of care.[452] This is corroborated by the fact that European criminal law can be characterised as focused on crime control and duty-based. The focus is not so much on the real conduct of the offender, but rather on his position or responsibility.[453] To counterbalance these tendencies, special heed needs to be paid to notions circumscribing the establishment of duties of care.

In regard to the limitations of duties of care, several notions need to be taken into consideration. First and foremost the principle of individual autonomy functions as a circumscription of duties of care. While social responsibility and solidarity is vital in modern society, one ought not to forget that notions based on social responsibility always contain some embedded authoritarian elements.[454] The criminal law should punish wrongdoing but should not enforce morality. The more social responsibility one allows the criminal law to enforce, the more authoritarian and paternalistic our society will become.

Furthermore the principle of reliance should act as a resistance to the expansion of duties to act.[455] This concept holds that everybody should prima facie be able to rely on the fact that the conduct of third parties or the victim conforms to their legal obligations. In other words, citizens should be able to rely on the fact that the conduct of their fellow citizens is in compliance with the law. This principle will be of particular importance in regard to duties of care enacted for reasons of crime control like the responsibility for the acts of people over which one exercises control, such as children, employees, etc. Accordingly, in situations where to the persons involved it was not foreseeable that a criminal offence would be committed by the person under his command, no duty of care can arise. But this evaluation would change, if the person in question was aware of the criminal proclivities of the

451 Regulation 466/2001 of 8 March 2001 setting maximum levels for certain contaminants in foodstuffs, OJ 2001 L 77/1.

452 Klip, 'Criminal Law in the European Union' (2005), p. 53.

453 Klip, 'Criminal Law in the European Union' (2005), p. 61.

454 Norrie, 'Crime, Reason and History – A Critical Introduction to Criminal Law' (2001), p. 131.

455 See: Vogel, 'Norm und Pflicht bei den unechten Unterlassungsdelikten' (1993), pp. 200–216.

other. The principle is, however, again pierced by the exception that in particular instances, such reliance is unreasonable. This might be the case in regard to road traffic, elderly, disabled people or minors.

Finally, the concept of impossibility of the required conduct limits the scope of duties. This concept has its origin in the principle *lex non cogit ad impossibilia* or *ultra posse nemo tenetur*.[456] Thus liability can be avoided where it was impossible for the person to comply with the duty (e.g. because (s)he was paralysed). Just as with affirmative actions an omission needs to reflect human agency in order to constitute the basis for the imposition of criminal liability, but it must furthermore be established whether or not in the particular situation it could have reasonably been expected by the person to fulfil his/her duty. It goes without saying that there is no general rule when this will be the case, but this is to be determined on a case by case basis. Much will also depend on the question whether the underlying rationale of duties of care is crime prevention or solidarity towards the victim. Duties based on solidarity towards the weak (i.e. the victim) appear more easily acceptable than duties based on the general prevention of crime.

After having discussed the doctrine of conduct with its two forms of manifestation, i.e. actions and omissions, this research will now turn its attention to the third and final basic ingredient of criminal liability namely the doctrine of causation.

4. Causality

4.1. Introduction

When something goes wrong and a (criminal) harm occurs, we intuitively ask what has caused it and whether or not someone can be held responsible for it. The public response and debate following high profile disasters such as the explosion of the oil rig Deep Water Horizon in the Gulf of Mexico is a fine example of this way of thinking. Surprisingly, in the converse situation when fortune favours us we generally do not initiate a search for the magic fairy to give her credit.

In the realm of criminal law causation plays a crucial role in the attribution of criminal liability. It is possible to approach the notion of causation from a variety of angles. Is causation in criminal law for instance concerned with uncovering some basic truth about the functioning of the world (ontology) or is it rather a purely legal/normative tool? In short, it is proposed here that the doctrine's essential task is to distinguish human causes from "Acts of God", i.e. accidents. Thus, criminal law seems on first sight less interested in unearthing general causal explanations but

456 De Jong and Knigge, 'Het materiele strafrecht' (2003), p. 69, Roxin, 'Strafrecht Allgemeiner Teil, Band II: Besondere Erscheinungsformen der Straftat' (2003), pp. 629–632, Wilson, 'Central Issues in Criminal Theory' (2002), pp. 121–125. See also: Vogel, 'Norm und Pflicht bei den unechten Unterlassungsdelikten' (1993), pp. 182–189.

rather in attributing liability to someone or something for the occurred harm. Yet, one will also have to acknowledge that the attribution of liability cannot be entirely decoupled from science and the laws of nature. As will become apparent below, the search for causal explanations and the attribution of criminal liability will often be connected in the sense that the former is seen as a prerequisite for the latter. It will furthermore become apparent that both approaches (i.e. the ontological and the normative) have their own inherent difficulties.

As previously outlined, the imposition of criminal liability requires as a basis the occurrence of a criminally relevant conduct. Pertinent to every result crime is additionally the issue of causation in order to establish the required casual link between the defendant's action and the ensuing result. Causation can however also play a role in regard to endangerment offences or even in regard to conduct crimes like theft, robbery, fraud, etc.[457] For instance, in many cases of fraud it will be necessary to prove that the occurred financial loss was caused by the deception in question. Furthermore, the doctrine plays a role in regard to offences where the manifestation of a certain result triggers an aggravation of punishment.[458] A pertinent example can be found in Art. 300 (2) DPC where in cases where serious bodily harm is caused as a result of physical abuse criminal liability is aggravated.[459] But also in regard to crimes of strict liability the doctrine of causation in connection with the requirement of voluntariness is of utmost importance in order to compensate for the missing mens rea element. Furthermore the requirement of causation is fundamental to one's understanding of the actus reus in criminal law as it provides the logically necessary linchpin between action and result. Finally, the doctrine is of importance in regard to crimes of negligence where the Public Prosecutor generally needs to prove that the violation of the duty of care by the defendant has caused the criminal harm.

Generally speaking, causation concerns the relationship between two phenomena, where the one phenomenon is the cause of the other (i.e. effect). At its loosest, the causal relationship may be merely an empirically observable relationship between two phenomena. "At its most analytical it may entail a full description of the conditions whose presence guarantees the occurrence of the event."[460] However, an event can have more than one cause and a cause more than

---

457 De Hullu, 'Materieel Strafrecht' (2006), p. 169, Wilson, 'Central Issues in Criminal Theory' (2002), p. 167, Ashworth, 'Principles of criminal law' (2006), p. 125, Schönke and Schröder, 'Kommentar zum Strafgesetzbuch' (2006), Vorbem §§13 Mn 71, 130.

458 De Hullu, 'Materieel Strafrecht' (2006), p. 169, De Jong and Knigge, 'Het materiele strafrecht' (2003), p. 73.

459 Art 300 reads as follows:
(1) Physical abuse is punishable by a term of imprisonment of not more than two years or a fine of the fourth category.
(2) Where serious bodily harm ensues as a result of the act, the offender is liable to a term of imprisonment of not more than four years or a fine of the fourth category. [...].

460 Wilson, 'Central Issues in Criminal Theory' (2002), pp. 163–164.

one effect.[461] The effect of one cause can moreover be the cause of a following event and so forth.

For instance, the cause of a forest fire is not only a carelessly thrown away cigarette; but also the oxygen in the air, the absence of moisture in the ground, the strong wind, etc. can be conceived as causes of the fire. Faced with such far-flung causal chains, one might realise that the establishment of a causal connection can constitute a daunting challenge at times. Furthermore, results need not always manifest immediately but can occur protractedly, which makes the identification of the relevant cause even more difficult. The victim of an assault may for instance only succumb to his injuries a year or two later.

In any case, in the logic of criminal law we however fade out other causes and focus instead on (human) conduct which we can identify as the cause of a respective criminal harm. Thus out of the multitude of causes for the manifestation of a criminal event, criminal law is only concerned with (human) conduct which has caused the prescribed result. The law is therefore involved in an artificial, though necessary oversimplification of reality. A further example might elucidate the matter. If an ancient vase falls from a shelf and breaks, we might blame gravity for the cause of this event. If however a human conduct is involved in the sequence of events leading to the breaking of the vase, we no longer focus on gravity, though still being a relevant cause, but rather turn our attention to the human conduct which potentially set in motion the chain of causation. Thus, while science strives for causal generalisation, the law in general is interested in singular causal statements. The law is not interested in what causes things to fall in general, but rather what caused *this* thing to fall. The reason for this is that the law's underlying purpose to engage in causal evaluations is the proper attribution of blame or liability to an agent for a particular event. If a particular harm has occurred, we look for factors responsible for its occurrence. Hart has termed this causal responsibility and distinguished it from role-responsibility, liability-responsibility and capacity responsibility.[462] The imposition of criminal liability requires a special connection between the occurred harm and the conduct of the defendant. This connection must be sufficiently strong so that one can see the occurrence of the harm as his doing.[463] Thus, the notion of causation is a multi-purpose tool which can have an explanatory as well as an attributive function. Accordingly, one can distinguish two levels of causation. At one level one is faced with the question whether a particular conduct was in fact causally connected with the result, but there remains the further question whether or not the person will be held liable in law for having caused the occurrence of the harm.[464] This raises the question whether the imposition of criminal liability requires a different conception of cause in law and in fact. Penal

---

461 Nieboer, 'Schets materieel strafrecht' (1991), p. 89.

462 Hart, 'Punishment and Responsibility' (2008), pp. 211–216.

463 Roxin, 'Strafrecht Allgemeiner Teil, Band I Grundlagen: Der Aufbau der Verbrechenslehre' (2006), p. 349, Wilson, 'Central Issues in Criminal Theory' (2002), p. 163.

464 Norrie, 'Crime, Reason and History – A Critical Introduction to Criminal Law' (2001), p. 134.

systems have found different solutions to this question, which will be discussed in more detail below; for the time being it is sufficient to note that, to think in terms of cause and effect, seems to be a characteristic trait of human beings.[465] We always look for the thing which makes the difference. Accordingly, thinking in causal terms is not an exclusive trait of the law alone, let alone criminal law. It is also, as indicated above, applied in natural sciences, humanities, etc.

Traditionally, the doctrine of causation is rooted in a liberal individualist concept of human agency, an expression of Enlightenment thought, where individuals are perceived as causal actors who are able to change, manipulate and control things and can be held criminally liable for the results they cause.[466] The doctrine of causation reflects the prevalent individualistic stance in our society that no one should be convicted for a consequence (s)he did not cause. As the criminal law perceives individuals to be responsible agents with the capacity to reason and to accordingly choose their acts and omissions, they should only be held responsible for the "normal" consequences of their own behaviour. As Ashworth rightly points out: "respect for individual autonomy and responsibility for conduct and consequences go hand in hand".[467] Criminal law, it has been argued, should only punish the blameworthy and imposing punishment on citizens for results they are not to blame for would ride roughshod over the principle of guilt. Accordingly, a doctrine of collective social responsibility as once prevalent in ancient Greece would not be reconcilable with the modern European society which is founded on respect for individual liberties.

In any case, human beings do become involved in chains of events which do not always permit the imposition of criminal liability. Often coincidences and abnormal contingencies can occur after the individual conduct, which makes it impossible to qualify the harm as the actor's deed. The main problem here is to impose criminal liability on an individual in the context of causal sequences that pre-date and post-date individual agency.[468] Despite these difficulties, together with the act requirement, the doctrine of causation forms the very backbone of criminal liability in all penal systems. This is well demonstrated by the fact that the existence of the rules on participation can partly be traced back to the doctrine of causation. As an aider and abettor can in law not be regarded to have caused the harm, the doctrines of complicity were invented to close the lacuna, so the argument goes.[469] The doctrine constitutes another threshold for the imposition of criminal liability and it has a safeguard as well as a crime control function. On the one hand it ought to prevent the imposition of criminal liability for harm for which the actor is not

465 Wilson, 'Central Issues in Criminal Theory' (2002), p. 164.

466 Norrie, 'Crime, Reason and History – A Critical Introduction to Criminal Law' (2001), p. 137.

467 Ashworth, 'Principles of criminal law' (2006), p. 123.

468 Norrie, 'Crime, Reason and History – A Critical Introduction to Criminal Law' (2001), p. 135.

469 Kadish, 'Complicity, Cause and Blame: A Study in the Interpretation of Doctrine' California Law Review (1985), pp. 323–410, Williams, 'Finis for novus actus?' Cambridge Law Journal (1989), pp. 391–416.

responsible and on the other hand it ought to ensure that people who have caused a certain result can be held responsible. Such are the safeguard and crime control function of the doctrine.

To be functional, a theory of causation must outline a criterion or criteria to establish a link between a specific conduct and a result in such a manner that similar situations will be governed by a uniform rule.[470] Theories of causation differ on the question whether the doctrine is a legal[471] or a metaphysical[472] concept. The latter derive their criteria from areas outside the law, while the former assume a legal evaluation process.[473] Here the question is essentially whether causal enquiries in law are designed to uncover some fundamental truth about the nature of the world, or whether their purpose is rather to provide the just basis for the imposition of criminal liability. The choice taken here will influence the factors which one allows to influence the establishment of a causal link. If one deems causation a metaphysical concept, one will probably reject the claim that a free and informed intervening act can break the chain of causation, or that the culpability of the defendant can affect the causal status of his actions.[474] For if one bases causation on a prelegal notion of cause and effect and views it as operative force it seems clear that a person's intention cannot have an impact on it. Minds do not have any causal powers; there is no telekinesis, so the argument runs. Furthermore, proponents of such an approach would generally doubt that causal relations suddenly break off with the intervention of some force rather than petering out over time and space.[475]

The former example triggers a further general question, namely whether the doctrine can be seen exclusively as an element of the actus reus or if considerations of mens rea can also play a role. While it was traditionally seen as a purely objective theory, it is submitted that factors of mens rea can play a role as well. Principles like 'intended consequences are never too remote' to be found in English[476] and Dutch[477] law point in this direction. Furthermore notions such as foreseeability which often play a role in the establishment of a causal link, introduce subjective elements into the evaluation process. The importance of foreseeablity in establishing a causal link is arguably linked to the aforementioned need to punish only the blameworthy.[478] It would be unjust to punish persons for harm which they

---

470 Ryu, 'Causation in Criminal Law' University of Pennsylvania Law Review (1958), p. 786.

471 Wilson, 'Central Issues in Criminal Theory' (2002), p. 165.

472 Moore, 'The Metaphysics of Causal Intervention' California Law Review (2000), pp. 827–877. See also: Moore, 'Causation and Responsibility' (2009), pp. 327–513.

473 Ryu, 'Causation in Criminal Law' University of Pennsylvania Law Review (1958), p. 786.

474 Moore, 'The Metaphysics of Causal Intervention' California Law Review (2000), p. 848. See also: Moore, 'Causation and Responsibility' (2009), pp. 254–280.

475 Moore, 'The Metaphysics of Causal Intervention' California Law Review (2000), p. 828.

476 Smith and Hogan, 'Criminal Law' (2008), pp. 90–91.

477 See for instance: HR 7 May 1985, *NJ* 1985, 821. See also: Buruma, 'Bestraft zonder iets gedaan te hebben', in Kempen, et al. (eds), De gedraging in beweging (2007), p. 24.

478 See: Padfield, 'Clean water and muddy causation a question of law or fact, or just a way of allocating blame?' Criminal Law Review (1995), p. 683.

could not foresee, and furthermore punishment would be futile as the law cannot exert a deterrent effect by censuring unforeseeable violations. The interrelatedness of the doctrine of causation and mens rea also becomes apparent in cases where the intended result was brought about by a freakish causal route or where there is an obvious mismatch between the type of harm intended and the actual harm occurred. The courts when assessing causation in these instances have to fit the offender's mental state to the actual harm occurred or causal route envisaged and determine if it was close enough to be subjected to punishment and public censure.[479] This puts the distinction between actus reus and mens rea into perspective, but does not diminish the worth of the concepts as conceptual tools.

In any case, it should also not be overlooked that as causation in criminal law is ultimately a problem of attributing responsibility, the test to establish a proper link between the conduct and the occurred result must be geared to this function and the choice of the proper test will therefore more likely be influenced by consideration of legal policy rather than natural science or philosophy. One would however, be mistaken to think that scientific and philosophical tests are accordingly irrelevant in determining the choice of policy, as for a legal policy to be sound it ought to be oriented and correspond as far as possible to scientific data and philosophical criteria.[480]

Finally a distinction can be drawn between individualising and generalising theories of causation. The former attempts to reach a single cause by a process of logical selection, while the latter claim that every particular causal statement is implicitly general. Each causal statement, so it is argued, is dependent on the truth of some general statement of regularities.[481] The theory of adequate causation for instance, can be seen as a generalising theory, while the theory of proximate cause can be classified as an individualising theory.[482] Thus, it seems fair to conclude that penal systems have a variety of choices to make when devising a coherent approach to causation. Regardless of this variety and the corresponding different approaches to causation in national penal law it should however be stressed that there are certain situations which have troubled all courts equally. These conundrums relate to contributory and intervening causes as well as self endangerment by the victim. This research will aim to analyse these common conundrums in due cause, but will first discuss at a meta-level four principles of causation and their inherent pitfalls which have proved to be highly influential for the development of national concepts of causation. These meta-principles capture a basic truth about the way criminal law looks at causality and are therefore in one way or another, reflected in national

479 Some have therefore argued that these issues ought not to bear on the establishment of a causal link but are better perceived as mens rea problems. See: Moore, 'Causation and Responsibility' (2009), pp. 98 et seq.

480 Ryu, 'Causation in Criminal Law' University of Pennsylvania Law Review (1958), p. 785.

481 Hart and Honoré, 'Causation in the Law' (1985), p. 433, Ryu, 'Causation in Criminal Law' University of Pennsylvania Law Review (1958), pp. 788–791.

482 Hart and Honoré, 'Causation in the Law' (1985), pp. 433–442, Ryu, 'Causation in Criminal Law' University of Pennsylvania Law Review (1958), pp. 788–796.

doctrines on causation. Afterwards the different concepts of causation to be found in national criminal law will be investigated.

4.2. The conditio sine qua non or the 'but for' test

The baseline from which all penal systems in the context of causation depart is the *conditio sine qua non* or the 'but for' test.[483] The cause of an event is deemed to be the whole set of factors that played a role in the bringing about of an event. Every condition which cannot be eliminated from this set of factors without eliminating the occurred result is regarded as a legal cause.[484] In other words, the conduct in question must have been an indispensable condition for the occurred result.[485] A causal relationship cannot be assumed if the result would have occurred without the respective conduct. This doctrine constitutes the lower limits of causation in criminal law. A factor that can be eliminated from the cluster of factors without eliminating the result cannot be a cause in criminal law. The 'but for' cause is often referred to as the factual cause and is thus based on the assumption that the notion of causality applied in natural science would apply in law as well.[486] However, the doctrine has some serious shortcomings. First and foremost the theory only appears to be a real scientific theory. In science the singling out of a cause usually leads to a hypothesis which has to be experimentally confirmed. In criminal law such a confirmation is not required, so that the evaluation stops basically with the formulation of a hypothesis. In other words, the scientists starting point is the lawyers finish line.[487] Furthermore the doctrine can be seen as under- and over-inclusive. Over-inclusive, as for many results a multitude of causal factors can be relevant if the crime is placed in a broader perspective. To illustrate this truism, consider the example of a murderer's ancestors. If it was not for their acts the murder would not have occurred. But is this really a valid conclusion? Should they really be blamed for their sons' misdemeanour? If one's imagination is vivid enough, one could with this line of argumentation even regard Adam and Eve as necessary conditions for the murder.

The doctrine is under-inclusive in regard to alternative sufficient causes. Consider the example of Claudia and Rose, independent of each other pouring lethal doses of arsenic into Luke's glass. In these cases the *conditio sine qua non* test fails, as it cannot be said that but for Claudia's actions Luke would be alive. Furthermore

483 De Hullu, 'Materieel Strafrecht' (2009), p. 175, Roxin, 'Strafrecht Allgemeiner Teil, Band I Grundlagen: Der Aufbau der Verbrechenslehre' (2006), p. 351, Smith and Hogan, 'Criminal Law' (2008), pp. 75–76, Wessels and Beulke, 'Strafrecht Allgemeiner Teil, Die Straftat und ihr Aufbau' (2008), pp. 55–56.

484 Remmelink, 'Inleiding tot de studie van het Nederlandse Strafrecht' (1995), pp. 175–176.

485 De Hullu, 'Materieel Strafrecht' (2006), p. 170.

486 De Jong and Knigge, 'Het materiele strafrecht' (2003), p. 77, Roxin, 'Strafrecht Allgemeiner Teil, Band I Grundlagen: Der Aufbau der Verbrechenslehre' (2006), p. 352.

487 Nieboer, 'Schets materieel strafrecht' (1991), p. 93.

the test is a thought experiment which is based on and presupposes a certain degree of knowledge about the cause and effect of certain factors. Thus, the test depends largely on actual scientific knowledge which sometimes may not exist. This is even more so if one conceives of causation as a metaphysic/ontological concept. This is nicely demonstrated by two German decisions dealing with product liability. In the *Leather spray* case it was established that the spray had caused bodily harm to consumers, but it could not be made out which chemical substance had caused the damage.[488] The German Supreme Court held that it was not necessary to establish which substance had caused the damage as long as it could be established that one of the substances in the spray was the cause. In the *Wood impregnation* case the Supreme Court went even further.[489] Here scientific opinion was so divided that a clear conclusion as to the effects of the compound could not be reached. The court nevertheless assumed a causal connection and held that the causal effects of other potential factors could, even without a comprehensive analysis of their qualities be disregarded if at least a partial causal link between the contact with the wood impregnation and the bodily harm could be proven. Without a doubt these cases are influenced by policy considerations regarding the responsibility of producers for their products, but they nicely demonstrate the difficulties that the *conditio sine qua non* can encounter. It is even arguable that with the decision in the *Wood impregnation* case, the court has sidestepped the *conditio sine qua non* and has adopted an approach based on statistical probabilities.[490] While in the modern risk society there might be good reasons for the establishment of a causal link, in these cases it should not be overlooked that a substantial amount of (objective) uncertainty remains. The difficult task here for criminal law is to pin harmful effects to individual (business, economic, etc.) actors which can hardly be isolated within the complex system of the industrial production process.[491] Accordingly, the isolation of single causes and responsibilities becomes a daunting challenge. As a result, in certain cases, in order to avoid indemnity, liability is increasingly separated from causality and can crop up anywhere.[492]

It becomes clear that the *conditio sine qua non*, despite capturing an important truth about the distinction between causes and (natural) events, cannot on its own create satisfactory and reliable results for the attribution of criminal liability. The shortcomings of the *conditio sine qua non* have led to the development of various theories and models in the different penal systems, which all possess advantages and disadvantages.

---

488 6 July 1990 BGH NStZ 1990, 587.

489 2 August 1995 BGH NStZ 1995, 590.

490 Roxin, 'Strafrecht Allgemeiner Teil, Band I Grundlagen: Der Aufbau der Verbrechenslehre' (2006), p. 358. For a Dutch decision based on a probability reasoning see: Hof Leeuwarden 22 January 2010, *LJN* BL0315.

491 Beck, 'Risk Society – Towards a New Modernity' (1992), pp. 32–33.

492 Giddens, 'Risk and Responsibility' The Modern Law Review (1999), p. 10.

4.3. The theory of proximate cause

The essential task of causation doctrines is to choose from the multitude of causes for a specific event, the criminally relevant cause. The theory of proximate cause chooses the most proximate indispensable condition to be the criminally relevant.[493] In other words the cause closest to the manifested result will be deemed to be the one relevant for criminal law. Thus, the basic truth encapsulated in this concept is that causal forces can sometimes be superseded by new causes. The theory is, however, also haunted by serious shortcoming, as the exclusive focus on the most proximate cause can lead to unsatisfactory results in practice. Consider for instance the cases where the victim of an assault subsequently dies in the hospital due to negligent treatment by a nurse. The proximate cause theory would in these cases attribute the death of the victim to the conduct of the nurse and would acquit the original wrongdoer. It is evident that this outcome will not always be satisfactory especially if the wounds inflicted by the perpetrator were severe and the mistake of the nurse minor. In spite of that, courts do apply the doctrine to circumscribe the broad results gained by the 'but for' test. Dutch courts, for instance, occasionally seem to have resorted to the doctrine to exclude remote causes from the chain of causation.[494] In the English penal system the theory of proximate cause is reflected in the notion of a *novus actus interveniens*.[495] Where the prohibited result is caused by a *novus actus*, the defendant's contribution is no longer regarded as a significant and operating cause. Conversely, the chain of causation will not be broken if the initial conduct remains a substantial and operative cause of the result.[496] This also by and large resembles the situation in Germany.[497] However, as will be discussed later, the doctrinal reasoning by which this result is achieved in Germany is diametrically opposed to the one in the English penal system. Due to the aforementioned shortcomings, courts have however struggled to produce a clear approach in this area. Decisions are also heavily influenced by policy considerations which can for instance be seen in cases where the causal link is upheld if the intervening act stems from a health care professional.[498]

---

493 De Hullu, 'Materieel Strafrecht' (2006), p. 170, Kelk, 'Studieboek materieel strafrecht' (2005), pp. 236–237, Remmelink, 'Inleiding tot de studie van het Nederlandse Strafrecht' (1995), pp. 176–177.

494 See for instance: HMG 18 February 1921, *NJ* 1921, 321 (slagkwikpijpjes).

495 Simester and Sullivan, 'Criminal Law: Theory and Doctrine' (2007), p. 84. See also: Williams, 'Finis for novus actus?' Cambridge Law Journal (1989), pp. 391–416.

496 Smith and Hogan, 'Criminal Law' (2008), p. 78.

497 Schönke and Schröder, 'Kommentar zum Strafgesetzbuch' (2006), Vorbem §13 Mn 78, Wessels and Beulke, 'Strafrecht Allgemeiner Teil, Die Straftat und ihr Aufbau' (2008), p. 56.

498 See: Chapter II. 4.8.3.

4.4. The theory of adequate causation

Another theory which is sometimes invoked is the theory of adequate causation. The theory used to be prevalent in Dutch jurisprudence and in Germany the theory is applied in civil law but has also found some support in criminal law doctrine and jurisprudence.[499] In England and Wales the theory is also partially reflected in the *novus actus* doctrine where foreseeability sometimes plays a role.[500] It uses the *conditio sine qua non* as a starting point but subsequently further circumscribes its results. Loosely formulated, this theory holds that "a condition is the adequate cause of a consequence if it has a tendency, according to human experience and in the ordinary course of events, to be followed by a consequence of this sort".[501] According to this theory the central aspect is whether the pertinent result was foreseeable in the case at hand.[502] This involves a judgment of probability which is based on general experience.[503] While this certainly corresponds to the common way of thinking about causal responsibility, how this judgment of probability is to be reached is contentious.[504]

Foreseeability can pursuant to the objective/subjective distinction be interpreted either subjectively or objectively. Accordingly one can distinguish two schools of thought here. The former hold that the perpetrator's knowledge, background etc. at the time of the commission of the offence should function as a yardstick to determine whether a specific result was foreseeable in the case at hand.[505] Such an approach effectively reveals the impact that subjective factors can have on the establishment of a causal link.

The latter approach however holds that foreseeability needs to be determined objectively *ex post*. This means that a result will be deemed foreseeable if considering all the circumstances in a case, the conduct of the perpetrator is

499 For an overview see: Roxin, 'Strafrecht Allgemeiner Teil, Band I Grundlagen: Der Aufbau der Verbrechenslehre' (2006), pp. 268–370, Wessels and Beulke, 'Strafrecht Allgemeiner Teil, Die Straftat und ihr Aufbau' (2008), pp. 58–59. See for instance: 29 August 1952 BGHSt 3, 62, where the Supreme Court acquitted a drunken cyclist of negligent manslaughter. The defendant in this case was wheeling his bicycle home at night when he fell in the road. A passing motorist stopped and removed him to the side of the road. As the motorist was returning to his car another (drunk) motorist from behind collided with the first motorist's car and killed his wife. The court of lower instance had convicted the cyclist of negligent manslaughter, but the Supreme Court held that it was not foreseeable and lay outside human experience that someone who comes to the rescue of an "injured" person would become himself the causality of an accident.

500 See: Smith and Hogan, 'Criminal Law' (2008), p. 78.

501 Hart and Honoré, 'Causation in the Law' (1985), p. 470. See also: Roxin, 'Strafrecht Allgemeiner Teil, Band I Grundlagen: Der Aufbau der Verbrechenslehre' (2006), pp. 368–370, Wessels and Beulke, 'Strafrecht Allgemeiner Teil, Die Straftat und ihr Aufbau' (2008), pp. 58–59, Schönke and Schröder, 'Kommentar zum Strafgesetzbuch' (2006), Vorbem §13 Mn 87/88.

502 Remmelink, 'Inleiding tot de studie van het Nederlandse Strafrecht' (1995), pp. 178–181.

503 Kelk, 'Studieboek materieel strafrecht' (2005), p. 238.

504 Schönke and Schröder, 'Kommentar zum Strafgesetzbuch' (2006), Vorbem §13 Mn 87/88.

505 Kelk, 'Studieboek materieel strafrecht' (2005), pp. 238–239.

objectively deemed to be the cause of it. Also intermediate positions are however conceivable, by evaluating foreseeability with the help of role models like the reasonable person, the cautious person, etc. In Dutch jurisprudence as well as in German legal theory foreseeability has predominantly been interpreted objectively.[506] For instance it was held that throwing a slipper with sole and heel against a wife's head during an argument who, unknown to the husband, suffered from an eggshell-skull defect was a suitable and predestined cause of death.[507] In a later judgment the Dutch Supreme court established a causal connection in a case where the defendant had been driving recklessly, i.e. had exceeded the speed limit on wet ground with worn-out tires, had crashed into a bollard and slithered onto the pavement where he crashed a man through a shop window. The falling glass of the shop window had subsequently slit the throat of another bystander which caused his death.[508] The Supreme Court deemed this chain of events a foreseeable result of the reckless driving.

These cases reveal some significant shortcomings of the adequate causation theory. First and foremost, the concept of foreseeability can be adapted to the "needs" of the case at hand. For instance if it is deemed appropriate to hold the husband who threw the slipper responsible for his wife's death one asks if it is foreseeable for a person suffering from an eggshell-skull defect to die from such a throw. If one aims to avoid liability one simply has to alter the question whether it was foreseeable in general for someone to die from a slipper being thrown at him.[509] Furthermore, it needs to be stressed that causal insights and therewith foreseeability judgments are subject to constant change in our society and are anything else but unequivocal. Finally, the doctrine of adequate causation seems to conceal the issue that is really at stake here, namely the question whether a certain result can be reasonably attributed to the conduct of the perpetrator. The theory, thus, enriches the concept of causality with normative criteria of attribution and is in reality not a theory of causation but rather a theory of objective attribution as it does not answer the question when a condition is to be seen as the cause of a result but which causal conditions are to be relevant for the attribution of liability.[510]

4.5. The relevance theory

Related to the theories of adequate causation and proximate cause is the so-called relevance theory which aims to select from the multitude of indispensable causes, the one which in the view of the legislator is deemed the most relevant cause of the

506 Schönke and Schröder, 'Kommentar zum Strafgesetzbuch' (2006), Vorbem §13 Mn 87/88.

507 Hof Amsterdam 14 June 1939, *NJ* 1940, 24.

508 HR 13 January 1970, *NJ* 1970, 144.

509 De Jong and Knigge, 'Het materiele strafrecht' (2003), p. 80.

510 Roxin, 'Strafrecht Allgemeiner Teil, Band I Grundlagen: Der Aufbau der Verbrechenslehre' (2006), p. 369.

offence in question.[511] It also takes the *conditio sine qua non* as a starting point but solves the issue of attributing criminal liability by focusing on the purpose of the underlying offence.[512] It has for instance been argued in regard to assaults causing death that the legislator had envisaged that the injuries of an assault can prove deadly after all, but not that the victim dies due to a fire in the hospital.[513] Arguably, the basic truth underlying this theory is that a causal link in law is never established in a vacuum, as the scope and wording of the underlying offence influences and predetermines the causal inquiry. The theory however advocates an overly casuistic approach and runs into problems in situations where the purpose of the underlying offence is ambiguous. Is the purpose of an offence proscribing kidnapping also to minimise the chance that the victim dies in the course of the abduction? In these situations the theory cannot produce workable results without having recourse to the aforementioned concept of foreseeability.[514]

It has been attempted to show that these four broad general concepts of causation, in one form or another shine through in all penal systems. Despite their inherent shortcomings they seem to contain some important basic guidelines as to when one can properly say that result x was caused by A's conduct.

After having discussed in broad strokes the most influential theories in regard to causation, it is now time to investigate how the different penal systems have approached the topic. Subsequently this research will discuss a few problematic areas that have traditionally troubled the courts.

4.6. Causation in Criminal Law in England, the Netherlands and Germany

On first sight, one is faced here with three completely different approaches to causation, based on largely different theoretical premises. The English approach to causation can be described as legal/principled, while the Dutch approach is a legal/normative one and in Germany a two-tiered meta-juridical approach seems prevalent. The English approach is termed legal/principled here, because, as will subsequently become clear, it is generally accepted that causation is a legal concept which requires something more than a 'but for' causation. Jurisprudence has developed a variety of principles that indicate that other aspects ought to also play a role in the attribution of liability. The Dutch approach is termed legal/normative on the other hand as traditional theories of causation have formerly been discarded in the Netherlands and the focus there rests on the normative enterprise of fairly attributing liability. Finally German courts generally conceive a cause as any act without which the occurred result would not have manifested and do not distinguish

511 De Hullu, 'Materieel Strafrecht' (2006), p. 170, Remmelink, 'Inleiding tot de studie van het Nederlandse Strafrecht' (1995), pp. 177–178.

512 Wessels and Beulke, 'Strafrecht Allgemeiner Teil, Die Straftat und ihr Aufbau' (2008), p. 59, Schönke and Schröder, 'Kommentar zum Strafgesetzbuch' (2006), Vorbem §13 Mn 90.

513 Remmelink, 'Inleiding tot de studie van het Nederlandse Strafrecht' (1995), p. 177.

514 Remmelink, 'Inleiding tot de studie van het Nederlandse Strafrecht' (1995), p. 178.

between proximate and more remote causes (i.e. they perceive causation mainly in ontological, meta-juristic terms). If a result can furthermore also be attributed to the actor is however a different question in which a multitude of (often also normative) aspects and notions can play a role. Despite these seemingly big differences, one will nevertheless discover that the solutions reached in the respective penal systems are often similar. These similarities regardless of the theoretical underpinning can probably be partially explained by the influence of common sense as well as general considerations of justice in the individual case at hand.

As already mentioned, the baseline from which views on causation depart, by and large is the formula of the *conditio sine qua non* or the 'but for test'. By the same token, all penal systems have recognised that the results of the basic rule would be boundless. As this would lead to an excessive scope of criminal liability, this has fostered the development of legal concepts of causation or conceptual restrictions on the attribution of criminal liability for physically causal acts.[515] English and Dutch law seem to have adopted the former approach by adopting doctrines such as the *novus actus intervienens* and the doctrine of reasonable attribution respectively.[516] German legal theory, as already indicated, has on the contrary adopted a strict separation of the notions of causation and attribution, which brings them closer to the second solution.[517]

In the following section a mixed approach will be followed. Although this research will take the national rules on causation as a starting point, similarities between the national penal systems will be highlighted immediately and discussed in an integrated manner. This approach will not only enable an analysis of the peculiarities of every system, but will also facilitate deducing a common set of principles regarding causation from these national penal systems. The discussion will commence with the English rules on causation and subsequently proceed to the German and Dutch approach.

4.6.1. The legal principled approach

The issue of causation is, whenever it arises in English criminal courts regarded as a question of fact that must be left to the jury. In answering the question the jury must apply legal principles, which the judge must explain to them.[518] But leaving this procedural peculiarity aside, the following discussion will aim to shed some light on some of the underlying concepts influencing this central notion of English criminal law. English courts have often claimed that causation is to be established

515 Bohlander, 'Principles of German Criminal Law' (2009), p. 45.

516 De Hullu, 'Materieel Strafrecht' (2009), pp. 177–184, Smith and Hogan, 'Criminal Law' (2008), pp. 74–93, Wilson, 'Central Issues in Criminal Theory' (2002), p. 165.

517 Roxin, 'Strafrecht Allgemeiner Teil, Band I Grundlagen: Der Aufbau der Verbrechenslehre' (2006), p. 350, Wessels and Beulke, 'Strafrecht Allgemeiner Teil, Die Straftat und ihr Aufbau' (2008), p. 53.

518 See: R v Pagett [1983] 76 Cr App R 279.

by the application of common sense. For instance, in *Alphacell Ltd v Woodward*, Lord Salmon held: " [...]what or who caused a certain event to occur is essentially a practical question of fact which can best be answered by ordinary common sense rather than by abstract metaphysical theory".[519] However, it seems now generally recognised that this constitutes an oversimplification.[520] English law has developed a multitude of principles in order to establish a causal link between the conduct and the result.[521] Highly influential on the English law of causation has been the work of Hart and Honoré who in their opus magnus "Causation in the Law" base their concept of causation on ordinary language philosophy rooted in a liberal individualist analysis of human agency.[522] Accordingly, it constitutes an expression and continuation of Enlightenment thought.[523] Their analysis is based on what people conceive as a "normal" result of a particular conduct or event, "[...] as part of the usual state or mode of operation of the thing under inquiry [...]".[524] We thus look for things that make the difference between the accident and things going as usual and consider these as causes.[525] The drawback of this common sense approach is that it introduces a degree of uncertainty in the evaluation process, as it relies on conventions which are subject to change. What we consider normal can change due to new scientific insights or changing social norms and values; what was not considered a cause yesterday might become one tomorrow and vice versa. Thus, while Hart and Honoré's approach seems to correctly outline the common human pattern of thought, from a legal point of view, and in particular from the perspective of legal certainty it seems problematic.

The English rules on causation are diverse and at times even appear incoherent, making it impossible to be precise and comprehensive about the underlying principles governing causation.[526] Furthermore the rich details of this extensive body of case law make the extraction of general rules a daunting challenge. Some decisions have adopted an approach emphasising the importance of a person's wrongful act and have thus adopted a narrow stance pertinent to intervening acts. Others again have emphasised the notion of culpability in establishing causation and therefore require only a minimum causal connection between the result and the conduct. These illustrations already emphasise that the English concept of causation is not a single, unvarying concept which is mechanically applied without regard to the context in which the question arises. Hence, the diversity pertinent to causation seems immense and the underlying considerations affecting the issue manifold. Nevertheless, some guiding principles of causation have crystallised over the years and will be outlined below.

---

519 [1972] AC 824 at 847.

520 See now the discussion in Empress Car Co Ltd v National Rivers Authority [1998] 1 All ER 481.

521 Smith and Hogan, 'Criminal Law' (2008), pp. 75–93.

522 Hart and Honoré, 'Causation in the Law' (1985), pp. 1–128, 325–430.

523 Norrie, 'Crime, Reason and History – A Critical Introduction to Criminal Law' (2001), p. 140.

524 Hart and Honoré, 'Causation in the Law' (1985), p. 35.

525 Hart and Honoré, 'Causation in the Law' (1985), pp. 35–61.

526 Ashworth, 'Principles of criminal law' (2006), p. 124.

The required weight of the cause in question

It has already been mentioned that causation in English law is seen as a legal concept and that the starting point of the inquiry is the *conditio sine qua non* or 'but for' test. Yet it has been shown that the *conditio sine qua non* or 'but for' test can give rise to an infinite number of causes. Moreover, a particular result can often be traced back to several causes, which raises the question how one can from a myriad of causes, single out the one suitable for the attribution of liability. As criminal law is traditionally concerned with human beings, naturally, the focus also in regard to causation is on human conduct. Thus, corresponding to the situation in Germany[527] and the Netherlands[528], the conduct of the accused in the English penal system need not be the sole or the main cause of the result.[529] Thus, other factors contributing to the occurrence of harm need not bar the assumption of a causal link. Contributing factors can be predispositions of the victim, conduct of third parties or the victim himself.[530] In a pragmatic manner, characteristic of the English legal system, it has as a general rule also been established that regardless of other active causes, the defendant's behaviour must contribute in some significant way to the occurrence of the actus reus.[531] In other words, English courts have developed a *de minimis rule* for causation. It is not necessary that the contribution is a substantial one, but it nevertheless must not be insignificant or insubstantial. As Lord Widgery CJ held in *R v Cato*: "As a matter of law, it is sufficient if the prosecution can establish that [the defendant's conduct] was *a cause*, provided it was a cause outside the de minimis range."[532]

The connection between the created risk and the criminal harm

English courts require that a connection between the fault and the result can be established in order for a result to be attributed to the defendant.[533] If the defendant's culpable conduct has in no way contributed to the result, the attribution of criminal liability seems unwarranted. Consider for instance the case of an intoxicated driver, who in spite of this fact, adheres to all traffic rules when suddenly a suicidal pedestrian steps in front of his car. Theoretically this type of case can also arise in regard to intentional crimes (resulting in attempt liability), however, it should be clear that the main area of application of this principle will be

527 Wessels and Beulke, 'Strafrecht Allgemeiner Teil, Die Straftat und ihr Aufbau' (2008), p. 56. See also: 20 May 1980 BGH NStZ 1981, 218.

528 See: De Hullu, 'Materieel Strafrecht' (2009), pp. 177–184, See also: HR 12 September 1978, *NJ* 1979, 60, HR 23 December 1980, *NJ* 1981, 534, HR 26 November 1986, *NJ* 1986, 368, HR 11 December 2001, *NJ* 2002, 62, HR 13 June 2006, *NJ* 2007, 48.

529 Smith and Hogan, 'Criminal Law' (2008), p. 76. See also: R v Pagett [1983] 76 Cr App R 279.

530 Smith and Hogan, 'Criminal Law' (2008), p. 76.

531 Simester and Sullivan, 'Criminal Law: Theory and Doctrine' (2007), p. 81.

532 R v Cato and others [1976] 1 All ER 260.

533 Smith and Hogan, 'Criminal Law' (2008), p. 77.

crimes of negligence. Methodologically speaking, a comparative hypothesis has thus to be construed and the unlawful behaviour has to be substituted with the (hypothetical) lawful behaviour.

The *modus operandi* of this principle is nicely demonstrated in the *Dalloway* decision.[534] In this case the defendant was driving a cart with reins not in his hands but loose on the horse's back when a three-year old ran into the road in front of his horse and was killed. The crucial question here was whether the fact that the driver did not hold the reins properly had contributed to the child's death. The driver was acquitted although he had physically caused the child's death, because the death could not have been prevented by holding the reins.

In Germany a similar category of cases is recognised, often subsumed under the second (normative) step of the evaluation process, i.e. objective attribution, where no connection between the violation of a duty and the actual result can be established. This exception is often termed "lawful alternative behaviour" (*rechtmäßiges Alternativverhalten*). The leading case in Germany is quite similar to the *Dalloway* scenario.[535] A lorry driver did not observe the proscribed side clearance while overtaking a cyclist and ran over and killed him. Afterwards it was discovered that the cyclist had been severely drunk. The Supreme Court acquitted the driver as, so it was argued no connection between the driver's violation of the law and the death of the cyclist could be proven, as it could not be established that a collision could have been avoided had the driver abided by the traffic rules.[536] A controversial question in this regard is with which degree of certainty it has to be established that the result would not have occurred had the defendant acted in accordance with the law. If it was absolutely certain that the result would have also occurred in case of law abiding conduct, than no causal link can be established and no criminal liability can be attributed. However, absolute certainty will rarely be achieved in practice. The prevailing opinion in scholarly writing as well as jurisprudence in Germany generally requires "a probability bordering on certainty" (*an Sicherheit grenzende Wahrscheinlichkeit*).[537] This rather stringent requirement is, however mitigated by the concept of *in dubio pro reo* which requires that in case

534 R v Dalloway [1847] 2 Cox CC 273. See also: R v Marsh [1997] 1 Cr App R 67; R v Clarke [1990] 91 Cr App R 69.

535 25 September 1957 BGH NJW 1958, 149.

536 For a more recent similar decision see: 24 March 2006 OLG Jena Beck RS 2006, 06007.

537 Schatz, 'Der Pflichtwidrigkeitszusammenhang beim fahrlässigen Erfolgsdelikt und die Relevanz hypothetischer Kausalverläufe – Zum Einwand rechtmässigen Alternativverhaltens bei fehlgeschlagener Lockerungsgewährung' NStZ (2003), p. 583, Schönke and Schröder, 'Kommentar zum Strafgesetzbuch' (2006), Vorbem §13 Mn 99a, Wessels and Beulke, 'Strafrecht Allgemeiner Teil, Die Straftat und ihr Aufbau' (2008), p. 72. The alternative view (Risikoerhöhungstheorie), developed by Roxin, which has found considerable support in the academic debate claims that a causal link can be established and liability attributed when the violation of the duty (merely) increased the risk of realization of the criminal harm. But see also: 12 January 2010, BGH NJW 2010, 1087, which can be interpreted as a rejection of the theory by the Supreme court (at paras 63–64).

of doubt a certain result may not be attributed to the defendant if lawful behaviour would have *possibly* led to the same result.[538]

In the Netherlands this sort of cases are more implicitly recognised in the prevalent concept of causation and are more often debated in the realm of negligence. However, it is accepted in scholarly writing that the establishment of a causal link requires a connection between the fault and the result.[539] This is not surprising, as the logic of the prevalent theory of reasonable attribution would dictate that the attribution of a result is unreasonable if it had also occurred regardless of the faulty conduct of the defendant.[540]

In a pertinent case the defendant had been driving under the influence of alcohol and had exceeded the allowed speed limit and crashed into another car which led to the death of two persons. He was however acquitted of the charge under the Road Safety Act as *inter alia* expert witnesses had testified that it might also have come to the collision had the defendant not exceeded the speed limit and reacted adequately before the accident.[541] A similar line of thought can be found in a judgment concerning a fire in the cell complex at Amsterdam airport. A detainee had carelessly thrown away a hand-rolled cigarette, which led to a fire in the complex, which caused eleven casualties. In the subsequent investigation the question arose as to whether the wards of the cell complex and their superiors were also responsible for the death of the inmates. The District court Amsterdam reached a negative conclusion as in its view a causal link could not be established as it could not be proven that less lives had been lost if the wardens had acted differently.[542]

The role of the underlying offence

A further principle of English law holds that the defendant's role must also be salient.[543] The same is recognised and probably plays an even stronger role in the Dutch penal system[544] as well as in the German system.[545] This principle excludes cases from the realm of causation in which the defendant's conduct was not causal

---

538 Roxin, 'Strafrecht Allgemeiner Teil, Band I Grundlagen: Der Aufbau der Verbrechenslehre' (2006), p. 393, Wessels and Beulke, 'Strafrecht Allgemeiner Teil, Die Straftat und ihr Aufbau' (2008), p. 72.

539 De Jong and Knigge, 'Het materiele strafrecht' (2003), pp. 86–91.

540 See: Chapter II. 4.6.3.

541 HR 18 May 2004, *NJ* 2004, 512.

542 Hof Amsterdam, 16 December 2009, *LJN* BK6788. But see: HR 29 April 2008, *NJ* 2008, 439 where the Court did not consider the issue of alternative lawful behaviour.

543 Simester and Sullivan, 'Criminal Law: Theory and Doctrine' (2007), p. 81. See also: Hart and Honoré, 'Causation in the Law' (1985), pp. lxiii-lxv, and R v Carey [2006] EWCA Crim 17.

544 See: De Hullu, 'Materieel Strafrecht' (2009), p. 183, De Jong and Knigge, 'Het materiele strafrecht' (2003), p. 87.

545 In doctrinal terms this category is systematically treated under the heading of reasonable attribution. See: Roxin, 'Strafrecht Allgemeiner Teil, Band I Grundlagen: Der Aufbau der Verbrechenslehre' (2006), pp. 390–392, Wessels and Beulke, 'Strafrecht Allgemeiner Teil, Die Straftat und ihr Aufbau' (2008), pp. 62–63. Also the courts have accepted this principle as a

for the occurred result. Imagine the example of a driver driving from Manchester to London. For most of his journey he exceeds the speed limit, but he slows down to the correct speed before he reaches London, where he is involved in an accident. If he had not been speeding he would not have arrived in London when he did and the accident would have been avoided. However, the driver's antecedent speeding was not causal for the accident. The risk of an accident would have been just as high had he arrived late. Briefly put, the harm must be within the risk. Thus, "if it is negligent to hand a child a loaded gun, and the child drops the gun on his foot and injures it, the injury to the foot is not within the risk that made it negligent to hand the child the loaded gun".[546] This can be seen as illustrating a wider principle that confines liability to the type of harm envisaged by the purpose of the rule of law violated (*Schuztzweck der Norm*), which highlights the crucial importance played by the wording of the underlying offence in the establishment of a causal link. The principle is most relevant in regard to crimes of negligence where it has to be established that the violated duty was meant to protect the interest covered by the underlying offence.

Intervening causes

Probably the most salient feature of the English concept of causation is the doctrine of *novus actus interveniens*. This doctrine is strongly rooted in the principle of individual autonomy and recognises people as causal actors who are primarily responsible for what they themselves do.[547] But individuals can be involved or set in motion chains of events which do not always warrant the attribution of liability to the individual actor. Thus, where an abnormal contingency occurs after the initial action or where another individual voluntarily intervenes in the chain of events, liability can no longer be attributed to the first actor.[548] His behaviour then no longer is a significant and operating cause. Where the intervening cause is a natural event the basic rule is that the defendant will be held to have caused the event, unless the intervening natural event was not reasonably foreseeable.[549] Hence, when Oscar assaults Fred and leaves his victim unconscious on a beach just below the high water mark, he will be held to have caused Fred's death if he subsequently drowns in the incoming tide. Conversely Oscar would not be considered having caused Fred's death if he left him above the high water mark and Fred drowns because of a freak tidal wave.[550] This basic rule is circumscribed by the judicial

normative limitation to the broad results gained by the theory of condition. See: 6 November 1984 BGH NJW 1985, 1350, 14 August 2002 BGH NStZ 2003, 90.

546 Hart and Honoré, 'Causation in the Law' (1985), p. lxiii.

547 Norrie, 'Crime, Reason and History – A Critical Introduction to Criminal Law' (2001), pp. 137–140, Williams, 'Finis for novus actus?' Cambridge Law Journal (1989), pp. 391–416.

548 Smith and Hogan, 'Criminal Law' (2008), p. 78.

549 Empress Car Co Ltd v National Rivers Authority, [1998] 1 All ER 481.

550 Simester and Sullivan, 'Criminal Law: Theory and Doctrine' (2007), p. 84.

disposition to ignore causal problems where an unforeseen or extraordinary event, nevertheless caused the intended result.[551] This is nicely reflected by the adage "intended consequences are never too remote".[552] This, however, does not amount to a general rule, as for instance a *novus actus* of a third party can stand in the way of attributing the intended result to the initial actor.[553] However, it can be stated that when for instance death occurs in the manner intended by the actor, the result will be attributed even if the chain of events was not as he expected. This would for instance be the case where Oscar aims for Fred's head with his pistol but misses and the ricochet kills Fred by striking him in the back.[554]

"The general principle is that the free, deliberate and informed intervention of a second person, who intends to exploit the situation created by the first, but is not acting in concert with him is held to relieve the first actor of criminal responsibility".[555] However, where the third party's intervention cannot be regarded as voluntary, the chain of causation will not be broken. In other words, a genuine involuntary act is not regarded as being capable of breaking the chain of causation.[556] Thus, if for instance the intervening act is one caused by an epileptic fit, the chain of causation will not be broken. The chain of causation will further not be broken if the defendant knowingly uses an innocent agent, i.e. a person who is below the age of criminal responsibility, insane or acts without the necessary mens rea. In these cases, the result will be imputed on the perpetrator behind the innocent agent; he has caused the result through the innocent agent.[557] By the same token will the chain of causation not be broken where the third party's actions are justified or excused because of the situation the defendant has created. In the case of *Pagett* the defendant used a girl as a human shield to escape his lawful arrest and fired at present policemen.[558] The police shot back and killed the girl. The defendant was held to have caused the girl's death. The principle that emerges from this case is that where the intervening act is one of compulsion, necessity or duty, the chain of causation will not be broken. To sum up, a result will not be attributed to the defendant if a third party's intervening act is one of a free, deliberate and informed nature, regardless of its foreseeability; or if not free, it is not reasonably foreseeable.[559] This fundamental principle has however given rise to difficulties in

551 Simester and Sullivan, 'Criminal Law: Theory and Doctrine' (2007), p. 85.
552 See: Smith and Hogan, 'Criminal Law' (2008), pp. 90–91.
553 See for instance R v Jordan [1956] 40 Cr App R 152, where the intended result was not attributed to the agent.
554 Smith and Hogan, 'Criminal Law' (2008), p. 91.
555 R v Latif [1996] 2 Cr App R 92. See also: R v Pagett [1983] 76 Cr App R 279.
556 Smith and Hogan, 'Criminal Law' (2005), p. 57.
557 See also: Chapter III. 7.3.1. and 7.3.2.
558 R v Pagett [1983] 76 Cr App R 279.
559 Smith and Hogan, 'Criminal Law' (2008), p. 78.

regard to joint drug administration cases[560] and has been factually circumscribed in regard to pollution offences.[561]

Intervening causes have puzzled the courts in all three investigated systems. This research will dwell further on the matter in a subsequent section when discussing the influence of the victim's conduct or medical interventions on the establishment of a causal link. For the time being it should be noted that especially in regard to intervening causes, subjective factors might play an important role. The causal link between an intentional harmful conduct and the occurred harm will, arguably in most instances not be broken if the intervening one is "merely" negligent. Think for instance of a doctor who, attending to the victim of an assassin with life-threatening injuries, fails to spot a small perforation of the stomach, due to which the victim dies. Conversely however, as mentioned above, matters will frequently be straight forward if the intervening conduct is intentional. But how about cases where the initial cause amounts to negligent conduct with the intervening cause being negligent as well? In this situation a careful weighing of the negligent actions will be required. Courts may thereby for instance be guided by the notion of reasonableness. This however may cause friction with the principle of legality, as foreseeability for citizens will be impeded. The more delicate the balancing exercise between these two notions in which the courts have to engage, the greater the need for more arguments that are formulated to substantiate the legal reasoning.

Contrary to the English legal concept of causation with its strong roots in the principle of individual autonomy, it will become apparent that the German notion of causation also has some ties to a social responsibility point of view. Furthermore, German lawyers tend to draw a strict line between causation in law and in fact and view the concept against the background of systematic philosophy.

4.6.2. The metaphysical/normative approach

In Germany the conundrum of causation has been addressed in a multitude of different doctrines and theories and due to that the matter is complex and a lot of doctrinal uncertainty exists. As already mentioned, German scholars generally adopt a strict separation between factual and legal causation. Accordingly, the causal evaluation process is a two-tiered process in which the broad results of the ontological, meta-juristic theory of condition (*Äquivalenztheorie*) are circumscribed by a second, normative step, the theory of objective attribution.[562] As an ontological

---

560 See: R v Kennedy [2007] UKHL 38.

561 See: Empress Car Co Ltd v National Rivers Authority [1998] 1 All ER 481; R v Kennedy [2007] UKHL 38.

562 Roxin, 'Strafrecht Allgemeiner Teil, Band I Grundlagen: Der Aufbau der Verbrechenslehre' (2006), p. 350, Wessels and Beulke, 'Strafrecht Allgemeiner Teil, Die Straftat und ihr Aufbau' (2008), p. 53, Schönke and Schröder, 'Kommentar zum Strafgesetzbuch' (2006), Vorbem §13 Mn 84, 91.

concept the nature of causation is in Germany often perceived in terms of mechanistic concepts of physics such as matter in motion, energy or force.[563]

In academic literature the doctrine of objective attribution has been widely accepted. Jurisprudence has however been a bit more reluctant to fully embrace the doctrine. In practice, objective attribution generally becomes most relevant in the realm of crimes of negligence but plays only a minor role in regard to intentional crimes.[564] This can be explained by reference to the German tripartite concept of crime, without which the German concept of causation cannot be understood. Circumscriptions to the potentially far-flung results of the German theory of causation in regard to intentional crimes are namely frequently dealt with in jurisprudence on the level of mens rea or wrongdoing. The courts thus generally still adhere to the theory of condition (*Äquivalenztheorie*) as the sole test for establishing a causal connection but have by and by accepted a number of normative correctives in the evaluation framework which brings them, closer to a version of objective attribution.[565]

Step 1: The theory of condition (*Äquivalenztheorie*)

The nucleus of the German theory of condition is perhaps contained in the notion of *versari in re illicta*, which holds that one who takes part in illegal activities is responsible for all harm which would not have occurred but for his participation. This, more social responsibility-orientated point of view stands in contrast to the English approach where the principle of individual autonomy seems to carry more weight. According to this theory every *sine qua non* or necessary condition of an event is its cause when it cannot be eliminated from the chain of events without eliminating the result.[566] The prevalent view also takes as the starting point of the theory the proposition that all conditions of a consequence which cannot be eliminated in thought without eliminating the consequences are equivalent in causal value.[567] Thus, a certain fact need not be the sole or the main cause of a result, it suffices that it is one of the number of causes.[568] This theory, as already mentioned, occasionally produces unsatisfactory results and courts and scholars have been at pains to mitigate those shortcomings. First, it has been established that the thought process of elimination must be based on the actual events and nothing can be added

---

563 Jescheck and Weigend, 'Lehrbuch des Strafrechts: Allgemeiner Teil' (1996), p. 618, Schönke and Schröder, 'Kommentar zum Strafgesetzbuch' (2006), §13 Mn 61.

564 Roxin, 'Strafrecht Allgemeiner Teil, Band I Grundlagen: Der Aufbau der Verbrechenslehre' (2006), p. 373.

565 See for instance: 11 April 2000 BGH NStZ 2001, 205, 14 February 1984 BGH NJW 1984, 1469, 6 November 1984 BGH NJW 1985, 1350.

566 13 November 2003 BGH NStZ 2004, 151, 30 March 1993 BGH NStZ 1993, 386.

567 Schönke and Schröder, 'Kommentar zum Strafgesetzbuch' (2006), Vorbem §13 Mn 76.

568 Wessels and Beulke, 'Strafrecht Allgemeiner Teil, Die Straftat und ihr Aufbau' (2008), p. 56. See also: 20 May 1980 BGH NStZ 1981, 218, 29 July 2004 BGH NJW 2005, 915.

or eliminated from these.[569] It follows that alternative hypothetical causes cannot bear on the establishment of a causal link. In a pertinent case two doctors of a psychiatric institution had, in violation of their duty of care, granted a known dangerous and mentally ill perpetrator leave from which he did not return and subsequently injured eight and killed two women. The defence had argued that the result could have also occurred as a result of the patient unlawfully escaping, which had happened several times before, enabled by the poor condition of the barred windows of the institution. The Supreme Court, however, gave the argument short shrift and convicted the doctors of negligent manslaughter as only the actual events could form the basis for the establishment of the causal connection.[570]

To solve the problem of alternative causation the courts have held that in situations where for instance Ashley and Beatrix both pour a lethal dose of poison into Camilla's drink, both should be deemed causally responsible for the result.[571] The same applies to cases of cumulative causation, i.e. where only the amount of venom from Ashley and Beatrix together cause Camilla's death.[572] This certainly is from a normative point of view a correct solution for the predicament at hand, but the result nevertheless seems inconsistent with the theory of conditions if elimination is taken as the test of whether an act is a causal condition for a result. The latter cases are, arguably less problematic as both actions are causal for the result as neither can be eliminated without eliminating the concrete result.

The issue of alternative and/or cumulative causation continues to puzzle the courts in regard to environmental offences and the criminal liability of decision making committees. The dilemma in the latter scenarios is that every board member who voted in favour of an activity resulting in harm can in theory claim that his or her vote was not causal if the required decision making threshold had already been exceeded.[573] However, according to the prevalent view, all who voted in favour are deemed causal for the ensuing result.[574]

A repercussion of the ontological/metaphysical concept of causation applied in Germany is that causation in the realm of omission liability can only be hypothetical, as one of the leading scientific principles of our time holds: *ex nihilo nihil fit*.[575] As omissions are ontologically speaking 'a nothing', they, so the

---

569 See: 13 November 2003 BGH NStZ 2004, 151. Thus, also the fact that the victim would probably have died anyway regardless of the conduct of the defendant, will not stand in the way of establishing a causal link. Every (although minimal) shortage of the lifespan by the conduct in question will be deemed causal. See also: 20 May 1980 BGH NStZ 1981, 218.

570 13 November 2003 BGH NStZ 2004, 151. See also: 15 October 1981 BGH NJW 1982, 292 where it was held that if one injures a person in a mass collision, it would be irrelevant that the same result would have been caused by the next following car.

571 See: 30 March 1993 BGH NStZ 1993, 386.

572 Wessels and Beulke, 'Strafrecht Allgemeiner Teil, Die Straftat und ihr Aufbau' (2008), p. 54.

573 Röckrath, 'Kollegialentscheidungen und Kausalitätsdogmatik – Zurechnung überbestimmter Erfolge in Straf- und Haftungsrecht' NStZ (2003), pp. 641–646.

574 6 November 2002 BGH NStZ 2003, 141.

575 Schönke and Schröder, 'Kommentar zum Strafgesetzbuch' (2006), §13 Mn 61.

argument goes cannot be seen as causes. By establishing a causal link between the omission and the occurred result the courts thereby apply the following rule of thumb. An omission will be deemed causal if the required action cannot, with a probability bordering on certainty, be added without eliminating the occurred result.[576]

From the fact that all causes are deemed equal in value it can also be deduced that coexisting conditions such as the susceptibility of the victim or other abnormal contingencies will generally not stand in the way of establishing a causal link.[577]

Contrary to the situation in England, an intentional, i.e. voluntary intervention will *prima facie* not break the chain of causation, unless the initial cause is superseded by the intervening cause and is thus no longer seen as an operating cause.[578] An intervening act could however, prevent the attribution of criminal liability on the level of objective attribution.[579] It is however, generally recognised that only if the initial conduct is still an operating cause, will the intervener's act even if it is free, deliberate and informed not break the chain of causation.[580] A case in point can be found in a case where a foster child in the course of a fight stabbed her foster mother 16 times in the abdomen and head. She left the scene of the crime but returned with her boyfriend to hide evidence linking her with the crime. When the boyfriend found out that the victim was still alive he smashed her head with a water bottle and finally strangled her. It could not be precisely established whether the victim died due to the stab wounds or the beating. The Supreme Court ruled that the causal chain was not broken by the boyfriend's actions and convicted the foster child for manslaughter.[581] By the same token, a person who had set fire to a house during a party was convicted for negligent manslaughter as the house owner's son had re-entered the burning building before the arrival of the fire brigade to rescue property or his little brother who he wrongly believed to be still inside the burning house and had died due to a carbon monoxide poisoning.[582] Despite the fact that it was the victim's free choice to re-enter the building the Supreme Court upheld the defendant's conviction. Thus, the deliberate intervening act of the son was not deemed to break the chain of causation. It should be noted that the line between still operating causes and interventions breaking the chain of causation is

576 12 January NJW 2010, 1087, 21 April 1959, OLG Hamm NJW 1959, 1551. See also: Engländer, 'Kausalitätsprobleme beim unechten Unterlassungsdelikt' JuS (2001), pp. 958–962.

577 Roxin, 'Strafrecht Allgemeiner Teil, Band I Grundlagen: Der Aufbau der Verbrechenslehre' (2006), p. 362.

578 Roxin, 'Strafrecht Allgemeiner Teil, Band I Grundlagen: Der Aufbau der Verbrechenslehre' (2006), p. 363. See also: 11 August 1999 OLG Rostock NStZ 2001, 199.

579 Wessels and Beulke, 'Strafrecht Allgemeiner Teil, Die Straftat und ihr Aufbau' (2008), pp. 67–68.

580 14 March 1989 BGH NJW 1989, 2479.

581 30 August 2000 BGH NStZ 2001, 29.

582 8 September 1993 BGH NStZ 1994, 83. See also 18 September 2002 OLG Nürnberg NJW 2003, 454, 15 May 1972 BGH NJW 1972, 1207.

blurred. As a rough yardstick, it can be stated that the less the defendant's acts continue to operate in the final result, the less likely they are considered as causal.

Step 2: Objective attribution

It has always been recognised in the German penal system that the far-flung results gained by the theory of conditions need to be further circumscribed. It has however been a bone of contention at which level this circumscription should take place i.e. at the level of causation, guilt or wrongdoing. The prevalent view in doctrinal writing is that this should take place at the level of causation. Therefore the normative theory of objective attribution has been conceived. Although there is a lot of dispute regarding the precise categorisation and terminology of the principles involved in the theory, the results reached by different writers are largely similar and it is generally agreed that the basic formula consists of two steps. (1) A result (which has factually been caused by the actor) is attributable if the actor has created a legally relevant danger which has manifested itself in the concrete result. (2) A result may despite the creation of a legally relevant danger and its subsequent manifestation not be attributable if the underlying offence was not intended to prevent the concrete danger and its result.[583] Both aspects of the formula are closely connected and cannot be neatly separated and at times overlap. Be that as it may, from this basic formula several categories can be derived where a particular result will not be attributed to the actor. First, as already mentioned, a result will only be attributed if the result falls within the type of harm envisaged by the purpose of the offence violated (*Schutzzweck der Norm*).[584]

Second, attribution is barred if the created danger does not exceed the general risk of life or constitutes a socially accepted risk. An example of the latter is the old chestnut, often to be found in textbooks, where Sam convinces his uncle, from whom he will inherit a fortune, to go on a plane trip to Hawaii, hoping he will die in a plane crash, which actually happens.[585] These cases can also be explained by the lack of controllability of the chain of causation by the actor.[586] If the occurred result was not within the sphere of influence controllable by the actor, but appears rather to be an (un)fortunate coincidence, it cannot be attributed to him as his deed, so it is argued. Paradigm cases of socially accepted risks are for instance, driving a vehicle

---

583 Roxin, 'Strafrecht Allgemeiner Teil, Band I Grundlagen: Der Aufbau der Verbrechenslehre' (2006), pp. 372–373.

584 Roxin, 'Strafrecht Allgemeiner Teil, Band I Grundlagen: Der Aufbau der Verbrechenslehre' (2006), pp. 390–392, Schönke and Schröder, 'Kommentar zum Strafgesetzbuch' (2006), Vorbem §13 Mn 95/96, Wessels and Beulke, 'Strafrecht Allgemeiner Teil, Die Straftat und ihr Aufbau' (2008), p. 62. See also: 30 July 1981 OLG Stuttgart NJW 1982, 295.

585 Roxin, 'Strafrecht Allgemeiner Teil, Band I Grundlagen: Der Aufbau der Verbrechenslehre' (2006), pp. 377–379, 382–384, Wessels and Beulke, 'Strafrecht Allgemeiner Teil, Die Straftat und ihr Aufbau' (2008), p. 63.

586 Schönke and Schröder, 'Kommentar zum Strafgesetzbuch' (2006), Vorbem §13 Mn 93, Wessels and Beulke, 'Strafrecht Allgemeiner Teil, Die Straftat und ihr Aufbau' (2008), p. 63.

in accordance with traffic regulations, participation in dangerous and risky sports as well as medical treatment carried out in accordance with *de lege artis*.[587]

Third, a result should not be attributed if what the actor attempted to do was to diminish a risk to a person or another legally protected interest. If Mike for instance deflects a stab with a knife directed towards Kurt's heart by his enemy Chris to Kurt's shoulder the result should not be attributed to him. However, if Udo in the course of rescuing little Berta creates a completely new danger, as for instance by throwing the child out of the window of a burning house an attribution seems more warranted.[588] Fourth, the aforementioned cases of lawful alternative behaviour bar the attribution of a result to the actor.[589]

A fifth and highly controversial category concerns cases of self-endangerment or self-harm.[590] Here the principle of personal responsibility plays a crucial role which is used to distinguish the different spheres of responsibility by the application of the doctrine of objective attribution.[591] As long as A's decision to self endangerment is free, deliberate and informed and as long as B merely assists A in this dangerous enterprise, he cannot be seen as causal or as a party to B's self endangerment.[592] However, the threshold into causality and thus criminal liability is crossed if B had (sole) factual control over the situation as A lacked the capacities to sufficiently comprehend the ramifications of his actions, due to her age, mental constitution, etc. By the same token will a result be attributed where B possessed superior knowledge of the danger that A put himself in.[593] A pertinent example here is the case of an illegal street race where after a reckless overtaking manoeuvre the co-driver of one of the participants died in a crash. The young men in this case belonged to a local scene which conducted street races with tuned cars where in turns both functioned as driver or co-driver respectively. The central question in

---

587 Roxin, 'Strafrecht Allgemeiner Teil, Band I Grundlagen: Der Aufbau der Verbrechenslehre' (2006), pp. 383–384, Wessels and Beulke, 'Strafrecht Allgemeiner Teil, Die Straftat und ihr Aufbau' (2008), p. 63.

588 Roxin, 'Strafrecht Allgemeiner Teil, Band I Grundlagen: Der Aufbau der Verbrechenslehre' (2006), p. 376, Schönke and Schröder, 'Kommentar zum Strafgesetzbuch' (2006), Vorbem §13 Mn 94.

589 Roxin, 'Strafrecht Allgemeiner Teil, Band I Grundlagen: Der Aufbau der Verbrechenslehre' (2006), pp. 392–399, Wessels and Beulke, 'Strafrecht Allgemeiner Teil, Die Straftat und ihr Aufbau' (2008), p. 73.

590 Kuhli, 'Objektive Zurechnung bei eigenverantwortlicher Selbstgefährdung' HRRS (2008), pp. 385–388, Puppe, 'Die Selbstgefährdung des Verletzten beim Fahrlässigkeitsdelikt' Zeitschrift für Internationale Strafrechtsdogmatik (2007), pp. 247–253.

591 Roxin, 'Strafrecht Allgemeiner Teil, Band I Grundlagen: Der Aufbau der Verbrechenslehre' (2006), pp. 401–417, Wessels and Beulke, 'Strafrecht Allgemeiner Teil, Die Straftat und ihr Aufbau' (2008), pp. 64–67.

592 Roxin, 'Strafrecht Allgemeiner Teil, Band I Grundlagen: Der Aufbau der Verbrechenslehre' (2006), pp. 401–417, Wessels and Beulke, 'Strafrecht Allgemeiner Teil, Die Straftat und ihr Aufbau' (2008), pp. 64–67.

593 See for instance: 15 September 2005 AG Saalfeld NStZ 2006, 100, where the owner of a liquor store was convicted for negligently causing bodily harm because he sold liquor to a 13 year old boy who subsequently went binge drinking. See also: 28 August 2002 BGH NJW 2003, 371.

the case was whether or not the driver could be convicted for negligently causing the co-driver's death despite the fact that the latter had freely participated in the race and was aware of the risks involved. The Supreme Court held the line between self endangerment of the co-driver and endangerment by the driver had to be drawn according to the hegemony over the act doctrine (*Tatherrschaftslehre*), which as will subsequently be discussed is a tool to distinguish perpetration from participation.[594] As the hegemony over the situation, i.e. the overtaking manoeuvre was deemed to lie with the driver alone, the defendant could not invoke self endangerment and was convicted for negligent manslaughter (§222 GPC).[595]

As already mentioned, German criminal law is opposed to recognising hypothetical alternative causes to affect the chain of causation, but this does not necessarily mean that they should also be excluded from the realm of objective attribution. However, the prevailing view here is very strict even for free, informed and deliberate alternative hypothetical causes. Thus mobster Toni cannot escape criminal liability for murder by arguing that had he not done it, another member of his syndicate would have stepped in.[596]

Finally, a lack of objective foreseeability of the result or the chain of causation can stand in the way of attribution.[597] This category has clear ties to the above-mentioned theory of adequate causation and the predicaments connected to this theory resurface in this category of objective attribution. A textbook example here would be the case where William with the intent to kill, shoots and wounds Stephen. Stephen is brought to the hospital where on the day of his admittance a fire occurs in which he dies.

From the German doctrine of objective attribution it is only a small step to the Dutch theory of reasonable attribution. In an attempt to free criminal law from the shortcomings and pitfalls of traditional theories of causation Dutch criminal law formally discarded these theories and reduced causation to its very essence, namely to a problem of attributing criminal liability.

4.6.3. The normative/legal approach

The doctrine of causation used to be a constant bone of contention in Dutch legal writing, but since the Dutch Supreme Court adopted the notion of "reasonable attribution" to establish causality the discussion has almost ceased. In 1978 the Dutch Supreme Court abandoned the then prevailing theory of adequate causation and in a landmark judgment replaced it with the doctrine of 'reasonable attribution'. In the case at hand the victim of a car accident died 12 days after the accident in the

594 See: Chapter III. 7.2.1.

595 20 November 2008 BGH NJW 2009, 1155. Note that also the other driver involved in the race which led to the crash was convicted of negligent manslaughter.

596 Schönke and Schröder, 'Kommentar zum Strafgesetzbuch' (2006), Vorbem §13 Mn 97–98.

597 Wessels and Beulke, 'Strafrecht Allgemeiner Teil, Die Straftat und ihr Aufbau' (2008), pp. 70–71.

hospital due to a pulmonary embolism which was caused by a thrombosis. The question arose whether the injuries caused by the accident could still be considered the cause of death. The court ruled that the occurrence of a pulmonary embolism as a result of injuries caused by a car accident was not of such a kind that the death of the victim could not be reasonably attributed to the defendant. In other words the death of the victim could despite the occurrence of medical complications be attributed to the defendant. Thus no longer was the foreseeablity of the result decisive, but instead the court posed the question if a result could be reasonably attributed to the perpetrator.[598]

This line of case law was confirmed later in 1980 where the victim of a stabbing died in the hospital because the medical staff had overlooked minor perforations of the aorta which led to the victim's death. The court ruled that for the establishment of a causal connection between the stab wound in the abdomen and aorta on the one hand and the death of the victim on the other, the decisive criterion was whether the result could be reasonably attributed to the perpetrator. This reasonable attribution was in the court's view not prevented by the defective medical treatment.[599]

It already becomes apparent that the doctrine of reasonable attribution is an empty phrase. This is the case because the doctrine does not give any criteria for the establishment of a causal link but only reveals what the criminal law does when establishing a causal link between a conduct and a result.[600] This is exactly the opposite of what one saw before in regard to the traditional doctrines of causation which effectively cloaked the process of causal attribution. In any event, regarding the doctrine of reasonable attribution it remains unclear which factors and considerations determine the establishment of a causal link. The undetermined nature of the doctrine could however cause problems in regard to legal certainty.

By adopting the theory of reasonable attribution the Dutch penal system has abandoned the view that causality is an ontological fact and has adopted the view that the establishment of a causal link in criminal law entails a normative judgment. The emphasis in this respect is on the word "reasonable". After all the attribution of a result has to be reasonable. It follows that for instance the attribution of insignificant or insubstantial causes would be unreasonable. Such a normative judgment is, however, always highly influenced by the historic context and the particular circumstances of the case in which it is taken. Accordingly, the doctrine is highly casuistic and flexible. This grants enough room to the courts to adapt the evaluation to the needs of the case at hand. In this process of evaluation however, the traditional doctrines of causation like the *conditio sine qua non*, proximate cause and the theory of adequate causation, i.e. foreseeability, continue to play an important role. Especially in cases where the Courts invoke general rules of

598 HR 12 September 1978, *NJ* 1979, 60.

599 HR 23 December 1980, *NJ* 1981, 534.

600 De Jong and Knigge, 'Het materiele strafrecht' (2003), p. 79.

experience is the doctrine of adequate causation still visible. In this evaluation process the quality and finality of the (criminal) conduct often play a vital role.[601] If the conduct in question was reasonably suited to cause the respective result, a causal connection between conduct and result will often be assumed.[602] It thus becomes apparent that especially in regard to the reasonableness of the attribution the traditional doctrines of causality still exert considerable influence.

Other factors that influence the reasonable attribution of a result are the severity of the inflicted injuries as well as the degree of fault of the perpetrator with which he carried out his conduct.[603] Finally, also the wording and scope of the underlying offence can influence the establishment of a causal connection.[604] The different factors playing a role in establishing a causal link can be summarised in the following evaluation scheme:

- Factual evaluation: is the conduct according to general experience the cause of a result? This includes expert opinion as well as generally known facts. This question will thus have to be resolved by the best science the courts can master.
- Normative evaluation: can the result be attributed to the perpetrator on the basis of a legal rule? Thereby the wording of the underlying offence needs to be taken into consideration.
- Casuistic evaluation: is the result in the case at hand attributable to an external factor which weighs heavier than the defendant's conduct? Thereby also the mens rea of the defendant can play an important role.[605]

This schema gives a good overview of which factors can play a role in regard to the reasonable attribution of consequences in the Dutch penal system. Although the doctrine seems very broad at first sight, an analysis of pertinent case law also unveils that the results reached are largely similar to the one reached in Germany and England. Furthermore, the underlying principles at work in their core largely correspond as well. It has already been mentioned, for instance that contributory causes need not stand in the way of an attribution of the result.[606] Thus, the fact that the victim's prior consumption of cocaine and ether contributed and maybe quickened her death due to the severe battering by the defendant[607], as well as the fact that the victim did not wear a seatbelt[608] did not prevent a reasonable attribution. Likewise are hypothetical alternative causes negligible in establishing a

601 See for instance: Hof 's-Hertogenbosch 11 June 2010, *LJN* BM7414.
602 See: Rb. Breda 12 August 2008, *LJN* BD9861.
603 See for instance: HR 30 March 2004, *LJN* AO3231.
604 De Hullu, 'Materieel Strafrecht' (2009), pp. 173, 183.
605 Rozemond, 'De methode van het materiele strafrecht' (2006), pp. 53–58.
606 HR 26 November 1985, *NJ* 1986, 368, Rb. Breda 12 August 2008, *LJN* BD9861.
607 HR 26 November 1985, *NJ* 1986, 368.
608 HR 11 December 2001, *NJ* 2002, 62.

causal link.[609] Finally, also intervening causes need not necessarily break the chain of causation.[610]

The doctrine has been criticised in literature due to its inherent vagueness and the fact that it turns a blind eye to the question how criminal liability arises.[611] However, by and large, the doctrine is accepted among Dutch legal scholars. This might be due to the fact that Dutch courts have used their room to manoeuvre, granted to them by the doctrine, diligently and have kept by and large within the "margin of reasonableness" in establishing a causal connection in the case at hands.[612] However, the focus on normative considerations in the context of reasonable attribution can sometimes overly simplify the task of the courts to establish a causal link, which in connection with the general and summary manner of argumentation of Dutch jurisprudence can cause frictions with the principle of legality. The vague nature of the doctrine may namely not always make it readily foreseeable for the citizens when a causal link will be established. A controversial decision highlighting some of the shortcomings of the doctrine revolved around sex parties in Groningen, in the north of the Netherlands. Four gay men were part of a circle of like-minded people who on a regular basis organised sex parties at which also dis-inhibiting drugs were consumed and which were attended by many people. At these happenings but also at other occasions the men practiced unprotected sex with changing sexual partners. The victims had contracted HIV and claimed that they had been injected with HIV infected blood by the defendant during one of these sex parties. The court acknowledged that the victims might have contracted the virus also by having unprotected sex with other persons before or after the party but argued that the chances that the defendants had contracted HIV by a blood injection were considerably higher than by unprotected sex. This was particularly so, as the court accepted that it had been the defendant's purpose to infect others with the virus.[613] Here one can see again the influence of subjective factors such as mens rea and blameworthiness on the finding of a causal connection. This in itself does not however pose a problem. It is the rather scant argumentation of the court as well as its reasoning solely based on probability which is arguably problematic. Simply stating that the result may also have been caused by other events but that this cannot stand in the way of attributing the result to the defendant is problematic.[614]

---

609 Hof Leeuwarden 22 January 2010, *LJN* BL0315.

610 De Hullu, 'Materieel Strafrecht' (2009), p. 178.

611 Nieboer, 'Schets materieel strafrecht' (1991), pp. 102–103. See also Kwakman, 'De causaliteit in het strafrecht. Het vereiste van conditio sine qua non als enige bruikbare criterium' Nederlands Juristenblad (2007), pp. 992–999. Kwakman argues for a return to the conditio sine qua non formula to determine causality in criminal law.

612 Rb. Alkmaar, 18 Oktober 2006, *LJN*, AZ0368.

613 Hof Leeuwarden 22 January 2010 *LJN* BL0315.

614 Claessen, 'Over hiv-jurisprudentie en Groningse seksfeesten' Strafbald (2010), pp. 150–157.

The Supreme Court seems to have shared these concerns as in a recent decision it quashed the judgment of the court of lower instance, holding that the establishment of a causal link had been insufficiently motivated. The court referred the case back and held that it had not been established in the quashed decision that it was highly unlikely that the HIV infection had been caused by consensual unprotected intercourse with a HIV infected partner. The fact that it was much more probable that the infection had been caused by the illegal conduct of the defendant rather than by a third party was considered insufficient by the Supreme Court to not address this alternative at all.[615] This decision, it is submitted, ought to be welcomed as it reminds the courts of their duty to furnish sufficient arguments when establishing a causal link, especially in the light of the vague and highly flexible as well as casuistic nature of the doctrine of reasonable attribution.

4.7. Evaluation

The three different conceptions of causation, outlined above, all possess their own strengths and weaknesses. The German meta-juristic approach has strong ties to empirical science and to notions of social responsibility which needs to be circumscribed by normative criteria. The English approach might be classified as principled-legal approach which is strongly rooted in the Enlightenment concept of individual autonomy. Adjustments take place here by reference to public policy reasons. The Dutch approach on the other hand can be described as legal-normative, reducing causation to its very essence, namely the question of whether or not it is just to attribute criminal liability in a particular case. While this approach, in the view of the author correctly captures the crux of causation, it can lead to frictions with the principle of legal certainty as it imposes only very limited restraints on the judiciary. Overall however, these frictions seem not to be greater than in other systems, adopting a different take on causation.

It has been demonstrated that the broad German approach encounters difficulties in cases where from a common sense point of view a causal link can be established and appears too strict in cases of voluntary interventions and intervening abnormal or coincidental acts or events. It is in such cases that normative criteria need to be applied in order to reach the desirable result. The individualistic English approach on the other hand encounters difficulties once the individual action is placed in the wider social context in which it took place. Thus, individual action is seen as causal unless something abnormal intervenes. But what is normal or abnormal strongly depends on common social perception and is subject to change.[616] Likewise a causal link is deemed to exist until the voluntary intervention of a third party

615 HR 23 March 2012, *LJN* BT6362.

616 Norrie, 'Crime, Reason and History – A Critical Introduction to Criminal Law' (2001), p. 140.

breaks that link. Yet what one considers as voluntary is elusive, depending on how much weight one wishes to give to the social context in which the conduct took place.[617] It might be this stern individualistic approach which leads to the invocation of public policy considerations in order to reach socially acceptable results.[618] It is at least questionable whether such an approach can still be upheld in our modern, interlinked society.[619]

One should despite the significant complexity of the theories and doctrines described, not overlook that in the majority of criminal law cases the establishment of a causal link between the conduct and the result will not pose a problem. The suspect will simply have done it. In the typical cases of murder, theft, rape, etc., it will be obvious that the suspect has caused the occurred result. Difficulties however arise in cases where consequences occur which are not normally associated with the type of conduct practiced by the defendant or when harm comes about unexpectedly or a different kind of harm than that intended or expected materialises.[620] It is especially in these cases where the connection of the doctrine of causation with subjective factors such as mens rea and blameworthiness becomes visible. It is often in the realm of causation that courts have to overcome a "fit problem" between the mental state the defendant had when he acted with the actual result achieved. Especially the quality of the offender's mens rea in a case at hand seems at times to effectively determine the scope of results reasonably attributable. The more blameworthy the offender's conduct, the more readily a causal link will arguably be assumed. This given, one may pose the question whether establishing the legal cause of a result is not better seen as a problem of mens rea rather than causation.[621] This however, it is submitted, would merely amount to a cosmetic change as it will not solve the problem that is examined here but simply relocate it. The connection between causation and blame arguably emphasises the relation of actus reus and mens rea as communicating vessels. In case a narrow concept of fault such as intention is present, the attribution of a wider scope of harmful results may be defendable. In contrast, if the required fault element is more sweeping as for instance in regard to recklessness, a narrower approach to causation seems warranted.

In any event, there are certain categories of cases which have troubled the courts in all penal systems, regardless of the theory of causation applied. They concern intervening causes, unexpected outcomes and joint drug use. From this line of case law four common principles of causation can be deduced and these are the common conundrums of causation discussed below.

617 Norrie, 'Crime, Reason and History – A Critical Introduction to Criminal Law' (2001), p. 140.
618 Norrie, 'Crime, Reason and History – A Critical Introduction to Criminal Law' (2001), p. 140.
619 Norrie, 'Crime, Reason and History – A Critical Introduction to Criminal Law' (2001), p. 140.
620 Wilson, 'Central Issues in Criminal Theory' (2002), p. 169.
621 See for instance: Moore, 'Causation and Responsibility' (2009), p. 102 Fn 69, p. 110.

4.8. Conundrums of causation

4.8.1. Predispositions of the victim

In these cases the occurred result is often perceived as puzzling, as it is generally not associated with the kind of conduct practiced by the defendant. Experience has for instance told us that death is not the common result of a slap in the face, but nevertheless every now and then such cases do arise. Often in these cases certain predispositions of the victim exacerbated the injury resulting from the conduct and led to the unexpected outcome. Cases falling into this category are for instance stabbing a haemophiliac, slapping a person with an egg-shell skull or where the victim was suffering from symptoms of old age. Consider for instance the following Dutch Case. A 84-year-old woman died due to heart failure caused by strong emotional distress during a robbery in her house, during which she was handcuffed and gagged with tape. The overall approach regarding these case in all systems is that the causal link will generally not be broken.[622] This is nicely conveyed in the English dictum "the defendant has to take its victim as he finds it".[623] Accordingly, the Dutch Court held that it was generally known that strong emotional distress can cause fatal results in regard to elderly people and that therefore her death could be reasonably attributed to the perpetrators.[624] While these cases may be deemed difficult from a strict doctrinal point of view, it is argued here that the results reached by the courts excellently reflect what is to be the essence of causation, namely the just attribution of criminal liability. The cardinal question namely is, is the defendant liable for the deed by which the particular consequence came about? This constitutes a normative evaluative inquiry and the implication of this normative inquiry is that someone who engages in dangerous and wrongful activities ought to bear the risk of injuries exacerbated by the victim's poor state of health.[625]

---

622 See: HR 12 November 1985, *NJ* 1986, 782.

623 R v Blaue [1975] 3 All ER 446; See also: R v Masters [2007] EWCA Crim 142. Also in Germany it is recognised that predispositions of the victim do not stand in the way of establishing a causal link. See: Roxin, 'Strafrecht Allgemeiner Teil, Band I Grundlagen: Der Aufbau der Verbrechenslehre' (2006), p. 362, Wessels and Beulke, 'Strafrecht Allgemeiner Teil, Die Straftat und ihr Aufbau' (2008), p. 56. See also: 31 May 1920 RGSt 54, 349, 3 July 1959 BGH GA 1960, 111. Likewise, in the Netherlands this is the prevailing view. See: Kelk, 'Studieboek materieel strafrecht' (2005), pp. 240–241, citing several cases where egg-shell skull defects did not prevent the attribution of (severe) consequences to the perpetrator. See also: HR 12 November 1985, *NJ* 1986, 782 and HR 20 March 2001, *NJ* 2001, 340. For a similar reasoning see: HR 20 September 2006, *NJ* 2006, 86.

624 HR 12 November 1985, *NJ* 1986, 782. For a comparable English decision see: R v Watson [1989] 1 WLR. 684.

625 See also: Wilson, 'Central Issues in Criminal Theory' (2002), p. 176.

4.8.2. Conduct of the victim breaking the chain of causation

Closely connected to the foregoing category of cases are instances where the particular result was caused by actions of the victim himself. In these cases the victim met his death by refusing to undergo a life saving surgery or the victim injures or kills himself by acts instinctively done out of self-preservation. Here it would seem that the most immediate cause of the result was the victim himself. However for reasons of social responsibility and penal policy even in these cases a causal link can be established under certain circumstances. Take for instance the illustrative Dutch case of a young woman who was shot by her boyfriend. The bullet damaged the spinal cord in the cervical spine and caused paraplegia from the neck downwards which would have made her furthermore dependent on artificial ventilation. In hospital the victim came down with pneumonia for which she refused treatment and subsequently died. The defence had argued that no causal connection between the injuries caused by the defendant and the victim's death could be proved, as the death was the result of the victim's own action i.e. a free and deliberate choice. The court stressed that the defendant had caused the circumstances which led the victim to opt for the lesser of two evils and that the victim's action, taking into account the entire chain of events, did not wield the kind of influence that prevented the death from being attributed to the perpetrator.[626]

Important factors in that judgment were the extremely severe injuries caused by the defendant and the fact that her decision, informed by the knowledge that her life expectation after the incident had decreased to a maximum of ten years, was deemed reasonable. It can be deduced from that reasoning that in cases where the injuries are less severe, a refusal of medical treatment may be considered less reasonable. In this case the victim's actions might break the chain of causation.[627]

A similar approach is prevalent in England where in *R v Blaue*, the principle that the defendant has to take his victim as he finds it was expanded to cover not only the body but also the victim's mind. In this case the defendant stabbed an eighteen year old girl in the leg. At the hospital she was told that she needed a blood transfusion to save her life. As a Jehovah's Witness she refused the transfusion as a result of which she died. The Court of Appeal argued:

> It has long been the policy of the law that those who use violence on other people must take their victims as they find them. This in our judgment means the whole man, not just the physical man. It does not lie in the mouth of the assailant to say that his victim's religious beliefs which inhibited him from accepting certain kinds of treatment were unreasonable. The question for decision is what caused her death. The answer is the stab wound. The fact that the victim refused to stop this end coming about did not break the causal connection between the act and death.[628]

626 HR 25 June 1996, *NJ* 1997, 563.

627 De Jong and Knigge, 'Het materiele strafrecht' (2003), p. 84.

628 R v Blaue [1975] 3 All ER 446.

Likewise, will the causal link not be broken in these cases in Germany, as long as the decision of the victim to refuse certain treatment is not considered daft.[629] The refusal to undergo surgery was, considering the mortality rate of 5–15% in regard to the particular surgery, not considered daft.[630] Thus, as a general rule only daft conduct of the victim will be able to break the chain of causation. Opinions may however differ as to what can be considered daft. Scholarly opinion in Germany generally seems to reject the attribution of liability in cases such has *Blaue* due to the conscious self-endangerment of the victim.[631] The Supreme Court however appears to adopt a slightly broader view as it for instance also accepted the establishment of a causal link in a case where a woman sustained serious injuries by her husband but refused hospital treatment despite being explicitly warned that her life was in danger.[632] Clearly here friction with the principle of individual autonomy and responsibility arise and the emphasis on the (unusual) result, i.e. death instead on the (life threatening) conduct can only be explained by evoking considerations of common sense or criminal policy. We simply conceive causes of death in terms of wounds and injuries rather than in terms of ideas and convictions, however absurd they may be.

Cases that overall receive similar treatment are those where the defendant's initial conduct so frightened the victim that he jumped out of a window or a car or behaved in some other self-destructive way. Here the test applied by all courts is based on the notion of foreseeability and asks whether or not the response fell within the range of reactions which could have reasonably been expected from a victim in this situation. Only when the victim's reaction is to be considered daft, will the chain of causation be broken. This line of reasoning is apparent from the Dutch case regarding the paralysed young woman and is also reflected in German[633] and English[634] case law. It should be clear that precise criteria as to when a particular conduct will be considered daft can hardly be established. Factors like the age, metal capacities and perhaps even the sex of the victim can play a role here. Furthermore, the potential dangerousness of the conduct and the fact that this conduct directly caused the harmful response can be relevant.

---

629 Roxin, 'Strafrecht Allgemeiner Teil, Band I Grundlagen: Der Aufbau der Verbrechenslehre' (2006), pp. 408 et seq, Wessels and Beulke, 'Strafrecht Allgemeiner Teil, Die Straftat und ihr Aufbau' (2008), p. 65.

630 14 November 2000 OLG Celle NJW 2001, 2816. See also: 9 March 1994 BGH NStZ 1994, 394.

631 See: Roxin, 'Strafrecht Allgemeiner Teil, Band I Grundlagen: Der Aufbau der Verbrechenslehre' (2006), p. 408.

632 9 March 1994 BGH NStZ 1994, 394.

633 30 September 1970 BGH NJW 1971, 152, 17 March 1992 BGH NJW 1992, 1708, 9 October 2002 BGH NJW 2003, 150.

634 R v Williams and another [1992] 2 All ER 183, R v Daley [1979] 69 Cr App R 39, R v Mackie [1973] 57 Cr App R 453.

4.8.3. Medical interventions

Often, in cases of serious wounding, etc., the conduct of third parties, i.e. medical professionals, contribute to the occurrence of the result. Consider for instance the aforementioned Dutch case where after being stabbed in the abdomen by A, the medical staff had overlooked minor perforations of the aorta which led to the victim's death.[635] The question that arises here in regard to the doctrine of causation is whether the involvement of maybe poor medical treatment can break the chain of causation and bar the attribution of criminal liability to the initial actor. One could certainly argue that in these cases the doctor's conduct was the most proximate cause of the result.

The general approach adopted in all countries is a very strict one, certainly influenced by policy reasons and by recognition of the fact "that doctor's who have emergency surgery thrust upon them cannot be expected to get it right all the time".[636] Thus, the general approach is that medical treatment carried out corresponding to *de lege artis* will not break the chain of causation. Only in exceptional cases, where the standard of treatment fell far below what one might reasonably expect, will the causal chain be broken.[637] Illustrative of the general approach is the English case of *R v Cheshire*.[638] In this case a rare complication was held to be a direct consequence of the appellant's act which remained a significant cause of death. The Court of Appeal held:

> Even though negligence in the treatment of the victim was the immediate cause of death, the jury should not regard it as excluding the responsibility of the accused unless the negligent treatment was so independent of his acts, and itself so potent in causing death, that they regard the contribution made by his act as insignificant.

Crucial in this category of cases is thus the aforementioned general principle of causation, captured in the question whether or not the wound was (still) an operating and substantial cause of death in the chain of causation.[639] Accordingly, a wound can no longer be seen as an operating and substantial cause if the treatment was 'palpably wrong', so that the second cause is more potent and overwhelms the causal salience of the original wound. There is some dispute in the respective countries regarding the degree of negligence required for the interruption of the causal link, but it is generally agreed that grossly negligent treatment will stand in

635 HR 23 December 1980, *NJ* 1981, 534.

636 Wilson, 'Central Issues in Criminal Theory' (2002), p. 180.

637 De Hullu, 'Materieel Strafrecht' (2009), p. 178, Roxin, 'Strafrecht Allgemeiner Teil, Band I Grundlagen: Der Aufbau der Verbrechenslehre' (2006), pp. 419–421, Smith and Hogan, 'Criminal Law' (2008), p. 84.

638 [1991] 3 All ER 670.

639 For similar German case law see: 8 July 2008 BGH NStZ 2009,92. For similar Dutch case law see: HR 23 December 1980, *NJ* 1981, 534, HR 7 May 1985, *NJ* 19985, 821.

the way of attributing criminal liability.[640] *A fortiori*, the causal link will be broken if the faulty medical intervention causing the death of the victim was carried out intentionally, for instance when the severely injured victim is "put out of his misery" by an angel of death.

4.8.4. Drug administration cases

Especially in England and Germany a long line of a case law has revolved around cases of joint drug use. The problem in these cases can be summarised as follows. A injects himself with what turns out to be a fatal drug dose. B has either supplied the drugs prepared the syringe, assisted by holding the tourniquet or otherwise encouraged A. In how far can B be deemed causal for A's death? While in the early days the courts assumed a causal link, the prevailing position of the courts is to deny a causal link in such cases by emphasising the principle of individual autonomy and personal responsibility. As long as the decision to endanger oneself is free, deliberate and informed B cannot be seen to be a causal influence in A's death.[641] This, arguably is the correct approach but these cases are criminalised through the backdoor by holding B responsible for his failure to call for medical assistance, etc.[642] This goes to show that the safeguarding function of the doctrine of causation can be circumvented by applying a duty of care reasoning. This may also be the reason why such cases of joint drug use are primarily dealt with under the heading of omission in the Dutch penal system. There the focus is more on the subsequent failure to call for medical assistance than on the active involvement during the drug consumption.[643]

4.9. Causation in European Union Law

In the European context the issue of causation crops up in several topics. Causation plays a mere auxiliary role in competition law[644] but is of considerable importance

---

640 De Hullu, 'Materieel Strafrecht' (2009), p. 178, Roxin, 'Strafrecht Allgemeiner Teil, Band I Grundlagen: Der Aufbau der Verbrechenslehre' (2006), pp. 419–421, Smith and Hogan, 'Criminal Law' (2008), p. 84.

641 The leading case in England is R v Kennedy [2007] UKHL 38. For similar German case law see: 14 February 1984 BGH NStZ, 1984, 410, 11 April 2000 BGH NStZ 2001, 205, 11 December 2003 BGH NStZ 2004, 204.

642 See: Chapter II. 3.2.2.

643 See: Rb. Groningen 24 August 2006, *LJN* AY6882.

644 Arguably, Art. 101 TFEU requires a causal connection between the concerted practices and the subsequent market conduct of the undertaking. However, competition law applies a presumption that a concertation has been followed by conduct. And indeed, it is hard to imagine circumstances where the behaviour of an undertaking will not have been influenced by information acquired through concerting with others. See: 4 June 2009, Case C-8/08, *T-Mobile Netherlands BV, KPN Mobile NV, Orange Nederland NV and Vodafone Libertel NV v Raad van bestuur van de Nederlandse Mededingingsautoriteit* [2009] ECR I-04529, para 44. See also:

in regard to Anti Dumping cases and environmental liability. This research will investigate areas of European Union law in order to establish how the ECJ and other European institutions generally approach the topic and to establish communalities and differences with the solutions found in national law. The areas of anti-dumping and environmental liability have been selected for investigation because there the doctrine of causation functions similarly as in national criminal law. This means that it establishes a causal link between the conduct of the defendant and the harmful result in order to make the attribution of liability possible. One should however keep in mind that in the context of European Union law the doctrine is arguably less concerned with individual but rather more with corporate or collective wrongdoing. Nevertheless some valuable insights for a European doctrine of causation can be gained here.

As already mentioned, areas of EU law where the concept of causation plays a role are anti-dumping measures and cases of environmental liability. To address the former first, a company is deemed to be dumping if it exports its goods to the European Union at a price lower than the normal value on their domestic market. It is the Commission's task to investigate such cases and if dumping measures can be proven, to impose anti-dumping duties. However, before any measures can be adopted to counteract dumping, certain conditions must be met. (i) It must be established that the imported commodity was effectively sold at a dumping price.[645] (ii) The community industry producing the like product must have sustained material injury[646] and (iii) the dumped imports must have caused the injury found.[647] Finally, (iv) the imposition of anti-dumping measures must not be against Union interests, in order to ensure that account is taken of the Union's overall economic interests in order to protect European industries using the imported product and ultimately the end consumer.[648] The EU law applied here is closely connected to measures agreed under the framework of the World Trade Organisation and has been encapsulated in Regulation 1255/2009.[649] Articles 3 (6)

Jones and Sufrin, 'EC Competition Law: Text, Cases, and Materials' (2004), p. 153. Also in regard to violations of Art 102 TFEU concerning the abuse of a dominant position on the market, the ECJ has repeatedly held that the abuse need not be connected to the dominant position. It is merely necessary that the conduct in question strengthened the dominant position and fetters competition in the market. See: 21 February 1973, Case C-6/72, *Europemballage Corporation and Continental Can Company Inc. v Commission of the European Communities* [1973] ECR 00214, para 26, 27.

645 Article 1, Regulation 1225/2009 of 30 November 2009 on protection against dumped imports from countries not members of the European Community, OJ 2009 L 343/51.

646 Article 3 (1), Regulation 1225/2009 of 30 November 2009 on protection against dumped imports from countries not members of the European Community, OJ 2009 L 343/51.

647 Article 3 (6), (7), Regulation 1225/2009 of 30 November 2009 on protection against dumped imports from countries not members of the European Community, OJ 2009 L 343/51.

648 Article 21, Regulation 1225/2009 of 30 November 2009 on protection against dumped imports from countries not members of the European Community, OJ 2009 L 343/51.

649 Regulation 1225/2009 of 30 November 2009 on protection against dumped imports from countries not members of the European Community, OJ 2009 L 343/51.

and (7) of that Regulation outline the approach to causation in this area of law. The former paragraph establishes that the dumped imports need to have caused the injury to the Community industry and that the impact of that cause has to be classified as material. The latter paragraph provides that other factors than the dumped imports which are at the same time injuring the European industry should also be carefully evaluated in order to ensure that injury caused by these factors is not attributed to the dumped imports. It follows from these provisions that the establishment of a causal link between the imports and the injury will take place in two steps. First a test needs to be carried out whether the imports have caused the injury in question. Therefore, it will not be necessary for the Commission to prove a causal link that the dumped imports were the sole cause; other factors might also contribute. Afterwards a negative test will be carried out to determine whether other factors might have broken the chain of causation. This will however only be the case when the dumped imports can no longer be seen as a substantial and operating cause, so that its effect is so slight compared with other factors that it can no longer be deemed material.[650] It should be clear that the establishment of a causal link here involves the assessment of complex economic, political and legal factors in which the Community institutions enjoy a wide margin of discretion.[651] Thus, an undertaking accused of dumping measures will have to produce clear and convincing evidence that the injury to the Community industry was caused by other factors than the dumped import.[652]

Finally, Directive 2004/35 on environmental liability with regard to the prevention and remedying of environmental damage contains rules on causation.[653] Article 4 (5) of Directive 2004/35 holds that the Directive "shall only apply to environmental damage or to an imminent threat of such damage caused by pollution of a diffuse character, where it is possible to establish a causal link between the damage and the activities of individual operators. Article 8 (3) lit. (a) subsequently circumscribes Article 4 (5) by holding that "an operator shall not be required to

---

650 See: 3 September 2009, Case C-535/06 P, *Moser Baer India Ltd v Council of the European Union*, [2009] ECR I-07051, para 87–91. See also: AG's Trestenjak's opinion in that case (at para 147–149), 4 March 2010, Case T-401/06, *Brosmann Footwear (HK)Ltd and others v Council of the European Union*, [2010] ECR II-00671, para 190.

651 3 September 2009, Case C-535/06 P, *Moser Baer India Ltd v Council of the European Union*, [2009] ECR I-07051, para 85–86. However, the Commission's assessment seems to come under increased scrutiny from the ECJ in this context. See: 2 February 2012, Case C-249/10 P, *Brosmann Footwear (HK)Ltd and others v Council of the European Union* [2012] not yet reported.

652 A successful claim can be found in 14 March 2007, Case T-107/04, *Aluminium Silicon Mill Products GmbH v Council of the European Union*, [2007] ECR II-00669, where it was held that the Council committed manifest errors in establishing a causal link between the import of silicon originating in Russia and the alleged injury suffered by the Community industry when not considering factors such as the concentration in demand on the relevant market, the increase in market share and sales volume and the change in the structure of sales (para 116).

653 Directive 2004/35 of 21 April 2004 on environmental liability with regard to the prevention and remedying of environmental damage, OJ 2004, L 143.

bear the cost of preventive or remedial actions taken [...] when he can prove that the environmental damage or imminent damage was caused by a third party and occurred despite the fact the appropriate safety measures were in place [...]". It should however be noted that the Directive aims only at minimum harmonisation and therefore allows Member States to adopt more stringent measures in relation to the prevention and remedying of environmental damage, such as strict liability offences or measures operating with a presumption of a causal link between the operators and the pollution. However, such a presumption must be justified by plausible evidence like the vicinity of the operator's installation to the pollution and correlation between the pollutants and the substances used by the undertaking.[654]

4.10. Conclusion

The foregoing discussion has shown that the doctrine of causation fulfils an important role in the attribution of criminal liability. It establishes a link between the person whose punishment and guilt is under evaluation and the occurred result. Furthermore, the doctrine of causation is demonstrated as constituting an important, although not exclusive tool in measuring a person's desert in regard to a criminal harm.

After having discussed the different approaches to causation adopted in penal systems, one can in general distinguish three different concepts which can be put on a continuum spanning from a purely metaphysical to a purely normative concept. The first approach has a strongly metaphysically-influenced approach, circumscribed and adapted with normative criteria. The second is a legal-principled approach and the third is a strongly normative influenced view. It has been shown that the approaches adopt a completely different *modus operandi* but despite that achieve largely similar results. It should however be pointed out that the closer one moves on the continuum to a legal/normative approach, the closer one will get to the cardinal function of the doctrine in the realm of criminal law, i.e. the attribution of criminal liability.

Corresponding to the shift in the doctrine of conduct towards a more mental concept of conduct, the doctrine of causation is increasingly seen as a legal concept detached from the traditional physical notions of causation. Likewise, it can be seen that the doctrine's traditional focus on individual actions is increasingly broadened to cater to requirements of social responsibility as well. The conduct of the individual is increasingly placed in the social context in which it occurs, which means that normative considerations become more and more important in establishing a causal link. All criminal law is essentially a compromise between two fundamentally conflicting interests. First and foremost, there is the social

654 See: 9 March 2010 Case C-378/08 *Raffinerie Mediterranee (ERG) SpA, Polimeri Europa SpA and Syndial SpA v Ministero dello Sviluppo economico and Others* [2010] ECR I-01919. See also AG Kokott's opinion to this case.

interest in general well-being and security, which would demand the meting out of punishment for every conduct which contributed to the occurrence of the (criminal) harm. On the other hand, there are the interests of the individual against the encroachment of his liberties for harm for which he was not responsible for. In order to strike a balance between these two interests, a careful balancing of interests is required which is often influenced by normative considerations.

Furthermore, it has become apparent that the doctrine of causation has close ties to and is often influenced by subjective criteria such as fault, or blameworthiness respectively. The notion of foreseeability often plays a prominent role in the context of causation, in particular in regard to intervening causes and a-typical causal chains. Moreover, adages such as "intended consequences are never too remote" highlight the fact that causation and fault cannot be neatly separated in the construction of criminal liability. This arguably demonstrates that the doctrine serves in criminal law not only to establish a link between the conduct and harm, but also to establish a link between fault and harm. This emphasises the relationship of the notions of actus reus and mens rea as communicating vessels, which leads to the following rough yardstick. In case the fault element of a given offence is narrow, a broad causal basis is defendable while a more narrow causal approach ought to be adopted in case the fault element is more sweeping as in the case of recklessness.

The establishment of a causal link in criminal law will arguably remain a difficult matter as it involves a delicate balancing of individual, societal and political interests. It is important therefore to bear in mind that one of the core functions of the doctrine is to attribute liability to citizens for conduct for which they are responsible. This is because in the risk society where the avoidance of future harms is central, the doctrine is often sidestepped or broadened in order to avoid indemnity of an occurred harm within a complex social structure. Without the doctrine one would however abandon the project of establishing an objective connection between conduct and harm which is central to the assignment of responsibility as well as criminal liability. This would dispense with an important safeguard protecting fundamental rights such as individual autonomy and responsibility, potentially creating a slippery slope towards punishing thoughts, mere association or status. Thus, if European criminal law is to become a bastion of the protection of the individual rather than a harsh, punitive instrument, causation ought to be an indispensable element in attributing liability for all result crimes.

Leaving those general considerations aside, the following common principles of causation can be established. It has already been pointed out that a legal/normative concept of causation is to be preferred over an ontological/metaphysical one, as it corresponds better to the very function the doctrine ought to fulfil in criminal law. Criminal law attempts to exert its influence on intelligent, rational individuals who are assumed to have the capacity to control their conduct. Accordingly, individuals ought only to be held responsible for the harm they caused by their individual conduct. This ought to be the vantage point of every doctrine of causation and should prima facie constitute the corner stone of the doctrine in order to avoid a slippery slope towards over-inclusive forms of collective responsibility. However, it has rightly been pointed out that humans "have learnt to extend the range of their actions and have discovered that [...] they can [...] bring about secondary changes not only in the objects actually manipulated, but in other objects".[655] In these cases, it is submitted that the general individualistic concept of causation should be supplemented by normative criteria in order to adapt it to the needs of modern society and criminal law. An approach strictly based on metaphysics transposes all uncertainties prevalent in natural science into the criminal law and should therefore be avoided. The establishment of a causal link ought to first and foremost correspond to considerations of legal policy rather than science. Yet, it would be a fallacy to think that scientific and philosophical tests are accordingly irrelevant in determining the choice of policy, as for a legal policy to be sound it ought to be oriented and correspond as far as possible to scientific data and philosophical criteria.[656] Arguably, such a legal approach would also correspond nicely to the increasing complexity of our society and to the increasing complexity of the regulatory framework in which the doctrine is supposed to operate in European criminal law. Especially in the economic context and in regard to crimes characterised by a high degree of organisation and division of tasks, a legal concept of causation seems more expedient.

Such a legal/normative approach would also have the advantage of allowing a better incorporation of omissions in the framework of criminal liability. This might also constitute an important advantage for European criminal law where omission liability can play an important role. The argument that non-events like failures to intervene cannot bring things about (*ex nihilo nihil fit*) has less force if causation is conceived as a legal concept guided by normative considerations. It has been argued here that, "causal inquiries in law, by contrast with philosophical or scientific inquiries are not designed to uncover some basic or empirical truth about the nature or workings of the world".[657] By and large, the prevalent concern of the doctrine is to distinguish human causes, i.e. causes for which a person can be blamed as distinct from natural causes or accidents.[658] The predicament accordingly lies less in the causal status of omission itself, but rather in determining the expected standards of behaviour from which a deviation can be seen as the cause of a harmful result. The concept of a duty of care can accordingly also influence the establishment of a causal link. The stronger and well-defined the duty of care of the defendant, the easier it can prima facie be concluded that a causal connection between the harmful result and the omission of the defendant existed. This means that it can then be assumed that the result would not have occurred had the defendant acted as required by law.

---

655 Hart and Honoré, 'Causation in the Law' (1985), p. 28.

656 Ryu, 'Causation in Criminal Law' University of Pennsylvania Law Review (1958), p. 785.

657 Wilson, 'Central Issues in Criminal Theory' (2002), p. 165.

658 Fletcher, 'Basic Concepts of Criminal Law' (1998), pp. 59–73, Wilson, 'Central Issues in Criminal Theory' (2002), p. 165.

In any event, the very threshold for establishing a causal link for any form of conduct should be the *conditio sine qua non* or 'but for' test. It provides a first yardstick for the establishment of causal responsibility, especially in paradigm cases. However, one should always bear in mind the shortcomings of the test and accept that this basic principle has exceptions, especially in regard to cumulative and alternative causes. Admittedly, such cases will only play a subordinate role in practice, but can produce unsatisfactory results. Therefore the test ought to function only as a preliminary test which provides a first indication of the (non) existence of a causal link. In case the test provides a positive result, further principles should be applied in order to fine-tune the attribution of liability in the case at hand. Likewise, in the converse situation the failure of the test need not necessarily stand in the way of the attribution of liability if normative considerations would require so, as is for instance the case in regard to cumulative causes. Despite the apparent shortcomings of the test, it is nevertheless worthwhile to maintain, as it also excellently captures what causation amounts to in criminal law and thereby fulfils an important communicative function.

The proposed baseline principle is further shaped by the common rule that the conduct in question need not be the sole or main cause of the result. This rule is a recognition of the fact that in principle the 'but for' test produces an infinite amount of causes. Yet, other factors contributing to the occurrence of the result need not stand in the way of the assumption of a causal link. The rule might be seen as an expression of the goal of the doctrine in criminal law, namely the attribution of criminal liability for the particular result in the case at hand. As the law aims at achieving a single causal statement, it is necessary to realise that this is an oversimplification and that in reality most of the time several causes will combine to bring about the harmful result.

Moreover, the establishment of a causal link should require a connection between the harm and the fault of the individual. This principle is of special importance in regard to crimes of negligence, where it has to be established that the violation of the underlying duty of care was the cause of the harm. Criminal law ought to hold people responsible only for harm they caused which could have been prevented by observance of the standard of diligence required by the law. Holding someone responsible for harm which would have occurred even though the person had acted in accordance with the law would ride roughshod over the fundamental principles such as individual autonomy and responsibility. Accordingly, it is necessary to establish a link between the violation of the law and the harm occurred.

Closely connected to the foregoing, but nevertheless distinct is the requirement that criminal liability should be confined to the type of harm envisaged by the purpose of the rule of law violated. A causal link in criminal law is never established in a vacuum. The outer boundaries for the attribution of liability are therefore always set by the purpose and scope of the offence in question.

Subsequently it should be established whether other known factors might have broken the causal chain. For this to occur, the intervening cause must however be a potent one. As long as the initial cause remains a substantial and operating cause, the causal link will not be broken. Predispositions of the victim, contributing to the result will on first sight not break the chain of causation. Someone who engages in criminal activities is "walking on thin ice" and must accordingly bear the risk of bad luck over the choice of the victim. In regard to intervening causes and events some further specifications can be made. First, the conduct of the victim, will generally not break the chain of causation unless his/her conduct is considered daft or his reaction falls outside the range of responses to be reasonably expected from a victim in a particular situation. Hence the notion of foreseeability is of crucial importance here. Second, the conducts of medical professionals will also prima facie not break the chain of causation. Only when the applied treatment falls significantly short of the general standard of diligence, as in being palpably wrong, will the causal link be broken.

In regard to intervening natural events, the notion of foreseeablity will again be crucial and will help to distinguish consequences which might be expected in the normal course of events which are thus controllable and foreseeable by the defendant, from freak consequences which could not have been expected and were beyond his/her control. Furthermore, the principle of individual autonomy and self-determination should be taken into consideration when attributing criminal liability. This will particularly be so in cases of self-endangerment such as joint drug administration cases. In cases of free, informed and deliberate self-endangerment, a causal connection should be rejected. Everything else would amount to imposing criminal liability for the acts of another.

Chapter III
Modes of liability – The multiple actor scenarios

1. Introduction

After having discussed the basic ingredients of criminal liability the discussion can now turn its focus to the central figure of crime, i.e. the perpetrator as well as to persons furthering and assisting the commission of the offence. Traditionally, the description of all criminal offences is built on the concept of the sole perpetrator. Corresponding thereto might be an orthodox conception of crime where the villain (personally) commits the criminal offence.

However, it is a well-known factual and social phenomenon that people frequently cooperate in one form or another in order to bring about a certain (criminal) result. On a factual level, there are different degrees of involvement conceivable in a criminal enterprise and one of the difficult tasks, which every criminal law system faces, is to determine the proper scope of liability for participation in a criminal offence. Several people can for instance co-operate to jointly commit a robbery. Yet it is also conceivable that one person orders or solicits another to commit a criminal offence, possibly promising a reward. Moreover, a person can simply provide aid or assistance, so that the criminal offence can be committed more easily, securely, etc. What emerges from these examples is a continuum of involvement in a criminal offence, reaching from "merely" providing aid or assistance to orchestrating, planning and initiating the respective offence.

What this research will be concerned with in this chapter is the basis upon which several people cooperating in one way or another to commit a criminal offence can be held criminally liable. Traditionally, the distinction between perpetrators and other participants is often closely linked to the interpretation of the actus reus of the crime in question. Conventionally, in many penal systems only the person(s) who directly fulfil the actus reus of the criminal offence were (and sometimes still are) held liable as perpetrators, whereas for other participants, different labels or categories had to be created. To impose liability also on people who have not themselves brought about the actus reus of the offence in question, criminal justice systems have devised rules "that buttress substantive offences by broadening the context in which the deterrent and retributive aims of those offences can be attained".[659] This can for instance be achieved by imposing liability on people for their blameworthy contribution towards the commission of a criminal offence by someone else (participation in crime). Thus, criminal justice systems have adopted different strategies, i.e. modes of liability, to respond to cooperative

659 Horder, 'Reforming the auxiliary Part of the criminal law' Archbold News (2007), p. 6.

criminal efforts and have conceived different notions and concepts to cover the whole continuum of possible involvement in a criminal offence, which frequently find expressions in the law of complicity. The central question which this research will aim to address in what follows can thus scantly be summarised to: what could a just division of liability among different participants in a criminal enterprise for European criminal law look like?

The aforementioned rather narrow approach to perpetration which focuses on the fulfilment of the actus reus can arguably be linked to the historically prevalent philosophy of legal positivism and is also closely tied to an orthodox conception of the principle of legal certainty.[660] Furthermore, it is submitted that this narrow approach to the concept of perpetration has also been shaped by the orthodox theory of causal action, which purported to introduce a naturalistic/ontological view of criminal wrongdoing and accordingly shaped and influenced other criminal law doctrines. It fits nicely in the criminal law of the 19th century where a physical involvement in the criminal enterprise constituted the paradigm of criminal liability. However, as will subsequently be shown, in the modern risk society the significance of physical involvement has diminished and this shift in paradigm has significantly influenced and altered modes of liability and the notion of perpetration in particular.

This chapter will analyse the different modes of liability adopted in the investigated systems in due course but before descending into *medias res*, it seems pertinent to first clarify the terminology to be applied and sketch the general outline of the discussion before commencing the analysis of the law on complicity at a macro level in order to lay the foundation for the subsequent discourse.

2. Terminology and outline

2.1. Terminology

A comparative analysis of participation in crime is for several reasons somewhat more difficult than the foregoing discussion on the objective elements of criminal liability. The terminology applied in different penal systems is diverse and can lead to confusion as similar terms need not necessarily refer to the same theoretical construct. It is therefore vital to be clear in the use of terms from the outset. It is proposed to use the following terms as indicated:

1. A perpetrator is a person whose liability is primary. This means that it can be established independent of all other parties involved in the commission of the offence.[661] His liability is direct and not derived from someone else's wrongdoing.[662]

---

660 Tiedemann, 'Grunderfordernisse einer Regelung des Allgemeinen Teils', in Tiedemann (ed), Wirtschaftsstrafrecht in der Europäischen Union (2002), p. 8.

661 For a more in depth analysis of the concept of perpetration see: Chapter III. 6.2.

662 See: Fletcher, 'Rethinking Criminal Law' (1978), p. 637.

2. Accessories or accomplices are all those whose liability is derived from the wrongdoing of the perpetrator. In juxtaposition to the perpetrator their liability is accordingly termed secondary. This category in national law includes assistants or aiders as well as the English notions of aiding, abetting, counselling and procuring and the civil law concept of instigation.[663]
3. A participant is any partner in crime. This encompasses (co-) perpetrators and accomplices.[664]

It seems pertinent now to take a closer look at these categories. In regard to perpetration three different categories will be further distinguished. The sole or direct perpetrator directly commits the criminal offence. Co-perpetrators on the other hand can be seen as equal partners in crime. Every co-perpetrator contributes significantly to the commission of the offence, which is carried out according to a horizontal framework of division of tasks.[665]

The notion of perpetration by means is, in contrast to the former two, a more subtle category. The perpetrator by means is usually not directly involved in the execution of the crime but is nevertheless considered to incur primary liability as he uses another person as a means to his ends; i.e. to commit the offence. The perpetrator by means is considered to commit the offence in question by proxy. The conduct of the person utilised is considered the means by which the perpetrator commits the offence.[666] Paradigmatic instances can be found in using a child or an insane person to carry out a criminal endeavour, but it will become apparent that this notion can be given a much wider scope of application. Be that as it may, characteristic of this vertical form of participation certainly is that the perpetrator by means can be considered to take a superior position in comparison to his intermediary. He exploits this superior position by using the intermediary as a means or instrument for his criminal purposes.[667]

The notion of instigation can at times appear very similar to the notion of perpetration by means, but it encompasses cases where one person induces another person to commit the offence. Contrary to the concept of perpetration by means the intermediary is in these cases however fully responsible for his conduct. The notion of instigation, which can also be seen as a vertical form of participation is traditionally a civil law concept, as a differentiation between someone who procures or abets the act from someone who assists it. As will be further explained below, the reason for this peculiarity is straightforward. Dutch and German law recognise a higher punishment for instigators as compared to

663 Fletcher, 'Rethinking Criminal Law' (1978), p. 637.
664 Fletcher, 'Rethinking Criminal Law' (1978), p. 637.
665 See: Chaper III. 8.1.
666 Fletcher, 'Rethinking Criminal Law' (1978), p. 639.
667 See: Chapter III. 7.3.

aiders, while English law does not.[668] Paradigmatic examples here include the hiring of a contract killer to dispose of one's enemy as well as persuading someone to steal a car.[669]

Finally this research will distinguish the concept of assisting a criminal offence. The assistant generally only plays an auxiliary or supportive role in the commission of the offence. He facilitates the commission but is not primarily responsible for the occurred criminal harm. Examples hereof are lending someone a gun, keeping a lookout, etc. Due to their generally subservient role in the criminal enterprise, assistants are in some countries eligible to a mitigation of punishment, but this is certainly not a necessity.[670]

2.2. Outline

After having discussed the terminology to be used in this discourse, the structure of the following discussion can now be sketched. This chapter will commence by discussing the two fundamentally different systematic approaches as regards participation in crime between which a European criminal law can choose (section 3). Subsequently the focus will turn to a closely connected issue, namely the nature of the accomplice's liability which is traditionally conceived to be derivative (section 4). To set the scene for the subsequent comparative analysis and for the sake of clarity it has been decided to present the English law on participation in a separate section (section 5) as it considerably differs from the approaches adopted in Germany and the Netherlands, which are much more similar.

The comparative discussion will commence by focusing first on fundamental choices and dilemmas for European criminal law in regard to primary responsibility, i.e. perpetration (section 6) and will subsequently focus on two variations of the concept, namely vertical (section 7) and horizontal (section 8) forms of liability. In this context attention will *inter alia* be paid to the conundrum of the perpetrator behind the perpetrator, and there will be an attempt to clarify to what extent unforeseen events can be attributed to parties in crime. Afterwards secondary liability and the scope of criminal liability for assistance will be discussed (section 9). In the following section some common limitations to participatory liability will be discussed (section 10). Subsequently the rules on participation in European Union law will be outlined (section 11) and finally the findings so far will be briefly summarized (section 12) before an attempt is made to transform the results of this analysis into a theory of participation for European criminal law (section 13).

---

668 Fletcher, 'Rethinking Criminal Law' (1978), p. 645.

669 See: Chapter III. 7.4.

670 See: Chapter III. 9.

3. Unitarian and differentiated concepts of participation

It has already been indicated that at a fundamental level, different theoretical solutions to the factual problem of co-operative criminal efforts are conceivable. On the one hand, it is possible to consider everyone participating in the criminal endeavour to have fulfilled the actus reus of the offence and leave the precise meting out of punishment to the discretion of the courts. On the other hand, a criminal justice system might strive to adopt a neat dogmatic categorization of participatory conduct into different modes, carrying varying degrees of punishment.

It follows that in regard to punishing participation in crime one can *de lege lata* distinguish two different approaches which penal systems may adopt. The first distinguishes between countries that recognise an obligatory mitigation of punishment for accessories (such as Germany[671] and the Netherlands[672]) and countries that do not officially impose a mitigated punishment for lesser forms of participation (such as England[673]). To be sure, this distinction is a mere superficial one, as it is still possible in the latter category of countries that punishment for accessories is mitigated at the sentencing stage by judicial or prosecutorial discretion.[674] As will subsequently be demonstrated, it will not always be appropriate to punish accessories less than the perpetrator, but nevertheless many countries have a mandatory mitigation of punishment for accessories enshrined in their criminal code. The reason for this may be found in classical considerations of just punishment. If one participates in the commission of a crime, depending on one's point of view, the wrongdoing or culpability of the participant's act is less than that of the perpetrator. In other words, the participant's objective contribution to the consummation of the crime is considered less than that of the perpetrator or his subjective posture is seen as subservient to the perpetrator.[675]

This distinction along the lines of punishment leads to a continuum where on one end of the scale one finds the so called "unitarian" systems and on the other end the "differentiated" systems. The unitarian systems treat all (causal) contributions to a criminal act equally, i.e. all accomplices are put on an equal footing with the perpetrator and distinguish between them only at the sentencing stage.[676] In other words, all parties are deemed to commit the crime and are considered perpetrators and the different degrees of responsibility are taken into consideration at the

671 See §27 GPC that enshrines a mitigation of punishment for the aider.

672 See Art 49 DPC that holds that the maximum sentence for aiding shall be reduced by a third.

673 See section 8 of the Accessories and Abettors Act 1861 which holds: "Whosoever shall aid, abet, counsel or procure the commission of any indictable offence, whether the same be an offence at common law or by virtue of any act passed or to be passed shall be liable to be tried, indicted, and punished as a principal offender."

674 Fletcher, 'Rethinking Criminal Law' (1978), p. 636.

675 Fletcher, 'Rethinking Criminal Law' (1978), p. 654.

676 Ambos, 'Is the development of a common substantive criminal law for Europe possible? Some Preliminary Reflections' Maastricht Journal of European and Comparative Law (2005), p. 183.

sentencing stage.[677] Thus, in a pure unitarian system all conceivable forms of participation in crime flow together like water drops on a glass plate and are all treated as perpetrators which manifests in a very broad and undifferentiated concept of perpetration.[678]

The differentiated systems on the other hand distinguish between the different forms of participation already at the level of attribution in terms of the nature or degree of responsibility. The level of responsibility is grouped in different degrees which diminish from the perpetrator to the accomplice; the instigator theoretically constitutes a middle position but is mostly put on an equal footing with the perpetrator.[679] Thus, in a differentiated system, normally a distinction between the liability of the perpetrator which is primary and the liability of other participants which is secondary is drawn.

Besides these considerations, the distinction between unitarian and differentiated systems reveals another peculiarity. In a differentiated system the deed of the perpetrator plays a central role, as only he fulfils the actus reus of the underlying offence, and the liability of the accomplice is derived from the deed of the perpetrator. It also follows that in a paradigmatic differentiated system, generally, participants are not held liable for their own wrongdoing but for the extrinsic wrongdoing of the perpetrator.[680]

In a pure unitarian system such a connection is absent. As all parties are deemed to be perpetrators there is no need to derive the accomplice's liability. It becomes apparent from this distinction that, generally speaking, in an unitarian system a broader concept of perpetration is applied while differentiated systems adhere to a restricted notion of perpetration which leads to a strict distinction between perpetrators and accessories.[681] If placed on this continuum, the penal systems of Germany and the Netherlands can be characterised as differentiated systems while English law effectively takes a medium position, combining characteristics of both sides.

---

677 It is often argued that an ontological concept of causal responsibility, i.e. causation, lies at the heart of all unitarian systems. While this might historically be correct it should not be overlooked that a unitarian approach to participation can also be inferred from other, more modern rationales. A crucial role will thereby be played by the conception of wrongdoing applied in a penal system as well as the accepted rationale for punishing participants and the role of harm played in a penal system. See: Hamdorf, 'Beteiligungsmodelle im Strafrecht' (2002), pp. 35–37, 43, Schöberl, 'Die Einheitstäterschaft als europäisches Modell' (2006), p. 41.

678 Kienapfel and Höpfel, 'Grundriß des österreichischen Strafrechts' (2003), p. 220.

679 Ambos, 'Is the development of a common substantive criminal law for Europe possible? Some Preliminary Reflections' Maastricht Journal of European and Comparative Law (2005), p. 183.

680 It should however be noted that in regard to the theoretical rationale underlying the criminal liability of participants a lot of variations are conceivable. See: Chapter III. 9.3.2. in which it will be shown that also in a differentiated system it is possible to conceive the liability of participants as completely or at least partly free-standing.

681 See: Chapter III. 6.2.

4. The derivative nature of the accomplices' liability

4.1. Introduction

Painted in broad strokes, the central point of contention between unitarian and differentiated systems in regard to the criminal liability of accessories can thus be found in the question whether the liability of the accessory is derived from the wrong committed by the perpetrator, or whether it is autonomous. Thus, criminal justice systems are faced with two diametrically opposed concepts when contemplating the criminalisation of participation in crime. On the one hand the secondary party's culpability, i.e. mental association with or indulgence in a criminal objective (as manifested in the outside world by his overt act) can be regarded as the root of the participant's liability. In this approach, the focus clearly lies on the secondary party, his liability is so to say primary and self-contained.

On the other hand it is possible to shift the applied focus to the perpetrator by making the secondary party, through his culpable actions share responsibility for the occurrence of the offence, i.e. the manifested harm. The former approach can be characterised as inchoate or endangerment based, by anchoring criminal liability in the accessory's demonstrated anti-social tendencies, or in his willingness to risk the commission of the main offence. In stark contrast, the latter approach can be described as derivative, by making the liability of the accessory dependent on the occurrence of the main offence, presupposing a variety of participation or sharing in the principal offender's criminality.

The answer to this question, which will subsequently become evident has far reaching implications for the scope and nature of secondary liability. Furthermore, it is also closely connected to the rationale underlying the imposition of liability in cases of complicit activities. In other words, the distinction between harm and culpability-centred criminal law may also in the context of participation in crime considerably shape and influence the doctrine. Thus, more fundamental tenets of criminal responsibility such as the moral basis for criminal liability with its inherent question of what makes us responsible subjects of law, the nature and function of harm in a penal system and the relevance and connection of such issues with the justifying aims of punishment wield influence in this respect.[682]

However, leaving these theoretical consideration aside, it seems to be a defining feature of accessorial liability in all investigated penal systems that it is commonly perceived as a category of 'derivative liability'. This is arguably linked to the rationales underlying the punishment of participants to which this research now turns.

682 Smith, 'A Modern Treatise on the Law of Criminal Complicity' (1991), pp. 64, 71.

4.2. Rationales for secondary liability

As accessorial liability by definition is based on some form of "collaboration" between the perpetrator and the accessory, the question arises as to the nature of the relationship between the liability of accessories and perpetrators. This relationship may be posited on a multitude of theories, some of which can exert important repercussions for all aspects of the law on complicity.

The prevalent view in England for instance, conceives this relationship in terms of civil law agency, whereby certain deeds of the agent are imputed to the principal.[683] By assisting the perpetrator, so it is often argued, the accessory implicitly, consents, ratifies or authorises the commission of the offence, thereby manifesting consent to his own liability.[684] This notion of authorisation is considered to be consistent with the prevalent derivative liability principles.[685]

Treating the accomplice in terms of punishment and guilt as if he were the perpetrator is accordingly explained by reference to civil law agency principles. Thus, the principal is considered to be the accomplice's agent and his actions are subsequently imputed to the accomplice. However, the analogy to civil law agency is arguably not entirely convincing. Civil law agency is based on consensus and control. The principal assents to the agent's actions and the agent consents to be the principal's agent. Furthermore the principal is deemed to control the actions of the agent. And it is here where the shoe pinches. To take the latter point first, while accessories may sometimes exercise a similar degree of control over the actions of the principal, the reverse is often true in criminal enterprises.[686] In civil law it is usually the agent who takes executive actions and the principal takes responsibility for his actions as he has accepted the agent as his legal embodiment. In paradigmatic cases of participation the situation is often reversed. Here it is the principal that takes executive actions, whereas the accomplice takes or shares criminal responsibility for the principal's conduct.[687] Furthermore, the notion of consensus on which the civil law concept of agency is founded does not lend itself to constitute the theoretical foundation of participatory liability. Consensus can namely not be seen as the basis of accessorial liability because, as will be shown below, accessorial liability can arise in all systems without the perpetrator's consent or even knowledge. Finally, it can be doubted whether concepts originating from civil law with its primary focus on restitution and the fair appropriation of commercial and financial burdens can readily be transferred to the realm of criminal law and as a matter of principle, support the imposition of punishment and social stigma.[688]

---

683 Wilson, 'Central Issues in Criminal Theory' (2002), p. 198.

684 Smith, 'A Modern Treatise on the Law of Criminal Complicity' (1991), p. 6, Wilson, 'Central Issues in Criminal Theory' (2002), p. 198.

685 Wilson, 'Central Issues in Criminal Theory' (2002), p. 198.

686 Wilson, 'Central Issues in Criminal Theory' (2002), p. 198.

687 Wilson, 'Central Issues in Criminal Theory' (2002), p. 199.

688 Smith, 'A Modern Treatise on the Law of Criminal Complicity' (1991), p. 76.

An alternative view therefore claims that it is forfeiture which constitutes the basis of accessorial liability. When people participate in a criminal enterprise, so it is argued, they forfeit their right to be treated as an individual.[689] According to this view, in contrast to the agency rationale, an accomplice by aiding, etc. a criminal endeavour is not seen as the embodiment of the principal but rather is considered to renounce his right to be treated by the law as a responsible individual agent.[690] Thus, moral distinctions between parties are rendered irrelevant, the accomplice is no more than an incorporeal shadow.[691] The forfeiture rationale nicely describes the functioning of English law in regard to participation in crime, by focusing on the conduct of the participant. However, it fits better in a system where the liability of the accessory is conceived as autonomous from the wrongdoing of the perpetrator, rather than derivative. Thus, the theory belongs to a group of theoretical explanations, which focuses on the wrong committed by the accessory, i.e. his culpable acts of participation. Participation alone serves as potent evidence of an accessory allying or associating himself with the principal's criminal enterprise.

The forfeiture rationale, accordingly, might be capable of explaining much of the prevalent state of affairs of the common law doctrine of complicity but falls short in providing a normative justification why it is appropriate to punish accomplices for the wrongdoing of another instead of imposing punishment for his own wrongdoing. In other words, it fails to explain why accomplice liability ought to be derivative rather than personal.[692] Furthermore, the forfeiture rationale shares one characteristic feature with the aforementioned agency doctrine which can cause frictions with the principle of individual responsibility and proportionate punishment in regard to personal moral desert. Both rationales brush aside moral distinctions between participants and claim that in regard to accomplice liability the law may treat several people as if they were one. Most importantly however, such an approach is in stark contrast to the criminal law's usual focus on individual agency and responsibility and may conceptually hinder the just apportionment of guilt and punishment in co-operative criminal endeavours.[693] Given the multitude of different conceivable degrees of involvement in a criminal offence, arguably a finer grained concept of participation, capable of taking into account the nature and degree of involvement of the participant seems to be preferable.

The prevalent view in Germany sees the relationship between the perpetrator and the accessory as a causal one. The accessory by his contribution becomes causal for the commission of the offence. He contributes to the violation of the norm

689 Dressler, 'Reassessing the Theoretical Underpinnings of Accomplice Liability: New Solutions to an Old Problem' Hastings Law Journal (1986), pp. 91–140.

690 Wilson, 'Central Issues in Criminal Theory' (2002), p. 199.

691 Dressler, 'Reassessing the Theoretical Underpinnings of Accomplice Liability: New Solutions to an Old Problem' Hastings Law Journal (1986), p. 111.

692 Wilson, 'Central Issues in Criminal Theory' (2002), p. 199.

693 Dressler, 'Reforming Complicity Law: Trivial Assistance as a lesser offence?' Ohio State Journal of Criminal Law (2008), p. 434 et seq.

by the perpetrator. Thus his liability is seen as derived from the liability of the perpetrator.[694]

In the course of time a variety of other theories have evolved. However for current purposes this research will not delve deeper into that issue here. The discussion will however return to this topic when analysing the notion of assisting a criminal offence.[695] The point that has been tentatively shown is that the rationales of punishing accessories have important implications for the nature of the liability. One can generally distinguish two extreme positions here.[696] First, one can see the accomplice's liability as derived and dependent on the liability of the principal, an approach often followed in differentiated systems. Second, one can see the accessory's liability as autonomous and hold him liable for his own culpable actions. The important difference between the two camps is accordingly that in the former approach the accessory is held liable for the wrong committed by the perpetrator, while in the latter he is held liable for the wrong he committed himself, i.e. assisting or encouraging a person.

As already mentioned, all three investigated systems formally adhere to a derivative model of accessorial liability.[697] They accordingly consider the distinction between perpetrators and accomplices crucial as an accomplice's culpability or objective wrongdoing will generally be less than that of the perpetrator. Such a derivative nature can, as will subsequently become clear, lead to doctrinal frictions and even result in unwanted lacunas of the law. To fill the gaps created by the doctrine of derivative liability, penal systems had to devise other concepts of participation in order to achieve the desired result. For instance, in order to prevent that participants go unpunished because the conduct of the perpetrator is not deemed sufficient to constitute the basis from which the liability of the participants is derived, e.g. in case the perpetrator can invoke a justification, etc., differentiated systems have developed different versions of the perpetration by means doctrine, which make it possible to hold a participant liable as perpetrator. In other words, a participant who would strictly speaking not be criminally liable due to a lack of a primary offence from which his liability can be derived, will be held liable as a perpetrator in case he used another person who is not criminally liable as a tool to commit the actus reus of the offence.[698] In Germany the version of perpetration by means is referred to as *mittelbare Täterschaft*, while in the

694 Roxin, 'Strafrecht Allgemeiner Teil, Band II: Besondere Erscheinungsformen der Straftat' (2003), pp. 136–138, Schönke and Schröder, 'Kommentar zum Strafgesetzbuch' (2006), Vorbem §§25 et seq. Mn 17.

695 See: Chapter III. 9.3.2.

696 Also medium or mixed views are conceivable: Roxin, 'Strafrecht Allgemeiner Teil, Band II: Besondere Erscheinungsformen der Straftat' (2003), pp. 130–131.

697 De Hullu, 'Materieel Strafrecht' (2009), p. 423, Schönke and Schröder, 'Kommentar zum Strafgesetzbuch' (2006), Vorbem §§25et seq. Mn 14–40, Smith and Hogan, 'Criminal Law' (2008), p. 180, Wilson, 'Central Issues in Criminal Theory' (2002), p. 196.

698 Schöberl, 'Die Einheitstäterschaft als europäisches Modell' (2006), p. 39.

Netherlands the doctrine is called *doen plegen* and in England the doctrine is frequently referred to as innocent agency.

4.3. The nature and quality of the derivative relationship

It has already been indicated that the term "derivative" here relates to the dependency of the accessory's liability on the violation of the law by the principal. The corollary of this is that unless the latter is committed, there can be no accomplice liability. In other words, the cardinal issue is the responsibility of the secondary party for the principal's violation of the law.[699] One important question in this respect is from what the liability of the accomplice is derived; from the offender or from the committed offence. Historically, liability was arguably derived from the offender which found expression in a strong derivative link in common law requiring conviction and even punishment of the principals before the question of secondary liability could arise.[700] If the principal had died, received pardon or was not convicted for any other reason, an accessory had to be acquitted. However, in the course of time the dependence on the wrongdoing of the offender diminished and it seems now common ground in all penal systems that the liability of the accomplice is derived from the wrongdoing of the criminal offence.[701]

As has been shown, accessorial liability is in all investigated countries not considered an offence in itself, but is derived from the main offence. Hence, as participation is intertwined with the commission of the main offence this inevitably raises the question which requirements are imposed on the main offence to constitute a sufficient basis to derive liability.

The derivative nature of accessorial liability dictates that no-one can be guilty of participation in an offence unless the offence has actually been committed. Behind this truism lurks a considerable range of possibilities, depending on which qualities the principal offence has to fulfil. The different solutions can be placed on a continuum with at its extreme poles the positions that the perpetrator must be guilty of the offence before any other party can be convicted, or the law could be satisfied with the "mere" commission of the actus reus by someone. A medium position would be to require that the perpetrator has at least acted wrongfully i.e. that his conduct was not justifiable.

In the Dutch penal system it is generally recognised that a criminal offence, viz. a criminal attempt or preparatory act, needs to be committed in order for accessorial criminal liability to arise. The instigator and the aider need to wait for the main perpetrator(s) to commit the envisaged offence in order to incur criminal liability. The derivative nature of these doctrines thus circumscribes the scope of liability for

699 Kadish, 'Complicity, Cause and Blame: A Study in the Interpretation of Doctrine' California Law Review (1985), p. 337.

700 Sayre, 'Criminal Responsibility for the acts of another' Harvard Law Review (1930), p. 695.

701 See also: Stewart, 'The End of "Modes of Liability" for international crimes' Leiden Journal of International Law (2012), p. 34.

participation in crime. The limitations flowing from the doctrine for different forms of participation are also visible in Art 46 a DPC which explicitly proscribes attempted instigation (i.e. no criminal offence has been committed yet). The legislator, thus, found the consequences flowing from the derivative nature of participation as unacceptable, and explicitly criminalised the conduct. Finally it should be mentioned here that also the insertion of Art 46 DPC proscribing certain forms of preparatory acts, has broadened the scope of the rules on participation in the Netherlands and has also diminished the relevance of the doctrine of derivative liability.[702] The latter differs from the approach taken in Germany and England where it is generally accepted that the perpetrator must at least have reached the attempt phase in order for liability to be derived.[703]

As to the quality of the underlying offence it seems common ground in the Netherlands that for liability to be derived, the perpetrator must not have acted in a justifiable manner. Thus, defences that are special and personal to the perpetrator himself do not sever the derivative link, while defences of general application do. Furthermore, if the prosecution is barred due to general procedural reasons, such as the statute of limitation, liability cannot be derived.[704]

The situation in the Netherlands is comparable to the one in Germany where the §§26, 27 GPC require an intentional participation in the intentional commission of an *unlawful* act. Intentionally in that context refers at least to the lowest form of intention, i.e. *dolus eventualis.* Hence also in Germany the perpetrator must not act justified, while in the case of an excuse, liability can be derived. From these two paragraphs it is clear that German unlike English or Dutch law does not know a concept of aiding a negligent, or even a strict liability offence, nor can one aid or instigate negligently.

But just like in the Netherlands, the German legislator found the implications flowing from a strict application of the doctrine of derivative liability unacceptable and attempted to circumscribe it. Accordingly, §30 GPC, much like Art 46 a DPC criminalises attempted instigation, a form of participation which would be excluded by a strict application of the doctrine of derivative liability. Likewise, §28 GPC contains some exceptions to the concept of derivative accomplice liability.[705]

---

702 De Jong, 'Vormen van strafbare deelneming', in van der Leij (ed), Plegen en Deelnemen (2007), p. 117.

703 Child, 'The differences between attempted complicity and inchoate assisting and encouraging – a reply to Professor Bohlander' Criminal Law Review (2010), p. 925, Simester and Sullivan, 'Criminal Law: Theory and Doctrine' (2007), p. 230, Wessels and Beulke, 'Strafrecht Allgemeiner Teil, Die Straftat und ihr Aufbau' (2008), p. 200. See also the English case of R v Dunnington [1984] QB 472.

704 De Jong and Knigge, 'Het materiele strafrecht' (2003), p. 225.

705 §28 (2) contains an exception to derivative liability by holding that special personal characteristics which aggravate, mitigate or exclude punishment shall only apply to the accomplice in whose person they are present. Thus, if for instance A instigates (or aids) the civil servant B to assault one of his clients during work, only the civil servant is liable pursuant to §340 GPC (causing bodily harm while exercising a public office), while the instigator's liability would be based on §§26 and 223 GPC (causing bodily harm). §28 (1) on the other hand dilutes

It has been demonstrated that in Germany and the Netherlands a restricted or circumscribed version of derivative liability is applied requiring non-justifiable conduct. Furthermore, statutory limitations circumscribe the scope of the principle. Conversely, in England at least formally a strict version of the principle is applied. The general principle in English criminal law seems to be that the principal needs at least to be guilty of the offence.[706] This general principle is however subject to three limitations, namely in cases where (i) the principal has a defence (ii) the principal is a minor or legally insane, and (iii) where the principal lacks the requisite mens rea to be convicted of the main offence; i.e. cases of perpetration by means, or innocent agency. Moreover, in case law, some further limitations of the principle have been carved out.

For instance, the logic of derivative liability would dictate that the liability of a secondary party cannot be greater than that of the perpetrator. After all, how can the greater possibly derive from the less? If A for instance wants to assist the robbery of jewellery, while the actual perpetrator does not rob, but steals the jewels, the aider can only be held criminally liable for assisting theft. Such is for instance the prevalent view in the Netherlands[707] and Germany.[708] However, in England there seems to be authority to the contrary. In *R v Richards* for instance, a woman hired two men to beat up her husband in order to put him in hospital for a view days.[709] The two men, however, inflicted less serious wounds as agreed and they were convicted of unlawful wounding, while the woman was convicted of wounding with intent to cause grievous bodily harm, the more severe offence.[710] Likewise in the conjoined cases of *Howe and Burke*, both cases of homicide, the question arose whether an accessory can be convicted of murder if the person committing the killing was only held liable for manslaughter, which the House of Lords seems to have answered affirmatively.[711]

Matters become even more complicated in cases where the principal is not guilty at all, so that there is effectively no basis from which liability could possibly derive. One can distinguish different scenarios with varying degrees of complexity here. The situation is quite clear in cases where the would-be perpetrator has not committed the actus reus of the crime in question. In this situation all systems

---

this general principle by holding that if personal characteristics that establish the perpetrator's liability are absent in the secondary party, their punishment shall be mitigated. Thus if A instigates or aids the civil servant B to a false certification (§348 GPC – making false entries in public records), A's sentence will be mitigated.

706 Simester and Sullivan, 'Criminal Law: Theory and Doctrine' (2007), p. 233. Lanham, 'Primary and derivative criminal liability: An Australian Perspective' Criminal Law Review (2000), p. 707.

707 Wolswijk, 'Medeplichtigheid', in van der Leij (ed), Plegen en Deelnemen (2007), p. 199.

708 Roxin, 'Strafrecht Allgemeiner Teil, Band II: Besondere Erscheinungsformen der Straftat' (2003), p. 129.

709 [1973] QB 776.

710 However on appeal her conviction was quashed and a conviction for unlawful wounding substituted.

711 R v Howe [1987] AC 417.

concur that no liability can be derived.[712] Things get more complicated in case the perpetrator committed the actus reus but without the required mens rea or acted justified or excused. In an illustrative English case a husband compelled his wife to have sex with a dog. His conviction of abetting buggery was upheld although it was assumed that the wife, if she had been charged, would have been acquitted on the ground of duress.[713] In the similar case of *R v Cogan & Leak*, Leak procured Cogan to have sexual intercourse with his wife. Cogan mistakenly believed that the wife was consenting but Leak was very much aware due to a long history of domestic abuse that she was not. Cogan's conviction was quashed but Leak's conviction was upheld.[714] The court citing *R v Humphreys*[715] held:

> It would be anomalous if a person who admitted to a substantial part in the perpetration of a misdemeanour as aider and abettor could not be convicted on his own admission merely because the person alleged to have been aided and abetted was not or could not be convicted. In the circumstances of this case it would be more than anomalous: it would be an affront to justice and to the common sense of ordinary folk.[716]

What these rather bizarre cases have in common is that in each case the would-be perpetrator was acquitted on the basis of an excusing factor (duress or lack of mens rea), which seems to point in the same direction as in Germany and the Netherlands, namely that if the perpetrator's conduct is excused liability can still be derived, whereas if his conduct is justified derivation is excluded.

What can be deduced from all these cases is that the principle of derivative liability can cause problems in practice. In certain cases it can unduly restrict the scope of criminal liability for participants, where the perpetrator for whatever reasons is not guilty but liability for the participant seems nevertheless warranted. All penal systems have therefore created devices to circumvent the implications of the principle or have watered down the principle all together. This point will become even clearer once this research turns its attention to the doctrine of perpetration by means, which often establishes liability as a perpetrator for someone who did not commit the crime himself but used another person who is not deemed guilty of its commission.

Regarding the quality of the derivative relationship the following can tentatively be stated. It seems to be common ground in all investigated systems that in order to

---

712 In Germany and the Netherlands this follows from the provisions in the penal code, namely §§26, 27 GPC and Art 48 DPC. For an English authority see: Morris v Tolman [1923] 1 KB 166, Smith and Hogan, 'Criminal Law' (2008), p. 225.

713 R v Bourne [1952] 36 Cr App R 125.

714 [1975] 2 All ER 1059.

715 [1965] 3 All ER 689.

716 This case would nowadays probably be solved by applying Section 47 (5) (iii) of the Serious Crime Act 2007, where it is also sufficient that D would have mens rea were he to commit the anticipated offence.

constitute a sufficient basis to derive liability, the perpetrator must at least have acted wrongfully and his conduct must at least amount to an attempt. In other words, the focus rests on the offence or wrongful act rather than on the offender. It is also common ground that if the would-be perpetrator cannot be considered to have committed the actus reus of the crime in question, no accomplice liability can arise. By and large it has been shown that defences such as excuses that leave the general wrongfulness of the deed intact do not stand in the way of deriving liability. However, if the law condones a certain deed due to the application of a justificatory defence it can no longer constitute a basis for deriving liability. In other words, personal defences that excuse the conduct of the perpetrator but maintain the wrongfulness of the offence do not bar the attribution of liability to the accomplice whereas general defences that remove the wrongful character of the deed stand in the way of attributing liability.

After having discussed the theoretical foundations of participation in crime as well as the concept of derivative liability, this research will now investigate the approach taken in regard to participation in crime in England. It has been decided to present the English system on participation in a separate section here, as it fundamentally differs from the Dutch and German approach. This should allow the reader to become acquainted with the common law approach in order to lay the foundation for the following comparative analysis.

5. The concepts of participation in England: a short introduction

The doctrinal differences between Germany, respectively the Netherlands and England can on the one hand be explained by the fact that the English penal system can by and large be classified as a functional unitarian system.[717] On the other hand, it is submitted that some apparent differences between the common law doctrine of complicity and its civil law counterparts can be traced back to different conceptions of mens rea applied in common or civil law countries respectively. Briefly stated, in the Netherlands and Germany the notion of intention is broader than in the English penal system, as it also encompasses the concept of *dolus eventualis*. Bluntly put, *dolus eventualis* will be established if the actor foresaw the possibility of the occurrence of a certain criminal harm and nevertheless acted, reconciling himself to the possible outcome. As a sub-species of intention, *dolus eventualis* is sufficient to establish accomplice and attempt liability.

In the English penal system, intention is however interpreted more narrowly encompassing only direct and indirect intention. The functional equivalent to *dolus eventualis* in the common law system can be found in the notion of recklessness, but as it is not considered to constitute a form of intention recklessness is generally

[717] See: Chapter III. 5.1.

not sufficient to give rise to accomplice or attempt liability.[718] The narrower scope of intention, it is argued here, considerably shaped the English doctrine of participation. The narrower scope in terms of subjective elements of liability, arguably was to some extent compensated by adopting broader objective requirements, a fact, as will be discussed in due cause, is effectively demonstrated by the English doctrine of joint criminal enterprise.

5.1. The English approach to participation

If several persons are involved in the realisation of a criminal deed, English criminal law distinguishes between primary parties, also called perpetrators or principals and secondary parties, also called accessories or accomplices. Perpetrators are the persons who directly bring about the actus reus of the offence. Their liability is directly based on the respective definition of the criminal offence. Accessories on the other hand "merely" contribute to the offence committed by the perpetrator.[719] The legal basis for accessories for indictable offences is enshrined in the Accessories and Abettors Act 1861 and for summary offences in Section 44 of the Magistrate Court Act 1980.[720] Section 8 of the Accessories and Abettors Act 1861 as amended by the Criminal Law Act 1977 reads as follows:

> Whosoever shall aid, abet, counsel or procure the commission of any indictable offence, whether the same be an offence at common law or by virtue of any act passed or to be passed shall be liable to be tried, indicted, and punished as a principal offender.

In *Attorney-General's Reference (No 1 of 1975)*[721] Lord Widgery held:

> We approach section 8 of the 1861 Act on the basis that the words should be given their ordinary meaning, if possible. We approach the section on the basis that if four words are employed here "aid, abet, counsel or procure", the probability is that there

718 For a more detailed analysis see: Blomsma, 'Mens rea and defences in European criminal law' (2012).

719 Smith, 'Strafbare Voorbereiding, Een rechtsverglijkend onderzoek' (2003), p. 166.

720 For procedural purposes English law distinguishes between indictable and summary offences. Summary offences encompass mainly minor offences like traffic offences, and are exclusively statutorily created and defined. Indictable offences are the more severe offences and are tried by the "Crown Court" with a jury. Conversely, summary offences are tried by "Magistrates Courts" (either by two or three magistrates whose powers of sentencing are limited by the Acts which govern the offence in question, or by a District Judge sitting alone) without a jury. Indictable offences can in turn be divided into most severe offences "triable only on indictment" and the category of offences of medium seriousness – called "triable either way". Within the latter category the defendant may elect trial in the magistrates court or in the Crown Court, unless the magistrates insist on a Crown Court trial or, in certain instances, where the prosecutor can and does so.

721 [1975] EWCA Crim 1.

> is a difference between each of those four words and the other three, because if there were no such difference, then Parliament would be wasting time in using four words where two or three would do.

Despite this fact not much heed is paid to a clear demarcation of the four notions in English law and neither is the distinction between principals and secondary parties regarded as vital. This blurred demarcation stems on the one hand from the fact that secondary parties are put on an equal footing with perpetrators and can be punished as such, i.e. each of them is deemed to be guilty of the full offence.[722] Thus, English law treats the participant as if he had committed the offence himself, although he has in fact not done so.[723] This peculiarity of unitarian systems makes a sharp distinction of the four notions superfluous. Accordingly in practice the four forms of participation, are not neatly separated in English criminal law and tend to overlap.[724] Furthermore this is compounded by the fact that judges are not obliged to state in their verdicts whether a person was found guilty as a perpetrator or as an accessory. "The crucial point is that the jury must be unanimous that the accused was either the principal or an accessory".[725] Also the prosecution is not required to specify in their indictment the nature of the participation. It suffices when guilt is alleged.[726] It is merely demanded that the adduced evidence proofs that the act of the defendant falls within one of the four categories.[727] Thus, in *R v Giannetto* it was deemed sufficient for the prosecution to allege that the defendant had either killed his wife or was an accessory to her death as he had hired a killer to do so. In this case it could not be established beyond reasonable doubt that the defendant had indeed killed his wife, but there was sufficient evidence to show that he was involved in plotting the killing.[728] Nevertheless it is regarded as desirable for the prosecution to specify the form of participation, wherever possible.[729]

It goes without saying that this rather pragmatic approach tremendously simplifies the task for the prosecution, as the sometimes difficult and cumbersome task to distinguish in the case at hand between perpetrators and accessories on the one hand and between the different forms of participation on the other is avoided. Thus, the aforementioned reveals a paradox. Despite the fact that the English penal system, strictly speaking, distinguishes four different forms of participation, practice often ignores this differentiation. Be that as it may, the different degrees of participation are, however, taken into consideration at the sentencing stage which

722 Simester and Sullivan, 'Criminal Law: Theory and Doctrine' (2007), p. 196.

723 Wilson, 'A rational scheme of liability for participating in crime' Criminal Law Review (2008), p. 4.

724 Simester and Sullivan, 'Criminal Law: Theory and Doctrine' (2007), p. 199, Smith, 'Strafbare Voorbereiding, Een rechtsverglijkend onderzoek' (2003), p. 167.

725 R v Giannetto [1997] 1 Cr App R 1.

726 Simester and Sullivan, 'Criminal Law: Theory and Doctrine' (2007), p. 196.

727 Smith, 'Strafbare Voorbereiding, Een rechtsverglijkend onderzoek' (2003), p. 167.

728 R v Giannetto [1997] 1 Cr App R 1.

729 Maxwell v DPP for Northern Ireland [1978] 3 All ER 1140.

can be deduced from several sentencing guidelines which mention for instance, planning the offence or being a ringleader as aggravating and playing a minor role in the commission of the offence as mitigating factors.[730]

Collapsing the distinction between perpetrators and accomplices and holding all participants accountable for the wrong committed by the perpetrator rather than their own wrongful behaviour (i.e. aiding, abetting, counselling and procuring) also allows for a necessary degree of flexibility and allows the imposition of punishment corresponding to the person's degree of responsibility for the committed offence. As will become evident, sometimes people who might not qualify as perpetrators bear greater or equal responsibility for the committed crime than the one actually committing it. This will often be the case in regard to organised crime which nowadays spans from small partnerships or gangs to substantial criminal organisations. To make things clear, consider for instance a mobster, Vito, playing a significant role in preparing a robbery but leaving the execution of the offence to other members of the syndicate. Convicting Vito as an accessory to the robbery, as he did not commit the actus reus of the offence would seem slightly out of tune with reality here. In a differentiated system these cases can prove problematic, as the assigned label does not appropriately express the responsibility of Vito in the robbery and the amount of punishment foreseen might be deemed insufficient as well. By collapsing the distinction between perpetrators and participants, English law has left these cases to prosecutorial and judicial discretion. This means that accessories to a crime can be punished as or more severely than the direct perpetrator(s), while also allowing in more typical cases of participation in crime the imposition of a mitigated punishment for the accomplice.[731]

Nevertheless it will occasionally be necessary to distinguish between principals and secondary parities. This is the case due to the fact that accessorial liability in England is in principle regarded as derivative and therefore depends on the existence of a principal who perpetrates the offence. What is more, is the fact that the enquiry into the liability of the principal takes a different form than the enquiry into the liability of the secondary party. As will be explained in more detail below, the actus reus and mens rea requirements for principals and secondary parties vary significantly. The elements of the principal offence are specific to every offence, while the requirements of secondary liability remain the same whatever the main offence. Thus, the offence definition of murder and fraud are by nature fundamentally different but participating in either of these offences is subject to the very same conditions enshrined in the law of complicity. Furthermore the distinction is of importance, as some offences are defined in a way that certain participants are exempt from liability.

730 See for instance the guidelines drafted by the Sentencing Guidelines Council, available at: www.sentencingcouncil.org.uk/guidelines/guidelines-to-download.htm.

731 Wilson, 'A rational scheme of liability for participating in crime' Criminal Law Review (2008), p. 4.

5.2. Secondary forms of participation

5.2.1. Actus reus

As already mentioned, the Court of Appeal held in *Attorney General's Reference No 1 of 1975* that the four terms were to be given their ordinary meaning, and this view still seems to be the prevailing one in jurisprudence.[732] A variety of verdicts exist that deal with the scope of the four terms. However, criteria for a possible demarcation of the different forms are hardly found in English legal literature. Due to this it might be regarded slightly artificial to deal with the four notions separately.[733] Nevertheless, this will be the approach adopted subsequently, because each of the notions contributes and shapes decisively the overall scope of participation in England covered by section 8 of the Accessories and Abettors Act 1861.

Leaving aside the notion of "procuring" it is generally accepted in English criminal law that the four different notions basically cover two different kinds of conduct, namely assistance and encouragement.[734] Accordingly, the Law Commission proposes to substitute the four terms by a statutory provision which describes the conduct element as "assisting or encouraging".[735] Assisting or encouraging can practically take any conceivable form: supply of weapons, tools, information, support and encouragement, keeping a lookout, filming an attack on a mobile phone[736], etc.[737]

AIDING

It is sometimes argued that "aid and abet" denote to one single concept, aid constituting the actus reus and abet the mens rea.[738] However, the judgment of, *Attorney General's Reference No 1 of 1975* is authority to the contrary. The notion of aiding is frequently interpreted to contain assisting, helping or giving support to the principal.[739] Obvious examples of aiding may *inter alia* include supplying an instrument or tool to the principal, keeping a look out and committing preparatory acts (provided the offence is subsequently at least attempted by the perpetrator).[740]

---

732 [1975] EWCA Crim 1.

733 Simester and Sullivan, 'Criminal Law: Theory and Doctrine' (2007), p. 199.

734 'Participating in Crime', LAW COM No 305 [2007], p. 29. Smith and Hogan, 'Criminal Law' (2005), p. 171.

735 'Participating in Crime', LAW COM No 305 [2007], p. 51.

736 R v A [2008] EWCA Crim 2193.

737 Smith and Hogan, 'Criminal Law' (2008), p. 185.

738 Ashworth, 'Principles of criminal law' (2006), p. 414, Smith and Hogan, 'Criminal Law' (2005), p. 171.

739 Smith and Hogan, 'Criminal Law' (2005), p. 200.

740 Ashworth, 'Principles of criminal law' (2006), p. 414.

The Courts have adopted a rather broad approach to aiding and it now seems that any form of assistance given will qualify as aid.[741] Once it has been established that the conduct of the participant helped, respectively. facilitated the offence or enabled the principal to commit it easier or with greater safety, it need not be established that the aid was a *conditio sine qua non* for the principal's offence.[742] Thus, aiding does in principle not require any causal connection.[743] Furthermore, aiding does not require any consensus between the principal and the participant.[744] This implies that a participant can be convicted of aiding an offence even if the perpetrator is unaware that he has been aided.[745] If Michael for instance sees that James is about to set fire to the house of Michael's enemy Craig and restrains a policeman who would have prevented James from committing the crime, Michael is guilty despite the fact that his help was unforeseen, unknown and maybe unwanted by James.[746]

ABETTING

The ordinary meaning of "abet" is to incite, instigate or encourage.[747] As this definition overlaps with other forms of participation, its typical connotation is nowadays, encouragement. However, there might still be an extensive overlap with other forms of participation as for instance encouraging the principal usually accompanies or is implicit in an act of aiding.[748] Similarly it is likely that encouragement to commit a respective offence will amount to counselling.[749] It has therefore even been submitted that there may not be any difference between counselling and abetting left in English law.[750] It is however crystal clear that either form of conduct will suffice to ground liability as a secondary party. The encouragement may be given by words, gestures or even by mere presence at the *locus delicti*.[751]

This rather broad approach is circumscribed by the requirement that the participant did *in fact* encourage the principal in the commission of the offence.[752] This requirement distinguishes the notion from aiding which as previously

741 Smith and Hogan, 'Criminal Law' (2005), p. 172. See also: R v Soloman [2009] EWCA Crim 48, where it was held that arranging for a man to attend a house where she knew that children were, violating the man's Sexual Offences Prevention Order constituted aiding and abetting.

742 Ashworth, 'Principles of criminal law' (2006), p. 415.

743 Smith and Hogan, 'Criminal Law' (2008), p. 186.

744 Smith and Hogan, 'Criminal Law' (2005), p. 172.

745 See: State v Tally [1894] 15 So 722.

746 Smith and Hogan, 'Criminal Law' (2008), p. 186. See also: R v Fury [2006] EWCA Crim 1258.

747 Simester and Sullivan, 'Criminal Law: Theory and Doctrine' (2007), p. 200.

748 Ashworth, 'Principles of criminal law' (2006), p. 415.

749 Simester and Sullivan, 'Criminal Law: Theory and Doctrine' (2007), p. 201.

750 Smith and Hogan, 'Criminal Law' (2005), p. 171.

751 For an oddity in regard to encouragement see: R v Gnango [2012] Cr App R 18. See also: Buxton, 'Being an accessory to one's own murder' Criminal Law Review (2012), pp. 275–281.

752 Simester and Sullivan, 'Criminal Law: Theory and Doctrine' (2007), p. 200.

discussed can be rendered without the principal's knowledge. Regarding encouragement however it is essential that it has been communicated successfully to the principal as otherwise there can be no encouragement in fact.

In any case, it finally needs to be stressed that it is not required that the encouragement made any difference to the outcome. In *R v Giannetto* for instance it was held that it would be sound to convict a secondary party of abetting murder if A had told B that he was about to kill B's (the secondary party's) wife and his response to this was as little as patting him on the back, nodding and saying "Oh goody".[753] What is important however, is that the encouragement was rendered in circumstances where P could have been aware of the encouragement.[754]

Counselling

Historically, the difference between counselling and abetting used to lie in the temporal manifestation of the act. While abetting took place at the time of the commission of the crime counselling occurred before the commission. However, the difference between the two notions seems to deteriorate. To 'counsel' means to advise or solicit or encourage. Generally counselling carries two different meanings. First it includes the provision of advice or information, although such conduct may also be categorised as aiding and abetting. Alternatively counselling may also encompass "urging" someone to commit an offence. Thus it seems safe to conclude that virtually every form of advice, aid, encouragement or moral support can be regarded as abetting or counselling.[755] Generally, counselling requires some connection between the counselling and the commission of the offence. More precisely, where the prosecution relies on counselling as the basis for secondary liability, it must establish that the commission of the offence was within the scope of the perpetrator's authority.[756] Thus, the perpetrator must be aware that he has the authority of the person counselling to commit the relevant acts. In other words, an accidental commission of the envisaged offence will not amount to counselling.

Generally, an attempt to counsel does not amount to counselling. Proffered advice or encouragement which has no effect on the mind of the principal offender is not counselling. Yet, a "but for" connection is certainly not required as the counselling participant may be liable, although, when he encouraged, he knew that the perpetrator had already made up his mind to commit the offence.[757]

---

753 [1997] 1 Cr App R 1.

754 'Participating in Crime', LAW COM No 305 [2007], p. 191. It is interesting to note that the Law Commission submits that the current law regarding encouragement should be interpreted to contain a rebuttable presumption of encouragement except in cases of joint criminal enterprises. The underlying rational for this seems to be forensic reasons. [...where violence is inflicted or sexual offending perpetrated in the presence of others, it would be a manifest nonsense to require proof that the principal were aware of the encouragement provided by each individual].

755 Smith, 'Strafbare Voorbereiding, Een rechtsvergelijkend onderzoek' (2003), p. 168.

756 See: R v Luffman [2008] EWCA Crim 1739.

757 Smith and Hogan, 'Criminal Law' (2008), p. 187.

Furthermore, as will be discussed in due course, liability may arise for encouragement, pursuant to section 44–46 of the Serious Crime Act, even if the offence is subsequently not committed or if A carries out acts capable of encouraging, which includes attempts by the participant to encourage the would-be perpetrator, which fail to do so.[758]

Procuring

Jurisprudence has interpreted procuring to mean "to produce by endeavour". You procure a thing by setting out to see that it happens and taking the appropriate steps to produce that happening".[759] In essence this amounts to bringing about the commission of an offence by another. Here a causal link is required, because "you cannot procure an offence unless there is a causal link between what you do and the commission of the offence […]".[760] Generally procurement will take the form of persuasion, inducement or threats.[761] One might for instance shame someone into committing an offence by calling him a coward. However, it is not necessary that the principal is aware of the procurement, i.e. that someone is trying to bring about a criminal offence. An example amply discussed in legal literature is *Attorney-General's Reference (No 1 of 1975)*, where the accused surreptitiously laced the drink of his friend. Subsequently the friend drove his car home and was stopped by the police and convicted for driving under the influence. As this offence is in England an offence of strict liability, the driver could not be regarded as an innocent agent and his friend could not be regarded as a principal but rather as the procurer of the committed offence.[762] In a similar case A had instructed his employee B to drive a poorly maintained tractor with a trailer close behind it. A knew that the hitching mechanism of the tractor was defective, but B was unaware of this fact. During the ride the trailer became detached, which resulted in a deadly accident with an oncoming vehicle. The court convicted A for having procured the offence committed by B by giving instructions to drive the defective vehicle.[763]

Ashworth has due to the causal requirement categorised cases of procuring as "the high water mark of causal connection among the various types of accessorial conduct, headed by the case of procuring an unwitting principal, where there is no meeting of minds between principal and accomplice".[764] Such a strong causal connection is for instance absent in regard to counselling.

The notion bears close resemblance with the notion of instigation (*Anstiftung,* or *uitlokken* respectively) as applied in Germany and the Netherlands. This becomes

758 Smith and Hogan, 'Criminal Law' (2008), p. 187.
759 Attorney-General's Reference (No 1 of 1975) [1975] EWCA Crim 1.
760 Attorney-General's Reference (No 1 of 1975) [1975] EWCA Crim 1.
761 Simester and Sullivan, 'Criminal Law: Theory and Doctrine' (2007), p. 203.
762 Attorney-General's Reference (No 1 of 1975) [1975] EWCA Crim 1.
763 R v Millward [1994] Crim. LR 527. See also: R v Wheelhouse [1994] Crim. LR 756.
764 Ashworth, 'Principles of criminal law' (2006), p. 421.

apparent when considering that a clear case of producing by endeavour is where A hires B to kill X, i.e. contract killings.[765] Such cases would be considered paradigmatic for instigation in Germany and the Netherlands. Yet, the strong link of procuring to causation has narrowed the scope of the application of the doctrine and the Law Commission proposes to abolish it all together and only retain an offence of intentionally causing a 'no fault offence', as it considers that assisting and encouraging will cover most cases of procuring.[766]

Omissions

As established in the previous chapter, English criminal law is reluctant to impose criminal liability for omission, and in general, English criminal law is more likely to impose criminal liability for an act rather than an omission.[767] The cardinal question raised in the ambit of the law on omissions re-occurs, *mutatis mutandis*, in the realm of the law of complicity. In a nutshell, the question is whether a person can be convicted as an accomplice merely for standing by idle while an offence is being committed.

The general principle here is that a failure to act does not ensue criminal liability.[768] However, this general principle is impinged by two categories of cases, which constitute exceptions to this general rule. First there are the well-established categories where the law imposes a duty to act on an individual. A failure to discharge this legal duty is capable of constituting complicity. The Law Commission presents the example of a security guard who deliberately omits to lock a door to enable burglars to enter the premises to clarify the issue.[769] In their view the duty to act in these cases originated from the security guard's contract of employment.

A second category of cases centres on circumstances when the person had *a right to control* the actions of another and (s)he deliberately refrains from exercising it. In these circumstances inactivity may be regarded as encouragement to another to perform an illegal act, and, therefore as aiding and abetting.[770] Thus, a person may be liable for aiding and abetting causing death by dangerous driving, if he leaves his car to someone he knows is unfit to drive and subsequently fails to intervene.[771]

---

765 Taylor, 'Procuring, Causation, Innocent Agency and the Law Commission' Criminal Law Review (2008), p. 45.

766 'Participating in Crime', LAW COM No 305 [2007], cl. 8(1), para 4.3.1, Smith and Hogan, 'Criminal Law' (2008), pp. 233–235, Taylor, 'Procuring, Causation, Innocent Agency and the Law Commission' Criminal Law Review (2008), p. 34.

767 'Participating in Crime', LAW COM No 305 [2007], p. 186.

768 Smith and Hogan, 'Criminal Law' (2005), p. 117.

769 'Participating in Crime', LAW COM No 305 [2007], p. 187.

770 Smith and Hogan, 'Criminal Law' (2005), p. 117.

771 See: R v Webster [2006] EWCA Crim 415. See also R v Gaunt [2003] EWCA Crim 3925, where D, a manager, failed to take steps to prevent his employees, P, racially harassing another employee, V.

Secondary liability of corporate officers

It is also worthwhile mentioning here that a great many specific statutes in English criminal law create an extended form of secondary liability for an offence committed by a body corporate. Many statutes creating offences likely to be committed by corporations frequently contain the following provision:

> Where an offence [...] committed by a body corporate is proved to have been committed with the consent or connivance of, or to be attributable to any neglect on the part of, any director, manager, secretary or other similar officer of the body corporate or any person who was purporting to act in any such capacity, he as well as the body corporate shall be guilty of that offence and shall be liable to be proceeded against and punished accordingly.

Thus, if a corporation is found guilty of a criminal offence, any director, manager, secretary, etc. by whose negligence or with whose consent, etc. this offence has been committed can be held criminally liable next to the corporation.[772]

Recent Developments

The law on accessoryship in England has recently been much disturbed by the decision of the Supreme Court (former House of Lords) in *R v Gnango*. In this case a 17 year old (A) had a dispute with another youth (B) which led to a public shoot out. In the crossfire of the gunfight an unfortunate Polish care worker was killed on her way home from work. Forensic evidence proved that the lethal bullet originated from B's gun. B was however able to flee and was never apprehended. The Court of Appeal had quashed A's conviction for participating in murder but the Supreme Court restored the conviction by a majority of six to one.[773] Although the majority in the Supreme Court may have agreed on the outcome, they disagreed on their reasoning. Not less than four different routes to convicting A were mooted, with varying levels of support. The leading judgment, given by Lord Phillips and Lord Judge, with whom Lord Wilson agreed, argued that A, by agreeing to the shootout, had aided and abetted B to shoot at him by encouraging him to do so. He was thus peculiarly perceived to be an accessory to his own attempted murder. As the doctrine of transferred malice equally applied to accessories he was found guilty for the death of the passer-by. In this case their Lordships *inter alia* disagreed to some extent if A's liability should be primary, i.e. if he should be seen as a joint principal in the killing, or as secondary, i.e. accessorial liability. As this dispute was however considered not to have any practical implications or affect the result, it was

772 Smith and Hogan, 'Criminal Law' (2008), pp. 253–254. See for instance: section 20 of the Trade Description Act 1968, section 36 of the Food and Safety Act 1990, or the even wider section 12 of the Fraud Act 2006.

773 R v Gnango [2012] Cr App R 18.

declared irrelevant. Arguably, this decision has unfortunately brought further uncertainly to an already complicated area of the law.[774] Furthermore, it can be questioned whether the uncertainty surrounding the different routes to conviction outlined in this decision can be reconciled with the requirements of Article 6 of the European Convention of Human Rights which requires that defendants can know why they have been convicted in order to have a fair trial.[775]

5.2.2. The fault element in complicity

The mental element takes a pivotal role in English criminal law pertinent to complicity. As the liability of accessories is in principle derived from the main offence of the perpetrator, the mental element functions as lynch pin between the act of the perpetrator and the act of his accomplice. Furthermore, as the acts of an accomplice can be innocuous at first sight, like lending someone a screwdriver, the fault requirement needs to compensate for the objectively "missing" culpable conduct. In other words, the further one expands the net of criminal liability beyond paradigm cases, the more emphasis needs to be put on the question how closely a person should be involved in the crime's commission if (s)he is to be held liable as an accessory?[776]

Furthermore the influence of chance regarding the determination of criminal liability hinges to some extent on the applied mens rea requirements. Chance plays a significant role in the law of complicity because on the one hand the liability of A turns on the uncontrollable and unpredictable behaviour of B. Moreover, in regard to complicity the whim of chance can influence the faith of a party at several stages. For instance the help may coincidentally not reach the principal or might be rejected by him.[777] These natural predicaments however might be acerbated or mitigated by the applied mens rea requirements in place in the respective penal system. Arguably the role of chance is diminished when an intentional or purposeful act of complicity is required (as is for instance the case in US law), while the role of chance might be strong where (as in English law) knowledge or subjective recklessness suffices.[778]

The mens rea requirements for secondary parties are complex and authorities are contradictory, nevertheless some general principles have emerged over time. Firstly, it is required that the secondary party must intend to assist or encourage the act of the principal, or in the case of procurement, to bring the offence about; and

774 Virgo, 'Joint enterprise liability is dead: long live accessorial liability' Criminal Law Review (2012), pp. 850–870.

775 See: *Taxquet v Belgium,* appl no 926/06, 16 November 2010. See also: Rogers, 'Shooting (and judging) in the dark?' Archbold Review (2012), pp. 8–9.

776 Duff, '"Can I help you?" Accessorial liability and the intention to assist' Legal Studies (1990), pp. 165–181.

777 Smith, 'A Modern Treatise on the Law of Criminal Complicity' (1991), p. 65.

778 Smith, 'A Modern Treatise on the Law of Criminal Complicity' (1991), p. 65.

secondly the accomplice must know the essential matters that constitute the objective elements of the offence.[779]

The first requirement is the less controversial of the two. In essence it holds that the secondary party must not only intend his (her) action, but must furthermore act with the intent to aid, abet, counsel or procure the main offence of the principal.[780] Hence the secondary party must have been aware that the aiding, abetting, etc. will be a virtually certain consequence of his conduct. In other words, recklessness is regarded as insufficient.[781] However, there are contradictory authorities as to the meaning of intention in this context. Generally one can distinguish two diametrically opposed approaches. One view regards it as sufficient that the secondary party intended to do acts capable of assisting or encouraging crime; i.e. knowledge is sufficient.[782] Another view rejects the aforementioned standard as over inclusive and asserts that the mental element in complicity should require direct intention, i.e. purpose to facilitate the offence. In other words, the participant must, so the argument goes, act in order to facilitate the commission of the crime.[783]

The prevalent view however is that knowledge is sufficient and that it is not necessary that the secondary party acted in order to assist or encourage the principal.[784] In some, although exceptional cases the courts seem to require more than knowledge of the principal's intention. In *Gillick v West Norfolk and Wisbech Area Health Authority* the question arose whether a doctor who prescribed the pill to a girl under 16 would assist the commission of the offence of sexual intercourse with a girl under 16.[785] The House of Lords held that even though the doctor knew of the crime his purpose was to protect the girl and not to assist the offence.[786] Thus, apparently it was purpose rather than knowledge that was required here. It is however submitted that these are hard cases and hard cases, it has frequently been observed, are apt to introduce bad law.

The second requirement is more contentious than the first one. The classical statement to this requirement can be found in *Johnson v Youden*: "Before a person can be convicted of aiding and abetting the commission of an offence he must at least know the essential matters which constitute that offence".[787]

---

779 Ashworth, 'Principles of criminal law' (2006), p. 422, Dennis, 'The mental element for accessories', in Smith (ed), Criminal law – Essays in honour of J C Smith (1987), pp. 40–67, Simester and Sullivan, 'Criminal Law: Theory and Doctrine' (2007), p. 207. See also: 'Participating in Crime', LAW COM No 305 [2007], p. 195.

780 Simester and Sullivan, 'Criminal Law: Theory and Doctrine' (2007), p. 208.

781 Simester and Sullivan, 'Criminal Law: Theory and Doctrine' (2007), p. 208.

782 Smith and Hogan, 'Criminal Law' (2005), p. 179.

783 Sullivan, 'Intent, Purpose and Complicity' Criminal Law Review (1988), p. 641 et seq.

784 'Participating in Crime', LAW COM No 305 [2007], p. 195.

785 [1994] QB 581, House of Lords [1986] AC 112.

786 Gillick v West Norfolk and Wisbech Area Health Authority [1986] AC 112.

787 [1950] 1 KB 544.

This statement immediately raises two further questions, namely:

1) what are the essential matters of the principal offence?
2) What state of mind is denoted by "know"?

The discussion will first address question 2.

The connotation of know

Although there seems to be ample authority that knowledge, in the true meaning of the word is required[788], the courts have adopted a broader reading of the term, covering intention, subjective recklessness and wilful blindness. Thus in *R v Bryce* the Court of Appeal held that it would be sufficient that the secondary party at the time of doing the act contemplated the commission of the offence by the principal, i.e. *he foresaw it as a real or substantial risk or real possibility*.[789] This amounts in essence to a recklessness test. Thus the courts have interpreted knowledge as tantamount to foresight of the probable existence of the essential matters of the main offence.[790] The Law Commission propels the view that the inclusion of recklessness is too far-reaching and proposes in its report that the secondary party should intend (directly or obliquely) that the principal will commit the conduct element of the offence.[791]

The essential matters of the principal offence

A further potential stumbling block in the English law on complicity is the question what counts as an essential matter which the secondary party must foresee? The case establishing the general principle and going beyond the requirement of *Johnson v Youden* mentioned above is *R v Bainbridge*.[792] In this landmark decision A supplied oxygen cutting equipment to B who later used it to break into the Midland Bank at Stoke Newington. A claimed that although he had suspected that the equipment might be used for some illegal purpose he had not foreseen that it would be used to break into a bank. The court held that the minimum condition for accomplice liability is knowledge that the principal intends to commit a crime of the *type* actually committed.[793]

This reasoning immediately triggers a further question namely what qualifies as the same type of offence? Marginal variations in the conduct element of the offence, such as time and place are immaterial, as they do not alter the type of offence.

[788] See for instance: R v Webster [2006] EWCA Crim 415, para. 21.
[789] R v Bryce [2004] EWCA Crim 1231, at para 71. [emphasis added].
[790] Simester and Sullivan, 'Criminal Law: Theory and Doctrine' (2007), p. 215.
[791] 'Participating in Crime', LAW COM No 305 [2007], pp. 69–73.
[792] R v Bainbridge [1960] 1 QB 129.
[793] See also: Ashworth, 'Principles of criminal law' (2009), p. 419.

However, if the variation concerns a specific aspect of the offence which the participant wanted to assist or encourage, this might affect the participant's liability. Thus, if for instance Ruben provides a gun to Ben in order to murder his uncle Albert, but in a sudden change of heart Ben kills Wyatt; Ruben will not be held liable. It however needs to be stressed that this principle does not apply to accidental or mistaken changes of the victim, as the doctrine of transferred malice is believed to apply also to secondary parties.[794] In other words only substantial variations are apt to relieve the participant from liability. Furthermore the circumstance and consequence elements of the principal offence are regarded as essential matters of which the participant must have knowledge.[795]

The House of Lords further developed and extended the principle mentioned above in *Maxwell*.[796] In this case A, a member of the Ulster Volunteer Force (UVF), a terrorist organisation, was asked to drive some combatants to a house knowing that an attack was planned but not knowing any particularities of the offence, let alone the exact means to be deployed. Lord Scarman delivering the judgment of the Court held: "An accessory who leaves it to his principal to choose is liable, provided always the choice is made from the range of offences from which the accessory contemplates the choice will be made". If the committed offence thus falls within the range of offences contemplated by the secondary party, liability will ensue.

It follows from the ruling in Maxwell that the Courts have departed from the requirement of full knowledge of the particular crime and have introduced a recklessness standard. The knowledge of a risk that the offence might be committed is sufficient to hold the secondary party liable.[797]

The mens rea of the principal

The requisite mens rea of the principal is regarded as an essential matter in regard to participation. The participant must foresee that the principal will act with the required mens rea for the main offence.[798] Finally it needs to be noted that the mens rea requirements for secondary parties also apply in situations where the main offence requires a lesser degree of mens rea, such as for instance, recklessness.[799]

5.3. An expansion of liability – The Serious Crime Act 2007

Quite recently the English rules on participation have been extended and altered by the introduction of the Serious Crime Act 2007. This Act *inter alia* abolished the

794 Simester and Sullivan, 'Criminal Law: Theory and Doctrine' (2007), p. 217.

795 'Participating in Crime', LAW COM No 305 [2007], p. 203.

796 DPP for Northern Ireland v Maxwell [1978] 3 All ER 1140.

797 Ashworth, 'Principles of criminal law' (2006), p. 424.

798 Simester and Sullivan, 'Criminal Law: Theory and Doctrine' (2007), p. 219. 'Participating in Crime', LAW COM No 305 [2007], p. 205.

799 Smith, 'Strafbare Voorbereiding, Een rechtsvergelijkend onderzoek' (2003), p. 171.

former common law and inchoate offence of incitement and substituted it with three inchoate offences which also significantly broadened the scope of participation rules. The impetus for the Act was a conceived gap and inconsistency in the law, namely that whereas criminal liability existed at an inchoate level for incitement (i.e. attempted instigation), criminal liability could, due to the derivative nature of secondary liability, not arise in cases where assistance was offered but where subsequently the assisted offence was not committed. Accordingly, if Roland had told David to go and murder his treacherous wife, Roland would have been liable for incitement regardless whether David went on to commit the murder or not; whereas if Roland handed David, whom he knew to be a contract killer, a gun he could not be prosecuted unless the murder was subsequently committed.[800] The Act is aimed to step into this lacuna, but at the same time brings about a significant expansion of criminal liability. In summary, the Serious Crime Act 2007 introduces criminal liability where:

a) A person does an act that is *capable* of encouraging or assisting the commission of an offence, *intending* to encourage its commission (Section 44)
b) A person does an act *capable* of encouraging or assisting the commission of an offence, *believing* that the offence will be committed and *believing* that his act will encourage or assist its commission (Section 45)
c) A person does an act *capable* of encouraging or assisting the commission of one or more of a number of offences, *believing* (i) that one or more of those offences will be committed (without having any belief as to which particular crime); and (ii) that his act will encourage or assist the commission of one or more of them (Section 46).

Thus, a broad scheme of inchoate liability is introduced, which overlaps considerably with the traditional scope of secondary liability. In many cases this might result in a choice for the prosecution of charging a person with aiding and abetting a less serious offence or assisting and encouraging a more serious one. For instance, the prosecution might have the choice between charging aiding and abetting wounding, or assisting and encouraging murder.[801]

The Act expands and affects criminal liability for participation in crime in several ways. First, the fault element in Sections 45–46 is lower than in regard to the traditional fault requirement regarding secondary liability.[802] The most salient changes are however brought about by the offence's inchoate nature. This means that a person will be liable as soon as he has performed any act capable of assisting

---

800 Spencer and Virgo, 'Encouraging and assisting crime: Legislate in haste, repent at leisure ' Archbold News (2008), pp. 7–9. See also: Spencer, 'Trying to help another person commit a crime', in Smith (ed), Criminal law – Essays in honour of J C Smith (1987), pp. 148–169.

801 Ormerod and Fortson, 'Serious Crime Act 2007: The Part 2 Offences' Criminal Law Review (2009), p. 393, Smith and Hogan, 'Criminal Law' (2008), p. 449.

802 See: Chapter III. 5.2.2.

or encouraging the commission of an offence irrespective of whether it had any effect on the commission of the offence or whether the offence has been committed.[803] Thus, intentional facilitation is now criminalised. Furthermore, liability will arise regardless whether the crime assisted and encouraged was committed. Thus, where Alvin supplies a gun to Barney, believing it to be used in murder, liability will arise in the instant the gun is supplied, even though Barney never committed the offence. As liability is not derivative under the Serious Crime Act 2007, there is no need to establish a primary offence from which the liability of the participant can be derived.[804] Finally, "the offences work both ways". Thus if William asks Lucas to lend him his crowbar to break into Charley's house and Lucas does so, both will be liable under the Act for a violation of Sections 45 and 44 respectively.[805]

It becomes apparent from this brief overview that the Act conceives the participant's liability as free standing, as opposed to derivative, which shifts the focus from the harm caused by the perpetrator to the participant's own conduct and wrongdoing.[806] Furthermore, it criminalises conduct taking place in the preparatory phase, thus far removed from the paradigm of blameworthy wrongdoing resulting in a proscribed harm. What is worrisome about this Act is on the one hand the considerable breadth of its conduct requirement as well as the fact that sections 45 and 46 in addition also lower the fault element for liability regarding participation in crime. To take the former point first, the defendant's conduct need only be capable of amounting to assistance or encouragement. Thus, as there is no requirement that the conduct in question did in fact assist and encourage, any act however small will suffice for liability to arise. Moreover, according to sections 45 and 46 it is sufficient if the defendant believes that the anticipated offence will be committed.[807] Thus, if a shopkeeper sells a kitchen knife to two customers who he overheard discussing using it to murder someone he will be liable under the Serious Crime Act if he has the necessary belief and does not think they were talking hypothetically.[808]

In light of the concept of actus reus and mens rea as communicating vessels, this constitutes an undesirable inconsistency. It has been argued that the conduct

803 Ormerod and Fortson, 'Serious Crime Act 2007: The Part 2 Offences' Criminal Law Review (2009), pp. 400–402, Smith and Hogan, 'Criminal Law' (2008), p. 449.

804 Ormerod and Fortson, 'Serious Crime Act 2007: The Part 2 Offences' Criminal Law Review (2009), p. 400, Smith and Hogan, 'Criminal Law' (2008), p. 449.

805 Smith and Hogan, 'Criminal Law' (2008), p. 449.

806 Ormerod and Fortson, 'Serious Crime Act 2007: The Part 2 Offences' Criminal Law Review (2009), p. 392.

807 Section 46 has recently been challenged as being too vague and uncertain in the light of Article 7 ECHR. The Court of Appeal adopted a restrictive construction of section 46. The prosecution should create separate counts in respect of each reference offence which the defendant allegedly assisted or encouraged. Interpreted in such a way the section 46 was deemed compatible with the ECHR. R v Sadique and Hussain [2011] EWCA Crim 2872. See also: [2012] Crim LR 449–453.

808 Ashworth, 'Principles of criminal law' (2009), p. 460.

requirement for liability may be lowered if this is compensated by a more stringent fault element and vice versa. Unfortunately however, the Act effectively lowers both requirements leading to an overall expansion of liability for participation in crime. Besides this problematic inconsistency it will subsequently be demonstrated that none of the other investigated penal systems has expanded liability for participation as far as the Serious Crime Act has in the English penal system. It is therefore submitted that such an approach should neither be transferred to European criminal law.

This research will refer in the following sections to the most important changes brought about by this Act and discuss the most important theoretical aspects of the Act in due course.[809]

6. Perpetration: Choices and Dilemmas

6.1. Introduction

After having discussed the theoretical underpinnings of the law of complicity in general as well as the current law on accessorial liability in England, it is now time to commence the comparative discussion of the law of complicity in England, Germany and the Netherlands. The beginning of the discourse will focus on different forms of primary responsibility, i.e. perpetration. Therefore the focus will rest on questions such as: How do penal systems distinguish between perpetrators and accomplices? At the outset the discussion will first focus on the notion of perpetration in an abstract manner and analyse the different connotations of the concept as well as its different conceptual scopes. Subsequently, special heed will be paid to vertical forms of participation in crime which are often encountered in an economic context. This will also provide the opportunity to introduce the doctrinal conundrum of the perpetrator behind the scenes and discuss the different solutions developed in the penal systems.

The German[810] and Dutch[811] conception of participation in crime can, at least formally, be seen as paradigmatically differentiated. They, crudely stated,

---

[809] See: Chapter III. 9.3.2.

[810] §25 of the German Penal Code distinguishes three forms of perpetration and reads as follows:
(1) Any person who commits the offence himself or through another shall be liable as a principal.
(2) If more than one person commit the offence jointly, each shall be liable as principal (joint principals).

[811] Art 47 of the Dutch Penal Code, contrary to common parlance mentions three forms of participation in crime which are put on an equal footing with the direct perpetrator, so that in total four forms of participation are eligible to full punishment. Art 47 reads as follows:
(1) The following are liable as principals:
   1. those who commit a criminal offence, either personally or jointly with another or others, or who cause an innocent person to commit a criminal offence;

distinguish between five basic categories of participation in crime, i.e. already at the level of attribution, depending on the level and degree of involvement. Furthermore, in both systems a mandatory mitigation of punishment for aiders is foreseen.[812] Despite minor differences in the classification and scope of the different forms of involvement both systems distinguish five forms of participation in crime.[813] In terms of punishment, the direct perpetrator, the co-perpetrators, the perpetrator by means and the instigator are eligible to full punishment for the committed offence while the aider is eligible to a mitigation of punishment. From this, it has already become apparent that these systems are faced with tricky issues of line drawing as four boundaries must be worked out. The direct perpetrator must be distinguished from the co-perpetrator and from the perpetrator by means as well as the aider needs to be distinguished from the instigator.[814]

It follows that in both civil law systems the notion of perpetration plays a crucial role. While English law has traditionally been more concerned with the modes and nature of complicity, in the differentiated systems of Germany and the Netherlands the focus rests on the central figure of a criminal enterprise. This central figure is then again distinguished from the residual categories of complicity. Despite these different emphases in the three investigated systems, the notion of perpetration is essential for the law of complicity in general. Not at least because the liability of the accomplice in all three countries is derived from the wrongdoing of the perpetrator.

---

2. those who, by means of gifts, promises, abuse of authority, use of violence, threat or deception or providing the opportunity, means or information, intentionally solicit the commission of the crime.

(2) With regard to the last category, only those actions intentionally solicited by them and the consequences of such actions are to be taken into consideration.

Art 48 of the Dutch Penal Code deals with accessories. It read as follows:

The following persons are liable as accessories to a serious offence:

(1) those who intentionally assist during the commission of the serious offence;

(2) those who intentionally provide the opportunity, means or information necessary to commit the serious offence.

812 In Germany, §27 DPC reads as follows:

(1) Any person who intentionally assists another in the intentional commission of an unlawful act shall be convicted and sentenced as aider.

(2) The sentence for the aider shall be based on the penalty for a principal. It shall be mitigated pursuant to §49 (1).

In the Netherlands Art. 49 DPC provides:

1. In the case of complicity as an accessory, the maximum of the principal penalty prescribed for the serious offense is reduced by one-third.
2. In the case of a serious offense carrying a sentence of life imprisonment, a term of imprisonment of not more than twenty years shall be imposed
3. The additional penalties for complicity as an accessory are as for principals.

Only those actions that were intentionally facilitated or promoted by the accessory and the consequences of such actions are to be taken into consideration in sentencing.

813 In Germany instigation is categorised as a form of secondary participation, but the code does not foresee a mitigation of punishment in §26 DPC, while the Dutch penal Code puts the instigator on an equal footing with the perpetrator.

814 Fletcher, 'Rethinking Criminal Law' (1978), p. 641.

The concept can however at times carry different connotations. It is therefore vital at the outset to highlight and outline the different meanings of the concept in order to avoid confusion.

6.2. A Restrictive or extensive conception of perpetration?

6.2.1. The different connotations of perpetration

The notion of perpetration can, depending on the context in which it is used, have at least four, at times overlapping meanings. Thus, the notion can refer to only one or a combination of these different meanings. Firstly, the notion can refer to the fulfilment of the offence definition enshrined in the actus reus of the underlying offence. This connotation of the concept of perpetration is central to the understanding of the different models of attribution of criminal liability applied in a system. The central point here is that a perpetrator is held responsible for the manifestation of the actus reus as his own doing.[815] Responsibility for the manifestation of the actus reus can be based on two foundations. First a person can have committed the actus reus himself, or liability for the conduct of another can be attributed to him due to his role and position in the commission of the offence. In the latter case he is treated as if he had committed the actus reus himself, while factually and ontologically he has not done so.

From the latter it follows that, secondly, the notion of perpetration can also be used to denote a model of attribution. If liability for the acts of another is attributed to someone, he is treated as if he had brought about the actus reus himself. In some penal systems as in Germany or the Netherlands, perpetration in the sense of a model of attribution is subdivided into further categories depending on the form of cooperation involved, i.e. (sole) perpetration, perpetration by means, also known as innocent agency, and co-perpetration.[816]

Thirdly, perpetration can also take the meaning of an independent and free-standing form of criminal liability. A perpetrator is someone whose liability can be always established independently of all other parties. His liability is direct and not derivative of someone else's committing the offense.[817]

Finally, the notion of perpetration can also be used to denote the person who is deemed to carry the main part of responsibility for the commission of the offence. This evaluation does not necessarily hinge on the question whether that person has committed the actus reus himself, as will become apparent for instance in the discussion on perpetration by means, below.[818]

---

815 Hamdorf, 'Beteiligungsmodelle im Strafrecht' (2002), p. 11.
816 Hamdorf, 'Beteiligungsmodelle im Strafrecht' (2002), pp. 13–14.
817 Fletcher, 'Rethinking Criminal Law' (1978), p. 637.
818 Hamdorf, 'Beteiligungsmodelle im Strafrecht' (2002), p. 16.

Leaving national peculiarities aside, one can generally distinguish two different conceptions of perpetration; a restrictive, and an extensive notion of perpetration which penal systems may adopt. Traditionally criminal law, *inter alia* for the sake of legal certainty, adopted a restrictive concept of perpetration but, it will become apparent that recent developments in doctrine and criminal policy have led to an inflation of the concept. In the remainder of this chapter, this research will first discuss the merits and shortcomings of these two approaches and will subsequently discuss how penal systems try to distinguish between perpetrators and accomplices, before turning the focus to doctrinal developments which prompted the emergence of a moderate extensive concept of perpetration in Germany and the Netherlands.

6.2.2. The restrictive concept of perpetration

First and foremost, it should be noted that traditionally the scope of perpetration is inextricably linked to the interpretation of the actus reus and the question when someone can be deemed to having brought about the actus reus of the respective crime. Traditionally, the interpretation of the actus reus rested, and in some countries still rests on an objective, physical basis. Accordingly, only the person whose own conduct fulfils all the requirements of the offence definition is deemed to be the perpetrator of the crime in question.[819] The foundation of perpetration is thus found in the definition of the criminal offence. The advantage of such an approach can be seen in its dogmatic clarity, as it will be relatively simple to demarcate the liability of the perpetrator from other participants and the arguably high degree of legal certainty it provides due to its link to objective facts.

A restrictive concept of perpetration is certainly a corollary of a causal theory of conduct, and fits nicely into a society where murder is predominately committed by dagger, sword or poison. Yet, in a highly complex, modern society where the possibilities to bring about a desired criminal result have become almost infinite, such an approach can prove problematic. While the vantage point of this approach, i.e. the underlying criminal offence is certainly correct and constitutes the foundation of perpetration in all penal systems, it has considerable shortcomings which makes it unfeasible especially in connection with a differentiated system of participation.[820] The shortcoming of this approach is that from a strict point of view it would eliminate the notion of perpetration by means, as the puppeteer who uses an innocent agent to commit the crime does not fulfil the elements of the definition[821] and is flawed in regard to result crimes, as the latter "merely" prohibits the manifestation of certain results and therefore do not encompass a specific

819 See: Roxin, 'Täterschaft und Tatherrschaft' (2006), pp. 34–51.

820 See: De Hullu, 'Materieel Strafrecht' (2009), pp. 149–151, Roxin, 'Strafrecht Allgemeiner Teil, Band II: Besondere Erscheinungsformen der Straftat' (2003), p. 7, Smith and Hogan, 'Criminal Law' (2008), p. 180, Wessels and Beulke, 'Strafrecht Allgemeiner Teil, Die Straftat und ihr Aufbau' (2008), p. 180.

821 Fletcher, 'Rethinking Criminal Law' (1978), p. 655.

definition of conduct that would allow a delineation of perpetration and complicity.[822]

Moreover, and maybe more crucially, such an approach also leads to a narrow concept of perpetration which may not always capture the actual division of labour and responsibility between the parties involved in the commission of the crime, as it is required that each participant at least brings about a part of the actus reus. Due to *inter alia* the shift in the doctrine of conduct, outlined above, the direct, physical commission of the offence has lost its paramount significance and exerts these days a mere indicatory function.[823] The main responsible or prime movers, frequently no longer take a hands on approach to crime but use their cunning, authority or power. The concentration of all reproach and responsibility in the person who physically brings about the actus reus can in some instances transform small-time criminals into prime movers.

Despite these shortcomings, this approach is still prevalent in the English legal system. In English law usually the principal is referred to as the one whose act is the most immediate cause of the actus reus.[824] At first sight, this will be the person who brings about the actus reus of the offence with the required mens rea. Thus, English law distinguishes perpetrators from accessories by resorting to the notion of directness or "immediacy of cause".[825] This approach has its roots in a stern concept of individual responsibility that criminal liability should only be imposed for wrongdoing for which a person himself is responsible.[826] Accomplices, so the argument goes, cannot be seen as a direct cause of the actus reus, which finds expression in a separate body of law on accessory liability.[827]

Be that as it may, it is furthermore acknowledged in English criminal law that more than one principal can be involved in the commission of the offence. Two variations are conceivable here. On the one hand it is possible that every party to the offence satisfies the required ingredients of the respective offence. Suppose for instance that Andrew and Brian assault Jesse by hitting him with clubs. If Jesse dies from the combination of blows, they will each be guilty of manslaughter or murder.[828] Thus, joint commission of an offence is seen as the parallel to the direct

822 Jescheck and Weigend, 'Lehrbuch des Strafrechts: Allgemeiner Teil' (1996), p. 648. See also: Schönke and Schröder, 'Kommentar zum Strafgesetzbuch' (2006), Vorbem §§25 et seq. Mn 53–55.

823 See: Chapter II. 2.

824 Smith and Hogan, 'Criminal Law' (2008), p. 180.

825 Smith, 'A Modern Treatise on the Law of Criminal Complicity' (1991), p. 79 et seq.

826 Smith and Hogan, 'Criminal Law' (2008), p. 181. See also: R v Kennedy [2007] UKHL, 38, where the House of Lords reaffirmed the concept of individual responsibility.

827 Kadish, 'Complicity, Cause and Blame: A Study in the Interpretation of Doctrine' California Law Review (1985), p. 327, Smith and Hogan, 'Criminal Law' (2008), p. 181, Williams, 'Finis for novus actus?' Cambridge Law Journal (1989), pp. 391–416.

828 Simester and Sullivan, 'Criminal Law: Theory and Doctrine' (2007), p. 196. Smith and Hogan, 'Criminal Law' (2008), p. 182.

commission of the offence definition, which by and large makes a concept of co-perpetration as applied in Germany and the Netherlands superfluous.

Furthermore each may satisfy some part of the actus reus with the requisite mens rea and the sum of their actions adds up to fulfil the complete actus reus requirement. It is however important to stress that the principal must contribute to the occurrence of the actus reus through his own act and must at least have fulfilled a part of the actus reus. If in the aforementioned example Jesse dies due to a particular blow distributed by Andrew then Brian cannot be convicted as a principal.[829] This line of reasoning also implies that one cannot be convicted as a principal to murder if one "merely" restrains the victim while the other stabs it with a knife. The actus reus of murder is intentionally killing or causing grievous body harm to a human being and does not contain any form of restraining.[830] Moreover, it follows from the focus of the approach on the actus reus of the underlying offence that if an offence definition requires a perpetrator with certain characteristics or qualities, the absence of these will bar the possibility of principal liability.[831]

The same is true, as will be further discussed below, for the German penal system, where the underlying offence definition is also seen as the foundation of perpetration.[832] In the Netherlands, however, a missing quality need not stand in the way of establishing perpetration in cases where another person is used to bring about the desired result. This was *inter alia* made possible by the ambiguous wording of Article 47 DPC[833], which made it possible to interpret it broadly.[834]

6.2.3. An extensive concept of perpetration

An alternative approach open to penal systems is to adopt an extensive concept of perpetration. An extensive concept of perpetration can take two forms; a strict one and a moderate one. The former is usually applied in paradigmatic unitarian systems. All participants are deemed to fulfil the actus reus regardless of their factual contribution to the crime. This makes other categories of participation besides perpetration redundant and leads to a monistic or unitarian concept of

---

829 Simester and Sullivan, 'Criminal Law: Theory and Doctrine' (2007), p. 196.

830 Smith, 'A Modern Treatise on the Law of Criminal Complicity' (1991), p. 80.

831 Smith, 'A Modern Treatise on the Law of Criminal Complicity' (1991), p. 28.

832 Wessels and Beulke, 'Strafrecht Allgemeiner Teil, Die Straftat und ihr Aufbau' (2008), p. 184.

833 Art 47 reads as follows:
(1) The following are liable as principals:
those who commit a criminal offence, either personally or jointly with another or others, or who cause an innocent person to commit a criminal offence;
those who, by means of gifts, promises, abuse of authority, use of violence, threat or deception or providing the opportunity, means or information, intentionally solicit the commission of the crime.
(2) With regard to the last category, only those actions intentionally solicited by them and the consequences of such actions are to be taken into consideration.

834 De Hullu, 'Materieel Strafrecht' (2009), p. 421, De Jong, 'Vormen van strafbare deelneming', in van der Leij (ed), Plegen en Deelnemen (2007), pp. 113–114.

participation. Anyone who has contributed to the commission of the criminal offence is seen as a perpetrator. Qualitatively all participants are in equal measures involved in the crime and merely participate quantitatively to different degrees.

An alternative to the strict extensive concept of perpetration can be found in a moderate extensive concept of perpetration. If one adopts this approach the notion of perpetration is generally used to denote the person(s) who has to shoulder the main share of responsibility for the occurred criminal harm. The vantage point of a moderate extensive concept of perpetration to imposing primary liability is identical to the one of a restrictive conception of perpetration. This means that someone will be deemed to be the perpetrator of an offence if he brings about the actus reus of the underlying offence. However, the bringing about of the actus reus is here no longer confined to direct physical involvement. Rather, by the application of particular doctrines, the actus reus of an offence is interpreted broadly as to allow the attribution of criminal liability to those deemed primarily responsible, i.e. the main or central figure.[835] Just like the strict restrictive conception of perpetration this leads to a dualistic model of participation, distinguishing between perpetrators and accomplices.

In the German as well as in the Dutch penal system a moderate extensive concept of perpetration is applied. Both systems apply a broad interpretation of the actus reus which makes it possible to conceive as perpetrators, also those who have not physically contributed to the commission of the actus reus. Thus, it will subsequently become apparent that in these countries the concept of perpetration has developed from a factual to a more normative concept. In Germany this shift has been prompted by the so-called hegemony over the act doctrine which by and large has also been accepted by the courts. In our society, organisations and social networks take a prominent role which materialises in "new" concepts of criminal liability where the focus is no longer exclusively on the individual, physical perpetrator but also on factual responsible perpetrators behind the screen.[836] In the Netherlands this is nicely illustrated by the doctrine of functional perpetration which, just like the hegemony over the act doctrine allows the attribution of criminal liability to persons deemed responsible for a criminal offence, despite the fact that they were not physically involved in the commission of the crime. This research will discuss these doctrines in more detail in due course. First, some space will be devoted to discussing along which lines one may try to distinguish perpetrators from accomplices and how the notion of perpetration can be defined.

6.3. A Subjective or objective approach to perpetration?

It has been demonstrated that the concept of perpetration takes an important place in criminal law. But how to define the concept precisely and how can one

835 Hamdorf, 'Beteiligungsmodelle im Strafrecht' (2002), p. 175.

836 De Hullu, 'Materieel Strafrecht' (2009), pp. 152–154, 171–173.

distinguish perpetrators from accomplices? In line with the objective/subjective distinction pervading the criminal law one can rely for that matter either on objective or on subjective factors. As outlined above, an objective approach to perpetration is heavily linked to a physical conception of criminal wrongdoing and generally leads to a restrictive concept of perpetration. Whether or not a person has brought about the actus reus of a crime and can thus be seen as the perpetrator is according to this approach assessed objectively.

Alternatively it is also possible to interpret the actus reus subjectively by taking the person's subjective attitude as a starting point for the interpretation of the actus reus.[837] Thus, the focal point becomes the intention with which the participant committed the act.[838] The subjective approach introduces a degree of flexibility, which provides room for the courts to impose a higher punishment on those who bear prime responsibility for the crime committed despite the fact that they have not committed the actus reus themselves. Conversely, they can also impose less punishment on those who only contributed auxiliary to its commission.[839] German criminal law adhered for a long time to this theory and although the courts have by now adopted a medium position between objective and subjective theories, the influence of the subjective theory remains perceivable. According to the subjective theory, the perpetrator conceives the act "as his own", i.e. he acts with *animus auctoris*, while the accessory conceives the act as the "act of another", i.e. he acts with *animus socii*.[840] The former *Reichsgericht* extensively applied the theory, taking it to extremes.

In its extreme form, the subjective approach can lead to peculiar outcomes, as it is possible that persons who directly brought about the actus reus are nevertheless treated as accessories when they did not conceive the act to be their own. Maybe the most notorious decision of the *Reichsgericht* in this respect is the so called bathtub case.[841] In this case the mother of a newborn begged her sister to drown the child in a bathtub. The sister fulfilled the wish and was convicted as an accessory, as, so it was argued, she only wished to further the mother's act.[842] Also the German Supreme Court has based quite a substantial number of judgments on the subjective approach. The most famous case in point here is the so called *Stashynskij* case.[843] During the decades of the cold war Mr. Stashynskij, a Russian spy, carried out two political assassinations in West Germany. In 1961 when the Berlin wall was built he fled to West Germany and was indicted for the assassinations. Even though Mr.

---

837 See: Roxin, 'Täterschaft und Tatherrschaft' (2006), pp. 51–57.

838 Roxin, 'Strafrecht Allgemeiner Teil, Band II: Besondere Erscheinungsformen der Straftat' (2003), pp. 11–12, Wessels and Beulke, 'Strafrecht Allgemeiner Teil, Die Straftat und ihr Aufbau' (2008), p. 182.

839 Hamdorf, 'Beteiligungsmodelle im Strafrecht' (2002), pp. 138–142.

840 Fletcher, 'Rethinking Criminal Law' (1978), p. 655, Jescheck and Weigend, 'Lehrbuch des Strafrechts: Allgemeiner Teil' (1996), p. 650.

841 19 February 1940 RGHSt 74, 84.

842 See: Fletcher, 'Rethinking Criminal Law' (1978), p. 658.

843 19 October 1962 BGH NJW 1963, 355.

Stashynskij carried out the killings with his own hands, he was regarded as being an accessory to the murders as he did not conceive his acts to be his own but rather the acts of the KGB.

The rationale underlying these kind of decision arguably is of a criminal policy nature. The courts tried to circumvent the mandatory life sentence enshrined in §211 GPC (murder) in circumstances where they regarded this harsh punishment as inappropriate. The same rationale led to the application of the subjective theory in cases of killings ordered by state authority during the Third Reich.[844] This historical peculiarity also to some extent explains why subjective factors at times still play a prominent role in German jurisprudence despite its formal abolishment by the Supreme Court.[845]

If one takes into consideration the aforementioned examples it is thus not surprising that the subjective theory has been criticised extensively, as the theory offers no rational reviewable criteria for the demarcation of perpetration and accessory liability. Thus the task, so it can be argued, is at the whim of the judge, and regarded as untenable and contrary to legal certainty.[846]

The discussion about objective and subjective approaches to perpetration reveals a crucial contentious point with respect to liability for participation in a criminal offence. The fundamental disagreement between these two diametrically opposed approaches is namely whether the demarcation of primary and secondary responsibility ought to take place along the objective/ontological lines of fulfilment of the actus reus or whether it should essentially be regarded as a question of guilt.[847] In an act-based criminal law where punishment is primarily imposed for wrongful and unlawful actions, objective factors seem to carry more weight as they make it possible to link criminal liability to objectively assessable external events rather than subjective, amoral and antisocial proclivities. However, it has already been noted in the beginning of this book that none of the investigated penal system can be considered to be exclusively act-based criminal law, but rather that subjective factors relating to the criminal tendencies of the suspect have become increasingly influential as well. This would from a systematic point of view indicate that subjective and objective factors should be combined in order to distinguish between perpetrators and accomplices.

Finally, it should not be overlooked that also practical considerations can play a role here. More precisely, the potential choice between an objective and a subjective approach to perpetration may also be influenced by one's view regarding the role of the judge in the criminal trial. An objective theory forces judges to adhere more closely to the wording of the law, i.e. the actus reus of the crime in question and evaluate whether or not the suspect has (objectively) fulfilled all the elements of the

844 Roxin, 'Täterschaft und Tatherrschaft' (2006), p. 647, Weisser, 'Täterschaft in Europa' (2011), pp. 27–32.

845 Roxin, 'Täterschaft und Tatherrschaft' (2006), pp. 646–654.

846 Jescheck and Weigend, 'Lehrbuch des Strafrechts: Allgemeiner Teil' (1996), p. 651.

847 Roxin, 'Täterschaft und Tatherrschaft' (2006), p. 651.

offence definition. The judge's margin of discretion is accordingly more limited than would be the case in regard to a subjective theory where it is left to the judge to evaluate the suspect's subjective postures, will and intention.[848] In other words, a subjective theory with its elusive concepts such as *animus auctoris*, intention and interest in the commission of the offence generally grants more leeway to judges than on objective theory with its focus on the commission of the actus reus.

6.4. Concluding remarks

In regard to the doctrine of perpetration European criminal law is faced with several crucial choices and dilemmas. First, a choice between a restrictive concept of perpetration, a strict extensive and a moderate extensive one will have to be made. The restrictive approach is inextricably bound up with a physical, or factual conception of crime. This will often be reflected in the requirement of a direct and immediate causal involvement in the commission of the offence by the person held responsible as a perpetrator. According to this view the law will focus on the moment of the commission of the actus reus and exclude factors from the evaluation scheme, which from a normative perspective may be considered crucial for the attribution of primary responsibility. The restrictive approach generally leads to a clear distinction between perpetrators and accomplices which may admittedly increase dogmatic clarity as well as legal certainty as the demarcation of primary from secondary responsibility takes place according to clear objective factors. Such an approach might however not always be able to reflect the actual division of labour and responsibility between the parties involved in the offence, as it will be necessary for each participant to bring about at least a part of the actus reus in order to be held liable as a perpetrator.

A strict extensive conception of perpetration avoids this pitfall by prima facie considering all participants in a criminal endeavour to be perpetrators regardless of their contribution. It thus leads to a monistic concept of perpetration. This also reveals that while a restrictive approach only takes a snapshot of the events to base primary liability on, an extensive concept makes a video of the entire criminal event and only subsequently distributes criminal liability to the participants according to their respective roles in the commission of the crime. If one were to adopt such a strict, extensive approach of perpetration then the different nature and quality of the participant's contributions will only be taken into consideration at the sentencing stage. While this would free legal doctrine from the difficult task of distinguishing a variety of different categories of participation, it may cause frictions with the principle of legality and legal certainty. The monistic concept of participation stemming from a strict extensive approach would not only make it difficult for the citizens to foresee when they might incur liability as a perpetrator but will also confer a considerable breadth of discretion to the judges as the

[848] Roxin, 'Täterschaft und Tatherrschaft' (2006), p. 646.

differentiation between the respective contributions of the participants will still have to be made at the sentencing stage.

Preferable seems therefore a medium position in the form of a moderate extensive concept of perpetration. This approach leads to a dualistic concept of participation, distinguishing primary from secondary responsibility. This approach combines the advantages of the restrictive concept, but avoids most of its drawbacks. It shifts the focus from the direct or physical perpetrator respectively, to a holistic conception of perpetration where also normative considerations of "substantial criminal energy" and control over the course of criminal events may enter the equation which is arguably crucial for a just attribution of liability. A substantial contribution to a criminal outcome arguably reflects considerable criminal energy which is more culpable than other minor contributions. Thus, while the perpetrator's contribution drives the wrongdoing, the aider's contribution is only of minor significance. This crucial insight ought to, it is submitted, also be reflected at a doctrinal level. The different nature and degree of responsibility for the criminal offence should find expression in different labels which will not only increase legal certainty but also fulfil an important communicative function for the public with regard to the different degrees of wrongdoing and culpability. In other words, fairness demands that offenders are labelled and punished in correspondence to their wrongdoing.

Given that one accepts that the distinction between perpetrators and accomplices is important, one is faced with a further dilemma namely with the question if perpetration ought to be filled in objectively or subjectively. A strict restrictive conception of perpetration is often linked to an objective interpretation of the notion. However it is also possible to invoke a person's subjective attitude in order to define the concepts of perpetration. This approach will broaden the scope of perpetration but arguably relies too heavily on an offender's subjective, antisocial tendencies. This, it is submitted shifts the focus too strongly to illusive subjective criteria. Punishment should only be imposed for the culpable commission of wrongful conduct. Wrongful conduct in turn, it has been submitted, ought to reflect on the offender in a way that makes the public censure contained in the imposition of liability appropriate and depicts him as a responsible agent. A strict reliance on subjective criteria may however lead to the punishment of thought-crimes or guilt by association. A mixed approach, combining objective and subjective criteria seems therefore preferable. Thereby the safeguarding function of objective factors can be maintained while overcoming the rigidness of this approach by the inclusion of subjective elements. One important factor which should be taken into account here is the actuality of modern crime. As the increasing division of labour in our society has also influenced the way how crimes are committed, it becomes crucial to distribute liability according to the actual blameworthiness of the respective participants. Often the arm-chair strategist behind the scene will deserve more reproach than the actual perpetrator who puts the former's plan into action.

After having discussed preliminary choices and dilemmas in the context of perpetration the following sections will focus on two different modes of attributing liability to perpetrators. Thus, the main focus will lie in the following on the establishment of primary responsibility in the case of involvement of multiple actors in the commission of the offence. A distinction may be drawn therefore between vertical and horizontal forms of perpetration. The latter refers to situations where all persons participate as equal partners in the commission of the offence, while the former refers to situations where the relationship between the parties involved is a vertical and more hierarchical one, denoting a relationship of subordination. The following section will commence with a discussion of vertical forms of perpetration (section 7) before the discussion will turn to horizontal forms (section 8).

7. Vertical forms of perpetration

7.1. Introduction

It has already been mentioned that all investigated countries formally depart from a restrictive concept of perpetration, as it is deemed to provide a high level of legal certainty and foreseeability. However, it has also been shown that a restrictive conception of perpetration will give rise to some legal lacunas, especially if applied in a differentiated system. A restrictive approach is for instance incapable of attributing liability to persons who were not themselves involved (physically) in the commission of the offence but are nevertheless deemed to be just as responsible for the outcome as their partners. Consider for instance the case of someone who played an instrumental role in conceiving and organising the commission of the offence, received a substantial cut of the booty, but was not present during the commission of the crime.

It seems only natural that in these situations primary responsibility should rest with the person in charge, who commands, orders, organises or controls the commission of the offence rather than with the direct perpetrator who is either unaware of the exact ramifications of his conduct, or obeys orders or commands. In these situations of vertical forms of participation it will become apparent once again that a shift in the paradigm of participation towards a more normative approach has taken place, connecting responsibility primarily to the power to command or control the commission of the offence.

Vertical forms of perpetration strive to assign primary responsibility to persons possessing (intellectual) authorship for an occurred criminal harm without having directly been involved in its commission. Frequently people rely on intermediaries to bring about a criminal result and holding them liable as accessories to their own criminal enterprise seems to strike the wrong chord in regard to the applied label as well as desert.

7.2. The Perpetrator behind the scene

An important variation of the aforementioned predicament can be described as the perpetrator behind the scene predicament. A restrictive conception of perpetration is incapable of holding the so called perpetrator behind the perpetrator responsible for his role in the commission of the crime. A variation of these cases can also arise in the economic and business context, where an employee might bring about some sort of criminal harm by e.g. releasing toxic waste into the ground water, yet, we deem his supervisor, manager, etc. who was in charge of and oversaw the operation as deserving more reproach than the employee, i.e. the direct, physical perpetrator.

With the increasing organisation and sophistication of criminal behaviour in the last decades, the focus of criminal law has shifted from the person who physically commits the crime to the grey eminence in the background who conceived, controlled and supervised the enterprise and which is accordingly considered functional responsible for the commission of the crime. We deem these persons who are in charge of an operation, conceive the plan, etc. often just as, if not more dangerous as the actual perpetrators. This change in the nature and perception of crime, in conjunction with the aforementioned shift in the doctrine of conduct towards a less physical concept, has led to an increasing focus on the leading figure within the co-operative framework. The corollary of this shift is that often people who procure the commission of a criminal offence through an intermediary are nowadays classified as perpetrators. When evaluating human conduct one ought not only look at its mere physical manifestation but one should also take into account factors like the social ramification of the conduct, as well as the function and sphere of influence of the person involved in the crime.[849] This line of reasoning also corresponds to general parlance, where we no longer conceive only the bricklayer as the builder of a house, but rather the building contractor or architect who is in charge of the whole construction.[850]

It follows that the scope of criminal offences has been broadened by this new conception of action, and that people that in the past could only incur criminal liability via participation rules, are nowadays conceived as (direct) perpetrators. This increased emphasis on forms of perpetration is particularly visible and problematic in countries formally adhering to a differentiated model of participation in crime.

This discussion will commence by dwelling on the German doctrine of hegemony over the act, and the Dutch doctrine of functional perpetration. These two doctrines have led to the adoption of a moderate extensive concept of perpetration in their respective systems. The hegemony over the act doctrine in Germany is *inter alia* seen as a concept by which perpetrators can be distinguished from other participants. It has already been mentioned that when distinguishing

849 Gritter, 'Functioneel plegen door een natuurlijke persoon', in van der Leij (ed), Plegen en Deelnemen (2007), p. 14.
850 De Hullu, 'Materieel Strafrecht' (2006), p. 149.

perpetrators from other participants, one can generally focus on objective or subjective criteria. The hegemony over the act doctrine, combines the objective and subjective theory and holds that next to the objective conduct also the intention of the participant should play a role in distinguishing (co-) perpetration from participation.[851] This approach resembles the situation in the Netherlands where also subjective and objective factors alike play a role in the demarcation of the notion of perpetration from other forms of participation.[852]

The Dutch doctrine of functional perpetration on the other hand is not so much seen as a tool of demarcation but rather as an additional basis of criminal liability for "the functional responsible". As will subsequently be shown, the two doctrines, despite being conceptually different, have by and large similar effects and aim to mitigate the very same shortcomings of the restrictive concept of perpetration outlined above. This research will first investigate the two doctrines on an abstract level, attempting to outline their main elements and underlying rationales. Subsequently it will focus on one important aspect of these doctrines, namely the liability of employers, mangers, etc, in the context of economic, business and employment relationships for the conduct of their employees. In all three countries special doctrines have been conceived to hold people responsible for the conduct of their subordinates. These different doctrines will be compared and subsequently the different modes and forms of attribution for participants in crime will be discussed more closely.

7.2.1. The German hegemony over the act doctrine

In German literature the so called hegemony over the act doctrine (*Tatherrschaftslehre*) is nowadays almost unanimously accepted.[853] This academic construction is often closely linked to the German scholar Claus Roxin who played an instrumental role in the doctrine's acceptance.[854] The decisive criterion of perpetration in this theory is, crudely stated, the hegemony and control over the execution of the criminal act.[855] Accordingly, a person will be held liable as a perpetrator if he controlled the commission of the offence, considerably influenced the shape and manner of the commission and can thus be seen as the central figure in the occurred crime.[856] Conversely an accessory is deemed not to be in a position to considerably shape the commission of the offence, despite his obvious influence

851 Van Toorenburg, 'Medeplegen' (1998), p. 207.

852 Van Toorenburg, 'Medeplegen' (1998), p. 208.

853 Roxin, 'Strafrecht Allgemeiner Teil, Band II: Besondere Erscheinungsformen der Straftat' (2003), pp. 9–11, Wessels and Beulke, 'Strafrecht Allgemeiner Teil, Die Straftat und ihr Aufbau' (2008), p. 181.

854 See: Roxin, 'Täterschaft und Tatherrschaft' (2006), pp. 1–539.

855 Fletcher, 'Rethinking Criminal Law' (1978), p. 655.

856 Schönke and Schröder, 'Kommentar zum Strafgesetzbuch' (2006), Vorbem §§25 et seq. Mn 62, Wessels and Beulke, 'Strafrecht Allgemeiner Teil, Die Straftat und ihr Aufbau' (2008), p. 181.

on the course of events.[857] This theory is a hybrid of the subjective dolus theories and the objective theories. Scholars have striven for a synthesis of the aforementioned theories and accordingly the doctrine encompasses subjective as well as objective criteria. Thus the intention of the perpetrator as well as his factual contributions to the manifestation of the actus reus need to be taken into consideration.[858]

As a vantage point the restrictive concept of perpetration is applied, which is subsequently extended by objective as well as subjective criteria. The objective criteria of the theory encompass the factual hegemony and control over the execution of the criminal act. This will be determined by taking into account the objective contribution of the person and its suitability to exert hegemony.[859] The subjective element of the hegemony over the act doctrine encompasses the intention of the person. The person must will to exert hegemony over the act and intend the manifestation of the objective offence definition.[860] In other words, perpetration can be depicted as the intentional hegemony over the conduct that leads to the manifestation of the offence definition.

Two conclusions can be drawn from this definition. Firstly it follows that the hegemony over the act doctrine is not applicable to negligent conduct, where by definition one cannot speak of intentional control over conduct. However, this has no practical repercussions, as the German penal system does not distinguish between perpetrators and accessories in crimes of negligence.[861] Secondly, it follows that the hegemony over the act doctrine is not a readily applicable notion for every crime, but rather that it needs to be adapted, substantiated and fleshed out in every case and offence at hand.[862] In other words the hegemony over the act doctrine needs to be adapted to every form of perpetration. Thus, the hegemony over the act manifests itself as hegemony over the misfeasance (*Handlungsherrschaft*) pertinent to direct perpetration (*unmittelbare Täterschaft*), in regard to perpetration by means (*mittelbare Täterschaft*) as hegemony over the will, or hegemony due to superior knowledge (*Willensherrschaft; Herrschaft kraft überlegen Wissens*) and in co-perpetration (*Mittäterschaft*) as functional hegemony over the act of the jointly acting perpetrators.[863]

---

857 Roxin, 'Strafrecht Allgemeiner Teil, Band II: Besondere Erscheinungsformen der Straftat' (2003), p. 10.

858 Fletcher, 'Basic Concepts of Criminal Law' (1998), p. 61, Schönke and Schröder, 'Kommentar zum Strafgesetzbuch' (2006), Vorbem §§25 et seq. Mn 62–63, Wessels and Beulke, 'Strafrecht Allgemeiner Teil, Die Straftat und ihr Aufbau' (2008), pp. 181–184.

859 Jescheck and Weigend, 'Lehrbuch des Strafrechts: Allgemeiner Teil' (1996), p. 652.

860 Jescheck and Weigend, 'Lehrbuch des Strafrechts: Allgemeiner Teil' (1996), p. 652.

861 See §§26, 27.

862 Roxin, 'Strafrecht Allgemeiner Teil, Band II: Besondere Erscheinungsformen der Straftat' (2003), p. 10, Wessels and Beulke, 'Strafrecht Allgemeiner Teil, Die Straftat und ihr Aufbau' (2008), pp. 181–185.

863 Wessels and Beulke, 'Strafrecht Allgemeiner Teil, Die Straftat und ihr Aufbau' (2008), p. 181.

Exemptions to the hegemony over the act doctrine

It is contentious in German literature whether the hegemony over the act doctrine is applicable to all forms of offences. The prevalent view however holds that the doctrine does not only take a different shape in regard to the different forms of participation, but also that it is inapplicable to some forms of crime.[864] As the doctrine is inextricable bound up with the respective offence definition, some offences, so the argument goes, are not susceptible to the teachings of the doctrine as some offences require particular attributes to be present in the perpetrator. For instance in regard to "*eigenhändigen Delikten*", i.e. offences that require the physical carrying out of the conduct requirement, only the person who carries out the respective conduct can be regarded as the perpetrator. Thus, the offence of perjury (§154 GPC) can only be committed by the witness and not by someone who has "merely" hegemony over the testimony.[865] Put differently, who is not physically involved in the carrying out of the offence definition, can despite his hegemony over the act not be regarded as a perpetrator. Furthermore, in regard to "*Pflichtdelikte*", which require a certain duty to act it has been argued that only the person to whom the duty is addressed can be regarded as the perpetrator.[866] This reasoning would *inter alia* apply to all improper crimes of commission, which pursuant to §13 GPC necessarily require a duty to act. It is common ground here that the duty to act must rest on the perpetrator, but it is disputed whether the duty to act requirement will supersede the hegemony over the act or will be required cumulatively with it.

Perpetration pursuant to contemporary jurisprudence

As has already been mentioned, the jurisprudence of the *Reichsgericht* applied a rather subjective approach. Despite heavy criticism from legal scholars, this approach was continued by the German Supreme Court (BGH). Also in more recent jurisprudence the BGH took a subjective approach as vantage point.[867] However, this stance is nowadays more and more pervaded and supplemented by objective requirements. Thus, it can be said that jurisprudence has progressed to a synthesis where objective as well as subjective requirements are of relevance. This recent developments show in essence a trend towards the hegemony over the act

864 Roxin, 'Strafrecht Allgemeiner Teil, Band II: Besondere Erscheinungsformen der Straftat' (2003), p. 10, Schönke and Schröder, 'Kommentar zum Strafgesetzbuch' (2006), Vorbem §§25 et seq. Mn 63.

865 Wessels and Beulke, 'Strafrecht Allgemeiner Teil, Die Straftat und ihr Aufbau' (2008), p. 185.

866 Wessels and Beulke, 'Strafrecht Allgemeiner Teil, Die Straftat und ihr Aufbau' (2008), p. 185.

867 Roxin, 'Strafrecht Allgemeiner Teil, Band II: Besondere Erscheinungsformen der Straftat' (2003), pp. 13–14, Wessels and Beulke, 'Strafrecht Allgemeiner Teil, Die Straftat und ihr Aufbau' (2008), pp. 182–183.

doctrine.[868] In recent case law the courts determine whether the accused had the *animus auctoris* by applying a comprehensive evaluation including the accused's objective influence and control over the commission of the offence, his interest and degree of involvement in the offence and his will to exert control.[869] The German Supreme court has for instance held that a member of a burglar gang who pursuant to an agreement had provided his van for transportation on two occasions but generally was only in charge of opening the safes which the other members had stolen could only be seen as an accessory as the commission of the burglaries was not depending on his participation. He only carried out supporting tasks and received only a minor share of the loot for his services.[870]

However, at times subjective criteria still seem to be decisive in jurisprudence. In particular the suspect's interest in the commission of the offence is sometimes invoked to distinguish between perpetrators and aiders. The Supreme Court for instance held in a pertinent case of a joint robbery that the partner who had provided his car, functioned as a driver, removed the ignition key from the money transport and held the guards at bay with a gas pistol could be seen as an aider, as he had only reluctantly agreed to assist in the robbery and contrary to his partner who was hard pressed for money did not have a strong interest in the commission of the crime.[871] The influence of subjective criteria however varies from case to case. While in regard to direct, co-perpetration and perpetration by means a clear tendency towards the hegemony over the act doctrine is discernible in regard to the demarcation of forms of perpetration from aiding and instigation subjective factors seem to feature more prominently.[872]

Evaluation

It has become apparent that a central aspect of the contemporary doctrine of perpetration is to hold the person who we deem functionally responsible for the occurred harm liable. This should be possible regardless of close temporal and spatial ties to the commission of the offence and even regardless of any physical contribution to the commission of the offence. The leaders of large crime syndicates

868 It is interesting to note here that in the case 26 July 1994 BGH NStZ 1994, 537 the BGH based the liability of members of the defence council of the former German Democratic Republic as perpetrators by means almost exclusively on the hegemony over the act doctrine and hardly mentioned subjective considerations in his verdict. It is however questionable to what extent this judgment is of general application as cases dealing with this chapter of German history follow their own logic.

869 See: 14 November 2001 BGH NStZ 2002, 200, 24 July 2008 BGH HRRS 2009 Nr. 626. See also: Roxin, 'Strafrecht Allgemeiner Teil, Band II: Besondere Erscheinungsformen der Straftat' (2003), p. 10, Fn 22.

870 24 July 2008 BGH HRRS 2009 Nr. 626.

871 6 November 1984 BGH NStZ 1985, 165. See also: 15 January 1991 BGH NStZ 1991, 280. For an overview of case law see: Roxin, 'Täterschaft und Tatherrschaft' (2006), pp. 558–642.

872 Roxin, 'Täterschaft und Tatherrschaft' (2006), pp. 642–646.

or arm-chair strategists like Adolf Eichmann, are only rarely involved in the actual commission of the crime, but can nevertheless be primarily responsible for it. Without their involvement the crime would possibly have been never committed or would have taken a completely different shape. To hold these key figures in a criminal enterprise liable as "mere" accessories to the crimes of their subordinates does not reflect their actual role and should therefore be avoided.

The doctrine of hegemony over the act provides one solution to the task at hand here. By combining objective and subjective criteria, it succeeds in moving away from the requirement of physical presence and contribution at the commission of the crime and therefore also covers the functional perpetrator behind the physical one. Due to modern developments in regard to telecommunication, the increasing division of labour and degree of organisation in crime etc. it is obvious that one can exert hegemony over a crime despite not being present during its commission.

The hegemony over the act doctrine is however by no means the only solution regarding liability for the conduct of subordinates. In the Netherlands and England, other, equally effective doctrines have been conceived in order to hold the functional perpetrator criminally liable for the acts of his subordinates.

7.2.2. The Dutch doctrine of functional perpetration

The Dutch courts have developed a concept to determine the criminal liability of a natural person by attributing liability to a perpetrator behind the scene. The notion of functional perpetration evolved gradually over time. Already in 1947 it was recognised in Dutch jurisprudence that also the (partial) bringing about of the offence definition through another could under certain circumstances amount to perpetration. The Dutch Supreme Court for instance convicted a Dutch citizen for the illegal importation of goods despite the fact that the goods were effectively imported by four English soldiers in their car whom the suspect had convinced to help him, while he was riding in a car behind them.[873] The court did not adopt a pure physical concept of conduct on the one hand, and gave the word "to import" a legal, more mental connotation.[874] This form of interpretation made it possible to assume perpetration in a case where the suspect had not himself brought about the actus reus of the offence but was nevertheless deemed responsible for its occurrence.

Even earlier had the Supreme Court convicted the director of a printing office for printing prohibited content in violation of Art 419 DPC[875], despite the fact that it

---

873 HR 22 July 1947, *NJ* 1947, 469.

874 Gritter, 'Effectiviteit en aansprakelijkheid in het economisch ordeningsrecht' (2003), p. 205.

875 Article 419 reads as follows:
A person who prints any written matter or any image of a criminal nature is liable to a term of imprisonment or of detention of not more than one year or a fine of the third category, where:
(1) the person who ordered the printing of the material is neither known, nor was disclosed upon the first written notice following initiation of the preliminary judicial investigation;

was not he who had operated the printing press.[876] In the courts reasoning a more mental concept of conduct is again clearly visible. Not only does the printer operating the press violate the law, but also the person "procuring" the commission of the offence can be held responsible as a perpetrator. The court also emphasised the function of the director within the company and in society and thus interpreted the norm broadly.[877] This case can be nicely compared to old English authorities regarding the doctrine of vicarious liability where it was held that the owner of a newspaper or magazine was liable for libellous publications in his paper despite the fact that he had neither authorised nor knowledge of the publication.[878] Thus, these cases bear witness to the fact that expediency can create strong pressure to relax the ordinary principles of individual liability.

The aforementioned cases are just some examples which attempt to sketch a shift in the conception of conduct in particular and criminal liability in general which led to a landmark decision in 1954. While in the aforementioned cases the Dutch courts had established criminal liability by interpreting offence definitions broadly, in a functional way, the Supreme Court in 1954 established conditions under which, if fulfilled, the functional responsible person who did not (physically) cause the actus reus of the offence could be held criminally liable.[879]

In the infamous *IJzerdraad* (iron wire) judgment, the question arose in which circumstances the conduct of an export manager could be seen as the conduct of the owner of the company.[880] The Supreme Court held that this could be the case, if (1) it was within the owner's power to control/determine the employee's conduct, and (2) the employee's act belonged to a category of acts "accepted" by the firm as being in the course of normal business operations.[881] Accordingly the *IJzerdraad* criteria are often dubbed the criteria of power and acceptance. In the context of the natural person the notion of power revolves around the factual control of the suspect over the (non-) manifestation of the criminal conduct. This aspect constitutes the normative core of the concept of power. The perpetrator with control over the factual perpetrator is in a (hierarchic) position to prevent the criminal conduct from occurring.[882] The power to control can for instance be grounded in an employment relationship or other variations of subordination as well as in close co-operation.

---

(2) the printer knew or might reasonably have expected that it was not possible to subject the person who ordered the printing to criminal prosecution at the time the printed matter was published, or where he knew or might reasonably have expected that person to be established outside the Kingdom within Europe.

876 HR 13 March 1933, *NJ* 1933, 1385.

877 Torringa, 'De rechtspersoon als dader; strafbaar leidinggeven aan rechtspersonen' (1984), p. 20.

878 Sayre, 'Criminal Responsibility for the acts of another' Harvard Law Review (1930), p. 710.

879 Gritter, 'Effectiviteit en aansprakelijkheid in het economisch ordeningsrecht' (2003), p. 208.

880 HR 23 February 1954, *NJ* 1954, 378.

881 Roef, 'Strafbare overheden – Een rechtsvergelijkende studie naar de strafrechtelijke aansprakelijkheid van overheden voor milieuverstoring' (2001), p. 331.

882 Gritter, 'Functioneel plegen door een natuurlijke persoon', in van der Leij (ed), Plegen en Deelnemen (2007), p. 20.

The notion of acceptance on the other hand is a much more subjective criterion which in essence requires an intentional involvement in the conduct factually committed by another actor.[883] Acceptance can for instance be assumed if the perpetrator was aware of the criminal conduct and embraced, tolerated or even encouraged it. At stake here is the acceptance of the occurred criminal conduct or conduct of a similar kind.[884] This includes systemic conduct patterns which often occur in an economic context. In the systematic acceptance or tolerance of the conduct, for instance in an economic relationship, one could therefore see the foundation of functional perpetration.[885]

The *IJzerdraad* criteria were developed to attribute criminal liability to the perpetrator behind the scene who did not (physically) cause the criminal harm. In doctrinal terms this notion is called functional perpetration. By virtue of the fulfilment of the criteria of power and acceptance, the conduct of the factual perpetrator is attributed to the functional perpetrator. The fulfilment of these criteria constitutes the basis for the liability of the functional perpetrator. Accordingly, functional and factual perpetration are generally not mutually exclusive.[886] However, in practice, a prosecution of the factual perpetrator will often be deemed unnecessary especially when the actual responsibility is perceived to lie with the functional perpetrator.[887]

To sum up, the main function of the doctrine is to hold a person liable as the perpetrator of an offence despite the fact that he has not physically brought about the actus reus, because he is deemed to be responsible for the occurred criminal offence.[888] By virtue of this doctrine he is deemed to have committed the offence himself.[889] In essence, the doctrine of functional perpetration constitutes an additional ground for attributing criminal liability. Not only can the physical perpetrator be held responsible but also the functional. Arguably this corresponds to common parlance, where for instance, we do not only conceive the trucker but also the ordering party as the importer of goods. Yet another example is baking. In our society it is not only the baker that bakes bread but also the company or the master baker who supervises the process. Accordingly, the doctrine is mostly, but not exclusively applied in situations where economic, organisational or professional conduct is at stake.[890] Against this backdrop it already becomes apparent that the doctrine of functional perpetration bears some resemblance with the notion of vicarious liability applied in England and other common law countries.

883 Gritter, 'Functioneel plegen door een natuurlijke persoon', in van der Leij (ed), Plegen en Deelnemen (2007), p. 28.

884 De Hullu, 'Materieel Strafrecht' (2006), p. 152.

885 De Hullu, 'Materieel Strafrecht' (2006), p. 152.

886 De Hullu, 'Materieel Strafrecht' (2006), p. 149.

887 De Hullu, 'Materieel Strafrecht' (2006), p. 149.

888 De Hullu, 'Materieel Strafrecht' (2006), p. 149.

889 De Hullu, 'Materieel Strafrecht' (2006), p. 149.

890 De Hullu, 'Materieel Strafrecht' (2006), p. 149.

The emergence of corporate liability in the realm of criminal law might have fostered and speeded up the further development of the doctrine. As will subsequently be demonstrated, although the doctrine was initially designed to tackle individual wrongdoing it nowadays plays a pivotal role in regard to corporate wrongdoing, where the doctrine is frequently invoked to establish corporate criminal liability. The criteria of power and acceptance are namely especially well suited to attribute conduct of employees, etc. which cause a criminal harm to the corporation as it had the power to control, supervise and guide the subordinates' conduct.

The scope of functional perpetration

Before liability can be attributed to the functional perpetrator by virtue of the criteria power and acceptance, the question of the scope of the underlying criminal offence arises.[891] In other words, it needs to be evaluated first, if the crime in question can be functionally perpetrated at all. This requires dwelling on the issue of the addressee of the underlying offence (norm).[892] Is murder for instance only committed by the doctor carrying out an abortion after the 24th week of pregnancy or can also the doctor who intentionally stated the week of pregnancy incorrectly, admitted the woman to hospital and ordered the termination of pregnancy be regarded as a murderer?[893]

Of particular importance therefore is the wording of the underlying offence. If an offence for instance requires the personal commission of the actus reus, functional perpetration seems at first sight impossible.[894] Some offences might thus be more susceptible to functional perpetration than others. Also in regard to crimes of omission it seems unnecessary to invoke the doctrine of functional perpetration as the perpetrator behind the scene can be held directly liable if he had a duty of care. When interpreting criminal offences one ought to take into consideration not only the intention of the legislator, but also the specific form of conduct prescribed in the offence, as well as the context in which the offence occurred (i.e. was the offence committed in an organised, hierarchical context?).[895] Furthermore the

891 Vellinga-Schootsstra, 'Het daderschap van de natuurlijke persoon', in van der Leij (ed), Daderschap en Deelneming (1999), p. 22.

892 Vellinga-Schootsstra, 'Het daderschap van de natuurlijke persoon', in van der Leij (ed), Daderschap en Deelneming (1999), p. 22.

893 See: HR 29 May 1990, *NJ* 1991, 217, where the doctor who "miscalculated" the week of pregnancy was convicted for murder.

894 See for instance: HR 2 June 1992, *NJ* 1992, 754 (Spruivliegtuig).The Dutch Supreme Court acquitted for instance a corporation in 1992 from an alleged violation of aviation rules (Besluit luchtvaarttoepassingen bestrijdingsmiddelen) because in the court's view, the norm was not addressed to the corporation but rather to the respective pilot.

895 De Hullu, 'Materieel Strafrecht' (2006), p. 154, Vellinga, 'Eenheid in Daderschap?', in Harteveld, et al. (eds), Systeem in ontwikkeling: liber amicorum G. Knigge (2005), pp. 527–546.

context of the law in which the provision is placed as well as our common parlance has to be taken into consideration.[896]

It becomes apparent from the foregoing that functional perpetration plays an important role, especially, but not exclusively in regard to offences committed in an economic context. Especially offences where economically-orientated conduct like importing, selling, building, causing or polluting plays a role are suited for functional perpetration. It should however be noted that functional perpetration can also play a role in regard to classical offences like murder[897], fraud or handling stolen goods.[898] Nevertheless, not all traditional crimes are open to functional perpetration, as some offence definition for instance require personal, physical perpetration. A paradigmatic example can for instance be found in the offence of rape which can according to the prevalent opinion not be functionally perpetrated, but requires a direct commission.

The criteria of power and acceptance

Once it has been established that a particular crime can be functionally-perpetrated liability needs to be established by application of the criteria of power and acceptance. As has already been noted, the criteria constitute a normative (power) and a subjective requirement (acceptance). The concept of power constitutes the foundation of the doctrine. Only if the functional perpetrator had the power to influence the conduct of the physical perpetrator, can he be deemed responsible for the harm occurred. What is important here is if the perpetrator had (factual) control over the (non) commission of the offence by another.[899] This does not however mean that the functional perpetrator cannot be involved in the commission of the offence at all, but in most cases, the physical involvement of the functional perpetrator will be rather minimal.[900]

While the requirement of power has proved to be rather uncontroversial the criterion of acceptance has caused multiple frictions. The criterion of acceptance has mostly been interpreted subjectively, in the sense that acceptance requires a form of intention, i.e. conditional intent (i.e. *dolus eventualis*).[901] Crucial here is the acceptance of a concrete conduct or the systematic acceptance of similar

---

896 Vellinga-Schootsstra, 'Het daderschap van de natuurlijke persoon', in van der Leij (ed), Daderschap en Deelneming (1999), p. 24–25.

897 HR 29 May 1990, *NJ* 1991, 217.

898 Rb. Amsterdam 27 June 2008, *LJN*, BF1083.

899 De Hullu, 'Materieel Strafrecht' (2006), p. 151, Gritter, 'Functioneel plegen door een natuurlijke persoon', in van der Leij (ed), Plegen en Deelnemen (2007), pp. 20 et seq.

900 De Hullu, 'Materieel Strafrecht' (2006), p. 151.

901 Gritter, 'Functioneel plegen door een natuurlijke persoon', in van der Leij (ed), Plegen en Deelnemen (2007), p. 21, Wolswijk, 'Functioneel daderschap en IJzerdraadcriteria' Delikt en Delinkwent (2001), pp. 1088–1114. A more objective interpretation would for instance deduce acceptance from the actual course of events.

conduct.[902] Thus, an awareness and willed acceptance of the criminal conduct is sometimes considered necessary to prove the requirement of acceptance. This interpretation can lead to a paradox in regard to the functional perpetration of crimes in cases where no intention is required for the physical perpetrator. Accordingly, functional perpetration would always require intention also in regard to crimes which require a lower form of mens rea or no mens rea at all. This is for instance the case in regard to misdemeanours which generally do not require fault in the Dutch penal system. This has led some scholars to plead for an abolishment of the *IJzerdraad* criteria.[903]

The arguments pro and contra the requirement of acceptance are manifold[904], but it is submitted that the Dutch Supreme Court might have ended the discussion in favour of a more objective interpretation of the criterion in 2003.[905] Ruling on corporate perpetration, the Supreme Court expanded the scope of the acceptance criteria, by holding that "acceptance" could also be assumed if the corporation had breached a duty of care (which could be reasonably expected of it) to prevent the conduct from occurring.[906] In other words, a corporation will be deemed to have accepted a particular criminal conduct, if this can be derived from the course of events, for instance if the company has neglected its duty to supervise. It is conceivable to say the least that this more objective approach will in future also apply in regard to natural perpetrators.[907] This would amount to a negligence standard, where acceptance can be assumed if the functional perpetrator did not apply the diligence reasonably expected of him. Some have even argued that this objective standard developed for legal persons ought to be applied to natural persons as well as otherwise, so the argument goes, an unjustified inequality in the law would arise.[908] In the light of social developments and the increased emphasis on duties of care in criminal law it would certainly not be surprising to witness such a cross-fertilisation of concepts. If such a development is however also desirable is another question.

---

902 De Hullu, 'Materieel Strafrecht' (2006), p. 152.

903 See for instance: Knigge, 'Doen en laten; enkele opmerkingen over daderschap' Delikt en Delinkwent (1992), pp. 128–154.

904 See: Wolswijk, 'Functioneel daderschap en IJzerdraadcriteria' Delikt en Delinkwent (2001), pp. 1088–1114.

905 HR 21 October 2003, *LJN* AF7938.

906 Gritter, 'Duidelijkheid omtrent corporatief daderschap' Tijdschrift voor Onderneming en Strafrecht (2004), p. 35.

907 De Hullu, 'Materieel Strafrecht' (2006), p. 152.

908 Gritter, 'Functioneel plegen door een natuurlijke persoon', in van der Leij (ed), Plegen en Deelnemen (2007), p. 29, Vellinga, 'Eenheid in Daderschap?', in Harteveld, et al. (eds), Systeem in ontwikkeling: liber amicorum G. Knigge (2005), pp. 527–546, Kessler, 'Beschikkingsmacht centraal bij functioneel plegen', in Keulen, et al. (eds), Pet af: liber amicorum D.H. de Jong (2007), pp. 201–223.

Functional perpetration in jurisprudence

Jurisprudence on functional perpetration of individuals is scarce in the Netherlands. As already mentioned the doctrine is mostly applied in an economic context where a clear hierarchical relationship is given. In other situations the courts mostly apply the broad general notions of participation to sanction the wrongdoing at stake.[909] The rare application of the doctrine also shows that individual wrongdoing can in many cases be sufficiently tackled with traditional criminal law concepts. Thus it can crudely be stated that the doctrine is only applied on an exceptional basis to individual wrongdoing. Furthermore, if the courts apply the doctrine, they often do not neatly distinguish between the notion of power and acceptance and often substantiate the finding of functional perpetration scarcely. Moreover the criteria are rarely explicitly mentioned in jurisprudence. This makes it difficult to deduce a prevalent interpretation of "power" and "acceptance" from Dutch case law. Nevertheless this research will dwell on some judgments subsequently and finally conclude this discourse with a brief evaluation of the doctrine.

In a pertinent case a plastic surgeon was accused of charging excessive rates in contravention of the law on health care tariff (*Wet tarieven gezondheidszorg*). The surgeon's claim was that not he had charged excessive rates, but rather the corporation, of which he was a joint director, in which name the bills were sent out. The court gave the argument short shrift and held that the surgeon was to be regarded as an officer of health care and had thereby functionally perpetrated the offence in question. The fact that he had used the corporation as an intermediary could not exculpate him.[910]

In 2005 the Supreme Court acquitted the owners of a ship for pollution of the water due to a defect valve of the ship. The Supreme Court held that mere ownership was insufficient to conclude that the owners could be held responsible for crimes committed by the captain or the crew respectively.[911] In essence the court seemingly held that mere ownership was insufficient to constitute "control" over the (non) commission of the criminal offence, but this has not been phrased by the court in such an unequivocal way. An exculpating factor in this case was that the crew could according to the court not be blamed for the pollution of the sea as they could not foresee the breaking of the valve. The court held that as not even the crew could be blamed for the occurred pollution, neither could the owners of the ship be held responsible as a perpetrator.

Finally the District Court Amsterdam convicted the owner of a business for handling stolen goods as he and his employees had repeatedly bought goods from what can at least be considered dubious origin for a price considerably below the regular market price. The court ruled that the owner had factual control over the purchases by the employees. The court deduced acceptance in this case from the

909 See also: De Hullu, 'Materieel Strafrecht' (2006), p. 156.
910 HR 31 August 2004, *LJN* AO643.
911 HR 24 May 2005, *NJ* 2005, 434.

fact that he, despite being aware of the risk of handling stolen goods purchased by his employees, did not take any measures or give appropriate instructions to prevent such conduct from occurring.[912]

Evaluation

The doctrine of functional perpetration constitutes a hotly debated issue within the Dutch penal system, where many facets remain unclear. Some authors view the doctrine as a special construction, while others claim that the doctrine fits into the traditional dogmatic structure of the law. Gritter for instance views the doctrine as a form of liability for omissions.[913] Moreover, as a creation of jurisprudence the doctrine's underlying theoretical construction remains unclear. It is possible to view the doctrine as a mere form of attribution where the physical conduct of the factual perpetrator is attributed to the functional perpetrator. On the other hand, the doctrine can be viewed as a form of (functional) interpretation of the offence definition so that not only the physical conduct is prescribed by the offence but also the commission of the offence by an intermediary.[914] Furthermore a mixed approach is conceivable where attribution as well as interpretation plays a role.

The choice for one or the other form of construction also has implications in practice as one could for instance pose the question whether one could assume a criminal attempt once the functional perpetrator has taken the decision that a specific conduct should be carried out. Whatever the answer to that question is, it can only arise if one follows the path of interpretation, so that the functional perpetrator can commit the crime himself. If one adheres to the idea of attribution the question of attempt liability cannot arise as the factual perpetrator has not yet committed any more than merely preparatory acts.[915] Most Dutch scholars view the doctrine as a form of (functional) interpretation or a mixture of interpretation and attribution.[916] The Dutch Supreme Court however has not yet taken a stance in this respect. It is submitted here that the doctrine is based on interpretation as well as attribution. To establish functional perpetration a two-step approach needs to be adopted. First the criminal offence needs to be interpreted in order to establish who the addressee of the norm is. Subsequently liability can be attributed to the

912 Rb. Amsterdam, 27 June 2008, *LJN* BF1083.

913 Gritter, 'Effectiviteit en aansprakelijkheid in het economisch ordeningsrecht' (2003), pp. 219–222, 226, Gritter, 'Functioneel plegen door een natuurlijke persoon', in van der Leij (ed), Plegen en Deelnemen (2007), pp. 22–24.

914 Wolswijk, 'Functioneel daderschap en IJzerdraadcriteria' Delikt en Delinkwent (2001), pp. 1088–1114.

915 Wolswijk, 'Functioneel daderschap en IJzerdraadcriteria' Delikt en Delinkwent (2001), pp. 1088–1114.

916 Wolswijk, 'Functioneel daderschap en IJzerdraadcriteria' Delikt en Delinkwent (2001), pp. 1088–1114. See also: Gritter, 'Functioneel plegen door een natuurlijke persoon', in van der Leij (ed), Plegen en Deelnemen (2007), pp. 22–24.

functional perpetrator but not for the acts of another but for his own (in) action expressed in the notions of power and acceptance.

Another important question regarding the doctrine of functional perpetration relates to its scope. Does the doctrine constitute an expansion of criminal liability or is it compared to other doctrines a mere *lex specialis*? Some have forcefully argued that acceptance of the doctrine in the Dutch penal system ought not to lead to an expansion of criminal liability.[917] According to this view the doctrine might apply in some situations where classical doctrines such as perpetration by means (*doen plegen*) or instigation (*uitlokking*) are inapplicable, but by and large it is argued that the doctrine constitutes an additional ground for criminal liability which greatly overlaps with traditional doctrines.[918] This assessment seems to be substantiated by the scarce use of the doctrine in practice. The broad interpretation given to different forms of participation in the Dutch penal system seems to sufficiently cover all manifestation of individual wrongdoing. Only in cases with an economic or organisational backdrop appears the doctrine to be relevant. To be sure, the doctrine unfolds much more influence in regard to corporate liability but is nevertheless an important tool to assure the effective application of the law.

The doctrine can be compared to the doctrine of hegemony over the act (*Tatherrschaftslehre*) applied in Germany. In essence the criteria of power and acceptance correspond to the objective and subjective criteria enshrined in the hegemony over the act doctrine. Thus, the approach taken by the Dutch penal system by and large resembles the one taken in Germany. While the Dutch legislator and courts have never made an explicit choice between the two theories (i.e. objective and subjective theories), it can be deduced from case law that the objective conduct of the participant alone rarely is decisive in practice, but that more and more emphasis is put on subjective criteria.[919] It follows that, similar to the situation in Germany, subjective and objective factors are combined in order to establish perpetration.

Yet, the main difference between functional perpetration and the hegemony over the act doctrine can be seen in the fact that the former constitutes an additional ground of criminal liability, while the latter, although expanding the realm of perpetration is primarily seen as a tool to distinguish perpetration from accessorial liability. Nevertheless, the doctrines can both be seen as an expression of the desire to hold people responsible for the acts of their partners or subordinates, even though they have not been physically involved in the commission of the offence. It is this desire which they share with the English doctrine of vicarious liability and to which this discussion now turns.

917 De Hullu, 'Materieel Strafrecht' (2006), p. 156.

918 De Hullu, 'Materieel Strafrecht' (2006), p. 156.

919 Van Toorenburg, 'Medeplegen' (1998), p. 208.

7.2.3. The English doctrine of vicarious liability

A functional equivalent to the doctrine of functional perpetration and hegemony over the act in the common law system is vicarious liability. Based on the maxim "*qui facit per alium facit per se*" (he who acts through another acts through himself), the doctrine of vicarious liability holds that one can be held responsible for the acts of another person as if they were one's own acts.[920] In other words, "vicarious liability is a mechanism by which the law attributes blame for the acts of another".[921] It also fulfils an important function in regard to corporate wrongdoing as, where a statute imposes vicarious liability or where courts have found the doctrine to be applicable, a corporation can be held vicariously liable for the acts of its employees or agents, just like a natural person would be liable in these circumstances.[922] The doctrine proceeds to the attribution of the act of the individual to the individual or corporation held liable for it in a two-step process. First, it needs to be established whether the conduct of the individual fulfils all the elements enshrined in the underlying offence. Once this has been established, the liability of the individual is imputed to the liable individual or corporation, based on the legal relationship between the individuals or the corporation, i.e. agency or employment. This imputation is based on the legal fiction that the actions and/or the state of mind of the individual are the actions or state of mind of the liable subject.[923]

It becomes already apparent from the foregoing that the doctrine militates against a fundamental principle in criminal law, the principle of individual responsibility. It can only be justified from the perspective of protecting societal interests like the protection of the environment or consumers, which could not be effectively protected from wrongdoing without the doctrine. Nevertheless due to its sweeping and harsh nature, the doctrine should be kept within strict limits.[924]

Identifying criminal vicarious liability

As a general rule in regard to criminal liability it can be stated that a person can only be held responsible for the acts of another where he participated in them pursuant to the rules governing accessorial liability.[925] However, in a penal system like England and Wales, which is based on the concept of sovereignty of parliament, it goes without saying that parliament is at liberty to impose vicarious criminal

920 Fletcher, 'Basic Concepts of Criminal Law' (1998), p. 190.

921 Smith and Hogan, 'Criminal Law' (2008), p. 258.

922 Smith and Hogan, 'Criminal Law' (2008), p. 248.

923 Lederman, 'Models for Imposing Corporate Criminal Liability: From Adaptation and Imitation Toward Aggregation and the Search for Self-Identity' Buffalo Criminal Law Review (2000), p. 652.

924 Smith and Hogan, 'Criminal Law' (2008), p. 258.

925 Smith and Hogan, 'Criminal Law' (2008), p. 258.

liability where it deems it necessary. Occasionally statutes explicitly impose vicarious liability for the acts of another. A case in point can for instance be found in section 64 (5) of the 1988 Road Traffic Offenders Act which provides that the owner of a vehicle (which can also be a corporation), shall be conclusively presumed to have been the driver at the time of the commission of certain offences and, "accordingly, that acts or omissions of the driver of the vehicle at the time were his acts or omissions". Likewise, section 59 of the Licensing Act 1964 provides that a licensee will breach the terms of his license should he "by himself or by his servant or agent sell or supply to any person in the licensed premises [...] any intoxicating liquor outside permitted hours".

However, as statutes are drafted notoriously vague in England, in practice, the imposition of vicarious criminal liability is to a large extent based on the interpretative work of the courts.[926] The courts have adopted a purposive construction of statutes in this regard and frequently impose vicarious liability where they "detect" such an intention of parliament in the respective legislation. The rationale forwarded by the courts to impose vicarious liability is mostly expediency based. The statute would be rendered nugatory, and the will of the parliament defeated, so the argument goes, if vicarious liability would not apply.[927] In *Mousel Brother Ltd v London and North-Western Railway Co* the court provided some guidance as to the identification of statutory vicarious liability:

> [...] To ascertain whether a particular Act of Parliament has that effect or not regard must be had to the object of the statute, the words used, the nature of the duty laid down, the person upon whom it is imposed, the person by whom it would in ordinary circumstances be performed, and the person upon whom the penalty is imposed.[928]

The application of vicarious liability

Two distinct principles have emerged in English law regarding vicarious liability. On the one hand, a person may be held liable for the acts of another to whom he has delegated the carrying out of certain duties imposed on him by an Act of Parliament (delegation principle). On the other hand an employer may be held liable for the acts of an employee which are deemed in law to be his own (attributed act principle).

The delegation principle

In cases, where a statute imposes liability on the owner, licensee or keeper of property (e.g. premises) he will be held vicariously liable for the conduct of any person to whom management of the premises has been delegated. This principle

926 Smith and Hogan, 'Criminal Law' (2008), p. 261.
927 Smith and Hogan, 'Criminal Law' (2008), p. 261.
928 [1917] 2 KB 836.

applies to corporations and individuals alike.[929] An illuminating example can be seen in the case of *Allen v Whitehead*.[930] The case dealt with section 44 of the 1839 Metropolitan Police Act which makes it an offence for a keeper of a refreshment house "to knowingly permit or suffer prostitutes or persons of notoriously bad character to meet together and remain therein". The defendant in this case had delegated his duties to a manager and only visited the premises once or twice a week. Despite the explicit instructions of the defendant, the manager had allowed prostitutes to remain on the premises. The court held that the defendant's ignorance of the facts was no defence and that the acts and guilty mind of the manager were to be imputed to him because the management had been delegated.

Consequently, for the principle to be applicable it needs to be shown that a duty has been effectively delegated. This is not always an easy task and there remain some uncertainties in English law as to the degree of delegation required in order to trigger the application of the principle.[931] However, in a leading case, *Vane v Yiannopoulos*, the court established the following rule of thumb: "It must be shown that the licensee is not managing the business himself but has delegated the management to someone else".[932] This would point in the direction of a complete delegation of functions, so that delegation will not be applied where the licensee has handed over control of merely a particular function or part of the licensed premises.[933] Furthermore, vicarious liability, arguably, can only arise if the employee or delegate acted within the scope of his employment or authority.[934] If he exceeds this scope, no liability can arise.

The rationale underlying this principle seems to be the assumption that such offences would otherwise not be enforceable, if a licensee could avoid liability by delegating his duties to another.[935] If that would be the case, the intention of Parliament to control the licensed activity would be thwarted.[936]

There is some doubt about whether or not the delegation principle can only be applied in regard to offences requiring mens rea as suggested by Lord Parker in *R v Winson*.[937] Yet, the prevalent view seems to limit the delegation principle to offences requiring mens rea, which means that cases of strict liability must be treated under the attributed act principle.[938]

---

929 Ashworth, 'Principles of criminal law' (2006), p. 116.
930 [1930] 1 KB 211.
931 Smith and Hogan, 'Criminal Law' (2008), p. 263.
932 [1965] AC 486.
933 Pace, 'Delegation – A doctrine in search of a definition' Criminal Law Review (1982), pp. 629–635.
934 Pace, 'Delegation – A doctrine in search of a definition' Criminal Law Review (1982), p. 635.
935 Ashworth, 'Principles of criminal law' (2006), p. 116.
936 Pinto and Evans, 'Corporate Criminal Liability' (2003), p. 316.
937 [1969] 1 QB 371.
938 See: Pace, 'Delegation – A doctrine in search of a definition' Criminal Law Review (1982), pp. 628–629.

THE ATTRIBUTED ACT PRINCIPLE

The second principle refers to situations, where the actus reus of an employee etc. is imputed to the defendant. Such cases arise in particular in situations where the legislation in question involves acts of selling, possessing, using, etc. An illuminating case in point here is *Coppen v Moore (No. 2)*.[939] The defendant in this case owned six shops in which he sold *inter alia* "American ham". He instructed his workforce that the ham should be sold as breakfast ham and not under any other name. In his absence and without his knowledge, one of the assistants nevertheless sold a ham as "Scots ham". He was charged and convicted for selling goods under a false description. The court held: "It can not be doubted that the appellant sold the ham in question, although the transaction was carried out by his servants. In other words he was the seller, although not the actual salesman".

In essence this means that as long as the assistant is acting as an agent, vicarious liability will be imposed.[940] In these cases, the courts interpreted the key words of the legislation in a way that they reflected the interpersonal nature of the commercial transactions they described.[941] Activities like selling and possessing are clearly technical terms in law, they derive their connotation from civil law. Thus it should not come as a surprise that, legally, one can sell or possess through another.[942]

7.2.4. Evaluation

As has already been pointed out, the doctrine of vicarious liability has the advantage of simple application. It has emerged due to pragmatic considerations that the law would not be effective if one could not under certain circumstances hold the person behind the physical perpetrator responsible for the acts of the other. The doctrine also carries a strong business or economic connotation as its primary field of application are employment relationships as well as cases of corporate liability. In these situations it can be argued that the virtue of the doctrine lies in the fact that by holding an employer or a corporation liable for the acts of its employees and agents it imposes a desirable "private policing role" on these subjects.[943] By holding these important economic actors responsible for the acts of their subordinates, they will exercise more care when hiring and supervising employees, so the argument goes. The two subspecies of vicarious liability slightly differ in their focus. The delegation principle for instance can be understood as ensuring the effective handling of offences requiring a particular quality of the offender. If

939 [1898] 2 QB 306.
940 Ashworth, 'Principles of criminal law' (2006), p. 116.
941 Pinto and Evans, 'Corporate Criminal Liability' (2003), p. 29.
942 Simester and Sullivan, 'Criminal Law: Theory and Doctrine' (2007), p. 253.
943 Gobert and Punch, 'Rethinking Corporate Crime' (2003), p. 56.

delegation can be proven, the delegator will be held liable for the acts of his subordinate and his actions as well as his mens rea will be imputed to him. The delegation principle can thus be seen as the corollary of the licensee's freedom to delegate the carrying out of the business to another. The attributed act principle, however, probably can best be understood as a case of extensive or functional interpretation of certain statutory terms.

Yet, one should not overlook that vicarious liability constitutes an exception to the principle of individual responsibility and can only be justified by the need to enforce modern regulatory legislation such as food and health regulations. The doctrine effectively introduces liability for the acts of another which may also explain why its scope of application is rather narrow and why English scholars generally view the doctrine with suspicion.

Compared to the doctrine of functional perpetration and hegemony over the act, vicarious liability seems to be the most far reaching. It introduces liability for the acts of another while the German and Dutch doctrines impose liability for own conduct. Moreover, vicarious liability also allows for the imputation of fault, which is not possible under the former doctrines. In the Dutch *IJzerdraad* judgment it was even explicitly stressed by the court that the concept of intention referred to an individual state of mind which was not transferrable. Thus, the doctrine of vicarious liability can cause frictions with the principle of *nulla poene sine culpa* as well as with Article 6 ECHR, as it allows for the attribution of liability regardless of the fault of the employer, licensee, etc.[944] It is submitted that such an approach might only be acceptable in regard to strict liability offences and that in regard to offences requiring mens rea, functional perpetration or the hegemony over the act doctrine should be preferred.

The common core of the three doctrines can be seen in their aim to hold the (factual) perpetrator behind the actual perpetrator responsible and that one of the main areas of application of these doctrines are vertical relationships of subordination as one often encounters them in the economic world. These three doctrines excellently demonstrate the contemporary desire of penal systems to countermand the shortcomings of a restrictive concept of perpetration in regard to vertical forms of participation in crime. They arguably bear witness to an ongoing paradigm shift towards a more normative conception of participation where an increased focus seems to rest on duties of the respective participant, such as duties to prevent the commission of offences by intermediaries, duties to decide about and control potential criminal conduct, as well as duties to control and diligently manage the conduct of subordinates. The focus of liability arguably has shifted to persons who are deemed to possess such duties of control such as heads of businesses, but also criminal masterminds, ringleaders and arm-chair strategists,

944 See: *Salabiaku v France*, appl. no. 10519/83, 7 October 1998, where it was implicitly held that irrebuttable presumptions of guilt would violate Article 6 ECHR.

which we deem to bare the lion share of responsibility in vertical forms of co-operation.[945]

This is also however where the commonalities end. As already mentioned, one crucial difference between the doctrine of vicarious liability and functional perpetration and hegemony over the act is that with the latter two doctrines, liability is not imposed for the acts of another but rather for the individual conduct of the functual perpetrator, i.e. his role and contribution in the commission of the offence. Thus, functional perpetration and hegemony over the act uphold the principle of individual liability and do not permit the attribution of guilt from one actor to another but rather establish liability according to the individual wrongdoing and culpability of the functional perpetrator. From this it also follows that vicarious liability is not so much a theory of perpetration but rather a far reaching theory of attribution designed for the sake of expediency and efficiency.

In regard to the hegemony over the act doctrine it is important to keep in mind that the backdrop of its creation was to countermand subjective tendencies in jurisprudence which led to unsatisfactory results. Furthermore, the doctrine contrary to vicarious liability and functional perpetration constitutes an overarching theory with its main goal to establish sound and reliable criteria to demarcate secondary from primary responsibility.

After having discussed the problematic surrounding the perpetrator behind the scene this research now turns to another variation of a vertical form of perpetration namely the doctrine of perpetration by means.

7.3. Perpetration by means

7.3.1. The traditional scope of the doctrine

If one views accessorial liability as derivative from the liability of the perpetrator, as formally all investigated countries do, the general theory of complicity will in some situations face serious challenges, testing the concept of derivative liability almost to its destruction. This will for instance be the case where the instigator of the offence completely dominates the behaviour of the actor at the scene, such as a child, a person acting under mistake or someone insane at the time of the commission of the offence. Thus, the traditionally derivative principles of complicity encounter difficulties where the ostensible perpetrator is not liable for some reason, but an apparent participant appears to be sufficiently culpable in relation to the occurrence of a criminal harm or wrongdoing to such an extent that he or she should be held liable.[946] Suppose that Bob threatens nine year old John

945 Vogel, 'Criminal Responsibility – Parties to the offence', in Cullen (ed), Enlarging the Fight against Fraud in the European Union: Penal and Administrative Sanctions, Settlement, Whistleblowing and Corpus Juris in Candidate Countries (2003), p. 47 et seq.

946 Taylor, 'Procuring, Causation, Innocent Agency and the Law Commission' Criminal Law Review (2008), p. 32.

with serious violence unless he burns down Alex's shed. John is scared and intimidated and sees no other solution and burns down the shed.[947] In this case John cannot be held criminally liable because he is below the age of criminal responsibility and possibly also acted under duress. These cases cause problems for a theory of derivative liability, as there is strictly speaking no basis from which liability can be derived.

The common solution of penal systems to this problem has been to treat the ostensible participant as the perpetrator of the offence and the innocent person on the scene merely as a puppet or instrument in the hands of the perpetrator. This concept is referred to here as perpetration by means, as the person in the background uses another as a means to his ends, i.e. the commission of the offence.[948] It seems intuitively right to punish those who manipulate innocent agents to achieve their goals for the harm brought about by these "instruments".

These cases, i.e. where the actus reus of the criminal offence was brought about by an innocent agent constitute the common core of the notion of perpetration by means in the three investigated countries. In England, the doctrine is referred to as innocent agency and is seen as an exception to the aforementioned rule that the principal must directly bring about the actus reus of the offence in question.[949] In cases where the actus reus was brought about by someone who acted without mens rea, or has a defence,[950] such as infancy or insanity, the ostensible participant is regarded as the perpetrator of the occurred criminal offence.

This by and large corresponds to the situation in Germany and the Netherlands where the doctrine is generally deemed applicable where the instrument acted without the necessary mens rea, guilt or lacked criminal capacity.[951] In the explanatory memorandum the Dutch legislator for instance stated that the doctrine would include situations where the offence was committed through an agent who due to his lack of information, an induced mistake or subdued by violence, acts without mens rea, guilt or culpability. One might see this as an exhaustive enumeration, as only in those cases can one properly speak of an innocent agent. However, the Dutch Supreme Court has given the doctrine a broader scope. In a pertinent case a land owner had ordered workers to dig off a knoll[952] in breach of municipal law. The workers were aware of the fact that they were engaging in

947 Taylor, 'Procuring, Causation, Innocent Agency and the Law Commission' Criminal Law Review (2008), p. 38.

948 The term has first been coined by Fletcher: Fletcher, 'Rethinking Criminal Law' (1978), p. 639, Fletcher, 'Basic Concepts of Criminal Law' (1998), p. 197 et seq.

949 Smith and Hogan, 'Criminal Law' (2008), p. 181.

950 Other than duress: R v Bourne [1952] 36 Cr App R 125.

951 For Germany see: Roxin, 'Strafrecht Allgemeiner Teil, Band II: Besondere Erscheinungsformen der Straftat' (2003), pp. 23–46, Schönke and Schröder, 'Kommentar zum Strafgesetzbuch' (2006), §25 Mn 6–60. For the Netherlands see: De Hullu, 'Materieel Strafrecht' (2009), pp. 451–457.

952 The specific word in Dutch is "terp" which refers to a man-made knoll on which houses were built to protect the inhabitiants from flodding.

conduct which was prohibited for land owners. The law was explicitly addressed to land owners, a quality, which the workers digging up the knoll, of course, lacked. Relying on the explanatory memorandum the defence had argued that the doctrine of perpetration by means was not applicable, as the workers could not be regarded as *manus mistrae* (serving hands) acting without mens rea, guilt or culpability. The Supreme Court, however, adopted a broader approach, and held that the doctrine of perpetration by means could be invoked also in cases where the non-liability of the "instrument" was due to the lack of a quality required by the underlying offence.[953] This was even the case where the workers knew that they were committing an act prohibited by law for the employer. As already mentioned, the peculiarity here is that in such a situation one cannot really say that the agent was innocent; he merely lacked a quality required for the commission of the offence. Nevertheless was the doctrine deemed applicable here. It will subsequently become apparent that the doctrine in the German legal system has been given an even broader scope.

The non-liability of the innocent agent in the Netherlands, must also not, due to the derivative nature of all forms of participation, stem from the fact that the underlying offence is not punishable, for instance due to an applicable justification. If the underlying offence is not punishable, than one cannot generally participate in the commission of this "crime". An attempt to induce an innocent agent is therefore not deemed punishable. However, Art 46 a DPC can provide the basis for exceptions in these circumstances. This is contrary to the situation in Germany, where the doctrine is deemed to be a form of perpetration. Direct liability can therefore also ensue in cases where the agent can invoke a justification, like for instance a permit.[954]

It should be noted at this point that in the Netherlands the issue which arose in the aforementioned case of the workers ordered to dig up the knoll in violation of the law would nowadays most likely be solved by invoking the doctrine of functional perpetration or the doctrine of co-perpetration, discussed below, as a physical presence or act is no longer required for the establishment of criminal liability. It already becomes apparent that the doctrine only plays the role of a residual category in the Dutch penal system. The broad concepts of (co-) perpetration have absorbed many of the cases dealt with under the doctrine of perpetration by means in earlier times. In other words, the development of the doctrine of functional perpetration as well as the broad approach taken in regard to co-perpetration has condemned the notions of instigation and perpetration by means to a shadowy existence. This goes even so far that it has been argued that the doctrine of innocent agency should be abolished.[955] A suggestion which also seems to find some support amongst practitioners.[956]

---

953 HR 19 December 1910, *W* 9122.

954 Roef, 'Strafbare overheden – Een rechtsvergelijkende studie naar de strafrechtelijke aansprakelijkheid van overheden voor milieuverstoring' (2001), p. 545.

955 De Hullu, 'Materieel Strafrecht' (2009), pp. 457, 466.

956 WODC report, 'Daderschap en deelneming doorgelicht', pp. 110 et seq.

An early example of the application of the doctrine in England can be found in *R v Michael* where a mother planned to kill her child by giving laudanum to the nurse boarding her son, claiming it to be medicine.[957] The nurse put the preparation of laudanum aside as she thought that the baby did not need any medicine. Unfortunately, however, the nurse's own young son administered the laudanum to the baby which caused his death. The court had no problems to convict the infant's mother of murder by an innocent agent. However, in the twentieth century the doctrine has somehow fallen into disfavour. This might *inter alia* be explained by the fact that the results of innocent agency doctrine can just as well be explained by the application of traditional concepts of causation. As the acts of the innocent agent due to threat, deception, etc. are not free, deliberate and informed, the causal link between the conduct of the ostensible participant and the occurred result is not broken and the participant therefore liable. Accordingly it has been argued that the doctrine is strictly speaking unnecessary.[958]

In the economic context, the doctrine will in England often be applied to punish a person who sets into motion actions by innocent fellow employees which result in financial harm. In a pertinent case a business manager of the company X arranged for a director of company Y to submit false invoices which were signed by a junior manager of X and passed for payment by another employee of X. The court convicted the business manager of theft by an innocent agent, as it was he who had a dishonest intention when he signed the invoices which initiated the series of events causing X's account to be debited with the material amounts.[959] Likewise, where A, a collector of money, makes false statements to his employer's account which he knows will be entered into the books by an innocent employee, he is liable as a principal of falsifying his employer's accounts.[960] The Law Commission has proposed to replace the doctrine with a specific offence where A will be liable as a perpetrator if he intentionally causes an innocent agent to commit the conduct element of an offence but he does not commit the offence because he is (i) under the age of 10, (ii) has a defence of insanity, or (iii) acts without the fault required to be convicted of the offence.[961]

7.3.2. The different designs and limitations of the doctrine

In general it can be said that the doctrine will take different shapes in different jurisdictions depending on whether the focus lies on the man behind the innocent agent or on the instrument, (i.e. focusing on the question whether or not the

957 R v Michael [1840] 173 ER 876.

958 Alldridge, 'The doctrine of innocent agency' Criminal Law Forum (1990), pp. 45–83, Smith, 'A Modern Treatise on the Law of Criminal Complicity' (1991), pp. 94–110.

959 R v Stringer [1991] Crim LR 639.

960 R v Butt [1884] 15 Cox CC 564.

961 'Participating in Crime', LAW COM No 305 [2007], pp. 99–106, Smith and Hogan, 'Criminal Law' (2008), p. 234.

"instrument" is criminally liable). The stance taken here can for instance influence the answer to the question whether the person behind the "instrument" must intend the agent to commit the principal offence. In England, it is unclear whether the perpetrator behind the scene must intend the innocent agent to commit the principal offence.[962] It has for instance been argued that innocent agency is restricted to intended acts because the notion rests on the civil law concept of agency, for which consensus is crucial.[963] The prevalent view of the Law Commission seems to be however that the doctrine is not confined to cases where the perpetrator behind the scene has intentionally or purposefully brought about the "instruments" action.[964]

By contrast, in the Netherlands the initiator must intend that the envisaged result is brought about by the innocent agent and must furthermore intentionally induce the innocent agent to commit the crime.[965] The person behind the scene needs however not act intentionally in regard to the non-liability of the agent. It is therefore conceivable that a person believes to be instigating a crime while he is in reality committing the crime through an innocent agent.[966] Generally the doctrine of perpetration by means, just like the doctrine of instigation requires some form of psychological inducement of the factual perpetrator. It is however possible that such an inducement takes place without any direct contact of the parties involved. Such a case arose for instance in 1961. Five young men had staged a shooting in the centre of Amsterdam. They had fired several shots from replica guns. One of them pretended to be wounded by cutting a package of pigeon blood which he was carrying with him. His colleagues had afterwards carried him to a car with which they "fled" from the scene. Worried eyewitnesses had contacted the police. The Supreme Court left the conviction for wrongly reporting a crime by means of innocent agents in tact and ruled that for the application of the doctrine a direct contact between the agent and the person behind the scene was not required. It was deemed sufficient that according to general experience it could be expected that the actions of the person behind the scene led to the occurred offence.[967] Thus, the actions of the puppeteer need not be goal orientated in order for criminal liability to arise. The requirements shaped by jurisprudence in the Netherlands, outlined in this chapter, have not been altered by more recent judgments. The focus is still on the innocent agent, with the cardinal question being whether (s)he can be held criminally liable for the occurred harm. A man who had for instance forced his

---

962 'Participating in Crime', LAW COM No 305 [2007], p. 180.

963 Kadish, 'Complicity, Cause and Blame: A Study in the Interpretation of Doctrine' California Law Review (1985), pp. 323–410.

964 'Participating in Crime', LAW COM No 305 [2007], p. 180. See also: Smith, 'A Modern Treatise on the Law of Criminal Complicity' (1991), p. 97 and R v Tyler and Price [1838] 173 ER 643 which seems to suggest that it is unnecessary for the perpetrator to blieve or know that the agent was in some way innocent.

965 De Hullu, 'Materieel Strafrecht' (2009), p. 445, Kelk, 'Studieboek materieel strafrecht' (2005), p. 345.

966 Harteveld, 'Doen plegen', in van der Leij (ed), Plegen en deelnemen (2007), p. 159.

967 HR 18 October 1960, *NJ* 1961, 415.

former girlfriend, by threatening to kill her or her children, to smuggle cocaine was convicted for importing illegal drugs through an innocent agent into the Netherlands. The court held that the threats were so severe that the woman could be regarded as an instrument in the hands of the perpetrator behind the scene.[968]

In a similar case a man was convicted for the importation of a considerable amount of hashish (190 kg) through an innocent agent. In this case a man had used a transport company to bring his boat, in which the drugs were hidden, from Spain to the Netherlands. The court had no problems in applying the doctrine and convicted the man for the importation of hashish.[969]

It is in theory also considered possible in the Netherlands to commit negligent crimes through the doctrine of innocent agency. It is for instance conceivable that a person induces an agent to commit certain acts which he knows are dangerous, but believes that the detrimental consequences will not occur.[970]

Conversely, in Germany, the notion is confined to intentional act, as the concept is conceived as a form of perpetration. Accordingly it is required that the perpetrator behind the scenes fulfils all requirements of perpetration, i.e. exerts hegemony over the acts of the "puppet". Thus, in Germany the doctrine is restricted to cases where the person in the background dominates or manipulates the agent, so that he can be considered to exert hegemony over the act of the agent. This can of course only be the case if the person intends the agent to commit the crime.[971] Accordingly, if the person behind the agent is not aware of the non-liability of the agent, hegemony cannot be established and the doctrine of perpetration by means will not be applicable.[972] Thus, in Germany the focus seems to lie on the perpetrator behind the instrument, while in England and the Netherlands, the emphasis is primarily on the instrument focusing on the question, whether or not the agent is innocent.

However, that the doctrine in England too has its roots partly in the soil of perpetration becomes apparent in offences where specific qualities or a prescribed status are needed to commit the crime (e.g. being a clerk officer or servant). The doctrine is namely not deemed to apply if the principle offence is one that can only be committed by persons meeting a particular description which the person behind the innocent agent does not meet.[973] A case in point would be bigamy. If Anton, a bachelor untruthfully but on reasonable grounds, persuades Wayne that Wayne's estranged wife died three years ago in the jungle of South America and encourages him to marry Charlotte, Anton cannot be held liable of bigamy by virtue of innocent agency, as only those who are married can commit bigamy as a principal offender.

---

968 Rb. Haarelm, 22 April 2009, *LJN* BI 3519.

969 HR 11 May 1982, *NJ* 1983, 3.

970 Harteveld, 'Doen plegen', in van der Leij (ed), Plegen en deelnemen (2007), p. 159, Kelk, 'Studieboek materieel strafrecht' (2005), pp. 345–346.

971 Roxin, 'Strafrecht Allgemeiner Teil, Band II: Besondere Erscheinungsformen der Straftat' (2003), pp. 39, 58–60.

972 Schönke and Schröder, 'Kommentar zum Strafgesetzbuch' (2006), §25 Mn 31.

973 'Participating in Crime', LAW COM No 305 [2007], p. 180.

This bears resemblance to the situation in Germany and the Netherlands where perpetration by means can be established even if the agent did not possess the required quality, as long as the perpetrator behind the instrument does so.[974] Yet, the new offence of innocent agency proposed by the Law Commission in England would also extend to such cases where the offence in question can only be committed by a person of a particular description (e.g. a licensee). Thus any difficulties about whether for instance a bachelor can commit bigamy as a perpetrator (through an innocent agent) or similarly whether a woman can commit rape (see below) would be removed by a provision that the perpetrator by means can be convicted even though he does not fulfil the description of those persons who are capable of committing the offence in question (i.e. married persons and men, in the examples given).[975]

In case the converse situation presents itself, i.e. the instrument possesses a necessary quality, but the person behind it does not, the differences in focus (i.e. on the instrument or the person behind) also lead to different results. In Germany, where the focus is on the perpetrator behind the instrument, all necessary qualities must be present in the person of the perpetrator by means.[976] Likewise the aforementioned English example of bachelor Anton inducing Wayne to commit bigamy shows that in such cases the doctrine will not be applicable according to the law as it currently stands.[977]

Conversely, in the Netherlands, the doctrine will be applicable in these cases as there, the ambiguous wording of Article 47 DPC made it possible for the courts to adopt a more flexible approach. In a pertinent case a mayor had requested a passport for someone but had intentionally filled in the wrong age in the request. A civil servant had issued the passport with the wrong age. The mayor had argued that only the civil servant was bestowed with the power to issue passports, so that he could not be held liable as a perpetrator by the doctrine of perpetration by means. The Supreme Court held that someone who causes an innocent person to commit a criminal offence was not deemed to be a perpetrator per se but was only put on an equal footing with the perpetrator and that the doctrine could therefore be invoked in cases where the initiator lacked a required quality.[978] It is however required that the initiator acted intentionally in regard to the presence of the quality in the person of the factual perpetrator.[979] Thus, in the Netherlands a dispersion of certain objective offence requirements is considered possible. One can therefore commit an offence requiring a certain quality through an innocent agent even though oneself

974 Roxin, 'Strafrecht Allgemeiner Teil, Band II: Besondere Erscheinungsformen der Straftat' (2003), pp. 107 et seq, Schönke and Schröder, 'Kommentar zum Strafgesetzbuch' (2006), §25 Mn 43–44.

975 Taylor, 'Procuring, Causation, Innocent Agency and the Law Commission' Criminal Law Review (2008), p. 35.

976 Schönke and Schröder, 'Kommentar zum Strafgesetzbuch' (2006), §25 Mn 44.

977 Smith, 'A Modern Treatise on the Law of Criminal Complicity' (1991), p. 107.

978 HR 21 April 1913, *NJ* 1913, 961.

979 De Hullu, 'Materieel Strafrecht' (2009), p. 454.

does not posses this quality and would therefore have been unable to commit the offence directly.[980] While admittedly this approach is at odds with the very nature of the doctrine as a form of perpetration, it is however submitted that the Dutch approach seems to be the favourable here. There seems nothing untoward in holding the person behind the scene responsible for a crime committed by an innocent agent, as long as the perpetrator behind the scene acted intentionally in regard to this fact.

There is a further set of cases in which the doctrine seems inapplicable. Attributing liability to the person behind the innocent agent namely seems impossible where the offence in question appears to require that the conduct requirement is performed personally. Naturally, whether or not this will be the case depends largely on the definition of the crime in question. In England this is deemed to be the case in regard to the crime of rape and other offences requiring sexual intercourse but also for instance in regard to driving offences.[981] This even despite the fact that the Court of Criminal Appeal in *Cogan and Leak* convicted Leak for rape as a principal offender by virtue of the doctrine of innocent agency.[982] In this case which has also important repercussions, as discussed above, for the principle of derivative liability Leak induced Cogan to have sexual intercourse with his wife who he made him believe consented to the act.[983] Leak however knew that his wife was not consenting. Cogan subsequently committed the cohabitation. The court acquitted Cogan of rape, but left Leak's conviction in tact. The majority of legal scholars, however, regard this line of reasoning as contrary to principle and to be a violent wrench of the English language.[984] In Germany it is generally recognised that offences requiring a personally performed conduct cannot be committed by perpetration by means nor in co-perpetration.[985] Yet, which crimes belong to this category is a contentious matter.[986] Also in the Netherlands the doctrine is considered inapplicable in some offences which require personal conduct by a person possessing a certain status (often civil servants).[987]

---

980 Roef, 'Strafbare overheden – Een rechtsvergelijkende studie naar de strafrechtelijke aansprakelijkheid van overheden voor milieuverstoring' (2001), p. 538.

981 Smith, 'A Modern Treatise on the Law of Criminal Complicity' (1991), p. 107, Taylor, 'Procuring, Causation, Innocent Agency and the Law Commission' Criminal Law Review (2008), pp. 42 et seq.

982 R v Cogan & Leak Leak [1975] 2 All ER 1059.

983 See: Chapter III. 4.3.

984 Simester and Sullivan, 'Criminal Law: Theory and Doctrine' (2007), p. 198. 'Participating in Crime', LAW COM No 305 [2007], p. 180, Smith and Hogan, 'Criminal Law' (2008), p. 182.

985 Roxin, 'Strafrecht Allgemeiner Teil, Band II: Besondere Erscheinungsformen der Straftat' (2003), pp. 114 et seq, Schönke and Schröder, 'Kommentar zum Strafgesetzbuch' (2006), §25 Mn 45–48.

986 Roxin, 'Strafrecht Allgemeiner Teil, Band II: Besondere Erscheinungsformen der Straftat' (2003), pp. 114 et seq.

987 Noyon, Langemeijer, Remmelink, Wetboek van Strafrecht, (2010) Art 47, note 8.

7.3.3. Extending perpetration by means

So far this research has focused on the common core of the doctrine in all three countries, namely on situations where the person committing the offence is for a variety of reasons not criminally liable. However, the German doctrine of perpetration by means is considerably broader and covers also situations in which the intermediary is considered not responsible for the committed criminal offence, thus is "innocent" for other reasons than lack of mens rea, criminal capacity or an excusatory defence. It is therefore worthwhile to have a closer look at the doctrine and its scope of application.

The German concept of perpetration by means (*mittelbare Täterschaft*) covers a big variety of scenarios where a person uses another as an instrument to commit a criminal offence. The perpetrator by means controls the situation or manipulates the instrument because he possesses superior knowledge or superior powers in relation to the agent. This implies a relationship of subordination between the perpetrator by means and the instrument, so that in German law the doctrine is frequently described as a vertical model of attribution.[988]

One way to establish such a relationship of subordination might be when the perpetrator behind the scene controls the will of the "instrument" (*Willensherrschaft*), e.g. by force, threat, or where the other person acts under duress.[989] Another form of subordination might be established by superior knowledge (*Wissensherrschaft*), where the other person acts due to a mistake. In this respect it is irrelevant whether the "instrument" erred in regard to a defence, the offence definition, the effect of his acts etc.[990]

A further form of perpetration by means is the use of an infant or insane person.[991] Finally a fourth form comprises cases where a persons exploits framework conditions prevalent in certain organisational power structures or hierarchies (*Organisationsherrschaft*) such as in businesses, corporations, crime

---

988 Schönke and Schröder, 'Kommentar zum Strafgesetzbuch' (2006), §25 Mn 6a.

989 Hamdorf, 'The concept of a Joint Criminal Enterprise and Domestic Modes of Liability for Parties to a crime: A Comparison of German and English Law' Journal of International Criminal Justice (2007), p. 211, Roxin, 'Strafrecht Allgemeiner Teil, Band II: Besondere Erscheinungsformen der Straftat' (2003), pp. 22–77, Schönke and Schröder, 'Kommentar zum Strafgesetzbuch' (2006), §25 Mn 6a.

990 Hamdorf, 'The concept of a Joint Criminal Enterprise and Domestic Modes of Liability for Parties to a crime: A Comparison of German and English Law' Journal of International Criminal Justice (2007), p. 211, Roxin, 'Strafrecht Allgemeiner Teil, Band II: Besondere Erscheinungsformen der Straftat' (2003), pp. 22–77, Schönke and Schröder, 'Kommentar zum Strafgesetzbuch' (2006), §25 Mn 6a.

991 Hamdorf, 'The concept of a Joint Criminal Enterprise and Domestic Modes of Liability for Parties to a crime: A Comparison of German and English Law' Journal of International Criminal Justice (2007), p. 211, Roxin, 'Strafrecht Allgemeiner Teil, Band II: Besondere Erscheinungsformen der Straftat' (2003), pp. 58–64, Schönke and Schröder, 'Kommentar zum Strafgesetzbuch' (2006), §25 Mn 6a.

syndicates, etc., which almost automatically lead to the commission of the offence.[992]

In cases where the perpetrator by means controls another person's will the prevalent theory in Germany resorts to the so-called principle of accountability (*Verantwortungsprinzip*) in order to establish hegemony over the act. According to this principle, a "deficient" will of the instrument will only lead to liability for the perpetrator, if due to the deficient will the responsibility of the instrument is excluded. Cases where the instrument does not fulfil all the elements of the offence definition encompass deficiencies on the subjective, as well as on the objective side of the offence definition. In the former scenario the instrument would for instance act without the requisite mens rea of the offence, while in the latter case the instrument lacks a particular quality required by the offence definition (for instance a public bearer position).[993] If liability for perpetration by means can also arise if the responsibility of the instrument is merely diminished is contentious in academic literature.[994] However, as will subsequently become clear, jurisprudence seems to have accepted this possibility.

Already from this brief overview it becomes apparent that the scope of the doctrine is much broader than its functional equivalent in the Netherlands and England. As will subsequently become apparent, the doctrine is not confined to cases where the instruments acts without mens rea, guilt or lacks criminal capacity (i.e. is an innocent agent), but it also covers cases where the instrument's conduct was justified and even scenarios where the agent is fully criminally liable.

Jurisprudence and commentators have accepted the following categories:

The instrument does not fulfil either the actus reus or mens rea of the offence

There are situations conceivable where the instrument or intermediary cannot even be considered to having committed the actus reus of an offence but where due to the superior position of the perpetrator by means, an imposition of liability nevertheless seems defendable.

The instrument will not be deemed to have fulfilled the actus reus of an offence if the perpetrator induced the instrument to harm an interest which legally is at the disposal of the instrument and its conduct can therefore not amount to a criminal offence. Accordingly, perpetration by means also covers (the unusual) scenarios where the instrument and the victim are one and the same person. This might be the case where an insane person is induced to inflict harm on or kill himself.

---

992 Hamdorf, 'The concept of a Joint Criminal Enterprise and Domestic Modes of Liability for Parties to a crime: A Comparison of German and English Law' Journal of International Criminal Justice (2007), p. 211.

993 Schönke and Schröder, 'Kommentar zum Strafgesetzbuch' (2006), §25 Mn 36–39, Smith, 'Strafbare Voorbereiding, Een rechtsvergelijkend onderzoek' (2003), p. 65.

994 Weisser, 'Täterschaft in Europa' (2011), pp. 150–156.

In case the perpetrator uses coercion to induce the instrument to inflict self harm or to commit suicide not only will situations be covered where the instrument could invoke necessity as an excuse (§35 GPC), but also in situations coming close to a justification. Thus perpetration by means will not only be assumed where Tony threatens Edgar to commit suicide (e.g. by violence, threats of torture, etc.) but also where Tony threatens a person close to Edgar (e.g. his wife, children, etc.).[995]

In case of deception, perpetration by means will be assumed if the instrument acted without mens rea, for instance where cunning Eric induces gullible Kenny to touch an electric cable claiming it not to be energised.[996] The German Supreme Court in one case even assumed that an error of the instrument about the motive of the deed was sufficient to trigger liability as perpetrator by means.[997] In this case an unfaithful wife who wanted to dispose of her depressive husband persuaded him to jointly commit suicide by drinking poison. The husband agreed with the words that this way they could forever remain together. She prepared the drink and handed it to the husband. After he had ingested a lethal dose of poison, she however refused to drink herself from the bottle. The Supreme Court convicted her of murder as perpetrator by means as she not only tricked the husband into committing suicide but also was in charge of the whole situation, i.e. exerted hegemony over the act.[998]

Another spectacular example of a deception leading to (attempted) suicide can be found in the fairy tail like *Sirius* case. In this case the defendant met the victim who suffered from an emotionally and intellectually retarded personality development at a disco. He soon became her spiritual and philosophical leader, and she totally enslaved to him. To get the money from her life insurance he told her that he was from the planet Sirius who's inhabitants were on a much higher plane of philosophical sophistication than mankind. He pretended that he could also elevate her to this level of sophistication but required that she would have to destroy her old body and acquire a new one. She would, he claimed, after killing herself awake in a new body as an artist in a red room on Lake Geneva. She was thus not completely aware that she was about to end her life. He instructed her to kill herself by dropping a hairdryer in the bath while she was in it, but the attempt failed. The Supreme Court convicted the defendant for attempted murder by perpetration by means arguing that he had used his superior knowledge to use the woman as an instrument against herself.[999]

Typically the instrument will act without the necessary mens rea if he is completely oblivious to the results of his conduct, as would for instance be the case

995 Schönke and Schröder, 'Kommentar zum Strafgesetzbuch' (2006), §25 Mn 10.

996 Schönke and Schröder, 'Kommentar zum Strafgesetzbuch' (2006), §25 Mn 11.

997 In scholarly writing opinions are divided. Some argue that any substantial threat or deception should be sufficient, while others like Roxin claim that a coercion or deception ought at least amount to necessity as an excuse (§35 GPC) to trigger the notion as people ought to resist threats, etc. below that threshold. See: Roxin, 'Strafrecht Allgemeiner Teil, Band II: Besondere Erscheinungsformen der Straftat' (2003), p. 27.

998 3 December 1985 BGH GA 86, 508.

999 5 July 1983 BGH NStZ 1984, 70.

when a nurse administers a lethal dose of poison to a patient believing it to be antibiotics, or if the intermediary envisages a different result than the perpetrator by means, i.e. when he believes to commit a less serious offence than intended by the perpetrator. In a pertinent case A wanted to kill his rival in love X, but decided to use other persons to carry out his plan. He convinced B and C to rob X promising a big loot and handed them a plastic bottle containing a strong sedative, so he claimed. In fact, however, he had filled the bottle with hydrochloric acid. Fortunately for X, B and C out of curiosity opened the bottle and noticing the acidic smell abstained from the deed. The Supreme Court convicted A for attempted murder by perpetration by means as he had used his superior knowledge to deceive B and C to believe that they were to commit a robbery when in fact they would have been committing murder.[1000]

The instrument is acting objectively lawful under an accepted defence

If the instrument's conduct is lawful, perpetration by means can come into play if the perpetrator has deceived the instrument to commit the lawful conduct. Consider for instance that Aaron untruthfully tells a police officer that Robin has just stolen his TV, which leads to Robin's arrest. In this case Aaron will be held liable for deprivation of liberty by perpetration by means.[1001]

The responsible instrument

Perpetration by means is not only considered applicable if the instrument acts justified or excused or lacks criminal capacity, but also if the instrument fulfils all requirements of the offence definition and is considered fully criminally liable. In these situations, one is accordingly confronted with two perpetrators and one can speak here of the perpetrator behind the perpetrator. On the one hand one can subsume here cases where the instrument has a wrong perception of the harm he causes, as is for instance the case when Howard induces Leonard to destroy Sheldon's antique vase claiming it to be a cheap replica. In this case Howard will be considered the perpetrator by means as Leonard is unaware of the factual consequences of his conduct.[1002] Furthermore, if the perpetrator provokes an *error in persona vel objecto* perpetration by means can come into play. If for instance Gordon is aware that Rudy hates and despises his enemy Harry and without Rudy's knowledge stages a situation where he believes to have his enemy Harry in front of him but in reality it is Bruce whom Gordon wants to see dead and who is subsequently shot by Rudy, Gordon will be liable for murder as perpetrator by means.[1003]

[1000] 26 January 1982 BGH NJW 1982, 1164.

[1001] Schönke and Schröder, 'Kommentar zum Strafgesetzbuch' (2006), §25 Mn 27.

[1002] Schönke and Schröder, 'Kommentar zum Strafgesetzbuch' (2006), §25 Mn 22.

[1003] Schönke and Schröder, 'Kommentar zum Strafgesetzbuch' (2006), §25 Mn 22.

Perpetration by means will further be applied in cases where the instrument acts under an unreasonable (avoidable) mistake of law. Such was the case in the so called *King Cat* case. In this case two women manipulated a psychologically weak and slightly gullible man into believing and fearing an evil "King cat". For reasons of jealousy the two women wanted to eliminate B, the new wife of one of the women's former lover. They convinced the man that the "King Cat" would claim a million victims if he did not kill B. The man realised that this was murder but thought that killing one person to save a million could be justified. He thus chose what was in his view the lesser of two evils and tried to kill B by stabbing her three times but did not succeed. The Supreme Court considered that perpetration by means was also applicable in cases where the actual perpetrator acted culpable and that all three could be considered perpetrators. The two women were considered perpetrators by means as they had manipulated the man and exploited his gullibility and thereby induced him to commit the offence.[1004]

A couple of years later the Supreme Court further developed this line of thought in the aftermath of the German reunification. The German Supreme Court, for example, applied the notion in a case where it convicted three members of the National Defence Council of the former German Democratic Republic for manslaughter of German civilians who had been shot by boarder guards when they attempted to escape to the West. The court convicted the members of the Defence Council, as this organ had given orders to the border guards to prevent flight to the West, "by any means necessary". The court in his verdict left the question whether the boarder guards could be regarded as fully responsible perpetrators unanswered, because in the view of the court, there can be situations, where perpetration by means is applicable despite the fact that the person carrying out the offence is fully culpable and responsible. Thus, the liability of the defendants was in this case solely based on their hegemony over the acts of the boarder guards, which stemmed form the organisational structure of the former German Democratic Republic and the position which the defendants fulfilled in this organisation. In several other cases dealing with the responsibility of boarder guards and their superiors for killing or injuring civilians trying to escape from East Germany the doctrine has been applied.[1005]

The notion has since then been further expanded and is now frequently applied in the economic context to hold business executives, managers, directors, etc. responsible for crimes committed by their subordinates.[1006] When the "mastermind" behind the offence exploits a certain framework, to be found in organisational structures or hierarchies (e.g. within state, business[1007] and business-

---

1004 15 September 1988 BGH NJW 1989, 912.

1005 For a good overview see: Rotsch, 'Tatherrschaft kraft Organisationsherrschaft' ZStW (2000), pp. 518–562, Rotsch, 'Einheitstäterschaft statt Tatherrschaft' (2009), pp. 376–388.

1006 Rotsch, 'Tatherrschaft kraft Organisationsherrschaft' ZStW (2000), pp. 518–562, Rotsch, 'Einheitstäterschaft statt Tatherrschaft' (2009), pp. 376–388, Roxin, 'Strafrecht Allgemeiner Teil, Band II: Besondere Erscheinungsformen der Straftat' (2003), pp. 46–58.

1007 6 June 1997 BGH NStZ 1997, 544.

like enterprises[1008], organised crime syndicates and military chains of command) within which his actions regularly set in motion a certain chain of events, he can be held liable as a perpetrator.[1009] The impetus for this expansion, arguably lies in the desire to hold executives, etc. primarily responsible for the wrong committed by subordinates who often are considered less culpable than the person in charge as they only carry out orders.[1010] This broad approach bears witness to the fact that a differentiated system encounters difficulties in achieving adequate results in economic and organisational structures which are characterised by a high degree of division of labour, as well as by complex hierarchical structures.[1011]

Be that as it may, the effect of this broad approach regarding perpetration by means is certainly that the boundaries between instigation and perpetration become more blurred. It allows for the attribution of liability as a perpetrator in situations which would traditionally be classified as instigation.[1012] For instance, in a pertinent case the defendant A controlled several companies amongst others the limited company I (GmbH). The warehouseman B was officially registered as director, but was factually bound by A's instructions. In spring 1994 the company encountered financial difficulties and A estimated that before the end of the year the company would be bankrupt. Despite this he ordered B to *inter alia* continue to buy supplies which resulted in financial loss for the company's creditors. The court of lower instance had convicted A for instigating fraud, but the Supreme Court quashed the conviction and held A liable for fraud as perpetrator by means.[1013]

7.3.4. Concluding remarks

It can be deduced from the foregoing that the notion of perpetration by means sidesteps problems traditionally flowing from the principle of derivative liability as it allows for the attribution of liability in cases where the deed of the perpetrator does not constitute a sufficient basis to derive liability from or where the person behind the scene could only be regarded as an accessory as the factual perpetrator acted with full responsibility. As a vertical form of perpetration it applies to situations where the perpetrator uses another as a means to bring about the desired (criminal) harm. As a prerequisite for liability the perpetrator needs to exert control over the conduct of the instrument in one form or another or otherwise significantly steer or influence its behaviour. This can take the form of almost total control as is the case for instance if the instrument is an innocent agent or otherwise completely unaware of the ramifications of his conduct. Yet it can also cover situations where

---

1008 13 September 1994 BGH NStZ 1995, 80.

1009 See: Schönke and Schröder, 'Kommentar zum Strafgesetzbuch' (2006), §25 Mn 6–60. See also: 26 August 1988 OLG Düsseldorf NStZ 1989, 370, 13 September 1994 BGH NStZ 1995, 80.

1010 Rotsch, 'Einheitstäterschaft statt Tatherrschaft' (2009), pp. 388–390.

1011 A fact which could certainly be mitigated by the introduction of corporate liability.

1012 Rotsch, 'Einheitstäterschaft statt Tatherrschaft' (2009), p. 372.

1013 11 December 1997 BGH NJW 1998, 767.

the element of control stems from the position of the perpetrator in an hierarchic organisational context. In these situations the instrument is perceived by criminal law as the avatar through which the offence is committed.

From a traditional doctrinal point of view however the conceptual danger inherent in the construct should not be overlooked. Perpetration by means, originally introduced to cover certain problematic cases could easily swallow the rule. The courts in the German differentiated system by attempting to fix the primarily responsible person for a criminal offence with the correct label and stigma of perpetration have in fact dissolved the boundaries between the different concepts of participation in crime and diminished the importance of derivative liability principles which leads to a more autonomous conception of the participant's liability. From the point of view of criminal policy the desire to brand the arm-chair strategist or primarily responsible person as perpetrator is understandable, but this is at odds with the very rationale of the doctrine and of differential systems in general. In a differentiated system the dogmatic classification of the conduct in question ought to determine the amount of punishment. However, considering someone a perpetrator despite the fact that another fully responsible person has committed the crime reverses this approach and allows considerations of just punishment and labelling determine the dogmatic classification of a certain conduct. This in essence inflates the notion of perpetration, sidesteps the doctrinal restrictions of a differentiated system and reflects an expansion of perpetrational liability.

The breadth of the doctrine can, however, also partially be explained by the absence of corporate criminal liability in Germany. As has been demonstrated, an important focus of the notion of perpetration by means is to hold those responsible who within an organisational framework ordered the commission of the act or supervised the unlawful behaviour. Such conduct would in the Netherlands for instance be covered by Article 51 (2) which introduces criminal liability for supervisors, managers, etc. for participating in a criminal offence committed by a corporation. A similar approach is also perceivable in English criminal law.[1014]

To isolate these cases from the traditional rules on participation would already considerably reduce the complexity of the doctrine. The same result could be achieved by introducing a rule in the vein of Art 12 Corpus Juris.[1015] This article introduces criminal liability for the head of business or persons with power of decision-making and control within the business and would exactly cover the vertical forms of participation in an organisational context, which led to the inflation of this doctrine in Germany. Thus a new, separate offence would help to keep the doctrine between proper boundaries and at the same time simplify the doctrine and make its application and demarcation more straightforward. Likewise, the struggle of differentiated systems to cope with systematic and organised

1014 See: Chapter III. 5.2.

1015 Roxin, 'Täterschaft und Tatherrschaft' (2006), p. 717.

wrongdoing which results in an expansion of the notion of perpetration could at least partially be mitigated by introducing corporate criminal liability.[1016]

7.4. Instigation

7.4.1. Introduction

Another form of participation, related to the doctrine of perpetration by means, is the notion of instigation. In essence, both forms deal with the inducement of one person by another to commit a criminal offence. The person being blamed for instigation or using an innocent agent, can thus be seen as the "*auctor intellectualis*" of the criminal offence. The reproach is accordingly in both situations that they have caused an intermediary to commit a criminal offence. They are the "*raison d'être*" of the occurred criminal harm. The difference between the two forms *inter alia* lies in the criminal status of the intermediary. While generally speaking by definition the intermediary must not be criminally liable (i.e. be an innocent agent) in regard to the doctrine of perpetration by means, the intermediary in regard to instigation must be criminally liable for the committed offence.

In Germany the doctrine is known as *Anstiftung* and is regulated in §26 GPC, while in the Netherlands the doctrine is called *uitlokking* and is regulated in Article 47 DPC. In the English penal system this form of conduct is by and large covered by the concepts of counselling and procuring. Dutch and German law thus distinguish on the one hand between instigation of an offence and aiding on the other. Such a distinction is alien to English law. English law includes both forms of participation under a broad category of accessorial liability. The reason for this difference is once again linked to the level of punishment. While German and Dutch law formally recognise a higher level of punishment for instigators than for aiders, such a distinction is absent in the English system where all participants are eligible to the same punishment than the perpetrator.[1017]

German unlike English[1018] and Dutch law[1019] does not know a concept of instigating negligence or strict liability offences, as §26 GPC requires the instigation of an intentional and unlawful act. However, instigating a negligence offence may result in the imposition of liability as a perpetrator, as German law applies a unitarian approach in regard to crimes of negligence.[1020]

1016 Rotsch, 'Einheitstäterschaft statt Tatherrschaft' (2009), pp. 335–337.

1017 Fletcher, 'Rethinking Criminal Law' (1978), pp. 644 et seq, 671 et seq.

1018 See: Section 44 of the Magistrate Court Act 1980.

1019 De Hullu, 'Materieel Strafrecht' (2009), p. 460, Krabbe, 'Uitlokking', in van der Leij (ed), Plegen en Deelnemen (2007), pp. 143–144.

1020 Also in the Netherlands where it is generally considered possible to instigate a crime of negligence, it is nevertheless also accepted that in many instances a conviction for (co-) perpetrating the criminal offence will also be possible. See: De Hullu, 'Materieel Strafrecht' (2009), p. 460.

The prevalent view in the Netherlands accepts that the intention of the instigator needs to be directed to the elements of the offence which he wishes to solicit. From this it follows that misdemeanours (which are often strict liability offences) can only be instigated if the intention of the instigator encompassed the elements of the offence. In other words, while the intermediary need not possess intention in order to commit the offence, the instigator must nevertheless act intentionally as to the elements of the crime. This underlines the nature of the instigator as the *"auctor intellectualis"* of the criminal offence and further assures that his actions are sufficiently culpable to warrant criminal punishment. By the same token, in the so called 'intent-negligence' combinations in German law such as assault occasioning death, the instigator will only be liable for the aggravating result if he was also negligent as to the result.[1021]

7.4.2. Instigation in Germany and the Netherlands

On first sight, the most salient difference between the concept of instigation in Germany and the Netherlands is that Article 47 DPC closely circumscribes the means by which one can instigate, while in §26 GPC such an enumeration is absent. Article 47 DPC enumerates nine means which can be used for instigation, namely gifts, promises, abuse of authority, use of violence, threat or deception; providing the opportunity, means or information. These means also play a role in regard to attempted instigation (Art 46 a DPC), as attempted instigation will only trigger criminal liability in the event that one of the means was used. The aim of the legislator was to limit the means by which one can instigate, but not the channels by which the instigator wielded his influence. This means that any medium, like the internet, newspapers etc., can be used to apply one of the means.

In Germany on the other hand the emphasis lies more on the indirect violation of the legally protected interest by the instigator who causes another to commit an intentional and unlawful act. This indirect violation is seen in the communicated inducement of the perpetrator.[1022] Accordingly, the means of instigation can take any form of an explicit or implied inducement. One can think here of orders, persuasions, requests or the promise of a reward as well as suggestions, questions, etc.[1023]

The instigator causes another to commit a criminal offence. Thus, the means of instigation must have caused a psychological change in the mindset of the intermediary.[1024] The instigator must have evoked the will to commit the criminal

1021 Schönke and Schröder, 'Kommentar zum Strafgesetzbuch' (2006), §26 Mn 22.

1022 Schönke and Schröder, 'Kommentar zum Strafgesetzbuch' (2006), §26 Mn 4.

1023 Schönke and Schröder, 'Kommentar zum Strafgesetzbuch' (2006), §26 Mn 5.

1024 De Hullu, 'Materieel Strafrecht' (2009), p. 464, Krabbe, 'Uitlokking', in van der Leij (ed), Plegen en Deelnemen (2007), p. 139, Roxin, 'Strafrecht Allgemeiner Teil, Band II: Besondere Erscheinungsformen der Straftat' (2003), p. 149, Schönke and Schröder, 'Kommentar zum Strafgesetzbuch' (2006), §26 Mn 1.

offence.[1025] Before the instigation the intermediary had no plans (or concrete plans) to commit the criminal offence, but afterwards the will to commit the crime had been formed and the offence has been committed. By contrasting juxtaposition it seems pertinent to recall here that English law does not require a factual causal link to find a person guilty as an accessory, be it on the basis of assistance or encouragement.[1026]

The fact that the instigator must be causal for the commission of the offence by the instigated person excludes cases where the person is already determined to commit the offence. The instigated is then called *omnimodo facturus*.[1027] It is however possible that the means used to instigate the *omnimodo facturus* can amount to aid and thus to liability as an accessory in the case at hand.[1028]

The liability of the instigator is in both countries derivative, but both legislators thought the repercussions of derivative liability principles, which would lead to non-liability of the instigator in case the instigated subsequently does not commit, or at least attempt the offence, unacceptable and therefore included provisions in their penal codes (Art 46 a DPC and §30 GPC respectively) criminalising attempted instigation. Thus, in the case of an *omnimodo facturus* also attempted instigation could be assumed. This corresponds to the situation in England where traditionally attempted instigation gave rise to liability for incitement (an inchoate offence) which has now been replaced by the Serious Crime Act 2007.

It has already been mentioned that the instigator must cause someone to commit a criminal offence, but this does not mean that the instigator must be the *conditio sine qua non* of the offence.[1029] An already existing proclivity of the instigated does thus not preclude instigation.[1030] This is a corollary of the simple practical fact that a person nourishing a certain criminal proclivity will be easier to persuade to commit an offence than someone whose mind constitutes a *tabula rasa*. Even in situations where the instigated person offers his services to the instigator in exchange for a reward, liability for instigation is conceivable, as his concrete decision is dependent on the conduct of the instigator.

Problematic here are cases where Jake instigates Allen to commit a more serious offence than the one Allen was planning to commit anyway. Such would for

---

1025 See: HR 22 February 1977, *NJ* 1978, 38. Schönke and Schröder, 'Kommentar zum Strafgesetzbuch' (2006), §26 Mn 1.

1026 See: Chapter III. 5.2. and 9.4.

1027 Schönke and Schröder, 'Kommentar zum Strafgesetzbuch' (2006), §26 Mn 7, Noyon, Langemeijer, Remmelink, Wetboek van Strafrecht, (2010) Art 47, note 32. See also: 8 August 1995 BGH NStZ 1996, 1.

1028 Schönke and Schröder, 'Kommentar zum Strafgesetzbuch' (2006), §26 Mn 7, See also: 8 August 1995 BGH NStZ 1996, 1, Noyon, Langemeijer, Remmelink, ‚Wetboek van Strafrecht', (2010) Art 47, note 32.

1029 Schönke and Schröder, 'Kommentar zum Strafgesetzbuch' (2006), §26 Mn 6, See also: 7 September 1993 BGH NStZ 1994, 29. Noyon, Langemeijer, Remmelink, 'Wetboek van Strafrecht' (2010) Art 47, note 32.

1030 See: HR 6 May 1986, *NJ* 1987, 77, Schönke and Schröder, 'Kommentar zum Strafgesetzbuch' (2006), §26 Mn 7.

instance be the case if he tells Allen to take a gun with him on his way to rob Berta.[1031] It is furthermore conceivable that Jake causes Allen to commit another offence than the one initially intended by Allen or that due to the influence of the instigator the same general act falls under another legal characterisation. The prevailing view in Germany assumes instigation in those cases. Thus, if Jake for instance, instigates Allen who has set his eyes on committing fraud to commit theft instead as this would be easier to commit and Allen subsequently does so, then Jake will be liable for instigation.[1032] In the converse situation however, where the instigator abets the intermediary to commit a less serious offence as for example if Jake induces Allen to leave the gun for committing a robbery at home, instigation will not be applicable, because Allen was already determined to commit the more serious offence which necessarily includes the lesser.

Another controversial question in the realm of instigation is the question whether or not the instigating act must be communicated to the perpetrator or if instigation also covers cases similar to the one covered by the English concept of procuring where the perpetrator is unaware that he or she is being manipulated into committing the offence. The answer to this question largely depends on which position a penal system chooses on the continuum regarding the necessary link between the instigator and the instigated and the corresponding rationale for punishing the instigator. This continuum has at one extreme, the sufficiency of any causal link between the conduct of the instigator and the decision to commit a criminal offence by the instigated person. This would make the housekeeper who intentionally leaves open a window, hoping a burglar will seize the opportunity and steal from the tyrannical landlord liable for instigation.

On the other extreme, views are situated which would require a sort of binding undertaking between the perpetrator and the instigator.[1033] The prevailing view in Germany and the Netherlands seems to include such non-communicated causal actions in the ambit of instigation, but nevertheless requires that the actions of the instigator had a decisive impact and increased the likelihood that the offence will be committed.[1034] Thus, the two systems effectively take a medium position on the aforementioned continuum. They view the collusive pact between the instigator and the perpetrator as the ground for punishing instigators with the significant weight of the instigator's conduct regarding the commission of the offence warranting to make the instigator eligible for the same amount of punishment as the perpetrator.

1031 For a German decision see: 3 June 1964 BGH NJW 1964, 1809.

1032 Roxin, 'Strafrecht Allgemeiner Teil, Band II: Besondere Erscheinungsformen der Straftat' (2003), pp. 158–164, Schönke and Schröder, 'Kommentar zum Strafgesetzbuch' (2006), §26 Mn 8.

1033 Roxin, 'Strafrecht Allgemeiner Teil, Band II: Besondere Erscheinungsformen der Straftat' (2003), pp. 153–158.

1034 Schönke and Schröder, 'Kommentar zum Strafgesetzbuch' (2006), §26 Mn 12, Noyon, Langemeijer, Remmelink, 'Wetboek van Strafrecht' (2010) Art 47, note 32–33.

7.4.3. The fault element of instigation

Instigation, just like aiding, requires double intention in Germany and the Netherlands. The instigator must intentionally induce the commission of the offence and must intend the offence to be committed. The instigator wishes that the offence will be committed by the intermediary and he wants to be the instigator of this crime. Art 47 (1) sub 2 of the Dutch penal code contains the requirement that the instigator intentionally solicits the commission of a crime. The importance of this requirement is underlined by Art 47 (2) which aims at situations where the intention of the instigator diverts from the intention of the intermediary. The instigator must thus intentionally solicit the commission of a crime, thereby using one of the nine means listed in Art 47. Furthermore, the instigator must act intentionally in regard to the particular offence which he wishes to be committed.[1035] Likewise, §26 of the German penal code holds that the instigator must intentionally induce another to intentionally commit an unlawful act. In both countries *dolus eventualis* will be sufficient. The knowledge of the instigator required in regard to the offence to be committed must encompass the essential elements but need not cover every detail.[1036] This essentially corresponds to the approach adopted by the English Court of Appeal in Bryce, mentioned above in regard to accessorial liability in general.[1037]

Taking into account the temporal distance between the instigation and the commission of the criminal offence, it becomes apparent that in theory frictions can emerge if the intermediary deviates from what the instigator initially had in mind. If the deviation is only minor, the broad concept of *dolus eventualis* will in the majority of cases bridge the gap between what the instigator had in mind and what the intermediary effectively brought about.[1038]

A nice illustration of the aforementioned can be found in a Dutch case, where A instigated B and C to steal a colour copier from a copy shop which he needed to forge money by promising B and C a financial reward. B and C set out to steal the copy machine but returned with a black and white copier. A sent them back to the copy shop to steal the colour copier, but they were arrested by the police at the scene. The defence had argued that A's intention was to instigate the theft of a colour copier and that he could not be held liable for instigating the theft of the black and white copier. The Supreme Court gave the argument short shrift, and held that A had accepted the considerable risk that a different copy machine to the one

---

1035 De Hullu, 'Materieel Strafrecht' (2009), p. 459, Kelk, 'Studieboek materieel strafrecht' (2005), pp. 348–350, Krabbe, 'Uitlokking', in van der Leij (ed), Plegen en Deelnemen (2007), pp. 141–144.

1036 21 April 1986 BGH NStZ 1986, 407. De Hullu, 'Materieel Strafrecht' (2009), p. 461. See also: 12 September 1996 BGH NStZ 1997, 281.

1037 R v Bryce [2004] EWCA Crim 1231.

1038 Schönke and Schröder, 'Kommentar zum Strafgesetzbuch' (2006), §26 Mn 17–18, 22, Noyon, Langemeijer, Remmelink, 'Wetboek van Strafrecht' (2010) Art 47, note 34.

intended by him might get stolen when he "hired" B and C to carry out the theft.[1039] Thus, due to the broad concept of *dolus eventualis*, it can be said that the crime committed must correspond in a general way to what the instigator intended.

That the correspondence in Dutch law only needs to be general in nature is further substantiated by the fact that the *dolus eventualis* of the instigator will usually encompass situations where the instigator convinces A to commit a crime, and A subsequently persuades B to commit the crime with him together.[1040] Consider for instance the following. Two men had promised a considerable amount of money and some heroin to A if he killed a Turkish shop owner. A had subsequently convinced B to commit the crime with him together. On the day when the killing took place, B went to A's home to pick him up. A was however not at home, as he had been arrested by the police this morning in a traffic control due to unpaid traffic fines. B decided nevertheless to carry out the crime, took the gun which he found in A's house and shot the victim a few hours later. The Supreme Court held that the intention of the two initiators, covered the possibility that A committed the crime together with another person or that he instigated another person to commit the offence. They were convicted of intentionally instigating the instigation of murder.[1041] This approach again reflects the presumed role of the instigator as *auctor intellectualis* of the crime. The instigator is interested in achieving his goal, i.e. that the criminal offence in question is committed. That the method of execution of this goal differed from what the instigator had in mind, does not affect his culpability and blameworthiness, as long as the result has been achieved.

The derivative liability principles at work within the realm of instigation have important repercussions in situations where the perpetrator deviates from what the instigator had envisaged. If for instance the perpetrator commits a less serious offence than envisaged, the instigator can, as his liability is derived from the offence of the perpetrator, only be liable for what was actually accomplished, provided it remains within the general category of offences that was contemplated by the instigator and not something completely different.[1042] It is however possible that the instigator will then be liable for attempted instigation. If in the reverse situation the perpetrator exceeds what was envisaged by the instigator one will have to distinguish. Generally, the instigator can only be held liable for the crime he intended.[1043] If however, the instigator was indifferent or negligent as to the occurred result, liability seems possible.

1039 HR 29 April 1997, *NJ* 1997, 654.

1040 De Hullu, 'Materieel Strafrecht' (2009), pp. 460–461.

1041 HR 31 March 1987, *NJ* 1988, 633.

1042 De Hullu, 'Materieel Strafrecht' (2009), p. 461, Schönke and Schröder, 'Kommentar zum Strafgesetzbuch' (2006), §26 Mn 22.

1043 Krabbe, 'Uitlokking', in van der Leij (ed), Plegen en Deelnemen (2007), p. 145. Schönke and Schröder, 'Kommentar zum Strafgesetzbuch' (2006), §26 Mn 22.

7.4.4. Errors of the perpetrator and their effect on the instigator

Finally scenarios are conceivable where the perpetrator due to a mistake commits another crime than the one the perpetrator had in mind. Consider for instance the case where Gregory instigates Patrick to kill Christina in a park where she takes a walk every evening. Patrick sets out to do so and in the twilight he sees a woman approaching which he believes to be Christina and shoots her. However, it subsequently turns out that the victim was not Christina but the innocent passerby Lisa. In Dutch criminal law the broad concept of *dolus eventualis* would most likely cover Patrick's mistake and also in German law a mistake which is irrelevant for the liability of the perpetrator will also have no effect on the liability of the instigator.[1044] In a pertinent case where the perpetrator had accidently shot a neighbour and not the instigator's son as planned, the German Supreme Court held that the perpetrator's mistake had no effect on the instigator's liability as such a mistake was considered foreseeable and corresponding to general experience.[1045]

7.4.5. The means of instigation in the Dutch penal system

One of the central features of the Dutch provision dealing with instigation is the exhaustive enumeration of means. It is by one of these means that the instigator must have induced the perpetrator to commit the offence. Art 47 closely circumscribes the means by which one can instigate. The law enumerates nine means which can be used for instigation. The form of a conclusive enumeration was initially chosen for the sake of legal certainty, but the broad interpretation given to these means in practice has diminished this endeavour.[1046] This goes so far that some have argued for the abolition of the enumeration of means.[1047] This in connection with the aforementioned proposed scrapping of the doctrine of innocent agency (*doen plegen*) would lead to a broad concept of instigation resembling to a certain extent the concept of perpetration by means as applied in the German penal system, as then the whole continuum of innocent and fully liable agents procured by a person to commit an offence would be covered by this new notion. Therefore, the requirement of intentional instigation is nowadays deemed to be the most limiting factor in attributing criminal liability for instigating a crime.

Jurisprudence has further shaped the meaning of the means of instigation which can be subdivided in two categories. In one category the intermediary retains his freedom of choice, but he is induced to commit the criminal offence. In the other category the intermediary's choice is circumscribed. The pressure exerted makes it difficult for him to choose for something else than the commission of the crime, although an alternative choice is still possible (otherwise the intermediary would

---

1044 Schönke and Schröder, 'Kommentar zum Strafgesetzbuch' (2006), §26 Mn 23.
1045 25 October 1990 BGH NStZ 1991, 123.
1046 See also: WODC report, 'Daderschap en deelneming doorgelicht', pp. 111 et seq.
1047 WODC report, 'Daderschap en deelneming doorgelicht', pp. 111 et seq.

not be criminally liable and the doctrine of perpetration by means would apply).[1048] Under the former category, means like: gifts, promise, providing the opportunity, means or information can be subsumed. Under the latter, fall cases of abuse of authority and use of violence, threat or deception.

The means of gifts and promises imply that some form of agreement between the instigator and the intermediary is achieved. The gift or promise must have induced the intermediary to commit the crime. A gift can be anything that the intermediary receives for committing the crime. A promise can be any undertaking which induces the intermediary to commit the offence (e.g. money, goods, services, etc.) which has not been fulfilled at the time of the instigation.[1049] For instance, the assurance to pay money and deliver drugs as a reward for the crime to be committed, will frequently be deemed to be a promise.[1050]

A demarcation of the notions of gifts and promises is elusive. A promise can for instance be the undertaking to fulfil an agreement and it is even deemed possible to tacitly promise something.[1051] Despite the elusive boundaries and overlap of the concepts it will be necessary to chose one of the two in practice. The Supreme Court has namely established that a reward given for committing a criminal offence cannot at the same time be classified as a gift or a promise.[1052] The decisive factor to distinguish a gift from a promise is generally seen in the moment of instigation. If someone is promised a gift in order to rob a bank, and he is thereby induced to commit the offence, and the gift is subsequently handed over, before the commission of the crime, than the means of instigation was the promise and not the gift.[1053]

The gift and promise need not be proportional rewards for the committed offence. Anything that induced the intermediary to commit the offence can qualify as a gift or a promise.[1054] Likewise, the gift, and promise need not consist of material goods, but can also consist of services or intangible advantages.

In cases of abuse of authority an authority to determine someone's conduct is used in a way which does not correspond to the scope of the authority in question.[1055] In many cases these relationships of authority will be based on either civil or administrative law provisions. Consider for instance relationships of authority based on family law (e.g. parents and under-age children) or relationships based on employment (e.g. employer and employee).[1056] In early jurisprudence, this category was strongly linked to these legally determined relationships of authority, but more recent jurisprudence has loosened this link and established that the authority need not necessarily flow from a legal relationship, but can also be rooted

---

1048 Krabbe, 'Uitlokking', in van der Leij (ed), Plegen en Deelnemen (2007), p. 146.
1049 Krabbe, 'Uitlokking', in van der Leij (ed), Plegen en Deelnemen (2007), p. 146.
1050 See: HR 5 December 2000, *NJ* 2001, 139.
1051 De Hullu, 'Materieel Strafrecht' (2009), p. 462.
1052 HR 27 March 1973, *NJ* 1973, 248.
1053 Krabbe, 'Uitlokking', in van der Leij (ed), Plegen en Deelnemen (2007), p. 147.
1054 Krabbe, 'Uitlokking', in van der Leij (ed), Plegen en Deelnemen (2007), p. 147.
1055 Krabbe, 'Uitlokking', in van der Leij (ed), Plegen en Deelnemen (2007), p. 147.
1056 Krabbe, 'Uitlokking', in van der Leij (ed), Plegen en Deelnemen (2007), p. 147.

in a relationship of factual subordination. A case at hand is the case of a legal person involved in fraudulent activities. The (legal) director of the company, who *inter alia* fraudulently filled out the companies wage books, wielded in fact no authority at all, but all the power was in the hands of the defendant who held no official position in the company. The Supreme Court looked through the legal veil and held that a relationship of authority existed between the defendant and the company director and convicted the defendant for instigating fraud by abuse of authority.[1057]

A relationship of authority needs however, be established before an abuse of this relationship can take place. In a pertinent case, a father was accused of having instigated his adult daughter to wrongly report her ex-boyfriend to the police for having raped her (Art 188 DPC). The Supreme Court juxtaposed legal with factual relationships of authority. The court held that a legal relationship could not be established, as the daughter was adult and that a factual relationship of authority could not be established, as the daughter was *inter alia* not living with her parents anymore.[1058]

The use of authority will amount to abuse in case the commission of a criminal offence is instigated.[1059] Abuse does however not imply that the intermediary was opposed to committing the offence at first. Also the unsuspecting intermediary, acting out of the wrong belief that his superior ordered him to commit legal conduct can be deemed to have acted due to an abuse of authority. It is furthermore not necessary that the instigator announces consequences in case of non obedience. Consider for instance the threat of resignation. In these situations, however, the means of instigation is not the abuse of authority but rather the use of a threat.[1060]

Finally, also the term "abuse" has been interpreted broadly by jurisprudence.[1061] Abuse can for instance be assumed if the instigator pretends to the intermediary that the commission of the crime is "nothing special".[1062] In these cases one can also see an overlap with the notion of deception, under which such conduct could also be subsumed. In a relationship of employment, the Supreme Court has held that the abuse of authority can also take place by making a request, rather than an order to commit a criminal offence. The context in which the request is posed, thus determines whether or not an abuse of authority has taken place.[1063]

When the means used is violence, threat or deception, it touches upon the ambit of perpetration by means. The extensive use of these means can in any case lead to the non-liability of the intermediary due to a justification or an excuse. But the legislator obviously thought that these means can also be applied without removing the liability of the intermediary. These three means are, however, not often applied

---

1057 HR 27 March 1973, *NJ* 1973, 248.

1058 HR 14 May 1991, *NJ* 1991, 769.

1059 Krabbe, 'Uitlokking', in van der Leij (ed), Plegen en Deelnemen (2007), p. 147.

1060 Krabbe, 'Uitlokking', in van der Leij (ed), Plegen en Deelnemen (2007), p. 148.

1061 De Hullu, 'Materieel Strafrecht' (2009), p. 463.

1062 De Hullu, 'Materieel Strafrecht' (2009), p. 463, Krabbe, 'Uitlokking', in van der Leij (ed), Plegen en Deelnemen (2007), p. 148.

1063 HR 29 May 1984, *NJ* 1985, 6.

in practice.[1064] The use of violence is not defined by the law, so that also a very low level of violence can be subsumed under art 47 DPC.

Threat is usually defined as a declaration of harm or distress to be inflicted on the intermediary or a third person, in case the crime in question is not committed. However, not only the threat of violence is subsumed under this category, but also a threat concerning other events can qualify as a means of instigation. The Supreme Court held for instance that the threat of a wife that she would leave her husband, if he would not bury the newborn child, which he had had with his stepdaughter, alive, would qualify as a threat pursuant to Art 47 DPC.[1065] Problematic in this regard are threats which are based on facts. The threat that if the crime was not committed, the company of the defendant would have to close and the intermediary would be released, was not considered a threat by the Supreme Court as it was based on true facts.[1066]

Deception encompasses situations where the intermediary acts on false pretences induced by the instigator. The deception can be related to an element of the criminal offence to be committed, but this is not always necessary. If Theodor for instance wrongly tells Basil that Constantine is having an affair with his wife and Theodor proposes to seek vengeance, this can qualify as a deception pursuant to Art 47 DPC.[1067]

The means, providing the opportunity, means or information, can also be found in Art 48 DPC in regard to assistance. The following paragraphs will therefore at this point only discuss the notion of providing information as recent jurisprudence has shed new light on the notion in regard to instigation.

Providing information must amount to more than a simple encouragement to commit the crime in question. It must consist of communicating facts or circumstances by which the commission of the offence is made possible or facilitated.[1068] While this definition still retains some value, in 2000 the Dutch Supreme Court adopted a new definition of providing information. In the case at hand, the Supreme Court held that providing information could *inter alia* be seen in a phone call of a mother to her son, telling him that an acquaintance had threatened to kill her, knowing that her son had a history of violent behaviour.[1069] The Supreme Court held that providing information encompassed factual statements which are important for the commission of the envisaged offence, in the sense that they are suitable in the circumstances of the case to procure the commission of the offence. This slightly limits the scope of the means, by requiring that the information constitutes a factual statement, but would make room for statements which only

---

1064 De Hullu, 'Materieel Strafrecht' (2009), p. 463.

1065 HR 25 June 1968, *NJ* 1969, 250.

1066 Krabbe, 'Uitlokking', in van der Leij (ed), Plegen en Deelnemen (2007), p. 150.

1067 Krabbe, 'Uitlokking', in van der Leij (ed), Plegen en Deelnemen (2007), p. 150.

1068 Wolswijk, 'Inlichtingen versus aansporingen', in Franken, et al. (eds), Constante waarden – Liber amicorum Prof. mr. Constantijn Kelk (2008), p. 263. See also: HR 29 October 1991, *NJ* 1992, 267.

1069 HR 27 February 2001, *NJ* 2001, 308.

morally facilitate the commission of the crime for the intermediary.[1070] The difference between providing information and simple encouragement, which is not a means of instigation is certainly an elusive one. The difference seems to lie in the fact that information is factual in nature, while this is not necessarily the case for simple encouragement.[1071] The reason for this elusive distinction is maybe related to evidentiary considerations, as factual statements seem to provide more certainty here. The information provided, must, however, be unknown to the intermediary. Information which the intermediary already possessed cannot function as a means of instigation.[1072]

The requirements for providing information are however interpreted broadly. Drawing someone's attention to the presence of heroin in a flat, and letting him know that he should remove it, can according to the Supreme Court already amount to providing information, instigating the transport of heroin.[1073]

While, as has been demonstrated above, the means of instigation are interpreted broadly in the Dutch penal system, some means are nevertheless excluded. Insufficient means of instigation are for instance, persuasion, encouragement, begging, provoking or daring.[1074] This is notably different to the situation in Germany, where any means of causing another to commit a criminal offence will be sufficient.

The obvious rationale underlying the exhaustive enumeration of means in the Netherlands is legal certainty. Yet, against the background of recent developments in regard to the notions of co-perpetration and functional perpetration which have extended the scope of perpetration considerably, the question can be posed if the argument of legal certainty can still be maintained. Not only are the means interpreted extensively by jurisprudence but also if the notion of instigation is compared to co- and functional perpetration it becomes apparent that the latter two concepts are guided by less clear and restrictive criteria. Arguably, a removal of the list of means would thus not considerably diminish legal certainty.[1075] On the contrary, it might remove a considerable degree of complexity from the doctrine and make its application easier. The boundaries of the doctrine would then be determined by the mens rea requirements applied and the doctrine of causation in the sense that only conduct that caused a person to wilfully commit a criminal offence can give rise to liability. It is submitted that such an approach would safeguard legal certainty as efficient as an enumeration of means but would require less doctrinal efforts which might in turn just as well foster legal certainty.

1070 Wolswijk, 'Inlichtingen versus aansporingen', in Franken, et al. (eds), Constante waarden – Liber amicorum Prof. mr. Constantijn Kelk (2008), p. 265.

1071 Wolswijk, 'Inlichtingen versus aansporingen', in Franken, et al. (eds), Constante waarden – Liber amicorum Prof. mr. Constantijn Kelk (2008), p. 267.

1072 De Hullu, 'Materieel Strafrecht' (2009), p. 462.

1073 HR 27 May 1986, *NJ* 1987, 278.

1074 De Hullu, 'Materieel Strafrecht' (2009), p. 464, Kelk, 'Studieboek materieel strafrecht' (2005), p. 347.

1075 WODC report, 'Daderschap en deelneming doorgelicht', p. 112.

8. Horizontal forms of perpetration

8.1. Co-perpetration

So far the focus of this comparative analysis has mainly been on situations where one perpetrator uses an intermediary to commit a criminal offence or where one person for his significant role in the commission of the offence incurs perpetrational liability despite a lack of physical involvement in committing the actus reus. However, frequently perpetrators will also co-operate as equal partners in a criminal endeavour. One might refer to these situations as cases of joint or co-perpetration. From the perspective of a restrictive conception of perpetration, several people may be classified as co-perpetrators where each of two or more parties does an act which is an element of, or part of the actus reus.[1076] It has already been mentioned that this corresponds to the prevalent view in the English legal system. For instance if in a robbery Alex wields a gun whilst his partner grabs the loot, or where Alex and Bob each forge a part of a banknote, both will be liable as perpetrators.[1077]

The latter two variations would in Germany[1078] and the Netherlands[1079] be subsumed under the notion of co-perpetration, a concept which is not to the same extent recognised in England. The form of liability which comes closest to the concept of co-perpetration applied in Germany and the Netherlands is the doctrine of a joint criminal enterprise. Just like in the Netherlands and Germany a common plan, purpose or design constitutes the central notion of the doctrine. One can roughly distinguish two variations. The first which has been termed the "plain vanilla version of joint enterprise" concerns cases where two or more people join in committing a single crime, such as three robbers who together rob a security men making a cash delivery.[1080] Thus, "where two or more persons embark on a joint enterprise, each of them may play a different part, but if they are in it together as part of a joint plan or a common purpose, each is held liable for the acts done in pursuance of that joint enterprise".[1081] In a pertinent case, A drove B, C and D to the victim's house, knowing that there were frictions between the parties, foreseeing that as probable consequence, violence might occur. As foreseen B, C and D assaulted the victim, while A stood in the doorway watching the attack. The court upheld the conviction, holding that A was a party to a joint criminal enterprise and that in those circumstances a defendant can be criminally liable for an offence, even

---

1076 Smith and Hogan, 'Criminal Law' (2008), p. 182.

1077 Smith, 'A Modern Treatise on the Law of Criminal Complicity' (1991), p. 28.

1078 See: Schönke and Schröder, 'Kommentar zum Strafgesetzbuch' (2006), §25 Mn 64, 65.

1079 Elzinga, 'Medeplegen', in van der Leij (ed), Plegen en Deelnemen (2007), p. 166, Kelk, 'Studieboek materieel strafrecht' (2005), p. 353.

1080 See: R v Rahman (House of Lords) [2008] UKHL 45, see also: R v Gnango [2010] EWCA Crim 1691.

1081 R v Rahman and others (Court of Appeal) [2007] EWCA Crim 342.

if she neither enters the premises in which the assault takes place nor strikes any blow nor provides any active encouragement while the offence takes place.[1082]

The common core of the English joint criminal enterprise doctrine and the concept of co-perpetration as applied in Germany and the Netherlands is that a person may be criminally liable for acts which his own hands did not physically commit, if those acts fall within the common purpose of the participants. Yet, the doctrine's main trust is revealed in the second category of a joint criminal enterprise where A and B set out to commit crime X but in the course of it A commits a second crime Y.[1083] This research will therefore address the doctrine in more detail below, when turning to the problematic cases of "collateral offences" which occur during the carrying out of a common plan. It is however important to note again the crucial difference in regard to the systematic approach towards participation in crime in England, Germany and the Netherlands respectively. In England all parties to a crime are eligible to the same punishment. Thus, at the level of attribution, no strict distinction between perpetrators and other participants is drawn. Accordingly, German and Dutch law attach much more weight to the distinction between perpetrators and (secondary) participants. Thus, while, as will become evident, the scope of liability, i.e. the different forms of behaviour covered by law, is by and large identical, in Germany and the Netherlands, a distinction is drawn between the different forms of participation in a joint criminal enterprise. A participant will only be regarded as a perpetrator if he can be regarded as direct perpetrator, co-perpetrator or perpetrator by means, each of this three models of attribution having their own prerequisites. Under English law where the distinction between perpetrators and other participants is less significant, the only peculiarity of joint criminal enterprise cases as a form of accessorial liability is that once a common purpose has been established, there is no need to look further for evidence of assistance and encouragement.[1084]

It has already been mentioned that English criminal law adheres to a very strict and limited concept of perpetration in which in general only the offender whose act is the most immediate cause of the actus reus is seen as a perpetrator. Thus, only the person whose conduct can be seen as the last act in the causal chain to bring about the actus reus of the offence in question will be deemed to be the perpetrator. As already indicated, the repercussion of this strict approach to perpetration is that it becomes impossible to hold the criminal mastermind, who orchestrated, but did not participate in the crime, as perpetrator. In other words, while such an approach leads to a clearly defined and circumscribed concept of perpetration, it cannot reach satisfactory results in situations where the lion's share of responsibility is believed not to lie with the person causing the actus reus. For differentiated systems who foresee a mandatory mitigation of punishment this poses problems, as the amount

---

1082 DPP v Nedrik-Smith [2006] EWHC 3015 (Admin).

1083 Buxton, 'Joint Enterprise' Criminal Law Review (2009), pp. 236–238.

1084 Smith and Hogan, 'Criminal Law' (2008), p. 207.

of punishment as well as attached label (i.e. accessory) cannot capture the role of the mastermind.

The paradigm of co-perpetration, in line with a restrictive approach to perpetration and recognised in all investigated systems, is the case where each participant fulfils the whole actus reus of the criminal offence.[1085] Thus, the very essence of the notion of co-perpetration can be seen in the joint commission of a criminal offence, with the emphasis traditionally lying on the (joint) physical commission of the actus reus. The restrictive approach to perpetration, however, runs into problems in cases where the offence is committed based on a certain (sometimes predetermined) division of labour, as in these cases not all participants might fulfil the actus reus, but only a part of it. In other words, situations where several people co-operate to achieve a common criminal goal. In these cases not everyone may contribute equally to the commission of the crime. In fact, the participants conduct might, if evaluated separately, amount to different crimes. Consider the example of Eli and Theo who together drive to a museum at night. There, Eli breaks the lock of the door and disables the alarm system, while Theo takes away two Vermeer paintings. In this case it seems appropriate to hold both liable for the theft of the paintings although their respective contributions only amount to destruction of property and theft. Thus, as co-perpetrators jointly bring about the actus reus of a criminal offence, it is not necessary that all of them fulfil the entire actus reus, but rather that their actions in total amount to an actus reus. This means that the objective elements of a crime can be dispersed among the partners in crime and that elements can be attributed to the partners also if they did not fulfil them themselves. It follows that the notion of co-perpetration is a horizontal model of attribution in which the conduct of other participants is attributed to the others.[1086]

This attribution is based on the common purpose, goal or plan according to which the crime has been committed. The participants have in one form or another reached an agreement about the common goal of the criminal endeavour and the allocation of roles therein. They are equal partners in crime and the success of the enterprise depends on the substantial contributions of each participant. This common purpose and division of labour, it is often argued, constitutes the basis for the reciprocal attribution of the acts of the other participants.[1087] Thus, the consequence of establishing that the offenders acted according to a common purpose or plan is that the factual contribution by each of them to the commission of the offence are attributed to all others without the need to establish the

1085 Elzinga, 'Medeplegen', in van der Leij (ed), Plegen en Deelnemen (2007), p. 166, Kelk, 'Studieboek materieel strafrecht' (2005), p. 353, Schönke and Schröder, 'Kommentar zum Strafgesetzbuch' (2006), §25 Mn 61, Smith and Hogan, 'Criminal Law' (2008), p. 182.

1086 Hamdorf, 'Beteiligungsmodelle im Strafrecht' (2002), pp. 30–31.

1087 Kelk, 'Studieboek materieel strafrecht' (2005), p. 353, Schönke and Schröder, 'Kommentar zum Strafgesetzbuch' (2006), Vorbem. §§25 et seq. Mn 81.

commission of a full offence as such by one of them.[1088] It can be deduced from the foregoing that the concept of co-perpetration bears witness to the fact that some crimes possess an actus reus which is made up of several distinctive elements, leaving room for a division of labour where each participant fulfils a separate part of the actus reus, while other offences consist of a single element which can however be satisfied jointly.[1089]

Neither, Article 47 DPC nor §25 GPC contain any criteria for the establishment of co-perpetration, but merely hold that those who commit the offence jointly shall be punished as perpetrators. In the Netherlands, the Supreme Court as early as 1934 began to flesh out the doctrine and to move from a restrictive concept of perpetration to a more open one. In the case at hand, two men had according to a common plan, set fire to a barn. The defendant in this case had held the ladder, which his partner in crime used to climb to the loft to set fire to the hay stored there. At first, they were unsuccessful, as the hay seemed wet and did not catch fire and also a second attempt with dryer hay from the ground floor, which the defendant handed to his partner failed. Eventually, however, the hay caught fire and the barn burned down. The defence had argued that the Court of lower instance had wrongly convicted the defendant as co-perpetrator to arson, as he had not committed any part of the actus reus of arson, but had merely provided help by holding the ladder, an argument based on a stern restrictive conception of perpetration. The Supreme Court held that despite the fact that the hay was kindled by the partner of the defendant, taking into account the common plan of the two arsonists, their cooperation was so complete and close (*volledig en nauw*), that it was in the end coincidental that the fire was effectively set by the defendant's partner. The conduct of the defendant, so the Supreme Court argued, could therefore not be qualified as providing help, but rather as co-perpetration.[1090] Thus, the Court established that an actual contribution to the manifestation of the actus reus was not required for the establishment of liability as co-perpetrator, as long as the co-operation was intentional (*bewust*), complete and close. This requirement (i.e. the complete and close cooperation) became the central requirement in the Dutch penal system. It evidently consists of two parts, an objective one, i.e. the complete and close cooperation and a subjective one, i.e. the cooperation has to be conscious. Thus, the emphasis came to lie on the intentional, close cooperation in the commission of the offence. The determining factor thereby seems to be the intensity of the cooperation and from this landmark decision it can be deduced that a common plan or the exchangeability of roles can both be used to establish a sufficiently close co-operation.[1091]

The constituent elements of an intentional, complete and close cooperation correspond in essence to the requirements applied in Germany, where the notion of co-perpetration rests on a particular role allocation according to a common

1088 Bohlander, 'Principles of German Criminal Law' (2009), p. 163.
1089 Krebs, 'Joint Criminal Enterprise' The Modern Law Review (2010), p. 586.
1090 HR 29 October 1934, *NJ* 1934, 1673.
1091 De Hullu, 'Materieel Strafrecht' (2009), p. 436, Van Toorenburg, 'Medeplegen' (1998), p. 126.

purpose or plan, and a (substantial) contribution to the (joint) commission of the offence.[1092] In case law this is often described as the requirement of a substantial, objective contribution to the commission of the offence based on a common purpose or plan.[1093] The German Supreme Court assumed for instance co-perpetration in the following case. The later victim V owed a substantial amount of money to his friend A who also supplied him with cocaine. V was at the time on the brink of bankruptcy and unable to settle his debt. This angered A who was also under pressure to pay his drug supplier in the Netherlands. He tried to contact V in order to regain his money but was unable to reach him. This agitated A even more and he decided to pay V a visit to finally collect the money. He contacted B and C and made it clear to them that he was planning to kill V in case he did not receive his money this time. The three men drove to V's house where A told B to go and talk to V as he suspected that V would not open the door for him. B did as he was told, entered the flat claiming to be "the supplier from the Netherlands" and asked for the money. V told him that he did not have it, whereupon, B asked V to open the front door as he needed some fresh air. This allowed A to enter the apartment where it came to an argument between A and V which ended with V being shot by A. The Court of lower instance had convicted B for aiding the homicide, but the Supreme Court held that he had contributed substantially to the commission of the offence according to a common plan and did furthermore possess hegemony over the act, as it was only due to his contribution that A was able to gain access to the victim's apartment.[1094]

The cases discussed so far can be qualified as paradigmatic and uncontroversial as they all involve physical contributions at the time of the commission of the offence. Recent developments in criminal doctrine have however, altered and expanded the notion of co-perpetration considerably in comparison to the traditional approach outlined above. The shift to the social theory of action, in accordance with the developments discussed in regard to functional perpetration and the hegemony over the act doctrine have diminished the necessity of a physical contribution to the actus reus by the co-perpetrator, so that nowadays hardly any physical contribution is required for the establishment of co-perpetration. Likewise, the temporal aspect of a contribution at the time of the commission of the actus reus has been broadened, so that nowadays also conduct taking place in the preparatory phase of a crime can, if significant enough, constitute the basis of co-perpetration. It is these developments that will now be investigated.

[1092] Roxin, 'Strafrecht Allgemeiner Teil, Band II: Besondere Erscheinungsformen der Straftat' (2003), pp. 77 et seq, Schönke and Schröder, 'Kommentar zum Strafgesetzbuch' (2006), §25, Mn 61–76c.

[1093] See for instance: 29 November 2007 BGH NStZ 2008, 273, 2 July 2008 BGH NStZ 2009, 25, 22 July 1992 BGH NStZ 1992, 545.

[1094] 29 November 2007 BGH NStZ 2008, 273.

8.1.1. Expanding the scope of mutual attribution

On first sight it seems clear that a physical contribution during the commission of the crime is not necessary as also a mental contribution can be seen as substantial to the commission of the crime. Think for instance of someone who competently instructs another at the *locus delicti* on how to steal a laptop from a store. However, matters become more complicated if one broadens the scope to encompass also contributions which took place during the preparatory phase of the crime. Nevertheless, it seems conceivable that a contribution of a participant during the preparatory phase is so substantial that it significantly shapes the modality of the commission of the crime.[1095]

The person who waits with his van in front of the house in order to make the transportation of the heavy safe as well as the getaway possible, takes a significant role in and shapes the commission of the crime and should arguably therefore be seen as co-perpetrator. Yet, if one accepts these propositions, the boundaries between perpetration and other, auxiliary modes of participation such as aiding become blurred and elusive, as it would now seem possible to subsume activities such as driving the getaway car, which were traditionally seen as aiding the commission of a crime, under the heading of (co-)perpetration. This becomes possible by applying a moderate extensive concept of perpetration which, due to the repercussions of doctrines such as functional perpetration and hegemony over the act allows to view the commission of a crime holistically.

In the Netherlands and Germany it is nowadays accepted that neither a physical contribution nor presence at the commission of the crime is necessary for the establishment of co-perpetration. The Dutch Supreme Court began developing this approach in 1981. The defendant in the case at hand had orchestrated the theft of semitrailers. He had planed the crime, chosen the trailers which should be stolen, had falsified letters of consignment to be shown to the police in the case of a traffic control, and provided a truck to transport the containers and a shed where the loot could be moved to. However, the defendant was not present at the theft of the trailers which was carried out by his partners. The Supreme Court left the conviction for theft in co-perpetration intact and ruled that a physical presence at the *locus delicti* was not required, as long as it could be proven that the defendant had cooperated completely and closely with his partners.[1096] However, the role of the absent perpetrator in the preparatory phase or after the fact must have been a significant one in order to justify the imposition of perpetrational liability. Mere knowledge and acquiescence of the criminal enterprise in connection with rendered auxiliary services is insufficient for holding a person liable as co-perpetrator. The Supreme Court in a pertinent case for instance quashed a woman's conviction for murder in co-perpetration as she had not been present during the commission of the

[1095] Schönke and Schröder, 'Kommentar zum Strafgesetzbuch' (2006), §25 Mn 66.
[1096] HR 17 November 1981, *NJ* 1983, 84.

crime and had neither played any part in its execution. She had however been aware of the plan to kill the victim, had programmed the mobile phones which were especially bought for this occasion to facilitate the communication between the partners and had cleaned the van, in which the body had been transported, with chlorine.[1097]

In a pertinent German case the defendants A, B, C and D were the owners of a local brothel and decided to take actions against their business rivals. A suggested to drive to their rivals' establishment and randomly fire at a person with a shotgun. The others agreed and B and C carried out the plan, severely injuring a customer, while A and D kept a lookout in their car in the vicinity. The Court of lower instance had convicted A and D for aiding attempted murder, but the Supreme Court held that presence at the *locus delicti* was not necessary for imposing liability as co-perpetrators especially taking into consideration the common plan of the participants and the important role that A and D played in the commission of the offence.[1098]

An additional reason for dispensing with the traditional requirements of a physical contribution at the commission of the crime can be found in the increasing degree of organisation in crime and the corresponding desire to also capture and punish the person who considerably shaped the commission of the offence but is not present at the *locus delicti*. Often the underlying rationale in these cases state that even the persons in the background shaping the criminal endeavour, should be held liable as a perpetrator and not as an accomplice. It is a well know fact that often the grey eminence in the back, that conceives and initiates the crime, wields the most influence and control over it, while the actual crime is carried out by others. These people ought not to receive the benefit of a mitigation of punishment merely because they were not present at the commission of the crime.

These judgments also show that conduct taking place before the commission of the crime, i.e. in the preparatory phase can play a role in establishing liability for co-perpetration. This line of reasoning was repeated by the Dutch Supreme Court in 1986. In this case, the defendant had planned the killing of the victim, determined the time and place of the murder and had provided the gun with which the victim was killed, but was not present when his plan was put into practice. The Supreme Court reiterated that physical presence, let alone a joint commission of the offence was not necessary to hold the defendant liable as a co-perpetrator, as long as an intentional, complete and close cooperation could be proven.[1099] This further reflects the view adopted by the Supreme Court in Germany, which merely requires that based on a common purpose or plan a significant contribution to the commission of the offence is made which can also take place in the preparatory phase.[1100]

1097 HR 9 March 2010, *NJ* 2010, 194.

1098 15 February 1995 BGH NStZ 1995, 285. See also: 17 October 2002 BGH NStZ 2003, 253.

1099 HR 15 April 1986, *NJ* 1986, 740.

1100 See: 14 November 2001 BGH NStZ 2002, 200, 26 October 1984 BGH NJW 1985, 1035, 18 January 1994 BGH NStZ 1995, 122.

Due to the fact that physical presence, let alone joint perpetration is no longer necessary for establishing liability as a co-perpetrator, and due to the possibility of taking into account preparatory acts to establish primary responsibility and to prove a criminal co-operation between the partners, the differences between the notion of co-perpetration and instigation and perpetration by means have arguably diminished in Germany and the Netherlands.

The expansion of co-perpetration has encroached on the scope of instigation and perpetration by means to such an extent that a sharp and clear demarcation of the concepts seems no longer possible. Consider for instance the example of a physically absent initiator of a crime. In theory, his conduct can easily, depending of course on the exact details, be classified as co-perpetration, instigation, or perpetration by means alike. While a (partial) convergence of the different concepts of perpetration need not necessarily be problematic as they all trigger the same level of punishment, the expansion of the concept of co-perpetration has also blurred the boundaries between perpetrators and accessories. Due to the fact that an intentional cooperation is, based on circumstantial evidence readily assumed by jurisprudence, former paradigm cases of participation can nowadays be qualified as perpetration, ensuing greater punishment. Consider for instance the example of the person on a look-out while his partner breaks into a house, car, etc. While this could be seen as a paradigm for accessorial liability, Dutch jurisprudence has also assumed co-perpetration in these cases. A woman, who was on the look-out while her friend was breaking into a car to steal the radio, was for instance held liable for theft in co-perpetration.[1101] The Supreme Court argued that taking into account the common plan of the two, an intentional, close and comprehensive cooperation could be established.

Comparable cases of this kind can also be found in German case law.[1102] The German Supreme Court for instance handed down a conviction for robbery carried out in co-perpetration where the participant had assisted in the theft of the car which his partner used to commit the robbery, provided his own car and functioned as a getaway driver and had received a share of the loot.[1103] This convergence of forms of perpetration with forms of participation, can be a cause of concern from the viewpoint of legal certainty and just desert. If the boundaries between perpetration and accessory liability become arbitrary, a fair attribution of criminal liability is no longer possible. In general, these developments seem to bear witness to a more stringent, zero-tolerance type approach towards participation in crime.

The aforementioned developments in the concept of co-perpetration were to a certain extent in Germany as well as in the Netherlands also fostered by evidentiary problems, which can be circumvented by a broad application of the doctrine. If

1101 HR 23 October 1990, *NJ* 1991, 328.

1102 See: Schönke and Schröder, 'Kommentar zum Strafgesetzbuch' (2006), Vorbem §§25 et seq. Mn 89–97.

1103 17 March 1977 BGH GA 77, 306. See also: Roxin, 'Täterschaft und Tatherrschaft' (2006), p. 578 et seq.

co-perpetration can be established, the courts no longer need to establish precisely which contribution was made by a respective participant as every contribution can be attributed reciprocally.[1104]

It has already been stated that the notion of co-perpetration rests on a common criminal plan, purpose or goal, or as applied in the Dutch penal system on a complete and close co-operation between the participants. Such can be established in a variety of ways. Aspects which might play a role in establishing such a common purpose or close and comprehensive cooperation are the intensity of the cooperation, the proof of a common plan[1105], the division of tasks, the exchangeability of roles, the role of the suspect in the preparatory phase, in the commission and the dispatch of the crime, as well as the general importance of his role and interest in the crime and the presence at the place of the crime at crucial moments.[1106] The requisite consensus among the participants can according to the prevalent German view be reached explicitly or implicitly before the commission of the offence, but can also emerge in the course of the execution of the offence.[1107] The common approach of all three investigated systems here is nicely summarised in the English case of *Rahman*:

> An agreement to commit an offence may arise on the spur of the moment; sometimes there may be planning, sometimes not; sometimes there may be acts of preparation, sometimes not. Parties to an agreement may join at different times; nothing may be said at all. An agreement or common purpose can be inferred from the behaviour of the parties.[1108]

8.1.2. Is mere presence sufficient to establish co-perpetration?

The mirror question of the fact that neither physical presence at the commission of the crime, nor any physical contribution constitutes a prerequisite for establishing liability as co-perpetrator is whether someone who is present during the commission of the offence and fails to leave or maybe even condones the crime can be held liable as co-perpetrator. While admittedly, (continued) presence at the scene can be seen as contributing to the commission of the crime, especially where a person is

---

1104 Puppe, 'Der gemeinsame Tatplan der Mittäter' Zeitschrift für Internationale Strafrechtsdogmatik (2007), p. 234.

1105 Note that a common plan in the Netherlands constitutes a clear sign of a close co-operation between the persons involved in the commission of the crime. However a common plan is not a necessity for the assumption of co-perpetration. A close co-operation can for instance also be assumed due to a tacit agreement or due to other circumstantial evidence.

1106 De Hullu, 'Materieel Strafrecht' (2009), p. 441. See also: Van Toorenburg, 'Medeplegen' (1998), pp. 146–149.

1107 Wessels and Beulke, 'Strafrecht Allgemeiner Teil, Die Straftat und ihr Aufbau' (2008), p. 186, Jescheck and Weigend, 'Lehrbuch des Strafrechts: Allgemeiner Teil' (1996), p. 678. See also: 9 June 2009 BGH HRRS 2009 Nr 796, 3 November 1995 BGH NStZ 1996, 227, 15 January 1991 BGH NStZ 1991, 280.

1108 R v Rahman and others (Court of Appeal) [2007] EWCA Crim 342.

present by virtue of a prearranged plan, it is submitted that if applied in a strict manner, such an approach would practically establish a form of collective responsibility in cases where several people cooperate to bring about a prohibited harm and would come close to the proverbial "cling together, swing together". It would further result in a shift in the burden of proof, as anyone present at the *locus delicti* would have to prove that he had distanced himself from the criminal enterprise.[1109] It seems generally accepted that mere presence during the commission of the crime is insufficient to amount to co-perpetration. Yet, there are situations conceivable where presence at the commission in connection with other circumstances can amount to co-perpetration.

The notion of a failure to distance oneself from the criminal conduct seemingly for the first time played a role in Dutch criminal law in the aforementioned murder case[1110], where the defence had argued that the suspect had distanced himself from the murder, as he had not been present at the time and place when the crime took place.[1111] The Supreme Court, however, emphasised the strong involvement of the defendant in the preparatory phase of the crime and concurred with the Court of lower instance that he had failed to distance himself from the murder, resulting in the defendant's liability for co-perpetration. The failure to distance oneself has since then gained importance and has become a forceful weapon in the armoury of the prosecution. The notion can function as a 'wild card' for the public prosecutor where unambiguous evidence is scarce but a conviction seems nevertheless appropriate.[1112]

The Dutch Supreme Court has seemingly recognised the potential danger of the concept and has adopted a restrictive approach regarding a failure to distance oneself from criminal conduct. The failure to distance oneself per se has been deemed insufficient to establish a complete and close cooperation, i.e. co-perpetration. It is merely an additional argument with which the intensity of the cooperation can be proven, in case the passivity of the defendant contributed to the manifestation of the criminal harm. Thus one can speak here of "the failure to distance plus x requirement".[1113]

The fact that a failure to distance per se is insufficient to establish co-perpetration is further substantiated by a judgment from 2008. From a bridge straddling a motorway, pieces of paving stone were flung onto the motorway. One of the pieces broke the windshield of a car, due to which the driver lost control of his vehicle and crashed into the crash barrier, which caused his death. Four adolescents were prosecuted for murdering the driver of the vehicle. But only two of

1109 De Hullu, 'Materieel Strafrecht' (2009), p. 443.

1110 HR 15 April 1986, *NJ* 1986, 740.

1111 Keupink, 'Enkele opmerkingen over niet-distantieren bij medeplegen', in Kempen, et al. (eds), De gedraging in beweging (2007), p. 88.

1112 Elzinga, 'Medeplegen', in van der Leij (ed), Plegen en Deelnemen (2007), p. 171.

1113 See for instance: HR 14 October 2003, *NJ* 2005, 183, Hof Arnhem, 21 October 2010, *LJN* BO1426.

the boys had effectively thrown the stones, while the others were merely present at the scene. The Court of lower instance had acquitted the latter two as the mere failure to distance themselves was deemed insufficient to amount to co-perpetration and the Supreme Court upheld the acquittal.[1114]

Generally, the Supreme Court has thus treated the concept of "failure to distance" with the necessary retentiveness. The court for instance requires that it has been actually possible for the defendant to distance oneself from the criminal enterprise. In which cases this was not possible highly depends on the facts of the case at hand as well as on the evidence submitted. The court has for instance held that the possibility to distance oneself was not given in case of the sudden escalation of violence. In this case the defendant was insulted by some comments of the victim about his mother and decided to "teach him a lesson". He therefore contacted his friend who carried a gun and arranged a meeting with the victim at a petrol station. When they arrived at the station the defendant approached the already present victim, but fled once he realised that the victim also was equipped with a gun. The defendant's friend subsequently fired several times at the victim which led to his death. The Court of lower instance had convicted the defendant as co-perpetrator of manslaughter for *inter alia* his failure to distance himself from the killing, but the Supreme Court squashed the judgment and held that given the sudden escalation of violence it was impossible for the defendant to distance himself from the murder.[1115] Thus, truly unforeseeable, unexpected or sudden criminal conduct by one of the members of the criminal enterprise cannot warrant the reproach of a failure to distance.

In the German penal system it is generally recognised that mere presence during the commission and endorsement of the crime is insufficient for the establishment of co-perpetration.[1116] Yet, much will depend on the exact content of the common plan and the relevance given to his contribution for the commission of the offence. In case law the defendant's degree of interest in the successful commission of the crime, the weight of his objective contribution and his hegemony or intent to exert hegemony over the commission of the crime are frequently mentioned as reference points for the establishment of liability as co-perpetrator.[1117] This essentially means that a participant will be seen as a co-perpetrator in accordance with the hegemony over the act doctrine, as long as his contribution has an impact on how the common plan is shaped or enforced and as long as he wants to influence the actual mode of commission. One might therefore be inclined to think that negligible contributions such as mere presence can never trigger criminal liability as co-perpetrator.

1114 HR 18 March 2008, *NJ* 2008, 209.

1115 HR 26 October 2004, *NJ* 2004, 682.

1116 See for instance: 26 June 2002 BGH NStZ 2003, 85. See also: Schönke and Schröder, 'Kommentar zum Strafgesetzbuch' (2006), Vorbem §§25 et seq. Mn 74.

1117 See for instance: 22 July1992 BGH NStZ 1992, 545. See also: 14 February 2012 BGH HRRS 2012 Nr 534.

Frequently negligible contributions will indeed rather lead to criminal liability for aiding than co-perpetration, but exceptions might arise. The explosives expert for instance who accompanies his partners to a bank can be liable as co-perpetrator even if his services were in fact not needed as the vault was opened with a duplicate key.[1118] Likewise is it conceivable that the mere presence of another strengthens the resolve to commit the crime of the actual perpetrator which could result in liability as co-perpetrator. This was for instance the case in the following decision. The defendant had two months before the deed not returned from prison leave. His partner A had convinced him to do so as he was wanted by the police for the very same reason. A planned to commit crimes together with the defendant and also gave him a gun which the defendant carried at all times. A was determined not to go back to prison again even if that would entail using lethal force to resist an arrest and he assumed that the defendant would do the same and support him. One night they were stopped by the police in their car. The defendant did initially not resist the arrest but A fired several shots and killed two police officers. The two were subsequently able to flee, but were arrested the next day. The Supreme Court held that the two had tacitly entered an agreement to forcefully resist an eventual arrest and that the defendant's presence contributed to the commission of the offence as it strengthened A's resolve to resist the arrest. He also, so it was argued, exerted hegemony over the crime as his armed presence constituted mental support and as he could have tried to persuade A not to shoot.[1119]

A comparable reasoning was applied in the following case. A had a relationship with B which she ended in order to start a new relationship with C. When B would not accept the break up, A and C agreed that he should be killed in case he were not to accept the end of the relationship. The three met for a final talk which took place in C's car and to which C brought a gun with A's knowledge. After an intense discussion C executed B when he was about to leave the car. The Court of lower instance had acquitted A as she neither had hegemony over the act nor contributed in any way to the commission of the crime. The Supreme Court, however, held that although she had not contributed to the commission of the crime she had a significant interest in its commission and also had hegemony over the act as she easily could have prevented the murder.[1120]

Knowing that the concept of co-perpetration does not exist as such in the English penal system it is necessary to turn to instances of assistance to gain some comparative insights. Keeping in mind that accessories are eligible to the same amount of punishment as the perpetrator, this may give an indication as to the role of physical presence in establishing liability.

1118 Schönke and Schröder, 'Kommentar zum Strafgesetzbuch' (2006), §25 Mn 73/74.

1119 15 January 1991 BGH NStZ 1991, 280.

1120 15 October 2003 BGH NStZ-RR 2004, 40.

In England it seems clear that mere presence of an actor very near the scene of a crime, for instance as a spectator, is not enough to prove participation.[1121] Yet it is equally clear that mere presence in certain situations can trigger criminal liability if it can be proved that it constituted encouragement or assistance. This will be the case when (i) the person was present in pursuance of an agreement that the crime be committed, or (ii) his presence constituted actual assistance or encouragement of the principal offence, which he intended.[1122] Thus, a person who stands outside a building while his friends vandalise the property inside cannot be held liable unless it can be proven that he assisted or encouraged the crime by for example acting as a lookout.[1123] Yet, the fact that a person was voluntarily present on purpose, witnessing the commission of a crime and afforded no opposition, though he might reasonably be expected to prevent it and had the power to do so, or at least express his dissent, might in some circumstances afford cogent evidence upon which assistance and encouragement can be inferred.[1124] Likewise, voluntary presence at an event can amount to prima facie evidence of assistance and encouragement. In *Wilcox v Jeffry*,[1125] for instance A visited the public performance of a renowned American saxophonist who had only been allowed to enter the UK under the condition that he would not take up employment. In combination with A's behaviour before and after the performance (he had met the musician at the airport and had praised the performance in his jazz periodical) this was deemed sufficient to constitute aiding and abetting the musician's contravention of the Aliens Order Act 1920.

This view seems to be confirmed by Lord Justice Hooper in a case where a 16 year old died from a stab wound during an attack on him by several persons. The judge instructed the jury regarding the responsibility of the attackers for participating in a joint criminal enterprise in the following way:

> Mere presence at or very near the scene of the attack, for example as a spectator, is not enough to prove participation. But if you find a particular defendant was there and intended and did by his presence alone encourage the others […] and he intended to kill […] (the victim) […], that would amount to participation in it (i.e. the joint criminal enterprise).[1126]

The picture that emerges from these judgments is that presence per se is insufficient for the establishment of co-perpetration. However, presence in addition to other

1121 See: R v Rahman and others (Court of Appeal) [2007] EWCA Crim 342, R v Ellis [2008] EWCA Crim 886.

1122 Smith and Hogan, 'Criminal Law' (2008), p. 191.

1123 See also: R v Rose [2004] EWCA Crim 764, where a conviction for causing grievous bodily harm was quashed, as the defendant's only actions at the scene were to discourage his friend from carrying out his attack.

1124 See: R v Ellis [2008] EWCA Crim 886.

1125 [1951] 1 All ER 464.

1126 R v Rahman and others (Court of Appeal) [2007] EWCA Crim 342, para 9.

circumstances such as a clear common plan, a significant interest in the commission of the crime or if his presence is deemed to have significantly shaped the mode of the commission, can result in a conviction for co-perpetration. This illustration aptly demonstrates that the concept of perpetration is increasingly interpreted normatively. It is no longer the empirical contribution that entails the reproach of co-perpetration, but rather that the defendant violated a duty of care, i.e. that he did not prevent something from happening which he should have.

8.1.3. The limits of mutual attribution

Contrary to the objective elements of crime, the subjective elements, according to the guiding principle of individual culpability, cannot be dispersed among the partners in crime. It follows that the acts of other participants can only be attributed insofar as they are covered by the intention of the participant to which they are attributed. Thus, everybody is liable for the occurred criminal harm only in so far as this corresponds to his intention. This represents by and large the situation in Germany and the Netherlands.[1127] In Germany intention regarding the circumstances constituting co-perpetration as well as an awareness of the joint realisation of the plan is generally required.[1128] In the Netherlands in regard to the fault element in co-perpetration two requirements are generally distinguished. First, every co-perpetrator has to act with the mens rea of the underlying offence. Second, every co-perpetrator has to cooperate intentionally in the commission of the criminal offence.[1129] In regard to the first requirement the same standard as applied in regard to (sole) perpetration, applies to co-perpetration as well. This means for instance that in order to be liable for manslaughter in co-perpetration every participant must have the intention to kill another human being. In regard to the second requirement it is necessary that the partners intentionally cooperate. In other words, they must intend to commit the crime together.

As a subspecies of primary liability, i.e. perpetration, it seems also clear that also in regard to offences committed in co-perpetration every participant must, if required, possess certain qualities, enshrined in the actus reus. This is the general rule in Germany as well as in England.[1130] If one of the participants lacks a certain quality necessary for the specific offence, he cannot be a co-perpetrator of that offence, but possibly of another, sometimes maybe a lesser included offence.

In the Netherlands where the prevalent view is that the persons mentioned in Article 47 DPC are not perpetrators per se but are simply put on an equal footing

---

1127 De Hullu, 'Materieel Strafrecht' (2009), pp. 444–446, Schönke and Schröder, 'Kommentar zum Strafgesetzbuch' (2006), §25 Mn 95.

1128 Schönke and Schröder, 'Kommentar zum Strafgesetzbuch' (2006), §25 Mn 94.

1129 De Hullu, 'Materieel Strafrecht' (2009), pp. 444–446, Elzinga, 'Medeplegen', in van der Leij (ed), Plegen en Deelnemen (2007), p. 169.

1130 See: Chapter III. 6.2.2.

with the perpetrator, a different approach has been adopted.[1131] Thus, as co-perpetrators are only put on an equal footing with the perpetrator, offences requiring a certain quality as well can be committed in co-perpetration, despite the fact that not all participants possess the required quality of the offence. In these situations it is required that the co-perpetrator knew that his partner possessed the required quality and acted intentionally in regard to this circumstance.[1132]

Another limit to attribution comes to the fore in cases where one of the co-perpetrators deviates from the common plan. Thus, doctrinal predicaments arise in the context of collateral crimes brought about as a side product of the commission of another offence deliberately embarked upon jointly. Consider for instance the case where Nick, Garry and Hyde agree to rob a jewellery store together. Nick and Garry insist that only replica guns should be used during the heist as they do not want anyone to get hurt. During the robbery however, Hyde, trying to force the shop owner to open the safe, produces a knife and stabs the shop owner in the heart. The question then is whether the death of the shop owner can also be attributed to Nick and Garry as the death occurred during the execution of their common goal, i.e. the robbery. Put differently, the cardinal question here is whether an individual might be held liable for actions of his associates which did not form part of their common plan or purpose.

As all participants can only incur liability for deeds that were covered by their (common) intention, i.e. the common plan or purpose, it seems to follow that unilateral deviations by one participant can generally not be attributed to the others. Yet, as the common intention or plan does not need to be elaborated in detail, some deviations from the common design can under certain circumstances be attributed, if they were of a kind which one could reasonably expect to occur in the execution of the crime.[1133] As will be shown, the notion of foresight of a real risk of commission of the collateral offence plays a crucial role in all penal systems. Therefore the inherent dangerousness of the conduct agreed upon as well as the dangerousness of the means and instruments applied (e.g. usage of blunt objects, a knife or a firearm) will be important factors in the consideration whether or not participants can be held liable for the occurred collateral damage.

The question whether or not a certain conduct is still covered by the common plan or intention of the participants is in Germany and the Netherlands highly influenced by the mens rea concept of *dolus eventualis*. The concept of *dolus eventualis* is a broad one and facilitates the attribution of deviations from the

---

1131 De Hullu, 'Materieel Strafrecht' (2009), p. 421, De Jong, 'Vormen van strafbare deelneming', in van der Leij (ed), Plegen en Deelnemen (2007), pp. 113–114.

1132 De Hullu, 'Materieel Strafrecht' (2009), p. 431. See also: HR 28 February 2006, *LJN* AU9096.

1133 Hamdorf, 'The concept of a Joint Criminal Enterprise and Domestic Modes of Liability for Parties to a crime: A Comparison of German and English Law' Journal of International Criminal Justice (2007), pp. 208–226, Roxin, 'Strafrecht Allgemeiner Teil, Band II: Besondere Erscheinungsformen der Straftat' (2003), p. 81. See also: HR 10 April 2007, *NJ* 2007, 224, where the court held that it was not necessary for the defendant to know exactly what his "partners" were doing.

common plan greatly. The Dutch concept of *dolus eventualis* can be established in case the defendant (knowingly and willingly) exposed himself to a considerable chance that a certain consequence will result from his actions. Thus, the concept consists of three elements: (i) the offender has to be aware of the possible consequence; (ii) there is a considerable chance that this consequence will occur; (iii) the offender acknowledged the chance of occurrence of that consequence knowingly and willingly.[1134]

In Germany, on the other hand the requirement of a considerable chance is missing, but *dolus eventualis* will be established if the offender foresaw the consequences as possible and approved them.[1135] Thus, crudely stated, the common core of the concept lies in the actor's awareness of a certain risk and its acceptance or indifference towards it.[1136] This broad concept allows in practice to attribute excesses of co-perpetrators exceeding the common plan, to the other partner, if it can, for instance due to a common plan, be proven that he accepted the chance of the occurrence of the unplanned consequence. Given the fact that crime is deemed to be risky business, it becomes apparent that the broad *dolus eventualis* concept makes it easy in practice to deem certain unforeseen results to be covered by the intention of the co-perpetrator.

Two Dutch cases might serve as an example here. After an argument with a group of Albanians in a nightclub, the brothers A and B went to A's house to pick up a gun and to subsequently confront the Albanians again. B had taken the gun and tried together with B to re-enter the nightclub, but the bouncers refused to let them in again. As a result, B randomly fired three shots at the closed door of the nightclub (allegedly to hit the bouncers) which caused the death of two young women standing behind the entrance door. The defence had argued that the defendant had not accepted the considerable chance that his brother would fire at the bouncers. The Supreme Court however concurred with the reasoning of the Court of lower instance and held that given the fact that he was aware that his brother was carrying a gun and that his brother under certain circumstance could act violently, the defendant had accepted the considerable chance that his brother would act violently and maybe use the gun on their return to the nightclub.[1137]

A further case in point is the case of a school shooting in Veghel. A Turkish father and his son had planned the honour killing of a boy who had compromised the honour of their daughter/sister. The son had located the boy at the school in Veghel and had contacted his father who came to the school equipped with a gun. The son took the gun from his father, in order to prevent him from going to jail and went inside the school. He was an inexperienced shooter but nevertheless fired

1134 See: De Hullu, 'Materieel Strafrecht' (2009), pp. 228–233.

1135 Badar, 'Mens Rea – Mistake of Law & Mistake of Fact in German Criminal Law: A Survey for International Criminal Tribunals' International Criminal Law Review (2005), p. 227, Bohlander, 'Principles of German Criminal Law' (2009), pp.63–67.

1136 See: Blomsma 'Mens rea and defences in European criminal law' (2012).

1137 HR 8 May 2001, *NJ* 2001, 480.

several shots at the victim in the crowded auditorium of the school, thereby wounding four other students and a teacher. The defence had argued that the intention of the father had not covered the wounding or killing of any bystanders. The Supreme Court, however, gave the argument short shrift and held that the father had accepted the considerable chance that bystanders got killed or wounded, by sending his son, who he knew to be an inexperienced shooter, equipped with a gun inside the school, which he also knew was crowded at the time.[1138] These examples nicely demonstrate that the broad concept of *dolus eventualis* will often mitigate the problem of differing intentions between co-perpetrators.[1139] In the Netherlands the mitigating function of *dolus eventualis* is even extended so far that classical English joint criminal enterprise cases can be subsumed under the concept. It seems that only the most blatant and unforeseeable deviations from what the perpetrators had in mind cannot be attributed to a co-perpetrator in the Netherlands.

The general principle in Germany on first sight seems to be slightly narrower as it holds that prima facie excesses of co-perpetrators exceeding the common plan cannot be attributed to the other participants.[1140] This is particularly so in cases where the perpetrator commits an entirely different deed then intended by the common plan.[1141] Each participant will only be liable as far as the actus reus of the crime in question is covered by his respective intent. Thus, if Scott and Gareth set out to burgle a house and Gareth unbeknown to Scott carries a gun with which he kills the house owner when caught in the act, Scott will not be liable for murder. If the deviation makes the participant causing it liable under another, more serious offence, the others can however still be liable for the lesser, included offence.[1142] In a pertinent case a mother had persuaded her son to jointly murder her aunt, so that the mother could inherit the aunt's fortune. Although reluctant, the son finally killed the aunt in the presence of his mother with a blunt object. The Supreme Court convicted the mother to life imprisonment for murder under specific aggravated circumstances (§211 GPC carrying the sentence of life imprisonment) as she fulfilled the constituent element of greed and killing by stealth, while the son was convicted to six years for simple murder (§212 GPC carrying a minimum sentence of 5 years).[1143]

1138 HR 17 September 2002, *LJN* AE6118.

1139 See also HR 14 October 2003, *NJ* 2004, 103, where it was planned to kill one man. The suspects waited for the victim outside a gym, only to find out that the victim was accompanied that night by another man. Eventually both men were killed and the Supreme Court held that the defendant had accepted the considerable chance that also the other man was killed, especially, as he continued to play his part in the crime even when it became apparent that the victim was not alone that night and when his partner attacked the second victim.

1140 Weisser, 'Täterschaft in Europa' (2011), pp. 368–373, Wessels and Beulke, 'Strafrecht Allgemeiner Teil, Die Straftat und ihr Aufbau' (2008), p. 189.

1141 Hamdorf, 'The concept of a Joint Criminal Enterprise and Domestic Modes of Liability for Parties to a crime: A Comparison of German and English Law' Journal of International Criminal Justice (2007), p. 215.

1142 See for instance: 27 January 2011 BGH HRRS 2011 Nr 375.

1143 25 July 1989 BGH NStZ 1990, 227. See also: 3 March 2011 BGH HRRS 2011, Nr 714.

Yet, matters become less clear if the committed collateral offence is not entirely different from what was initially envisaged. It is generally accepted that deviations which were reasonably foreseeable to occur in the course of committing the crime can be attributed. Likewise, if the participant is aware of the relevant fact or risk and was indifferent towards it (e.g. if he generally condones the commission of the offence and is indifferent as to the *modus operandi* of his partners) the deviation can be attributed.[1144] Hence the cardinal question in this context, barring a remarkable resemblance with the stance taken in English criminal law in regard to the notion of a joint criminal enterprise, is "whether the act committed by one of the perpetrators was fundamentally different from the performance of the common plan as foreseen by the co-perpetrator".[1145] The German Supreme Court has formulated the principle in the following way: "co-perpetrators will be liable for any acts that lie within a range of typical offences that one can expect to be committed given the circumstances of the case, namely if these (acts) will reach the aim of the other co-perpetrator to a similar extent, e.g. if one steals goods instead of money, if the goods can easily be sold".[1146] In another case the Supreme Court held: "all deviations from the common plan that one has to expect given the circumstances of the case and all deviations where the agreed performance is replaced by an act that is equally severe and dangerous, are covered by the co-perpetrator's intent, even if he has not reflected on them".[1147] Thus, if the deviation from the common plan was to be expected by the other participants, given the specific circumstances of the case at hand, or if the common plan can be interpreted to cover the deviation occurred, an attribution will be possible.

When evaluating whether or not a certain deviation was foreseeable, the concrete circumstances of the case at hand are to be taken into consideration. Thus, the severity and dangerousness of the situation and the conduct agreed upon have to be considered. It was for instance held that an attack carried out with blunt objects and superior numbers (5 vs. 1) already carried an inherent danger of a lethal escalation which made the fact that the participants were not aware that one of them carried a knife irrelevant for the attribution of liability.[1148] If the deviation fell

1144 Roxin, 'Strafrecht Allgemeiner Teil, Band II: Besondere Erscheinungsformen der Straftat' (2003), pp. 80–81. See also: 16 September 2009 BGH NStZ 2010, 81, 10 June 2009 BGH HRRS 2009 Nr 747, 15 September 2004 BGH NStZ 2005, 261, 15 June 2000 BGH NStZ-RR 2000, 327, 9 July 2002 BGH NStZ 2002, 597.

1145 Hamdorf, 'The concept of a Joint Criminal Enterprise and Domestic Modes of Liability for Parties to a crime: A Comparison of German and English Law' Journal of International Criminal Justice (2007), p. 216.

1146 Quoted in: Hamdorf, 'The concept of a Joint Criminal Enterprise and Domestic Modes of Liability for Parties to a crime: A Comparison of German and English Law' Journal of International Criminal Justice (2007), p. 216.

1147 2 December 2004 BGH NStZ-RR 2005, 71.

1148 10 June 2009 BGH HRRS 2009 Nr 747. For a more restrictive approach see: 3 March 2011 BGH HRRS 2011, Nr 714.

outside the common plan and was not reasonably foreseeable, it can however not be attributed to the other participants.

Whether negligent deviations from the common plan are to be attributed to other participants is contentious in Germany. The mistake of one co-perpetrator about the object of his conduct's impact *(error in persona vel objecto)* which is irrelevant for his liability is likewise irrelevant for the other participants.[1149] In a tragic-comic case with a rather peculiar legal twist, three robbers had agreed to shoot at anyone who would hinder their escape. During their escape from the scene of the crime one of the robbers shot at a person following them (with the *dolus eventualis* to kill), believing the pursuer to be a policeman. In fact he shot at one of his partners in crime, who was injured but not killed. The Supreme Court convicted the shooter, but more surprisingly also his injured partner for an (impossible) attempt to murder.[1150] The usage of weapons constituted part of the common plan and the fact that the shooter mistook the victim for a policeman was regarded as an irrelevant *error in persona*. Finally, in the so called intent negligent combinations, such as assault causing death (§226 GPC), each perpetrator must be negligent as to the more serious result that upgrades liability.[1151]

In England, where the broad and flexible concept of *dolus eventualis* is absent and where in general only (direct or indirect) intention is sufficient to trigger the liability of participants it has already been mentioned that in cases where a carrying out of a common resolution or agreement takes place, English criminal law applies the notion of "joint criminal enterprise".

8.2. The English doctrine of joint criminal enterprise

It has already previously been discussed that the doctrine of joint criminal enterprise in English law serves two distinct purposes. On the one hand it covers cases best referred to as forms of co-perpetration, i.e. cases where several persons agree to commit a criminal offence and subsequently do so. On the other hand it applies to scenarios where several people set out to commit crime X in the course of which another, unplanned crime Y is committed.[1152] The doctrine has emerged as a "jack of all trades", coping *inter alia* with mob and gang violence, linking crimes to a multitude of actors (perpetrators and accomplices) and blaming criminal actors for collateral damage caused in the course of bringing about a common criminal plan. One underlying rationale of the doctrine seems to be that crimes committed by groups are more dangerous than "ordinary" criminal enterprises and that these joint criminal ventures unfortunately only too readily escalate into the commission

---

1149 Schönke and Schröder, 'Kommentar zum Strafgesetzbuch' (2006), §25 Mn 96, Wessels and Beulke, 'Strafrecht Allgemeiner Teil, Die Straftat und ihr Aufbau' (2008), p. 190.

1150 23 January 1958 BGH NJW 1958, 836.

1151 17 October 1996 BGH NStZ 1997, 82.

1152 Krebs, 'Joint Criminal Enterprise' The Modern Law Review (2010), p. 584 et seq.

of greater offences.[1153] While this argument certainly carries some force and admittedly the law ought to address and deter these forms of collective wrongdoing, it should not be overlooked that as will be demonstrated in due course, the doctrine only just falls short of the notorious felony murder rule which held participants vicariously liable for the acts of another but which was formerly abolished in England in 1957.[1154]

The doctrine has been a permanent bone of contention and inconsistent decisions have contributed to the dispute among scholars.[1155] It is disputed whether the doctrine of joint criminal enterprise amounts to a separate form of participation (beyond aiding, abetting, counselling and procuring) or whether it was merely a descriptive term entailing no legal consequences.[1156] Also in these cases, so the argument goes, the secondary party engages in nothing more than assisting and encouraging the perpetrator by aiding, abetting, counselling or procuring the commisson of the offence.[1157] According to this stance, the peculiarity of the doctrine of joint criminal enterprise is that proof of a common purpose to commit an offence absolves the prosecution from adducing evidence of assisting and encouraging.

However, there also seems to be some support for the stance that the two doctrines are distinct. Professor Simester has for instance forcefully argued for the distinctiveness of the two doctrines. He argues that a joint criminal enterprise is distinct from standard forms of participation, both doctrinally and normatively.[1158] The Law Commission has considered both approaches and concluded that the differences produced by the two stances would not be sufficiently significant enough to matter in practice.[1159] The Court of Appeal seems to have endorsed the former view in the controversial decision of *R v Stewart & Schofield.* The court ruled:

> The allegation that a defendant took part in the execution of a crime as a joint enterprise is not the same as an allegation that he aided, abetted, counselled or procured the commission of that crime. A person who is a mere aider or abettor, etc. is truly a secondary party to the commission of whatever crime it is that the principal has committed although he may be charged as a principal. [...] In contrast, where the

---

1153 'Participating in Crime', LAW COM No 305 [2007], pp. 88–89, para 3.144 et seq.

1154 Fletcher, 'Basic Concepts of Criminal Law' (1998), p. 192.

1155 Parsons, 'Criminal Liability for the act of another: Accessorial Liability and the doctrine of joint enterprise' Journal of Criminal Law (1998), pp. 352–359.

1156 Defending the latter view: Smith and Hogan, 'Criminal Law' (2005), pp. 190–200. Smith, 'Criminal Liability of Accessories: Law and Law Reform' The Law Quarterly Review (1997), pp. 453 et seq. Reed, 'Joint Participation in Criminal Activity' Journal of Criminal Law (1996), pp. 310–324. Reed however acknowledges that there might be differences between aiding, etc. and a joint criminal enterprise.

1157 Smith and Hogan, 'Criminal Law' (2008), p. 207.

1158 Simester and Sullivan, 'Criminal Law: Theory and Doctrine' (2007), pp. 228–230.

1159 'Participating in Crime', LAW COM No 305 [2007], p. 61–64, para 3.56.

> allegation is joint enterprise, the allegation is that one defendant participated in the criminal act of another. This is a different principle.[1160]

It is submitted that this view seems to be correct. Not only do the doctrines rest on different rationales, but they, as will be shown subsequently also differ in regard to their actus reus and mens rea requirements.[1161]

A first difference becomes apparent when one juxtaposes the actus reus requirements of the two doctrines. While for secondary participation it needs to be proved that the participant assisted or encouraged the main offence, the decisive point in joint criminal enterprises is that the parties entered an agreement, or reached a reciprocal understanding to pursue the crime.[1162]

As already mentioned, the agreement that establishes a common purpose or plan does not need to be explicit. It suffices if an agreement (common plan) can be deduced from the acts of the parties.[1163] However, the doctrine's main thrust comes to the fore when one of the participants deviates from the common plan and commits an offence which was not an object of the joint venture. If secondary participation rules would apply to a criminal joint venture, the general principles outlined above would require the parties to have the aforementioned fault requirements (i.e. for aiding, abetting, etc.). However, as will be shown below, in a joint criminal venture foresight of the possibility that another offence will be committed in the course of the undertaking is sufficient.

In regard to deviations from the common plan several distinctions need to be drawn. In circumstances where the miscarriage was unexpected for A as well as for B, the doctrines of transferred malice, unintended mode, etc. remain applicable and apply to principals and accomplices.[1164]

The notion of joint criminal venture however becomes relevant where A deviates intentionally from the agreed course of conduct. The general principle here, which has been confirmed by the House of Lords[1165] is that B will be held liable for the collateral offence if he foresaw it as an incident of the joint enterprise.[1166] The test applied here is, similar to the test outlined before in the *Maxwell* case a (subjective) test of foresight of a significant possibility. Thus it is safe to conclude that foresight, or contemplation is the key ingredient here.[1167] In essence it is the foresight of a real risk of commission of the collateral offence and participation in the joint venture with that foresight that determines the culpability of the participant.

1160 R v Heather Stewart & Barry John Schofield [1994] EWCA Crim 3.

1161 For the opposite view see: R v Ian Bryan Stringer [2011] EWCA Crim 1396.

1162 Simester and Sullivan, 'Criminal Law: Theory and Doctrine' (2007), p. 221.

1163 Simester and Sullivan, 'Criminal Law: Theory and Doctrine' (2007), p. 222.

1164 Ashworth, 'Principles of criminal law' (2006), p. 428.

1165 R v Powell and English [1999] AC 1.

1166 Simester and Sullivan, 'Criminal Law: Theory and Doctrine' (2007), p. 223.

1167 See for instance: R v Starfield Badza [2009] EWCA Crim 1363, DPP v Nedrik-Smith [2006] EWHC 3015 (Admin), Attorney General's Reference (No 3 of 2004) [2005] EWCA Crim 1882.

In *R v English* the House of Lords elaborated on this principle.[1168] In this case A and B agreed to attack a police officer with wooden posts. In the course of the beating A drew a knife of which B was allegedly unaware and killed the officer. The court held that the stabbing would fall outside the scope of the joint criminal venture. Lord Hutton delivering the speech held: "to be guilty under the principle stated in *Chan Wing-siu v R* the defendant must foresee an act of the type which the principal committed, and that in the present case the use of the knife was fundamentally different to the use of a wooden post."[1169] Thus, the House of Lords has created a two step test for joint ventures. If the act of the perpetrator was not foreseen by the participant, he will not be held liable for the collateral offence, provided that the act was fundamentally different.

In the law of homicide, where the extended reach of this doctrine becomes most obvious, much emphasis will lie on the perpetrator's weapon of choice and whether or not this can be regarded as a lethal or non-lethal weapon. However, the assessment of dangerousness must be made in context and across all the evidence and not just focusing on the abstract nature of the weapon. In *R v Rahman* the defendants participated in an attack on a 16 year old boy as part of a mob, using several blunt objects.[1170] In the course of the attack one of the participants produced a knife and stabbed the boy fatally. The participants were convicted for murder and the Court of Appeal ruled that the jury could infer from the particular circumstances of the case that they had foreseen the use of the knife and the stabbing considering that the ferocity of the attack was not fundamentally different to what was contemplated by the appellants.[1171]

The defendants in this case had also argued that they had been unaware that anyone within the group carried a knife and furthermore were they unaware that anyone would kill with the intent to kill. Therefore, so the argument went, the fundamentally different act rule should apply. The court rejected the argument and held that it was not necessary that the perpetrator's intent to kill was known to others in the joint enterprise but that it was sufficient if they knew that there was a real risk of death or grievous bodily harm being caused intentionally. The decision was later confirmed by the House of Lords.[1172] This seems to confirm that the focal point of the doctrine is the foreseeable objective conduct of the perpetrator; i.e. an objective act, the possible commission of which was contemplated. This arguably objectifies the participant's liability, which leads to a broader scope of liability in this context than in Germany and the Netherlands.[1173] Yet, in these cases where the mens rea of the principal was different to the one of the secondary party, some

1168 R v Powell and English [1999] AC 1.
1169 R v Powell and English [1999] 1 AC 1, 28.
1170 R v Rahman and others (Court of Appeal) [2007] EWCA Crim 342.
1171 R v Rahman and others (Court of Appeal) [2007] EWCA Crim 342, para. 71–88, 91.
1172 R v Rahman (House of Lords) [2008] UKHL 45.
1173 Weisser, 'Täterschaft in Europa' (2011), pp. 436–439.

authorities now point to the availability of manslaughter as an alternative verdict for the secondary party.[1174]

If however the accomplice is not held liable for the perpetrator's conduct because he did not foresee it or it was fundamentally different, the question arises if the participant can be held liable as an accomplice to manslaughter while the principal committed murder. This would correspond to the prevalent approach in Germany, outlined above. The case law on this issue is however contradictory. Cases like *Stewart & Schofield*[1175] seem to endorse the possibility whereas cases like *Attorney General's Reference (No 3 of 2004)*[1176] reject it. The Law Commission, acknowledging the uncertain character of the authorities propounds the view that there ought to be no liability for manslaughter. In their view there should be no halfway house as far as liability for the victim's death is concerned.[1177]

8.3. Concluding remarks

In horizontal forms of perpetration several persons as equal partners set out to commit a criminal offence according to a common plan or purpose. Therefore often a certain division of labour will be agreed upon in advance. To hold them all primarily responsible for the occurred criminal harm the law aggregates the participants conduct so that in total it amounts to an actus reus. It follows that the objective elements of a crime can be dispersed among the different participants. The question however is how far this dispersion may reach for the attribution of liability. May the different elements be spatially and chronologically dispersed indefinitely? While generally neither a physical contribution to the commission of the crime nor physical presence will be necessary for liability to arise, mere presence alone will not suffice. Guilt by association ought to be anathema to any liberal society based on the rule of law. While a hard and fast rule seems hard to formulate, here it can be stated that the participant's contribution or role should be substantial or essential to the commission of the offence. Furthermore his intention must be the one laid down in the respective criminal offence and not merely directed at providing aid. This rough yardstick underlines once again the nature of actus reus and mens rea as communicating vessels as a minor objective contribution can be compensated by a more on the culpability side and vice versa.

As previously mentioned, the common plan underlying the criminal enterprise forms an essential pillar for attributing primary responsibility to the members of the criminal joint venture. This leads one to the outskirts of criminal liability and to the question to what extent individuals should be held liable for actions of their partners in crime, which fall outside the common plan or purpose. On first sight,

1174 See: R v Carpenter [2011] EWCA Crim 2568.
1175 R v Heather Stewart & Barry John Schofield [1994] EWCA Crim 3.
1176 Attorney General's Reference (No 3 of 2004) [2005] EWCA Crim 1882.
1177 'Participating in Crime', LAW COM No 305 [2007], p. 221.

the approaches taken regarding excesses occurring during the commission of a common plan seem quite different if one juxtaposes the Dutch and German with the English approach. The English concept of a joint criminal enterprise seems to come close to introducing collective responsibility at times, especially if one takes into consideration that the not very demanding test of subjective foresight in practice is sometimes further diluted to one of (objective) foreseeability.[1178] The Dutch and German approach on the other hand seems on first sight to remain firmly rooted in the principle of individual responsibility and culpability. However, the fact that deviations that were not entirely different from the acts that the participant intended and that the notion of *dolus eventualis* is in practice often interpreted objectively, so that it effectively amounts to foresight assimilates the stances taken by the three countries. It follows that the approach taken in regard to collateral offences committed in the course of the execution of a common plan and the basic principles of attribution applied are largely similar in all countries.

Generally (subjective) foresight of the occurrence of the collateral offence will be of crucial importance. Therefore the common plan or purpose and the inherent dangers it contains as well as the knowledge and awareness of the participant in regard to the likelihood of the occurrence of the collateral offence will be important factors. In the civil law traditions of Germany and the Netherlands, the notion of intention and in particular the broad and flexible notion of *dolus eventualis* provide room for the courts to attribute certain deviations from the common plan to all participants. The central question thereby is whether the deviation was still covered by the common purpose or plan of the partners in crime.

In the English common law system, where the concept of *dolus eventualis* is absent, the doctrine of joint criminal enterprise is applied to hold participants liable for collateral crimes. The principle applied there, just like in Germany and the Netherlands turns on contemplation and foresight. It meets the case of a crime foreseen as a possible incident of the common unlawful enterprise. Thus, a subjective test of foresight seems to be applied in all penal systems.[1179] It should however not be overlooked that this constitutes a rather broad approach to criminal liability and marks a departure from the general principle that liability is only imposed for conduct accompanied by the requisite intention, which in these cases is watered down to the purely cognitive concept of foresight. This can lead to harsh and draconian results in practice, especially in situations where the collateral offence is murder which in some penal systems such as England carries a mandatory minimum sentence.[1180]

Certainly, considerations of penal policy have contributed to the width of the law here. If one were to restrict liability to harm done in pursuance of the common

---

1178 Krebs, 'Joint Criminal Enterprise' The Modern Law Review (2010), p. 584.

1179 The less significant the deviation is from what was initially intended, the easier foresight will most likely be assumed.

1180 Sullivan, 'First degree murder and complicity – conditions for parity of culpability between principal and accomplice' Criminal Law and Philosophy (2007), p. 284.

goal, arguably gaps in the law could arise as joint criminal endeavours can arise spontaneously, are fast moving and have the tendency to escalate. If the prosecution had to prove every participant's individual conduct and intention, it would arguably become increasingly difficult to assure convictions in cases of joint criminal wrongdoing. Furthermore, from the viewpoint of the risk society or the culture of control it seems almost obvious that we would like to "encourage" our robbers to be careful robbers and to minimise the risk flowing from their criminal enterprise.

However, although one might be sympathetic towards these aims, efficiency arguments alone should never be able to justify an expansion of liability but rather such a step should require a justification in terms of principle as well. Therefore one can for instance focus on the participant's previous conduct. One possibility would therefore be to invoke a variation of the thin ice principle which in essence holds that those who skate on thin ice take the risk of falling in.[1181] According to this logic, a participant by joining forces with others assumes the risk that he will be held responsible for all the wrongs that are committed in realising this goal.[1182] While this argument certainly has some merits, especially where the collateral offence belongs to the same "family of offences" as is for instance the case where Martin and William set out to injure Laura but Laura unforeseen dies in the process, it cannot justify the imposition of liability where the connection with the collateral offence is more loose as for instance in regard to a burglary resulting in murder.

A related justification claims that by participating in crime X the participant has enhanced the risk of crime Y occurring.[1183] However, this justification suffers from the same shortcoming than the "acceptance of risk" rationale namely that it can account for the imposition of liability where the risk of the collateral offence is strictly speaking inherent in the original enterprise but that it encounters difficulties in case the link to the collateral offence becomes more tenuous.[1184]

Finally, a justification similar to the imposition of omission liability due to the creation of a dangerous situation can be invoked. Liability would then be imposed for the participant's failure to prevent his partner from acting as he did. His duty of care would stem from the creation of a dangerous situation which can be seen in joining the criminal enterprise which created the opportunity for the commission of the collateral offence.[1185] Arguably, the latter justification provides a sound rationale for imposing liability in situations where Arthur and Boris set out to burgle Hugh's house in the course of which Hugh is killed by Boris. Arthur is punished for failing to prevent the commission of the collateral offence which lay outside the common purpose, due to the fact that his own conduct created the dangerous situation which subsequently manifested in criminal harm. Despite the fact that this view provides a sound rationale for imposing liability in general it

1181 Ashworth, 'Principles of criminal law' (2006), pp. 73–74.
1182 Krebs, 'Joint Criminal Enterprise' The Modern Law Review (2010), p. 594.
1183 Krebs, 'Joint Criminal Enterprise' The Modern Law Review (2010), p. 595.
1184 Krebs, 'Joint Criminal Enterprise' The Modern Law Review (2010), p. 596.
1185 Krebs, 'Joint Criminal Enterprise' The Modern Law Review (2010), p. 597.

cannot explain why foresight of the occurred crime should suffice for the imposition of liability instead of the requisite intention of the crime in question. Omission liability, next to a violation of a duty of care still requires the presence of the mental element of the committed offence. Thus, while this approach in general can explain the imposition of liability in the case of collateral offences, it cannot explain why foresight should generally suffice for the imposition of liability.

In criminal law foresight is generally relied on as a means to infer volition in regard to fault elements but in regard to collateral offences foresight is used as a cognitive concept, which more or less on its own is deemed sufficient for the imposition of criminal liability. This however militates against general principles of criminal law as liability is imposed for crimes for which the participant lacked the required degree of culpability. The fact that the participant possesses the culpability for the initially envisaged crime and could foresee the commission of the collateral offence is not sufficient to establish the culpability for another, more serious crime. It is therefore submitted that not mere foresight but rather a recklessness standard as to the commission of the collateral offence should be required for the imposition of liability. Accordingly liability for a collateral offence could only be imposed when it stems from the conscious disregard of a substantial and unjustifiable risk whose disregard entails a gross deviation from the standard of care that a reasonable person would observe. Thus, the commission of the collateral offence must be a foreseeable, substantial and unjustifiable risk. In this case one could normatively establish acquiescence on the part of the participant and under these circumstances imposing liability for the collateral offence seems warranted and justified. As the collateral offence must constitute a substantial and unjustifiable risk this would exclude cases from liability where A is for instance unaware of B's violent proclivities or unaware that B brought a gun to the burglary. Thus, a certain degree of likelihood of the commission of the collateral offence should be established accompanied by acquiescence of its commission.

Such an approach would limit the scope of liability in these situations and make sure that liability is not only imposed for conduct accompanied by foresight but bring the imposition of liability back in line with the fundamental requirement of criminal law requiring that liability is only imposed in situations where the relevant conduct is accompanied by a sufficient degree of culpability.[1186] Although this approach would be narrower than the one prevalent in the English penal system, the proposed solution would still make the attribution of minor deviations from the common plan which according to common experience are likely to occur possible, as the substantial risk of committing these minor deviations will be inherent in the commission of the initial offence but would require a higher standard of fault in regard to loosely connected collateral offences as seems currently to be the case.

[1186] Krebs, 'Joint Criminal Enterprise' The Modern Law Review (2010), pp. 578–604.

9. Assisting a criminal offence

9.1. Introduction

Paradigmatically, in a framework of criminal liability the aider of a criminal offence takes an auxiliary position. His conduct, if analysed detached from the committed underlying offence is often innocuous, like handing someone a pack of matches or a screwdriver, and does not fulfil the actus reus of the criminal offence, while his intention is to "merely" assist the perpetrator.[1187] Furthermore, assisting or furthering the commission of an offence constitutes the outer limit of criminal liability regarding the scope of people involved in the commission of a crime. It has already been mentioned that this auxiliary position of the aider is in differentiated systems, such as Germany and the Netherlands, expressed in a mandatory mitigation of punishment for these forms of conduct. This also corresponds to the fact that the requirements regarding the weight and significance of the contribution for the commission of the offence are in comparison much less than for instance in regard to (co-) perpetration and instigation. Contrary to the instigator, the assistant does not cause, viz. induce somebody to commit an offence and neither closely cooperates with others to commit the offence jointly as would be the case in regard to co-perpetration. The assistant merely furthers the commission of the offence in one way or another.

9.2. Assistance in the Netherlands, Germany and England/Wales

Art 48 of the Dutch Penal Code outlines that aiding a criminal offence entails criminal liability:

> The following persons are liable as accessories to a serious offence:
>
> (1) those who intentionally assist during the commission of the serious offence;
> (2) those who intentionally provide the opportunity, means or information necessary to commit the serious offence.

From the wording of this provision one can already distil some important features. Firstly, the article distinguishes between two different forms of aiding. Art 48 (1) deals with so-called concurrent forms of aiding; the accessory assists *during* the commission of the criminal offence. Art 48 (2) on the other hand deals with preceding forms of aiding; the accessory provides the opportunity, means or information necessary *to* commit the criminal offence. The distinguishing factor between Art 48 (1) and (2) is thus the temporal aspect of when the aid was provided.

[1187] Van der Wilt, 'Ontwikkeling van nieuwe deelnemingsvormen' Delikt en Delinkwent (2007), p. 147.

§27 (1) of the German criminal code on the other hand provides generally that any person who intentionally assists another in the intentional commission of an unlawful act shall be convicted and sentenced as an aider. The German penal code does thus, contrary to the situation in the Netherlands, not distinguish between concurrent and preceding forms of aid. The point in time when assistance is provided is not considered important in German criminal law. It is generally accepted that both forms, i.e. concurrent[1188] and preceding[1189] assistance can give rise to liability pursuant to §27 (1) GPC.[1190] What is however considered crucial is that the provided assistance had an effect on the commission of the offence.[1191]

Another formal difference between the Dutch and the German approach is that assistance will only give rise to criminal liability in the Netherlands in cases where a felony was furthered. Facilitating a misdemeanour does not constitute a criminal offence.[1192] In Germany and also England such a limitation is absent. What matters in the German penal system is that the intentional commission of an unlawful act has been assisted, which excludes liability for aiding a negligence-based offence. This is contrary to the situation in England[1193] and the Netherlands[1194] but can be explained by the fact that the German penal system takes a unitarian approach in regard to participation in negligent offences. Everyone involved in the commission of the negligence-based offence is considered to be a perpetrator. Considering the fact that offences of negligence feature prominently in the German system, this peculiarity also puts the strict differentiated stance in regard to intentional crimes, generally prevalent in Germany into perspective.[1195]

The Dutch distinction between preceding and concurrent assistance bears some resemblance to the former English approach, where the term aid was commonly used to describe someone assisting the perpetrator at the time of the offence. However, this restriction has vanished and it is nowadays generally accepted that liability for providing aid can arise for any act of assistance before or at the time of the offence.[1196] Be that as it may, it follows from the foregoing that the prevalent view in all countries is that no temporal limitation regarding the provision of assistance applies for imposing liability in general. For the classification of a person's conduct as assistance to murder, it is immaterial whether the helper handed the perpetrator the gun the day before or at the killing. It should, however, be

1188 6 November 1984 BGH NStZ 1985, 165.

1189 1 August 2000 BGH NJW 2000, 3010.

1190 Roxin, 'Strafrecht Allgemeiner Teil, Band II: Besondere Erscheinungsformen der Straftat' (2003), p. 219.

1191 Roxin, 'Strafrecht Allgemeiner Teil, Band II: Besondere Erscheinungsformen der Straftat' (2003), p. 205, Schönke and Schröder, 'Kommentar zum Strafgesetzbuch' (2006), §27 Mn 10.

1192 This follows implicitly from Art 48 and explicitly from Art 52 DPC.

1193 Simester and Sullivan, 'Criminal Law: Theory and Doctrine' (2007), p. 216.

1194 Noyon, Langemeijer, Remmelink, 'Wetboek van Strafrecht' (2010), Art 48, note 8.

1195 Rotsch, 'Einheitstäterschaft statt Tatherrschaft' (2009), pp. 192 et seq.

1196 Smith and Hogan, 'Criminal Law' (2008), p. 186. See also: Attorney-General v Abel and Others [1984] QB 795, Sungarapulle Thambiah v The Queen [1966] AC 37.

pointed out here once more that the crucial difference between the different national notions of assistance is that in Germany and the Netherlands, the offence carries a mandatory mitigation of punishment, while in England *all* (four) forms of participation are formerly eligible to the same amount of punishment.[1197]

The majority of acts of assistance will certainly take place before the commission of the offence, as is for instance the case in regard to supplying the weapon for a robbery. Yet, if aid is provided at the time of the offence, demarcation problems between the notion of co-perpetration and aiding arise in differentiated systems, which prescribe a mandatory mitigation of punishment for assistance. Consider for instance the case of keeping a lookout. Depending on the importance and weight of this contribution for the commission of the offence, both liability for assistance and co-perpetration are conceivable. It is here where the boundaries between primary and secondary responsibility become blurred and elusive, and doctrinal friction in differentiated systems can arise. When discussing the concept of co-perpetration above, it has already been demonstrated that conduct that would traditionally have been perceived as providing assistance can nowadays also give rise to liability as a perpetrator.[1198] This arguably contradicts to some extent the very essence of a differentiated system of participation which considers the proper classification of different degrees of responsibility at the dogmatic level of attribution as vital for the just imposition of criminal liability.

There is however another important aspect which makes any added value of a distinction between concurring and preceding assistance doubtful. This aspect is the fact that the dividing line between the two is elusive and not always easy to draw in practice. It can for instance be difficult to subsume the conduct of the aider under a respective category. Is the lending of a knife with which the victim is subsequently killed, a preceding form of aid or a concurrent form, as the knife was used *at* the commission of the crime? Further problems can arise where it remains unclear which conduct of the aider triggered accessorial liability. Does the aider who, according to an agreement, drives the perpetrator to the vicinity of the *locus delicti*, and waits for him to return, so that he can subsequently escape, provide concurrent or preceding aid? These examples already illustrate that a hard and fast separation of the two categories of aid is not always achievable. The two forms can constitute polar opposites in certain situations, but in borderline cases the distinction becomes elusive.[1199]

In the Dutch penal system, the distinction between concurrent and preceding assistance has been watered down by a broad interpretation given to the means in Art 48 (2) DPC by jurisprudence. Scholars have also criticised the distinction and have argued that the circumscription of preceding assistance does not correspond anymore to the modern conception of criminal wrongdoing.[1200] Furthermore, a

---

1197 See also: Chapter III.3.

1198 See: Chapter III. 8.1.1.

1199 De Hullu, 'Materieel Strafrecht' (2009), p. 496.

1200 Wolswijk, 'Medeplichtigheid', in van der Leij (ed), Plegen en Deelnemen (2007), pp. 193–194.

distinction along chronological lines, so the argument goes, would not correspond to the developments in the realm of (co-) perpetration, outlined above, in which the role of temporal aspects in the attribution of liability has been considerably diminished.[1201]

The Dutch Supreme Court seems to have taken the aforementioned criticism to heart and started in recent jurisprudence to pay less and less attention to the distinction between the two forms of assistance.[1202] This development culminated in a decision where the Supreme Court declared the distinction between preceding and concurrent aid irrelevant for establishing secondary liability. The Supreme Court argued that as the relevance of physical conduct diminished in the framework of criminal liability in general, it would seem artificial to strictly distinguish between different forms of conduct in the context of aiding a criminal offence. In the opinion of the court this conclusion was further substantiated by the fact that the label attached to the offender in cases of aid was the same for both categories (i.e. guilty of aiding crime X) and that the level of punishment prescribed by Article 48 DPC was identical as well.[1203]

In the light of the foregoing, it is submitted that a distinction between preceding and concurrent aid *de lege lata* seems neither feasible nor warranted. It introduces a considerable degree of dogmatic complexity which is strictly speaking unnecessary and furthermore does not correspond to the modern conception of criminal wrongdoing. It is the weight and significance of the contribution for the commission of the offence that we consider important rather then the time when it is rendered. It is therefore proposed that *inter alia* for the sake of doctrinal simplification a European criminal law should not distinguish between concurrent and preceding aid but should rather prescribe in general terms the rendering of assistance.

9.3. The scope and nature of assistance

9.3.1. The scope of assistance

The concept of facilitation is an abstract one and under it a myriad different forms of conduct may be subsumed. One may facilitate the commission of an offence in a variety of ways and it seems impossible to neatly outline all forms of behaviour giving rise to liability. In general terms it can be stated that any conduct that furthered or made the commission of the offence easier, securer or swifter can be qualified as assistance. Lending a jemmy to a known burglar or providing weapons for a robbery, certainly constitute textbook examples. But also opening a bank account under a false name for a friend, in order to provide a vehicle for realising

---

1201 De Hullu, 'Materieel Strafrecht' (2009), p. 475.

1202 See: HR 24 March 2009, *LJN* BG4831. See also: WODC report, 'Daderschap en deelneming doorgelicht', p. 47.

1203 HR 23 March 2011, *LJN* BO2629.

the proceeds of forged cheques, hiring cars to be used in a robbery, transporting someone to or from the scene or lending a helping hand during the commission of the crime, as for instance holding a security guard at bay may all give rise to liability for assistance.

Generally one can draw a distinction here between material and immaterial aid and, as is the case in the German penal system between physical and psychological aid. Handing someone a knife clearly constitutes material help, while providing someone with the combination of a vault constitutes immaterial aid. The question is whether the means of aiding and abetting are confined to these types of cases. It is namely easily conceivable that a criminal offence is furthered by other means, as for instance by additional encouragement to commit the crime. This raises the question in how far moral support can constitute assistance. Prima facie one might not want to exclude these cases from the scope of liability as it is certainly conceivable that a form of rendered assistance did not physically influence the commission of the crime in the sense of (actively) lending someone a helping hand but nevertheless constituted assistance to the criminal offence. The inherent danger here is however that these, certainly exceptional cases, might swallow the rule and that criminal liability will be imposed for every contribution, however insignificant for the commission of the offence. Even worse, it could then also be argued that mere presence should trigger liability as it can be argued that the perpetrator felt reassured and encouraged to carry out the offence. The issue of moral or psychological assistance is also closely linked to the question whether or not the provided assistance must have had to some extent, a causal effect on the commission of the offence. The discussion will therefore return to that issue shortly in the context of causality.

It is generally accepted in all penal systems that assistance can also be provided by omission.[1204] However, in accordance with the requirements for omission liability discussed above, this can by and large only be the case when the assistant was under a duty of care and violated this duty. Thus, if a person had a duty of care due to his special relationship to the victim (e.g. parent-child), because he undertook a duty of care, because of his specific qualities (e.g. doctor), or because he created a dangerous situation, or was responsible for a source of danger, he can incur liability for assistance in case of nonfeasance. That can for instance lead to liability where a person was under a duty of care if he previously created a dangerous situation, which would have required him to intervene into the wrongdoing committed by another. The German Supreme Court convicted for instance a cell-mate for facilitating the infliction of bodily harm by inmate A to another (B) by omission, as he had contributed to the "atmosphere of violence" prevalent in the cell, as he had

---

[1204] De Hullu, 'Materieel Strafrecht' (2009), pp. 469–470, Roxin, 'Strafrecht Allgemeiner Teil, Band II: Besondere Erscheinungsformen der Straftat' (2003), p. 201, Schönke and Schröder, 'Kommentar zum Strafgesetzbuch' (2006), §27 Mn 15–16, Smith and Hogan, 'Criminal Law' (2008), pp. 190–191, Wolswijk, 'Medeplichtigheid', in van der Leij (ed), Plegen en Deelnemen (2007), pp. 190–191.

participated in the afflictions and degradations against the weak fellow-inmate. He had *inter alia* in this long lasting history of abuse failed to intervene when on one occasion A had tied B with his hands behind his back to a chair and pulled a plastic bag over his head. B however managed to free himself and remove the bag from his head.[1205]

On the other hand, not every omission can lead to accessorial liability. This was for instance established by the Dutch Supreme Court when it was held that the mere knowledge that a crime will be committed was insufficient to create a duty of care and trigger criminal liability.[1206] This did however not mean that the defendant could not be held responsible in this case at all. He was aware of the perpetrator's plan to kill his grandmother, and had bought together with him two hammers, with which the victim was killed. The Supreme Court might have rejected the attribution of accessorial liability by omission, but nevertheless convicted the defendant for actively aiding the offence. Further examples might include a security guard who deliberately omits to lock a door to enable burglars to enter or looks the other way during the theft of a big shipment of coffee as had been agreed beforehand with the thieves.[1207]

As already mentioned, especially in the English penal system accessorial liability can also arise in cases where A has the power or right to control the actions of another and he refrains deliberately from exercising it. In these circumstances, A's inactivity may be regarded as encouragement and therefore as aiding. Thus if A lets the intoxicated B drive his car, which he subsequently drives recklessly he may be found guilty of aiding dangerous driving.[1208]

9.3.2. The nature of assistance

It has already been discussed that the perceived nature of liability and rationale of punishment regarding participation in crime has important repercussions on the scope of liability as well as the guise of the rules of participation.[1209] Traditionally the liability of the participant is in all investigated penal systems considered to be derived from the wrongdoing of the perpetrator. Participation is thus perceived to amount to involvement in someone else's criminal conduct and not as an autonomous form of wrongdoing.

It is, however, also possible to conceive of assistance as a separate offence; an autonomous form of wrongdoing. The aforementioned English Serious Crime Act 2007 constitutes an example of such an approach, as it *inter alia* puts facilitation on

---

1205 12 February 2009 BGH NStZ 2009, 231. For a comparable Dutch decision see: HR 12 December 2000, *NJ* 2002, 516.

1206 HR 27 November 2001, *NJ* 2002, 517. For a comparable German decision see: 17 November 2009 BGH NStZ 2010, 224.

1207 HR 21 February 1921, *NJ* 1921, 465, 'Participating in Crime', LAW COM No305 [2007], p. 187.

1208 See: R v Webster [2006] EWCA Crim 415.

1209 See: Chapter III. 4.2.

an inchoate/endangerment rationale. The crucial difference between the two approaches thus lies in their respective focus. If liability is derivative then the focus rests on the harm committed by the perpetrator, from which the liability of the participant is derived. If liability is however inchoate, then the focus turns to the conduct of the participant and the prospect of harm, albeit remote, that his behaviour may cause.

The focus would be similar if participation, and more particularly facilitation, were to be perceived in terms of endangerment. If one perceives the increase in risk regarding the successful commission of the primary offence as the rationale for punishing participants, facilitation would evolve into an offence of abstract endangerment.[1210] One can also take this line of reasoning one step further and consider the abstract endangerment of the underlying protected legal interest as the rationale for punishing facilitation. This would be tantamount to an inchoate liability approach, as liability would already arise from the moment that aid was provided (regardless of whether the assistance had any impact on the commission of the offence and regardless of whether the perpetrator carries out the offence). Finally a medium position between the derivative and the autonomous conception of the assistant's liability can be opted for as well. It could for instance be argued that liability is derivative as the wrongdoing committed by the perpetrator is attributed to the participant, but at the same time autonomous; as such an attribution of liability can only take place if the participant's contribution can be seen as an autonomous attack on the protected legal interest.[1211]

Depending on which view one adopts here regarding the rationale of punishment, this will have implications in regard to the scope and guise of liability. First, it will determine the scope of liability concerning the issue of attempted aid and second, it will shape the guise of liability as to the question whether or not the provided assistance must have exerted a causal effect on the commission of the primary offence committed by the perpetrator in order for liability to arise. The latter question will be discussed in more detail in the subsequent section.

Regarding the former question, the essential issue concerns cases where aid or assistance has been provided, but the perpetrator subsequently does not commit the offence. If liability is considered to be derivative or based on a concrete endangerment rationale, liability is generally excluded in those cases due to the lack of a sufficient base for liability to be derived from or due to the lack of a concrete endangerment of the underlying protected legal interest respectively. If liability is however inchoate or based on an abstract endangerment rationale, then attempted aid, prima facie, will be punishable. This will be the case, because if the wrongdoing of the participant is considered to be autonomous, then criminal liability will arise

1210 Roxin, 'Strafrecht Allgemeiner Teil, Band II: Besondere Erscheinungsformen der Straftat' (2003), pp. 195–196, Schönke and Schröder, 'Kommentar zum Strafgesetzbuch' (2006), §27 Mn 9.

1211 Roxin, 'Strafrecht Allgemeiner Teil, Band II: Besondere Erscheinungsformen der Straftat' (2003), pp. 130–132.

as soon as he provides assistance, irrespective of the subsequent conduct of the perpetrator.

Traditionally, attempted aid fell outside the scope of liability in all investigated penal systems, but considerations of crime control, as evidenced by the Serious Crime Act 2007 in England, might shed some doubt on this seemingly evident exclusion of liability. If the focus of criminal law were to exclusively rest on the criminal proclivities of citizens or their disrespect for the legal order, as expressed in their conduct, it seems at least debatable that attempted aid should give rise to liability. A person who intentionally assists the prospective commission of a criminal wrong, arguably has manifested his or her criminal proclivities and disrespect for the legal order and should therefore incur criminal liability. While such an approach might correspond well to the social sentiments in a risk society or culture of control, where crime prevention and the detection, control and management of risk factors such as antisocial and lawbreaking citizens has become the paramount interest, it should not be overlooked that focusing on the criminal attitude or proclivities of citizens carries an inherent risk of overcriminalisation. It is submitted that criminal law should only come into play when the conduct in question had a significant impact on the legal order and the protected legal interest to justify the imposition of criminal punishment and stigma. With inchoate liability punishment is generally not imposed for causing harm but rather for creating or increasing a risk of harm. This form of liability however carries an inherent danger of criminalising conduct only remotely connected to the harm prescribed by law. It is therefore proposed here that liability for assistance should, just as in national law, in the context of European criminal law best be considered derivative in order to avoid criminalisation of conduct at an unwarrantably early stage.

Inchoate liability in regard to criminal attempts and preparation will be discussed in chapter IV in greater detail. In this context suffice it to say that inchoate liability for participation shifts the focus from the wrong committed by the perpetrator, to the risk of harm created by the accessory's conduct and his individual dangerousness.

9.4. The furthering effect of aid (causality)

It has already been mentioned that with the notable exception of the Serious Crime Act 2007 in England, all investigated penal systems regard liability for assisting a criminal offence to be derived from the liability of the perpetrator. A repercussion of the derivative nature of liability for assistance is that it is generally thought that liability for assistance requires a connection between the act of assistance and the commission of the offence by the perpetrator. The idea that some connection between the provided assistance and the occurred criminal wrong should be established is based on the general view that assistance constitutes involvement in the criminal offence of another and not a separate, autonomous offence. If one were to dispense with the causal connection as a prerequisite for liability for assistance, this would transform the offence into an offence of either abstract or concrete endangerment and thus in a separate offence, consummated with the provision of assistance.[1212]

However, the precise quality of this connection is elusive and a bone of contention among scholars and practitioners. Consider for instance the following example. Max, aware of Kieran's intentions to kill his diabolical neighbour Michele, lends Kieran his gun which he puts into his coat pocket. The next day Kieran persuades Michele to accompany him to a bar in order to sort out their differences. However, Kieran has no intentions to resolve his quarrels and drives to a secluded place in the forest. When Michel realises that he has been deceived an argument follows, resulting in a fight in which Kieran suffocates and kills Michele without making use of the supplied gun.[1213]

Intuitively one might argue here that Max should not incur liability as his acts of assistance did not have any bearing on the actual outcome of the offence. Yet, on second thought, it might be arguable that although the gun played no tangible or physical causal role in the commission of the offence, it might nevertheless have strengthened Kieran's resolve or given him more security to commit the offence.[1214] Whether or not one favours the imposition of criminal liability in these situations depends on the required quality of the causal link between the assistance and the commission of the offence. An extreme position here would require that the provided assistance was a *conditio sine qua non* (or 'but for' connection) for the commission of the offence. This however, would cast the net of criminal liability too narrowly, as assistance can be a 'but for' condition for the occurred criminal result as is for instance the case if the assistant provides the combination of a bank vault without which the criminal enterprise would have been bound to fail; however, this does not necessarily always have to be the case. A person who helps a burglar to carry his equipment and a leather to the scene of the crime and secures it while the burglar climbs into the building assists the criminal offence, even though the perpetrator could have carried the equipment himself and would have managed to enter the building without the provided assistance anyway.[1215]

In Germany, the prevalent view among scholars requires a causal link between the assistance and the offence, in the sense that the assistance must at least partially have had a causal effect on the commission of the offence.[1216] Thus, the provided assistance must have at least influenced the mode or manner of the commission of the offence. Jurisprudence, however has, presumably to overcome evidentiary difficulties, adopted a different approach and merely requires that the assistance has

1212 Schönke and Schröder, 'Kommentar zum Strafgesetzbuch' (2006), §27 Mn 10.

1213 Example from: Bohlander, 'Principles of German Criminal Law' (2009), p. 172.

1214 Bohlander, 'Principles of German Criminal Law' (2009), p. 172.

1215 Roxin, 'Strafrecht Allgemeiner Teil, Band II: Besondere Erscheinungsformen der Straftat' (2003), p. 193.

1216 Roxin, 'Strafrecht Allgemeiner Teil, Band II: Besondere Erscheinungsformen der Straftat' (2003), pp. 192–195, Schönke and Schröder, 'Kommentar zum Strafgesetzbuch' (2006), §27 Mn 7, Wessels and Beulke, 'Strafrecht Allgemeiner Teil, Die Straftat und ihr Aufbau' (2008), p. 208.

furthered the offence. A causal link between the assistance and the commission of the offence is not required by the courts. An illustration of this approach can be found in the case of a student network involved in the 9/11 terrorist attacks in New York. The defendant in this case, a Moroccan citizen, studied electrical engineering at the University of Hamburg. He joined a group of radical Islamic students to which *inter alia* also Mohamed Atta and Marwan Alshehhi belonged who in September 2001 carried out the attacks on the World Trade Centre. Under the leadership of Atta the group evolved into a hierarchical organisation. When Atta and others left Germany to commence their pilot training, the defendant *inter alia* kept up the appearance that the men still resided in Germany and when the men encountered financial difficulties, he remitted, following the orders of another combatant 5000 Marks to the American bank account of the terrorists. However, the transaction proved to be cumbersome and before the money arrived in the United States the account had already been topped up by another combatant. The Supreme Court held that for assistance to be proven it sufficed that the conduct in question furthered or facilitated the offence and that a causal link was not required. Therefore it was considered immaterial that the terrorist attacks might also have taken place without the efforts of the defendant, as the preparations, etc. might not have been detected anyway. By the same token the Supreme Court regarded as immaterial that the remittance of the 5000 Mark in hindsight proved superfluous, as the terrorists had already received money from another source to continue their preparations in the US.[1217]

Whether or not the different approaches taken by German scholars and jurisprudence will make much of a difference in practice is open for debate. The two approaches seem at odds with each other on first sight, but on closer scrutiny the differences between the two seem marginal. Because arguably, if the provided assistance must have furthered the commission of the offence, then there must have been some impact on the offence itself and thus some sort of causal connection.[1218] Requiring "merely" a furthering effect, introduces a degree of flexibility and diminishes the circumscription of liability as it will often be possible to argue that a particular form of assistance had an impact on the commission of the offence and thus a furthering effect, despite the absence of a clear causal link. This makes it possible for the courts to circumvent evidentiary problems in practice as it makes the imposition of liability easier especially in cases of so-called psychological aid, respectively moral support and assistance by omission, where a clear causal link is often difficult to establish.

The approach taken by German jurisprudence seems to correspond to the one taken by their counterparts in the Dutch penal system. According to jurisprudence it needs to be established in regard to Art 48 (1) that the aid furthered or facilitated

[1217] 16 November 2006 BGH NJW 2007, 384. See also: 8 March 2001 BGH NJW 2001, 2409.

[1218] Bohlander, 'Principles of German Criminal Law' (2009), p. 172, Roxin, 'Strafrecht Allgemeiner Teil, Band II: Besondere Erscheinungsformen der Straftat' (2003), p. 194.

the commission of the offence[1219] and in regard to Art 48 (2) that the aid facilitated or made the commission of the offence possible.[1220]

An illustration of the approach taken in the Netherlands can be found in the so called *Van Anraat* case. Van Anraat, a Dutch business man had during the 1980's exported approximately 1400 metric tons of chemicals to Iraq or respectively Iraqi companies, which he knew constituted a precursor for the production of mustard gas. The gas was subsequently used in attacks against the Kurdish minority in Iraq resulting in a high death toll. In this case the question arose which role the defendant's shipment of chemicals played in the production of mustard gas and its subsequent use on the battle field, taking into account that also other entities from all over the world had delivered chemicals to Iraq and that the chemicals could also be used for other, legal purposes i.e. the textile industry. The court rejected the latter argument holding that it was unlikely that the chemicals were used in Iraq's underdeveloped textile industry. In regard to the usage of the chemicals for the production of mustard gas, the court, taking into consideration several factors such as the total quantity of chemicals exported to Iraq as well as the amount confiscated and destroyed by allied forces after the end of the war, concluded that at least 38% of the chemical precursor for mustard gas between the year 1980 and 1988 had been supplied by the defendant. The court reiterated that regarding liability for assistance it was not necessary that the provided aid constituted a *conditio sine qua non*. It was sufficient that the conduct in question had furthered the commission of the offence and convicted the defendant for assisting the production of chemical weapons.[1221]

It has already been mentioned that in the English penal system, aid generally does not require any causal connection.[1222] However, some sort of connection between the assistance and the commission of the offence seems to be required, which in the case of aiding finds expression in the requirement to demonstrate that assistance of some sort was *in fact* provided.[1223] This view is also shared by the Law Commission which in its 2007 report on Participating in Crime holds that although some authorities seem to imply a causal link, this would be by no means clear and the precise nature of the connection would be elusive.[1224] The pivotal point in the Law Commissions view is that the conduct of the secondary party has made a contribution to the commission of the offence.[1225] What is vital is thus that there was actual assistance.

Yet, even if no actual assistance can be established, a person might nevertheless incur criminal liability by virtue of sections 44–46 of the Serious Crime Act 2007.

1219 HR 7 April 1998, *NJ* 1998, 558.

1220 HR 10 June 1997, *NJ* 1997, 585.

1221 Hof 's-Gravenhage, 9 May 2007, *LJN* BA4676; HR 30 June 2009, *NJ* 2009, 481.

1222 See: Chapter III. 5.2.1. Smith and Hogan, 'Criminal Law' (2008), p. 186.

1223 Simester and Sullivan, 'Criminal Law: Theory and Doctrine' (2007), pp. 199, 203. See also: A-G v Able [1984] QB 795, 812.

1224 'Participating in Crime', LAW COM No 305 [2007], p. 32.

1225 'Participating in Crime', LAW COM No 305 [2007], p. 32.

As already mentioned, these provisions provide for liability in cases where acts capable of assisting and encouraging have been performed, irrespective of whether the offence is committed by the perpetrator. This in essence amounts to the imposition of criminal liability for attempted aid and potentially broadens the scope of criminal liability considerably.

It follows from the foregoing that if one leaves certain doctrinal peculiarities aside the approach taken in all investigated penal systems regarding the furthering effect of assistance is largely similar. As a corollary of the assistant's derivative liability some connection between the assistants' conduct and the commission of the offence must be proven. However a 'but for' connection, or put differently, proof that the assistance constituted a *conditio sine qua non* for the commission of the offence is not required.

To summarise, it can be stated that liability for assistance is generally imposed for a person's loose association with the offence committed by the perpetrator rather than for a person's direct instrumentality.[1226] The prevalent view of the courts seems not to require that the offence would not have occurred 'but for' the assistant's conduct but rather that the assistant's conduct 'might have' furthered the commission of the offence.[1227]

Moral support or psychological assistance

A problematic issue in regard to the furthering effect of assistance concerns cases which in the penal systems of Germany and the Netherlands are dubbed moral support or psychological assistance. Moral support, such as encouragement or the promise of help, can further the commission of a crime if the perpetrator was actually supported in his decision to commit the criminal offence.[1228] It arguably constitutes the lower limits of accessorial liability with the cardinal question being: of which quality a contribution must be in order to warrant the imposition of punishment. This form of aid does thus not influence the way in which the crime was committed but rather works on the mind of the perpetrator. What these civil law systems usually construe as psychological assistance will in the English penal system often amount to encouragement.[1229] Therefore this form of conduct could amount to abetting or counselling in the English penal system as well as it may give rise to inchoate liability under the Serious Crime Act 2007. However, it should be pointed out here that under this category in Germany and the Netherlands, not only

1226 Wilson, 'Central Issues in Criminal Theory' (2002), p. 191.

1227 Wilson, 'Central Issues in Criminal Theory' (2002), pp. 191–193. See also: Fletcher, 'Rethinking Criminal Law' (1978), pp. 581–682.

1228 Wolswijk, 'Medeplichtigheid', in van der Leij (ed), Plegen en Deelnemen (2007), p. 196. Schönke and Schröder, 'Kommentar zum Strafgesetzbuch' (2006), §27 Mn 12–14. See also: Charalambakis, 'Zur Problematik der psychischen Beihilfe', in Schünemann, et al. (eds), Festschrift für Claus Roxin (2001), pp. 625–639.

1229 Hart and Honoré, 'Causation in the Law' (1985), p. 386, Fn 19.

psychological means of aid, like encouragement, can be subsumed, but also material aid, like the lending of burglary tools can be pigeon-holed under this category. Consider for instance cases, where the provided aid was not used in the commission of the criminal offence. The burglar might for instance not need the tools provided, as to his surprise the front door of the house he wants to break-in is unlocked. The provided tools can nevertheless be seen to have furthered the commission of the offence, as the aid constituted moral support and backup for the perpetrator.[1230]

While this solution seems right in general, there is an intrinsic danger in accepting psychological assistance as a way of furthering the commission of an offence. As moral support is a notoriously vague concept, a broad interpretation of the term could result in an expansion of liability, where every approval of a criminal enterprise would result in accessorial liability. It is arguably here where the line between culpable conduct and guilt by association becomes rather thin. And in fact, in the past this form of assistance has often functioned as a catch-all clause under which, cases of concealed instigation were subsumed for evidentiary reasons or where cases of attempted aid or mere presence at the scene were pigeon-holed as these cases were considered to warrant the imposition of punishment.[1231] Accordingly this form of assistance can in practice be difficult to distinguish from instigation and can lead to the blurring of boundaries between the two concepts. As psychological assistance influences the mind of the perpetrator as instigation would, although to a qualitatively lesser extent, it should be pointed out here that it can sometimes be difficult in practice to establish whether the desire to commit the offence was induced (instigation) or whether the pre-existing desire was corroborated by the aider.[1232]

It has already been said that cases of counselling as for example providing technical advice for the commission of the offence can be subsumed here. More controversial are however cases where the contribution is considered to have strengthened the resolve of the perpetrator to commit the offence. Here one can encounter considerable evidentiary difficulties. However this does not generally negate the fact that such cases can give rise to criminal liability. The German Supreme Court for instance convicted a defendant for aiding rioting (§125 GPC) as he had marched together with 25 fellow skinheads, some of them were equipped with blunt objects, to a local bar which in their view was a meeting point of "leftist imbeciles", to teach them a lesson. Some members of the group entered the bar and assaulted the customers, but the defendant remained outside the premises. The defence had argued that merely marching together could not constitute aid but the court rejected the argument and ruled that the conduct of the defendant indicated

1230 Wolswijk, 'Medeplichtigheid', in van der Leij (ed), Plegen en Deelnemen (2007), pp. 196–198.

1231 See for instance: 7 May 1982 BayObLG NJW 1982, 1891. In this case a husband was convicted for (psychologically) assisting his wife in driving without a license as she had transported him to the nearest local pub to do him a favour. See also: 8 August 1995 BGH NStZ-RR 1996, 1.

1232 Wolswijk, 'Medeplichtigheid', in van der Leij (ed), Plegen en Deelnemen (2007), p. 198.

the defendant's solidarity with the criminal enterprise and thereby strengthened the resolve of those carrying out the assault.[1233]

In a comparable English decision A had killed V during a fight with a knife. B and C had joined the chase with hostile intent but allegedly took no part in the fight nor in the stabbing. The Court of Appeal however upheld their conviction for murder and argued that there was sufficient evidence that A was encouraged and assisted in the attack which he carried out on V by the conduct of the appellants in joining in the chase. He "had the comfort and spur of knowing that he was not on his own, but had the support of the appellants and the reasonable expectation that they would come to his aid if he needed it".[1234]

The not always unambiguous jurisprudence in Germany requires in contemporary decisions some form of active contribution in order for liability to arise. Mere presence and approval is therefore considered insufficient.[1235] The German Supreme Court for instance acquitted a defendant who had accompanied his friend on a trip from Düsseldorf to Utrecht and back in January 2009. The driver had not informed the defendant of the purpose of the trip, namely the importation of 827g of cocaine nor had he explained to him that his presence should make him feel more secure. He had initially promised him a "free night-out" in Düsseldorf as well as a visit to a local brothel at his expense. Only on their way back from Utrecht, approximately 30 minutes from the German border had the driver informed the defendant that they were transporting drugs. The Court of lower instance had convicted the defendant for aiding the importation of drugs, but the Supreme Court quashed the conviction and acquitted the defendant as he had not actively contributed to the commission of the offence, due to the fact that he was only a passenger in the car.[1236] The court however pointed out that in the case of a driver, the situation would be different as he would, if he continued the ride then actively further the commission of the offence.

This case can be compared to the English case of *R v Coney*.[1237] The defendants in that case watched an illegal price fight and were in first instance convicted of aiding and abetting assault. However, there was no evidence that they took any part in the management or that they said or did anything. The court therefore quashed their conviction since nothing they had done could be construed as encouragement to fight or continue fighting. The underlying principle therefore seems to be the same in both cases. There must be some form of active (psychological) assistance or encouragement in order to give rise to liability. To avoid the imposition of liability by mere association the law should arguably require that the assistant's conduct

1233 21 March 2000 OLG Naumburg NJW 2001, 2034. See also: 15 July 1999 BGH NStZ 1999, 609, where it was held that also the mere promise of assistance could give rise to liability.

1234 R v Ian Bryan Stringer [2011] EWCA Crim 1396.

1235 Schönke and Schröder, 'Kommentar zum Strafgesetzbuch' (2006), §27 Mn 12.

1236 17 November 2009 BGH NStZ 2010, 224. See also: 13 January 1993 BGH NStZ 1993, 233, 17 March 1995 BGH NStZ 1995, 490, 24 October 2001 BGH NStZ 2002, 139, 14 November 2006 BGH NStZ-RR 2007, 37.

1237 R v Coney and Others [1882] 8 QBD 534.

furthered the commission of the offence, provided it falls outside a certain de minimis range.

Such a restrictive approach is certainly necessary as otherwise failures to act even without a corresponding duty of care could give rise to criminal liability, which would amount to an expansion of criminal liability through the backdoor. However, as the aforementioned case of drug trafficking shows, the line between liability and non-liability is a fine one and sometimes minor difference in circumstances can tip the scale in one direction or another.

In Germany the concept seems to enjoy the strongest support. At least in theory, here even the provision of an additional motive to someone who is already determined to commit a criminal offence can give rise to liability.[1238] Yet, in the Dutch penal system, the Dutch Supreme Court seems to look at these cases with more reluctance. In a pertinent case, where a mother was accused of aiding by providing information as she had told her sons that they would obtain a substantial amount of money from a life insurance if they would kill their violent father, the Supreme Court held that her statement had not furthered or facilitated the commission of the crime, as it merely provided an additional ground to commit the offence.[1239] In the eyes of the court, providing additional grounds, thus, does not mean that the commission of the offence has been furthered. Such an effect has however to be proven in order to establish accessorial liability.

9.5. The fault element of assistance

The fault element plays an important role in the realm of accessorial liability. As the liability of accessories is in principle derived from the main offence of the perpetrator, the mental element functions as a lynch pin between the act of the perpetrator and the act of his accomplice. Furthermore, as the acts of an accomplice can be innocuous on first sight, like lending someone a screwdriver, the fault requirements need to compensate for the objectively "missing" culpable conduct. In other words, the further one expands the net of criminal liability beyond paradigm cases, the more emphasis needs to be put on the question how closely a person should be involved in the crime's commission if (s)he is to be held liable as an accessory.[1240]

On first sight, the mens rea standards regarding assistance are remarkably similar in the investigated countries. It is generally required that (i) a person intends to assist the act of the principal and (ii) that he knew the essential matters that constitute the objective elements of the offence. Thus, one can in general terms speak here of a requirement of double intention. Discrepancies in regard to the first

1238 Schönke and Schröder, 'Kommentar zum Strafgesetzbuch' (2006), §27 Mn 12.

1239 HR 10 June 1997, *NJ* 1997, 585.

1240 De Hullu, 'Materieel Strafrecht' (2009), p. 471, Duff, '"Can I help you?" Accessorial liability and the intention to assist' Legal Studies (1990), pp. 165–181.

requirement seem to emerge here due to the different mens rea standards applied in the civil law countries of Germany and the Netherlands and the common law system of England. The former, as already mentioned, include in their concept of intent, the notion of *dolus eventualis*, while in the latter system only direct and indirect intent are covered by the concept of intention. The functional equivalent to the civil law notion of *dolus eventualis* is the concept of recklessness, which however constitutes a form of blameworthiness distinct from intention.[1241] In Germany and the Netherlands *dolus eventualis* generally suffices for liability for assistance to arise.[1242] This could suggest that the scope of liability in England is narrower as the prevalent view requires that the secondary party must not only intend his(her) action, but must furthermore act with the intent to aid abet, counsel or procure the main offence of the principal.[1243] Hence the secondary party must have been aware that the aid, etc. will be a virtual certain consequence of his conduct.[1244] In other words, recklessness is regarded as insufficient.[1245]

Although the situation seems different in Germany and the Netherlands where *dolus eventualis* is deemed sufficient for the establishment of liability, on closer scrutiny the three systems might not differ so drastically in their approaches after all. This is because generally speaking, *dolus eventualis* will be established if it can be proven that the assistant according to the circumstances of the case could not reasonably believe that the offence will not be committed. Thus, in a pertinent German case the Supreme Court convicted a lawyer for aiding the taking of hostages as she had smuggled a gun inside a prison in order to facilitate, or so she believed, the suicide of one of her clients. He however pulled the gun during an interrogation, took a recording clerk hostage and shot the prosecutor before he turned the gun against himself. The court argued that by providing the gun she had intentionally aided the taking of hostages.[1246]

Regarding the second requirement the prevalent state of affairs in all investigated penal system is nicely summarised by the English case of *Johnson v Youden* where it was held that: "Before a person can be convicted of aiding and abetting the commission of an offence he must at least know the essential matters which constitute that offence".[1247] In the leading English case of *R v Bryce*, which further developed the general rule set out in *Johnson v Youden* the Court of Appeal held that it would be sufficient that the secondary party at the time of doing the act contemplated the commission of the offence by the principal, i.e. *he foresaw it as a*

1241 See: Blomsma 'Mens rea and defences in European criminal law' (2012).

1242 De Hullu, 'Materieel Strafrecht' (2009), pp. 471–472. See also: HR 4 March 2008, *NJ* 2008, 156. Schönke and Schröder, 'Kommentar zum Strafgesetzbuch' (2006), §27 Mn 19. See also: 21 May 1999 BayObLG NStZ 1999, 627.

1243 Simester and Sullivan, 'Criminal Law: Theory and Doctrine' (2007), p. 208.

1244 Smith, 'Strafbare Voorbereiding, Een rechtsvergelijkend onderzoek' (2003), p. 170.

1245 Simester and Sullivan, 'Criminal Law: Theory and Doctrine' (2007), p. 208. See also: Chapter III. 5.2.2.

1246 28 November 1989 BGH NJW 1990, 1055.

1247 [1950] 1 KB 544.

real or substantial risk or real possibility.[1248] This amounts in essence to a recklessness test. Thus the courts have interpreted knowledge as tantamount to foresight of the probable existence of the essential matters of the main offence.[1249]

This corresponds to the situation in Germany where it is generally accepted that the assistant must at least expect and accept that his conduct furthers the commission of the offence by the perpetrator. If the assistant is aware however that the criminal offence despite his involvement can never materialise, then no liability can arise. Thus, in a case where the defendant had in a spirit of revenge wrongfully convinced his friend A that he could supply several kilos of heroin, which A in turn planned to sell on and therefore entered into negotiations with potential buyers, the German Supreme Court acquitted the defendant of assisting the selling of illegal drugs, as he was aware that the envisaged offence could never be committed as he was not in a position to supply the promised heroin.[1250] This also excludes cases from liability where Wallace seemingly agrees to help his friend Steward to murder his unfaithful wife by handing him a bottle allegedly containing arsenic whereas Wallace knows that the bottle contains only a harmless cough syrup.

Concerning the degree of knowledge of detail as to the criminal offence required by the assistant one can generally say that a generic form of knowledge or intention is required. The assistant's knowledge must encompass the essential factual elements, but need not cover every detail. Thus bluntly stated, the mens rea necessary is quite similar to that required for instigation, however the degree of knowledge required is lower in cases of assistance, as the instigator is actually involved in shaping a person's intent to commit an offence, while the assistant plays a less influential role and has less impact on the commission of the offence.

Generally, the assistant needs to know the *type of crime* that will be committed. Therefore it is immaterial that he did not know the exact particulars of the respective plan. Those were the merits of the English landmark decision in *R v Bainbridge* which also reflect the prevalent view in Germany and the Netherlands.[1251] In a pertinent German case for instance, the defendant had sold special equipment to the perpetrator to empty slot machines of brand X. He had also demonstrated the usage of this equipment to the perpetrator in a local pub. With this equipment the perpetrator had during a period of three months emptied several slot machines in the region. The Court of first instance had acquitted the defendant as he did not know the exact time, place and other circumstances of the commission of the thefts subsequently carried out by the perpetrator. The Court of Appeal however overruled the decision and held that the assistant only needed to posses a generic knowledge of the essential factual elements but not every detail.[1252]

[1248] [2004] EWCA Crim 1231 at para 71, (emphasis added).

[1249] Simester and Sullivan, 'Criminal Law: Theory and Doctrine' (2007), p. 215.

[1250] 24 October 2006 BGH NStZ 2007, 531.

[1251] R v Bainbridge [1960] 1 QB 129.

[1252] 27 March 1991 BayObLG NJW 1991, 2582. See also: 7 November 2001 BGH NStZ 2002, 145; Schönke and Schröder, 'Kommentar zum Strafgesetzbuch' (2006), §27 Mn 19.

In a comparable Dutch decision, the defendant had assisted three of his friends in an attempt to kill the victim. He had provided the means of transportation for finding the victim and had functioned as a driver. He did however not know the precise manner of the planned attack. In the course of the attack one of the perpetrators had pulled a gun and fired several shots at the victim. The Court of Appeal had acquitted the defendant but the Dutch Supreme Court, quashed the acquittal and held that in order for liability for assistance to arise, it was not necessary for the defendant to know the precise manner of the commission of the offence, but that it was sufficient that he was generally aware of the type of crime he was assisting.[1253]

Crucial is therefore that the crime committed fell within a spectrum of wrongdoing envisaged by the assistant. Thus, marginal variations in the conduct element of the offence, such as time and place are immaterial, as long as the assistant is generally aware of the dimension of wrongdoing strived for by the perpetrator. It follows that if a variation would occur which affects a specific aspect of the offence that the participant wanted to assist, this can stand in the way of a conviction for assistance. Accordingly, if Walter hands Hank a duplicate key to steal widow Diana's jewels, but in a sudden change of heart he assaults and rapes her, Walter ought not to incur liability for assisting Hank in the assault/rape.[1254] From this it can also be deduced that if the assistant leaves it to the perpetrator to choose which offence shall be furthered by his contribution, the assistant will be liable as long as the committed offence falls within a range of offences from which the assistant contemplated that the choice would be made.[1255]

A pertinent example here can be found in a German decision concerning an official expert in the field of jewellery. He had knowingly issued a false certificate in which he estimated the value of the perpetrator's jewellery at approximately 300.000 Marks, while he knew that the inferior quality of the stones meant that they were not worth more than 36.500 Marks. The expert knew that his certificate could be used to sell the stones for an excessive price or that it could alternatively be used to lend an excessive amount of money against the security of the jewellery. The perpetrator used the certificate for the latter purpose. He pawned the stones at his local bank and subsequently withdrew approximately 266.000 Marks from his bank account. On appeal the defendant had argued that he had not known the exact purpose for which his certificate would be used and that therefore his conviction for assisting fraud should not be allowed to stand. The Supreme Court however upheld his conviction and ruled that liability for assistance could arise if the assistant provided a means which increased the risk that by its usage a criminal offence, typically furthered by this means, will be committed.[1256]

1253 HR 4 March 2008, *NJ* 2008, 156.

1254 It should however be noted that liability could arise if the collateral offence was a foreseeable consequence of B's attempt to burgle the house.

1255 DPP for Northern Ireland v Maxwell [1978] 3 All ER 1140.

1256 18 April 1996 BGH NStZ 1997, 272.

A further illuminating example can be found in a Dutch case where a phone booth in a shopping mall was blown up by a firework bomb on New Years eve, which the suspect had built together with his partners. The defence had argued that the defendant had not foreseen the blowing up of the phone booth and that therefore his intention did not cover the destruction of the phone booth. The Supreme Court rejected the argument and held that given the nature of the bomb, which he helped to build, and given the fact that it was to be detonated within the shopping mall, the defendant had accepted the considerable chance (i.e. he had acted with *dolus eventualis*) that property would be destroyed by the detonation of the bomb.[1257] Another case in point is the one of two brothers who were threatened by two acquaintances. Before the four met again brother A handed B a gun and it was agreed that he should hold the two acquaintances at bay. However, the situation escalated and B killed one of the visitors. The defence had argued that A had not intended the killing of the visitor, but the Supreme Court held that when handing his brother the gun he had accepted the considerable chance (*dolus eventualis*) that his brother would use it to kill.[1258]

Thus, it follows that only in the most blatant and obvious cases of differing intentions no criminal liability will arise. In most cases where the intention of the aider and the perpetrator at least partially corresponded, the civil law notion of *dolus eventualis* will make the attribution of criminal liability possible. This also means that cases where in the English penal system the doctrine of joint criminal enterprise would be applied, will be covered in the Netherlands and Germany by the broad *dolus eventualis* concept and thus also lead to criminal liability. In other words the notion of *dolus eventualis* is broad and flexible enough to cloak normative considerations in seemingly factual assessments.[1259]

However, a provided assistance cannot indefinitely give rise to liability for any offence furthered by it. In regard to the commission of several offences furthered by the assistance, the assistant should therefore, at least in broad outline, be aware of the pertinent period and number of offences to be committed by the perpetrator.[1260] This is because it is quite likely that in these situations the intention of the aider does not exactly correspond to the factually committed crime. The Dutch legislator has foreseen this possibility and has laid down in Art 49 (4) DPC that "only those actions that were intentionally facilitated or promoted by the accessory and the consequences of such actions are to be taken into consideration in sentencing". From this it can be deduced that the aider follows the qualification of the offence effectively committed by the perpetrator, but that his punishment will be determined according to the crime he intended to promote or

1257 HR 13 November 2001, *NJ* 2002, 245. See also: HR 4 March 2008, *NJ* 2008, 156.

1258 HR 26 February 1985, *NJ* 1985, 651.

1259 See also: Knigge, 'Het opzet van de deelnemer', in Groenhuijsen, et al. (eds), Glijdende Schalen – Liber amicorum J. de Hullu (2003), p. 294. See also: Blomsma 'Mens rea and defences in European criminal law'(2012).

1260 See: 14 November 2001 BGH NStZ 2002, 200.

facilitate. If for instance the aider intends to aid the commission of theft (Art 310 DPC), but the perpetrator commits a robbery (Art 312 DPC), the aider will be deemed to have aided the robbery, as his intention included the unlawful appropriation of property, but his punishment will be determined according to the crime he intended to aid (Art 310 DPC). The German solution effectively resembles the Dutch approach in this respect, with the notable difference that if the offence actually committed does not constitute a complete *aliud* the participant will be liable for assisting the offence he envisaged.[1261] The same seems to apply in the English penal system. If the assistant contemplates theft and the perpetrator commits robbery, the assistant is not guilty of robbery but may be convicted of theft, which is included in it.[1262]

However, if the intention of the assistant went further than the crime actually committed (he thought he aided murder, but the victim was "merely" assaulted), the derivative nature of the doctrine would dictate that he can only be responsible for assisting the crime that had effectively been committed. While this seems to be the prevalent approach in Germany[1263] and the Netherlands,[1264] it was however mentioned before that the situation is a bit more complex in the English penal system where some authorities seem to endorse the possibility to convict the assistant of the intended, more severe offence.[1265]

"Neutral conduct" – criminal liability for everyday activities?

The subjective requirement that the assistant must know the essential matters that constitute the offence, i.e. he foresaw a substantial risk of an offence being committed, can lead to intricate questions in scenarios where the perpetrator seeks to exploit the natural course of events in everyday or business life. This might for instance be the case where the conduct of the would-be assistant is what one might call "neutral conduct", i.e. completely innocuous in itself. Should for instance a shopkeeper who sells a gun to a shady looking person incur liability for assisting murder which was committed with this weapon? Should a bank clerk be liable for assistance if he, following the wishes of a customer, transfers money to an anonymous bank account in Switzerland despite the fact that this is done in order to commit tax evasion? The predicament here in general is similar to the one encountered in the realm of omissions. The question in essence here is to what extent private actors in their day-to-day activities should be considered to have a duty to prevent or at least not to further the criminal conduct of others. In other

1261 Schönke and Schröder, 'Kommentar zum Strafgesetzbuch' (2006), §27 Mn 21.
1262 Smith and Hogan, 'Criminal Law' (2008), p. 204.
1263 Schönke and Schröder, 'Kommentar zum Strafgesetzbuch' (2006), Vorbem §§25 et seq. Mn 25.
1264 De Hullu, 'Materieel Strafrecht' (2009), p. 472.
1265 See: Chapter III. 4.3.

words, the doctrinal predicament here by and large is to distinguish "lending support to crime from more basic cases of poor citizenship".[1266]

What one is dealing with here are thus generally ordinary and ordinarily lawful, everyday activities, as for instance normal commercial transactions, such as the selling of guns, weapons, etc., which were later found to facilitate or assist a criminal offence. The central question raised by these cases in regard to criminal liability essentially is how closely should a person be involved in the crime's commission and how much knowledge should (s)he possess of the perpetrator's criminal enterprise in order to be held liable for assisting a criminal offence. Thus, as the conduct of the assistant in these cases is innocuous and often part and parcel of ordinary business transactions, much depends here on the knowledge, respectively mens rea of the person involved. Essentially the predicament at hand here can be traced back to a general problem of standards of fault concerned with the imposition of liability for risk-taking or the awareness of risk.

Accordingly when discussing this problem in the context of participation in crime the different mens rea standards applied in the investigated Member States again play an important role. While the broad concept of *dolus eventualis* applied in the civil law systems of Germany and the Netherlands potentially leads to a broad scope of criminal liability, the confinement of assistance to intentional acts in England in the sense of direct or indirect intent prima facie leads to a narrower scope of liability. However, many of these forms of conduct will in the English penal system nowadays be covered by the Serious Crime Act 2007 which adopts a lower mens rea standard for inchoate liability for assistance and encouragement in comparison to the traditional scheme of accessorial liability.

An inherent risk in criminalising these forms of behaviour is that the force of criminal law will impact more severely on economic actors with a vivid imagination or pessimistic mindset than on more naïve or even simple-minded ones, a distinction which is of course arbitrary and should not influence the imposition of criminal liability in a system based on the rule of law. As already stated, the problem at stake here, arguably has close ties to the duty of care predicament in regard to omissions liability.[1267] The defendants in these cases often legitimately operate in certain business sectors in which particular business standards, work ethics and diligence standards apply. These factors together with the defendant's knowledge and mens rea will play a role in the assessment of liability and need to be carefully weighed. Think for instance of a hotelier who lets a room to a man who obviously intends to use it to have unlawful sexual intercourse with his under-age companion.[1268] It is certainly arguable here that the hotelier should incur liability for assisting the unlawful sexual intercourse if one takes the view that he had a responsibility to

1266 Wilson, 'A rational scheme of liability for participating in crime' Criminal Law Review (2008), p. 16.

1267 See: Chapter II. 3.2.2.

1268 Duff, '"Can I help you?" Accessorial liability and the intention to assist' Legal Studies (1990), p. 174.

attend to such consequences of his business activities.[1269] In our modern culture of control in which risk prevention is pivotal, economic actors are deemed to have a duty to attend to foreseen effects of their commercial activity. Therefore, they must accept liability for any part which they knowingly play in facilitating an offence, so the argument goes. The problem is however where to draw the line.

If one incorporates the conceivable range of cases in a continuum, the extreme poles prove to be uncontroversial. In the case where the whole business operation is aimed at facilitating criminal activities, as will for instance be the case in regard to a shopkeeper who sells untraceable guns or specially adapted burglary equipment, the imposition of criminal liability seems a forgone conclusion. On the other hand, in cases where the actor was unaware of and also could not reasonably have know the (illegal) use to which the items he provided were put, it seems clear that no liability should arise. More problematic are however cases where the actor was aware of the criminal intent of the buyer or where he merely expected it.

There are different approaches conceivable to deal with that matter and once again one is faced with the question whether imposing criminal liability should be driven by objective or subjective factors. A purely subjective approach will place emphasis on the intention of the assistant. The cardinal question will then become whether the defendant intentionally assisted the perpetrator's criminal endeavour. Can it be deduced from his knowledge or intention that he voluntarily associated himself with the criminal offence committed by the perpetrator? Simply foreseeing the possibility that a crime might be committed will certainly not be sufficient in order for criminal liability to arise. Otherwise the law would indeed punish pessimists more severely than optimists. Something more than foreseeing the possibility will therefore be necessary. How high the degree of foreseeability should be set is however open to debate. If one were to opt for a narrow scope of liability one ought to require purpose to assist in order to exclude cases where the person merely suspected that an offence will be committed. As already mentioned, this, however, does not sit well with the current focus on risk minimisation and prevention. The purpose standard in this context would arguably place the emphasis on individual autonomy and on the safeguard function of criminal law, while the lower knowledge standard would promote the crime control function of the law.[1270]

The Dutch penal system generally tries to solve these cases by focusing on the mens rea of the participant. As previously discussed, it is generally not necessary for an assistant to know every exact detail of the criminal enterprise he is assisting. It suffices if he is aware of the main features of the criminal enterprise and is aware that he furthers a criminal offence. This rather broad approach together with the broad concept of *dolus eventualis* makes it possible to impose liability also in the case of 'neutral actions'. The already mentioned *Van Anraat* case can serve as an

---

1269 Duff, '"Can I help you?" Accessorial liability and the intention to assist' Legal Studies (1990), p. 176.

1270 Stewart, 'The End of "Modes of Liability" for international crimes' Leiden Journal of International Law (2012), pp. 36 et seq.

example here.[1271] In this case the business man was simply indifferent to the consequences of his conduct, as long as he could generate a profit. The court held that the evidence proved that the defendant knew that in the ordinary course of events his chemicals would be used for the production of mustard gas which in turn would be deployed in combat. The defendant had therefore intentionally assisted the deployment of chemical weapons.

The English penal system on the other hand seems to take a broader approach in regard to traditional accessorial liability. "At present, English authorities suggest a general rule of liability for sellers".[1272] This will be even more so in the case of lenders or letters of articles or premises for unlawful purposes as here the owner has a right to control the property.[1273] Yet, one doctrinal limitation to impose accessorial liability for minor assistance arguably flows from the concept of recklessness. This notion consists of an objective as well as a subjective element. Thus, the risk must not only be subjectively foreseen, but it must furthermore also be unreasonable to run it. This, in principle constitutes a useful devise to limit criminal liability for minor forms of assistance.

However, as has already been mentioned, the Serious Crime Act 2007 will now apply to many of these cases, regardless of whether the perpetrator subsequently commits the criminal offence and regardless of whether the provided assistance had any effect on the commission of the offence. Liability will arise as soon as an act capable of assisting or encouraging the perpetrator has been performed. According to sections 44 and 45 for instance, criminal liability will arise if an act capable of assisting or encouraging the commission of an offence is performed and the person either intends to assist or encourage (s 44) or where he believes that the offence will be committed and that his act will encourage or assist its commission (s 45). This would however result in a very broad scope of liability, as it would potentially make a motorist A liable under English law if he changes lanes, to allow a following motorist B to overtake, knowing that B is speeding. Therefore the act introduces an interesting defence of acting reasonable to keep the offence within reasonable limits.[1274] This defence especially caters for the sort of cases discussed here. Thus, it applies to acts in which the would-be assistant could reasonably have expected to be able to engage, free from any taint of criminality. Section 50 of the Serious Crime provides:

(1) A person is not guilty of an offence under this part if he proves
   a) that he *knew* certain circumstances existed; and
   b) that it was reasonable for him to act as he did in those circumstances

---

1271 Hof 's-Gravenhage, 9 May 2007, *LJN* BA4676, HR 30 June 2009, *NJ* 2009, 481.
1272 Smith and Hogan, 'Criminal Law' (2008), p. 198.
1273 Smith and Hogan, 'Criminal Law' (2008), p. 198.
1274 Ormerod and Fortson, 'Serious Crime Act 2007: The Part 2 Offences' Criminal Law Review (2009), p. 411.

(2) A person is not guilty of an offence under this part if he proves
  a) that he believed certain circumstances to exist
  b) that his believe was reasonable; and
  c) that it was reasonable for him to act as he did in the circumstances as he believed them to be.

(3) Factors to be considered in determining whether it was reasonable for a person to act as he did include:
  a) the seriousness of the anticipated offence [...]
  b) any purpose for which he claims to be acting;
  c) any authority by which he claims to be acting

A drawback of this defence is certainly its inherent vagueness and open-ended nature which could cause frictions with the principle of legal certainty, but it constitutes a good summary of the legal predicament at stake and at the same time outlines in broad strokes the essential factors that play a role.

An alternative approach to the problem places the emphasis on objective factors. Therefore factors such as diligent standards and customs in a respective sector are invoked to exclude liability in certain cases. If a respective conduct was carried out according to *de lege artis* and corresponded to the applicable professional standards, liability will be excluded.[1275]

Preferable are however mixed approaches, combining objective and subjective factors, as can for instance be seen in Section 50 of the Serious Crime Act. Objective factors such as business and diligence standards, etc. provide a good indication of what a respective economic actor should have foreseen and how he was supposed to conduct his business. However, also subjective factors ought to play a role as they allow evaluating the actor's individual culpability and blameworthiness. Here the nature of actus reus and mens rea resurfaces. The less in regard to the assistant's objective wrongdoing can arguably be compensated by a more on the subjective side. Thus, as in this context the objective conduct is innocuous, a higher standard in regard to the assistant's knowledge seems defensible.

Modern jurisprudence in Germany has adopted the following guidelines. If the conduct of the perpetrator is exclusively aimed at committing a criminal offence and the assistant is aware of that fact, liability for assistance will arise as the conduct of the assistant is then deemed to lose its innocuous, every-day character and is then considered to signify solidarity with the wrongdoing of the perpetrator. If the assistant however considers it merely possible that his conduct may be used to further a criminal offence, then prima facie no liability will arise. Only in cases where he was aware of a considerable risk that the perpetrator will commit an offence, so that he can be reproached with assisting a person bent on committing a criminal offence can liability be imposed.[1276]

1275 Schönke and Schröder, 'Kommentar zum Strafgesetzbuch' (2006), §27 Mn 10 b.

1276 Roxin, 'Strafrecht Allgemeiner Teil, Band II: Besondere Erscheinungsformen der Straftat' (2003), pp. 216–219, Schönke and Schröder, 'Kommentar zum Strafgesetzbuch' (2006), §27 Mn

Thus, a lawyer who creates selling/advertisement brochures despite his awareness that they will be used for fraudulent activities in connection with commodities futures may be held liable for providing assistance.[1277] Likewise, a notary who assisted a couple, who recently moved to Paraguay as they were wanted in Germany for tax evasion and bribery, by transferring money to bank accounts in Switzerland and Luxembourg and arranging an investment adviser for his clients in order to carry out high risk cross currency swaps, can incur liability despite the fact that he merely carried out his normal business activities.[1278]

Yet, someone who hires a carpenter to renovate his house, of whom he knows that he does not declare his income to the tax office, is not guilty of aiding tax evasion, as the conduct of the carpenter is not exclusively aimed at committing a criminal offence.[1279] Similarly the German Supreme Court acquitted a former training supervisor of the East German army who drafted standing orders under the border security regime of the former German Democratic Republic. Included in the border security regime was also the maintenance and deployment of minefields and spring guns, which killed several people trying to flee to West Germany. However, the defendant in that case was not involved in the training of the people maintaining the mines and was thus not actively involved in the organisation of the landmines. The Supreme Court held that he had not aided those in charge of the minefield, as the general organisation of the border regime for which he was responsible, remained useful and legal even if one excluded the illegal minefield issue.[1280]

In regard to these "neutral actions" which effectively contribute and further a criminal offence generally, a certain degree of adjustment or impact on the commission of the criminal offence by the perpetrator should objectively be required. Otherwise, all the perpetrator does is to exploit the natural course of events in everyday or business life. Therefore the focus should arguably primarily lie on the quality of the contribution of the assistant rather than the general usefulness of his conduct for the commission of the offence.[1281] In this evaluation general diligence standards and customs in the respective business sector should be taken into consideration as well as other professional standards, the seriousness of the anticipated offence, the purpose for which the defendant claims to have been acting and any authority by which he claims to have been acting.

At the subjective level of mens rea, a certain form of intent regarding the commission of the offence should be required. It is debatable whether *dolus eventualis* or recklessness as to the commission of the offence should suffice

10a, Hartmann, 'Sonderregeln für die Beihilfe durch "neutrales" Verhalten?' ZStW (2004), p. 596. See also: 18 June 2003 BGH NStZ 2004, 41.

1277 20 September 1999 BGH NStZ 2000, 34.

1278 26 October 1998 BGH NStZ-RR 1999, 184.

1279 23 June 1992 BGH NStZ 1992, 498.

1280 8 March 2001 BGH NJW 2001, 2409.

1281 Schönke and Schröder, 'Kommentar zum Strafgesetzbuch' (2006), §27 Mn 10b.

here.[1282] Clear-cut cases will include circumstances where the assistant knew or was aware that he will assist an offence through his conduct. More difficult cases which should nevertheless trigger criminal liability are, where the assistant did not possess actual awareness of the ramifications of his conduct but should have done so according to pertinent business and diligence standards. If a relatively low mens rea standard were to be adopted either in these cases or regarding participation in general, the introduction of a defence of acting in a reasonable manner as introduced by the Serious Crime Act 2007 in England, should arguably be adopted in order to avoid hardship and to avoid the introduction of risk liability. As already mentioned, the innocuous nature of the objective conduct in these cases should, it is submitted, be compensated by a higher mens rea standard. What should however be avoided is that one of these elements completely replaces the other. This would arguably militate against the general requirement that (for imposing criminal liability) actus reus and mens rea need to be established.

10. Limitations to participatory liability – Withdrawal

In the English penal system it is thought that the derivative nature of complicity offers an accessory special exculpatory possibilities, not available to the principal.[1283] If the accomplice has a sudden change of heart before the perpetrator has reached the attempt phase, English common law recognises that accomplice liability can be undone. This will however not affect liability for any inchoate offences. This is a corollary of the inchoate nature of these offences and is entirely to be expected. As liability in regard to these offences immediately arises with the occurrence of the participatory conduct, no room for a withdrawal remains. Accordingly also the Serious Crime Act 2007 does not foresee a defence of withdrawal.[1284] However, some have advocated the inclusion of the defence in the Act to keep liability within reasonable limits and the Law Commission in earlier proposals had sought to incorporate such a defence.[1285]

Unlike many other countries English criminal law explicitly recognises that the accomplice can withdraw her participation.[1286] This approach is contrary to the stance that English criminal law takes in regard to attempts and conspiracy where the possibility of voluntary withdrawal is generally rejected. The different

1282 See also: Kadish, 'Reckless Complicity' The Journal of Criminal Law & Criminology (1997), pp. 369–394.

1283 Smith, 'Withdrawal in Complicity: A Restatement of Principles' The Criminal Law Review (2001), pp. 769 et seq.

1284 Ormerod and Fortson, 'Serious Crime Act 2007: The Part 2 Offences' Criminal Law Review (2009), p. 411.

1285 Ormerod and Fortson, 'Serious Crime Act 2007: The Part 2 Offences' Criminal Law Review (2009), p. 411.

1286 Smith, 'Withdrawal in Complicity: A Restatement of Principles' The Criminal Law Review (2001), pp. 769 et seq.

approaches here are often explained by the distinctive features of the doctrines. Attempt liability, so the argument goes, requires something of manifest wrongdoing or dangerousness to have occurred, as a more than merely preparatory conduct must have taken place.[1287] Complicity however requires no proximity between the conduct of the secondary party and the offence. An act of assistance or encouragement suffices, which can in itself be entirely innocuous and which possibly will only exert influence at a much later stage, depending on the conduct of the perpetrator. Due to the fact that accessorial liability is deemed not to require proximity or manifest dangerousness, it is thought that an avenue for the accessory needs to be open to redeem himself in case of a change of heart.[1288]

While it is certainly true that a participant will often be far removed from the actual occurrence of harm, it is nevertheless questionable whether the differences between the doctrines of attempt and complicity are strong enough to support these different approaches. It is submitted that the same arguments allowing the defence in the realm of complicity would also apply in regard to criminal attempts. The fact that the conduct of the participant at times is further removed from the criminal wrongdoing and furthermore dependent on the conduct of the perpetrator would only seem to provide an additional argument in favour of the defence in such cases and not necessarily exclude its application from the law of attempt. This tension arguably is nicely reflected in the rationales brought forward in the English penal system for recognising a withdrawal defence in complicity which almost entirely resemble the arguments proposing a withdrawal defence for attempts. A first argument focuses on the power of the defence to function as an incentive for an accessory to take action to revoke his assistance and encouragement, thereby reducing the risk of the principal offence being carried out.[1289] The second rationale regards the accomplice's withdrawal as diminishing his culpability or future dangerousness.[1290] However, the exact scope of the defence seems to be unclear as well as quite restricted.

10.1. Withdrawal from participation in a joint enterprise

Where the participant has joined the common purpose of a joint criminal enterprise he may generally withdraw from the enterprise by timely and unequivocally communicating his withdrawal to the other participants.[1291] Merely leaving the crime scene or simply not turning up will however not constitute a sufficient basis

1287 Wilson, 'Central Issues in Criminal Theory' (2002), pp. 212–218.

1288 Wilson, 'Central Issues in Criminal Theory' (2002), pp. 212–218.

1289 Ashworth, 'Principles of criminal law' (2006), p. 437, Wilson, 'Central Issues in Criminal Theory' (2002), pp. 212–218.

1290 Ashworth, 'Principles of criminal law' (2006), p. 437, Wilson, 'Central Issues in Criminal Theory' (2002), pp. 212–218.

1291 Simester and Sullivan, 'Criminal Law: Theory and Doctrine' (2007), p. 240.

for a withdrawal.[1292] However, if one searches for clear guidelines as to the requirements of a withdrawal, one searches in vein. Much will depend on the scope and guise of the assistance or encouragement provided by the accessory and how close to the actual commission of the offence by the principal his change of mind took place. The further events have advanced, the more the accomplice will have to do to countermand his participation. In essence the courts seem to apply a sort of proportionality test where they weigh the inculpatory action of the accomplice against the exculpatory factors.[1293] If for instance Ralph has provided Peter with poison in order to kill his wife, it will not be sufficient if Ralph subsequently tells Peter that he wants nothing more to do with the offence, while in other cases where the assistance was petty, this might well suffice.

10.2. Withdrawal from assistance and encouragement

Where A has assisted or encouraged the commission of a crime, a mere cessation of further participatory activity, as might be sufficient in some cases of joint criminal ventures, will not constitute a sufficient basis for withdrawal. Here it will be required to take effective steps to counteract the repercussions of the participant's previous act.[1294] The greater the participant's involvement the more the law will require to effectuate his withdrawal.

The German Penal Code in a similar manner provides that accomplice liability will be excluded if the participant voluntarily prevents the commission of the offence. If the offence has not been completed due to circumstances independent of the participant's influence or independent of his previous contribution it is required that the participant earnestly and voluntarily tried to prevent the commission of the offence.[1295] As attempted facilitation is not punishable under German law, the German Penal Code only provides for the possibility of voluntary withdrawal in regard to attempted instigation. §31 GPC provides that no liability should arise in cases where the defendant voluntarily abandons the attempt to instigate another to commit a felony (this is because attempts to instigate other offences is not criminal

[1292] Reed, 'Case Note: Joint Enterprise: Withdrawal' Journal of Criminal Law (2005), pp. 467–471.

[1293] Reed, 'Case Note: Joint Enterprise: Withdrawal' Journal of Criminal Law (2005), pp. 467–471.

[1294] See: R v Croft [1944] KB 295, R v Grundy [1977] Crim LR 543, R v Arthur Armour Mallie Whitefield [1984] 79 Cr App R 36.

[1295] §24 GPC reads as follows:

(I) Whoever voluntarily abandons the further execution of the act or prevents its completion shall not be punished for attempt. If he act is not completed without contribution by the person withdrawing from the attempt, then he will be free from punishment if he voluntarily and earnestly seeks to prevent the completion.

(II) If several persons participate in the act, then anyone who voluntarily prevents the completion is not punished for attempt. However, to be free from punishment it suffices that he voluntarily and earnestly seek to prevent the completion of the act if it is not completed without his contribution or independent of his previous contribution to the act.

under German law), and diffuses any danger that the instigated person commits the offence.[1296]

In Dutch criminal law it is generally recognised that a person can voluntarily withdraw from an attempt or a preparatory offence, but the possibility of withdrawal is not explicitly discussed in regard to complicity. Of course, members of a joint criminal enterprise (i.e. co-perpetrators) can withdraw from an attempt to commit the offence or from its preparation. In these situations the general rules and jurisprudence pertinent to Article 46 (b) DPC will be applicable which excludes liability in cases where the commission of the offence has been prevented "by reason only of circumstances dependent on the perpetrator's will". The same rules will arguably be applied in regard to attempted instigation.

To conclude this section, it can be stated that all systems in one way or another recognise (voluntary) withdrawal as a defence in complicity cases. The question can however be posed if it is strictly necessary to design specific rules on withdrawal for complicity cases. This may only be necessary if one rejects the defence in regard to attempt liability, as is the case in the English penal system. In regard to forms of perpetration, it is otherwise arguable that the normal rules concerning withdrawal in the realm of attempts should be applicable and that in regard to assistants or facilitators only a complete renunciation or retraction of the provided contribution ought to be able to prevent liability from arising. There will be more discussion on voluntary withdrawal in general in the context of attempt liability where the different constitutive elements of the doctrine will be examined. For the time being, suffice it to say that in regard to participation in crime as a rule of thumb, the more directly and actively involved a participant is in the commission of the offence, the more active and direct steps ought to be required from him to effectively withdraw. Much will therefore depend on the nature and scope of participation. The law should require different actions in regard to an instigator who has induced another to commit the offence than in regard to someone who lends his friend a jemmy or the criminal mastermind who has set in motion the wheels of a criminal organisation, bound on committing criminal offences.

1296 §31 GPC reads as follows:

(I) Whoever voluntarily

1. abandons the attempt to induce another to commit a felony and averts any danger that the other commit the act
2. after having declared himself ready to commit a felony, abandons his plan or,
3. after having planned with another, or having acceded to another's request, to commit a felony, prevents the act,

is not punished according to §30.

(II) If the act does not occur without contribution by the person withdrawing from the attempt or if it is committed independent of his previous behavior, then his voluntary and earnest effort to prevent act suffices for him to be free from punishment.

11. THE NOTIONS OF PERPETRATION AND PARTICIPATION IN EU LAW

11.1. Introduction

After having discussed the rules on participation in national law, this research can now turn to European Union law. The notions of perpetration and participation have not yet been extensively dealt with in the realm of Union law. Although, the European Union frequently requires Member States in legal instruments to criminalise also conduct concerned with the participation in a criminal offence, it does so in a rather haphazard and inconsistent manner. Article 4 of the Directive on the protection of the environment[1297] for instance holds that "Member States shall ensure that inciting, aiding and abetting the intentional conduct [...] is punishable as a criminal offence".[1298] Other instruments such as Directive 2005/60/EC on the protection of the use of the financial system for the purpose of money laundering and terrorist financing seem to adopt a more fine grained approach by holding that the intentional participation in, association to commit, attempts to commit and aiding, abetting, facilitating and counselling the commission of an offence outlined in the directive shall trigger criminal liability.[1299]

Already from these different wordings it can be deduced that a coherent definition of participatory conduct is yet to be found in European criminal law. None of these concepts are further defined and it is left to the implementing Member States to lay down the conditions under which one of these forms of participation will be applicable. Generally speaking, the legislative technique applied by the Union in regard to criminalising perpetration and participation is to draft in some detail the primary offence and subsequently establish in generic terms that participation in the newly-created offence shall be punishable as well. This is the approach to be found in the aforementioned Framework Decisions but can also be found in other European instruments such as the Convention on the protection of the European Communities' financial interests (a.k.a. PIF Convention) and its protocols.[1300]

1297 Directive 2008/99 of 19 November 2008 on the protection of the environment through criminal law, OJ 2008 L 328/28.

1298 The same phrase can also be found in Article 3 of Framework Decision 2005/667 of 12 July 2005 to strengthen the criminal law framework for the enforcement of the law against ship-source pollution OJ 2005, L 255/164 and Article 3 of Directive 2011/36 of 5 April 2011 on preventing and combating trafficking in human beings and protecting its victims, and replacing Council Framework Decision 2002/629/JHA, OJ 2011, L 101/06.

1299 Article 1 (2) lit. d of Directive 2005/60 of 26 October 2005 on the prevention of the use of the financial system for the purpose of money laundering and terrorist financing, OJ 2005, L 309/15.

1300 Convention of 26 July 1995, on the protection of the European Communities' financial interests, OJ 1995 C 316/49, Protocol of 27 September 1996, on the protection of the European Communities' financial interests, OJ 1996 C 313/02, Second Protocol of 19 July 1997 to the Convention on the protection of the European Communities' financial interests, OJ 1997, C 221.

Article 1 (1) of the Convention in some detail sets out the offence definition of fraud affecting the financial interests of the Union, while Article 1 (3) in a general manner proscribes that certain preparatory acts such as for instance the falsification of documents shall be punishable as well if they are not already punishable as a principal offence or as participation in, or instigation of fraud.[1301] Article 2 of the PIF convention then makes it clear that "each Member State shall take the necessary measures to ensure that the conduct referred to in Article 1 (1), and participating in, instigation, or attempting the conduct referred to in Article 1 (1) shall be punishable by effective, proportionate and dissuasive criminal penalties".[1302] Finally, Article 3 (3) of the Second Protocol to the Convention mentions perpetrators, instigators or accessories whose criminal liability should not be excluded by the liability of a legal person in the case at hand.[1303]

It can be deduced that the common approach of the European Union in regard to participation in crime at least formally distinguishes perpetrators from accessories, i.e. formally adopts a differentiated or pluralistic model of participation. But whether these different forms are part of a unitarian or differentiated model of participation is open for debate. Yet, the details are arguably deliberately left vague by the European legislator, so that national systems are able to fit the provisions in their national participation scheme, as long as an effective, proportionate and dissuasive protection of the Union's financial interests is guaranteed.[1304] However, as has become apparent from the foregoing discussion, the approaches taken regarding participation in crime in different Member States are diverse and can lead to varying scopes of liability, a situation which is undesirable in a "Common Area of Freedom, Security and Justice".[1305] More importantly maybe, a European concept of perpetration which will influence the scope and guise of all other forms of participation has not yet emerged. This will become an even more crucial aspect in case of the establishment of a European Public Prosecutor's office as foreseen in Article 86 TFEU. In order to ensure a proper functioning of the office it will be vital to establish who or what will be qualified as a perpetrator or as an accomplice at Union level.[1306]

Notwithstanding the general underdevelopment of the doctrine at Union level, there are some authorities to be found which can constitute the foundation for

---

1301 Convention of 26 July 1995, on the protection of the European Communities' financial interests, OJ 1995 C 316/49.

1302 Convention of 26 July 1995, on the protection of the European Communities' financial interests, OJ 1995 C 316/49.

1303 Second Protocol of 19 July 1997 to the Convention on the protection of the European Communities' financial interests, OJ 1997, C 221.

1304 Vogel, 'Criminal Responsibility – Parties to the offence', in Cullen (ed), Enlarging the Fight against Fraud in the European Union: Penal and Administrative Sanctions, Settlement, Whistleblowing and Corpus Juris in Candidate Countries (2003), p. 59.

1305 See also: Schöberl, 'Die Einheitstäterschaft als europäisches Modell' (2006), pp. 229–246.

1306 Klip, 'European Criminal Law' (2012), p. 460.

discussion here. First, the Council in its draft on guidelines and model provisions of criminal law for instance held that the criminalisation of inciting, aiding and abetting of intentional offences should normally follow the criminalisation of the main offence and subsequently in its model provisions establishes that "each Member State shall ensure that inciting, aiding and abetting the intentional conduct referred to in an Article [...] is punishable as a criminal offence".[1307] From these statements one can clearly deduce one thing. The Council's insistence on intentional conduct in regard to inciting, aiding and abetting clearly points to the exclusion of aiding a negligent offence from the scope of criminal liability. A crucial question left unaddressed however is whether negligent aid can give rise to liability in European criminal law as well. Unfortunately however, the model provisions do neither contain any further elaboration on the content and scope, nor on the theoretical and doctrinal foundation of criminal liability for participation in crime. This is however understandable, given the fact that these provisions were merely meant to set out a common denominator and to guide future legislation as well as to achieve thereby coherent and consistent criminal law provisions.[1308]

Second, the Corpus Juris 2000 project, aiming at the protection of the financial interests of the European Union has opted for a differentiated approach in regard to participation in crime. The Project strives to establish an autonomous European model of participation for offences against the financial interests of the Union.[1309] Article 11, titled "individual criminal responsibility" distinguishes the main offender from the inciter and the accomplice and entails a mandatory mitigation of punishment for accomplices.[1310] Pursuant to Article 11 a main offender either commits the offence himself, jointly with others or by means of an innocent agent. The inciter is defined in the draft as one who knowingly provokes a natural person or organisation to commit the illegal act and an accomplice is deemed to knowingly help a natural person or organisation to commit the illegal act.[1311] Thus, it can be stated that also the Corpus Juris introduces a pluralistic or differentiated model of participation, distinguishing perpetrators from accomplices. Liability as a perpetrator will arise if the offence is committed directly either by himself or jointly with others or indirectly by means of an innocent agent. The requirements for indirect participation are however unclear. The term innocent agent would suggest that the agent must have acted without culpability (i.e. lack of mens rea,

---

1307 Draft Council conclusions on model provisions, guiding the Council's criminal law deliberations, Brussels, 27 November 2009, 16542/2/09 REV 2.

1308 Draft Council conclusions on model provisions, guiding the Council's criminal law deliberations, Brussels, 27 November 2009, 16542/2/09 REV 2.

1309 See also: Hamdorf, 'Beteiligungsmodelle im Strafrecht' (2002), p. 385, Schöberl, 'Die Einheitstäterschaft als europäisches Modell' (2006), p. 252.

1310 Delmas-Marty and Vervaele, 'The implementation of the Corpus Juris in the Member States – Volume I' (2000), p. 192.

1311 Delmas-Marty and Vervaele, 'The implementation of the Corpus Juris in the Member States – Volume I' (2000), p. 192.

insanity, etc.) so that a wider interpretation of the notion in the sense of the German doctrine of perpetration by means seems on first sight excluded.[1312]

The decisive criterion for the categorisation of the scheme as a differentiated one can be found in the provision's final sentence which holds that "the maximum penalty for the accomplice shall not exceed three-quarters of the penalties under Article 14".[1313] Thus, a mandatory mitigation of punishment is foreseen for accomplices. Moreover, negligent instigation or facilitation falls outside the scope of criminal liability as both forms can only be committed intentionally (Article 11 refers to *knowingly* provoking or helping someone to commit the illegal act). The wording of the rules on instigation and facilitation (i.e. to provoke or help the commission of the criminal offence) furthermore points in the direction of a derivative nature of criminal liability.[1314] This assessment is supported by Article 11 bis on criminal attempts which provides that participation in an attempt shall be punishable. It follows *a contrario* that attempted instigation and facilitation shall under the Corpus Juris not give rise to criminal liability.[1315] Thus, the facilitation or instigation of an offence is not punishable unless the main offence has either been committed or attempted. Accordingly, liability regarding these two modes of participation is derived and dependent on the commission or attempt to commit the criminal offence. An autonomous conception of instigation or facilitation seems therefore not reconcilable with the wording of the Corpus Juris 2000. It follows that the rules on participation can be considered to adopt a differentiated model which would most likely also introduce the intricate demarcation problems inherent to these models, as discussed above in the context of Dutch and German law.

Despite the fact that the doctrines of perpetration and participation have not received thorough treatment in Union law yet, the concepts have been discussed in the realm of competition law. Of particular interest for the purposes of this research is Article 101 TFEU.[1316] This provision is of particular interest as it covers agreements, decisions or concerted practices involving more than one undertaking.

1312 Vogel, 'Criminal Responsibility – Parties to the offence', in Cullen (ed), Enlarging the Fight against Fraud in the European Union: Penal and Administrative Sanctions, Settlement, Whistleblowing and Corpus Juris in Candidate Countries (2003), p. 64.

1313 Delmas-Marty and Vervaele, 'The implementation of the Corpus Juris in the Member States – Volume I' (2000), p. 192.

1314 See also: Hamdorf, 'Beteiligungsmodelle im Strafrecht' (2002), p. 385.

1315 Delmas-Marty and Vervaele, 'The implementation of the Corpus Juris in the Member States – Volume I' (2000), p. 73.

1316 Article 101 TFEU reads as follows:

1. The following shall be prohibited as incompatible with the internal market: all agreements between undertakings, decisions by associations of undertakings and concerted practices which may affect trade between Member States and which have as their object or effect the prevention, restriction or distortion of competition within the internal market, and in particular those which:
   (a) directly or indirectly fix purchase or selling prices or any other trading conditions;
   (b) limit or control production, markets, technical development, or investment;
   (c) share markets or sources of supply;

Thus, by its very nature it is concerned with co-operative conduct of at least two undertakings which potentially prevents, restricts or distorts competition within the internal market. In order for liability pursuant to Article 101 TFEU to arise, all its elements must be established. In other words there must be (i) an agreement between undertakings, or (ii) decisions by associations of undertakings, or (iii) concerted practices, which (iv) may affect trade between Member States and (v) which have as their object or effect (vi) the prevention, restriction or distortion of competition within the common market.[1317]

11.2. The notions of agreement and concerted practices

The terms agreement and concerted practices have been given a broad reading by the Court of Justice and encompasses all forms of coordination between undertakings which might restrict competition. The discussion will first focus on the notion of agreement and subsequently shed some light on the concept of concerted practices. Afterwards the focus will turn to the model of attribution applied in competition law.

An agreement generally includes all legally enforceable agreements, both written and oral, while the term concerted practices refers to what might be called 'gentlemen's agreements', i.e. agreements that are not legally enforceable. The term 'agreement', thus "is merely another way of indicating coordinated/collusive conduct which is restrictive of competition, or a cartel in the wider sense, in which at least two distinct undertakings participate after expressing their joint intention of conducting themselves on the market in a specific way".[1318] What is accordingly decisive here is that the conduct of at least two undertakings constitutes an

---

(d) apply dissimilar conditions to equivalent transactions with other trading parties, thereby placing them at a competitive disadvantage;

(e) make the conclusion of contracts subject to acceptance by the other parties of supplementary obligations which, by their nature or according to commercial usage, have no connection with the subject of such contracts.

2. Any agreements or decisions prohibited pursuant to this Article shall be automatically void.
3. The provisions of paragraph 1 may, however, be declared inapplicable in the case of:
   - any agreement or category of agreements between undertakings,
   - any decision or category of decisions by associations of undertakings,
   - any concerted practice or category of concerted practices,

   which contributes to improving the production or distribution of goods or to promoting technical or economic progress, while allowing consumers a fair share of the resulting benefit, and which does not:

   (a) impose on the undertakings concerned restrictions which are not indispensable to the attainment of these objectives;

   (b) afford such undertakings the possibility of eliminating competition in respect of a substantial part of the products in question.

1317 Jones and Sufrin, 'EC Competition Law: Text, Cases, and Materials' (2004), pp. 102 et seq.

1318 8 July 2008, Case T-99/04, *AC-Treuhand AG v Commission of the European Communities*, [2008] ECR II-01501, para 118.

expression of the concurrence of wills, the form of which not being important per se.[1319] Thus, the proof of an agreement pursuant to Article 101 TFEU is based on the existence of the subjective criterion which lies at the heart of all agreements, namely a "concurrence of wills".[1320]

The concept of a concerted practice on the other hand:

> refers to a form of coordination between undertakings which, without having been taken to the stage where an agreement properly so-called has been concluded, knowingly substitutes practical cooperation between them for the risk of competition. The criteria of coordination used to define that term must be understood in the light of the concept inherent in the provisions of the Treaty relating to competition, according to which each economic operator must determine independently the policy which it intends to adopt on the Common Market.[1321]

Once an agreement or a concerted practice has been established, an infringement of Article 101 TFEU can be attributed to a company and give rise to liability if the Commission can prove two conditions; the first being of an objective and the second of a subjective nature.

11.3. The objective requirement

According to the case law of the ECJ this objective requirement is met where it can be established that the participating undertaking has contributed to the implementation of the cartel, even when it only fulfilled a subsidiary, accessory or passive role therein.[1322] Thus, it needs to be established that the undertaking intended through its conduct to contribute to the common objectives of the cartel and that it was aware of the planned or implemented conduct of the other

---

1319 8 July 2008, Case T-99/04, *AC-Treuhand AG v Commission of the European Communities*, [2008] ECR II-01501, para 118.

1320 Jones and Sufrin, 'EC Competition Law: Text, Cases, and Materials' (2004), p. 130. See also: 8 July 2008, Case T-99/04, *AC-Treuhand AG v Commission of the European Communities*, [2008] ECR II-01501, para 125, 26 October 2000, Case T-41/96, *Bayer AG v Commission of the European Communities*, [2000] ECR II-03383, para 173. See also: 6 January 2004, Joined Cases C-2/01 P and C-3/01 P, *Bundesverband der Arzneimittel-Importeure eV and Commission of the European Communities v Bayer AG*, [2004] ECR I-00023.

1321 15 March 2000, Case T-25/95, *Cimenteries CBR and Others v Commission of the European Communities* [2002] ECR II-00491, para 22. See also: 14 July 1972, Case C-48/69, *Imperial Chemical Industries Ltd. v Commission of the European Communities*, [1972] ECR 00619, para 64 et seq. 16 December 1975, Joined Cases C-40–48, 50, 54–56, 111, 113 & 114/73, *Coöperatieve Vereniging "Suiker Unie" UA and others v Commission of the European Communities*, [1975] ECR 01663, para 173.

1322 8 September 2010, Case T-29/05, *Deltafina SpA v European Commission*, [2010] not yet reported, para 58, 8 July 2008, Case T-99/04, *AC-Treuhand AG v Commission of the European Communities*, [2008] ECR II-01501, para 133.

participants in pursuance of the common objectives, or that it could reasonably have foreseen that conduct and that it was ready to accept the attendant risk.[1323]

The threshold to establish such an objective contribution is however considerably low and comes close to an establishment of guilt by association. It is namely in this regard sufficient for the Commission to prove that the undertaking in question attended meetings at which anti-competitive agreements were concluded without manifesting its opposition to such meetings.[1324] If attendance at such meetings can be established, a shift in the burden of proof will take place as it will then be for the undertaking concerned to demonstrate that it participated in those meetings without any anti-competitive intentions. Therefore it must be demonstrated that it made it apparent to its competitors that it was participating in those meetings in a spirit that was different from theirs.[1325]

If the undertaking has not publicly distanced itself from the anti-competitive conduct as previously described, or reported it to the administrative authorities, it will be assumed that the undertaking tacitly approved of the unlawful initiative and that the effect of its behaviour is to encourage the continuation of the infringement and to compromise its discovery.[1326] The undertaking in question is then considered to engage in a passive form of participation in the infringement. Thus, in the realm of competition law, there seems to be not only a duty to retreat from unlawful behaviour but an even more far-reaching requirement to publicly distance oneself from the anti-competitive behaviour or to report it to the administrative authority.

This stringent standard is further exacerbated by the fact that even if an undertaking did not act according to the outcome of such meetings having an anti-competitive object, i.e. it did not implement the agreement, liability will still arise

---

1323 8 September 2010, Case T-29/05, *Deltafina SpA v European Commission*, [2010] not yet reported, para 59, Case T-99/04, *AC-Treuhand AG v Commission of the European Communities*, [2008] ECR II-01501.

1324 28 June 2005, Joined Cases C-189/02 P, C-202/02 P, C-205/02 to C-208/02 P and C-213/02 P, *Dansk Rørindustrie and others vs Commission of the European Communities*, [2005] ECR I-05425, para 142–144, 8 September 2010, Case T-29/05, *Deltafina SpA v European Commission*, [2010] not yet reported, para 59, Case T-99/04, *AC-Treuhand AG v Commission of the European Communities*, [2008] ECR II-01501, para 130. See also: 7 January 2004, Joined Cases C-2004 P, C-205/00 P, C-213/00 P, C-217/00 P and C-219/00 P, *Aaborg Portland and others v Commission of the European Communities*, [2004] ECR I-00123, para 81.

1325 28 June 2005, Joined Cases C-189/02 P, C-202/02 P, C-205/02 to C-208/02 P and C-213/02 P, *Dansk Rørindustrie and others vs Commission of the European Communities*, [2005] ECR I-05425, para 142. See also: 7 January 2004, Joined Cases C-2004 P, C-205/00 P, C-213/00 P, C-217/00 P and C-219/00 P, *Aaborg Portland and others v Commission of the European Communities*, [2004] ECR I-00123, para 81.

1326 28 June 2005, Joined Cases C-189/02 P, C-202/02 P, C-205/02 to C-208/02 P and C-213/02 P, *Dansk Rørindustrie and others vs Commission of the European Communities*, [2005] ECR I-05425, para 142–144, 8 September 2010, Case T-29/05, *Deltafina SpA v European Commission*, [2010] not yet reported, para 59, 8 July 2008, Case T-99/04, *AC-Treuhand AG v Commission of the European Communities*, [2008] ECR II-01501, para 130, 7 January 2004, Joined Cases C-2004 P, C-205/00 P, C-213/00 P, C-217/00 P and C-219/00 P, *Aaborg Portland and others v Commission of the European Communities*, [2004] ECR I-00123, para 83 et seq.

unless it has publicly distanced itself from what was agreed at the meeting.[1327] Thus, if an undertaking attends meetings in which anti-competitive conduct is discussed and it was aware of the object of these meetings it can only prevent incurring liability if it either publicly in a clear and unequivocal manner distanced itself from the collusion or blew the whistle on the other participants. Regarding the awareness of the undertaking concerning the anticompetitive object of meetings, a stringent diligent standard will be applied due to which the Commission may infer from the economic activity and professional expertise of the undertaking in question that it cannot but be aware of the anti-competitive nature of the conduct at issue.[1328] These stringent standards set the bar in avoidance of liability very high indeed and arguably border on a "cling together, swing together" rationale. The objective requirement thus can be considered as rather sweeping, advocating a broad approach to the imposition of liability. But it is now time to dwell on the second, subjective requirement.

11.4. The subjective requirement

The subjective condition in essence holds that the attribution of an infringement of the competition rules depends on the manifestation of the undertaking's intentions. According to the ECJ this subjective requirement is inherent in the rules on tacit approval and failure to publicly distance oneself from the content of a cartel, as in these rules an assumption is implied that the undertaking will continue to endorse the objectives of the cartel and support its implementation.[1329] According to the subjective requirement it is necessary to establish that the undertaking intended to contribute through its own conduct to the common objectives of the cartel and that it was aware of the anti-competitive conduct of the other participants, or could reasonably have foreseen that conduct and was ready to accept that risk.[1330] This subjective requirement is thus easily inferred from thc objcctive conduct of the undertaking concerned, especially if one takes into consideration that a sufficient manifestation of the undertaking's intentions can be inferred from its tacit approval of and its failure to publicly distance itself from the cartel.

1327 28 June 2005, Joined Cases C-189/02 P, C-202/02 P, C-205/02 to C-208/02 P and C-213/02 P, *Dansk Rørindustrie and others vs Commission of the European Communities*, [2005] ECR I-05425, para 144 et seq.

1328 8 September 2010, Case T-29/05, *Deltafina SpA v European Commission*, [2010] not yet reported, para 63, 8 July 2008, Case T-99/04, *AC-Treuhand AG v Commission of the European Communities*, [2008] ECR II-01501, para 136.

1329 8 September 2010, Case T-29/05, *Deltafina SpA v European Commission*, [2010] not yet reported, para 62, 8 July 2008, Case T-99/04, *AC-Treuhand AG v Commission of the European Communities*, [2008] ECR II-01501, para 134.

1330 8 September 2010, Case T-29/05, *Deltafina SpA v European Commission*, [2010] not yet reported, para 62. See also: 7 January 2004, Joined Cases C-2004 P, C-205/00 P, C-213/00 P, C-217/00 P and C-219/00 P, *Aaborg Portland and others v Commission of the European Communities*, [2004] ECR I-00123, para 83.

11.5. The model of participation in competition law

In the realm of competition law the ECJ also had the opportunity to discuss the system of participation in more detail and has thereby clearly opted for a unitarian approach. In the *AC-Treuhand* case the question arose whether or not a consultancy firm, which was not active on the relevant organic peroxide market on which the cartel in question was operating could infringe Art 101 TFEU and be considered a perpetrator of the infringement.

The consultancy firm had contributed to the cartel in a mere accessorial or auxiliary manner by *inter alia*, collecting and monitoring figures, establishing statistics, organising meetings, respectively reserving meeting rooms for unofficial meetings of the colluding companies, but allegedly without attending the meetings nor being aware of their content.[1331] The ECJ held that in the absence of a rule distinguishing perpetrators from participants all undertakings who fulfilled the conditions outlined above could be deemed to have infringed Article 101 TFEU.[1332] It reiterated that tacitly approving the cartel or failing to report it to the authorities will be sufficient, since the limited importance of that contribution may be taken into consideration for determining the level of the fine.[1333] Thus an undertaking might be considered to have violated Article 101 TFEU (former Art 81 EC), even if it has not itself restricted competition. It follows that European Union law in this context clearly seems to favour a strict unitarian approach.

11.6. Evaluation

The question one must now attempt to answer is which lessons can be drawn from the European approach in competition law for the purpose of establishing a European framework of participation in crime. First, it should be mentioned that in the realm of competition law it is a general rule that natural or legal persons may be penalised only for acts imputed to them individually.[1334] However under existing case law it is on an exceptional basis also possible to attribute liability to a legal entity for conduct it has not itself committed. Parent companies can for instance be held liable for the conduct of their subsidiaries, even if they possess a distinct legal

1331 8 July 2008, Case T-99/04, *AC-Treuhand AG v Commission of the European Communities*, [2008] ECR II-01501.

1332 8 July 2008, Case T-99/04, *AC-Treuhand AG v Commission of the European Communities*, [2008] ECR II-01501, para 103 et seq.

1333 8 July 2008, Case T-99/04, *AC-Treuhand AG v Commission of the European Communities*, [2008] ECR II-01501, para 133. This line of reasoning was later confirmed in: 8 September 2010, Case T-29/05 *Deltafina SpA v European Commission*, [2010] not yet reported. See also: 7 January 2004, Joined Cases C-2004 P, C-205/00 P, C-213/00 P, C-217/00 P and C-219/00 P, *Aaborg Portland and others v Commission of the European Communities*, [2004] ECR I-00123, para 86.

1334 Montesa and Givaja, 'When Parents pay for their children's wrongs: Attribution of liability for Antitrust infringements in Parent-Subsidiary scenarios' World Competition (2006), p. 558.

personality. This will be possible where the parent company exerted considerable control over the subsidiary. The test applied thereby is whether the subsidiary does not independently decide its own conduct on the market but carries out in all material respects, the instruction given to it by the parent company.[1335] This in effect largely resembles the situation in national law regarding vertical forms of perpetration, outlined above. Regarding the requirement of control, competition law however, adopts a broad approach as case law has established a rebuttable presumption that a parent company exercised decisive influence over the wholly-owned subsidiary at the time of the infringement.[1336]

Besides this, it is however submitted that the substantive rules pertaining to participatory conduct in competition law should be treated with caution and are not easily transferrable to the realm of wrongdoing committed by natural persons. This is for several reasons. First, in the view of the Commission and the ECJ, competition law despite its punitive nature is formally considered to be administrative law. This means that general principles of community law such as the principle of legality or guilt need not necessarily have the same scope as when they apply to a situation covered by criminal law in the strict sense.[1337]

Furthermore, the rather broad approach to participation adopted here can be explained by the broad offence definitions of Articles 101 and 102 TFEU as well as by the underlying protected legal interest, i.e. the unrestricted competition within the internal market. The protected legal interest in competition law is highly abstract. It is not an individual interest such as life and limb but rather a collective good – the functioning of the internal market. Accordingly, every contribution is seen as a harmful attack on the protected interest.[1338] A member of a cartel, regardless of his contribution is considered to be a perpetrator. This also corresponds to the view of the commission which considers infringements under Art 101 TFEU (former Article 81 EC) by their very nature to be abstract endangerment offences, in the sense of "an offence consisting in the creation of a state of affairs which is dangerous, where no specific danger need be statutorily defined".[1339] This is particularly so since Article 101 TFEU is concerned with the restriction of competition and a cartel poses a general danger for competition, quite apart from the individual case.[1340] Finally, it should be kept in mind that competition

1335 16 November 2000, C-286/98 P, *Stora Kopparbergs Bergslags AB v Commission of the European Communities*, [2000] ECR I-9945.

1336 Montesa and Givaja, 'When Parents pay for their children's wrongs: Attribution of liability for Antitrust infringements in Parent-Subsidiary scenarios' World Competition (2006), pp. 555–574.

1337 8 July 2008, Case T-99/04, *AC-Treuhand AG v Commission of the European Communities*, [2008] ECR II-01501, para 113.

1338 Hamdorf, 'Beteiligungsmodelle im Strafrecht' (2002), p. 356.

1339 8 July 2008, Case T-99/04, *AC-Treuhand AG v Commission of the European Communities*, [2008] ECR II-01501, para 107.

1340 8 July 2008, Case T-99/04, *AC-Treuhand AG v Commission of the European Communities*, [2008] ECR II-01501, para 107.

law is of course concerned with the liability of legal entities, which adheres at times to a slightly different logic than the rules regulating the conduct of natural persons.

Nevertheless, an evaluation of the competition rules is valuable for the purposes of this research as it provides insights on possible solutions on how to deal with concerted practices in criminal wrongdoing. It can for instance be deduced from the foregoing that the core of the notion of co-perpetration is a common plan or purpose, or in the words of the ECJ a "concurrence of wills". This corresponds well to the approach taken by national criminal law outlined above and can therefore be seen as the common foundation for the imposition of liability as co-perpetrators. However, this is not the end of the matter.

In order to be held liable as a co-perpetrator, one must according to European and national law furthermore contribute through its own conduct to the common objective of the criminal enterprise. It is therefore irrelevant if this contribution took place at a preparatory stage (as is for instance the case when a consultancy firm organises meetings, etc. but is not involved in restricting competition on the relevant market) or at the time of the commission of the offence (i.e. in competition law terms the implementation of the anti-competitive agreement or concerted practice and thereby the effective restriction of competition on the relevant market). Furthermore, another common trait that emerges from the comparison of competition with national law is that an individual can only be held liable for conduct committed by its partners in crime of which he was either aware or could reasonably have foreseen that conduct and that it was ready to accept the attendant risk.

Presence at the scene of the crime can be an indication for assistance and encouragement but it is submitted that a stringent duty to retreat or to disclose as it applies in competition law should not be applied to individual wrongdoing. Undertakings are arguably much more rationally calculating economic actors than individuals. Given their economic activities and professional expertise and the applicable diligence and business standards in their operational sector a stricter duty to refrain from illegal activities seems defensible in regard to corporate liability but should not be imposed on the individual.

Competition law first and foremost deals with conduct of professionals, i.e. business and economic actors for which a considerable degree of skills and knowledge is required. Our everyday life on the other hand is much less regulated than the economic world and the conduct of our fellow citizens is most likely less predictable than the one of economic operators. Furthermore individuals might be much more susceptible to peer pressure than undertakings. For all those reasons it is submitted that for individual wrongdoing, something more than mere presence should be required for the imposition of criminal liability. Moreover a stringent duty to retreat or report should not be imposed on individuals as it is much more likely for them to become implicated in criminal wrongdoing by chance, bad luck or coincidence than is arguably the case in the business world.

12. Preliminary conclusion

Before proceeding to discuss a potential European concept of participation in crime it seems pertinent to first pause for a moment and recapitulate the foregoing findings. In short, it is possible to distinguish horizontal forms of participation where all persons involved can be considered as equal partners (e.g. co-perpetration), from vertical forms of participation where the primary responsible utilises another person to achieve his goals. A final category can be distinguished from the aforementioned, namely the notion of facilitation where the participant often takes an auxiliary or subservient role.

Perpetrational liability, it has been shown, has traditionally been linked to a strict restrictive concept of perpetration. Based on an empirical or naturalistic view of participation, perpetration is according to this stance, closely linked to the direct and immediate fulfilment of the actus reus. However, this does not correspond anymore to the actuality of modern crime and can lead to frictions, especially in differentiated systems and in particular in situations where the crime has been committed in some sort of organisational context. Such an approach might namely not always capture the actual division of labour and responsibility between the parties involved in the commission of the crime, as it is required that each participant at least brings about a part of the actus reus. Yet, from a moral or culpability point of view criminal responsibility does not necessarily diminish as the distance from the *locus delicti* increases, but rather one may even consider it to grow. The concentration of all reproach and responsibility in the person who physically brings about the actus reus can in some instances transform small-time criminals into prime movers.

In a unitarian system, on the other hand, where all participants are meted out to the same punishment, a restrictive conception of perpetration is maintainable as the different degrees of responsibility, and culpability can be taken into consideration at the sentencing stage. This might explain why only the English penal system strictly applies such a restrictive approach. There the focus lies on the different modes of participation rather than on the concept of perpetration. By contrast, in Germany and the Netherlands, the restrictive approach has been supplemented firstly by the legislator who added the notion of co-perpetration and perpetration by means to the direct perpetrator and secondly by doctrines which expand the concepts of perpetration to situations where the main responsible has not himself, i.e. physically committed the actus reus of the underlying offence.

Therefore, it can be said that in formally differentiated systems a clear paradigm shift towards a normative concept of participation is discernible. The imposition of liability seems to increasingly focus on duties of control of the respective participant. If a duty to control or prevent a potentially criminal conduct can be established for a participant he will be regarded as primary responsible for the occurred criminal harm. Thus, the focus has shifted from the physical perpetrator to the person "in charge" of the criminal enterprise. This shift towards a more normative conception of participation can also be linked to the rise of the social act requirement and the emergence of doctrines such as hegemony over the act and functional perpetration. The creation of these doctrines has however had a distortive effect on these differentiated participation systems.

One effect of these developments is namely that many forms of involvement in the commission of the crime that were traditionally classified as instigation or aiding are nowadays often considered as forms of perpetration resulting in a higher punishment. Consider for instance the example of a physically absent initiator of a crime. In theory, his conduct can easily, depending of course on the exact details, be classified as co-perpetration, instigation, or perpetration by means alike. A brief look at pertinent case law confirms this tendency. Consider for instance the example of the person on a lookout. While this could be seen as a paradigm for accessorial liability, Dutch and German jurisprudence has also assumed co-perpetration in these cases.[1341]

This convergence of forms of perpetration with forms of participation can be problematic from the viewpoint of legal certainty and just desert. If the boundaries between perpetration and accessory liability become arbitrary, a fair attribution of criminal liability is no longer possible. It already becomes apparent that one of the alleged core functions of a differentiated system, namely the neat and fair categorisation of participatory conduct into different categories linked to different degrees of punishment is not always possible in practice. In the German penal system the boundaries between instigation, aiding and perpetration have further been blurred by the expansion of the notion of perpetration by means. The notion has its roots in the doctrine of innocent agency which allows for the establishment of liability as a perpetrator in cases where the participant has caused an innocent person to commit the criminal offence. However, the doctrine is interpreted broadly in Germany to encompass also situations where the person committing the crime is not innocent but fully criminally liable.[1342]

One driving force behind this expansion arguably lies in the desire to hold executives, etc. primarily responsible for the wrong committed by subordinates who often are considered less culpable than the person in charge as they only carry out orders.[1343] This broad approach bears witness to the fact that a differentiated system encounters difficulties in achieving adequate results in economic and organisational structures which are characterised by a high degree of division of labour, as well as by complex hierarchical structures.[1344] Be that as it may, the

[1341] See: Chapter III. 8.1.1.

[1342] In the Netherlands the doctrine of instigation seems to have taken a similar development, as it seems no longer required for instigation that the person committing the offence acted with full responsibility. See: De Hullu, 'Materieel Strafrecht' (2009), p. 458. However, instigation (uitlokking) in the Netherlands has also lost its importance as the application of functional perpetration in the economic context and the broad concept of co-perpetration cover most of the classical situations of instigation.

[1343] Rotsch, 'Einheitstäterschaft statt Tatherrschaft' (2009), pp. 388–390.

[1344] A fact which could certainly be mitigated by the introduction of corporate liability.

effect of this broad approach regarding perpetration by means is certainly that the boundaries between perpetrational and accessorial liability become more blurred. This can arguably cause problems with regard to foreseeability and legal certainty as it might not be easy to determine for a defendant in advance whether his conduct will give rise to primary or secondary responsibility.

The corollary to the developments outlined above is that the notion of perpetration in countries adhering to a differentiated approach to participation, becomes inflated due to a more normative and holistic conception of the notion, which in turn encroaches on and diminishes the importance of other traditional categories like instigation and aiding. It has been demonstrated that conduct traditionally classified as instigation in Germany nowadays is often seen as perpetration and a similar development is visible in the Netherlands. There the development of the doctrine of functional perpetration as well as the broad approach taken in regard to co-perpetration has diminished the relevance of the notions of instigation and perpetration by means. This goes even so far that it has been argued that the doctrine of innocent agency could be abolished.[1345]

In summary it can be stated that differentiated systems increasingly move away from the strict dogmatic separation and demarcation of the different forms of participation in crime. The increasing normative tendencies in regard to perpetration arguably bear witness to a more social conception of liability. Criminal liability has discarded its stern individualistic conception of wrongdoing and more frequently assesses wrongdoing in the social context in which it occurs. Moreover, the shift in focus to less tangible forms of conduct is also discernible in the context of perpetration. As the importance of an objective involvement in the commission of the actus reus diminishes, it however becomes necessary to invoke other safeguards to adhere to the principle of individual responsibility and culpability flowing from the principle of guilt. In order to assure that the punishment imposed matches the wrongdoing and culpability of the offender, the emphasis comes to rest on more subjective elements such as the concept of control. The more control, hegemony or dominion a person is deemed to possess over the commission of the offence the severer the quality and degree of his liability will arguably be. Yet, it should also be noted here that one further reason for this development can certainly also be found in evidentiary difficulties that courts encounter with organised and systemic wrongdoing as well as in cases where participants refuse to cooperate with the court and rely on their right to remain silent.[1346]

1345 De Hullu, 'Materieel Strafrecht' (2009), pp. 457, 466.

1346 See for instance: HR 12 April 2005, *NJ* 2005, 577. The victim in this case was found strangled in his apartment and the DNA of one of the two suspects was found on the carrier strap with which the victim was suffocated. Regarding the defendant in this case, it could only be proven that he was present in the flat at the time of the crime and from a confiscated letter it could be deduced that he knew what had exactly happened on the night of the murder. The court held that the fact that he was present at the murder, did nothing to deter his partner from killing the victim and did not distance himself from the criminal enterprise was sufficient to indicate a conscious, close and comprehensive cooperation of the two partners.

This shift in the conception of liability also finds expression in the severity of the sentences imposed. This is arguably a corollary of the prevalent culture of control which imposes high demands and diligent standards on its citizens. The higher and more demanding the social standards, the more severe a breach of these standards will arguably be assessed by society.

From the foregoing one can infer that the different models of participation, outlined above, all have their different shortcomings. In Germany and the Netherlands the demarcation of the different notions of participation in crime has proven cumbersome and has given rise to sophisticated and intricate doctrines. Yet despite these doctrinal efforts, the boundaries between the different concepts remain vague and are often ignored by the courts.

The English approach on the other hand, at times adopts an overly broad approach in regard to accomplice liability. Not only is the accomplice guilty of the same offence, which can lead to harsh results in regard to crimes where a mandatory minimum sentence is foreseen, as for instance in regard to the offence of murder, but furthermore, the doctrine of joint criminal enterprise allows convictions on the basis of foreseeability despite the absence of any assistance or encouragement in regard to the crime for which the participant is convicted.[1347] This arguably can create a mismatch between the culpability of the accessory and the underlying criminal offence of which he is found guilty. Crudely put it seems peculiar, to say the least, that a perpetrator must act with intention to kill in order to be found guilty of murder while an accomplice merely needs to participate in a criminal enterprise with the foresight that this consequence will occur.[1348]

There is, yet another potentially problematic aspect of the English functional unitarian approach which is worthwhile mentioning and which will considerably influence the following discussion on a European model of participation. One may recall that in the English model of participation the distinction between perpetrators and accomplices only plays an auxiliary role.[1349] This hallmark of the English law on participation has however some important practical implications. It has been discussed that due to the fact that all participants in the English penal system are formally eligible to the same amount of punishment, it is not necessary for the prosecution to specify in advance whether the suspect is charged for being a perpetrator or an accomplice. Neither is it necessary for the prosecution to clearly outline which form the alleged complicity took.[1350]

While this certainly is of great convenience for, and simplifies the task of the prosecution significantly in certain cases, it causes frictions with Art 6 (3) (a) of the

1347 See also: Sullivan, 'First degree murder and complicity – conditions for parity of culpability between principal and accomplice' Criminal Law and Philosophy (2007), pp. 271–288.

1348 Stewart, 'The End of "Modes of Liability" for international crimes' Leiden Journal of International Law (2012), pp. 3–73.

1349 See: Chapter III. 5.

1350 See for instance: R v Giannetto [1997] 1 Cr App R 1; Ashworth, 'Principles of criminal law' (2006), p. 412.

European Convention of Human Rights. This Article holds that everyone charged with a criminal offence has the right to be informed promptly, in a language which he understands and in detail, *of the nature and cause of the accusations against him.*[1351] Accordingly it could be argued that such an approach is also incompatible with the right to a fair trial under Article 6 of the ECHR. A formal unitarian system where all participants are deemed to be perpetrators regardless of their precise role in the commission of the offence could be seen to be in contradiction of this article as the defendant will not be informed in detail about the nature and cause of the accusation against him. The same point could be advanced against the English model of participation. In *R v Mercer*, English law escaped the invalidation of the system as it was found that Article 6 (3) was not violated in a case where it was alleged that the defendant was part of a joint criminal enterprise in regard to a robbery without specifying his precise role.[1352] Yet, in a comparable Belgian case the European Court of Human Rights found a violation of the right to a fair trial pursuant to Article 6 (1) where an aggravating circumstance (the death of the victim during the robbery), proved against one person, had been attributed to all members of the joint criminal enterprise.[1353]

Two conclusions can be drawn from this. On the one hand, it is arguable that as a matter of principle a penal system should set up at least some form of categorisation, in order to provide the suspect with a fair warning of the allegations against him and to allow him to exercise his defence rights in a practical and effective manner. On the other hand, it follows that the attribution of collateral offences to other participants in the context of a joint criminal enterprise may in certain cases well be contrary to the principle of individual criminal liability and therefore incompatible with Article 6 ECHR.

Arguably some form of categorisation or distinction respectively between primary and secondary responsibility seems also necessary from the viewpoint of legal certainty and the principle of legality as enshrined in Article 7 ECHR. Article 7 *inter alia* embodies the principle that the criminal law ought not to be construed extensively to the detriment of the accused. "It should be construed and applied, as follows from its object and purpose, so as to provide effective safeguards against arbitrary prosecution, conviction and punishment".[1354] This requirement will be fulfilled if a person can reasonably foresee the consequences of his actions.[1355] If without exception even remote causal contributions were to result in perpetrational liability this could arguably be seen as an extensive interpretation of the underlying criminal offence, undermining the foreseeability of the consequences flowing from the conduct of the defendant. Thus also from this

1351 Italics added.

1352 R v Mark John Leslie Mercer [2001] EWCA Crim 638.

1353 *Goktepe v Belgium*, appl. no. 50372/99, 2 June 2005.

1354 *Kononov v Latvia*, appl. no. 36376/04, 17 May 2010, para 185–187. See also: *Van Anraat v the Netherlands*, appl. no. 65389/09, 6 July 2010.

1355 See: *Cantoni v France*, appl. no. 17862/91, 11 November 1996.

perspective a distinction between primary and secondary responsibility seems desirable.

13. Towards a European concept of participation

13.1. Introduction

The foregoing discussion has shown that differentiated systems of participation such as the Netherlands and Germany encounter particular difficulties in regard to vertical forms of co-operation as well as in regard to some forms of horizontal co-operation where a part of the participants is not actively involved in the commission of the offence. In other words, they struggle to cope with contemporary forms of criminal wrongdoing which is characterised by an increasing division of labour, high degree of organisation as well as systematisation.

Increasingly human beings use intermediates (often due to an increase in the division of labour) to bring about a certain result and do not bring it about directly despite being in control and thus blameworthy for the criminal conduct.[1356] In such circumstances, the person carrying out the offence might seem less culpable than the mastermind organising the scheme. Likewise, the person who during the crime functions as a lookout or getaway driver, traditionally seen as a form of auxiliary participation, might be the driving force behind the criminal enterprise, deserving more or just as much punishment as his partners actually committing the crime.

Due to the significant breadth of the doctrine of participation, it will not be possible here to address, let alone attempt to solve all conundrums and predicaments surrounding it. This research will however attempt to outline in broad strokes an alternative to traditional concepts of participation. It will strive to develop a skeleton argument and leave it for subsequent discussions to flesh out the concept proposed here.

13.2. A normative concept of participation in crime

In order to countermand the friction caused by the orthodox, strict, restrictive conception of perpetration, the notion of participation is increasingly interpreted normatively in order to respond to contemporary challenges in criminal law, such as organised and white collar crime. It is therefore submitted that in European criminal law the focus on the individual, physical perpetrator should be substituted by a holistic concept of perpetration in which not only the physical, viz. direct perpetrator of the actus reus may be considered the primary responsible, but also

1356 Gritter, 'Functioneel plegen door een natuurlijke persoon', in van der Leij (ed), Plegen en Deelnemen (2007), p. 14.

other persons, if their conduct, contribution or role in the commission of the offence establishes that he bears substantial responsibility for the wrong committed.

Accordingly the empirical or naturalistic conception of participation should be replaced by a normative one, distributing liability according to the criteria of (substantial) authorship for a criminal harm or outcome respectively. It has already been discussed that one of the central tasks of the concept of actus reus is to establish a link between a person and a criminal outcome.[1357] Naturally also several persons can be involved in bringing about a prescribed criminal harm and can therefore incur liability for this outcome. Thus, criminal liability could arguably be imposed when some form of "outcome responsibility" for the criminal harm can be established.[1358]

The question then of course becomes when it would be adequate to hold that someone bears responsibility for a criminal outcome. This could be the case if the occurrence of a criminal outcome can be linked to the agency of the person in question.[1359] Therefore it will be necessary to establish a linkage between the agent and the (criminal) outcome.[1360] However, this linkage must be sufficiently material or salient in order to warrant the imposition of liability as a perpetrator. In other words, there must be some material connection between the contribution, role, etc. of the defendant and the committed offence. He must bear "substantial responsibility" for the occurred criminal outcome. In order to establish such a link and in order to achieve a holistic concept of perpetration, a shift in perspective will be required. Traditionally criminal law focuses on the main character, i.e. the perpetrator and takes a forward-looking perspective by enquiring what the participants intended, what they foresaw, how the division of tasks was negotiated, etc.

A holistic concept of participation, it is submitted, requires however a retrospective approach. The vantage point for the attribution of criminal liability is the occurred criminal outcome. From this outcome one reasons backwards to attribute outcome responsibility to those participants that due to their role, significant contribution, control, duty to control, etc. possess authorship for the outcome.[1361] Such an approach also introduces a social component into the evaluation by not only focusing on the principal, but on the committed deed and its inherent social wrongdoing.[1362]

This evaluation is a normative one as it does not focus on empirical or naturalistic facts such as the direct commission of the actus reus but rather

---

1357 See: Chapter II.1.

1358 The term outcome responsibility has been coined by Honoré for whom it represented the most basic form of accountability in civil and criminal law. See: Honoré, 'Responsibility and fault' (1999), pp. 7–40. The term is however given a slightly different meaning here.

1359 Sullivan, 'First degree murder and complicity – conditions for parity of culpability between principal and accomplice' Criminal Law and Philosophy (2007), p. 276.

1360 Sullivan, 'First degree murder and complicity – conditions for parity of culpability between principal and accomplice' Criminal Law and Philosophy (2007), p. 276.

1361 See also: Weisser, 'Täterschaft in Europa' (2011), pp. 497, 506–511.

1362 Lampe, 'Tätersysteme: Spuren und Strukturen' ZStW (2007), pp. 482, 517.

distributes liability according to the requirement of a material or substantial connection between the person and the criminal harm.[1363] The normative core of attribution in criminal law can be seen in ascribing responsibility for a criminal harm to its author, i.e. the perpetrator.[1364] The general norm or duty, resting on all citizens, not to participate in criminal wrongdoing constitutes the foundation of this attribution. Therefore the term perpetration is interpreted normatively in the sense that a direct fulfilment of the actus reus may be a sufficient but not a necessary requirement for the imposition of primary liability. The connection between a criminal outcome and its author(s) must rather be established by analysing the conduct of every participant in the context of the realisation of a criminal wrong in a co-operative manner. If such a connection can be established, the person arguably bears substantial responsibility for the criminal outcome and imposing liability as a principal seems justified. In this evaluation also social factors such as the participant's vested interest in the commission of the offence, the organisational framework in which the conduct took place, the prevalent chain of command, the presence of duties to supervise or control, etc. have to be taken into consideration in order to obtain an overall picture of the criminal enterprise and to arrive at a holistic concept of perpetration.

Furthermore, also conduct taking place and contributions rendered in the preparatory phase or after the fact can play a role in the evaluation process. However, these contributions should have had a significant impact and must have considerably shaped and influenced the commission of the offence in order for substantial responsibility to arise. In other words, if the defendant was not actively involved in the commission of the offence, substantial responsibility can nevertheless be established if he played an active, initiating, organising or co-ordinating role in the preparatory phase. This reflects the nature of actus reus and mens rea as communicating vessels, as a less objective involvement in the commission of the offence can be compensated via more involvement on the subjective side, i.e. the preparatory mens rea and vice versa. Conduct taking place after the fact can be of relevance in two ways. On the one hand it is conceivable that the conduct after the fact is part and parcel of a prior agreement or division of labour. The getaway driver, arguably can incur substantial responsibility if he for instance devised the plan for the heist. Furthermore, conduct after the fact can indirectly shed some light on the respective roles of the participants. Thus, the fact that someone received an even share of the loot could be an indication that he participated in the deed as an equal partner. Mere presence at the scene of the crime should generally not suffice to establish primary responsibility but might nevertheless be a factor that taken in connection with additional circumstances could be seen as an indication of substantial responsibility.

The most obvious material linkage where one can speak of "substantial responsibility" will arguably exist in cases where the contribution, influence, etc. of

---

1363 See also: Weisser, 'Täterschaft in Europa' (2011), p. 509.

1364 De Jong, 'Daad-Schuld' (2009), p. 61.

the defendant constitutes a *conditio sine qua non* for the commission of the offence.[1365] Thus, there must at least be sufficient evidence that the person was a major participant and not merely "a pawn in a complex game of criminal chess". In other words, as already mentioned, the attribution of primary responsibility ought to require that the link between an occurred criminal outcome and a participant should be substantial rather then tenuous. Therefore the discussion will now turn to the question of when it can be held that a person should bear substantial responsibility for an occurred harm.

Generally speaking criminal law always comes into action when a legally protected interest, such as life and limb, sexual integrity, property rights, etc. has been harmed, or at least endangered.[1366] The concept of a legally protected interest could to a certain extent be derived in the realm of European law from the general principles of Union Law such as the common European values of the European Convention of Human rights or the Charter of Fundamental rights of the European Union as a well as the fundamental rights and freedoms enshrined in the treaties and as they flow from the constitutional traditions common to the Member States.[1367]

A legal interest may be harmed or endangered either directly or indirectly.[1368] Either the conduct of the principal causes the violation of the norm directly, i.e. without the intervention of another, or the violation has been brought about indirectly by the conduct of another person (an intermediary) over which the primarily responsible principal exerted control and in addition possessed culpability regarding the commission of the offence. The notion of control in this context constitutes an important threshold for imposing primary liability as it assures that people will only be held liable for harm which can be seen as an expression of their agency. It prevents the creation of collective responsibility and assures that the imposed punishment by and large corresponds to the culpability of the individual.

The question that subsequently arises in regard to indirectly harming a protected legal interest accordingly is when it can be said that a person exerted control over another. This arguably will to a large extent depend on the relationship between the principal offender and the intermediary. In relationships of subordination, where a duty to control, or prevent rests on the person in charge, as is frequently the case in business or economic relationships (e.g. employer – employee, etc.) control will often be easily established. An employer, executive manager, etc., due to his social role and position is under a duty to diligently control and supervise the conduct of his employees. He is obliged to conduct the daily business operations in accordance with the law and prevalent diligence standards in a given economic sector. Where he severely neglects these duties by for instance turning a blind eye to certain forms

1365 Sullivan, 'First degree murder and complicity – conditions for parity of culpability between principal and accomplice' Criminal Law and Philosophy (2007), p. 277.

1366 See also: Chapter I. 4.3.2.

1367 See: Article 6 TEU.

1368 Rotsch, 'Einheitstäterschaft statt Tatherrschaft' (2009), p. 422 et seq.

of conduct, or abuses his authority, control can arguably be assumed. Thus, where for instance the CEO of a company orders his employees to open a tank containing waste oil, the CEO can be considered to bear substantial responsibility for the pollution and can therefore be considered a perpetrator.

Yet, there are further situations conceivable where it can be said that a person exerted control over another. In these situations, special heed will have to be paid to the peculiarities of the case at hand. Consider for instance the situation that ruthless John might for instance pressurise weak-willed James into robbing a bank. In this case the primary responsible violates the legal norm indirectly by using another to directly commit the offence. Comparable thereto are cases where the primary offender instigates or abets another to commit the offence. Accordingly also cases where a person can be considered to possess intellectual authorship for the crime in question can give rise to substantial responsibility. Intellectual authorship for an occurred criminal harm can arguably be established in a variety of ways. The inducement can either take place through personal contact, but also through other channels or mediums such as the internet or newspapers. Therefore, any form of implicit or explicit inducement, such as orders, persuasion, request, suggestion, etc. can give rise to substantial responsibility. What is however crucial is that the conduct of the intellectual author had a decisive impact on the person factually committing the actus reus and increased the likelihood of the commission of the offence considerably in order to establish primary responsibility.[1369] Thus, if for instance accountant Saul induces Walt to falsify documents in order for Walt's business to be eligible for subsidies, Saul can be considered to share substantial responsibility together with Walt. The same reasoning can be applied to cases where Marcus persuades or offers Charles a reward to kill Marcus's nagging wife.

However, a person can also posses a more complete form of control over the intermediary's conduct, namely in cases where the harm is caused by an "innocent agent" acting without mens rea, justified or excused. Under these circumstances the exerted control can be considered so complete that the person behind the "innocent agent" will be deemed directly responsible for the occurred criminal harm. Thus, under this category *inter alia* situations can be subsumed where one person assumes a superior position in comparison to the one directly bringing about the actus reus due to superior knowledge or due to the fact that he controls the intermediary's will. An indication for the establishment of control and thus substantial responsibility can in the latter cases often arguably be found in the utilisation of means such as force, threat or deception.

In case the person to be deemed to carry substantial responsibility for the criminal harm lacks a required quality for the commission of the offence, liability can arguably still be imposed if he acted intentionally in regard to the presence of the quality in the person of the factual perpetrator. In this case his culpability encompasses the presence of the quality as he deliberately selected an intermediary

---

1369 See also: Weisser, 'Täterschaft in Europa' (2011), pp. 513–516.

possessing this quality for the commission of the offence. The same would apply to offences that formally require the physical carrying out of the conduct requirement, as is for instance the case in regard to perjury. As the normative concept of perpetration proposed here is not linked to the physical commission of the actus reus but rather focuses holistically on establishing substantial responsibility for a criminal offence, these cases can arguably easily be dealt with.[1370]

Finally, several persons can bear responsibility for a criminal wrong if they acted according to a common purpose or plan. They will share responsibility for the occurrence of the criminal offence. A mutual attribution of conduct will however become unnecessary in the context of a normative concept of perpetration which takes the occurred criminal offence or harm as a starting point. Due to the overall assessment adopted by this approach, a distinction between liability for own conduct and attribution of conduct carried out by partners in crime becomes redundant.[1371]

To establish whether a criminal offence has been committed for which several persons bear substantial responsibility, different aspects might be taken into account, such as for instance a common plan or purpose. It seems vital here that a concurrence of will can be established, regardless of whether this was reached explicitly or tacitly, prior or during the commission of the crime. Therefore the division of tasks, the exchangeability of roles, the role of the suspect in the preparatory phase, in the commission of the offence, as well as the general importance of the participants' role for the manifestation of the offence can be important factors.

In this context one could further raise the intricate question whether and to what extent such a common purpose or plan can generate responsibility for an unplanned, collateral offence committed in the course of carrying out the initial offence. Naturally, the scope of the envisaged offence as well as the foreseeability of the occurrence of the collateral offence will play a role here. It is submitted that the general rule here should be that prima facie only intended consequences can be attributed. This follows from the fundamental principles of individual responsibility or guilt. Yet, an attribution of liability could still be possible where the committed conduct is not entirely different from what was intended by the participants or the common plan. In other words, one would have to establish whether or not the collateral offence can be regarded as being covered by the respective intent or common plan. As a yardstick a recklessness standard could be applied here which would lead to the attribution of liability if a conscious disregard of a substantial and unjustifiable risk whose disregard involves a gross deviation from the standard of conduct that a law-abiding person would observe can be established. It should however in these cases still be possible for the judge to distinguish between the different parties on the sentencing level according to their individual guilt and wrongdoing.

1370 See: Weisser, 'Täterschaft in Europa' (2011), pp. 529–533.

1371 See: Weisser, 'Täterschaft in Europa' (2011), pp. 511–512, 542.

To briefly summarise, it can be said that such a normative approach would thus lead to a broad concept of primary responsibility, capable of catering to the actuality of crime and all its manifold variations. Not only the person directly fulfilling the actus reus would be considered a principal, but every participant who carries "substantial responsibility" for the criminal outcome will be deemed to have committed the offence himself. Furthermore such an approach would be able to achieve satisfactory results in the context of systemic and organised wrongdoing. Given the fact that the European Union's focus will be exactly on those areas of criminal behaviour, such as organised crime, trafficking in human beings, money laundering, corruption and computer crime, a normative approach arguably also seems to correspond well to the scope and requirements of a European criminal law. These are crimes which are rarely committed single headedly and often involve large crime syndicates, operating on an international level, characterised by a high degree of structural complexity.

13.3. Trivial assistance

The aforementioned approach, however, leaves a small category of cases unaccounted for, which can be termed forms of "trivial assistance". These cases could be covered by a separate offence of "trivial assistance".[1372] Under this category would fall cases of minor assistance, which fall below the substantial responsibility standard outlined above. Here traditional cases of providing aid such as lending a known burglar a screwdriver, or giving instructions on how to crack a safe, can be pigeon-holed. Thus, any kind of conduct that furthered or made the commission of the crime easier, swifter or "securer" can be subsumed here.

A complex and intricate question here concerns the applicable mens rea standard. The doctrinal predicament here by and large is to distinguish "lending support to crime from more basic cases of poor citizenship".[1373] It is common ground that liability for assistance requires an 'intention' to assist the offence in question. But what exactly intention should mean in that context is a bone of contention.[1374] Generally speaking, one could adopt two different approaches. On the one hand it could be argued that as the conduct of the aider in this category of cases will often be innocuous, an increased standard of fault should compensate for the less in objective wrongdoing. Thus, according to such an approach a direct intention to facilitate the commission of the offence should be required. The

1372 The term "trivial assistance" is taken from: Dressler, 'Reforming Complicity Law: Trivial Assistance as a lesser offence?' Ohio State Journal of Criminal Law (2008), pp. 427–448.

1373 Wilson, 'A rational scheme of liability for participating in crime' Criminal Law Review (2008), p. 16.

1374 See also: Blomsma, 'Mens rea and defences in European criminal law' (2012). Naturally also the fundamental question as to which conduct qualifies as intentional conduct, on which common and civil law countries generally adopt different approaches, will have significant implications for the law of complicity.

assistant in other words must act *in order* to facilitate the commission of the offence.[1375] Such a standard of fault would exclude cases from liability where the person in question merely suspects or fears that his conduct will contribute to the commission of the offence. Thus, a shopkeeper who sells a crowbar to a shady person would in this case not incur liability.

Another view would however claim that such a strict approach would cast the net of criminal liability too narrowly. It would therefore be preferable, so the argument runs, to adopt a lower standard of fault but exclude from liability scenarios where the aid was provided unwittingly. Thus, according to this approach intention will be assumed as long as the assistant acts in a way which (s)he knows will facilitate the commission of the offence. On this view, knowledge is thus sufficient since the assistant need only have intended acts, which he knew to be capable of assisting or encouraging the commission of the crime.[1376] As this could give rise to hardship cases as is demonstrated by the aforementioned shopkeeper example who would according to such an approach *prima facie* incur criminal liability, an escape route from liability in the form of a defence such as acting in the ordinary course of business supply, etc. could be introduced to exclude cases of poor citizenship from the realm of liability.[1377] An alternative to the introduction of such a defence for assistance by neutral conduct would be to closely evaluate subjective as well as objective factors on a case by case basis. In these cases the focus should arguably rest on the quality of the assistant's contribution rather than the general usefulness of his conduct for the commission of the offence. Prevalent diligent standards and business customs, as well as the seriousness of the anticipated offence and the purpose for which the defendant claims to have been acting could all be taken into account in order to develop a yardstick for imposing liability.

An additional question that would warrant further investigation here is if derivative liability principles should be applied or if liability should be inchoate. Applying derivative liability principles would circumscribe the scope of criminal liability, as depending on the link between the offence of the perpetrator and the aider required, attempted aid would not trigger criminal liability. If one however prefers to view the liability of the aider as free standing and autonomous, the creation of an inchoate offence would seem more appropriate. Conduct aiding the commission of the criminal offence would then trigger liability regardless whether or not the perpetrator subsequently committed the criminal offence, thus criminalising attempted aid. Such an autonomous concept of assistance would arguably fit nicely in an increasingly individualised society.

1375 Duff, '"Can I help you?" Accessorial liability and the intention to assist' Legal Studies (1990), pp. 165–181.

1376 Duff, '"Can I help you?" Accessorial liability and the intention to assist' Legal Studies (1990), pp. 165–181.

1377 Wilson, 'A rational scheme of liability for participating in crime' Criminal Law Review (2008), p. 16.

However, this predicament defies an easy solution and is further complicated by the fact that often considerations of penal policy will wield a considerable influence here. From the perspective of fair labelling as well as the safeguard and expressive function of criminal law it would arguably be preferable to view the facilitator's liability as derivative from the liability of the substantially responsible principal. This would on the one hand circumscribe the scope of criminal liability in line with the *ultima ratio* principle, as a clear link between the provided assistance and the committed offence would be required, and attempted aid would fall outside the scope of criminal liability. This would stress the safeguard function of European criminal law and help to avoid criminalisation of conduct at an unwarrantably early stage, far removed from the commission of the offence.

Furthermore, such an approach would also correctly express the social reproach in its label. Criminal law and criminal convictions ought to reflect as clearly and closely as possible on the different degrees of wrongdoing and the nature and magnitude of the occurred law-breaking. This *inter alia* serves to devise a proportionate response to law-breaking.[1378] It is a general principle of justice in any liberal penal system that offenders be labelled and punished in proportion to their wrongdoing; a requirement that also European criminal law must adhere to. To convict John the hunter who lends his rifle to Bob so that he can shoot his nagging wife of "trivial assistance" as an inchoate model of facilitation would do, arguably understates John's culpability and does not communicate the gravity of the offence involved.[1379] As the label of the crime is a key element in the punishment inflicted "trivial assistance" arguably understates the wrongdoing committed by the assistant. If as defended here the outcome, as in harm, matters for criminal liability it seems preferable to convict John in this case of providing trivial assistance to murder.

Such a two-pronged approach consisting of a broad normative concept of perpetration and an auxiliary offence of assistance would possess several advantages. First it would dispense with the difficult problem of line drawing between the different concepts of participation and would shift the focus from the internal boundaries to the arguably more important outer limits of criminal liability. This would not only make the system of participation in crime more effective and easier to apply for the courts but would arguably also improve individual justice, as the exact degree of the participants wrongdoing and culpability can now easier be taken into consideration by the judge at the sentencing stage. Here courts could also obtain guidance by the adoption of sentencing guidelines.

Furthermore, a normative approach to perpetration would correspond to the actuality of crime in which often other persons than the direct perpetrator play an influential and determining role and thus bear (substantial) responsibility for the harmful outcome. To properly reflect their degree of responsibility a holistic

---

1378 Ashworth, 'Principles of criminal law' (2009), pp. 78–80.

1379 See also: Stewart, 'The End of "Modes of Liability" for international crimes' Leiden Journal of International Law (2012), pp. 32 et seq.

conception of crime and not a strict focus on the individual perpetrator seems warranted.

The auxiliary offence of trivial assistance would cover all contributions falling below the substantial responsibility threshold outlined above. Here contributions which had an impact on the commission of the offence but were not crucial or indispensable for it could be subsumed. As these participants cannot be deemed to carry substantial responsibility for the commission of the offence, but at best peripheral responsibility; a mitigation of punishment for these participants seems defensible.

To adopt a separate offence for auxiliary assistance would appropriately reflect the role and culpability of this category of participants. Moreover, such a two-pronged approach would also be in line with the requirements of Article 6 ECHR as defendants would receive sufficient information concerning the nature and cause of the accusations against them, which would allow them to develop an effective defence against the charges. Additionally, it would increase legal certainty in line with the requirements of Article 7 ECHR as it would arguably be more foreseeable to an offender whether his conduct will give rise to primary or secondary responsibility. Finally, it would allow for the individual assessment of a participant's wrongdoing and culpability and thereby fulfil an important safeguard function against collective responsibility and arbitrary punishment.

After having discussed multiple actor scenarios, the discussion can now turn to another subsidiary mode of liability, i.e. inchoate liability where the conventional scope of liability is expanded to cover also cases where the criminal offence was not consummated, contrary to the intention of the offender.

Chapter IV
Inchoate offences: Attempt and preparation

1. Introduction

Traditionally the focus of criminal law has been retrospective with a stern focus on retribution; one of its primary goals being to reduce criminality i.e. harm by imposing punishment for wrongdoing. Yet, in the course of time the focus of criminal law has widened and the common consensus nowadays is that criminal law is not only appropriately invoked to reduce harm, but furthermore also to reduce the risk of harm.[1380] This means that criminal law in the culture of control becomes more and more concerned with the task of preventing crime.[1381] For this reason new offences have been devised whose purpose is rather preventive than retributive. An example of the former can be found in the category of inchoate offences. This research has already touched upon the concept of inchoate offences in the previous chapter on participation in crime, but now it is time to shed a bit more light on these offences. Textbook examples of inchoate offences generally include the notion of attempt, as well as preparatory offences.

The term inchoate generally means 'just begun, undeveloped, incipient'.[1382] Accordingly a central feature of these offences is that they are committed although the substantive offence envisaged by the perpetrator was not completed and no harm in the ordinary sense of the word has emerged.[1383] Therefore, it seems fair to assume that the main objective of inchoate offences is the prevention of harm. They proscribe the creation of a risk of harm and thereby expand the functional scope of criminal law.[1384]

A central ingredient for criminal liability, namely the occurrence of harm in the ordinary meaning of the word in these offences is by definition absent. A fundamental question pervading the analysis of these offences accordingly becomes: how can one justify the existence of these offences and how should they be punished in comparison to the complete offence?[1385] First and foremost, one should note that although the paradigm of inchoate offences does not involve any harm in the strict sense, this need not always be the case. Attempt liability can for instance arise in cases where James shoots at David with the intent to kill, but due to a stroke of luck the bullet misses David's heart and only damages his shoulder. In

---

1380 Husak, 'Overcriminalization' (2008), p. 159.

1381 See also: Chapter I. 3.2. and 5.4.

1382 Ashworth, 'Principles of criminal law' (2006), p. 444, Smith and Hogan, 'Criminal Law' (2008), p. 379.

1383 Ashworth, 'Principles of criminal law' (2006), p. 444.

1384 Husak, 'The nature and justifiability of nonconsummate offences' Arizona Law Review (1995), pp. 164 et seq.

1385 See also: chapter I. 4.3.2.

this scenario clearly some tangible harm has manifested which is punishable pursuant to the inchoate offence of attempt.[1386] Yet, in the majority of cases of inchoate liability, the search for harm in the ordinary sense of the word will prove in vain as can easily be demonstrated by altering the foregoing example so that James is now arrested by the police before he can fire a single shot. Also in these instances penal systems generally impose attempt liability despite the absence of any tangible harm.

In regard to the justification of these offences in the absence of harm, i.e. where no person needs to be injured or no proprietary interest needs to be damaged the different justifications of punishment again come to the fore as they attach different weight to the role of harm played in the imposition of criminal liability and punishment.[1387] Retributivists generally attach more weight to the manifestation of harm and have therefore strived to identify some sort of harm in inchoate offences. It has for instance been argued that inchoate offences cause intangible harm, namely a threat to security, the endangerment of the underlying protected legal interest or a disturbance of the social order.[1388] In utilitarian terms, on the other hand, criminal liability in the absence of harm may be justified as long as the occurred conduct bears witness to the person's general dangerousness/ blameworthiness and wickedness, which warrants the imposition of punishment. Furthermore utilitarians often argue that the police should be given sufficient powers in order to prevent crime rather than simply to detect it. One can deduce from this that inchoate offences can generally be justified by either of these rationales.

However, it should be reiterated that no investigated system exclusively adheres to one of these theories of punishment and that generally a combination of rationales is invoked to explain the whole realm of criminal law. Therefore it is also not necessary here to make a selection between these rival justifications as the purpose of this research is to describe and devise a coherent account of criminal liability for attempts and preparatory offences, which may in whole or in part rest on retributive or utilitarian reasoning. Furthermore, regardless of whichever justifying reason for punishing inchoate offences one is willing to accept, both camps concur that in regard to attempt, or preparatory liability respectively, the major part of responsibility flows from the actor's mental culpability as expressed by some form of overt conduct. Thus, there seems to be agreement as to the central ingredient of criminal liability in these cases, from which the following discussion can commence.

The fact however remains that, in regard to inchoate offences the conduct committed by the perpetrator might, if viewed objectively, seem completely innocuous. To take an example from the law of attempt, consider for instance a

---

1386 Smith and Hogan, 'Criminal Law' (2008), p. 379.

1387 Smith, 'A Modern Treatise on the Law of Criminal Complicity' (1991), p. 71.

1388 Clarkson and Keating, 'Criminal law: Text and Materials' (2003), p. 465, Smith, 'A Modern Treatise on the Law of Criminal Complicity' (1991), p. 71.

person with a newspaper in his hands and a lighter in his pocket walking towards a barn. It seems impossible to draw any conclusions regarding the person's enterprise. He might be an arsonist on his way to the *locus delicti* or an innocent civilian who likes to read his newspaper on the bench in front of the barn while smoking a cigar. Regarding preparatory conduct matters become even more ambiguous. It is virtually impossible to objectively determine whether a person buying fertiliser or a hunting rifle does so in order to manure his lawn, respectively indulge in his hobby of hunting or plans to manufacture a bomb or kill his vicious neighbour.

These examples serve to draw attention to a crucial practical problem underpinning inchoate offences, namely, how far can one legitimately expand criminal liability without unduly infringing individual freedoms. Therefore it is important to keep in mind that the scope of liability is inextricably linked to the powers of the police in this area of the law. The broader the scope of liability, the earlier the police will be able to intervene. The narrower the scope on the other hand, the longer the police will have to delay their intervention in order to secure a conviction. Merely focusing on the protection of individual liberties will accordingly almost certainly not do, because once we curtail the possibility of early police intervention to arrest and punish those who are about to commit a crime "we threaten public safety and expose others to a significant risk of harm".[1389] Since both of these underlying rationales, i.e. the protection of public safety and individual liberties are however legitimate aims and boundaries of any penal system, it becomes apparent that a proper balancing of these considerations is vital to circumscribe the scope of inchoate offences.[1390]

Nevertheless, it is first and foremost important to note here that the contours of the law will vary depending on which of the two rationales is emphasised. This will particularly become apparent in the subsequent discussion on attempts and especially in regard to the actus reus requirement, impossible attempts and the corresponding appropriate punishment. For the moment, the focus will however rest on a tension between different patterns of criminality which pervades a wide field of the criminal law but which becomes most visible in regard to inchoate offences and exerts significant influence on their scope and guise. This tension arises between what Fletcher has termed the pattern of manifest criminality in contrast to the pattern of subjective criminality.[1391] By dwelling on these two patterns an important interpretative tool in order to better understand the disputes and conundrums raised by attempts and preparatory offences will be unearthed. Against the backdrop of this tension an attempt will finally be made at the end of this chapter to create a European framework of attempts and preparation. But first, a closer look at these different patterns is warranted.

1389 Mathis, 'Criminal Attempts and the Subjectivism/Objectivism Debate' Ratio Juris (2004), p. 329.

1390 Mathis, 'Criminal Attempts and the Subjectivism/Objectivism Debate' Ratio Juris (2004), p. 329.

1391 Fletcher, 'Rethinking Criminal Law' (1978), Chapter 3, pp. 115–234.

2. Two patterns of criminality

2.1. The pattern of manifest criminality a.k.a. the harm-centred view

The distinction between manifest and subjective criminality by and large corresponds to the already mentioned difference between act-based and guilt- or attitude-based criminal law.[1392] In essence the dispute between the two patterns centres around the question what is punishment imposed for. In the pattern of manifest criminality the main emphasis lies on the occurred criminal conduct. The notion of intent only takes a subsidiary position in the analysis of criminal liability.[1393] This corresponds to the requirements of what has been called act-based criminal law. Criminal liability, so the argument goes, ought to require an act that is objectively criminal. The conduct ought to betoken criminality.[1394] The focus thus rests on the harm or evil of the respective criminal offence. Applied to the notion of inchoate offences, this pattern would impose criminal liability only when the actor comes close to bringing about a tangible harm or evil.[1395] This pattern of criminality, as will subsequently become evident, leads to a narrower scope of liability than the subjective pattern, as the manifestly criminal conduct is considered to constitute a substantive condition of liability. It arguably has its roots in a liberal theory of legality in which it was thought that criminal law should only come into play once the actor's conduct had manifestly endangered society.[1396] As already mentioned, the act requirement in criminal law dictates that mere thoughts should not be punishable, as they occur in the private sphere of the citizens.[1397] The state may only proceed against the citizen and ençroach on his autonomy, if his conduct manifests danger to the community.[1398] The pattern of manifest criminality thus begins with liberty and insists that citizens in a liberal state ought not to be punished unless they commit a wrongdoing which constitutes an unreasonable risk of harm to others.[1399] The emphasis rests therefore on the wrongful conduct rather than the criminal actor. This retentive approach towards criminality arguably constituted the vantage point of traditional criminal law as it emerged from the enlightenment movement.[1400] It is based on the simple assumption that "we know a

1392 See: Chapter I. 5.2. and Chapter II. 2.1.

1393 Fletcher, 'Rethinking Criminal Law' (1978), p. 117.

1394 Fletcher, 'Rethinking Criminal Law' (1978), p. 232, Fletcher, 'Constructing a theory of impossible attempts' Criminal Justice Ethics (1986), p. 55.

1395 Robinson and Darley, 'Objectivist versus Subjectivist Views of Criminality: A Study in the Role of Social Science in Criminal Law Theory' Oxford Journal of legal Studies (1998), p. 414.

1396 Fletcher, 'Rethinking Criminal Law' (1978), p. 117, Fletcher, 'Constructing a theory of impossible attempts' Criminal Justice Ethics (1986), p. 64.

1397 See: Chapter II. 2.

1398 Fletcher, 'Rethinking Criminal Law' (1978), p. 117, Fletcher, 'Constructing a theory of impossible attempts' Criminal Justice Ethics (1986), pp. 64–65.

1399 Garvey, 'Are attempts like treason?' The New Criminal Law Review (2011), p. 181.

1400 De Jong, 'Daad-Schuld' (2009), p. 64.

thief when we see one". In other words that crime is readily recognisable by members of the community. The retrospective and retributive approach of traditional criminal law is based on the liberal maxim that the freedom and private sphere of the citizen ought to be respected and protected as much as possible.[1401] Contemporary criminal law has however, especially in regard to inchoate offences, increasingly moved away from the pattern as it is considered too narrow and nowadays shows a rise of subjectivist tendencies.[1402] As the notion of crime prevention became increasingly important in our society and the focus of criminal law more forward looking and pre-emptive the pattern of manifest criminality lost influence on doctrinal thinking. In other words, recent developments seem to suggest that the foundational substance of the criminal law has changed and not just its form of application.[1403]

2.2. The pattern of subjective criminality a.k.a. the culpability-centred view

Conversely to the pattern of manifest criminality where the criminal conduct lies at the focal point of criminal law, the pattern of subjective criminality departs from the diametrically opposed assumption that the core of criminal conduct is the actor's intention to harm a legally protected interest (i.e. culpability).[1404] Criminal law, so it is argued, ought to protect specific legal interests, and people who intent to harm such interests are dangerous and therefore deserve punishment.[1405] The driving force behind this pattern arguably is the concern that people should only be held responsible for those criminal outcomes over which they exerted control.[1406] The reason why criminal law generally requires some form of conduct for the imposition of liability, so the proponents of this pattern state, is to assure the firmness of the actor's evil intention. Thus, in the pattern of subjective criminality, conduct only fulfils an evidentiary function, while in the pattern of manifest criminality, it constitutes a substantive requirement.[1407] This distinction becomes especially important in the realm of inchoate offences where the outward conduct often appears objectively innocuous. If the manifest criminality of the conduct is a substantive requirement of the pattern of criminal law, then no proof of intent can function as a substitute and make up for the missing manifest criminality. If conduct however only plays an evidentiary role than the lack of a manifestly wrong conduct

1401 De Jong, 'Daad-Schuld' (2009), p. 64.

1402 Fletcher, 'Rethinking Criminal Law' (1978), p. 115, Robinson and Darley, 'Objectivist versus Subjectivist Views of Criminality: A Study in the Role of Social Science in Criminal Law Theory' Oxford Journal of legal Studies (1998), pp. 411–415.

1403 See: Chapter I. 4.3.2. and 5.4. See also: Chapter IV. 3. and 4.

1404 Fletcher, 'Rethinking Criminal Law' (1978), pp. 118–119.

1405 Fletcher, 'Rethinking Criminal Law' (1978), p. 233.

1406 Garvey, 'Are attempts like treason?' The New Criminal Law Review (2011), p. 192.

1407 Fletcher, 'Rethinking Criminal Law' (1978), p. 119, Roef and Prakken, 'Strafbare Voorbereiding in Nederland: Juridische Overkill', in Verbruggen, et al. (eds), Voorbereidingshandelingen in het Strafrecht (2004), pp.231–244.

may be remedied by the proof of a substitute criminal intent.[1408] Thus, the focus in this pattern primarily rests on the person or the actor rather than his conduct. It can be deduced from the foregoing that the pattern of subjective criminality in regard to inchoate offences results in a broader scope of criminal liability. As the conduct in question need not betoken criminality, it is not required that the actor came close to the manifestation of the proscribed harm. Rather, any conduct that signalises the actor's willingness to act on his criminal intentions will suffice to trigger criminal liability. It is the actor's subjective culpability that is decisive.[1409]

2.3. The communalities of the two patterns

The two patterns of criminality are often entwined in contemporary thinking about criminal law. It would therefore be a fallacy to view those patterns as a strict dichotomy. In fact, as both currents influence our way of thinking about criminal law and criminal liability in particular, it is possible that one follows the manifest pattern on some issues but prefers the subjective on others.[1410] This is even more so if we remind ourselves that we frequently distinguish in our thinking about criminal law between the level of attribution, i.e. the assessment of minimum requirements for liability and the level of grading wrongdoing, i.e. punishment. It therefore seems perfectly conceivable that one might prefer a subjectivist view in regard to the analysis of criminal liability but endorses the pattern of manifest criminality in regard to meting out punishment.[1411]

Furthermore, one would also be mistaken to overstate the differences between the two patterns. The different labels namely cloud what is in fact a rather subtle distinction. Both patterns share the same doctrinal foundation and concur that the imposition of criminal liability generally presupposes (1) conduct, (2) blameworthiness, i.e. mens rea and (3) a concurrence of conduct and blameworthiness. Thus, both patterns adhere to the fundamental tenets of *nulla poena sine culpa* and *nulla poena sine actione*. However, these tenets are assigned different meanings and significance within the two patterns. In the pattern of manifest criminality the notion of conduct must give expression to the perpetrator's criminal plan. In the pattern of subjective criminality, however, the requirement of conduct is not invoked to establish the content of the actor's intent but rather the firmness of the actor's determination to violate the law.[1412] The results of these different accentuations are differing scopes of liability. This is because "while only

1408 Fletcher, 'Rethinking Criminal Law' (1978), p. 119.

1409 Robinson and Darley, 'Objectivist versus Subjectivist Views of Criminality: A Study in the Role of Social Science in Criminal Law Theory' Oxford Journal of legal Studies (1998), p. 412.

1410 Robinson and Darley, 'Objectivist versus Subjectivist Views of Criminality: A Study in the Role of Social Science in Criminal Law Theory' Oxford Journal of legal Studies (1998), pp. 415–416.

1411 Robinson and Darley, 'Objectivist versus Subjectivist Views of Criminality: A Study in the Role of Social Science in Criminal Law Theory' Oxford Journal of legal Studies (1998), pp. 409–447.

1412 Fletcher, 'Rethinking Criminal Law' (1978), p. 120.

some acts are manifestly criminal, any voluntary act can establish the actor's commitment to do harm".[1413] Thus, while both patterns accept that thoughts ought to be free and that criminal law should not be concerned with punishing thought crimes, the realm of thought takes different connotations in both patterns. In the pattern of manifest criminality one is free to think whatever one pleases as long as the accompanying conduct does not bespeak criminality. In other words, all routine, innocuous and unthreatening conduct is insufficient to ground criminal liability.[1414] In the pattern of subjective criminality on the other hand, the realm of thought is reduced to the world of fantasy and other purely subjective experiences. Once these thoughts are translated into actions, they will come under scrutiny of the criminal law.[1415]

It has already been noted that in modern criminal law, both patterns continue to play an important role, but that by and large subjective criminality seems to prevail in many areas of the law. From this it can be deduced that the development of responsibility attribution (from objective to subjective criminality) is not a linear trajectory. It is rather a complex and shifting configuration of principles which combine to form the foundation for attributing liability.[1416] Thus, what one arguably can conceive is not the replacement of one pattern by another but a merger and combination of different patterns in order to fulfil the needs of modern criminal law.

3. The Objective – Subjective Debate

Before attempting to sketch the prevalent pattern of criminality in the modern risk society or culture of control, it seems first appropriate to revisit another debate which informs and steers the doctrinal discussion throughout the criminal law. Related and linked to the two different patterns of criminality is another, already discussed dichotomy which influences and shapes the fundamental debate concerning the proper foundations and principles of criminal liability.[1417] This distinction permeates the criminal law as many aspects of the discussion on criminal liability can be categorised as being informed by either an objective or a subjective point of view. The value of this distinction for the discussion here is that it provides another analytical tool, just like the dichotomy of actus reus and mens rea or the pattern of manifest or subjective criminality, through which one can assess and better understand the doctrinal tensions running through the criminal law. The distinction is particularly valuable for the subsequent discussion of attempt

1413 Fletcher, 'Rethinking Criminal Law' (1978), p. 120.
1414 Fletcher, 'Rethinking Criminal Law' (1978), p. 121.
1415 Fletcher, 'Rethinking Criminal Law' (1978), p. 121.
1416 Lacey, 'Psychologising Jekyll, Demonising Hyde: The strange case of criminal responsibility' Criminal Law and Philosophy (2010), p. 131.
1417 See: Chapter I. 5.2.

liability where the repercussions of the different approaches will become most visible. As will later become clear, the tension between manifest and subjective patterns of criminality culminate in the law of attempts, as the emphasis on the actor's intention as the core of the offence conflicts with the manifest criminality pattern which stresses the importance of objective criteria as a condition and constitutive element of criminal liability.[1418] Hence, it can be said that, the dispute about the proper scope, structure and guise of the law of attempts can be traced back to the uncertainties and disagreements about the foundations of criminal liability.[1419] On the other hand, the vivid controversy between objective and subjective conceptions of criminal liability, scantly stated, has as its central point of contention the question whether doctrines and principles of criminal law ought to be fleshed out in subjective or objective terms. This can for instance be seen in the discussion whether concepts such as mens rea or perpetration respectively, should be interpreted objectively or subjectively.[1420]

It is however important to stress that although the objective – subjective debate has close ties to the two aforementioned patterns of criminality, it nevertheless constitutes a distinct subject. As will subsequently become apparent, adherence to the pattern of manifest criminality for instance does not necessarily entail an objective interpretation of doctrine. On the contrary, as will become evident in the discussion on criminal liability for preparatory conduct in the Netherlands, it is possible to subscribe to the subjective pattern of criminality, but despite this choice interpret the doctrine of preparation objectively

4. The pattern of criminality in the culture of control

The social shift from the welfare state to the risk society or culture of control, outlined above[1421], has also had a considerable influence on the criminal law as well as on the pattern of criminality invoked and applied by scholars, politicians, legislators and the like.[1422] One important effect of this shift can be seen in the fact that we conceive crime no longer exclusively as harm or wrong, which has to be remedied retrospectively by the imposition of punishment. Rather, in the culture of control, crime is essentially seen as a form of risk.[1423] As risks are by definition located in the future, the focus of criminal law has increasingly come to rest on the concept of crime prevention. Accordingly, the focus of criminal justice systems more and more shifts towards the reduction of criminal opportunities in everyday life. Multiple tools have been put in place to minimise the occurrence of criminal

1418 Fletcher, 'Rethinking Criminal Law' (1978), p. 135.

1419 Duff, 'Criminal Attempts' (1996), p. 145.

1420 See: Chapter III. 6.3.

1421 See: Chapter I. 5.4.

1422 In general see: Roef, 'Strafrechtelijke Verantwoordelijkheid in de Risicomaatschappij', in Vos and Calster (eds), Risico en voorzorg in de rechtsmaatschappij (2004), pp. 201–226.

1423 Zedner, 'Pre-crime and post-criminology' Theoretical Criminology (2007), p. 261.

behaviour and to assure that fewer crimes will end successfully.[1424] Thus, a temporal shift in perspective, seems to have taken place, so that we are nowadays at times even more concerned with anticipating and forestalling future risks instead of responding to wrongs done.[1425] Moreover, the preoccupation of criminal law with individual offenders is increasingly substituted by the desire to identify and classify suspects and potentially dangerous segments of the population in order to manage the risk they collectively pose.[1426]

It seems at times that criminal law for the sake of crime prevention has turned to "targeting and managing through disruption, restriction and incapacitation, those individuals and groups considered to be a risk".[1427] In other words, it is the pursuit of security which more and more influences and drives the application of criminal law.[1428] Security has become the magic word and is what citizens crave for and expect from state authorities. As Garland observes: "Today, there is a new and urgent emphasis upon the need for security, the containment of danger, the identification and management of any kind of risk. Protecting the public has become the dominant theme of penal policy".[1429] However, what is often overlooked is that security is an ideal and an inherently normative concept. It is the indefinite pursuit of the unattainable.[1430]

As the focus increasingly shifts to crime prevention and the reduction of criminal opportunity, criminal law is more and more often invoked to tackle conduct far removed from the occurrence of harm in the ordinary sense of the word. Criminal law is nowadays applicable to ever earlier stages of a criminal enterprise in order to ensure that the law can intervene before any harm has actually occurred. Polemically speaking, it seems as if the dystopia of Steven Spielberg's 'Minority Report' has become the utopia of modern society. A pre-crime unit or a 'thought police' as in George Orwell's 1984 appears as the pinnacle of a modern security policy.[1431] Central to, as well as a paradigmatic expression of this shift in focus is the increasing criminalisation of preparatory conduct. In order to fulfil the demand of security, the remit of criminal law is expanded and used to justify earlier and earlier intervention in order to reduce criminal opportunity.[1432]

1424 Garland, 'The Culture of Control – Crime and Social Order in Contemporary Society' (2006), p. 103–139.

1425 Zedner, 'Pre-crime and post-criminology' Theoretical Criminology (2007), p. 262.

1426 Zedner, 'Pre-crime and post-criminology' Theoretical Criminology (2007), p. 265.

1427 McCulloch and Pickering, 'Pre-Crime and Counter-Terrorism' British Journal of Criminology (2009), p. 631.

1428 Zedner, 'Pre-crime and post-criminology' Theoretical Criminology (2007), p. 262.

1429 Garland, 'The Culture of Control – Crime and Social Order in Contemporary Society' (2006), p. 12.

1430 Zedner, 'Pre-crime and post-criminology' Theoretical Criminology (2007), p. 274.

1431 See also: Schuilenburg, 'Technologie en Misdaad – Over de opkomst van een protocollaire samenleving' Flexmens (2006), pp. 22–25.

1432 McCulloch and Pickering, 'Pre-Crime and Counter-Terrorism' British Journal of Criminology (2009), p. 633, Zedner, 'Pre-crime and post-criminology' Theoretical Criminology (2007), p. 265.

This also denotes a shift in the prevalent pattern of criminality, which conflicts with the fundamental tenet of criminal law that thoughts are free or the *nulla poena sine actione* principle. This is because contrary to the pattern of manifest criminality, liability is no longer exclusively imposed for the blameworthy commission of wrongful conduct, but rather the commission of seemingly innocuous conduct carried out with bad intentions suffices for imposing liability. Thus, clearly the subjective pattern of criminality seems to be embraced by modern penal and security policy. But, arguably in the culture of control, the pattern is at times even further distorted and taken to extremes.

It is the dangerousness of unruly subjects that we are concerned with. The increased significance of the subjective pattern of criminality shifts the focus in criminal law from the wrongful conduct to the actor whose (potential) dangerousness forms the centre of attention. Hence one can speak of a shift from an act to an actor-based criminal law.[1433] The goal of traditional criminal law namely to protect the individual from the whims of state authority has been substituted by the modern goal of social control.[1434]

Purely focusing on the actor can however lead to frictions in the law as it would purport to impose heavy punishment on recidivists of minor offences such as fare dodging, but on the other hand allow the imposition of low punishment on one time offenders.[1435] Thus a person who commits murder due to a particular family crisis could according to the logic of an actor-based criminal law, escape punishment or receive mitigation, if it could be established beyond reasonable doubt that a repetition of the deed is virtually impossible and that the actor can therefore not be considered dangerous.[1436]

Yet, there arguably is also a change in the manifest pattern of criminality perceivable. Advancements in sciences and medicine namely seem to provide new methods to establish patterns of manifest criminality. Technologies geared to indentify (potential) criminals such as crime statistics, policing through Lombrosian criminology, profiling, neurosciences and gene technologies are on the rise and are more and more frequently invoked to detect and signal manifest criminality.[1437] Thus, perhaps, in the modern culture of control we do not see so much of a shift from one pattern to another, but a reformulation and reinterpretation of these intertwined patterns of criminality.

In essence, we thus witness a temporal expansion of the scope of criminal liability as well as a renewed focus on the criminal actor. Therefore it should be remembered that it is not the expansion of liability alone that could be seen as a cause for concern, but that these developments in substantive criminal law also

---

1433 De Jong, 'Daad-Schuld' (2009), p. 68.

1434 De Jong, 'Daad-Schuld' (2009), p. 68. See also: Chapter I. 4.3.2.

1435 Heinrich, 'Die Grenzen des Strafrechts bei der Gefahrenprävention' ZStW (2009), p. 118.

1436 Heinrich, 'Die Grenzen des Strafrechts bei der Gefahrenprävention' ZStW (2009), p. 118.

1437 Lacey, 'Psychologising Jekyll, Demonising Hyde: The strange case of criminal responsibility' Criminal Law and Philosophy (2010), p. 130.

have counterparts in procedural law. The trends, namely those outlined above, go hand in hand with the expansion of the legitimate use of investigation and evidence-gathering techniques. Phone tapping, undercover surveillance, dragnet investigations, are just some examples of modern investigation techniques which can be applied once a person is suspected to be in the course of, for instance, preparing an offence. All these measures severely encroach on individual liberties and add a further punitive twist to the outlined developments.[1438] Beyond the intrusive nature of these investigation techniques, they also risk the entanglement of innocent actors with the law, due to for instance, erroneous factual interpretations by the police. Furthermore, they contain a danger of misuse and the waste of law enforcement resources.[1439] The cause of concern thus lies in the fact that preventive logic expands: who wants to prevent, never possess enough information.[1440]

To countermand these punitive tendencies and inflation of criminal law, it is submitted that legal theory should strive to develop constraints which set boundaries to criminal liability. Therefore traditional, fundamental principles of criminal law such as the principle of legality, harm, guilt, proportionality or the act requirement can play a decisive role.[1441] Yet, arguably, much more work is needed and other principles ought to be devised in order to create a respectable theory to keep criminal law within acceptable limits.[1442] The focus here will however be much more modest. This research will attempt to unearth principles that have guided penal justice systems when imposing inchoate liability, and to pinpoint doctrinal frictions as well as crossroads for European criminal law.

5. Attempt versus preparation

Traditionally, all investigated penal systems defined the threshold for criminal liability along the lines of the distinction between an attempt and mere preparation. In short, once a person had reached the attempt stage, criminal liability would arise while preparatory conduct which was far removed from the legislative defined offence or harm would fall outside the scope of criminal law. To fully understand this distinction, one has to bear in mind that generally in the course of the commission of a criminal offence one can in most cases distinguish different

---

1438 See also: Heinrich, 'Die Grenzen des Strafrechts bei der Gefahrenprävention' ZStW (2009), pp. 94–130.

1439 Ohana, 'Desert and Punishment for Acts preparatory to the commission of a crime' Canadian Journal of Law and Jurisprudence (2007), p. 141.

1440 Deckers and Heusel, 'Strafbarkeit terroristischer Vorbereitungshandlungen – rechtsstaatlich nicht tragbar' ZRP (2008), p. 171. This trend is arguably also visible on the European level. See for instance: Directive 2006/24 of 15 March 2006 on the retention of data generated or processed in connection with the provision of publicly available electronic communications services or of public communications networks and amending Directive 2002/58, OJ 2006 L 105/54.

1441 See: Chapter I. 4.3.2.

1442 For an admirable attempt see: Husak, 'Overcriminalization' (2008), pp. 55–177.

chronological stages before the crime in question is finally consummated. For instance: conceiving the plan, acquiring necessary materials and information for the coup at hand, making one's way to the intended target, deploying the materials, and finally, executing the crime.[1443]

Thus, to use an oversimplification if vengeful John shoots at his enemy Bob, but misses he has come close enough to the violation of the protected legal interest to warrant the imposition of punishment, while at the time when John purchases the rifle his conduct is too far removed from the actual offence to warrant criminal censure. Criminal law therefore carved out conduct that was adjacent to the proscribed harm and constituted a clear danger while excluding conduct temporarily and qualitatively further removed. Accordingly, it has once been said, "the distinction between preparation to commit a harm and an attempt to do so can be stated in terms of the difference between 'collecting' forces and 'discharging' them".[1444] Gathering vital information, reconnoitring the site of the crime, obtaining materials and tools (such as procuring means to avoid detection (e.g. a balaclava) or to overcome the resistance of the victim (e.g. rope, ether) could therefore be seen as instances of 'collecting' forces which traditionally fell outside the scope of criminal law.

The liberal tendencies in traditional criminal law with their emphasis on individual autonomy militated against the idea of punishing conduct far removed from the commission of the offence.[1445] In a democratic society, based on the rule of law it was sought that it was not only unacceptable to punish thoughts, but that one should also refrain from imputing liability for conduct that only poses a distant threat. It has already been mentioned that this restrictive approach is however more and more discarded in the contemporary culture of control for the sake of a policy of early intervention and crime prevention. Therefore, as will subsequently be attempted to show, the distinction between attempt and preparation has lost some significance in determining the outer limits of criminal liability. This is nicely demonstrated by the fact that the distinction since 1994 does not hold anymore in the Netherlands, which now sentences attempts and preparation to criminal punishment.[1446] While the penal systems of Germany and England still formally uphold the distinction, the expansion of inchoate as well as endangerment offences and the legislative trend to increasingly criminalise conduct far removed from harm also sheds some doubt on the usefulness of this distinction to peg the limits of

---

1443 In some crimes the chronological stages are clearly visible, as for instance in an intricate fraud scheme which requires diligent preparation. However, in other crimes such as traffic offences or affray, which occur at the spur of the moment and are not methodically executed, different stages are much harder to discern.

1444 Ohana, 'Desert and Punishment for Acts preparatory to the commission of a crime' Canadian Journal of Law and Jurisprudence (2007), p. 133.

1445 Fletcher, 'Rethinking Criminal Law' (1978), p. 136. For a contemporary rejection of some preparatory offences on the ground of individual autonomy see: Duff, 'Criminal Attempts' (1996), pp. 189–190, 386–393.

1446 See: Chapter IV. 6.3.2.

criminal liability. Yet, the distinction is useful and of significance for distinguishing and defining preparation and criminal attempts in general, as well as distinguishing and identifying the relevant set of principles applicable to these doctrines.

6. Preparation

6.1. Introduction

Generally speaking, one can define preparation as conduct, carried out with the intention and in order to engage in future criminal behaviour, yet still temporarily and qualitatively removed from the commencement of the execution of the offence.[1447] Despite the reluctance of traditional criminal law to criminalise these forms of conduct, it should be noted that certain preparatory offences always were part and parcel of the criminal law, although on an exceptional basis.

One situation where preparatory conduct was and often is criminalised is when the underlying protected legal interest is considered especially worthy of protection. An instance where this was considered to be the case were offences threatening national security or the integrity of the democratic state. Preparing treason or endangering national security has therefore always constituted criminal conduct in the investigated penal systems.[1448]

Furthermore, legislators have always and nowadays increasingly criminalise certain preparatory conducts which typically precede the commission of certain offences or which are considered to increase the risk of the commission of a related offence. These forms of conduct are frequently enshrined in specific offences in the special part of criminal law. They especially bolster police powers by creating more room for controlling the dangerous and maintaining public order, rather than that they penalise wrongs committed against others.[1449] Due to the big variety of these offences it will not be possible to provide the reader with an exhaustive evaluation here. Instead, this research will confine itself to point at some specific forms of legislation such as possession offences as well as endangerment offences. These two are of particular relevance as their very aim is to prevent wrongs or harms by penalising conduct before the harm is actually perpetrated.

1447 See: Ohana, 'Desert and Punishment for Acts preparatory to the commission of a crime' Canadian Journal of Law and Jurisprudence (2007), pp. 115–120, Roef and Prakken, 'Strafbare Voorbereiding in Nederland: Juridische Overkill', in Verbruggen, et al. (eds), Voorbereidingshandelingen in het Strafrecht (2004), p. 212.

1448 See for instance: Treason Act 1351 and 1702, §§83, 87, 98, 90 GPC and Articles 92–107a DPC.

1449 Ashworth, 'The Unfairness of risk-based possession offences' Criminal Law and Philosophy (2011), p. 2.

6.2. Offences criminalising preparatory conduct

6.2.1. Introduction

There is a multitude of offences that criminalise preparatory conduct. §149 GPC for instance prohibits the preparation of counterfeiting money, official stamps, etc. Thus, obtaining counterfeit machinery is explicitly criminalised in Germany.[1450] Also the Dutch penal system knows similar offences which are enshrined in Articles 214, respectively 234 DPC and section 17 (1) of the English 1981 Forgery and Counterfeiting Act prohibits the possession of instruments with the intent to use for forgery. Furthermore, in the Netherlands Article 140 DPC (participation in a criminal organisation) plays an important role in imposing liability for preparatory acts.[1451]

Other examples can for instance be found in the English Sexual Offences Act 2003 which in its section 15 prohibits grooming, i.e. seducing a child to a meeting or in the 1953 Prevention of Crime Act which penalises the carrying of offensive weapons without lawful authority. Likewise the Dutch law on prevention of money laundering and financing of terrorism (*Wet ter voorkoming van witwassen en financieren van Terrorisme*) or the law on weapons and ammunition (*Wet Wapens en munitie*) as well as the law on the prevention of the abuse of chemicals and strategical goods (*Besluit strategisch goederen*) criminalise a multitude of preparatory conduct. And similar goals are pursued by some provisions of the German Weapons Act[1452] and the Narcotics Act. Reference should also be made here to the already discussed English Serious Crime Act 2007. One may recall that this Act *inter alia* criminalises participatory conduct taking place in the preparatory stage of the main offence, thereby expanding the scope of liability to cover also the remote risk of harm inherent in the participant's conduct.

Finally, a universally valid example which should be mentioned in this respect can also be found in the notion of conspiracy which criminalises preparatory conduct by proscribing the formation of an agreement to commit a serious crime. The notion traditionally plays an important role in covering preparatory conduct in the English legal system, where it is generally interpreted broadly.[1453] Conspiracy in England consists as a statutory as well as a common law offence. The former is enshrined in section 1 (1) of the Criminal law act and essentially criminalises agreements between two or more people to commit a crime.[1454] What is required is

---

[1450] See also: §§80, 83, 149, 202 (c), 234 (a), 275, 263 (a) and 303 (a), (b) for offences in the German penal code criminalising preparatory conduct.

[1451] De Hullu, 'Materieel Strafrecht' (2009), p. 406. Furthermore, Articles 132, 134 and 234 DPC as well as Article 10 (a) of the Dutch Narcotics Act are important provisions, covering preparation.

[1452] In particular see: §§40–42.

[1453] Smith and Hogan, 'Criminal Law' (2008), pp. 399–437.

[1454] Section 1 (1) of the Criminal law Act 1977 reads as follows:
Subject to the following provisions of this part of this Act, if a person agrees with any other person or persons that a course of conduct shall be pursued which, if the agreement is carried out in accordance with their intentions, either:

that the parties involved agree on a course of conduct, which if carried out necessarily amounts to or involves the commission of a criminal offence. The parties must intend that the agreement will be carried out and the crime committed by one or more of the conspirators. The required fault element of the offence is intention; recklessness will not be sufficient to impose liability.[1455] In addition three very broad versions of common law conspiracy exist. Probably the broadest and most controversial of the three is the conspiracy to defraud which will be committed as soon as an agreement to deprive another dishonestly of something can be proven. It can cover a wide variety of (preparatory) fraudulent activities and even criminalises conduct by two or more persons that would not be criminal or even tortious when performed by an individual.[1456] Finally, a conspiracy to corrupt public morals, respectively a conspiracy to outrage public decency also constitute common law offences.[1457] It becomes apparent that the offence of conspiracy in English law has an astonishingly broad scope which is able to cover a wide variety of preparatory conduct, i.e. conduct carried out with the purpose of effecting some other offence.

Conversely, in Germany and the Netherlands the scope of the offence was traditionally interpreted more narrowly, but has been rediscovered in the age of terrorism.[1458] Be that as it may, an in-depth analysis of the English law on conspiracy, let alone a comprehensive comparative analysis of the rules of conspiracy in all three investigated countries, would however exceed the scope of this book and will therefore be excluded from this research.

Last, but not least, it should be noted here that the myriad of Anti Terrorism legislation that mushroomed after the 9/11 attacks in all Western countries contain a multitude of provisions that seek to criminalise typically preparatory conduct.[1459] In this respect, one should also not overlook the influence of European Union law

---

a) will necessarily amount to or involve the commission of any offence or offences by one or more of the parties to the agreement, or

b) would do so but for the existence of facts which render the commission of the offence or any of the offences impossible,

he is guilty of conspiracy to commit the offence or offences in question. […].

1455 See: Ashworth, 'Principles of criminal law' (2009), pp. 449–457, Smith and Hogan, 'Criminal Law' (2008), pp. 399–419.

1456 See: Ormerod and Williams, 'Smith's law of theft' (2007), pp. 205–225. Many of these fraudulent acts would now also be covered by the Fraud Act 2006.

1457 Smith and Hogan, 'Criminal Law' (2008), pp. 429–431.

1458 De Hullu, 'Materieel Strafrecht' (2009), pp. 407–408, Roxin, 'Strafrecht Allgemeiner Teil, Band II: Besondere Erscheinungsformen der Straftat' (2003), pp. 303–319.

1459 See for instance: §89 a, penalizing the preparation of serious violent offences endangering the state, §89 b and §91. See also: Sieber, 'Legitimation und Grenzen von Gefährdungsdelikten im Vorfeld terroristischer Gewalt – Eine Analyse der Vorfeldtatbestände im "Entwurf eines Gesetzes zur Verfolgung der Vorbereitung von schweren staatsgefährdenden Gewalttaten"' NStZ (2009), pp. 353–364. See further: Sections 5, 6 of the 2006 Terrorism Act, criminalising the preparation of terrorist acts and terrorist training, the 2001 Anti-Terrorism, Crime and Security Act and the 2005 Prevention of Terrorism Act as well as the 2004 Dutch law on terrorist offences.

on national criminal law which by many legislative acts has contributed to and shaped national measures.[1460]

6.2.2. Specific offences: Possession and endangerment

The brief overview given above demonstrates that specific legislation is nowadays often enacted to protect people from (novel) ways that harm might be risked. One might therefore term them offences of risk prevention.[1461] These offences prohibit the possibility of harm and penalise conduct that is not per se harmful but remote from the ultimate harm to be prevented.[1462] An important role in regard to these offences of risk prevention in all penal systems but most importantly in England is played by possession offences.[1463] Arguably, possession offences share many characteristics with inchoate offences and can even be considered as essentially inchoate by nature. It is namely not so much the mere possession that is criminalised by these offences but the main reason for their criminalisation is probably more what the actor might do with the article or substance; thus a future risk.[1464] There is a multitude of possession offences, especially in the English system, which differ in the purpose they intend to fulfil. Possession of drugs is possibly the best known example here, but more significant for the purpose of this research are what have been called risk-based possession offences.[1465] These offences criminalise the possession of certain instruments such as weapons or burglary tools and thereby link the suspect to the creation of risk or danger.[1466] They effectively penalise the creation of a risk of harm, such as the risk of burglary, terrorism, death or serious injury. Section 25 (1) of the 1968 English Theft Act penalises for instance the possession of burglary tools and sections 16–22 of the 1968 Firearms Act criminalise the possession of firearms with the intent to commit certain criminal offences.[1467] Likewise, section 6 of the Fraud Act 2006 imposes liability on someone who has in his possession or under his control any article for use in the course of or in connection with any fraud. This constitutes a very wide offence

1460 Veegens, 'A disrupted balance? Prevention of terrorism and compliance with fundamental legal rights and principles of law – The Dutch anti-terrorism legislation' (2011), pp. 1–554.
See for instance: Framework Decision 2002/475 of 13 June 2002 on combating terrorism, OJ 2002 L 164/3.

1461 Husak, 'Overcriminalization' (2008), p. 38.

1462 Husak, 'Overcriminalization' (2008), pp. 38 et seq.

1463 For a detailed analysis see: Dubber, 'Policing possession: The war on crime and the end of criminal law' Journal of Criminal Law and Criminology (2001), pp. 829–996.

1464 Ashworth, 'Principles of criminal law' (2006), p. 444.

1465 Ashworth, 'The Unfairness of risk-based possession offences' Criminal Law and Philosophy (2011), pp. 1–21.

1466 Ashworth, 'The Unfairness of risk-based possession offences' Criminal Law and Philosophy (2011), p. 3.

1467 Section 16 of the 1968 Firearms Act criminalizes for instance the possession of a firearm with intent to endanger life and section 16 a criminalises the possession of a firearm with the intent to cause fear of violence.

under which the possession of a printer and computer or even a humble pen and paper might give rise to criminal liability, provided the necessary mens rea can be proven.[1468]

Underlying the criminalisation of possession offences is the concern about what harm or violation of a protected legal interest might be caused by the prohibited article in the future. The exact source of danger however often remains unspecified. Often it will be thought that the harm will be brought about by the possessor himself, but some possession offences take a more sweeping approach and extend to future harm to be committed by others. Thus, making it an offence to leave a prohibited article such as a gun or other weapons visible in the back seat of a car essentially criminalises the risk of future harmful conduct of others, where the traditional doctrine of complicity would be inapplicable.[1469] Especially this latter category raises difficult questions in regard to liability for acts of another and also leads one back to the crucial question, already touched upon, namely how stringent duties of care based on ownership, or to be more precise, on possession should be interpreted.[1470] It seems easy to agree that people who lawfully deal with explosives or nuclear materials should be subjected to stringent duties, given the scale of potential harm that can be brought about by these materials. Yet, waters already become murkier when one extends this reasoning to knives or other offensive weapons.

Thus, the rationale underlying possession offences is very much crime prevention. This draws upon the essential task of criminal law in the culture of control, namely the provision of public safety and the dangerousness inherent to the article in question in terms of its potential to cause serious harm.[1471] One encounters these considerations also in regard to endangerment offences which are related to possession as well as inchoate offences. It can even be argued that risk-based possession offences can best be conceptualised as offences of endangerment.[1472] Endangerment offences constitute yet another legislative tool by which it is possible to criminalise conduct remote from harm and thereby expand the net of criminal liability to the preparatory phase.

Endangerment offences generally occur in two variations. Less problematic are offences of concrete endangerment where a concrete endangerment of the protected legal interest is considered a prerequisite for imposing liability.[1473] An example can

---

1468 See: Ormerod and Williams, 'Smith's law of theft' (2007), pp. 284–295.

1469 Ashworth, 'The Unfairness of risk-based possession offences' Criminal Law and Philosophy (2011), p. 11.

1470 See: Chapter II. 3.3.2.

1471 Ashworth, 'The Unfairness of risk-based possession offences' Criminal Law and Philosophy (2011), p. 13.

1472 Ashworth, 'The Unfairness of risk-based possession offences' Criminal Law and Philosophy (2011), pp. 1–21.

1473 Faure and Visser, 'How to punish environmental pollution? Some reflections on various models of criminalization of environmental harm' European Journal of Crime, Criminal Law and Criminal Justice (1995), p. 328.

for instance be found in §324 of the German penal code, which penalises the pollution of water. Here it is required that the pollution must amount to a negative change in the quality of water before liability can arise.[1474]

More controversial are offences of abstract endangerment, where liability is imposed irrespective of any specific damage or threat of harm. They criminalise conduct which in general can cause harm to the underlying protected legal interest. Furthermore, no intention to cause harm is required by the suspect.[1475] Possession offences can be equated with this latter category where the possession of the prohibited article, material or substance is deemed to create the risk that either the possessor or a third party will use it in the future to bring about harm.[1476] Although frequently used, abstract endangerment offences are however problematic in regard to the principle of individual autonomy and responsibility. This is because the link between the conduct of the possessor and the potential harm is not the possessor's intention as is usually the case in criminal law, but rather an empirical prediction about what people might do in the future.[1477] Thus, these offences should arguably be applied restrictively.

Inchoate offences in general, such as attempt or preparation can be considered to constitute an allied species of endangerment offences as they prescribe the endangerment of an underlying protected legal interest. Yet, there is one vital difference that distinguishes inchoate offences from the aforementioned endangerment offences. In regard to the latter, punishment is imposed for the creation of an objective danger to the legal interest. If actual harm occurs in these cases is beyond the perpetrator's influence and in fact a matter of luck or coincidence.[1478] Consider for instance a possession offence imposing liability for leaving a handgun visible in the back of the car. If another person seizes the opportunity and causes harm with this weapon, is entirely beyond the control of the perpetrator.

In regard to the inchoate offences of attempt and preparation, which could be dubbed "planning offences", the endangerment stems not so much from an objective danger created by the perpetrator, but rather from his (subjective) intentions. These intentions need however to have somehow objectively manifested themselves by

1474 Faure and Visser, 'How to punish environmental pollution? Some reflections on various models of criminalization of environmental harm' European Journal of Crime, Criminal Law and Criminal Justice (1995), p. 336.

1475 Faure and Visser, 'How to punish environmental pollution? Some reflections on various models of criminalization of environmental harm' European Journal of Crime, Criminal Law and Criminal Justice (1995), pp. 319–328.

1476 Ashworth, 'The Unfairness of risk-based possession offences' Criminal Law and Philosophy (2011), p. 13.

1477 Duff, 'Answering for Crime' (2007), p. 165.

1478 Heinrich, 'Die Grenzen des Strafrechts bei der Gefahrenprävention' ZStW (2009), p. 125, Sieber, 'Legitimation und Grenzen von Gefährdungsdelikten im Vorfeld terroristischer Gewalt – Eine Analyse der Vorfeldtatbestände im "Entwurf eines Gesetzes zur Verfolgung der Vorbereitung von schweren staatsgefährdenden Gewalttaten"' NStZ (2009), p. 359.

some sort of overt conduct. Here some further intentional conduct by the perpetrator is needed in order to bring about the envisaged harm.[1479] Thus, in regard to inchoate offences, the perpetrator remains in control of the occurrence of harm. Contrary to the (primarily objective) endangerment offences, the intention of the perpetrator exceeds what has objectively been accomplished.

Nevertheless, endangerment offences can play an important and legitimate role within the criminal law. One just needs to take the endangerment offence of driving under the influence into consideration. It should however not be overlooked that they considerably depart from the traditional patterns of criminal liability. By removing the requirement that a certain conduct has brought about harm, one also removes the necessity of proving a causal link between conduct and harm. Therefore a dogmatic constraint is removed, which increases the chance of conviction and complicates the task of the defence.[1480]

To conclude, it can be stated that endangerment in general and possession offences in particular deviate from the normal patterns of imposing criminal liability in order to criminalise conduct far removed from harm and to protect public safety. Possession offences can probably best be categorised as offences of abstract endangerment based on a duty of care imposed on someone who knowingly has control over a dangerous object.[1481] This however brings the discussion right back to the predicament which has already been touched upon in the realm of omission liability. What weight should be assigned to individual liberties and fundamental freedoms as compared to the collective goods such as public safety, national security and crime prevention? It seems that at times of global crisis and increasing social anxiety, influenced by economic and social insecurity, the public is more willing to surrender individual rights for the (ultimately unattainable) goal of security.

6.3. Preparation as a doctrine of the general part

6.3.1. Introduction

So far the discussion has been primarily concerned with specific offences criminalising preparatory conduct. All investigated systems, it has been shown, use offences in their own right to expand the scope of criminal law to attain the ultimate goal of the culture of control, the prevention of crime. One red thread running through the foregoing discussion was that traditionally penal systems have been

---

1479 Heinrich, 'Die Grenzen des Strafrechts bei der Gefahrenprävention' ZStW (2009), p. 125, Sieber, 'Legitimation und Grenzen von Gefährdungsdelikten im Vorfeld terroristischer Gewalt – Eine Analyse der Vorfeldtatbestände im "Entwurf eines Gesetzes zur Verfolgung der Vorbereitung von schweren staatsgefährdenden Gewalttaten"' NStZ (2009), p. 359.

1480 Hassemer, 'Sicherheit durch Strafrecht' HRRS (2006), p. 136.

1481 Ashworth, 'The Unfairness of risk-based possession offences' Criminal Law and Philosophy (2011), p. 19.

reluctant to incorporate these sorts of offences into their framework of liability, but that this attitude seems to have changed recently. The concern for individual liberties and the general conviction that in a liberal democratic society the private sphere ought to be protected and an attitude-based criminal law avoided, also prevented the introduction of a general doctrine of preparation into the general part of criminal law in many systems. As the weight of these arguments however diminished in contemporary society, certain systems that were examined, notably the Netherlands have recently taken the step to introduce a doctrine of perpetration into their general part.

On first sight, such an approach might create the impression of an escalating punitiveness in a penal system. As discussed above, there is certainly a kernel of truth in such an assumption, but the doctrine should not be investigated and probably cannot be fully understood without taking into account the approach taken by Dutch scholars and courts towards attempt liability. As will be discovered in due course, the Dutch penal system in regard to attempts adheres to a rather objective approach or manifest pattern of liability. This resulted in a narrow conception of criminal attempts, which in turn led to some lacunas in the law which produced unsatisfactory results. Thus, partly due to this perceived legal lacunas created by the objectivistic approach, the need was felt in the Netherlands to create a new inchoate offence that would permit law enforcement intervention earlier than the law of attempt did.

The systems of Germany and England have not yet adopted such a general doctrine, but with the introduction of more and more endangerment offences and new legislation such as the Serious Crime Act 2007, a tendency to extend the scope of criminal law to preparatory conduct is perceivable in these systems as well.

6.3.2. The Dutch doctrine of preparation

In 1991 the Dutch government introduced a proposal regarding the criminalisation of preparatory acts in Parliament. After a long and heated discussion the bill entered into force in 1994.[1482] In its short history, the provision already has undergone several changes. Initially, preparation was for instance only punishable in regard to joint preparatory efforts of two or more perpetrators, as those were thought to constitute a bigger general threat to society.[1483] However, in 2002 the legislator removed the requirement of joint preparation and thereby expanded the scope of liability to crimes prepared by individual perpetrators.[1484] A further expansion of liability occurred in 2007 when the legislator removed the requirement that the means applied must be "manifestly intended" for the commission of an offence.

1482 De Hullu, 'Materieel Strafrecht' (2009), p. 395, Pelser, 'Preparations to commit a crime – The Dutch approach to inchoate offences' Utrecht Law Review (2008), p. 63.

1483 Strijards, 'Strafbare voorbereidingshandelingen' (1995), pp. 42 et seq.

1484 De Jong and Knigge, 'Het materiele strafrecht' (2003), p. 208.

This removed an objective requirement from the provision and reinforced the focus on the suspect's subjective intentions.

In the build up to the legislation also the possibility of creating a new conspiracy offence, modelled on the common law concept of conspiracy, was discussed, but rejected for reasons of principle. The penalisation of intentions that have not yet materialised, so the argument went, would militate against the fundamental principle of Dutch penal law that offences must penalise acts or behaviour.[1485] The law triggered a fierce discussion whether the new provision constituted a general shift towards a more subjectivist conception of crime and the provision was criticised for being too vague and too wide.[1486] The new provision, so the argument went, placed the emphasis on the offender's intentions while putting everyday objects to a specific use. Moreover, it was argued that the offence is strongly influenced by law enforcement arguments rather than by reasons of criminal liability and retribution.[1487] In the explanatory memorandum to the bill the legislator therefore explicitly emphasised that with the criminalisation of certain preparatory acts, no general shift towards a culpability based approach towards crime was envisaged and that Dutch criminal law remained act-based.[1488]

The legislator tried to achieve this by strongly linking the new provision to the law of attempts. The provision regarding voluntary withdrawal is applicable for preparatory acts as well as attempts, and participation in the preparatory phase is just like participation in an criminal attempt punishable.[1489] Furthermore, the distinction between absolute and relative unsuited means and objects is applicable to preparatory offences as well.[1490] It follows that, at least at the outset the new preparatory offence was indeed based on an act-based approach towards crime.[1491] This can be deduced from the fact that the defence of voluntary withdrawal is applicable to preparatory offences as well and that offenders receive a lesser punishment than they would, had their efforts resulted in a criminal attempt or a complete offence.[1492]

It seems now pertinent to take a closer look at Art 46 DPC, criminalising preparatory acts. After several amendments of the law, which gradually removed some objective safeguards, the provision now reads as follows:

1485 Pelser, 'Preparations to commit a crime – The Dutch approach to inchoate offences' Utrecht Law Review (2008), p. 63.

1486 For a good overview of the critique see: Strijards, 'Strafbare voorbereidingshandelingen' (1995), pp. 102–116.

1487 Pelser, 'Preparations to commit a crime – The Dutch approach to inchoate offences' Utrecht Law Review (2008), p. 64.

1488 De Hullu, 'Materieel Strafrecht' (2009), p. 396.

1489 See: Art 78 DPC.

1490 De Hullu, 'Materieel Strafrecht' (2009), p. 397.

1491 Pelser, 'Preparations to commit a crime – The Dutch approach to inchoate offences' Utrecht Law Review (2008), p. 64.

1492 The maximum sentence for the substantive crime is reduced by one-half in case of a preparatory offence whereas it is "only" reduced by one third in case of an attempt.

1. Preparation to commit a serious offense which, by statutory definition, carries a term of imprisonment of not less than eight years, is punishable, where the perpetrator intentionally imports, transits, exports or has at its disposal, objects, substances, information carriers, concealed spaces or means of transport intended for the commission of the serious offence.
2. In case of preparation, the maximum principal penalty prescribed for the serious offence is reduced by one half.
3. In case of serious offenses carrying a sentence of life imprisonment, a term of imprisonment of not more than fifteen years shall be imposed
4. The additional penalties for preparation are as for completed offences.
5. The term objects refers to all material and immaterial goods.

From the wording of the law one can already deduce some important features of this new inchoate offence. From a doctrinal point of view, paragraph 1 which refers to 'having at its disposal objects, substances, etc.' reveals the close connection and allied nature of the provision to the aforementioned possession offences. If system internally compared to the Dutch law of attempts, it becomes apparent that Art 46 DPC is much more detailed and thus more closely circumscribed than Art 45 DPC. Art 46 exhaustively lists the criminalised preparatory acts, as well as means, which is in stark contrast to the open wording of Art 45 which only requires the "initiation of the serious offence". While this detailed circumscription was certainly aimed at grounding the offence in an objectivist approach, it will subsequently be shown that the preparatory acts and means are interpreted so broadly in practice that they de facto no longer have a limiting effect.

One clear limitation of the scope of the offence can however be found in the requirement that the preparatory acts must concern a crime that carries a term of imprisonment of not less than eight years. This limits the offence to the preparation of serious offences like: arson, counterfeiting, rape and sexual assault, deprivation of liberty, murder and manslaughter, extortion, etc. From this it also follows that the prepared criminal offence must be outlined in the indictment and that it needs to be proven in court that the defendant prepared a crime punishable with at least eight years imprisonment.[1493]

Before dwelling on the constituent elements of this inchoate offence, a closer look at the nature of the offence seems appropriate first.

The nature of Art 46 DPC

It has already been pointed out that in comparison to the law of attempt, the social harm is much more distant in preparatory offences. Whereas in traditional criminal law, punishment is imposed for the harm inflicted to a legally protected interest, the aim of a preparatory offence is to allow an early intervention by the law to prevent

[1493] See: HR 17 September 2002, *NJ* 2002, 626.

the infliction of harm.[1494] Inchoate offences like attempts and preparatory acts, where by definition no criminal harm has yet occurred, are therefore in the Netherlands characterised as endangerment offences. They criminalise the endangerment and not the impairment of a legally protected interest.[1495] However, there is a crucial difference between attempts and preparatory acts. While the endangerment for the underlying legal interest stems from the initiation of the commission of the offence in regard to attempts, the endangerment in regard to preparatory acts is primarily deduced from the evil intentions with which the perpetrator carried out the preparations.[1496]

This, however, should not come as a surprise, if one takes into consideration that preparatory acts are far removed from the actual manifestation of criminal harm and that preparatory acts are even more innocuous and ambiguous than criminal attempts. Buying a hammer, a kitchen knife, or a pack of matches and other everyday actions, could for instance all be categorised as preparatory actions if carried out with the required intent.

The actus reus of preparatory acts

Also in regard to criminal preparation it is required that the intention to commit the offence has manifested itself in the preparatory acts. Thus, to ensure that thoughts remain free a certain externalisation of the criminal intent, i.e. an overt act is required.[1497] This externalisation of the intent or the overt act must be related to the underlying criminal offence. As a doctrine of the general part just like criminal attempts, preparatory acts are not punishable per se but only the preparation of a particular offence will lead to the imposition of criminal liability. The commission of a crime must actually have been prepared. It has for instance been argued that the preparatory acts must have actually brought the underlying offence closer to completion.[1498]

The law outlines several preparatory means and acts which were intended to circumscribe the scope of the offence. Thus, the offence contains two objective criteria. The perpetrator must (a) obtain, import, transit, export or have at his disposal (b) objects, substances, information carriers, concealed spaces or means of transport. However, the means are interpreted broadly. Already paragraph five of Article 46 holds that the term objects refers to all material and immaterial goods

---

1494 Roef and Prakken, 'Strafbare Voorbereiding in Nederland: Juridische Overkill', in Verbruggen, et al. (eds), Voorbereidingshandelingen in het Strafrecht (2004), pp. 231–234.

1495 Roef and Prakken, 'Strafbare Voorbereiding in Nederland: Juridische Overkill', in Verbruggen, et al. (eds), Voorbereidingshandelingen in het Strafrecht (2004), pp. 231–234.

1496 Roef and Prakken, 'Strafbare Voorbereiding in Nederland: Juridische Overkill', in Verbruggen, et al. (eds), Voorbereidingshandelingen in het Strafrecht (2004), pp. 231–234.

1497 De Hullu, 'Materieel Strafrecht' (2009), p. 399, Pelser, 'Preparations to commit a crime – The Dutch approach to inchoate offences' Utrecht Law Review (2008), p. 68.

1498 Buruma, 'Bestraft zonder iets gedaan te hebben', in Kempen, et al. (eds), De gedraging in beweging (2007), pp. 33, 37.

which includes any means of payment. Furthermore, it is not required that the objects already possess an instrumental character at the time the preparations are discovered. It is for instance possible that the members of a criminal group all possess or work on certain parts of a device which in total forms the detonator of a bomb.[1499]

Thus, under *preparatory means* a multitude of every day objects can be assumed. It has for instance been argued that a stone, a rope, a pin, or a kitchen knife could all constitute preparatory means, provided the required intention can be proven.[1500] The Supreme Court has for instance, *inter alia*, forged license plates, burglary tools, weapons and mobile phones classified as objects.[1501]

Under *substances* fall material(s), energy, etc., from which things can be created, developed or designed. Contrary to the category of objects, substances require further processing in order to become instruments of human conduct. Think for instance of fertiliser, etc. which can be transformed into explosives, or ether which is vital for many drug producing processes.[1502] The Supreme Court has for instance considered fertiliser, electric circuits and chemicals as substances.[1503]

Under the notion *information carrier*, any means to store information is subsumed. These means can reach from cd-roms, hard and floppy disks, usb sticks, e-mails etc. but also more traditional means like blueprints, letters, notes, etc. can be subsumed.[1504]

Under *concealed spaces* everything from a room or an apartment to large suitcases (for instance to transport a kidnapped person) can be subsumed. Also a car or a boat could function as a concealed space. In this case, the dividing line between this category and means of transport is drawn by the intention with which the perpetrator uses the means to prepare the offence.[1505]

The aforementioned examples already show that the listed preparatory means will hardly circumscribe the scope of the offence. The essence of criminal liability in regard to preparatory acts is simply situated in the criminal intention with which the means are deployed.

That the intention of the perpetrator plays a crucial role can also be deduced from a case where the Supreme Court acquitted the defendant from preparing a robbery on a money transport. During a house search a letter was discovered in a winter jacket which contained detailed information of how to rob a money transport. The defendant had stated that he had received the letter from an inmate during a previous stay in a correctional facility. He claimed to have read the letter and put it into his winter jacket, where it had remained for several months, until it was

---

[1499] De Hullu, 'Materieel Strafrecht' (2009), p. 400.

[1500] Strijards, 'Strafbare voorbereidingshandelingen' (1995), p. 125.

[1501] HR 18 November 2003, *LJN* AJ0517.

[1502] Strijards, 'Strafbare voorbereidingshandelingen' (1995), pp. 125–127.

[1503] HR 20 February 2007, *LJN* AZ0213.

[1504] See for instance: HR 17 February 2004, *NJ* 2004, 400, where a letter containing instructions on how to rob a money transport was considered an information carrier.

[1505] Strijards, 'Strafbare voorbereidingshandelingen' (1995), pp. 134–136.

discovered by the police. Despite the fact that the defendant had a previous conviction for similar offences, the Supreme Court acquitted the defendant and held that the mere possession of such a letter was insufficient to prove that the defendant was intentionally preparing a robbery.[1506] This case furthermore shows that the conduct requirement of Article 46 is relatively broad, especially as due to the notion of 'having at ones disposal' even omissions can constitute the basis for liability for preparatory acts.

A last objective element in the wording of Article 46 DPC can be found in the requirement that the preparatory means must be intended for the commission of a serious offence. How can it for instance be established that a cell phone, a car or a rope is intended for the commission of an offence. Is this to be determined by objective factors, like the outward manifestation of the conduct like in the Dutch law of attempts, or can the intention of the perpetrator with which he deploys the means also play a role? This used to be a hotly debated issue, but since 2007 it is clearly established that the intentions can play a role in the evaluation process.[1507] Before 2007 the law required that the means were "manifestly intended" for the commission of the offence, but in 2007 the word manifestly was removed. This of course, raises the question whether this change introduced a far-reaching shift towards subjectivism and an attitude-based criminal law.[1508] Although the legislator seemingly aimed at introducing a subjective approach with Article 46 and despite the fact that the intentions of the perpetrator will per definition play a crucial role in regard to preparatory offences it is submitted that jurisprudence seems to adopt a moderate objectivist approach. A (potential) objective endangerment still needs to be proven even though the subjective perception of the perpetrator, i.e. his intentions, can play an important role here.[1509]

Intentions alone are still considered insufficient to ground criminal liability in these cases. The offender's intentions must have objectively manifested themselves in an overt act. In addition it is still necessary to prove that the means were deployed to prepare a particular criminal offence. However, it should be made clear here that the objective tenor of Art 46 DPC has become diminished. If the required intention can be proven, a few, (minor) overt acts will suffice in practice to establish liability for preparatory acts. This can for instance be illustrated by a case in which the Supreme Court held that the purpose of preparatory means may be deduced from

---

1506 HR 17 februari 2004, *NJ* 2004, 400.

1507 De Hullu, 'Materieel Strafrecht' (2009), p. 401, Rozemond, 'De algemene strafbaarstelling van voorbereidingshandelingen in het licht van de pogingsjurisprudentie van de Hoge Raad' Delikt en Delinkwent (1994), pp. 667–675, Smith, 'Strafbare Voorbereiding, Een rechtsverglijkend onderzoek' (2003), pp. 202–207.

1508 See for instance: Rozemond, 'De Subjectivering van het Nederlands Strafrecht' Nederlands Juristenblad (2007), pp. 2301–2305. For the opposite view see: Gritter and Sikkema, 'Van kennelijke bestemming naar daadwerkelijke voorbereiding: subjectivering van het Nederlandse strafrecht?' Nederlands Juristenblad (2008), pp. 99–101.

1509 Gritter and Sikkema, 'Van kennelijke bestemming naar daadwerkelijke voorbereiding: subjectivering van het Nederlandse strafrecht?' Nederlands Juristenblad (2008), pp. 99–101.

the entirety of the objects seized, combined with their use and the criminal goal of the offenders. In this case a conviction for preparing a robbery by having at his disposal a vehicle intended for committing this crime was upheld. Two men had been "casing" a bank using a Ford Transit van. It had been proven that the defendant had parked the van across the street, and sitting in the car he and his partner had observed the bank for some time. Then they had driven off and pulled over somewhere else, got out of the van, walked around the bank building and got back into the van again. The Supreme Court upheld the conviction ruling that the Court of Appeal had rightly evaluated the van as to its outward manifestation, its use and the criminal purpose that the offenders had in mind concerning the van.[1510] From this case it can already be deduced that the objective requirements of the offence can in practice be satisfied very easily.

An important decision in regard to criminal preparatory acts is the so called Samir A. decision. Although the judgment concerned the old version of Art 46 where "manifestly" was still an element of the offence, the Supreme Court ruled that in determining the criminal purpose of preparatory means by their outward manifestation one cannot abstract from the criminal goal which the defendant aims to reach by using these means.[1511] With this judgment the Supreme Court anticipated and also paved the way for the subsequent removal of the word "manifestly" from the offence definition.

In the course of an investigation concerning the robbery of a supermarket, a house search was carried out in the flat of a 17-year old Muslim teenager, Samir A. who was suspected to be an accessory to the robbery. During the search the police found a cartridge clip, a silencer, an imitation firearm, a bulletproof vest, night-vision goggles, several handmade floor plans of public buildings like the Lower House of Parliament, a nuclear power plant and the Amsterdam airport, including notes on security measures and potential escape routes, as well as chemical and electronic equipment which was intended to manufacture a bomb. Samir had, before that incident, already attracted the attention of the Dutch secret service as he had travelled to Chechnya where he intended to support his "Muslim brothers" in the fight against Russia, but was detained by border guards and sent back to Amsterdam.[1512] As the 2004 Terrorist Offences Act was not yet in force, Samir A. was charged with the criminal preparation of murder, arson and causing an explosion.[1513] One characterising feature of this case was the amateurish nature of the preparatory acts, as well as the very early stage in which the criminal endeavour was discovered. Experts had concluded that the objects discovered (a plastic bottle with electric fibre made from Christmas-tree lights and filled with chemicals) were

1510 HR 18 November 2003, *LJN* AJ0535.

1511 HR 20 Februari 2007, *LJN* AZ0213.

1512 Pelser, 'Preparations to commit a crime – The Dutch approach to inchoate offences' Utrecht Law Review (2008), p. 67.

1513 Pelser, 'Preparations to commit a crime – The Dutch approach to inchoate offences' Utrecht Law Review (2008), p. 66.

not at all suited for causing an explosion, *inter alia* because the fertiliser used to construct the device lacked the necessary ammonium nitrate. Also the discovered blueprints and plans showed the amateurish nature of the enterprise, as most information was simply gathered from the internet. The Court of first instance had acquitted the defendant of preparing a terrorist attack but convicted him for the illegal possession of arms and ammunition. The court argued that the defendant lacked the necessary mens rea and that the primitive nature of the seized objects made it factually impossible that the crime be committed.[1514] The Court of Appeal subsequently upheld the acquittal but applied a slightly different reasoning. It held that despite the defendant's (terrorist) intention it was not only a question whether the means could contribute to the commission of the offence in the abstract, but also whether manufacturing materials or having materials at his disposal amounts to a concrete or actual danger. The Court ruled that despite the clear terrorist intention of the defendant, the amateurish and primitive means did not amount to an actual threat, nor could they do so in the near future.[1515] The Court of first instance thus saw the factual impossibility of the preparations as the determining factor, while the Court of Appeal placed the dangerousness of the conduct and the likelihood that the offender might be successful in committing the underlying offence first.[1516]

As already mentioned, the Supreme Court however squashed the acquittal and held that means of preparation had to be evaluated whether they, separate or together, by their outward manifestation, *can* be suitable for the criminal purpose the defendant has in using them. Thus, the evaluation need not be based on preparatory acts that provide a real possibility that the crime is committed, but a hypothetical possibility that the offender might ever reach that point is now sufficient. The exact content of this test remains to be seen in future, but this judgment underlines that intentions can play an important role in establishing the purpose of preparatory means.

Yet, the general tenor in jurisprudence arguably remains objective-orientated. In line with the prevalent approach in the law of attempt, the outward manifestation of the conduct in question plays a pivotal role in the Netherlands. In essence this amounts to an objective reasonable person standard. Also in regard to the means applied, reference is made to the criterion of outward manifestation, although thereby the subjective perspective of the perpetrator can play a role in the evaluation process. Furthermore it needs to be proven that the offender actually prepared a concrete serious offence and that the respective means were applied for that purpose.[1517] All these requirements can arguably be classified as objective,

---

1514 Rb. Rotterdam 6 April 2005, *LJN* AT3315.

1515 Hof Den Haag 20 November 2005, *LJN* AU6181.

1516 Pelser, 'Preparations to commit a crime – The Dutch approach to inchoate offences' Utrecht Law Review (2008), p. 67.

1517 See also: Gritter and Sikkema, 'Van kennelijke bestemming naar daadwerkelijke voorbereiding: subjectivering van het Nederlandse strafrecht?' Nederlands Juristenblad (2008), pp. 99–101.

counterbalancing the by-definition heavy influence of the perpetrator's intentions in regard to preparatory conduct. This goes to show that while a doctrine of preparation will generally have its roots in the subjective pattern of criminality, it is nevertheless possible to interpret the doctrine objectively in order to maintain reasonable boundaries to criminal liability.

Be that as it may, another interesting point raised by this case is the issue of impossibility, which is connected to the required (criminal) purpose of the preparatory means. Presumably, the issue of impossibility applies to preparatory acts as well as to the law of attempts. However, as will subsequently be shown, the matter only plays an auxiliary role in the law of attempts and this might be even more so in regard to preparatory acts. One reason for this might be that in regard to preparatory actions, the intentions of the defendant carry even more weight than in regard to attempts and in addition, the preparatory phase is even further removed from the completion of the offence which might give the defendant ample opportunity to amend or adjust unsuitable means.[1518]

It should however be kept in mind that the Samir A. saga constitutes an exceptional case, for it concerns the very serious endeavour of committing a large scale terrorist attack, and because the criminal enterprise was discovered at such an early stage that the preparatory means had not (yet) reached a high level of sophistication.

The general approach in Dutch jurisprudence regarding preparatory acts is quite casuistic where depending on the case at hand sometimes subjective and sometimes objective factors can be determining. In a recent case, the police were informed about two suspicious cars with foreign license plates parked in a residential area with three persons in it. The police searched the vehicles and found a large amount of potentially criminal objects like *inter alia* several weapons, cable ties, a baseball bat, pepper spray, masks, rubber gloves, and a note with the phone number and address of a person on it living in the vicinity of where the cars were parked. Furthermore another note was found which read: 800 Euro expenses, 1000 Euro in case of failure, 5000 in case of success. In the course of the investigation it became apparent the case was related to drugs and concerned drug money (30.000 Euro), which the person named in the note owed to the principal. The court had no problem in this case to deduce from the many and mostly clearly criminal preparatory means found in the two cars that the defendants were preparing the robbing of the person mentioned in the note.[1519] In this case the outward manifestation of the preparatory means was thus sufficiently clear to warrant a conviction, which might also have to do with the fact that the defendants had already come very close to the attempt stage and that the criminal purpose of the means was evident.

In another case, the clear criminal intent of the perpetrators was the determining factor in establishing criminal liability. The police had become aware of a plan to rob a store, as they had been tapping the phone of one of the defendants in

[1518] De Hullu, 'Materieel Strafrecht' (2009), p. 403.

[1519] Hof 's-Hertogenbosch 22 January 2008, *LJN* BC2604.

connection with a previous robbery. The police arrested four men in a car in the vicinity of the store and found a replica (air) gun inside the car. The court, in line with the aforementioned case law, held the driving to the *locus delicti* and the possession of the replica gun as sufficiently strong for a conviction of preparing a robbery.[1520]

These cases show that by and large the preparatory conduct remains central in the establishment of liability for preparatory acts and that the criminal intention has to be deduced from the outward manifestation of the preparatory conduct. However, the test is flexible enough to be completed in rather subjective terms as well. In borderline cases, the criminal intention of the perpetrator can become the all-determining factor which will outweigh shortcomings regarding objective elements. Thus, the further the criminal law "intrudes" into the preparatory phase of crime, the more pivotal subjective elements will become in order to ground criminal liability. The objective elements of the offence, i.e. the preparatory conduct and means, as well as the criminal purpose of these means will then only play an auxiliary role in the establishment of criminal liability.

The mens rea of preparatory acts

Art 46 DPC explicitly refers to an intention to prepare a criminal offence. This would on first sight also include the broad notion of *dolus eventualis* to establish liability for a preparatory offence. Placed in the broader context of the offence however, it seems that the word intention needs to be construed more restrictively in the realm of preparatory acts. This is understandable, if one considers the prominent role that intentions play here and that the objective conduct discernible is often innocuous and ambiguous. The less instructive the occurred conduct, the more weight one should place on the fault requirement.[1521] In almost every household you will find objects, like for instance a car, chemicals, etc. which could be regarded as means for preparing a criminal offence. But only if, independent of this means, a criminal purpose or enterprise can be proven, is the fault requirement of the offence fulfilled.[1522] The intention of the perpetrator needs furthermore be directed towards the commission of a particular crime. This is because preparatory acts are only punishable in regard to some serious offences. This requirement is not always easily satisfied in practice which constitutes an important circumscription of the scope of the offence. After all, if one sees 4 persons in a car wearing masks, one can easily come to the conclusion that they are up to no good, but what exactly they are doing is hard to deduce. To satisfy this requirement it will be necessary to prove, a more or less concrete plan, to commit a particular criminal offence. The Supreme Court has for instance held that it has to be established which category of a criminal

1520 Rb. Alkmaar, 10 September 2009, *LJN* BJ8580.

1521 De Hullu, 'Materieel Strafrecht' (2009), p. 404, Smith, 'Strafbare Voorbereiding, Een rechtsverglijkend onderzoek' (2003), pp. 212–224.

1522 De Hullu, 'Materieel Strafrecht' (2009), p. 404.

offence (carrying a punishment of not less than eight years) has been prepared. It is sufficient that it becomes clear that the acts were performed in the preparation of such crime (carrying a punishment of at least eight years).[1523]

6.4. Evaluation

The criminalisation of preparatory acts reveals some interesting modern tendencies not only in the Dutch penal system but in the criminal law in general. First and foremost, it once more shows that the criminal law increasingly is concerned with crime prevention instead of retribution. To achieve this goal and to provide security for society, the foundations of criminal liability are altered. This trend results in an alteration of safeguards and underlying principles which have shaped the criminal law for centuries. The (ultimately) futile quest for crime prevention and security has for instance led to a reversal of the ten to one principle which holds that it is better that ten guilty escape (the criminal law) than that one innocent person suffers.[1524] Analysed critically, the criminalisation of preparatory actions bears witness to this change. The preparatory acts are by definition far removed from the occurrence of criminal harm which would give the would-be perpetrator ample opportunity to rethink his endeavours and maybe ultimately change his mind. The criminalisation of these acts increases the possibility that people will get caught in the net of criminal law who would ultimately have never committed the crime in question.

However, it should be pointed out that in regard to Dutch criminal law one ought to distinguish between two different constellations here. First, there are cases that directly adjoin to the attempt phase but which fall outside the scope of attempts due to the objectivist approach taken therein. In these cases the imposition of criminal liability seems warranted as the perpetrator has come sufficiently close to the commission of the criminal offence and has shown strong criminal proclivities and energies.

Yet, the further one moves away from these cases situated at the outskirt of criminal attempts, the more problematic things become. The emphasis on the mens rea in these cases is reason for concern as criminal law moves further towards the punishment of thoughts and attitudes. The act requirement, i.e. that criminal liability ought to be based on some form of harmful conduct, is a fundamental principle, limiting the scope of criminal law and protecting society from arbitrariness and safeguarding individual liberty, which must not be discarded. Furthermore, it can be stated that modern criminal law becomes increasingly engaged in a balancing act between two abysses. On the one hand risk liability, i.e. liability without the proof of mens rea, is invading the traditional criminal law, while on the other hand an attitude-based criminal law, i.e. criminal liability

---

1523 HR 17 September 2002, *NJ* 2002, 626.

1524 Generaly see: Van Sliedregt, 'Ten to one – A contemporary reflection on the presumption of innocence' (2009), pp. 1–56.

without the proof of an actus reus equally increasingly undermines and alters traditional safeguards and principles.[1525] While it is understandable that the perpetrator's intentions play a prominent role in cases where the occurred conduct does not betoken harm or danger to society, it is important to stress that the notion of actus reus must remain an important part in the framework of liability for preparatory offences.[1526] This is in order to prevent a far reaching shift towards a culpability-centred approach. Thus the dangerous nature of a certain deed needs to be established by subjective and objective elements alike in order to respect the bedrock principles of legality as well as to ensure that thoughts remain free even in the risk society of the 21st century.[1527]

It has been attempted to show that criminal liability becomes more controversial when harm is risked rather than caused. Yet this does not mean that all offences criminalising preparatory conduct are per se objectionable. This raises the question when a legislator may legitimately design such offences without being accused of overcriminalisation. Some guidelines can thereby be derived from general principles of criminal law. First and foremost, in the light of the *ultima ratio* principle, it is arguable that conduct that only poses a remote danger to the protected legal interest and where the endangerment is still factually and temporally uncertain, should not be subjected to criminal sanctions.[1528] Furthermore, liability may only be imposed if the offender's conduct can in some sense be considered wrongful.[1529] This arguably follows from the *nulla poena sine actione* principle. The foundation of criminal liability ought to rest on a person's conduct and not on his evil thoughts, dangerousness or attitude.

Beyond that the underlying protected legal interest ought to be substantial in order to warrant an expansion of criminal liability. As trivial interests should not be protected by threat of criminal sanctions, it follows that preparatory offences ought to only be accepted if they are designed to reduce a substantial risk.[1530] Imposing liability to prevent an insubstantial risk would arguably punish individuals who are less culpable, than those who are negligent. This is because negligence generally requires the failure to attend to a substantial or considerable risk. Thus, liability for an insubstantial risk would fall below this standard which in terms of

---

1525 Roef and Prakken, 'Strafbare Voorbereiding in Nederland: Juridische Overkill', in Verbruggen, et al. (eds), Voorbereidingshandelingen in het Strafrecht (2004), pp. 210–269.

1526 See: Roef and Prakken, 'Strafbare Voorbereiding in Nederland: Juridische Overkill', in Verbruggen, et al. (eds), Voorbereidingshandelingen in het Strafrecht (2004), pp. 210–269.

1527 Roef and Prakken, 'Strafbare Voorbereiding in Nederland: Juridische Overkill', in Verbruggen, et al. (eds), Voorbereidingshandelingen in het Strafrecht (2004), pp. 209–269.

1528 Deckers and Heusel, 'Strafbarkeit terroristischer Vorbereitungshandlungen – rechtsstaatlich nicht tragbar' ZRP (2008), p. 171.

1529 Husak, 'Overcriminalization' (2008), pp. 73 et seq, Sieber, 'Legitimation und Grenzen von Gefährdungsdelikten im Vorfeld terroristischer Gewalt – Eine Analyse der Vorfeldtatbestände im "Entwurf eines Gesetzes zur Verfolgung der Vorbereitung von schweren staatsgefährdenden Gewalttaten"' NStZ (2009), p. 356.

1530 Husak, 'Overcriminalization' (2008), p. 162.

blameworthiness would fall outside the scope of criminal law.[1531] Finally, flowing from the principle *nulla poena sine culpa,* liability for preparatory offences seems only justified in case the person creating a risk of harm, possesses a significant culpability for the ultimate harm.[1532] This requirement, it is submitted, may in the case of criminalising risk of harm amount to a culpability standard of direct or indirect intention and exclude the application of *dolus eventualis.*

On a more general note, it should be stressed that the general goal of crime prevention most importantly ought to respect the fundamental principle of any community based on the rule of law namely proportionality. Adherence to these, admittedly vague, under-developed and rather crude guidelines, could assure that the fundamental criminal law principles of *nulla poena sine culpa et actione* would be respected also in regard to preparatory offences and could call a halt to the ongoing expansion of criminal law.

The foregoing propositions also by and large seems to correspond to the approach adopted by the Council of the European Union in its model provisions which holds that:

> Criminal provisions should focus on conduct causing actual harm or seriously threatening the right or essential interest which is the object of protection; that is, avoiding criminalisation of a conduct at an unwarrantably early stage. Conduct which only implies an abstract danger to the protected right or interest should be criminalised only if appropriate considering the particular importance of the right or interest which is the object of protection.[1533]

7. Criminal attempts

7.1. Introduction

Adjacent to the preparatory stage is the realm of attempt liability. Once the actor has transgressed the preparatory stage, i.e. has obtained the necessary materials, tools or expert knowledge, etc. and approaches the executory stage of the envisaged criminal enterprise, the law on criminal attempts comes into play. Thus, in comparison to the preparatory stage, the offender has come several steps closer to the commission of the offence in the attempt phase. It has already been mentioned that traditionally the distinction between attempts and preparation constituted the borderline between liability and non-liability. As preparatory conduct was (and in many jurisdictions still is) considered to be too far removed from the occurrence of harm to justify the imposition of punishment only conduct beyond mere preparation

---

1531 Husak, 'Overcriminalization' (2008), p. 162.

1532 Husak, 'Overcriminalization' (2008), pp. 174 et seq.

1533 Draft Council conclusions on model provisions, guiding the Council's criminal law deliberations, Brussels, 27 November 2009, 16542/2/09 REV 2.

was deemed to trigger criminal liability. Yet, the foregoing discussion has shown that this distinction, due to contemporary legislative trends increasingly loses relevance and becomes more and more elusive.

However, the fact remains that criminal attempts are historically the older concept which provided the battleground for the discussion on the proper scope of criminal liability for many years. In England and Germany, the distinction is still a crucial one as these systems do not accept a general doctrine of preparation. Conversely, in the Netherlands, where the doctrine of preparation has been enshrined in the penal code, the distinction nowadays merely plays an auxiliary role.

Generally speaking, attempts can be viewed as cases of failure. A burglar is apprehended by the neighbourhood watch before he can break into a house. Marc, who wants to shoot his uncle Barnaby to inherit his fortune pulls the trigger but misses, or the weapon jams. The pickpocket puts his hand into the pocket of the potential victim, but to his disappointment finds it to be empty. Or suppose that vicious John intends to kill his wife clumsy Kati for making his life miserable. He pours arsenic into her evening tea, but Kati spills the tea before she can take one sip. All these cases of failed criminal behaviour are candidates for attempt liability. Thus, at a more abstract level, criminal attempts can be conceived as conduct carried out with the intent to commit a crime, but which fails to achieve the envisaged result.

Many of the objections and predicaments which apply *a fortiori* to the criminalisation of preparatory conduct first came to the fore in and shaped the realm of criminal attempts. Traditionally, criminal law adopted a narrow approach regarding liability for attempts, because attempts, just like preparatory offences run the risk of introducing what liberal penal systems abhor the most: the punishment of thoughts. After all, what attempts and even more so preparatory offences punish is not what an actor has done, but rather, what he intends to do in the future. This traditional reluctance to impose punishment also in cases where no legal interest has been violated and no harm has occurred, which contradicts the old proverb 'No harm – no wrong', is still discernible in the general approach taken towards criminal attempts in all investigated penal systems. All three systems namely concur that an attempt should only be punishable in cases where the underlying protected legal interest seems significant enough to justify an expansion of criminal liability. Accordingly the penal codes or statutes of Germany, the Netherlands and England and Wales generally confine attempt liability to serious crimes, excluding attempt liability for misdemeanours.[1534]

The very essence of an attempt is that the defendant has for whatever reason failed to commit the full offence but would have acted with the necessary mens rea. In criminal endeavours, just like in other spheres of life, things do not always work out as planned or envisaged. However, should the criminal law abstain from

[1534] See: §23 GPC, Article 45 DPC and Section 1 of the 1981 Criminal Attempts Act. However, special legislation may create exceptions to this general rule.

intervention because the criminal enterprise has failed and no harm has occurred? After all the, difference between failure and success is often determined by factors such as luck, chance and misjudgement. It goes without saying that it would be regarded as untenable by modern societies if a person would escape criminal liability merely because of the fortuitous failure of its criminal endeavour. The view that people who attempt to commit a crime but fail should not escape criminal liability is further corroborated if one takes into consideration that in regard to moral culpability, there should be no distinction made between a person who attempts to bring about the prohibited result and fails, and the person who succeeds.[1535] They have both manifested their willingness to break the law and should therefore be punished.

It can be deduced from these initial points that in the law of attempts the tensions between the pattern of manifest and subjective criminality resurface. The emphasis on the actor's intentions causes frictions with the requirement of objective wrongdoing as a requirement of criminal liability. These tensions are particularly visible in the doctrinal disputes surrounding the law of attempts which has traditionally provided the battleground for subjectivists and objectivists with their different conceptions of criminal liability. The dispute between the two camps shapes and determines the scope of liability significantly in this area of the law. It plays a role at four different levels at least. First, it influences the shape and guise of the doctrine on a fundamental level in regard to the rationale for punishing attempts (section 7.2). Second, it influences the creation of proper criteria for conduct-ascription (section 7.4). Third, the different views may lead to different results in regard to impossible attempts, i.e. attempts which by their very nature cannot lead to fruition (section 8). Finally, the distinction is of relevance at the level of punishment, in regard to the question of just how much punishment attempts should warrant.

7.2. The rationale for punishing attempts

7.2.1. Introduction

In the German penal system with its focus on systematic thinking, the underlying rationale for attempt liability plays an important role, while in the Netherlands and England it only is of auxiliary importance. In practice these theoretical considerations only play a minor role, but it should not be overlooked that the underlying rationale may influence the interpretation of the doctrine in some areas.

The rationale for punishing attempts can probably best be understood by drawing a theoretical distinction between two different forms of attempts. Although not all jurisdictions recognise this distinction, it will help to structure the subsequent discussion. First, there are incomplete attempts. These are cases where

1535 Ashworth, 'Principles of criminal law' (2006), p. 445.

the defendant has not yet done all the acts to commit the offence. The case of an assassin lurking with the gun in hands might serve as an example here. The assassin still needs to aim and pull the trigger to complete the attempt. Once the shot has been fired, but has missed the target, one can speak of a complete attempt. The assassin has done all that he intended but the envisaged result (i.e. the death of the victim) has not followed.[1536] Generally, complete attempts might be easier to justify than incomplete, because in the former cases it can be said that the defendant actually endangered the protected legal interest or is just as culpable as a person who is successful in committing the substantive offence.[1537] Incomplete attempts however, arguably require some further justification as there the actor's culpability might be less than that of the actor who completed the attempt and because the actor here still needs to carry out several steps before an actual danger to the underlying legal interest emerges.[1538]

7.2.2. Objective rationales

Objective theories of punishing attempts focus on the dangerousness or wrongfulness of conduct.[1539] They can take a variety of forms but most require a concrete endangerment of the underlying protected legal interest.[1540] Objectivist theories generally stress the importance of legal certainty and protecting individual liberties and therefore tend to draw the line of liability as close as possible to the consummation of the offence. Corresponding to the pattern of manifest criminality, they try to establish objective wrongdoing by striving to define a required act of attempting independently of the actor's intentions. An example of such an endeavour can arguably be found in the classic phrase that the offender must have commenced with the execution of the criminal offence in order to incur liability.[1541]

A slightly broader scope of liability can be achieved here if one replaces the endangerment of a protected legal interest with the wider concept of endangering the legal order.[1542] In this case as well conduct which according to its external manifestation is directed towards the commission of the offence can trigger liability, despite the fact that one cannot yet speak of a beginning of execution of the offence

1536 Ashworth, 'Principles of criminal law' (2006), pp. 445–446, De Hullu, 'Materieel Strafrecht' (2009), pp. 379–380, Roxin, 'Strafrecht Allgemeiner Teil, Band II: Besondere Erscheinungsformen der Straftat' (2003), pp. 360, 395.

1537 Ashworth, 'Principles of criminal law' (2006), pp. 446.

1538 Ashworth, 'Principles of criminal law' (2006), pp. 446.

1539 Remmelink, 'Inleiding tot de studie van het Nederlandse Strafrecht' (1995), pp. 394–395, Roxin, 'Strafrecht Allgemeiner Teil, Band II: Besondere Erscheinungsformen der Straftat' (2003), pp. 340–342, Wilson, 'Central Issues in Criminal Theory' (2002), p. 230.

1540 Schönke and Schröder, 'Kommentar zum Strafgesetzbuch' (2006), Vorbem §22 Mn 18, Noyon, Langemeijer, Remmelink, 'Wetboek van Strafrecht' (2010), Art 45, note 2.3. See also: Duff, 'Criminal Attempts' (1996), pp. 193–236.

1541 See: Fletcher, 'Rethinking Criminal Law' (1978), p. 139.

1542 Noyon, Langemeijer, Remmelink, 'Wetboek van Strafrecht' (2010), Art 45, note 2.3.2.

which would be necessary to speak of an endangerment of the protected legal interest. In any case, however, the scope of liability for attempts remains limited according to objective rationales. Furthermore, if one entirely embraces this rationale, impossible attempts ought to escape criminal punishment due to a lack of objective dangerousness of conduct. None of the investigated penal systems embraces a purely objective rationale for punishing attempts, which is demonstrated by the fact, as will subsequently be shown that all systems, although to varying degrees, recognise the imposition of punishment for impossible attempts.

7.2.3. Subjective rationales

Subjective rationales on the other hand focus on the dangerousness or culpability of the actor.[1543] They see the reason for punishing attempts in the criminal disposition of the actor, the exercise of his criminal intentions or his hostile attitude towards the law.[1544] Subjective rationales also generally stress the importance of crime prevention. The actual occurred conduct is only relevant as far as it verifies the firmness of the intent. In other words, subjectivist rationales do not require any form of objective wrongdoing. The conduct requirement according to these theories merely fulfils an evidentiary function. Thus, for subjectivists, the evil in criminal attempts lies in the manifestation of the offender's deviant proclivities.[1545] For them, the fact that no criminal harm has actually occurred is only ancillary. Subjectivists thus assert the so-called "moral equivalence thesis" which holds that the culpability of an actor is not determined by the occurrence or non-occurrence of harm.[1546] The occurrence of harm, so the argument goes, is always dependent on luck, i.e. factors outside human control, and should therefore not influence a person's culpability.[1547] The corollary of this approach is that subjectivists generally claim that the punishment imposed for attempts should be just as severe as for the completed offence.[1548] By the same token, subjectivists argue that no impossibility whatsoever should preclude attempt liability.[1549]

The general vantage point of this rationale that the intention constitutes the central ingredient of criminal attempts is certainly correct, which also objectivists will have to concede. It is in practice namely virtually impossible to speak of an attempt without knowledge of the actor's intention. Consider for instance the barber who approaches his soaped customer with a razor in hand. Without knowledge of

1543 Wilson, 'Central Issues in Criminal Theory' (2002), p. 230. See also: Duff, 'Criminal Attempts' (1996), pp. 147–192.

1544 Roxin, 'Strafrecht Allgemeiner Teil, Band II: Besondere Erscheinungsformen der Straftat' (2003), pp. 342 et seq, Schönke and Schröder, 'Kommentar zum Strafgesetzbuch' (2006), Vorbem §22 Mn 21.

1545 Fletcher, 'Basic Concepts of Criminal Law' (1998), p. 174.

1546 Duff, 'Criminal Attempts' (1996), p. 335.

1547 Duff, 'Criminal Attempts' (1996), p. 335.

1548 Duff, 'Criminal Attempts' (1996), pp. 151 et seq.

1549 Duff, 'Criminal Attempts' (1996), pp. 154 et seq.

his intentions it is impossible to distinguish here between an attempt to shave and an attempt to kill. Yet, overemphasising the subjective element generally results in a broad scope of attempt liability *ratio temporis* and *ratio materiae*. This is because any form of conduct that manifests the actor's dangerousness will suffice for incurring criminal liability.

As will be demonstrated below, English law, by and large takes such a subjectivist approach.[1550] In the realm of attempts, English law focuses more on the deviant proclivities of the actor, manifested by his criminal attempt, rather than on considerations based on (potential) harm and wrongdoing.[1551] Yet, arguably, English law does not follow a purely subjective approach as some objective factors still play a role in the theory of attempts. For instance, the occurred conduct must constitute a vivid danger or threat of harm, which implies that the defendant must have come close to committing the crime.[1552] Yet, the fact remains that the English penal system as a primarily guilt-based criminal law places emphasis in the law of attempts on subjective criminality patterns. In Germany and the Netherlands, pure subjectivist rationales have generally been rejected by the prevalent opinion as they, for one, cannot be reconciled with the respective wording of the provisions in the penal code.[1553] Furthermore, the requirements flowing from an act-based criminal law militate against a pure subjective approach in these systems, which in the more culpability-centred English penal system, however, causes hardly any problems.

7.2.4. Mixed rationales

Due to the fact that both pure objective and subjective rationales have clear shortcomings, an intermediate rationale seems preferable to justify the punishment of attempts. These mixed rationales emphasise the social dimension of the conduct in question. Although it might be difficult or even virtually impossible to construe an endangerment of a protected legal interest in some cases (as is for instance the case when Gary tries to kill Lars by adding sugar, which he believes to be arsenic, into his drink) it might nevertheless be possible to consider these forms of conduct as jeopardising society by undermining the citizens trust in the legal order, so the argument runs. Mixed rationales straddle the objective, subjective dichotomy by not only invoking the actor's criminal intentions or proclivities to justify punishing attempts, but in some variations also the (objective) impression that the occurred conduct makes on society as a whole, without requiring any endangerment. These

1550 See for instance: 'Conspiracy and Attempts', LAW COM No 318 [2009], para 8.66, where an objective endangerment rationale is apparently rejected.

1551 A notable exception is R.A. Duff who advocates an "objective" harm-oriented theory of attempts. See: Duff, 'Criminal Attempts' (1996), pp. 1–400.

1552 See: 'Conspiracy and Attempts', Consultation Paper, LAW COM No 183 [2007], para 12.16, 15.6.

1553 Roxin, 'Strafrecht Allgemeiner Teil, Band II: Besondere Erscheinungsformen der Straftat' (2003), pp. 342–346. Noyon, Langemeijer, Remmelink, 'Wetboek van Strafrecht' (2010), Art 45, note 2.1.

variations, thus, include a standard of community apprehension in order to justify the imposition of punishment for criminal attempts. The question in which cases the community experiences apprehension is however a value judgment and carries the danger of achieving unjust results in case one puts too much emphasis on the community's fears and irrational sentiments.[1554] For a criminal justice system based on the rule of law and respect for human dignity, it would be unacceptable to allow for example racist sentiments or other prejudices prevalent in a community to determine the scope of liability. Furthermore, the requirement of apprehension experienced by society rests on a questionable empirical assumption, to say the least. Can an attempt to commit one criminal offence really cause fear and undermine society's trust in the legal order? It would seem as only an increase in certain forms of criminal behaviour would be able to do so, but never a single attempt.[1555]

Nevertheless such a mixed rationale has become the prevalent view in Germany and the Netherlands.[1556] However, as will become apparent, the two systems assign different weight and significance to the objective and the subjective limb of the theory which results in quite different conceptions of the rationale. In Germany, subjective factors such as the actor's plan and intentions seem to carry more weight while in the Netherlands the focus lies primarily on objective factors such as endangerment. Also in England some objective factors seem to play a role, although the prevalent view seems to put the main thrust on subjective factors.[1557] A notable exception in the English legal system can be found in the ideas of the legal philosopher Anthony Duff. He proposes a mixed theory of attempts by conceiving them as attacks on legally protected interests.[1558] He argues that attacks cause harm to the victim, even if the attack fails, as the victim has been seriously wronged by an attack directed towards him/her.[1559] Yet, he acknowledges that subjective factors are crucial for attempt liability but by adding the objective dimension of an attack to his evaluation pattern, he arrives at a mixed rationale for punishing attempts, which constitutes the counterpart to the prevalent subjective conception in the English law of attempts. This objective component is invoked to prevent an undue expansion of liability and to exclude radically inapt conduct (such as killing by black magic) from the realm of attempt.

It is submitted that an intermediate rationale for punishing attempts seems to be preferable in order to keep the law of attempts within acceptable limits on the one side and to account for all cases where contemporary criminal law currently

---

1554 Fletcher, 'Rethinking Criminal Law' (1978), pp. 145 et seq.

1555 Hirsch, 'Untauglicher Versuch und Tatstrafrecht', in Schünemann, et al. (eds), Festschrift für Claus Roxin (2001), pp. 714 et seq.

1556 De Hullu, 'Materieel Strafrecht' (2009), p. 380, Roxin, 'Strafrecht Allgemeiner Teil, Band II: Besondere Erscheinungsformen der Straftat' (2003), p. 347, Schönke and Schröder, 'Kommentar zum Strafgesetzbuch' (2006), Vorbem §22 Mn 22.

1557 See for instance: Ashworth, 'Principles of criminal law' (2006), pp. 445–447.

1558 Duff, 'Criminal Attempts' (1996), p. 221.

1559 Duff, 'Criminal Attempts' (1996), p. 368.

imposes punishment for. Arguably, an attempt can hardly ever be conceived purely objectively, as the occurred conduct will often be innocuous. An exclusive reliance on subjective factors would however make a demarcation from preparatory conduct elusive and in general, expand liability too widely. It is therefore argued that an objective endangerment rationale in combination with the subjective criminal proclivities of the actor as manifested by his conduct could constitute the basis of attempt liability. The notion of endangerment should therefore however carry more weight in the evaluation scheme.[1560] This could enhance legal certainty and safeguard individual liberties by requiring that the actor came close to the commission of the offence. Arguably, the conduct in question need not endanger the protected legal interest, but rather the legal order in general. Therefore also certain conduct which is only remotely connected to the protected legal interest can be seen as an attempt, if the conduct was geared towards the commission of the offence. This endangerment rationale will arguably account for the majority of cases, but on an exceptional basis, also subjective elements will be necessary to account for the current state of affair of the law. This will especially be the case in regard to so called impossible attempts, where an objective endangerment is difficult to construe. The fact that all investigated penal systems accept that certain forms of impossible attempts warrant punishment can only be explained by emphasising the fact that the actor by, for instance attempting murder by pouring sugar into his victim's tea, believing it to be arsenic, has unequivocally manifested his criminal proclivities and deserves punishment from the viewpoint of special prevention, despite the fact that his conduct objectively does not amount to an endangerment.[1561]

7.3. Analysing the legislative starting point of attempt liability

7.3.1. Introduction

After having discussed the rationales for punishing attempts in an abstract manner, the discussion can now turn to the legislative foundations for punishing attempts in Germany, the Netherlands and England. The ongoing discussion in any penal system with regard to the law of attempts is of course highly influenced and dependent on the wording the legislator gave to the criminal attempt statute. The legislator's view on the nature of attempt liability and a respective preference for one of the aforementioned rationales is often mirrored in the wording of the offence itself. The following investigation will set the scene for the subsequent discourse on the general requirements for attempt liability by deducing the general vantage point (i.e. objective, subjective or mixed) of a penal system from black-letter law.

1560 For a similar approach see: Roxin, 'Strafrecht Allgemeiner Teil, Band II: Besondere Erscheinungsformen der Straftat' (2003), pp. 335–340.

1561 See also: Roxin, 'Strafrecht Allgemeiner Teil, Band II: Besondere Erscheinungsformen der Straftat' (2003), p. 338.

7.3.2. Germany

§22 GPC contains a definition of attempts. It provides:

> A person attempts to commit an offence if he takes steps which will immediately lead to the completion of the offence envisaged by him.

§23 GPC subsequently deals with liability for attempts in general. It holds:

> (1) Any attempt to commit a felony entails criminal liability; this applies to attempted misdemeanours only if expressly so provided by law.
> (2) An attempt may be punished more leniently than the completed offence (section 49 (1)).
> (3) If the offender due to gross ignorance fails to realise that the attempt could under no circumstances have led to the completion of the offence due to the nature of its object or the means by which it was to be committed, the court may order a discharge, or mitigate the sentence as it sees fit (section 49 (2)).

From §22 GPC one can deduce that the legislator adopted a mixed rationale in order to justify the punishment of attempts. The objective limb can be found in the requirement that the actor needs to take steps which will immediately lead to the completion of the offence. Thus, there must be a certain imminence about the actor's conduct leading to the commission of the offence. The subjective criterion is reflected in the fact that this has to be established according to how the person envisaged the commission of the offence.[1562] It follows that the subjective component clearly seems to be prevalent in German law. It is the would-be perpetrator's expectations that define the attempted conduct. It is his subjective horizon, i.e. his intentions that determine whether he has already begun with the execution of the offence. The subjective theory has been prevalent in Germany in scholarly debate and jurisprudence ever since the end of the Second World War.[1563] To countermand some of the far-flung results of a subjective theory of attempts §§22 and 23 were introduced, which led to the rise of the mixed theory in the scholarly debate.[1564] However, as will subsequently become clear, the courts still predominantly adhere to a subjective rationale, viewing the actor's criminal intentions as the reason for punishing attempts.[1565]

1562 Schönke and Schröder, 'Kommentar zum Strafgesetzbuch' (2006), §22 Mn 1, Wessels and Beulke, 'Strafrecht Allgemeiner Teil, Die Straftat und ihr Aufbau' (2008), p. 216.

1563 Hirsch, 'Untauglicher Versuch und Tatstrafrecht', in Schünemann, et al. (eds), Festschrift für Claus Roxin (2001), p. 712. See also: 29 April 1958 BGH NJW 1958, 1051.

1564 Hirsch, 'Untauglicher Versuch und Tatstrafrecht', in Schünemann, et al. (eds), Festschrift für Claus Roxin (2001), p. 712, Schönke and Schröder, 'Kommentar zum Strafgesetzbuch' (2006), §22 Mn 25.

1565 Hirsch, 'Untauglicher Versuch und Tatstrafrecht', in Schünemann, et al. (eds), Festschrift für Claus Roxin (2001), p. 716.

In any case, further hints demonstrating that a mixture of objectivist and subjectivist considerations guide German law can be found in the fact that attempts *may* be punished more leniently according to §23 (2). Objective rationales would namely press here for a mandatory mitigation of punishment due to the absence of harm, while subjectivists would punish attempts as severely as completed crimes as the culpability of the actor appears equivalent to the one of the successful perpetrator. On the other hand, objective tendencies are reflected in §23 (3) which foresees the possibility to mitigate punishment or order a discharge in case the offender fails due to gross ignorance that his attempt is bound to fail.

7.3.3. The Netherlands

In the Dutch penal system an attempt is defined by Art 45 of the Dutch Penal Code (DPC). It reads as follows:

1. An attempt to commit a serious offense is punishable where the perpetrator manifests his intention by initiating the serious offense.
2. In case of attempt, the maximal principal penalty prescribed is reduced by one-third.
3. In cases of a serious offense carrying a sentence of life imprisonment a term of imprisonment of not more than twenty years shall be imposed
4. The additional penalties for attempt are as for the completed serious offence.

Similar to the German provision a mixed approach can be distilled from Art 45 DPC. The objective limb can be seen here by the requirement that the perpetrator must have initiated the offence, while the subjective component is contained in the requirement that the occurred conduct must manifest the would-be perpetrator's intention. However, it has already been mentioned that contrary to the situation in Germany, the prevalent component in the Dutch penal system is the objective one. A clear indication of this strong objective proclivity in the Dutch penal system can be found in Art. 45(3) DPC which foresees a mandatory reduction of the maximum penalty which can only be explained by an objectivist conception of attempts.

7.3.4. England

In England the law of attempt is since 1981 regulated in the Criminal Attempts Act. Section 1 (1) provides: "If with intent to commit an offence to which this section applies, a person does an act which is more than merely preparatory to the commission of the offence, he is guilty of attempting to commit the offence."

This phrase does not however provide the reader with much insight into the rationale underlying the English law of attempt. It contains a formula by which a line between attempt and preparation has to be drawn. The enshrined mens rea element is intention, which in literature and jurisprudence is often termed the principle ingredient of the crime.[1566] This already hints at a subjective conception of attempts. The subjective rationale is however more clearly revealed by Section 1 (2) of the Criminal Attempts Act 1981 which provides that: A person may be guilty of attempting to commit an offence to which this section applies, even though the facts are as such that the commission of the offence is impossible." Thus, the provision makes it clear that the actor's criminal proclivities or subjective conception of the deed is what constitutes the central focus of the law of attempts.

Furthermore, the subjective stance of the English penal system on first sight seems to be reflected in the fact that the 1981 Act has attributed no significance regarding punishment to the mere fact of failure. Thus, theoretically attempted and completed offences can be punished alike in England. The Law Commission thought a certain degree of flexibility to be desirable, as attempts may range from an offence being frustrated at the very last moment, to very remote acts of preparation which can only just be regarded as an attempt.[1567] However, it needs to be stressed here that English courts have retained the old common law practice of imposing lighter sentences for attempts, and continue to impose lighter sentences than for complete offences.

It should moreover be noted here that in practice, the law of attempt in English law, contrary to the situation in Germany and the Netherlands, is often sidelined by, first, the big variety of specific preparatory offences such as the aforementioned possession offences.[1568] Another pertinent example in this context can be found in section 7 (1) of the Fraud Act 2006 which makes it a criminal offence to make, supply or offer to supply articles for use in fraud.[1569]

Second, the broad definition of important criminal offences such as theft and fraud often make the law of attempt largely redundant as the breadth of these offences also covers conduct which in other penal systems would be seen as preparing or attempting the offence in question. For instance, section 1 (1) of the Theft Act 1968 defines theft as any dishonest appropriation of property belonging to another with the intention of permanently depriving the other of it. Section 3 (1) subsequently defines appropriation as "any assumption by a person of rights of an owner". Jurisprudence in this context has established that an assumption of the rights of the owner does not mean all the rights but rather the assumption of *any* right of an owner.[1570] It follows that A will commit theft as soon as he switches the

---

1566 Ashworth, 'Principles of criminal law' (2006), p. 447, Duff, 'Criminal Attempts' (1996), p. 5. See also: R v Whybrow [1951] 35 Cr App R 141.

1567 Duff, 'Criminal Attempts' (1996), p. 116.

1568 See: Chaper IV. 6.2.

1569 Ormerod and Williams, 'Smith's law of theft' (2007), pp. 295–302.
Section 7 (1) of the Fraud Act 2007 reads as follows:
A person is guilty of an offence if he makes, adapts, supplies or offers to supply any article:
(a) knowing that it is designed or adapted for use in the course of or in connection with fraud, or
(b) intending it to be used to commit, or assist in the commission of, fraud.

1570 R v Morris [1984] AC 320.

labels on two articles lying on the shelf of a supermarket, with the intention of buying the more expensive one for the price of the less expensive one.[1571] This goes to show that the broad definition of the offence leaves little, if any, room for an offence of attempt. Already the first dishonest act of the defendant will complete the offence of theft.[1572]

Finally, the broad concept of conspiracy in English law, as outlined above, often also diminishes the relevance of the rules on attempt, as conduct preceding the completion of an offence may already be covered by the offence of conspiracy.[1573] It should however be noted that this will of course only be possible in case two or more people are involved in preparing, respectively attempting the offence in question. Yet, these peculiarities should be kept in mind when subsequently comparing the law of attempt in England to the one of Germany and the Netherlands.

Be that as it may, it should also be noted here that the wording of legal statutes in general can only provide a first indication as to the exact approach adopted in a penal system. After all, the provisions cited above merely constitute a rough yardstick for imposing attempt liability which need to be fleshed out by the courts and scholarly writing. More crucial in this respect is therefore the manner in which the courts interpret the statutes in order to determine the dividing line between attempts and preparation. It is to this aspect the discussion now turns.

7.4. The actus reus of criminal attempts

7.4.1. Introduction

The central question in regard to the conduct requirement of attempts essentially is how close to the consummation of the criminal offence an actor must have proceeded in order to speak of a criminal attempt. As mere intentions are not punishable (*cogitationis poenam nemo patitur*) a threshold needs to be established in order to demarcate attempts from conduct falling short of an attempt (i.e. preparation). The only thing that can be stated with relative certainty is that somewhere between the moment where the actor decided to commit the offence and the subsequent manifestation of harm, lies the realm of attempts. Buying a rifle to assassinate a politician at an opening ceremony, a month from now, might be considered to fall into the preparatory phase, (which in Germany and England is still generally exempt from liability), while firing a shot but missing could be seen as an example of a criminal attempt. But besides these extreme poles, the dividing line between attempt and preparation is elusive. This is because the notion of attempt as a doctrine of the general part ought to apply to all (serious) crimes enshrined in the special part. But this is exactly where the shoe pinches.

1571 See: Ormerod and Williams, 'Smith's law of theft' (2007), p. 21.

1572 Ormerod and Williams, 'Smith's law of theft' (2007), p. 56.

1573 See: Chapter IV. 6.2.

The special part of criminal law contains a multitude of different offences which all possess their own peculiarities. To conceive criteria which would fit all of these different crimes therefore seems almost impossible. Furthermore, the fact that some crimes occur at the spur of the moment while others take lengthy preparations as well as the fact that some crimes take a longer time to be consummated or can be committed in several steps (e.g. robbery,) while others can take immediate effect and turn on one act (e.g. killing or wounding), complicates the matter further.[1574] Consider for instance the offence of fraud. It is possible that a cunning fraud scheme requires lengthy preparation. The forging of an official document may for instance be necessary in order to make a deception possible. Does the forging of this document then already constitute an attempt, although it has not yet been presented to the potential victim? Rape would be another case in point here. Should it suffice for attempt liability if the would-be perpetrator uses force against the victim to subdue her, but subsequently fails to consummate the sexual intercourse? On the other hand, a simple affray or acts of vandalism are usually immediately consummated, do not require lengthy preparation and are neither particularly well-suited to be committed in several steps. From this it follows that the actus reus of attempts is largely dependent on the offence definition of the underlying crime. Thus it is essential to take the substantive offence which the defendant allegedly intended to commit as a vantage point.[1575]

It becomes apparent that the law of attempts probably constitutes a form of necessary vagueness in the law as a magic formula which will produce workable results for all variations of attempts may be almost impossible to achieve. Nevertheless, one can distil some guiding criteria and guidelines from the jurisprudence of the investigated Member States.

7.4.2. Drawing the line between attempt and preparation

From the aforementioned rationales for punishing attempts, not much guidance for demarcating the realm of attempts from preparation can be gained regardless of whether one deems the actor's criminal intentions, the endangerment of a protected legal interest or another criterion as the justification for punishing attempts. This is, on the one hand, because all these aspects, at least theoretically, can also be interpreted to apply to preparatory liability as well.[1576]

Thus, these theoretical rationales are incapable of providing precise and workable criteria in order to determine how far an actor must have progressed with the commission of a criminal offence before he will incur liability. Yet, one guiding principle in regard to criminal attempts, which by and large can be reconciled with

1574 See: Smith and Hogan, 'Criminal Law' (2008), p. 390.

1575 Bohlander, 'Principles of German Criminal Law' (2009), p. 141, De Hullu, 'Materieel Strafrecht' (2009), pp. 377 et seq, Smith and Hogan, 'Criminal Law' (2008), p. 381.

1576 See: Roxin, 'Strafrecht Allgemeiner Teil, Band II: Besondere Erscheinungsformen der Straftat' (2003), p. 361.

all respective rationales for punishing attempts, is that the actor must have come sufficiently close to the commission of the actus reus of the offence in question. This follows from the fundamental principle *nulla poenae sine actione*, which arguably constitutes the cornerstone of every penal justice system based on the rule of law. Accordingly, criminal attitudes, proclivities, plans or thoughts ought to be of no concern to criminal law. In other words, as criminal liability, in short always requires the commission of an actus reus accompanied by the corresponding mens rea, a person should have come close to the consummation of the offence in order to avoid imposing punishment for thought crimes. In this sense criminal attempts constitute an expansion of traditional liability patterns by including conduct closely connected to the commission of the offence.[1577] However, it should be clear that the requirement of a close connection to the commission of the actus reus cannot provide sufficiently clear criteria to distinguish attempts from preparation either. It rather provides a rough yardstick which needs to be substantiated and fleshed out by other criteria and on a case by case basis.

The harm vs. culpability debate revisited

Corresponding to the tensions between the manifest and subjective pattern of criminality, the conduct requirement of criminal attempts constitutes another battleground for the competing views on how to substantiate criminal liability between objectivists and subjectivists. Simply put, the disagreement between objectivist and subjectivists in regard to attempts can best be depicted as a disagreement concerning the proper criteria for action-ascription.[1578]

Subjectivists argue that actions ascribed to an individual must be described in subjective terms, and require that the relevant act unequivocally manifest the dangerousness of the individual.[1579] By laying the emphasis on the intention (i.e. the culpability) of the actor and turning a blind eye to the actual conduct occurred, this view allows an early intervention of the criminal law if sufficient evidence for the dangerous intention of the suspect is furnished. Thus the primary concern of this approach can be seen in the early prevention of harm in order to protect public safety. This approach has, as already mentioned, far-reaching implications as it degrades the actual conduct manifested in the outside world to a mere evidentiary means to prove mens rea. In its most extreme form, this approach would come very close to the unwanted result of punishing thoughts.

Objectivists on the other hand, stress the importance of the actual criminal conduct occurred. For objectivists, a dangerous intent is not sufficient to establish

1577 Horder, 'Reforming the auxiliary Part of the criminal law' Archbold News (2007), p. 6, Roxin, 'Strafrecht Allgemeiner Teil, Band II: Besondere Erscheinungsformen der Straftat' (2003), p. 362.

1578 Duff, 'Criminal Attempts' (1996), p. 146.

1579 Mathis, 'Criminal Attempts and the Subjectivism/Objectivism Debate' Ratio Juris (2004), pp. 330 et seq.

criminal liability as long as no overt criminal conduct has occurred.[1580] In other words, they hold that liability needs to be ascribed (at least partly) in objective terms.[1581] Thus, according to this view the conduct is partly constitutive of the wrong which the law aims to punish.[1582] As already mentioned, strict, formal objective theories of attempts would for the sake of legal certainty require that the perpetrator already partially embarked on the commission of the actus reus. This would in essence mean that mounting a weapon in order to shoot at the victim would not trigger attempt liability as the occurred conduct does not yet constitute a partial fulfilment of the actus reus. An example of such a restrictive approach can be found in the following Dutch decision. The perpetrators in this case had first removed all valuable objects from a house, had then poured out petrol in several areas and had further arranged rags, soaked in petrol within the house. Their plan was to set the rags on fire with an electric igniter which they could activate from outside the house by pulling on a rope. The plan however failed as neighbours became suspicious of the strong petrol smell and informed the police. The Dutch Supreme Court held that this was not a case of attempted arson, as the perpetrators had not yet pulled on the rope. The court held that for attempt liability to arise, an act had to be carried out, which without the intervention of the perpetrator would lead to the commission of the offence.[1583]

It should be clear that such an approach by emphasising the requirement of legal certainty produces very narrow and unsatisfactory results in practice. Accordingly, none of the investigated penal systems nowadays adopts such an approach. This test, while certainly giving ample opportunity to the defendant to change his mind and abandon the attempt, arguably tilts the balance too far in the direction of protecting the interests of the individual. If one could escape criminal liability as long as the last act to commit the crime has not been done, this would greatly diminish the preventive effect of the law of attempts and would make it utterly difficult for police forces to intervene before the harm has occurred. For these reasons the judgment has been severely criticised in the Netherlands and already some years later the courts moved away from the strict formal objective approach towards a moderate objective approach.

It becomes apparent that the two approaches in the context of the law of attempts mirror the tension between the necessary social protection and the protection of individual liberty. However, it needs to be stressed that the two approaches constitute extremes and that both approaches are frequently applied in criminal law. The subjective goal of increased crime control is as much a legitimate and necessary aim of any penal system as is the objective goal of safeguarding individual

1580 Mathis, 'Criminal Attempts and the Subjectivism/Objectivism Debate' Ratio Juris (2004), pp. 330 et seq.

1581 Duff, 'Criminal Attempts' (1996), p. 146.

1582 Duff, 'Criminal Attempts' (1996), p. 35.

1583 HR 19 March 1934, *NJ* 1934, 450.

liberties.[1584] As already mentioned, what is needed is a careful balancing of the two opposites.

Accordingly, there are also mixed theories which combine subjective and objective factors to draw the line between attempts and preparation. Therefore the endangerment of the underlying protected legal interest, as well as the actor's criminal intentions are invoked to determine when criminal liability will arise. All investigated penal systems seem nowadays to combine these factors in order to determine when an actor has crossed the line to (attempt) liability. However, they do assign different weight to the respective factors. As the subsequent discussion will reveal, English penal law has taken a fluctuating course between mixed and more subjectivist theories, while Germany can be seen to constitute the clearest example of an intermediate approach. The Netherlands on the other hand can be seen as the most objectively orientated of the investigated penal systems, despite the fact that also in the Netherlands, subjective factors occasionally play a role. This slightly narrower conception of attempts in the Netherlands is however compensated by the fact that, as outlined above, preparatory conduct in the Netherlands can give rise to criminal liability.

Demarcation formulas

A common method to distinguish attempts from preparation in jurisprudence and scholarly writing is the application of formulas to substantiate when the threshold to attempt liability has been passed. §22 GPC requires steps which immediately lead to the completion of the offence, which is the equivalent to 'more than merely preparatory' in English law and 'initiation of the commission of the offence' under Dutch Law. All these notions are however notoriously vague and have encountered definitional difficulties in practice. All that can be said is that attempt liability in all penal systems seems to require a sort of imminence of the commission of the offence. Yet, this does not mean that it will be necessary that a part of the actus reus has already been brought about.[1585] A partial fulfilment of the actus reus can at times be a sufficient condition for attempt liability, but is certainly not a necessary one. And even if the perpetrator has already fulfilled parts of the actus reus, attempt liability may not yet arise if the temporal link to the final result is too tenuous. This might for instance be the case if Clark, several days before a planned robbery disables the security system of a bank in order to make the execution of the plan easier and securer but is subsequently arrested before he can carry out his plan.

1584 Mathis, 'Criminal Attempts and the Subjectivism/Objectivism Debate' Ratio Juris (2004), pp. 332 et seq.

1585 See: Roxin, 'Strafrecht Allgemeiner Teil, Band II: Besondere Erscheinungsformen der Straftat' (2003), pp. 362–368, Schönke and Schröder, 'Kommentar zum Strafgesetzbuch' (2006), §22 Mn 37–44, Noyon, Langemeijer, Remmelink, 'Wetboek van Strafrecht' (2010), Art 45, note 2.5, Smith and Hogan, 'Criminal Law' (2008), pp. 391 et seq.

The different tests can be put on a continuum with its extreme poles the first and the last act test. The least demanding test, which subjectivist might favour is the first act test, which would merely require some act towards carrying out the criminal intention.[1586] The first act test, has the advantage of simplicity of application on its side, as courts need merely establish that some act in furtherance of the criminal enterprise has occurred.[1587] Furthermore it is capable to achieve a high degree of security as it provides ample leeway for police forces to intervene at a very early stage of a criminal enterprise. However, on the other hand, the test is much too broad. Such a test would for instance convict the would-be assassin as soon as he sets out to buy the gun. This would surely strike the wrong balance between individual freedoms and community interests. Thus, such a test would not only lead to intrusive and oppressive police practices by granting executive authorities too much leeway, but would also leave insufficient room for an individual to determine its own conduct and maybe voluntarily desist from the completion of the crime.[1588]

The most demanding standard on the other hand would be set by the last act test, according to which the would-be offender can only be held liable after he has done all that he can do to commit the crime.[1589] It is this test that the Dutch Supreme Court seems to have applied in the aforementioned attempted arson case. This test, advocated by some disciples of the objective approach would certainly give ample opportunity to the defendant to change his mind and abandon the attempt, but arguably tilts the balance too far in the direction of protecting the interests of the individual.[1590] If one could escape criminal liability by not carrying out the last act required to commit the crime, this would greatly diminish the deterrent effect of the law of attempts and would make it utterly difficult for police forces to intervene before the harm has occurred.[1591]

In Germany, the courts frequently combine objective and subjective criteria in a test that assumes that attempt liability will arise once the perpetrator has subjectively passed the "Here we go" threshold and objectively commenced his attack on the legal interest, protected by the underlying offence, so that his conduct will without further steps lead to the commission of the actus reus.[1592] This means

1586 Duff, 'Criminal Attempts' (1996), p. 33.

1587 Duff, 'Criminal Attempts' (1996), p. 36.

1588 Ashworth, 'Criminal Attempts and the role of resulting harm under the code and in the common law' Rutgers Law Journal (1988), p. 750.

1589 Duff, 'Criminal Attempts' (1996), p. 37.

1590 Ashworth, 'Criminal Attempts and the role of resulting harm under the code and in the common law' Rutgers Law Journal (1988), p. 751.

1591 Ashworth, 'Criminal Attempts and the role of resulting harm under the code and in the common law' Rutgers Law Journal (1988), p. 751.

1592 Roxin, 'Strafrecht Allgemeiner Teil, Band II: Besondere Erscheinungsformen der Straftat' (2003), p. 370, Schönke and Schröder, 'Kommentar zum Strafgesetzbuch' (2006), §22 Mn 41–45, Wessels and Beulke, 'Strafrecht Allgemeiner Teil, Die Straftat und ihr Aufbau' (2008), p. 217.

that any conduct which on the basis of the perpetrator's plan is objectively suited to bring about, without any further essential steps necessary, a violation of the legal interest protected by the actus reus, can be interpreted to constitute a criminal attempt.[1593] This also includes conduct taking place before the 'last act' if it is necessarily connected to or if not interrupted would lead to the commission of the actus reus.[1594]

The focus on essential steps, necessarily connected to the commission of the actus reus, however makes the distinction between attempts and preparation a highly casuistic one, which is also strongly influenced by the offence in question. This becomes especially visible concerning cases where the criminal conduct from an objective point of view, is one continuous, uniform course of events.[1595] In regard to drug importation cases, for instance, this approach leads to different results depending on the chosen means of transport. Should the import take place by train or plane, the perpetrator will enter the attempt phase when he checks in his luggage, or passes the last customs control before the border. Should the import however take place by car, bike, or on foot, the attempt phase will only be reached once the perpetrator has come close to the German border, as is for instance the case when he passes the last exit on the motorway before entering German territory.[1596]

To demonstrate the functioning of the test in practice, consider the following case. The defendants had agreed to rob the owner of a petrol station. They drove to his house and rang the doorbell, gun in hand and wearing ski masks. However, the door remained closed and after a neighbour had spotted them, they abandoned the attempt. The Supreme Court, applying the aforementioned formula convicted the defendants of attempted robbery, as they had subjectively transgressed the "Here we go" threshold and had objectively commenced the attack on the legal interest as their conduct would without further steps have led to the commission of the actus reus (threatening the person opening the door with the gun).[1597]

It has already been mentioned that in German law the would-be perpetrator's subjective horizon, i.e. his plan or expectations as to the chain of events, is of utmost importance. This is well illustrated by the following case. Three defendants had planned to rob a local supermarket. First, two of them entered the supermarket carrying a gas pistol and a stun gun and wearing woollen caps in which they had cut slits. They kept their weapons concealed and had not pulled down their masks yet. The third defendant had first called the branch manager from a near by phone booth to distract him and had subsequently also entered the Supermarket. Due to

---

1593 Schönke and Schröder, 'Kommentar zum Strafgesetzbuch' (2006), §22 Mn 39.

1594 Schönke and Schröder, 'Kommentar zum Strafgesetzbuch' (2006), §22 Mn 41. See also: 30 April 1980 BGH NJW 1980, 1759.

1595 Schönke and Schröder, 'Kommentar zum Strafgesetzbuch' (2006), §22 Mn 41.

1596 See: 6 September 1998 BGH NJW 1990, 654.

1597 16 September 1975 BGH NJW 1976, 58. See also: 13 August 1996 BGH NStZ 1997, 83, 11 June 2003 BGH NStZ 2004, 38, 9 August 2011 BGH NStZ 2012, 85.

the presence of several customers they however abandoned their attempt as they thought it impossible to keep the entire crowd at bay. The Court of lower instance had convicted the men of attempted robbery, but the Supreme Court quashed the conviction. The Supreme Court held that it could not be established beyond reasonable doubt that the men, according to their conception of the course of events had already passed the "Here we go" threshold, as the men made their plan dependent on the assessment of whether or not the situation inside the supermarket would allow the commission of the offence.[1598]

On a more objective note, German jurisprudence sometimes requires that the perpetrator's conduct must have created a concrete or immediate danger for the protected legal interest. Such a danger to the legal interest is for instance not yet present when a HIV-positive person approaches prostitutes in a brothel (who are unaware of his infection) and enquires if it would be possible to have unprotected intercourse with them in exchange for a significantly high payment.[1599] This endangerment factor also plays an important role in German jurisprudence in cases where the perpetrator has set a trap for the victim.

In a pertinent case, burglars had broken into a pharmacist's home, had helped themselves to some food and drinks in the kitchen and had moved several entertainment electronics to the attic. Therefore it was assumed that the criminals could possibly return the next day to finally remove the items. For this reason, several police officers remained in the house the following night. The disgruntled pharmacist had however prepped a bottle of Schnapps with a highly poisonous substance and left it on the floor in case the burglars should return. Later he became however concerned with the fact that also the present police officers might drink from the bottle and warned them. The burglars themselves, never returned to finish their job. The prosecutor strived for a conviction for attempted murder, but the Supreme Court rejected the appeal, holding that in cases where it was merely possible but still uncertain whether or not and when the victim would come in contact with the trap, that an immediate danger for the protected legal interest had not been created.[1600]

The importance of the subjective sphere of the perpetrator in the German law on attempts is however further substantiated by the fact that the question whether or not it was uncertain if and when the victim would come in contact with the trap ought to be determined according to the perpetrator's expectations of the course of events. In other words, whether or not one can already speak of an endangerment of the protected legal interest is to be determined according to the conception of the perpetrator. Thus, if the perpetrator believes that the victim will come into contact with the trap in the foreseeable future, attempt liability will arise.

For this reason the Supreme Court for instance convicted several perpetrators of attempted murder, as they, had at night attached hand grenades to the cars of the

1598 7 April 1995 BGH NStZ 1996, 38.
1599 26 October 1989 BayObLG NJW 1990, 781.
1600 12 August 1997 BGH NStZ 1998, 241.

victims, which were meant to be detonated by wires connected to the wheels of the car. In one instance the bomb was detected by the victim before entering the car, and in another, the trigger mechanism malfunctioned and the grenade did not detonate. The Supreme Court distinguished the case from the aforementioned pharmacist case and held that in the case at hand, the perpetrators knew that the victims would use their cars in the foreseeable future and that they had even come within the sphere of action of the trap.[1601] Similarly, in a case where a peeved lodger had manipulated the sockets of his apartment, so that the disliked landlord or another tenant would receive a what would have been a potentially lethal shock, the Supreme Court held that he had transgressed the preparatory stage, as he was aware that within the foreseeable future it was almost certain that someone would get into contact with the sockets. The trap was however discovered before any harm could materialise after the caretaker of the building had also discovered manipulations on the house's central heating system.[1602]

What these examples demonstrate is that in Germany the temporal element combined with the question whether the perpetrator according to his point of view still has to take further essential steps or even a further decision before embarking on a certain course of conduct, plays a crucial role in determining the outer limits of attempt liability.[1603]

To turn to the Dutch approach, in a landmark decision very similar to the aforementioned German decision concerning the attempted robbery of the owner of a petrol station, the Dutch Supreme Court established a test to distinguish an attempt from mere preparation which is regularly applied until the time being. Two masked men, carrying weapons and a big bag had rung the doorbell of an employment agency. However, the door was subsequently not opened but the men were arrested by the notified police. The Supreme Court upheld the conviction for attempted robbery and held that the acts of the two men could be seen as the initiation of the commission of the offence as they, due to their outward manifestation, can be considered to be aimed at the completion of the offence.[1604] Thus, the test to distinguish attempts from preparatory acts is whether to its outward manifestation the offender's behaviour can be considered to be aimed at the completion of the offence. Accordingly, the Dutch Supreme Court seems to place special emphasis on the objective impression or meaning of the occurred conduct, a stance which arguably largely corresponds to a pattern of objective criminality, or rather objectivism.[1605] However, this does not mean that the would-be perpetrator in the Netherlands must have already brought about part of the actus reus or must have committed the last act. On the contrary, just like in Germany and England also conduct taking place before the 'last act' can amount to

---

1601 7 October 1997 BGH NStZ 1998, 294.

1602 8 May 2005 BGH NStZ 2001, 475.

1603 Bohlander, 'Principles of German Criminal Law' (2009), p. 143.

1604 HR 24 October 1978, *NJ* 1979, 52.

1605 See also: Mols and Wöretshofer, 'Poging en voorbereidingshandelingen' (1994), pp. 26–36.

a criminal attempt, if it is necessarily connected to the commission of the actus reus.[1606]

This test, which contains subjective and objective elements, was further developed in a case regarding the attempted robbery of an exchange office. Two men were sitting in a stolen car with forged licence plates in front of an exchange office. They were wearing wigs, and the engine of the car was running. They were waiting for the teller to open the exchange office, but when he arrived he recognised the car, grew suspicious and informed the police who arrested the men. The Supreme Court held that no attempt liability could be established, as the suspects had not initiated the commission of the robbery, as they had not yet left the car nor acted in a way, which according to its outward manifestation could be considered to be aimed at the completion of the offence. The court reached this conclusion despite the fact that the police found weapons, handcuffs, rope and tape in the suspects' car. The court seemingly put the emphasis in this case on the objective elements of criminal attempts. The outward manifestation of the offender's behaviour must be aimed at the completion of the offence. For a criminal attempt, it is thus important how a third person, interprets the deed. The literal outward manifestation seems to have been pivotal in this case. The social connotation of the conduct is the determining factor here. The danger inherent in the conduct has to be evaluated by the impression of an observer.[1607] The fact that the car was stolen, had forged licence plates and that the occupants of the vehicle were armed, etc. was not discernible for an observer and therefore not part of the outward manifestation of the behaviour.[1608]

The fact that the Dutch penal system puts emphasis on objective criteria in the law of attempts is further substantiated by the fact that the actually-occurred conduct plays a special role in Dutch jurisprudence. The Supreme Court had for instance no problem to uphold a conviction for attempted burglary in a case where a group of persons drove into the parking area of a supermarket at 4 o'clock in the morning with dimmed lights. The day before they had already cased the supermarket and its security system; this had alarmed the manager of the supermarket who had informed the police. They drove towards the back entrance of the supermarket where two men stepped out of the car and began to instruct the driver to slowly back up in the direction of the door. When the light in a nearby apartment went on the men yelled at the driver and they fled from the scene at high speed. The defence had argued that the conduct of the defendants did not amount to an initiation of the commission of the offence, but the Supreme Court rejected the claim and held that the outward manifestation of the defendants conduct was clearly aimed at the completion of the offence.[1609]

1606 Noyon, Langemeijer, Remmelink, 'Wetboek van Strafrecht' (2010), Art 45, note 2.5.

1607 De Hullu, 'Materieel Strafrecht' (2009), p. 382.

1608 Rozemond, 'De algemene strafbaarstelling van voorbereidingshandelingen in het licht van de pogingsjurisprudentie van de Hoge Raad' Delikt en Delinkwent (1994), p. 660.

1609 HR 3 March 2009, *NJ* 2009, 138.

The exact scope and interpretation of the criterion of outward manifestation was at the core of a case concerning attempted fraud. Two men in a car had approached a passerby on the street and asked him if he wanted to buy video recorders. In the trunk of the car were several boxes of video recorders which were filled with sand. Unfortunately for the two men, the passerby had already been deceived once by such a scam and informed the police. The Supreme Court ruled that the conduct of the suspects by its outward manifestation was aimed at the completion of fraud and convicted the two men. According to the court, this was the case, despite the fact, as the defence had argued that the boxes with sand were stored in the trunk of the car, where they were objectively not discernible to an observer.[1610] This judgment clearly is at odds with the aforementioned judgment regarding the attempted robbery of a border exchange office, where the Supreme Court only took the objectively discernible means and conduct into consideration and therefore acquitted the suspects.

Two possible interpretations of this case are conceivable. First, in line with the "exchange office judgment" it is arguable that the Supreme Court regarded the conduct of the defendants even without the knowledge of the boxes filled with sand hidden in the trunk, as sufficiently clear to assume an initiation of the commission of the offence.[1611] In this case one would have to take the criterion of outward manifestation literally.

A more convincing interpretation of the judgment would however be that the Supreme Court has slightly adjusted the scope of the criterion and that outward manifestation ought not to be equated with "visible".[1612] In this interpretation also, objective facts which only subsequently come to the fore can play a role in establishing attempt liability. This seems to be a sensible, objective interpretation of the criterion of outward manifestation. A literal interpretation would arguably seem overly-restrictive. The more neutral and innocuous the occurred conduct, the more important the role of other (objective and subjective) factors besides the discernible outward manifestation of the conduct will become to establish attempt liability.[1613] Thus in practice a big variety of facts and circumstances can play a role in establishing the outward manifestation of a criminal intent.

In England, the leading decision on what constitutes acts which are 'more than merely preparatory' is *R v Gullefer* where it was ruled that the defendant had to have 'embarked on the crime proper'. In this case, the defendant was acquitted of attempted theft, after he had jumped on a greyhound racing track in order to stop

---

1610 HR 8 December 1992, *NJ* 1993, 321.

1611 De Hullu, 'Materieel Strafrecht' (2009), p. 384.

1612 Pelser, 'Preparations to commit a crime – The Dutch approach to inchoate offences' Utrecht Law Review (2008), p. 62, Rozemond, 'De algemene strafbaarstelling van voorbereidingshandelingen in het licht van de pogingsjurisprudentie van de Hoge Raad' Delikt en Delinkwent (1994), p. 663, Rozemond, 'De methode van het materiele strafrecht' (2006), p. 118.

1613 Machielse, 'De opmars van de uit uiterlijke verschijningsvorm', in Franken, et al. (eds), Constante waarden, Liber amicorum Prof. mr. Constantijn Kelk (2008), p. 235.

the race when he realised that the greyhound he had bet on, was falling behind. His goal was to force the stewards to declare the race void, which would have allowed him to recover his stake (£18). The Court held that his act was merely preparatory, as he had not yet approached the bookmaker to claim back his stake. In this case Lord Lane CJ announced the now-generally accepted test. When dealing with the question of attempt he said:

> It begins when the merely preparatory acts come to an end and the defendant embarks on the crime proper. When that is will depend [...] upon the facts in any particular case.[1614]

This test was also applied in the more recent case of *R v Dagnall*.[1615] In this case the defendant was convicted of attempted rape. He had met the victim at a bus stop at night and a conversation followed, in which it became apparent that he wished to have sexual intercourse with her. As the victim attempted to move away from the bus stop, the defendant followed her, grabbed her by the hair from behind, pulled her forcibly towards him and finally forced her against a fence. Fortunately at this point the police arrived at the scene and arrested the defendant. The court concluded that the acts taken by the defendant had brought him beyond the merely preparatory stage. "He had virtually succeeded in achieving all that he needed. He had overcome her resistance and it was only [...] the arrival of the police car that prevented the ultimate offence from taking place". It becomes apparent that English law essentially strives for a midway course between the first and the last act test.[1616]

Unfortunately, however, English courts have failed to adopt a consistent approach here and fluctuate between a mixed approach with more weight on objective factors and a subjective approach.[1617] More restrictive or objective are decisions such as *R v Campbell*[1618] and *R v Geddes*.[1619] In *Campbell* the defendant was arrested in the vicinity of a post office, which he intended to rob, carrying a replica gun and a threatening note. The police had received a tip about the planned robbery and arrested him as he approached the door of the post office. His conviction for attempted robbery was quashed because "he had not even gained access to the place where he could be in a position to carry out the offence".

A similar restrictive approach was taken in *Geddes*, where the defendant was found in a boys lavatory block at a school in Brighton. He was carrying a rucksack, containing a large kitchen knife, some lengths of rope and a roll of masking tape,

1614 R v Gullefer [1990] 3 All ER 882.

1615 [2003] EWCA Crim 2441.

1616 See: Smith, 'Proximity in attempt: Lord Lane's "midway course"' Criminal Law Review (1991), pp. 576–582.

1617 Ashworth, 'Principles of criminal law' (2009), pp. 444 et seq. See also: Brockhaus, 'Die strafrechtliche Dogmatik von Vorbereitung, Versuch und Rücktritt im europäischen Vergleich' (2006), pp. 327–330.

1618 R v Campbell [1991] 93 Cr App R 350.

1619 R v Geddes [1996] Crim LR 894.

thus all articles that pointed towards an attempt at false imprisonment. His conviction however, was quashed and it was held that his acts were merely preparatory, as he did not have any contact or communication with any pupil, and had never confronted any pupil in the school.

More subjective tendencies, on the other hand, can be found in *R v Griffin* dealing with attempted child abduction.[1620] The defendant in this case wanted to take her children out of England without the permission of the local authority in whose care they were. She had bought ferry tickets to Ireland and then tried to take the children from school saying that they were to go to the dentist. The teacher however refused to let the children leave. She was convicted of attempted child abduction and the Court of Appeal upheld her conviction arguing that it was immaterial that the children had not been given into her custody and that she had neither embarked on the journey. In asking the school if she could take the children she had manifested her intentions which amounted to an act of attempted abduction.

A further example of a more subjective approach can be found in *R v Tosti*. The Court of Appeal convicted the defendants in *Tosti* for attempted burglary.[1621] The defendants were caught examining the bolt on the door of a barn, and oxyacetylene equipment was found hidden in a nearby hedge, yet not directly at the *locus delicti*. The Court of Appeal convicted the defendants, even though they had not taken any steps to enter the barn or break the lock open. Lord Justice Beldam recognised that: "there may be actions which are preparatory but which are not merely so and which are essentially the first steps in the commission of the offence". This judgment can be interpreted to encompass a more subjective approach as the defendants were merely examining the lock of the barn and were only planning to commit the offence at a later point in time which can be deduced from the fact that they had not yet transported their equipment to the scene of the crime.[1622]

In the view of the Law Commission the dictums in *Tosti* and *Dagnall* should be regarded as paradigms, as in the view of the Commission these cases strike the right balance between individual freedoms and the countervailing interest of society.[1623] The Law Commission regards the judicial interpretation of the phrase "more than merely preparatory act" as so defective that they propose the drafting of specific guideline examples as can be found for instance in the Model Penal Code. However, preferably the Law Commission proposed a complete statutory revision, thereby creating an offence of attempt which would adhere to the last act test and would thus be narrower than the present English law. This offence, again, it is proposed should be accompanied by an offence of criminal preparation, limited to

---

1620 R v Griffin, [1993] Crim LR 515.

1621 R v Tosti & White [1997] Crim LR 746.

1622 See also: Brockhaus, 'Die strafrechtliche Dogmatik von Vorbereitung, Versuch und Rücktritt im europäischen Vergleich' (2006), p. 326. Further examples of a more subjective approach can be found in R v Jones [1990] 1 WLR, 1057 and Attorney-General's Reference (No.1 of 1992) [1993] 96 Cr App R 298.

1623 'Conspiracy and Attempts', Consultation Paper, LAW COM No 183 [2007], p. 188, para 14.15.

acts of preparation which are properly to be regarded as part of the execution of the plan to commit the intended offence.[1624] Such a solution would to some extent mirror the approach adopted by the Dutch penal system. However, the Law Commission seems to have abandoned the project as their recommendations did not receive sufficient support and thought it would therefore be inappropriate to strive for a change of the law.[1625]

One possible explanation for the fluctuating approach of English law in regard to criminal attempts can arguably be found in the fact that the determination of when conduct can be considered to be 'more than merely preparatory' is in the English penal system seen as a question of fact, to be decided by the jury. Under current English law, both the judge and the jury have to decide whether the act was more than merely preparatory. The judge must rule whether the stage of mere preparation has been passed, and must then leave the very same question to the jury.[1626] It follows that in practice the demarcation of attempts from preparation in English law can be perceived as a procedural rather than a substantive law problem.[1627] Scholars and the Law Commission have denunciated this state of affairs as an insensible duplication of labour which might lead to inconsistencies and proposes that the question should be one of law, reserved for the judge.[1628]

Difficult cases and additional demarcation criteria

Arguably, the formulas for distinguishing attempt from preparation are in need for additional criteria in order to clarify and facilitate the demarcation of the two areas. Two factors which often seem to influence courts thereby are on the one hand a close temporal connection to the commission of the actus reus and an "intrusion" of the perpetrator's conduct into the sphere of the victim (in cases of attempted rape, injury/death, kidnapping, false imprisonment, etc.) or the property (in cases of attempted burglary, criminal damage. etc.). In other words, an intrusion into the sphere of the protected legal interest and a close temporal connection seems to be required.[1629]

1624 'Conspiracy and Attempts', Consultation Paper, LAW COM No 183 [2007], p. 208.

1625 'Conspiracy and Attempts', LAW COM No 318 [2009], para 8.69 et seq.

1626 Section 4 (3) of the 1981 Act reads as follows:
Where, in proceedings against a person for an offence under section 1 above, there is evidence sufficient in law to support a finding that he did an act falling within subsection (1) of that section, the question whether or not his act fell within that subsection is a question of fact.

1627 Brockhaus, 'Die strafrechtliche Dogmatik von Vorbereitung, Versuch und Rücktritt im europäischen Vergleich' (2006), p. 318.

1628 'Conspiracy and Attempts', Consultation Paper, LAW COM No 183 [2007], p. 20. See also: Clarkson, 'Attempt: The Conduct Requirement' Oxford Journal of Legal Studies (2009), p. 41.

1629 See also: Clarkson, 'Attempt: The Conduct Requirement' Oxford Journal of Legal Studies (2009), pp. 25–41, Roxin, 'Strafrecht Allgemeiner Teil, Band II: Besondere Erscheinungsformen der Straftat' (2003), pp. 374–389.

If one, as proposed here, at least partially sees the rationale for punishing attempts (objectively) in an endangerment of or attack on a protected legal interest, it becomes clear that an intrusion of the perpetrator's conduct into the sphere of the victim (the protected legal interest respectively) can play an important role. This is because one can hardly speak of an endangerment of or an attack on the protected legal interest without the causal chain having reached the pertinent sphere. While admittedly, this criterion might not reach satisfactory results in all cases, it can nevertheless constitute a useful tool to make the demarcation of attempts and preparation more concrete. The outcome of many English and German cases can be explained by invoking this criterion while it will also fit the Dutch definition of attempts, as an intrusion into the sphere of the victim will often correspond and substantiate the finding that the occurred conduct due to its outward manifestation can be considered to be aimed at the completion of the offence.

The requirement that an intrusion into the sphere of the protected legal interest must have taken place, can for instance explain why in cases where the defendant feigns theft in order to collect the insurance money generally lead to an acquittal, as long as the theft has not yet been reported to the insurance company. Pertinent examples can be found here in the aforementioned English decision of *R v Gullefer*, where the defendant had yet to reclaim his money from the bookmaker and the more recent decision of *R v Bowles & Bowles*. In this case a husband and his wife allegedly tried to exploit their elderly neighbour, who was suffering from dementia. The police found a draft form of will fully complete, except for the signatures in a drawer of the house of the defendants. The Court of Appeal acquitted the couple as it could not be proven that the two had taken any further steps to have the will executed and that the evidence presented disclosed no more than preparatory acts.[1630] Likewise German jurisprudence generally assumes that the staging of theft cannot yet amount to an attempt to commit insurance fraud.[1631]

On the other hand, if an intrusion into the sphere of the protected legal interest has taken place the courts seem more likely to impose liability for an attempt. If the would-be perpetrator has for instance already poured petrol over the door of a house[1632], over the victim itself[1633], had already entered the premises where they intended to set fire[1634] or has already damaged the door or window to a house[1635], an intrusion can be construed and accordingly an attempt can be assumed. In the aforementioned situations which stem from all three investigated penal systems, the respective courts have therefore assumed that the threshold to attempt liability has been passed. If however the perpetrator has already arrived at the scene but has yet to embark on his endeavour, as he wants to scout the location, or *a fortiori*, still has

1630 R v Lewis Bowles, Christine Bowles [2004] EWCA Crim 1608.
1631 11 January 1951 BGH NJW 1952, 430.
1632 R v Mihailis Litholetovs [2002] EWCA Crim 1154.
1633 HR 14 December 1993, *NJ* 1994, 293.
1634 9 March 2006 BGH NStZ 2006, 331.
1635 R v Boyle [1987] 84 Cr App R 270, HR 22 June 1999, *NJ* 1999, 636.

to drive several kilometres until he reaches the scene of the crime, no impact on the sphere of the protected legal interest has occurred and an imposition of liability seems more unlikely.

Approach cases

The multiple possibilities and different ways in which perpetrators can approach either the scene of the crime or the victim respectively can cause many demarcation problems in practice. However, with the requirement of an interference with the sphere of the protected legal interest in combination with the criterion of a close temporal connection, these cases can by and large be solved satisfactorily. The criterion of close temporal connection to the commission of the offence can play an important role here as it is conceivable that a certain interference with the sphere of the protected legal interest has already taken place but due to the remoteness of the conduct from the commission of the offence, the imposition of attempt liability seems nevertheless unwarranted. Consider for instance the case of a burglar who prepares his deed by leaning a ladder against a house, but only intends to put his plan into action several hours later, after dawn.

The aforementioned case of *R v Tosti* can also be subsumed here. There the English courts, implicitly putting subjective criteria to the foreground come to the conclusion that the threshold to attempt liability had been crossed despite the fact that the perpetrators had not yet brought all their equipment to the scene of the crime but were only inspecting the lock of the barn.[1636] This case can be interpreted in such a way that in examining the padlock with a view to gaining entry, an interference with the sphere and thus an endangerment of the protected legal interest had taken place.[1637]

In a similar German decision, two burglars were caught red-handed when they were standing next to their car on a parking space in front of a petrol station which they intended to burgle, smoking a cigarette. They had already fetched the bolt-cutter from their van and had placed it on the ground next to their car. Corresponding to the emphasis placed in German law on the subjective plan or horizon of the perpetrators, the Supreme Court acquitted the defendants as they were not yet 'on the job' as their plan encompassed to pause first and smoke a cigarette. Whether or not such a strong focus on the plan of the perpetrator is desirable, can be debated as it might lead to difficult evidentiary questions in practice especially in regard to non-cooperative criminals. Yet, corresponding to the view proposed here, the Supreme Court, stated that the threshold to attempt liability would only have been crossed when the perpetrators would have approached the building with the bolt-cutter in hands.[1638] Only then

1636 R v Tosti, [1997] Crim LR 746.

1637 See: Clarkson, 'Attempt: The Conduct Requirement' Oxford Journal of legal Studies (2009), p. 27.

1638 26 July 1989 BGH NStZ 1989, 473.

would an interference with the sphere of the protected legal interest have commenced.

Similarly, the German Supreme Court convicted a defendant for the attempted murder of A which he suspected to find in the living room of his parents-in-law. He punched through the living room door with the end of his rifle which A had barricaded upon his arrival. He subsequently entered the living room but A had already managed to flee through the window. The Regional Court had acquitted the defendant as in its view the attempt would only begin once he aimed at the victim. The Supreme Court overruled the Regional Court and argued that the defendant had passed the 'Here we go' threshold and had thereby commenced the execution of the offence.[1639] This result seems defensible. In this case the defendant's forceful intrusion into the living room certainly constitutes an interference with the sphere of the victim, or rather the protected legal interest and also a close temporal connection can be assumed as he correctly assumed that the victim could be found in the living room and as he intended to immediately execute his plan upon entry. This corresponds to the English case of *R v Boyle* where a conviction for attempted burglary was upheld as the defendants had already broken down the door of a house as well as to a Dutch case where the defendant had already interfered with and damaged the roof window of a shop.[1640]

Lying-in-wait cases

The so-called lying-in-wait cases are an equally frequently encountered type of cases in practice. In these situations, the perpetrator waits for the victim to arrive to carry out his deed. Generally speaking, it seems common ground that merely lying-in-wait is considered to fall under the preparatory phase. In the Netherlands for instance, lying-in-wait cases, will most likely not give rise to attempt liability as it seems difficult to consider the conduct due to its objective, outward manifestation to be aimed at the completion of the offence.[1641] Yet, the conduct may give rise to liability for preparatory conduct pursuant to Article 46 DPC.

In Germany, it is generally accepted that lying in wait will not yet give rise to liability.[1642] However, the more subjective orientation of the German penal system can lead to another result where the perpetrator expects the victim to appear within a moments. Thus, in cases where the victim actually approaches the designated scene of the crime or where the perpetrator expects that this will soon be the case, German courts have imposed attempt liability.[1643]

1639 26 August 1986 BGH NStZ 1987, 20.

1640 R v Boyle [1987] 84 Cr App R 270, HR 22 June 1999, *NJ* 1999, 636.

1641 See also: Noyon, Langemeijer, Remmelink, 'Wetboek van Strafrecht' (2010) Art 45, note 2.5.1.

1642 Roxin, 'Strafrecht Allgemeiner Teil, Band II: Besondere Erscheinungsformen der Straftat' (2003), p. 382, Schönke and Schröder, 'Kommentar zum Strafgesetzbuch' (2006), §22 Mn 44–46.

1643 Schönke and Schröder, 'Kommentar zum Strafgesetzbuch' (2006), §22 Mn 44. See also: 20 November 1953 BGH NJW 1954, 567.

In England lying in wait cases also seem to be considered to lie outside the scope of attempts. In the case of *R v Jones* the matter was addressed indirectly. The defendant (A) in this case was a married man, but started an affair with another woman B. She however started another relationship with C and broke off the relationship with A; a fact he could not accept. He bought a gun, shortened it and jumped into C's car in disguise. He pointed the gun at the victim, but with the safety catch still on and said "You are not going to like this". The victim however grabbed the gun and after a struggle managed to flee. The defence had argued that no attempt liability could be construed as he had not come close enough to the commission of the offence (in the sense of performing the last act), as he would have had to perform at least three more acts before the full offence could have been completed, i.e., removing the safety catch, putting his finger on the trigger and pull it. The Court, upholding the conviction but reducing his sentence from 12 to 8 years imprisonment concluded:

> Clearly [the defendant's] actions in obtaining the gun, in shortening it, in loading it, in putting on his disguise and in [lying] in wait could only be regarded as preparatory acts. But, in our judgment, once he had got into the car, taken out the loaded gun and pointed it at the victim with the intention of killing him, there was sufficient evidence for consideration of the jury on a charge of attempted murder.[1644]

This clearly suggests a narrow ambit of attempt, corresponding to the approach taken in *Gullefer.* Accordingly, lying in wait for the absent victim may pursuant to this *obiter dictum* fall outside the scope of attempt liability. Yet it should be recalled that liability may in these cases nevertheless arise on the basis of specific offences such as a possession offence.

7.4.3. Concluding remarks

If one puts the approach regarding attempt liability of the three investigated countries on a continuum it can be stated that the Netherlands seem to adopt the most restrictive, respectively objective approach, which is however supplemented by a general doctrine of liability for preparatory conduct. English law, *inter alia* due to the influence of lay participation, has adopted an inconsistent approach and fluctuates between a mixed and a subjective approach. German law on the other hand, already due to the wording of §22 GPC, adopts a mixed approach with a strong emphasis on the subjective criterion of the perpetrator's plan or intentions.

From a comparative point of view it can therefore be stated that by and large a mixed subjective/objective approach for the demarcation of attempts from

1644 R v Jones [1990] 1 WLR, 1057. See also: Smith, 'Proximity in attempt: Lord Lane's "midway course"' Criminal Law Review (1991), pp. 576–582.

preparatory conduct seems acceptable.[1645] Thus, a combination of subjective and objective factors ought to arguably be invoked in order to determine when a person has crossed the threshold to attempt liability. Accordingly, the plan and subjective horizon of the perpetrator as well as the immediate and imminent endangerment of the protected legal interest should play a decisive role here.[1646]

For the sake of legal certainty and in order to avoid an undue expansion of liability, it is submitted that objective factors such as the actual and imminent endangerment of the protected legal interest should carry more weight. There ought to be a certain imminence about the actor's conduct leading to the commission of the offence. This is because, to put it in the words of the English court in *R v Eagleton*: "Acts remotely leading towards the commission of the offence are not to be considered as attempts to commit it, but acts immediately connected with it are [...]".[1647] Yet, it has been established that already partially bringing about the actus reus of the envisaged offence should not be a prerequisite for attempt liability. Fulfilling a part of the actus reus can be considered a sufficient, but certainly not a necessary condition surely for imposing attempt liability. In many situations the offender will have come sufficiently close to causing harm to deserve criminal censure once he has committed parts of the actus reus. Yet, this does not always need to be the case, as when he is for instance still temporarily far removed from bringing his criminal enterprise to an end.

Objective and subjective factors should further be combined in order to strike a fair balance between the competing interests of providing an effective social defence (i.e. crime prevention) and the need to protect fundamental rights and more generally citizens from intrusive and pre-emptive state powers. This however, should not diminish the fact that the perpetrator's intentions will generally constitute the primary ingredient of attempt liability. Yet, which role the perpetrator's conception of the envisaged course of events should play is up for debate. The strong emphasis on this element in the German penal system is not reflected to the same extent in England nor the Netherlands. Due to its primarily objective stance the perpetrator's conception only plays an auxiliary role in the Netherlands. In England, however, they can arguably play a role, which can be deduced from the fact that the intention is often conceived to constitute the principal ingredient of the offence.[1648]

Admittedly, the perpetrator's conception of the course of events can play a role in certain cases, but making it the foundation of the evaluation process seems capable of causing friction in practice. It might namely be difficult to effectively

[1645] See also: Brockhaus, 'Die strafrechtliche Dogmatik von Vorbereitung, Versuch und Rücktritt im europäischen Vergleich' (2006), pp. 453–461.

[1646] Brockhaus, 'Die strafrechtliche Dogmatik von Vorbereitung, Versuch und Rücktritt im europäischen Vergleich' (2006), p. 457.

[1647] R v Eagleton [1855] 6 Cox CC 559.

[1648] See: Brockhaus, 'Die strafrechtliche Dogmatik von Vorbereitung, Versuch und Rücktritt im europäischen Vergleich' (2006), p. 457, Smith and Hogan, 'Criminal Law' (2008), p. 381.

establish the perpetrator's view on the course of events, especially in cases where he chooses to rely on his right to remain silent. To make the demarcation of attempt and preparation dependent on the perception of the perpetrator might introduce a degree of arbitrariness into the law which is undesirable. In order to make the said distinction however more concrete, it is submitted that the requirements of a close temporal connection to the commission of the actus reus and an intrusion of the perpetrator's conduct into the sphere of the victim may provide a useful yardstick to determine the scope of liability.

It has been demonstrated that for a variety of reasons a clear dividing line between attempts and preparation is sometimes hard to come by. A further complicating factor thereby is that the line arguably will have to be drawn slightly differently depending on whether one is concerned with a complete or an incomplete attempt. The crucial difference between the two here is that in regard to complete attempts, the causal chain need not yet have reached the sphere of the victim. For instance, the parcel bomb has been built and is now on its way to the victim, or the poisonous bottle of whisky has been placed on a shelf, but the victim is not due to return from his vacation until a week later. Is criminal law nevertheless justified in imposing attempt liability in these cases or should liability not arise until there is an objective intrusion in the sphere of the victim or protected legal interest by the perpetrator's conduct, i.e. when the parcel is delivered or when the victim picks up the whisky bottle from the shelf to pour himself a drink, as would be suggested by this requirement?

Arguably, the attempt stage will be reached, once the perpetrator has relinquished control over the causal chain of events, i.e. he has posted the parcel and placed the whiskey on the shelf without the intention to return to the premises before the victim returns. This is, because from a normative point of view, these cases mirror the same imminence of the commission of the actus reus. The possibly increased distance to the sphere of the victim in comparison to incomplete attempts is namely compensated by the actor's decision to give up dominion over the chain of events and let events run their course. Thus, attempt liability will in these cases generally arise once the perpetrator has given up the dominion over the course of events.

This seems to be the prevalent view among German scholars and arguably also in Dutch jurisprudence.[1649] In a pertinent Dutch decision, the defendant had cut the brake pipes of a car late in the evening and had written "death" in the snow in front of a house. When the writing was detected, the victim, who suspected that he knew the author of the death threat, had called the defendant and asked him what he knew about it. The defendant confessed that he had written the death threat and also confessed that the family should not use the car as he had also cut the brake pipes of the car. The Supreme Court considered it established that the threshold towards attempt liability had been crossed. This although it acknowledged that given the

---

1649 Roxin, 'Strafrecht Allgemeiner Teil, Band II: Besondere Erscheinungsformen der Straftat' (2003), p. 397.

late time of the attempt (the brake pipes were cut sometime between 2100 hrs and 2300 hrs; the aforementioned phone call took place around 2400 hrs) it was unlikely that the car would still have been used on that day and that the likelihood of the occurrence of harm was until that time thus minimal. However, precisely that factor in connection with the perpetrator's "confession" on the phone prompted the court to accept that the defendant had subsequently voluntarily withdrawn from the attempt.[1650]

7.5. The fault element in attempts

7.5.1. Introduction

It has already been mentioned that in the context of attempt liability, the fault element traditionally plays an important role. As the desired result is per definition absent in criminal attempts, one is often left with only the perpetrator's intentions to determine what he actually set out to achieve and how. In other words, the emphasis of the offence lies on the criminal intent as the manifested conduct might be completely innocent and innocuous.[1651] Here one is confronted once again with the different approaches as to mens rea standards adopted in the English common law tradition and in the civil law countries of Germany and the Netherlands.[1652] As already mentioned, the most crucial difference between common and civil law traditions here is that the latter recognises the concept of *dolus eventualis* as part of the concept of intention, while the former does not. As will become evident, this has repercussions for the scope of liability. To fully understand these differences it seems pertinent to first briefly outline the different connotations given to intention in the English penal system before subsequently juxtaposing the fault requirements for attempt liability in England, Germany and the Netherlands.

The English penal system knows several variations of the notion intent. First and foremost the English system distinguishes between direct and indirect (or oblique) intention. Direct intention constitutes the purest form of the notion. A person acts with direct intent if (s)he acts in order to bring about a certain result.[1653] In other words, a person acts with direct intent, if the non-occurrence of the intended result would mark at least the partial failure of his/her enterprise.[1654]

1650 HR 3 March 2009, *LJN* BF8844. Also earlier case law seems to suggest that attempt liability will arise from the moment when control over the course of events is relinquished. This would for instance be the case once the perpetrator has posted a parcel containing a poisonous cake. See: HR 19 June 1911, *W* 1911, 9203.

1651 This might be especially the case in English criminal law, as it does not know the notion of impossible attempt.

1652 See generally: Blomsma 'Mens rea and defences in European criminal law'(2012).

1653 Duff, 'Criminal Attempts' (1996), p. 17.

1654 Duff, 'Criminal Attempts' (1996), p. 17.

Conversely a person is said to have acted with indirect (or oblique) intent if a result is, although not considered constitutive for the success of the enterprise, anticipated as a virtually certain side effect of the directly intended action.[1655] A frequently mentioned textbook example to elucidate the matter is the case of a person planting a bomb on an airplane in order to collect the insurance money, well aware that in the course of this misdeed, passengers might be harmed. This form of intent can be roughly compared to the German notion of *dolus indirectus*.

Another subcategory of intention can be seen in conditional intent (this notion is not to be mistaken with the German notion of *dolus eventualis*). Sometimes a person is willing to commit a crime but his/her intention is hinging on a particular condition to materialise. Take for instance the thief rummaging the lockers in a gym meaning to steal in case (s)he finds something which (s)he considers worth stealing.[1656] Such cases frequently occur in an offence involving ulterior intent. The general rule here is that an intention hinging on a condition is in English law regarded as an intention.

7.5.2. The fault element in England/Wales

The fault element for attempt as outlined by section 1(1) of the 1981 Act requires "intent" to commit the substantive offence. This requirement seems straightforward on first sight, but the position is more complex as will subsequently be shown.

As the mens rea requirements of a particular offence can vary in regard to the different elements of the actus reus (i.e. conduct, circumstances and consequences), so too can the fault requirements for these elements differ in the law of attempts. This distinction might however give rise to complications in practice as it might not always be easy to categorise the actus reus of an offence into one of the three categories.[1657]

Intentional conduct

The first element causes the least problems in the law of attempts. It is generally accepted that the defendant must intend to bring about the relevant, more than merely preparatory act.[1658] This requirement will rarely prove problematic in practice. Leaving aside the rare cases of automatism, e.g. altered states of consciousness induced by drink or drug, the intentionality of conduct will mostly be easily established.[1659]

1655 Duff, 'Criminal Attempts' (1996), p. 17.

1656 Simester and Sullivan, 'Criminal Law: Theory and Doctrine' (2007), p. 132.

1657 See: Smith, 'Two Problems in Criminal Attempt' Harvard Law Review (1957), pp. 422–429.

1658 Smith and Hogan, 'Criminal Law' (2008), p. 381.

1659 Simester and Sullivan, 'Criminal Law: Theory and Doctrine' (2007), p. 312.

Intention as to consequences

Where the substantive offence requires the occurrence of a result or consequence (e.g. the death of a human being by murder), the doctrine of attempt will require proof of an intention regarding this consequence.[1660] This stance has repercussions on crimes of "constructive liability" like murder. Whereas in the complete crime of murder, an intention to cause grievous bodily harm is sufficient to warrant a conviction, attempted murder requires an intention to kill.[1661] What is disputed in this regard is whether direct intent should be required or if indirect (or oblique) intention should suffice for an attempt. In the view of the Law Commission, oblique and conditional intent should be sufficient to ground a charge of attempts.[1662] Also the courts seem to have endorsed this view and applied the *Wollin* doctrine of oblique intent to attempts.[1663] Thus, although the manifestation of a particular consequence was not directly intended by the defendant, the courts may nevertheless infer intention in circumstances where the defendant foresaw the occurrence of the consequence as a virtual certainty.[1664] In a pertinent case the defendants were involved in a fight with the victim. They threatened to kill him and finally dropped him from a third floor balcony. He survived the fall, severely injured. They were convicted of attempted murder and the Court of Appeal upheld the conviction holding that the jury was entitled to draw the inference that they were intending or trying to kill the victim given that they foresaw that the victim's death was a virtual certainty of their conduct.[1665] It should however be noted here that the jury is merely entitled to draw this inference in these situations but is not obliged to do so.

Intention as to circumstance

Where the substantive offence requires intention or knowledge as to circumstances, it is clear that the same will apply for attempts.[1666] The picture however gets more blurred if the substantive offence requires less than intention or knowledge. Although an attempt requires an intended result, it is clear that an intention as to circumstances is not required, a long as the substantive offence does not require intent.[1667] A case in point here is the offence of rape. In *R v Kahn* the Court of Appeal after carefully considering the conflicting opinions came to the conclusion that

---

1660 Smith and Hogan, 'Criminal Law' (2008), p. 381.
1661 Duff, 'Criminal Attempts' (1996), p. 5.
1662 'Conspiracy and Attempts', Consultation Paper, LAW COM No 183 [2007], p. 226, para 16.68.
1663 R v Wollin [1998] 4 All ER 103.
1664 'Conspiracy and Attempts', Consultation Paper, LAW COM No 183 [2007], p. 191, para 14.27.
1665 R v Walker [1990] 90 Cr App R 226.
1666 Smith and Hogan, 'Criminal Law' (2008), p. 383.
1667 Smith and Hogan, 'Criminal Law' (2008), p. 383.

> a man may commit the offence of attempted rape, even though he is reckless whether the woman consents to sexual intercourse since the attempt relates to the physical activity and his mental state of recklessness relates, as in the offence of rape itself, not to that activity but to the absence of the woman's consent and therefore no question of attempting to achieve a reckless state of mind arises in such circumstance.[1668]

This conclusion seems right in principle, as it is hardly conceivable to recklessly have sexual intercourse. Furthermore, a ruling to the contrary might have severely curtailed the protection offered to citizens by the law of attempts, as it seems a more than daunting challenge for the prosecution to prove that the defendant intended that the woman with whom he had sexual intercourse did not consent.[1669] This principle has arguably been extended in *Attorney-General's Reference (No 3 of 1992)* where the defendants had thrown petrol bombs at an occupied car but missed.[1670] In this case the Court of Appeal muddied the waters of criminal attempts by applying what might be termed the "missing element test". This test had been proposed in literature and essentially holds that one should distinguish in the law of attempts between the missing element of the actus reus and the other elements and while the missing element must be intended, the other elements should require only the mens rea required for the full offence.[1671] The court stated:

> A defendant, in order to be guilty of an attempt, must be in one of the states of mind required for the commission of the full offence, and did [sic] his best, so far as he could, to supply what was missing from the completion of the offence. It is the policy of the law that such people should be punished notwithstanding that in fact the intentions of such a defendant have not been fulfilled.[1672]

This decision goes beyond the aforementioned case of *Kahn* by holding recklessness sufficient for any present consequence element of the actus reus of the full offence, provided the defendant intended to bring about any missing consequence or other element (e.g. a circumstance).[1673] In other words, where the underlying offence "merely" requires recklessness, the same would be sufficient regarding present consequences (or circumstance) for the charge of attempt. This clearly militates against the wording of the 1981 Act which explicitly requires intent.[1674] Furthermore the dictum might have opened the flood gates for attempted strict liability offences

---

1668 R v Kahn and others [1990] 2 All ER 783.

1669 Smith and Hogan, 'Criminal Law' (2008), p. 384.

1670 [1993] 98 Cr App R 383.

1671 Stannard, 'Making up for the missing element – a sideways look at attempts' Legal Studies (1987), pp. 194–204.

1672 Quoted in: Smith and Hogan, 'Criminal Law' (2008), p. 384.

1673 Simester and Sullivan, 'Criminal Law: Theory and Doctrine' (2007), p. 316.

1674 Smith and Hogan, 'Criminal Law' (2008), p. 385.

or offences requiring only negligence with regard to a circumstance element. As some of these offences carry great stigma upon a conviction such an extension should be handled with great care and should not be too easily accepted.

The exact repercussions of the dictum in *Attorney-General's Reference (No 3 of 1992)* are however subject to a fierce debate among scholars and it remains to be seen how English courts will interpret it in the future. The judgment does highlight the intricate nature and lack of legal certainty regarding the mens rea requirements of the English law on attempts. It furthermore shows the struggle of the English judiciary to come to terms with the fact that English law dispenses with a general offence of reckless endangerment. To a certain extent the confusion caused by the dictum can be traced back to this lacuna in the law and the endeavour of the courts to close this gap by interpreting the law of attempts extensively.

Conditional intention

An early case which shook the English law of attempts in general and the law of burglary in particular was the decision of *R v Husseyn*.[1675] The Court of Appeal, oddly enough, concluded that it could not be said that someone who sets out to cabbage something, but only if (s)he finds something worth stealing has a present intention to steal. It is more than obvious that this might lead to a stalemate position in the law of burglary, as most people who set out to commit the crime do not intend to steal some particular thing, but anything they find worth stealing. The Court of Appeal was subsequently at pains to mitigate the effects of the judgment and held in *Attorney-General's Reference (No 1 and 2 of 1979)* that the dictum in *Hysseyn* should only apply where the indictment named the specific thing which was attempted to steal.[1676] Thus, in this respect, English law outsources the solution of a problem of substantive criminal law completely to the realm of procedural law. This procedural distinction has been heavily criticised, but it remains nevertheless part of the law.[1677]

Generally it can be said that most forms of conditional attempt have been (and rightly so) accepted in English criminal law. The Law Commission argues that the decision in *Husseyn* was wrong and that conditional intent should be sufficient to be liable for an attempt. In the Commission's view if someone breaks into a car with the intention to steal something if (s)he finds something worth stealing (s)he has an intention to steal.[1678]

1675 [1978] Crim LR 219.

1676 [1980] QB 180.

1677 Smith and Hogan, 'Criminal Law' (2008), p. 387.

1678 'Conspiracy and Attempts', Consultation Paper, LAW COM No 183 [2007], p. 228, para. 16.74.

7.5.3. *The fault element in the Netherlands*

The mens rea of the perpetrator does not play a prominent role in Dutch jurisprudence on criminal attempts.[1679] This is because Art 45 requires that the perpetrator's intention has manifested itself by the initiation of the execution of the offence. This formulation places the emphasis in the law of attempts on objective factors, i.e. the initiation of the execution.[1680] The intention of the perpetrator must be directed towards the execution of a specific offence.[1681] After all, an attempt is not punishable per se but only in regard to a specific underlying criminal offence. This can sometimes prove problematic in practice, as it is not always easily deducible from the occurred conduct which crime the perpetrator envisaged to commit. The occurred conduct can namely be ambiguous and open to different interpretations. This is because, strictly speaking one cannot deduce from the conduct of breaking into a house if the perpetrator intends to steal, destroy property, assault, or worse. This requirement, however, assures that the notion of a criminal attempt remains closely connected to the completion of the underlying offence and prevents the expansion of attempt liability to the preparatory phase.[1682]

It is generally accepted in the Netherlands that the lowest form of intention, i.e. *dolus eventualis*, is sufficient to trigger attempt liability.[1683] The Dutch Supreme Court has accepted *dolus eventualis* as a sufficient mens rea standard for attempt liability in the case of a car driver who attempted to run over a police officer. The police officer, in the last moment jumped out of harm's way, and the driver was convicted for attempted manslaughter, as in the court's opinion he had accepted the considerable chance that the police officer could get killed by his actions.[1684]

Also in more contemporary jurisprudence, *dolus eventualis* is frequently deemed sufficient to establish attempt liability. In a pertinent case, the suspect had shot at A in a crowded café. Two witnesses attempted to apprehend the suspect in order to prevent further bloodshed and in the ensuing struggle a second shot was fired which hit another guest, B. The Supreme Court convicted the suspect for the attempted manslaughter of B and held that by holding on to his weapon during the struggle, the suspect had accepted the considerable chance that further shots were fired and other people injured.[1685]

However, *dolus eventualis* will only be sufficient for an attempt if it is also sufficient for the commission of the underlying offence. In case the underlying offence requires a higher mens rea standard like purpose or malice aforethought,

---

1679 De Hullu, 'Materieel Strafrecht' (2009), p. 378.
1680 De Hullu, 'Materieel Strafrecht' (2009), p. 379.
1681 De Hullu, 'Materieel Strafrecht' (2009), p. 379.
1682 De Hullu, 'Materieel Strafrecht' (2009), p. 379.
1683 De Hullu, 'Materieel Strafrecht' (2009), p. 379, Kelk, 'Studieboek materieel strafrecht' (2005), p. 311.
1684 HR 6 February 1951, *NJ* 1951, 475.
1685 HR 10 October 2000, *NJ* 2001, 4. See also: HR 21 November 2000, *NJ* 2001, 160, HR 7 July 2009, *LJN* BH9030.

the same standard will apply in case of an attempt.[1686] Conversely, the intention of the perpetrator need not encompass elements of the underlying offence which need also not be covered by the perpetrator's intention in case of completion of the crime.

7.5.4. The fault element in Germany

In Germany it is generally required that an unconditional decision of the perpetrator to act can be established. On the cognitive side it is therefore required that the perpetrator envisaged circumstances which in case of manifestation would amount to the commission of the actus reus of the aspired offence. This includes any aggravating subjective requirements. Thus, in order to be liable for aggravated murder pursuant to §211 GPC, the perpetrator must have the intention to kill and have acted out of one of the subjective criteria mentioned therein, for instance bloodlust. If this is not the case only liability for attempted manslaughter pursuant to §212 GPC can arise.[1687]

As the perpetrator's decision to act ought to be unconditional, qualms and reservations of the offender may negate such a finding. Thus, attempt liability can for instance not arise in situations where the perpetrator is still in need of a 'final push' to commit the offence. Thus, if the perpetrator plans to threaten and intimidate his victim with a gun at point blank range but also accepts the possibility that he might also shoot the victim, an attempt to murder cannot be assumed.[1688]

These cases need however be distinguished from scenarios where the perpetrator has fully made up his mind but makes the commission of the offence dependent on occurrence of certain objective conditions. Thus, if the perpetrator intends to burgle a house, but makes the execution of his plan dependent on whether or not the watchdog will eat his poisonous bait an unconditional decision to act can be assumed as the perpetrator was subjectively firmly determined to commit the offence. His intent to do wrong was firm, only the occurrence of an objective condition independent of his will was still uncertain.[1689] This category also covers those cases of 'conditional intent' that caused frictions in the English penal system. Thus, in Germany and also in the Netherlands entering a house with the intention to steal but making the decision on what to steal dependent on what he finds, will be sufficient to establish an unconditional decision to act.[1690] Likewise, merely

---

1686 De Hullu, 'Materieel Strafrecht' (2009), p. 379, Pelser, 'Preparations to commit a crime – The Dutch approach to inchoate offences' Utrecht Law Review (2008), p. 60.

1687 Bohlander, 'Principles of German Criminal Law' (2009), p. 140.

1688 Roxin, 'Strafrecht Allgemeiner Teil, Band II: Besondere Erscheinungsformen der Straftat' (2003), p. 356. See also: 20 September 2004 BGH NStZ-RR 2004, 361.

1689 Schönke and Schröder, 'Kommentar zum Strafgesetzbuch' (2006), §22 Mn 19.

1690 Remmelink, 'Inleiding tot de studie van het Nederlandse Strafrecht' (1995), p. 391, Roxin, 'Strafrecht Allgemeiner Teil, Band II: Besondere Erscheinungsformen der Straftat' (2003), p. 359, Schönke and Schröder, 'Kommentar zum Strafgesetzbuch' (2006), §22 Mn 19.

examining an object to determine whether or not it constitutes an adequate object for theft can be sufficient to establish the decision to act.[1691]

In effect, the mens rea requirements for an attempt are thus equivalent to the fault requirements for the full offence.[1692] There is further no need that the perpetrator acted deliberately and premeditated his deed. Spontaneous ad hoc knowledge will suffice, so that also 'crimes of passion' can be attempted.[1693] On the volitive side and resembling the situation in the Netherlands, the perpetrator must possess the same form of intent as required by the offence in question. This may be as little as *dolus eventualis*.[1694] The solution in Germany and the Netherlands is notably different from the approach of English law, outlined above, where the corresponding problem of recklessness in attempt has been solved in such a way that recklessness can only suffice for attempt liability in regard to cognitive elements (such as the knowledge that the intercourse is non-consensual) while volitive elements will always require intention. Occasionally, however, a similar approach is also defended in Germany. Some scholars have argued that an attempt committed with *dolus eventualis* should not be punishable, but the prevalent view, including the courts accepts *dolus eventualis* as sufficient.[1695]

The concept of recklessness or *dolus eventualis* respectively is admittedly problematic in regard to criminal attempts. This is because the ordinary meaning of attempt in the sense of "actually trying" seems not reconcilable with this standard of fault. It may appear far fetched to describe someone as attempting to do X if he failed to see a serious risk occurring (recklessness) or that he foresaw the risk and accepted it (*dolus eventualis*). A strict adherence to the ordinary meaning of attempt would even point in the direction that attempt liability will require purpose. Unless your intent in acting was to do X, you cannot have attempted to do X, so the argument runs.[1696] Yet, this would arguably draw the scope of liability far too narrow. While the ordinary meaning of a word certainly carries some weight in the interpretation of the law they are ultimately not vey helpful here, as the substantial question is whether or not the law should impose punishment on those who knowingly or recklessly impose a risk on others, which however subsequently does not materialise.[1697]

1691 Roxin, 'Strafrecht Allgemeiner Teil, Band II: Besondere Erscheinungsformen der Straftat' (2003), p. 359, Schönke and Schröder, 'Kommentar zum Strafgesetzbuch' (2006), §22 Mn 19.

1692 Roxin, 'Strafrecht Allgemeiner Teil, Band II: Besondere Erscheinungsformen der Straftat' (2003), p. 353.

1693 Schönke and Schröder, 'Kommentar zum Strafgesetzbuch' (2006), §22 Mn 14–15.

1694 Schönke and Schröder, 'Kommentar zum Strafgesetzbuch' (2006), §22 Mn 17.

1695 See: Herzberg, 'Strafverzicht bei bedingt vorsätzlichem Versuch' NStZ (1990), pp. 311–318, Puppe, 'Der halbherzige Rücktritt' NStZ (1984), pp. 488–491.

1696 Chiao, 'Intention and attempt' Criminal Law and Philosophy (2010), p. 39.

1697 Chiao, 'Intention and attempt' Criminal Law and Philosophy (2010), p. 40.

7.5.5. Conclusion

It has become apparent that the mens rea requirements among the investigated penal systems are complex and diverse. All penal systems generally concur that only intentionally committed attempts can give rise to criminal liability. In other words, negligent attempts are alien to criminal law. By and large, the mens rea requirements for an attempt correspond to the fault requirements in place for the completed offence. From this it has to be concluded that the applicable mens rea standard for criminal attempts overall constitutes essentially a general mens rea problem which can only be solved in the broader context of a general discussion as to the definition of fault elements within the European context, which would exceed the scope of this book.[1698]

8. Impossible attempts

8.1. Introduction

If it is impossible to commit a crime, it is obvious that no one can be convicted for committing it. This does not however mean that one cannot attempt to commit this crime. This happens when the defendant does not realise that what he attempts is impossible that he is making a mistake, as when he tries to rape a corpse. There are a multitude of textbook examples which illustrate this situation. Suppose for instance that Brian wants to kill his uncle and therefore pours a white powder which he beliefs to be arsenic into his tea. Contrary to his belief however, the white powder is not arsenic, but harmless sugar. Thus, an impossible attempt can be defined as an attempt that could under no circumstances have led to the envisaged result. An attempt may be considered impossible due to the inaptness of the object or means or because the perpetrator as the subject of the crime lacks a certain quality (e.g. civil servant status) for the commission of the offence. In essence, impossible attempts are mistakes of the perpetrator. He imagines circumstances which in reality are inexistent, but which would make his conduct criminal were they really true. Usually, the problem of impossibility mainly arises in regard to complete attempts.[1699]

Classic examples of the inaptness of the object of the crime are cases where the perpetrator with the intent to kill stabs a person which he believes to be alive, but who in fact is already dead or shoots at a scarecrow believing it to be his enemy. In regard to property offences, one could mention situations where the perpetrator with intent to steal takes away an umbrella from a pub, which in fact belongs to himself, or where he destroys what he believes to be the property of Alex but what in reality is a *res nullius*. In all these cases an attempt is impossible due to the

1698 See however: Blomsma 'Mens rea and defences in European crimninal law' (2012).
1699 Ashworth, 'Principles of criminal law' (2006), p. 452.

inaptness of the object of the attempt. Yet, because of a mistake of fact the perpetrator fails to realise this.

An attempt may further be impossible due to the inaptness of the applied means. Here the aforementioned example of an attempt to kill with sugar, believing it to be arsenic can be categorised. Likewise, situations where the perpetrator attempts to shoot his victim with a replica gun, wrongly thinking it to be a loaded firearm.

An attempt can moreover be impossible as the perpetrator believes to possess a certain quality required for the offence in question, which he effectively lacks. A classic textbook example here would be a cleaning lady who believes to be an office bearer as she cleans the rooms in the local court, who accepts money from a friend, whom she promises to dispose of his case file in regard to a drunk-driving charge. Should the cleaning lady be liable for attempting §332 GPC (taking bribes meant as an incentive to violating one's official duties)? These cases are however of low practical relevance, which might explain the fact that they are not discussed in the English penal system at all. This despite the fact that such cases could in theory well arise as offences requiring a certain quality of the offender are not unknown to the English system. If these cases should warrant punishment is however a contentious topic in Germany.[1700] If one places the emphasis on the subjective sphere or plan of the perpetrator, then such cases might be considered to warrant punishment. Because if it is the perpetrator's beliefs that are decisive for attempt liability, then the same must apply to mistaken beliefs.[1701] According to this view a person who mistakenly considers himself an office bearer, could incur liability for attempting an offence which he can objectively not commit. The debate is however ongoing in Germany.[1702] Jurisprudence has adopted an uneven approach, but by and large shows strong subjective tendencies. Attempt liability for leaving the scene of an accident without cause (§142 GPC) was for instance imposed where a driver wrongly believed that he had caused an accident but nevertheless left the scene.[1703]

In the Netherlands, where the general approach to attempts is much more objectively orientated than in Germany these cases seem to be excluded from attempt liability. The objective impossibility of the offence is deemed decisive which also corresponds to the requirement of the outward manifestation of the conduct in question as a criterion for attempt liability.[1704]

Finally, one can distinguish two further subcategories of impossibility. On the one hand are ranged what may be termed imaginary offences. The offender in these scenarios believes that what he is doing is a criminal offence when in reality it is not. Thus, if Amil believes that adultery constitutes a criminal offence in Europe

---

1700 See: Roxin, 'Strafrecht Allgemeiner Teil, Band II: Besondere Erscheinungsformen der Straftat' (2003), pp. 446–451.

1701 Schönke and Schröder, 'Kommentar zum Strafgesetzbuch' (2006), §22 Mn 75–77.

1702 See: Roxin, 'Strafrecht Allgemeiner Teil, Band II: Besondere Erscheinungsformen der Straftat' (2003), pp. 446–451.

1703 25 August 1977 OLG Stuttgart NJW 1978, 900.

1704 De Hullu, 'Materieel Strafrecht' (2009), p. 387.

and nevertheless cheats on his wife can it then be said that he is attempting adultery? On the other side superstitious attempts are situated where the impossibility stems from the fact that the actor is attempting to achieve his goal by applying superstitious means such as curses or invoking demons.

In regard to impossible attempts, once again the competing rationales of punishing attempts play a decisive role. Objectivist and subjectivist perspectives of liability stress different factors here. Subjectivists argue that the perpetrator ought to be judged on the facts or circumstances as he believed them to be. That he was mistaken about these facts or circumstances is considered irrelevant. If a person pours sugar into the tea of his victim, which he believes to be arsenic, his state of mind is just as blameworthy as if the facts were as he believed them to be and the substance actually constituted poison. A strict adherence to the subjective approach would arguably cast the net of criminal liability very wide, as also superstitious attempts would in theory give rise to criminal liability. A person sticking pins into a voodoo doll or invoking black magic or divine powers to kill his victim would under such a view also incur liability. Yet, it is common ground in all penal systems that these cases should not trigger liability. In these cases the perpetrator applies paranormal means which do not belong to the ontological world and lie beyond the perception, logic and most importantly control of human conduct. Therefore they are considered not serious enough to justify the application of criminal sanctions.[1705] Again, these cases are of low practical relevance and in many instances will never reach the courts, especially in penal systems applying the opportunity principle to prosecutions where the prosecutor can use his discretion to drop the case beforehand.

Objective approaches, on the other hand, point to the absence of actual danger in these cases. From an objective point of view, a person shooting a scarecrow, or pouring sugar into tea does not endanger any protected legal interest. His conduct is objectively innocent, maybe even squarely in line with prevalent social conventions. It does not bespeak criminality and it is objectively unsuited to bring about the envisaged result. Thus, a strict adherence to this view would exclude impossible attempts completely from the realm of liability. One consideration behind such an approach might be the concern for the protection of individual freedoms which might be jeopardised if the law were to punish its citizens for objectively innocent conduct.[1706]

Yet, there are important grounds that arguably justify imposing punishment for some forms of impossible attempts. Not only does the blameworthiness of the perpetrator who pours sugar into the tea of his victim believing it to be poison correspond to the one actually using poison but also from the point of view of

---

1705 Ashworth, 'Criminal Attempts and the role of resulting harm under the code and in the common law' Rutgers Law Journal (1988), p. 763, Schönke and Schröder, 'Kommentar zum Strafgesetzbuch' (2006), §23 Mn 13–13a, Wilson, 'Central Issues in Criminal Theory' (2002), p. 254, Noyon, Langemeijer, Remmelink, 'Wetboek van Strafrecht' (2010), Art 45, note 2.6.2.

1706 See: Ashworth, 'Principles of criminal law' (2006), p. 453.

special prevention may punishment be warranted. The offender's conduct went beyond the preparatory stage and he has thereby demonstrated his willingness and capability to commit the offence.[1707] Furthermore, allowing such acts to go unpunished may jeopardise social interests by encouraging repetition, by the initial perpetrator or by others. Arguably the real danger here lies in future similar acts when the actor has learned from his mistakes and this time for instance chooses an ingredient which is actually poisonous.[1708] Accordingly, it is generally accepted that some forms of impossible attempts ought to be punished. The scope of liability varies however, depending on the prevalent rationale for punishing attempts in a respective system. This research will now investigate the approaches taken towards impossible attempts in the Netherlands, England and Germany, which as will subsequently become apparent nicely reflect the different underlying rationales for punishing attempts and their repercussions for the realm of impossibility.

8.2. The objective approach: Impossibility in the Netherlands

As already mentioned, if one accepts an objective rationale as the foundation of attempt liability and therefore requires an actual endangerment of protected legal interests, as is the case in the Netherlands, then difficulties arise in cases of impossible attempts. Sometimes a means or an object is so unsuited that one cannot speak of a concrete endangerment. The question in these cases thus is, if besides the criminal intent of the perpetrator there are sufficient objective reasons to nevertheless warrant the imposition of criminal liability. In older jurisprudence, the Dutch Supreme Court, clearly adopting an objective approach, declared *obiter* that an attempt to kill a corpse or an attempt to steal property which effectively belongs to the perpetrator should fall outside the scope of liability.[1709] Yet, more recent jurisprudence seems to indicate that the courts in regard to impossible attempts not only look at the suitability of the object or means, but that they rather take into account the entire criminal enterprise of the perpetrator. This also corresponds to the prevalent criterion of the outward manifestation, which in many cases will not be diminished by unsuitable means or objects.[1710]

Traditionally a distinction is drawn between relative and absolute impossible attempts.[1711] The general approach taken by the Dutch penal system is that relative impossible attempts will give rise to criminal liability, as relative impossible attempts nevertheless carry an inherent danger of causing harm. Absolute

[1707] Roxin, 'Strafrecht Allgemeiner Teil, Band II: Besondere Erscheinungsformen der Straftat' (2003), p. 338.

[1708] Sayre, 'Criminal Attempts' Harvard Law Review (1928), p. 850.

[1709] See: HR 28 December 1864, *W* 2663, cited in: Remmelink, 'Inleiding tot de studie van het Nederlandse Strafrecht' (1995), p. 402. See also: Noyon, Langemeijer, Remmelink, 'Wetboek van Strafrecht' (2010) Art 45, note 2.6.2, Fn 8.

[1710] De Hullu, 'Materieel Strafrecht' (2009), p. 387.

[1711] De Hullu, 'Materieel Strafrecht' (2009), p. 386.

impossible attempts on the other hand will not give rise to criminal liability, as they pose no danger. Relative impossible attempts are attempts where the means or the object is generally suitable to bring about the envisaged harm, but due to extrinsic factors the means/object was unsuitable in the case at hands.[1712] Think for instance of a case where someone tries to kill his mother-in-law with a non-lethal doses of strychnine. An absolute impossible attempt, on the other hand, is an attempt which under no circumstances can lead to the envisaged result, like for instance killing a corpse.

Accordingly one can distinguish four different forms of impossibility: (a) the object is absolutely unsuited (e.g. killing a corpse), (b) the means is absolutely unsuited (e.g. lacing a drink with sugar instead of arsenic), (c) the object is relatively unsuitable (e.g. trying to steal from an empty pocket), (d) the means is relatively unsuitable (e.g. administrating a non-lethal doses of poison).[1713]

The difference between absolute and relative impossible attempts however can be elusive at times. Crucial therefore is the chosen starting point of the evaluation. A till can be full or empty and an empty till is per definition an absolute unsuitable object for theft, and the same reasoning can be applied to the pickpocket who reaches into an empty pocket. However, the reasoning frequently applied in the Netherlands is that tills are generally full and that an empty till can be filled a few hours later.[1714] Thus an empty till or pocket is deemed only a relative unsuitable object.[1715] Characteristic for this approach is that object and means will generally be assessed as to their suitability for committing an offence in an abstract manner, independent of the circumstances of the case at hands.[1716] How far one may go with this abstraction is however up for debate.

Absolute impossible attempts play only a limited role in practice.[1717] Absolute impossibility is only rarely accepted by the courts, and if evidently so, the case would never reach the courts, as the public prosecutor would use his discretion and drop the case beforehand. The Supreme Court ruled for instance that an attempt to break into a jewellery store by destroying the shop window with a shovel was merely a relative impossible attempt, despite the fact that behind the regular window, another layer of bullet-proof glass was installed. The court argued that due to the fact that there was also another window which was not equipped with bullet-proof glass, the attempt was only relatively impossible.[1718] In another case, it was held that the attempt to draw money with a stolen cash card was only relatively

1712 De Hullu, 'Materieel Strafrecht' (2009), p. 386, Strijards, 'Strafbare voorbereidingshandelingen' (1995), pp. 30–31.
1713 Kelk, 'Studieboek materieel strafrecht' (2005), p. 325.
1714 HR 25 August 1932, *NJ* 1932, 1255.
1715 Kelk, 'Studieboek materieel strafrecht' (2005), p. 325.
1716 Brockhaus, 'Die strafrechtliche Dogmatik von Vorbereitung, Versuch und Rücktritt im europäischen Vergleich' (2006), p. 472.
1717 Pelser, 'Preparations to commit a crime – The Dutch approach to inchoate offences' Utrecht Law Review (2008), p. 61.
1718 HR 15 January 1980, *NJ* 1980, 245.

impossible despite the fact that the perpetrator did not know the pin-code.[1719] Thus, the courts will only accept a defence of absolute impossibility in cases where the attempt is so daft that it never, not even under the most favourable conditions can lead to the completion of the offence.[1720]

A related subcategory in the realm of impossible attempts in the Netherlands is the category of legal impossibility. In this category fall cases where the would-be perpetrator has completed all of his intended acts, but his endeavour was bound to fail from the very beginning due to other reasons than the unsuitability of the means or the object.[1721] Here two variations are discussed in legal literature. First, it is conceivable that an attempt is bound to fail due to a lack of elements which constitute the underlying offence. If for instance someone lacks a specific quality required by the underlying offence (e.g. the status of a civil servant), his attempt to commit this offence is bound to fail from the outset. It has already been mentioned that this is contrary to the situation in Germany. Likewise if someone engages in sexual intercourse with a person he believes to be under 16 but in reality is not, he is unable to consummate the offence of Art 245 DPC which prohibits sexual intercourse with children under the age of 16.

Furthermore, there is the category of cases where the perpetrator(s) believe that they are committing a criminal offence while in reality they are not. This can either be due to the fact that a change in the law has recently taken place, or if the persons are unfamiliar with the penal system they are in. Consider the example of two foreign men having sexual intercourse in The Hague, believing homosexual intercourse to be prohibited in the Netherlands.[1722] Should in these situations, where the offender commits what one might call an imaginary offence, liability arise? The issue is a bone of contention in the Netherlands, but the prevalent view seems to reject this possibility, because the consummation of the presumed criminal offence is legally impossible.[1723] This is in line with the underlying objectivist theory of attempts, where the objective element plays a more important role than the subjective, i.e. the evil intentions. In Germany and England, where a more subjectivist approach is prevalent, many of these cases which would probably lead to an acquittal in the Netherlands would trigger criminal liability there. However, the fact that these cases are also considered controversial in the Netherlands is evidence of the fact that the law of attempt can never be purely objectivist, but, by

---

1719 HR 7 October 2003, *NJ* 2004, 63. See also HR 23 January 2007, *LJN* AZ3587 for a case of attempted computer fraud where liability was assumed despite the fact that the device with which the crime was supposed to be carried out was malfunctioning.

1720 De Hullu, 'Materieel Strafrecht' (2009), p. 387.

1721 De Hullu, 'Materieel Strafrecht' (2009), p. 387, Kelk, 'Studieboek materieel strafrecht' (2005), p. 328.

1722 Kelk, 'Studieboek materieel strafrecht' (2005), p. 328.

1723 De Hullu, 'Materieel Strafrecht' (2009), p. 387, Kelk, 'Studieboek materieel strafrecht' (2005), p. 328, Pelser, 'Preparations to commit a crime – The Dutch approach to inchoate offences' Utrecht Law Review (2008), p. 61.

definition rests upon both objective and subjective elements. In practice, these cases are however of only minor importance.[1724]

It has been argued here that the dogmatic distinction between relative and absolute impossible attempts is elusive and seems arbitrary at times. The assessment hinges to a large extent on the applied degree of abstraction as well as on the question which factors are allowed to play a role. If in the examples discussed above, a pocket or a till is considered an absolute or a relative unsuitable object, depends whether or not one allows the fact that it was empty to enter the equation. If one refers to the thief reaching into an empty pocket that would arguably constitute an absolute impossible attempt, while if one refers to pockets in general, the attempt might seem only relatively impossible. The same predicament arises in the hypothetical case of a perpetrator shooting at someone with an unloaded rifle. An absolute impossible attempt can only be construed if one includes in the evaluation that the rifle was not loaded. If one however chooses to ignore this fact, then only a relative impossible attempt is conceivable.[1725] Further it finally seems slightly odd that an attempt to kill with one sleeping pill should be considered a relative impossible attempt and accordingly constitutes an endangerment, only because twenty sleeping pills could potentially be lethal.[1726] It is therefore submitted that a distinction between absolute and relative impossible attempts should not be introduced into European criminal law as it causes dogmatic predicaments in regard to demarcating the two notions and can, as the examples mentioned demonstrate, produce unsatisfactory results in practice. It could lead to the exclusion of liability in situations where considerations of criminal policy would certainly point towards an imposition of punishment, as for instance in the case of shooting with an unloaded rifle or reaching into an empty pocket.[1727]

8.3. The Subjective approach: Impossibility in England and Wales

The topic of impossibility in attempts used to constitute a hotly-debated topic in English criminal law. The current English rule was introduced after much discussion, in which prominent subjectivists such as Glanville Williams took the

---

1724 For a borderline case between legal and factual impossibility see: HR 17 March 1987, *NJ* 1988, 166. A man had attempted to kill a woman by strangulation but the woman had, so autopsy reports showed, died at some point during the strangulation from alcohol intoxication. The Supreme Court, however upheld the conviction of attempted murder, as, so it was argued, the death of the woman due to alcohol intoxication must be considered the extrinsic fact that the strangulation did not lead to her death.

1725 Brockhaus, 'Die strafrechtliche Dogmatik von Vorbereitung, Versuch und Rücktritt im europäischen Vergleich' (2006), p. 472.

1726 Roxin, 'Strafrecht Allgemeiner Teil, Band II: Besondere Erscheinungsformen der Straftat' (2003), p. 341.

1727 Brockhaus, 'Die strafrechtliche Dogmatik von Vorbereitung, Versuch und Rücktritt im europäischen Vergleich' (2006), p. 472.

lead.[1728] The subjectivist approach in regard to impossible attempts is now firmly rooted in English law. Section 1(2) and (3) of the 1981 Criminal Attempts Act reads as follows:

> (2) A person may be guilty of attempting to commit an offence to which this section applies even though the facts are such that the commission of the offence is impossible.
> (3) in any case where –
>   (a) apart from this subsection a person's intention would not be regarded as having amounted to an intent to commit an offence; but
>   (b) if the facts of the case had been as he believed them to be, his intention would be so regarded, then, for the purposes of subsection (1) above, he shall be regarded as having an intent to commit that offence.

What matters thus is whether on the facts as the defendant believed them to be, the agent's conduct was *ex hypothesi*, more than merely preparatory. Generally, English law distinguishes two categories of impossible attempts. On the one hand there is the category of legal impossibility, wherein the defendant achieves everything that he set out to do, but contrary to what he believes the intended result does not constitute a criminal offence.[1729] In other words, an imaginary offence is committed. This category has proved uncontroversial in English criminal law. There seems to be a consensus that legal impossibility should not lead to criminal liability.[1730] The House of Lords endorsed this view in *R v Taaffe*.[1731] In this case the defendant, imported what he believed to be foreign currency into the United Kingdom, which he thought constituted a criminal offence. Effectively it did not and furthermore it turned out that the packages he attempted to smuggle did not contain currency but cannabis. The Court held:

> When the state of an accused person's mind and his knowledge were ingredients of the offence with which he was charged, he has to be judged on the facts as he believed them to be. Accordingly, since the respondent mistakenly believed that by clandestinely importing currency he was committing an offence, his mistake of law could not convert his action into the criminal offence of "being knowingly concerned" in the importation of a controlled drug […] since he had no guilty mind in respect of that offence.

The second category which has proved much more controversial over the years is the doctrine of factual impossibility. Under this category, cases are subsumed where

---

1728 Williams, 'The Lords and impossible attempts, or quis custodiet ipsos custodes?' Cambridge Law Journal (1986), p. 37, Fn 8.

1729 Arenson, 'The Pitfalls in the Law of Attempt: A new Perspective' The Journal of Criminal Law (2005), pp. 162 et seq.

1730 Simester and Sullivan, 'Criminal Law: Theory and Doctrine' (2007), p. 324.

1731 [1984] 1 AC 539.

the intended objective would have constituted a criminal offence but the completion of the crime was scuppered due to the existence of facts unbeknownst to the defendant.[1732] The House of Lords had to deal with such a case in *R v Shivpuri*.[1733] In this case the defendant was apprehended by custom officials while in possession of a suitcase. He admitted that it contained heroin, but analyses showed that the substance in the suitcase was snuff. The accused was charged with attempting to distribute heroin. On appeal the question arose whether factual impossibility would amount to a defence. The House of Lords gave the argument short shrift and held that the defendant intended to smuggle heroin, and that his conduct was more than merely preparatory in furtherance of this objective.

In the light of this decision it becomes clear that factual impossibility is no defence to the crime of attempt in the English penal system. It is sometimes argued that this amounts to punishing mere thoughts, or that a conviction in such cases would infringe the principle of legality.[1734] However, viewed from the subjectivist perspective, this outcome is absolute defensible, as the culpability of the actor for taking the risk that certain circumstances exist is not diminished by the objective fact that they do not.[1735] The actor has manifested his/her deviant proclivity and should accordingly be punished.

Form the foregoing it can be derived that English law utilises for the demarcation of (punishable) impossible attempts and (non-punishable) imaginary offences the distinction between mistakes of law and mistakes of fact. This distinction already follows from the wording of section 1 (2) of the 1983 Criminal Attempts Act which makes it clear that a given mistake must relate to *facts*. The rationale behind this distinction is arguably the following: if a mistake of fact generally negates mens rea (i.e. Simon shoots at what he believes to be a scarecrow, while in reality it is Paul), then a 'reverse' mistake of fact (i.e. Simon shoots at a scarecrow believing it to be Paul) will establish mens rea.

Is a mistake however generally irrelevant for criminal liability (mistake of law) also a reverse mistake of law cannot lead to liability.[1736] In other words, as it is generally irrelevant for imposing liability that one believed that sexual intercourse with a man would not constitute a criminal offence, also the reverse mistake that homosexual intercourse is prohibited by law cannot ground liability.

This theory thus strives to exclude from the realm of attempts all cases in which the object or the means lack the qualities enshrined by law. In other words, it

---

1732 Arenson, 'The Pitfalls in the Law of Attempt: A new Perspective' The Journal of Criminal Law (2005), pp. 162 et seq.

1733 [1986] 2 All ER 334.

1734 Hogan, 'The Criminal Attempts Act and Attempting the Impossible' Criminal Law Review (1984), pp. 584 et seq.

1735 Duff, 'Criminal Attempts' (1996), p. 163.

1736 Brockhaus, 'Die strafrechtliche Dogmatik von Vorbereitung, Versuch und Rücktritt im europäischen Vergleich' (2006), p. 368.

attempts to circumscribe the law of attempts by invoking formal factors.[1737] This reasoning based on an *argumentum a contrario*, however, also possesses some weaknesses.[1738] The problem here is that the distinction between factual and legal impossibility is not a hard and fast one but can sometimes be elusive. Much depends on the exact description of the case at hand. While the House of Lords in Shivpuri argued that the defendant erred about a factual component, it is also in theory possible to describe the facts in a way so that they would constitute legal impossibility. If one views Shivpuri's conduct as an attempt to evade a prohibition on the importation of a controlled drug, then he arguably committed a mistake of law as he was mistaken about whether the material in his possession was a controlled drug.[1739] Thus, an agreement about the proper description of an occurred conduct is necessary. Otherwise one will encounter difficulties to refute the claim that a certain analysis of a case is arbitrary.[1740]

8.4. The mixed approach: Impossibility in Germany

Corresponding to the prevalent mixed rationale for punishing attempts in Germany also the approach taken towards impossible attempts in this system shows an influence of objective as well as subjective factors. Subjective considerations come to the fore in the generic rule which follows from §23 (3) GPC that impossible attempts ought to be punishable. Objective considerations, on the other hand are discernible in the fact that imaginary offences, i.e. legal impossibility is not considered punishable as well as in the fact that pursuant to §23 (3) the courts may order a discharge, or mitigate the sentence if the offender due to gross ignorance about the causal facts and circumstances of the case fails to realise that his attempt could under no circumstances have led to the completion of the offence.[1741] One might refer to this category as impossible attempts due to a gross lack of judgment by the perpetrator (*Versuch aus grobem Unverstand*). This latter category however, has to be distinguished from superstitious attempts which in correspondence to the situation in England and the Netherlands is also thought not to give rise to criminal liability.[1742]

From this general outline it can already be deduced that the German approach to impossible attempts is characterised by a high degree of doctrinal complexity.[1743]

1737 Brockhaus, 'Die strafrechtliche Dogmatik von Vorbereitung, Versuch und Rücktritt im europäischen Vergleich' (2006), p. 479.

1738 See also: Roxin, 'Strafrecht Allgemeiner Teil, Band II: Besondere Erscheinungsformen der Straftat' (2003), pp. 466–469.

1739 Fletcher, 'Constructing a theory of impossible attempts' Criminal Justice Ethics (1986), p. 55.

1740 Fletcher, 'Constructing a theory of impossible attempts' Criminal Justice Ethics (1986), p. 56.

1741 Schönke and Schröder, 'Kommentar zum Strafgesetzbuch' (2006), §22 Mn 65.

1742 Roxin, 'Strafrecht Allgemeiner Teil, Band II: Besondere Erscheinungsformen der Straftat' (2003), pp. 455 et seq.

1743 This high degree of doctrinal complexity is of course not confined to impossible attempts. It is discernible throughout the whole German penal system.

The impossible attempt has to be distinguished from the imaginary offence, which in turn is distinguished from impossible attempts due to a gross lack of judgment, which is again distinct from the category of superstitious attempts. None of the investigated systems has adopted such a fine-grained approach towards impossible attempts, and it is submitted that it is overly complex and prone to give rise to intricate demarcation problems.

An attempt may be considered impossible in the German penal system, due to the unsuitability of the object, means or subject.[1744] While the first two categories are generally accepted to give rise to liability despite impossibility, the latter is a bone of contention, with the prevailing opinion seemingly favouring the imposition of liability. An attempt can for instance be considered impossible due to the unsuitability of the applied means if one attempts an abortion by administering a laxative. The Supreme Court for instance assumed an impossible attempt due to the unsuitability of the object in a case concerning the handling of stolen goods. The defendant in this case had bought heating oil below the regular market price. The oil was always delivered outside the supplier's business hours and he never received any delivery receipts, which strongly indicated that the oil stemmed from an illegal origin, which the defendant knew and was willing to accept. The exact origin of the oil could not be established which made it possible that the goods were in fact not stolen. The Supreme Court nevertheless upheld the conviction for attempted handling of stolen goods, because given the defendant's mens rea, it held that even if the goods were not stolen, this would still constitute a punishable impossible attempt due to the unsuitability of the object.[1745]

As already mentioned, impossible attempts need to be distinguished from imaginary offences. In short, the former are based on a misconception about facts, while the latter are based on a misconception about the law. While in impossible attempts, the perpetrator tries to achieve a result which would constitute a criminal offence were it not for the unsuitability of the object, means or subject, in an imaginary offence the perpetrator aims at a result that does not amount to an offence. Thus, one who shoots at a tree stump, believing it to be a human commits an impossible attempt, while one who shoots at a tree stump believing that this will amount to an offence commits an imaginary offence. That imaginary offences ought not to give rise to criminal liability is in Germany often deduced from the fundamental principle *nullum crimen sine lege*. Conduct, which the law does not proscribe, can never give rise to criminal liability it is said.[1746] Yet, an imaginary offence cannot only be based on a wrong assumption that certain behaviour has been criminalised, it can also be based on a mistake about the existence or scope of

---

[1744] Roxin, 'Strafrecht Allgemeiner Teil, Band II: Besondere Erscheinungsformen der Straftat' (2003), pp. 446–456, Schönke and Schröder, 'Kommentar zum Strafgesetzbuch' (2006), §22 Mn 71–72.

[1745] 2 February 1983 BGH NStZ 1983, 264.

[1746] Roxin, 'Strafrecht Allgemeiner Teil, Band II: Besondere Erscheinungsformen der Straftat' (2003), p. 458, Schönke and Schröder, 'Kommentar zum Strafgesetzbuch' (2006), §22 Mn 79.

a defence. It is at least conceivable that a person is unaware of the existence of an applicable justification or errs about its scope. If Jack for instance wounds a fleeing thief (by shooting him in the leg) to protect his property this may qualify as self-defence according to §32 GPC. If Jack however mistakenly believes that self-defence only covers cases where life or limb is threatened, he is not deemed to attempt to cause bodily harm, but rather commits an imaginary offence.[1747]

Closely connected to the cases of an assumption of a non-existent offence are scenarios in which the offence envisaged by the perpetrator does exist, but he mistakenly extends the scope of the offence so that it also covers his conduct. These cases are complex and problematic and have given rise to many doctrinal difficulties which have made the distinction between impossible attempts and imaginary offences even more difficult in the German penal system. The problem here is that if a person mistakenly extends the meaning or scope of a normative element of an existing offence, a (punishable) impossible attempt as well as a (non-punishable) imaginary offence can in theory be assumed. Consider for instance the example where a person mistakenly believes that according to German civil law, property rights will be transferred as soon as the buyer and seller have reached an agreement, despite the fact that the property has not been handed over yet. He has reached such an agreement with Norman about the purchase of a laptop. Soon after, Roy offers him more money for the laptop and he agrees to sell it to him and also hands over the laptop. As he believes that the property rights have already been transferred to Norman after reaching a selling agreement with him, he wrongly believes to commit an unlawful appropriation pursuant to §246 GPC. This is however not the case, as the chattel did legally not belong to another, as the property has not yet been handed over.[1748] Is one now dealing here with an impossible attempt of unlawful appropriation or with an imaginary offence? As a general rule it is accepted that mistakes of the perpetrator about circumstances will lead to the assumption of an impossible attempt, while mistakes about the exact content of the law lead to the finding of an imaginary offence.[1749] Yet, in cases such as the one above the perpetrator does not simply err about circumstances but neither entirely about the law's content. These difficulties can also arise in regard to omission liability. If the perpetrator for instance errs about the circumstances or facts of the case which could give rise to a duty to act and does not act, he will commit an impossible attempt. However, if he perceives the facts and circumstances correctly but wrongly assumes that he is under a duty to act on this basis, he will commit an imaginary offence.[1750]

1747 Roxin, 'Strafrecht Allgemeiner Teil, Band II: Besondere Erscheinungsformen der Straftat' (2003), p. 459. See also: 18 July 1985 BayObLG NJW 1986, 1504.

1748 See: Roxin, 'Strafrecht Allgemeiner Teil, Band II: Besondere Erscheinungsformen der Straftat' (2003), p. 461.

1749 Schönke and Schröder, 'Kommentar zum Strafgesetzbuch' (2006), §22 Mn 83.

1750 Bohlander, 'Principles of German Criminal Law' (2009), p. 145. See also: 15 May 1997 BGH NStZ 1997, 485.

The doctrinal difficulties arising from these cases have led some to plead for a simplification of the law in a similar way to the prevalent English approach, namely that any mistake of law should be considered to give rise to a (non-punishable) imaginary offence.[1751] Corresponding to doctrinal uncertainties the courts have taken an uneven and sometimes contradicting course in this area of the law. In a case where the defendant crashed his car under the influence of alcohol and sustained considerable injuries, but did not injure any property or other interests of third parties, the Supreme Court held that despite the fact that the defendant believed that he violated §142 GPC (leaving the scene of an accident without a cause) he had merely committed an imaginary offence as §142 only applied to accidents where other parties sustained injuries or damages.[1752] In another situation, where a woman had given wrongful statements under oath during the legal declaration of death of her brother, the Supreme Court assumed an impossible attempt. She wrongly assumed that by her statements she had committed perjury (§154 GPC), but the problem was that the authority in this proceedings was not competent to administer oaths. The court emphasised that she believed she was actually committing perjury and convicted her of an attempt.[1753]

Finally, German law distinguishes attempts where the offender due to gross ignorance about the causal facts and circumstances of the case fails to realise that the attempt could under no circumstances have led to the completion of the offence. This category is distinguished from superstitious attempts and imaginary attempts which are considered not punishable. As already mentioned, pursuant to §23 (3) the Courts may in these cases order a discharge or mitigate the sentence as it sees fit under §49 (2). This category is unknown to the Dutch as well as the English penal system. Presumably, more pragmatic and case-by-case orientated systems deem such a complex, dogmatic differentiation as unnecessary, especially given the low practical relevance of this category. It is submitted that considering the considerable dogmatic efforts necessary to distinguish this category from superstitious attempts in particular and the low practical relevance of these cases that such a distinction should not be made in a European criminal law. This is substantiated by the fact that until the time being, no case has ever reached the German Supreme Court where an attempt due to gross ignorance of causal facts has been accepted.

In any case, included under this category are scenarios which no person in his right mind would take seriously. The perpetrator in these cases fundamentally errs about the laws of nature, so that an impartial observer would figuratively speaking, shake his head in disbelieve and shout: "You moron!"[1754] One could thus subsume here cases where the perpetrator tries to shoot down an airplane travelling at high altitudes with his airgun or tries to poison his wife by using mint tea. The dividing

---

1751 Schönke and Schröder, 'Kommentar zum Strafgesetzbuch' (2006), §22 Mn 89.

1752 26 May 1955 BGH NJW 1955, 1078.

1753 16 September 1958 BGH NJW 1958, 1881.

1754 Roxin, 'Strafrecht Allgemeiner Teil, Band II: Besondere Erscheinungsformen der Straftat' (2003), p. 452, Schönke and Schröder, 'Kommentar zum Strafgesetzbuch' (2006), §23 Mn 17.

line between this category and superstitious attempts is sometimes elusive, but arguably, the difference lies in the fact that in superstitious attempts the offender tries to wield supernatural powers while in this category he "merely" errs about the laws of nature.

In England, such attempts could arguably be conceived as garden-variety impossible attempts without the possibility of a mitigation of punishment or a discharge. It is however more than questionable if a jury would ever consider a conviction in these cases.[1755] It is moreover debatable if such cases do deserve punishment at all. Arguably these cases are not grave enough, also taking into account their impression on a reasonable person, and do not constitute any endangerment of a protected legal interest to warrant the imposition of punishment.[1756] This also seems to correspond to the approach in the Netherlands where such attempts would most likely be qualified as absolute impossible attempts, as the applied means can under no circumstances and against no one, lead to the commission of the offence. In a pertinent case a woman tried to kill her husband by serving him a tea made of warm beer, sassafras and copper coins, six times a day during a three week period. The Supreme Court held that this would not amount to an attempt as she had applied means which were absolutely unsuitable to achieve the envisaged result.[1757] It is therefore submitted that this category of cases in a European context ought not to give rise to criminal liability, but should rather be seen as trifles with which the law is not concerned.

8.5. Concluding remarks

The foregoing discussion has shown that the approaches to impossible attempts are diverse and that large doctrinal differences exist. Therefore, it is exactly in this area of the law where the need for doctrinal discussion and at times unification would be the most pressing. Although, some common ground among the investigated penal systems can be discerned, it is submitted that the different doctrinal solutions adopted are irreconcilable. Large differences can especially be found in regard to the underlying rationale for punishing impossible attempts. The subjective English approach can arguably be described as forward-looking, focusing on crime prevention, while the more objectively orientated systems of Germany and the Netherlands adopt a more retrospective approach, focusing on retribution for the given wrongfulness of the defendant's conduct. It is submitted here that this rationale for the sake of coherence should correspond to the rationale for punishing attempts in general. Corresponding to the findings above, a mixed objective/

1755 See also: Brockhaus, 'Die strafrechtliche Dogmatik von Vorbereitung, Versuch und Rücktritt im europäischen Vergleich' (2006), pp. 484 et seq.

1756 Brockhaus, 'Die strafrechtliche Dogmatik von Vorbereitung, Versuch und Rücktritt im europäischen Vergleich' (2006), p. 485, Roxin, 'Strafrecht Allgemeiner Teil, Band II: Besondere Erscheinungsformen der Straftat' (2003), p. 454.

1757 HR 7 May 1906, *W* 8372.

subjective rationale is advocated here. Subjective factors will play a prominent role as the perpetrator's mens rea per definition, constitutes the primary ingredient of attempt liability. Moreover, arguably, the blameworthiness of a person who tries to kill by pouring sugar into his victim's tea because the pharmacist sold him icing sugar instead of arsenic is equivalent to the person who actually uses a poisonous substance. Furthermore, significant utilitarian reasons, i.e. to protect the public and social interests as well as considerations of crime prevention speak for the criminalisation of impossible attempts. Corresponding to this line of thought it is common ground that impossible attempts generally give rise to criminal liability in all investigated penal systems.

This general liability ought however to be circumscribed by objective factors to exclude cases where a need for punishment is absent as they, due to their very nature, are inapt and even inept to achieve the desired result under any circumstances. Under this heading superstitious and grossly daft attempts can be subsumed. They arguably are exempt from liability in all penal systems. The former are excluded as the law is not anymore concerned with supernatural events. Since the time of the inquisition criminal law abstains from punishing magic. *A fortiori* it should therefore neither impose punishment for attempted magic. The latter, it is submitted, should be excluded from liability as due to their daft nature they pose no conceivable threat for the legal order and will neither be considered threatening by the public and should therefore be considered trifles with which the law is not concerned.

Excluded from liability in all penal systems are further what one might term imaginary offences. This already follows from the principle *nullum crimen sine lege*. Even if the perpetrator's mind is guilty as he believes to be committing an offence, criminal liability cannot arise if the conduct is in fact not proscribed by law. If Amil wrongly believes that homosexuality constitutes a criminal offence in Europe and thinks to be liable for sleeping with his boyfriend Mark, he is nevertheless not criminally liable. As the envisaged offence is non-existent, it cannot be attempted either.

To demarcate punishable impossible attempts from non-punishable imaginary offences several distinct approaches have emerged in national law. One solution could thereby be to invoke the dichotomy between mistakes of law and mistakes of fact. While mistakes of fact generally negate mens rea, a reverse mistake of fact leads to the imposition of liability for an impossible attempt. Likewise, while a mistake of law generally does not exclude liability, a reverse mistake of law leads to the exclusion of liability for an imaginary offence.[1758] It has been argued that such an approach is to be preferred over a distinction along the lines of absolute and relative impossible attempts as the borderline between the two is vague and at times elusive. This is because it highly depends on the degree of abstraction allowed to enter the evaluation process and on which facts of the case at hand are to be taken

[1758] Brockhaus, 'Die strafrechtliche Dogmatik von Vorbereitung, Versuch und Rücktritt im europäischen Vergleich' (2006), p. 486.

into consideration. Such doctrinal insecurity may however be problematic from the point of view of legal certainty and foreseeability and should therefore be avoided.

Although the demarcation along the line of mistakes is also problematic as it is dependent on an agreement on the relevant description of the occurred conduct, it arguably provides a more reliant tool than the dichotomy of absolute and relative impossible attempts. The results achieved by the 'mistake approach' are seemingly also reconcilable with the situation in the Netherlands, where in effect the distinction between factual and legal impossibility is also accepted. The simplest solution to the problem at hand here would arguably be to prima facie declare all impossible attempts punishable but provide for a defence in case of legal impossibility and superstitious attempts. The European legislator could therefore clearly establish that impossible attempts generally ought to give rise to criminal liability.

9. Voluntary Withdrawal

9.1. Introduction

The absence of any tangible form of harm as a characteristic feature of attempt liability and the fact that the conduct occurred will frequently be innocuous and not signify manifest criminality, can raise the question of how to deal with cases where the would-be perpetrator experiences a sudden change of heart and voluntarily abandons his attempt. Should a person for instance profit from remorse which led him to desist after having the victim already in his aim? Or how about the shoplifter who after remembering the commandment "thou shall not steal" places the goods he had put in his rucksack, back on the shelf?

It has already been mentioned that one crucial rationale for punishing attempts in all penal systems is to allow timely intervention by law enforcement before any harm has manifested and to seize and restrain the socially dangerous. Arguably a genuine change of heart proves that intervention and restraint were unnecessary in that situation. Furthermore, on a more subjectivist note, it could be said that voluntary withdrawal shows that the actor is not as dangerous as initially thought, as his criminal will was insufficiently strong to carry through and is therefore not the type of person the law should be concerned with.[1759] Yet, whether or not one is willing to accept these arguments hinges to a large extent on ones generic conception of (attempt) liability. It is here where the differences between the English common law and the civil law approach to inchoate offences and more particularly, attempt liability become most visible.

In England once an actor has committed more than merely preparatory acts with the required mens rea, criminal liability is triggered unless a pertinent justification or excuse can be evoked. Thus, once the actus reus and mens rea of a criminal

1759 Fletcher, 'Rethinking Criminal Law' (1978), pp. 186, 190.

attempt are present, liability will ensue. Criminal attempts are accordingly seen as an offence in itself. Hence, once a person has exceeded the threshold of merely preparatory acts, it cannot make a difference whether the crime was not completed because of voluntary desistance or for any other conceivable reason.[1760] The general approach of English law is well-articulated by Lord Hailsham in *Haughton v Smith*:

> First, (the defendant) may simply change his mind before committing an act sufficiently overt to amount to an attempt. Second, he may change his mind, but too late to deny that he had got so far as an attempt. [...] In the first case no criminal attempt is committed. At the relevant time there was no mens rea since there had been a change of intention, and the only overt acts relied on would be preparatory and not immediately. In the second case there is both mens rea and an act connected immediately with the offence. [...] It follows that there is a criminal attempt.[1761]

Thus, if the actus reus and mens rea of an attempt can be established the actor has reached the point of no return and liability will be imputed.[1762]

Conversely, however, in the Netherlands and Germany, attempt liability is seen as a stage of development in the consummation of the offence, creating room for a person to change his mind and abandon the criminal enterprise. Corresponding to these different conceptions of attempt liability, English law does not acknowledge voluntary withdrawal as a defence.[1763] It needs however be noted that voluntary withdrawal is an important factor at the sentencing stage and frequently leads to mitigated punishment.[1764] In a pertinent case the defendant had desisted from his attempt to rape a young woman after she had forcefully told him to abstain from his deed. The Crown court had meted out three years imprisonment, which the Court of Appeal reduced to two, noting that "the fact that an assailant abandons his attack at a stage prior to grave sexual interference is clearly something to be taken into account in his favour".[1765]

Furthermore, also the generic question of what punishment is imposed for arguably plays a role here. If punishment is thought to be imposed for evil character then the relevance of voluntary withdrawal diminishes. As a person's character is usually not subject to sudden change and a voluntary withdrawal is unlikely to remove evil character traits, the idea of granting someone immunity in these cases becomes less convincing. If it is however choice and control for which punishment is imposed then it seems clear that an actor can and may change his mind while perusing a given task, creating more room for the defence. In accordance with the

---

1760 Smith and Hogan, 'Criminal Law' (2005), p. 419.

1761 Haughton v Smith [1975] AC 476.

1762 Simester and Sullivan, 'Criminal Law: Theory and Doctrine' (2007), p. 319.

1763 Simester and Sullivan, 'Criminal Law: Theory and Doctrine' (2007), p. 319, Smith and Hogan, 'Criminal Law' (2008), pp. 398–399.

1764 Arenson, 'The Pitfalls in the Law of Attempt: A new Perspective' The Journal of Criminal Law (2005), p. 162.

1765 R v Keith Neville Rackley [1994] 15 Cr App R (S) 794.

image of man advocated in a previous chapter, it is submitted that the latter view is to be preferred.[1766] To treat humans as responsible subjects of the law arguably requires accepting that they are responsible for their choices over which they exerted control, which necessarily entails that they can choose to change their mind which should be reflected in their degree of liability. It is therefore submitted that the law should generally provide room for a defence of voluntary withdrawal. The exact scope of the defence is however open to debate depending on the chosen rationale as well as pertinent considerations of criminal policy.[1767]

Conversely to the situation in the English penal system, in the Netherlands, the concept is recognised and has been enshrined in Article 46 (b). Article 46 (b) DPC provides that "neither preparation nor an attempt to commit a serious offense obtains where the serious offence has not been completed by reason only of circumstances dependent on the perpetrator's will".

Likewise §24 of the German penal code provides:

> (1) A person who of his own volition gives up the further execution of the offence or prevents its completion shall not be liable for the attempt. If the offence is not completed regardless of his actions that person shall not be liable if he has made a voluntary and earnest effort to prevent the completion of the offence.
> (2) If more than one person participate in the offence, the person who voluntarily prevents its completion shall not be liable for the attempt. His voluntary and earnest effort to prevent the completion of the offence shall suffice for exemption from liability, if the offence is not completed regardless of his actions or is committed independently of his earlier contribution to the offence.

Both systems thus allow a person to escape liability in case he forestalls the consummation of the criminal offence and therefore the occurrence of harm initially envisaged. Preconditions for this escape route are in both systems that the actor has entered the attempt phase and that at the time of the withdrawal the offence in question could still be completed. If the latter is due to certain factors impossible, one speaks of a failed attempt, where the issue of voluntary withdrawal cannot arise.

9.2. Rationales for accepting voluntary withdrawal

The reasons for allowing someone to withdraw from an attempted offence, resulting in a full acquittal for the attempted offence are controversial. Over the years a multitude of diverse theories have emerged, which cannot all be discussed here. This research will confine itself to providing a brief overview of the most prominent rationales before further investigating the requirements of voluntary withdrawal.

1766 See: Chapter II. 2.2.
1767 See: Chapter IV. 9.2.

One popular argument discussed in all three penal systems is that the promise of immunity from sanctions will provide an incentive for attempters to desist from committing the offence.[1768] The Dutch legislator for instance when introducing Article 46 (b) DPC claimed that the safest way to prevent the commission of an offence is to grant immunity to the person who freely chooses to abandon his criminal endeavour. For this reason the law ought to pave the way for the offender's reintegration into society.[1769] Without the incentive of immunity from punishment, a person who has already progressed to the attempt phase with his conduct would more or less be forced to consummate the offence as he would know that remorse will not affect his liability in any way, so it is argued. The idealistic appeal of this argument certainly lies in the fact that it seems to recognise and respect the intrinsic value of the offender as a responsible agent. However, this argument, it is submitted is not entirely convincing and might in essence rather constitute a criminal policy orientated wishful thinking. It is highly doubtful that criminal offenders when embarking on a criminal enterprise are aware when they pass the threshold of attempt liability, let alone are aware of the possibility and effects of a voluntary withdrawal.[1770]

Another argument in favour of voluntary withdrawal is that abandonment demonstrates that the actor's intent to commit the criminal wrong was not as firm as to warrant criminal liability.[1771] This argument has close ties to subjective rationales of attempt. This goes to show that a subjective approach generally does not entirely foreclose the acceptance of voluntary withdrawal. Some English authors have therefore sought to create room for the defence by relying on the notion of mens rea, which in case of withdrawal is perceived as half-formed or provisional.[1772] The prevalent English view however rejects this approach by adopting a forward-looking view, geared at crime prevention and emphasises the actor's culpability once he has committed more than merely preparatory acts. In any case, while this approach would, as stated, sit nicely with a pure subjective conception of attempt liability it seems less convincing if, as is advocated here, one also deems objective factors relevant for attempt liability. Yet, it is submitted that the different theories need not be mutually exclusive and that a wide combination of factors may explain the immunity granted for voluntary withdrawal. Therefore the rationales for

1768 Roxin, 'Strafrecht Allgemeiner Teil, Band II: Besondere Erscheinungsformen der Straftat' (2003), pp. 482–484, Smith and Hogan, 'Criminal Law' (2008), pp. 398–399.

1769 See: Noyon, Langemeijer, Remmelink, 'Wetboek van Strafrecht' (2010), Art 46b, note 2.

1770 Roxin, 'Strafrecht Allgemeiner Teil, Band II: Besondere Erscheinungsformen der Straftat' (2003), p. 484, Smith and Hogan, 'Criminal Law' (2008), p. 399.

1771 De Hullu, 'Materieel Strafrecht' (2009), pp. 414–415, Fletcher, 'Rethinking Criminal Law' (1978), pp. 186 et seq, Machielse, 'Vrijwillig terugtreden in Nederland en Duitsland', in Harteveld, et al. (eds), Systeem in Ontwikkeling – Liber amicorum G. Knigge (2005), pp. 417–418.

1772 Brockhaus, 'Die strafrechtliche Dogmatik von Vorbereitung, Versuch und Rücktritt im europäischen Vergleich' (2006), p. 382, Williams, 'Criminal Law: The General Part' (1953), p. 620.

punishing attempts, as will soon become apparent, can exert a reversed influence to ground immunity.

One argument, combining different rationales is that if a person abandons his enterprise before any harm is caused, this shows that the threat of criminal punishment has had a deterrent effect. The offender's will was not firm enough to go through with the crime and to punish him despite his change of heart would be futile. Thus, neither considerations of special prevention nor of general prevention would make the imposition of punishment necessary, as the offender has not proven as dangerous as first feared and needs therefore not be deterred from committing crimes in the future. Furthermore, the voluntary withdrawal mitigates the social apprehension felt by society (in regard to criminal attempts) and leads to a feeling of relief which warrants impunity. In short, in case of a withdrawal there is nothing warranting punishment conceivable in legal reality. This approach seems to be the prevalent in German literature and is also the one frequently invoked by the Supreme Court.[1773] However, it fits also the more objective orientated Dutch law of attempts, where the apprehension felt by society by a criminal act often plays a significant role.[1774] Perhaps in combination with the 'incentive' theory outlined above, these rationales can provide a sound doctrinal as well as a criminal policy rationale in favour of accepting immunity for voluntary abandonment in a European criminal law.

9.3. The nature of the exception

Besides the rationale for accepting voluntary withdrawal in a respective penal system the nature of this exemption from liability is crucial from a systematic point of view. Depending on which of the rationales one wishes to follow the character of the withdrawal changes. If one thinks for instance that by voluntarily withdrawing the actor cancelled out his culpable attempt then withdrawal becomes a factor extinguishing guilt.[1775] On the other hand, if one believes that by withdrawing the wrongfulness of the deed is diminished, withdrawal becomes a factor generally removing wrongfulness. Especially this latter view is problematic as it would mean that in multiple actor scenarios participants could profit from the withdrawal of the principal, as by removing the wrongfulness of the deed also the basis for deriving liability of the participants would be removed. This would however, it is submitted be an unacceptable outcome. It seems difficult to justify why participants who themselves may remain fully committed to the criminal enterprise should profit

[1773] Roxin, 'Strafrecht Allgemeiner Teil, Band II: Besondere Erscheinungsformen der Straftat' (2003), pp. 478–481, Schönke and Schröder, 'Kommentar zum Strafgesetzbuch' (2006), §24 Mn 2b. See also: 28 February 1956 BGH NJW 1956, 718.

[1774] Machielse, 'Vrijwillig terugtreden in Nederland en Duitsland', in Harteveld, et al. (eds), Systeem in Ontwikkeling – Liber amicorum G. Knigge (2005), p. 419.

[1775] Schönke and Schröder, 'Kommentar zum Strafgesetzbuch' (2006), §24 Mn 4.

from the change of heart of one of their partners in crime with which they had nothing to do.

If one, as is proposed here, merely denies the concrete necessity to impose punishment in the case of withdrawal, the exception becomes a personal reason for exemption from punishment. If immunity constitutes a reward for the actor for returning to the 'righteous path' then it follows that those who do not achieve such an accomplishment cannot profit from the reward.[1776] This constitutes the prevalent view in the German penal system.[1777]

The exact nature of the exception used to be a bone of contention in the Netherlands. The legislator attempted to end the discussion in 1994 by inserting Article 46 (b) into the criminal code. In the explanatory memorandum the legislator pointed out that Art 46 (b) would exclude liability as a perpetrator which had to lead to an acquittal. If the perpetrator voluntarily withdraws the wrongdoing of the deed would be diminished to such an extent that no imposition of punishment was warranted. This approach was however criticised in literature, as already mentioned, a removal of wrongdoing would also affect the liability of potential accomplices.[1778] It is therefore often submitted that voluntary withdrawal should "merely" function as an exemption from punishment which would exclude accessories form the effects of a withdrawal.[1779] The Dutch Supreme Court seems to have perceived these far flung effects and adopts the prevalent view in literature nowadays.[1780]

9.4. The constituent elements of withdrawal

9.4.1. Categories of attempts

In order to determine at which stage voluntary withdrawal is still open to the criminal actor and what exactly will be required from him to be able to invoke the exemption several factors play a role. First and foremost, it is a prerequisite that the criminal result or harm has not yet occurred. This means that an actor will not be able to rely on the exemption if the criminal harm has manifested itself even despite his efforts to prevent it. Thus, if Jim, with the intent to kill shoots at Pavel and subsequently regrets his actions when he sees his injured victim and drives him to

---

1776 Machielse, 'Vrijwillig terugtreden in Nederland en Duitsland', in Harteveld, et al. (eds), Systeem in Ontwikkeling – Liber amicorum G. Knigge (2005), p. 421.

1777 Schönke and Schröder, 'Kommentar zum Strafgesetzbuch' (2006), §24 Mn 4.

1778 De Hullu, 'Materieel Strafrecht' (2009), p. 411, Kelk, 'Studieboek materieel strafrecht' (2005), p. 321.

1779 De Hullu, 'Materieel Strafrecht' (2009), p. 411, Kelk, 'Studieboek materieel strafrecht' (2005), p. 321.

1780 See: HR 12 April 2005, *LJN* AS6095. The situation is however not yet entirely resolved. For a recent verdict in which the Supreme Court *obiter* held that instigators and aiders may profit from the perpetrator's withdrawal see: HR 12 April 2011, *NJ* 2011, 358.

the hospital but Pavel's injuries are beyond remedy and dies, Jim will nevertheless be liable for the homicide. From this it also follows that the exemption will be excluded when the result materialises despite the withdrawal of the offender. Accordingly, if Lee plans to kill his vicious mother in law by spiking her morning coffee with mercury and believes that at least five dosages will be needed to get rid of her, but subsequently abandons his attempt after administering only two dosages, Lee will be liable for murder if his mother in law dies after the second dosage as the heavy metal was more potent than expected. Arguably, the futile efforts of the principal can however be taken into consideration at the sentencing stage and lead to a mitigation of punishment.[1781]

Furthermore, a voluntary withdrawal will not be possible if the offender's attempt has failed. This is the case when the offender's goal can no longer be achieved. For instance, Manny has fired all his shots at Alice but Alice stands unharmed, the oxygen cutting equipment with which Omar tries to open a safe has broken down, or the victim of a robbery realises that the gun pointed at him is a replica and refuses to hand over his wallet.[1782]

Failed attempts, i.e. where the intended goal can no longer be achieved, have to be distinguished from complete and incomplete attempts respectively. This distinction is crucial here in order to set out the requirements for accepting a claim of voluntary withdrawal. The distinction is well expressed in §24 GPC which holds that "a person who of his own volition gives up the further execution of the offence or prevents its completion shall not be liable for the attempt". It follows that in case of an incomplete offence, simple desistance might suffice to be granted immunity, while in the case of a complete attempt, a concrete "*actus contrarius*" will be required.[1783]

Distinguishing complete and incomplete attempts

In practice it can sometimes be difficult to distinguish between complete and incomplete attempts. Which criteria should be used to distinguish these two notions? Should the evaluation take place *ex ante* or *ex post*? Also here a subjective and an objective approach are distinguishable. The objective approach claims that the distinction between complete and incomplete attempts should be drawn by looking at the objective impression, the outward manifestation, the occurred conduct made on society, i.e. the legal order. Conversely, a subjective approach places the emphasis on the subjective plan, i.e. the intention, of the perpetrator.

The two approaches lead to different scopes of the exemption which can be adequately demonstrated by comparing the German and the Dutch approach to

---

1781 See: Roxin, 'Strafrecht Allgemeiner Teil, Band II: Besondere Erscheinungsformen der Straftat' (2003), p. 521.

1782 Roxin, 'Strafrecht Allgemeiner Teil, Band II: Besondere Erscheinungsformen der Straftat' (2003), pp. 502 et seq. See also: AG Vellinga in HR 21 Augustus 2007, *LJN* BA5019.

1783 See also: De Hullu, 'Materieel Strafrecht' (2009), p. 412. HR 3 March 2009, *NJ* 2009, 236.

voluntary withdrawal. Corresponding to their respective rationales for penalising attempts, the Netherlands adopt an objective approach to demarcate the different categories of attempts, while in the German penal system a subjective approach is prevalent. In line with the general subjective approach to attempt liability in Germany, the subjective view of the offender is also determinative in regard to voluntary withdrawal and not whether the attempt is objectively complete, incomplete or failed. In this context German law speaks of the 'withdrawal horizon'.

This means that an attempt will be considered incomplete with the result that simple desistance will suffice for voluntary withdrawal as long as the offender at the moment when the withdrawal takes place, has in his view not done everything necessary to achieve his goal, but believes, even if mistakenly, that by simply continuing to act he could reach it.[1784] In other words, he believes that the envisaged result will not yet manifest. It follows that a complete attempt can transform into an incomplete and vice versa, depending on the perpetrator's view. If the offender for instance, after his last action thinks that he has done everything to bring about the envisaged result, but subsequently reassesses the situation and now believes that the result will not manifest without further steps, he can withdraw by merely desisting from further conduct. The converse situation can present itself if the offender first believed that he has not done everything to bring about the desired result, but subsequently realises that his conduct thus far proved sufficient to achieve his goal. This can become especially relevant in regard to homicide where it will often be difficult for the offender to determine whether the inflicted injuries are already lethal or not.

To shed some light on this subjective approach, consider the following case. The defendant had stabbed the victim with *dolus eventualis* to kill in the neck. The victim however remained conscious and a fight followed after which the victim lay on the ground, but was still able to speak to the defendant. The defendant subsequently left the room which allowed the victim to flee through the living room window. Despite life-threatening injuries, the doctors managed to save the victim. The German Supreme Court held that the facts of the case constituted an incomplete attempt from which the defendant could withdraw by desistance (as he had not pursued the victim). It stressed that in regard to the demarcation of complete and incomplete attempts, the view of the offender was decisive. Even though, the defendant at some point might have thought that he had done everything necessary to kill the victim, he must have changed his assessment of the situation at the moment when the victim managed to flee through the window, so the argument went.[1785]

1784 See: Schönke and Schröder, 'Kommentar zum Strafgesetzbuch' (2006), §24 Mn 12 et seq. Roxin, 'Strafrecht Allgemeiner Teil, Band II: Besondere Erscheinungsformen der Straftat' (2003), p. 528.

1785 16 February 1993 BGH NJW 1993, 2125. See also: 21 January 1998 BGH NStZ-RR 1998,134, 8 February 2007 BGH NStZ 2007, 399.

Such a subjective approach thus provides offenders with more room to invoke voluntary withdrawal and constitutes a withdrawal-friendly approach by jurisprudence. To justify such a withdrawal-friendliness the Supreme Court often invokes the interests of the victim. Arguably, if the victim survives the initial attack, it is in his interest to deter the offender from continuing his efforts by allowing him to withdraw by mere desistance. This applies especially to homicide attempts where an offender might be inclined to finish what he started in order to rid himself of a potential witness and to cover up his deed.[1786]

This approach can however lead to peculiar results, especially in regard to particularly dangerous acts of violence. Is it really acceptable that an offender who hits his victim on the head with a hammer but then desists from finishing what he started and leaves the victim to his fate, profits from voluntary withdrawal only because he believed that the injuries were not yet lethal? Although the German Supreme Court has always been quite strict in these cases, in recent jurisprudence it seems as if the court has increased the stringency of the applied standard in those scenarios. Seemingly the court has taken a more normative approach and nowadays considers not only the offender's conception of the situation as decisive, but rather the (reasonable) conception which he should have had according to the circumstances of the case.

In a pertinent decision, A and B set out to assault C, the owner of a local pub. A stabbed C in the arm and B, an amateur boxer, hit C with *dolus eventualis* to kill with a barstool on the head. C sustained a base skull fracture and collapsed behind the bar. Subsequently A and B left the Pub and C was rescued by the emergency services that were called by two guests who had witnessed the attack. The Court of lower instance had assumed an incomplete attempt as the defendants at the time they left the pub had not thought that C was dead and accepted voluntary withdrawal by desistance. The Supreme Court however overruled the decision and held that in regard to especially dangerous acts of violence carried out with *dolus eventualis* to kill, an incomplete attempt can only be assumed if circumstances can be proven that in an overall assessment allow the conclusion that the offender after his final action did not consider the manifestation of the deadly result possible.[1787]

The approach taken in these cases and in general to the conundrum of demarcating complete from incomplete attempts, is notably different in the Netherlands. As already mentioned, the Dutch penal systems also in the realm of voluntary withdrawal takes a much more objective approach than the German penal system. A more objective approach will for the demarcation at stake here look more at what the perpetrator has already done to achieve his goal, while the more

1786 See for instance: 19 May 1993 BGH NStZ 1993, 433. See also: Puppe, 'Die Rechtsprechung des BGH zum Rücktrittshorizont' Zeitschrift für Internationale Strafrechtsdogmatik (2011), pp. 524–530.

1787 8 December 2010 BGH NStZ 2011, 209. See also: Puppe, 'Die Rechtsprechung des BGH zum Rücktrittshorizont' Zeitschrift für Internationale Strafrechtsdogmatik (2011), pp. 524–530.

subjective approach in Germany will ask if the perpetrator after he completed his action knew that he did not need to take any further steps to achieve his goal.[1788]

For instance, in a case where the defendant attempted to kill his brother with a crowbar and severely injured him, but in the course of the beating changed his mind and stopped the beating, the Dutch Supreme Court held that given the actions of the perpetrator and the serious injuries inflicted (the victim had *inter alia* suffered a pneumothorax) that the attempt was completed and that simple desistance would not suffice for withdrawal here. Conversely, in Germany, as has been shown, such cases can be seen as incomplete attempts, with the result that desistance will suffice to invoke voluntary withdrawal. Thus, an objective approach will often at an earlier point in time conclude that the attempt was complete, thereby excluding the possibility of withdrawing by mere desistance, leaving only the possibility to withdraw by an *actus contrarius*.

Distinguishing incomplete and failed attempts

A further crucial difference between an objective and a subjective approach to withdrawal comes to the fore in the context of distinguishing failed from incomplete attempts. As already mentioned, this distinction is crucial as in regard to failed attempts generally no withdrawal is considered possible. One can distinguish different approaches here. It is for instance possible to view every single act which the offender deems suited to achieve the desired result as a separate attempt.[1789] If the desired result is not brought about by this act, the attempted is considered to have failed with the result that no withdrawal is subsequently possible. Thus, if the offender believed he could kill the victim by striking his head with a wooden post, then the attempt has failed if the result did not ensue, even if he had in mind from the very beginning to suffocate the victim should the first means fail. More clearly stated, an offender shooting at his victim with a revolver, loaded with six bullets, would have committed a failed attempt from which no withdrawal is possible after the first bullet has missed its target.

Another approach focuses on the offender's plan before he embarked on the commission of the offence. Once he has taken the last step in his plan and the desired result has not occurred the attempt is considered to have failed. Thus, if in the aforementioned example the offender had planned to kill the victim with the wooden post, his attempt would have failed after the strike failed to achieve the result. If he had however contemplated from the beginning that he might also strangle the victim, the attempt would be considered to be incomplete leaving the offender with the possibility to voluntarily withdraw from the enterprise. As a result, the offender with a well-conceived plan would be able to invoke the exception

[1788] Machielse, 'Vrijwillig terugtreden in Nederland en Duitsland', in Harteveld, et al. (eds), Systeem in Ontwikkeling – Liber amicorum G. Knigge (2005), pp. 417–428.

[1789] Roxin, 'Strafrecht Allgemeiner Teil, Band II: Besondere Erscheinungsformen der Straftat' (2003), p. 535.

while an offender with an ill-conceived plan would be deprived of this opportunity. As will subsequently become apparent, this seems to be the approach adopted by Dutch jurisprudence

Finally, it is possible to adopt a holistic approach and to consider an attempt as incomplete, even if singular actions of the offender have failed, as long as his conduct is part of a coherent event, directly connected to his previous steps and the offender can continue his attempt with a chance of success.[1790] The focus in this approach thus lies on the point in time when the decision to withdraw was made rather than focusing on the plan of the defendant when he initially set out to commit the offence. Holistically viewed, the aforementioned example regarding the assault with a wooden post and the subsequent attempt to suffocate the victim would be seen as a coherent event from which the offender could withdraw by simple desistance. In the case of the shooter firing a revolver loaded with six bullets, the offender can withdraw by desistance even after several bullets have missed the target, as long as he gave up the possibility to fire, with a chance of success, further shots at the victim. This approach thus broadens the concept of incomplete attempts by adopting a holistic approach, granting offenders much room to withdraw. Thus, if the perpetrator after taking all the steps in his (failed) initial plan sees another possibility to achieve his goal but does not take it because of a sudden change of heart, he will be able to invoke voluntary withdrawal to escape attempt liability. As already mentioned, this situation may frequently be the case in homicide cases.

The latter approach is the prevalent in the German penal system, where the courts have considered a withdrawal possible, as long the offender's conduct can be seen as a coherent event, in the sense of a close temporal and spatial proximity between the already-performed actions and those from which he desisted.[1791]

In a pertinent case A intended to force a slot machine to be handed over by using violence if necessary. Together with two friends he drove to the warehouse of the company equipped with a knife and a loaded pump gun. Initially, the gun was left behind in the car. First he threatened the owner of the company and an employee with the knife, but as this proved to be unsuccessful he fetched the pump gun to intensify his efforts. Yet, the victims were not threatened and resisted the offenders which forced them to retreat. The Court of lower instance had rejected the claim of withdrawal, as the offenders' initial plan, according to its view had failed. Yet, the Supreme Court overruled the Court of lower instance and emphasised that the offenders' initial plan was not decisive in determining whether or not an attempt had failed, but that it was rather the defendant's subjective perception of the situation at hands. If he was of the opinion that he could still achieve his goal, albeit maybe by applying other means (e.g. firing the rifle, etc.), then the attempt was to be

[1790] Roxin, 'Strafrecht Allgemeiner Teil, Band II: Besondere Erscheinungsformen der Straftat' (2003), p. 535.

[1791] Schönke and Schröder, 'Kommentar zum Strafgesetzbuch' (2006), §24 Mn 13–17c.

considered incomplete with the result that desistance form further steps would amount to a voluntary withdrawal.[1792]

This decision is a good comparison to a similar Dutch case which will reveal the repercussions of the different approaches taken in the two systems on the scope of the exemption. In this case three girls had attempted to rob a cigar store in Amsterdam. They had entered the store and threatened the shopkeeper with a gun. The shopkeeper was however not intimidated by the weapon and remarked belittlingly: "and now?" Flabbergasted the three girls subsequently left the shop. The Court of lower instance had rejected the claim of withdrawal as the girl's initial plan had failed and the Dutch Supreme Court upheld the judgment.[1793] Thus, by taking the plan of the attempter as a starting point, an attempt has failed and no withdrawal is possible anymore in the Dutch penal system, if the perpetrator has taken all the steps of his plan and the envisaged result has not followed. In these cases, Dutch jurisprudence will come to the conclusion that the result has not occurred due to circumstances *independent* of the perpetrator's will and exclude the possibility of voluntary withdrawal. This will also be the case if the perpetrator after taking all the steps in his initial plan sees another possibility to achieve his goal but does not take it because of a sudden change of heart.

The differences are perhaps revealed even more clearly if one juxtaposes two pertinent cases of attempted homicide. In a Dutch case a man had attempted to kill a sleeping woman by connecting two wires of a cable to her toes and plugging the cable in the socket. The woman awoke from the pain, but did not die from the electricity and the man unplugged the cable.[1794] The Supreme Court rejected the plea of voluntary withdrawal, because the man had only unplugged the cable after his attempt had failed due to circumstances independent of his will, i.e. that the woman had not died from the electric shock.

In a similar German decision A had poured petrol over his wife because she threatened to divorce him. He however did not manage to ignite the petrol with his matches and after a short struggle the wife was able to flee. A pursued her and subsequently strangled the victim until she temporarily lost consciousness. Yet, allegedly due to a sudden change of heart he desisted from finishing what he had started and left the scene. The Court of lower instance had rejected voluntary withdrawal but the German Supreme Court overruled the judgment and held that despite the fact that his initial plan had failed the offender had realised that he could still accomplish his goal by applying another means (strangulation) from which he had voluntarily withdrawn.[1795] The court thus adopted a holistic approach and viewed the two attempts as a coherent event which amounted to an incomplete attempt.

1792 26 September 2006 BGH NStZ 2007, 91.

1793 HR 21 August 2007, *LJN* BA5019.

1794 HR 19 April 1983, *NJ* 1983, 573.

1795 7 February 1986 BGH NStZ 1986, 264.

It becomes apparent that Dutch jurisprudence would assume in those cases that the attempt had failed and exclude voluntary withdrawal, while in Germany, where a more subjective stance is taken withdrawal would still be possible if the perpetrator had realised that he can still achieve his goal by another means. Thus, Dutch jurisprudence which focuses more on the initial plan of the offender will be more inclined to divide what in Germany is seen as a coherent event, into separate parts. The fact that the offender in this case did not succeed in igniting the petrol would in the Netherlands most likely be seen as an event independent of the perpetrator's will and thus lead to the finding of a failed attempt, from which no withdrawal will be possible.[1796]

It can be deduced from the foregoing that Dutch jurisprudence generally adopts a more objective approach to voluntary withdrawal which substantially limits the availability of the exemption in practice. Due to the focus on the offender's subjective 'withdrawal horizon' German law provides more room than Dutch law for incomplete attempts with the result that desistance will more often exempt the offender from liability in Germany than in the Netherlands. Conversely, by emphasising the initial plan of the offender Dutch law will more easily assume a failed attempt, while in Germany, where a holistic approach is prevalent, a failed attempt is less readily found.

9.4.2. Voluntariness

As already mentioned, the core issue in the realm of withdrawal is whether it was voluntary, which finds expression in the Dutch penal system in the phrase that the offence must not have been completed by reason only of circumstances dependent on the perpetrator's will. Also §24 GPC makes it clear that the offender must give up the further execution of the offence out *of his own volition*.[1797] Thus, the crucial point here is to distinguish and prove a bona fide change of heart from withdrawal prompted by outside forces such as fear of police presence or surveillance. This distinction, admittedly, is not always easy to draw. This difficulty is sometimes used in the English system to reject the possibility of voluntary withdrawal altogether. It would be too difficult for a court to satisfy itself of the voluntary nature of the withdrawal that the matter is much better dealt with at the sentencing stage, so the argument runs.[1798] The English penal system thus is of the opinion that the incentive for abandonment created by the defence would be outweighed by prospective struggles created by the difficulties to be encountered by courts.[1799] While there arguably is some truth in this argument, there are nevertheless certain

1796 Machielse, 'Vrijwillig terugtreden in Nederland en Duitsland', in Harteveld, et al. (eds), Systeem in Ontwikkeling – Liber amicorum G. Knigge (2005), p. 426.

1797 Emphasis added.

1798 Ashworth, 'Principles of criminal law' (2006), p. 467.

1799 Arenson, 'The Pitfalls in the Law of Attempt: A new Perspective' The Journal of Criminal Law (2005), p. 162.

theories available which can be invoked to separate bona fide changes of heart from withdrawals prompted by other factors which negate voluntariness. Furthermore, it is submitted that an exploration of voluntariness is perhaps more adequately dealt with in a trial setting rather than at the sentencing stage.

Generally, one can distinguish a psychological and a normative approach in regard to voluntariness. According to the psychological approach, a withdrawal is voluntary if the offender acted free from psychological coercion. On the other hand a withdrawal is considered involuntary if the circumstances of the situation exerted such pressure on the offender that he had no other choice than to withdraw.[1800] The theory thus draws a distinction between autonomous and not autonomous motives from withdrawal. If the decision to withdraw emanated from the offender's own free will, voluntariness will be assumed. If the decision was however prompted by external stimuli, the withdrawal will be involuntary.

Yet, for the normative approach, a psychological evaluation is not necessary. What is decisive for distinguishing voluntariness from involuntariness is rather an assessment of the withdrawal motive. A withdrawal will only be considered voluntary if it can be seen as an 'inversion', an expression of a changed attitude, i.e. a return to the righteous path.[1801] The normative theory is often defended in German literature, but jurisprudence largely adopts the psychological approach, which is also the prevalent approach in the Netherlands.[1802] Thus, as a yardstick in both systems one can apply the following formula: a withdrawal will be considered voluntary if the offender thinks 'I do not wish to carry on even if I could', while it will be involuntary if he thinks 'I cannot carry on even if I wanted to'.[1803]

According to this approach, a withdrawal will certainly not be accepted if the attempt has failed or was impossible. The burglar whose jemmy breaks during the attempt to force a door open or is fought off by the victim clearly does not abandon the attempt voluntarily.[1804] Furthermore, a withdrawal is generally deemed involuntary if the perpetrator has abandoned the criminal enterprise because of the intervention of the police[1805], fear of detection[1806], detection by the victim, etc. In regard to the latter one will however have to differentiate. If it was the offender's

1800 Roxin, 'Strafrecht Allgemeiner Teil, Band II: Besondere Erscheinungsformen der Straftat' (2003), p. 591.

1801 Roxin, 'Strafrecht Allgemeiner Teil, Band II: Besondere Erscheinungsformen der Straftat' (2003), p. 591.

1802 Schönke and Schröder, 'Kommentar zum Strafgesetzbuch' (2006), §24 Mn 43. 26 September 2006 BGH NStZ 2007, 91. Noyon, Langemeijer, Remmelink, 'Wetboek van Strafrecht' (2010), Art 46b, note 4.

1803 This formula is the so called Frank's formula, named after a well known German academic.

1804 Schönke and Schröder, 'Kommentar zum Strafgesetzbuch' (2006), §24 Mn 46 et seq. Noyon, Langemeijer, Remmelink, 'Wetboek van Strafrecht' (2010), Art 46b, note 4.

1805 HR 25 October 1988, *NJ* 1989, 456. 1 February 2005 BGH NJW 2005, 1205.

1806 HR 12 April 2005, *LJN* AS6095. Schönke and Schröder, 'Kommentar zum Strafgesetzbuch' (2006), §24 Mn 57.

plan from the outset to commit the deed in the open detection need not necessarily lead to an involuntary withdrawal. If it was however the offender's plan to act stealthily, then detection may indeed indicate involuntariness.[1807]

To achieve reasonable outcomes and to make the evaluation process more concrete one could invoke here a more normative criterion and base the assessment of voluntariness on the view of a 'reasonable criminal'. Thus if an offender withdraws without any reasonable grounds from the viewpoint of a criminal mind (e.g. because of remorse) from his enterprise, the withdrawal can be considered voluntary. If his conduct is however prudent from the point of view of a reasonable criminal, then the withdrawal will most likely be involuntary.[1808] In a Dutch case a withdrawal was for instance deemed involuntary in the case of a sailor who after the captain had ordered a cabin search to investigate some petty theft had confessed to the captain that he had 8 kilos of cocaine in his cabin. The court held that given the fact that the sailor, had no chance to hide the cocaine after the cabin search was ordered, the completion of the offence had been prevented by circumstances independent of the defendant's will, namely the likely detection of his cargo during the search.[1809]

The difference between the German and Dutch approach to voluntariness is however once again that the Dutch penal system generally adopts a more objective approach while in Germany voluntariness is determined according to the view of the perpetrator at the time when the decision was made. Yet, this may also in Germany be inferred from external circumstances and may be based on general experience.

It is in any case however not necessary that the defendant withdrew out of morally praiseworthy motives. The law is not interested whether or not the defendant withdrew due to a moral epiphany, but the law's focus is rather to prevent the occurrence of harm.[1810] Neither is it necessary that only internal factors played a role in the withdrawal. Also external factors can play a role, as long as the contribution of the perpetrator remains significant. A pertinent example of such a case in the Dutch penal system is one of attempted rape. The defendant had introduced himself to the seventeen year old victim as a movie producer and had lured her to his flat. There he told the victim to re-enact a bank robbery due to which the victim agreed to being tied up. The victim only grew suspicious when he dragged her on a mattress and began to undress her. The victim tried to resist and

---

1807 Mallens and Hornman, 'Vrijwillige terugtred bij poging' Delikt en Delinkwent (2010), pp. 78 et seq. See also: 8 February 2007 BGH NStZ 2007, 399.

1808 Mallens and Hornman, 'Vrijwillige terugtred bij poging' Delikt en Delinkwent (2010), pp. 78 et seq, Roxin, 'Strafrecht Allgemeiner Teil, Band II: Besondere Erscheinungsformen der Straftat' (2003), p. 600. Noyon, Langemeijer, Remmelink, 'Wetboek van Strafrecht' (2010), Art 46b, note 4.

1809 HR 25 October 1988, *NJ* 1988, 456.

1810 De Hullu, 'Materieel Strafrecht' (2009), p. 414, Roxin, 'Strafrecht Allgemeiner Teil, Band II: Besondere Erscheinungsformen der Straftat' (2003), p. 599. See also: 23 August 1979 BGH NJW 1980, 602.

finally asked the perpetrator "what sense would it make to rape me?" This statement seemingly brought the man to his senses and he desisted from raping the woman. The Supreme Court accepted the claim of voluntary withdrawal given the fact that he could have gone through with the crime.[1811] The Supreme Court apparently thought that the external factor of the woman's statement was not the decisive reason that had led to the (internal) change of heart of the defendant. It was thus deemed that the crucial factor in this withdrawal was the perpetrator's conscience.

In a pertinent German decision A had hit B, the new lover of his former girlfriend, with *dolus eventualis* to kill, several times on the head with a baseball bat. He left the severely injured victim on the bed and dragged his ex-girlfriend C outside and forced her to step into his car and left the scene. During the drive the girlfriend begged him to turn around as B was in desperate need for help. After approximately two minutes the defendant gave in, turned around and returned to the place of the crime, where he told C to call an ambulance and inform him of further developments. B survived but sustained lasting physical damages. The Supreme Court held that it was irrelevant that also external factors had contributed to the withdrawal (persuasion by C) and added that it was sufficient in these cases that the offender had set in motion a new causal chain of events which was at least concurrently causal for the non-consummation of the offence.[1812]

9.4.3. The actus contrarius in complete attempts

As already mentioned, in case of a complete attempt, a voluntary withdrawal remains possible but requires an *actus contrarius* which consists of conduct that is suitable to prevent the completion of the offence or the occurrence of the initially envisaged result.[1813] In the Dutch penal system it is in these situations required that the offender's conduct is at the relevant point in time of such a nature that it is suitable to prevent the manifestation of the result.[1814] To determine whether or not this is the case a risk assessment has to be carried out as well. The more likely it is that the result could have occurred after the defendant had completed his attempt and before the conduct took place, which is claimed to amount to a voluntary withdrawal the less likely it is that the claim will be successful.[1815] If this assessment has to be carried out *ex tunc* or *ex nunc* is however not entirely clear.[1816] It arguably corresponds to the objective approach to attempt liability in the

---

1811 HR 15 December 1992, *NJ* 1993, 333. See also: HR 19 December 2006, *NJ* 2007, 29, HR 22 December 2009 *LJN* BJ9244. For a very similar German decision see: 14 April 1955 BGH NJW 1955, 915.

1812 9 December 1998 BGH NStZ 1999, 128.

1813 De Hullu, 'Materieel Strafrecht' (2009), p. 412, Schönke and Schröder, 'Kommentar zum Strafgesetzbuch' (2006), §24 Mn 58 et seq.

1814 HR 19 December 2006, *NJ* 2007, 29.

1815 HR 3 March 2009, *NJ* 2009, 236.

1816 Mallens and Hornman, 'Vrijwillige terugtred bij poging' Delikt en Delinkwent (2010), pp. 78 et seq.

Netherlands where the outward manifestation of the conduct is considered decisive, to determine also the suitability of the *actus contrarius* objectively.

In any case, the impact of this required risk assessment can effectively be demonstrated by juxtaposing two decisions. The first case has already been discussed in a previous section, so that the facts need only be described briefly.[1817] The defendant had cut the brake pipes of a car, wrote 'death' in the snow, confessing later to the family when identified as the culprit, and warning them against using the car. The Supreme Court accepted voluntary withdrawal in this case as, so the argument went, given the late time of the attempt (the brake pipes were cut sometime between 2100 hrs and 2300 hrs; the aforementioned phone call took place around 2400 hrs) it was unlikely that the car would still have been used on that day and that the likelihood of the occurrence of harm was until that time thus minimal.[1818]

In another case, however, the court considered the likelihood of the occurrence of harm between the conduct of the perpetrator and the withdrawal more likely and therefore dismissed the claim of voluntary withdrawal. The defendant had removed all security rings from his gas oven, so that the gas could discharge freely and had left the apartment. Three hours later he went to a police station where he handed over his keys with the words that he had turned on the gas in his apartment. The Supreme Court considered the likelihood of the occurrence of harm as high, given the high concentration of gas in the apartment detected by the fire brigade, and the fact that already one spark from, for example the refrigerator, could have led to an explosion.[1819] In other words, the risk of an explosion had become so high that merely reporting it to the police was at the point in time and by its nature, considered unsuited to prevent the result from occurring. Perhaps if the offender had stopped the gas himself from escaping and defused the situation the court would have been more willing to accept his defence.[1820]

What exactly the formula referring to the likelihood of the occurrence of the result denotes is however not entirely clear. Arguably, the Dutch Supreme Court intended to interpret Art 46 DPC restrictively and thought that the probability of the occurrence of harm has to be taken into consideration when determining whether or not the prevention of the completion of the offence was really the result of the defendant's conduct and not merely a fortunate coincidence.[1821] Thus, it seems that conduct that was not at least partially causal for the prevention of the result, would not be accepted as withdrawal in the Netherlands.

This corresponds to some extent to the situation in Germany where it is required that in order to withdraw from a completed attempt, the offender exerted conduct that was aimed at preventing the harm from occurring. His conduct must be

1817 See: Chapter IV. 7.4.3.
1818 HR 3 March 2009, *NJ* 2009, 236.
1819 HR 13 March 2007, *NJ* 2007, 171.
1820 See: Keijzer, in his gloss under HR 3 March 2009, *NJ* 2009, 236.
1821 Keijzer, in his gloss under HR 3 March 2009, *NJ* 2009, 236.

deliberately aimed at breaking the causal chain, set in motion by his previous conduct, which excludes unwitting and accidental prevention of the completion of the offence. Overall the defendant's conduct must reflect his desire to desist from the offence entirely. Therefore, the defendant must carry out actions that objectively or at least from his point of view have a reasonable prospect of success and does not leave it to chance whether the result is avoided. In case he has fulfilled this minimum requirement it is irrelevant that he did not choose the optimal means.[1822] Finally, his efforts must be causal in preventing the result and must have actually prevented it.[1823] Thus, the fact that he need not necessarily choose the optimal means to prevent the completion of the offence is counterbalanced by imposing on the offender to bear the risk should the offence despite his efforts be completed. Should his conduct however not be causal for preventing the harm enshrined in the offence (i.e. where the attempt for instance was *ab initio* impossible or has failed but the defendant is not aware of this and believes that the completion is still possible) it will still be possible to profit from the exemption pursuant to §24 (1) second sentence, if he can prove that he has made a voluntary and earnest effort to prevent the completion of the offence.[1824]

The difference between the German and the Dutch approach in regard to the suitability of the defendant's conduct to prevent the completion of the offence lies here once again in the chosen perspective. While in the Netherlands suitability is determined objectively, in Germany it is the subjective view of the offender that is decisive. He has to take steps that are at least from his point of view sufficient and have a reasonable prospect of success.[1825] In case a human life is at stake the German Supreme Court frequently requires a strict standard.[1826] However, the foregoing has also revealed a further difference between the German and the Dutch approach to withdrawal. While in Germany §24 (1) second sentence provides for the possibility to rely on the defence also in case his conduct proved non-causal for the non-occurrence of harm, it seems that such conduct would not be considered sufficient in the Netherlands.[1827]

A different set of problems constitute situations where the defendant relies on third parties to prevent the completion of the offence, such as a doctor, etc. This is closely connected to the question which degree of diligence is required in order to rely on the defence. A prerequisite here is of course that the involvement of third parties can be attributed to the defendant's conduct and that they have not been called into action by other persons, such as witnesses, etc. The most obvious area of

---

1822 See: 26 September 2002 BGH NJW 2002, 3720, 12 November 1998 BGH NStZ-RR 2000, 42.

1823 See: 22 August 1985 BGH NStZ 1986, 25, where the conduct of the offender was regarded as insufficiently causal for the prevention of the completion of the offence.

1824 See: Schönke and Schröder, 'Kommentar zum Strafgesetzbuch' (2006), §24 Mn 58–72.

1825 27 April 1982 BGH NJW 1982, 2263, 12 November 1998 BGH NStZ-RR 2000, 42, 11 December 2007 BGH NStZ 2008, 329.

1826 13 March 2008 BGH NStZ 2008, 508.

1827 See: De Hullu, 'Materieel Strafrecht' (2009), p. 412. Stating that the defendant's conduct ought to be causal for the non-consummation of the offence.

application here is the realm of attempted homicide offences where the defendant after having injured the victim calls the emergency services. In Germany it is accepted that the offender need not necessarily prevent the completion of the offence himself, but may also rely on third parties. The involvement of emergency services will therefore generally be considered sufficient for voluntary withdrawal.[1828] In a pertinent case a father had thrown his sixteen year old daughter from the balcony of their 4th floor apartment (approximately 8,8 m). She landed on the roof of a garage where she lay motionless. Through the fall she had sustained severe but not life-threatening injuries. The father however thought his daughter was fatally injured and ran downstairs. On his way down he told his wife to call for an ambulance as their daughter had attempted to commit suicide. The Court of lower instance had rejected his claim of voluntary withdrawal but the Supreme Court quashed the judgment, referred the case back and stressed that the suitability of means had to be determined from the point of view of the defendant and that ordering his wife to call an ambulance was generally a suitable means to prevent the completion of the offence.[1829] However, not any step to make the provision of help possible will suffice. What seems to be crucial is that the successful intervention of third parties was not merely a sham but sincere and that it was the offender's purpose to rescue the endangered legal interests.[1830]

Dutch jurisprudence, on the other hand seems to be more reluctant in these situations, although a coherent approach is difficult to detect. This reluctance might to some extent be explained by the more objective approach of Dutch jurisprudence. Decisive seems the objective suitability of the defendant's conduct to prevent the completion of the offence after the decision to withdraw. The degree of probability with which the fatal result may ensue, will arguably also play a decisive role in determining whether the calling of emergency services will be considered sufficient. Further, in these cases a risk assessment will play a crucial role. If the probability of death is considerable due to the injuries the defendant previously inflicted, simply calling an ambulance will most likely not suffice. If the probabilities are however considerably low, then an intervention by help and rescue services may be considered sufficient.[1831] In a pertinent case a man stabbed his partner in the chest and his side, due to which he fell down the stairs where he lay breathing stertorously. Due to this and the considerable blood loss, the defendant became aware of the life-threatening situation, called emergency services and opened the entrance door. The Regional court rejected voluntary withdrawal, as the fact that the victim survived until the ambulance arrived was considered a fortuitous

1828 Roxin, 'Strafrecht Allgemeiner Teil, Band II: Besondere Erscheinungsformen der Straftat' (2003), pp. 548 et seq, 557 et seq, Schönke and Schröder, 'Kommentar zum Strafgesetzbuch' (2006), §24 Mn 66.

1829 11 February 2007 BGH NStZ 2008, 329.

1830 20 December 2002 BGH NJW 2003, 1058. See also: Neubacher, 'Der halbherzige Rücktritt in der Rechtsprechung des BGH' NStZ (2003), pp. 576–581.

1831 Mallens and Hornman, 'Vrijwillige terugtred bij poging' Delikt en Delinkwent (2010), pp. 78 et seq.

external factor which was independent from the defendants will.[1832] It did however take into account that the defendant had dialled 112 at the sentencing stage.

It seems that Dutch jurisprudence focusses in these cases more on the initial conduct of the defendant and the severity of the injuries the victim sustained, as well as on the objective conduct after the decision to withdraw, which has the effect that when the probabilities of a fatal result are objectively high, a fortuitous prevention of the outcome will not benefit the defendant. German jurisprudence on the other hand appears to focus more on the actual outcome which in these cases is generally that the victim's death could be prevented and according to the motto 'all's well that ends well' allows the defendant to invoke voluntary withdrawal.

Thus, Dutch law seems to require a higher standard of diligence from the defendant than German law. It is however submitted that the standard applied here ought not to be too stringent. Generally, informing emergency services will be the most suitable means in these cases to save the victim's life and will therefore also serve his interests best. Given the fact that the offender in any case bears the risk that the availability of the defence will be excluded should the result materialise despite his efforts it seems overly strict to additionally require that he choose the optimal means to prevent the completion of the offence. It is, however, difficult to create generally applicable rules in this context as the respective requirements in regard to an *actus contrarius* will highly depend on the facts of the case. The exact content of the required *actus contrarius* will largely depend on the severity and scope of the offender's previous actions and how far towards the completion of the offence he has already progressed. As a rule of thumb it can be stated that the further events have advanced, the more the offender will have to do to successfully withdraw from the offence. In essence, one may require a certain proportionality between the inculpatory actions of the offender and the conduct he claims to amount to voluntary withdrawal.

9.5. Voluntary withdrawal from preparation?

In case one were to opt for the inclusion of liability for preparatory offences in the general part of criminal law, as is the case in the Netherlands, the question arises whether the rules on withdrawal should apply to preparation as well. What is unclear in this respect is whether the nature of preparatory acts should lead to a more stringent interpretation of voluntary withdrawal. Is it for instance sufficient to simply stop the preparatory phase in order to invoke withdrawal? As preparatory acts are far removed from the commission of the offence the potential risk exists that the perpetrator will return to his criminal plan at a later time. It is therefore

1832 Rb. 's-Hertogenbosch 22 October 2008, *LJN* BG1023. See also: Hof Arnhem 22 December 2008, *LJN* BG8807. In Rb. Alkmaar 26 June 2001, *LJN* AB2375 it was however considered sufficient that the defendant after having poured alcohol over the victim and setting it on fire had extinguished the flames, placed the victim under the shower and had called emergency services.

conceivable that jurisprudence would in these instances require more than simple desistance. Nevertheless the Dutch legislator seems to have decided to apply the same rules to attempts and preparation in Article 46 (b) DPC.

In the realm of preparation the defence has so far only played an auxiliary role in the Netherlands, but it appears as if the same standards for withdrawal from attempt liability also apply to preparatory acts. The Supreme Court rejected for instance the defence where the defendants were arrested in the vicinity of several jewellery stores equipped with two weapons, a hammer, and a shawl to cover their faces around the neck on a previously stolen scooter. The defendants had argued that they had voluntarily withdrawn from their preparations because they were intimated by the high police presence on that day. The Supreme Court gave the argument short shrift and ruled that external circumstances independent from the defendants' will had prevented the completion of the offence.[1833] That the same rules apply to withdrawal from an attempt as well as from preparation was subsequently confirmed by the Regional Court Amsterdam in a case where the defendant was *inter alia* charged with attempted blackmailing as well as preparing blackmailing. The defendant had sent letters to Heineken threatening to poison beer and employees with sarin should the company not pay one million Euro. After approximately one week he had however reported himself to the police, making a full confession. The court stressed that withdrawal equally applied to attempts and preparation and acquitted him from preparing and/or attempting to blackmail the company but instead convicted him for threatening employees of Heineken.[1834]

10. Inchoate offences in the European Union

In regard to inchoate offences in European Union law, the picture that emerges is similar to the one described in the context of multiple actor scenarios. The concept has not yet been extensively discussed in the realm of Union law, despite the fact that EU legislation at times requires Member States to criminalise preparatory conduct and attempts to commit certain offences. In the realm of European competition law the broad offence definitions of Articles 101 and 102 TFEU may arguably facilitate the subsumption of attempt or preparatory conduct under competition rules. In regard to Article 101 TFEU the broad approach of competition law becomes particularly visible as all agreements are prohibited that have as their *object (i.e. intentionally) or effect (i.e. by default)* the prevention, restriction or distortion of competition. Thus, if it can be proven that the object of an agreement was to prevent, restrict or distort competition, there is no need to examine the effect of the agreement.[1835] Accordingly, if the undertakings intended to restrict

1833 HR 7 September 2004, *LJN* AP2570.

1834 Rb. Amsterdam, 1 July 2005, parketnr. 13.529008.05; Nieuwsbrief Strafrecht 2005, 380.

1835 Jones and Sufrin, 'EC Competition Law: Text, Cases, and Materials' (2004), p. 158. See also: 13 July 1966, Joined Cases C-56 & 58/64 *Établissements Consten S.à.R.L. and Grundig-*

competition, the occurrence of harm need not be proven by the Commission. This, it may be submitted, can essentially lead to the imposition of liability as soon as the undertakings in question have reached an agreement, covering conduct only remotely connected to the effective restriction of competition, i.e. inchoate offending.

More generally in regard to inchoate offences the Union's legislative technique is to define in some detail the primary offence(s) and subsequently to establish in generic terms that attempting, respectively preparing the offence in question shall be punishable as well. This approach has already been described in regard to the PIF Convention where the offence definition is set out in Article 1 (1) and where Article 2 of the PIF Convention then makes it clear that "each Member State shall take the necessary measures to ensure that the conduct referred to in Article 1 (1), and [...] attempting the conduct referred to in Article 1 (1) shall be punishable by effective, proportionate and dissuasive criminal penalties".[1836] Likewise Article 3 of the Directive on preventing and combating trafficking in human beings and protecting its victims provides that "Member States shall take the necessary measures to ensure that [...] attempting to commit an offence referred to in Article 2 is punishable.[1837] A further definition of the notion has however not yet emerged.

Less frequently, the Union legislator also obliges Member States to criminalise preparatory conduct. Article 1 (3) of the PIF convention for instance holds "[...] each Member State shall take the necessary measures to ensure that the intentional preparation or supply of false, incorrect or incomplete statements or documents having the effect described in paragraph 1 constitutes a criminal offence [...]".[1838] Although not especially indicated as such, certain other Union instruments also prescribe preparatory acts.[1839] Article 1 (f) of the Framework Decision on combating terrorism for instance holds that manufacture, possession, acquisition, transport, supply or use of weapons, explosives, [...] shall give rise to liability.[1840] Likewise, Article 4 of the Framework Decision on combating fraud proscribes the fraudulent making, receiving, obtaining, sale or transfer to another person or

Verkaufs-GmbH v Commission of the European Economic Community, [1966] ECR 299.

1836 Convention of 26 July 1995, on the protection of the European Communities' financial interests, OJ 1995 C 316/49. See also: Chapter III. 11.

1837 Directive 2011/36 of 5 April 2011 on preventing and combating trafficking in human beings and protecting its victims, and replacing Council Framework Decision 2002/629/JHA, OJ 2011, L 101/06. Similar provisions can also be found in Article 1 (d) of Directive 2005/60 of 26 October 2005 on the prevention of the use of the financial system for the purpose of money laundering and terrorist financing, OJ 2005, L 309/15. See also Article 5 of Framework Decision 2005/222 of 24 February 2005 on attacks against information systems, OJ 2005 L 69/67.

1838 Convention of 26 July 1995, on the protection of the European Communities' financial interests, OJ 1995 C 316/49.

1839 See also: Klip, 'European Criminal Law' (2012), p. 207.

1840 Framework Decision 2002/475 of 13 June 2002 on combating terrorism, OJ 2002 L 164/3. See also Art 2 of Framework Decision 2004/757 of 25 October 2004 laying down minimum provisions on the constituent elements of criminal acts and penalties in the field of illicit drug trafficking, OJ 2004 L 335/8.

possession of instruments, articles, computer programmes and any other means particularly adapted for counterfeiting or falsification of a payment instrument in order to be used fraudulently.[1841] From these instruments it is also possible to gain some insight into the relationship between preparatory acts and attempt liability in EU law.[1842] This is because both instruments make it clear that attempting a preparatory offence shall not give rise to criminal liability.[1843] It follows that double inchoate liability is not considered possible. Given the fact that inchoate liability is already by definition some steps removed from the full offence, it would constitute an undue expansion of the scope of criminal law to double inchoate liability. Such a limitation is therefore certainly to be welcomed.

Leaving preparatory offences aside, in regard to criminal attempts some further guidance as to a European approach can be found in the Council's draft on guidelines and model provisions for criminal law which hold that "Attempts to commit an intentional offence should be criminalised if it is necessary and proportionate in relation to the main offence" and in its model provisions establishes that "Each Member State shall ensure that attempting the intentional conduct referred to in Article […] is punishable as a criminal offence".[1844] Despite the basic nature of the provisions some guiding principles for this investigation can be deduced.

First, the Council seems to recognise that criminal attempts constitute an expansion of liability which should, to avoid over criminalisation, only be criminalised if it is necessary and proportionate in relation to the underlying protected legal interest enshrined in the main offence. Such a cautious approach is arguably to be welcomed, taking into account the *ultima ratio* principle and the fact that an expansion of liability can only be justified if the underlying protected legal interest is significant enough to accept a limitation of individual rights and freedoms. A further limitation can be found in the Council's choice to limit attempt liability to intentional crimes. It follows that first, attempting something negligently cannot give rise to liability. This corresponds to the natural meaning of the word attempt and makes it clear that to attempt means to act intentionally. What however is to be understood by the concept of intent in the realm of European Union law is another question. The choice taken by the Council to allow attempt liability in regard to all intentional offences, is at first sight notably different from the one adopted by the three investigated penal systems, which have all opted to limit liability to attempts to commit serious offences, excluding misdemeanours. If this different approach would however lead to significantly different results in practice is up for debate.

1841 Framework Decision 2001/413 of 28 May 2001 on combating fraud and counterfeiting of non-cash means payment, OJ 2001 L 149/1.

1842 See also: Klip, 'European Criminal Law' (2012), p. 207.

1843 See: Article 4 of Framework Decision 2002/475 of 13 June 2002 on combating terrorism, OJ 2002 L 164/3 and Article 5 of Framework Decision 2001/413 of 28 May 2001 on combating fraud and counterfeiting of non-cash means payment, OJ 2001 L 149/1.

1844 Draft Council conclusions on model provisions, guiding the Council's criminal law deliberations, Brussels, 27 November 2009, 16542/2/09 REV 2.

Besides the Council's model provisions, attempt liability has been discussed in the Corpus Juris project. In its original versions no article on attempt liability had been included which was strongly criticised by the rapporteurs which lead to the inclusion of Article 11 bis in the Corpus Juris 2000. Article 11 bis reads as follows:

> Attempts to commit an offence under articles 1 to 3 and 5 to 8, and participation in such an attempt (Article 11), are punishable. The maximum penalty is three-quarters of the penalty applicable, under Article 14, to the completed offence.
> A person is guilty of a criminal attempt if, with intent to commit an offence under Article 1 to 3 and 5 to 8 he performs an act which constitutes the commencement of the commission of a criminal offence.
> A person who has attempted to commit an offence shall not be punished if he voluntarily desists from completion or voluntarily forestalls completions. If the offence is not completed for other reasons, it is sufficient that the person voluntarily and seriously tries to desist from completion or forestalls completion.

The Corpus Juris thus defines the conduct element of criminal attempts by reference to the concept of the beginning of the execution. This originates from French law and by and large also resembles the definition of attempts to be found in Article 45 of the Dutch Penal Code, which itself was strongly influenced by the Code Penal. In essence the provision is intended to adopt a mixed approach combining objective and subjective factors, which is in line with the approach advocated here.[1845] The subjective element can be seen in the reference to the intent to commit the offence which is connected to the more objective requirement that a commencement of the commission of the offence must have occurred. In any case, the Corpus Juris makes it clear that a mixed approach seems to be suitable for European Union law as it is to be preferred by most systems.[1846] To what extent the perception of the perpetrator ought to play a role in the evaluation process is however not clear. As has been discussed above, the perpetrator's perception will certainly have to play a role in the evaluation process, as especially his intentions will be decisive. Yet, if the subjective element has to be emphasised as strongly as in the German penal system is debatable. In an alternative version for Art 11 bis the perspective of the perpetrator comes more clearly to the foreground as it strives for a merger of the German and English concept of attempts. It reads as follows:

1845 See: Brockhaus, 'Die strafrechtliche Dogmatik von Vorbereitung, Versuch und Rücktritt im europäischen Vergleich' (2006), p. 420. See also: Delmas-Marty and Vervaele, 'The implementation of the Corpus Juris in the Member States – Volume I' (2000), p. 73.

1846 Delmas-Marty and Vervaele, 'The implementation of the Corpus Juris in the Member States – Volume I' (2000), p. 73.

> A person is guilty of attempt if he, with intent to commit an offence under Article 1 to 7, does an act which is, according to his plans and notions, more than preparatory to the commission of the offence. [...][1847]

In essence this provision seems to favour a mixed approach as well, but here more emphasis rests on the subjective element, which by and large represents the German approach outlined above. Be that as it may, the reference to the objective requirement of the beginning of the execution makes it clear that preparatory conduct generally falls outside the scope of liability. Yet, the Corpus Juris itself contains several special provision which effectively extend liability in turn again to the preparatory phase.[1848]

The question whether or not impossible attempts ought to be punishable as well has not been explicitly addressed by the Corpus Juris, which is to be regretted. An explicit choice by the legislator as can for instance be found in the 1983 Criminal Attempts Act would have been preferable. Yet, it is arguable that the wording of Article 11 bis indicates that impossible attempts can give rise to liability, which would be in line with the findings above, which have shown that by and large impossible attempts give rise to liability in all penal systems.[1849] The alternative provision, mentioned before would bring more clarity here as it explicitly provides that: "It is immaterial whether the act is apt or likely to bring about an offence under Articles 1 to 7".[1850]

A more objective approach of the Corpus Juris is revealed by turning the focus to the sentencing of attempts. Article 11 bis does not, as a subjectivist approach would favour, provide for the possibility to punish attempts as severely as the completed offence, but foresees a mandatory mitigation of punishment. Article 11 bis provides that the maximum penalty shall be three quarters of the penalty applicable. This corresponds along general lines to the approach adopted by the Dutch penal system, while in Germany a mitigation is merely facultative and the English Criminal Attempts Acts formally allows for the imposition of equal punishment.

Finally, Article 11 bis contains a provision dealing with voluntary withdrawal. The wording of the provision (A person [...] shall not be punished [...]) may be interpreted in such a way that withdrawal constitutes a personal exemption from punishment from which other participants who have not withdrawn may not

---

1847 Delmas-Marty and Vervaele, 'The implementation of the Corpus Juris in the Member States – Volume I' (2000), p. 272.

1848 Brockhaus, 'Die strafrechtliche Dogmatik von Vorbereitung, Versuch und Rücktritt im europäischen Vergleich' (2006), p. 423 et seq.

1849 See: Brockhaus, 'Die strafrechtliche Dogmatik von Vorbereitung, Versuch und Rücktritt im europäischen Vergleich' (2006), p. 426.

1850 Delmas-Marty and Vervaele, 'The implementation of the Corpus Juris in the Member States – Volume I' (2000), p. 272.

profit.[1851] Apart from this slight uncertainty paragraph three of Article 11 bis constitutes an almost exact replica of §24 GPC. It distinguishes voluntary desistence from completion from forestalling the completion, which corresponds to the dichotomy of complete and incomplete attempts. Furthermore, the paragraph also provides that non-causal withdrawal will exempt the offender from liability. Art 11 bis is however more lenient in regard to non-causal withdrawals than §24 GPC as it even allows an offender to invoke the exemption if the offence is not completed for other reasons (than his conduct) but has voluntarily and seriously tried to desist from completion. In Germany however impunity in these situations will only arise if the offender has made a voluntary and earnest effort to prevent the completion of the offence.

11. Conclusion

11.1. Preparation

It has been attempted to show that preparatory conduct increasingly comes into the focal point of criminal law. In modern criminal law more and more specific offences emerge which have as their goal the prevention of a risk of harm. The question which now needs to be addressed is whether this legislative trend justifies the inclusion of a general doctrine of preparation into the general part. A recurrent theme of the foregoing discussion has been that legal doctrine is generally faced with two theories (i.e. subjective and objective) but only one law of attempts, which necessarily leads to frictions. One advantage of adopting a separate general law doctrine of preparation could therefore arguably be that criminal law could better accommodate the legitimate concerns of both theories by casting them in two separate offences (attempt and preparation), which recognise the competing traditions.[1852] Yet, while the former approach may have some advantages from a doctrinal and theoretical point of view, it is submitted that a case by case approach fits better into the prevalent common traditions of the European Union and the Member States. Therefore the European Union may criminalise preparatory conduct by adopting special offences such as possession or endangerment offences. Such, a case by case approach may arguably also provide a better restraint to overcriminalisation, as the legislator would be obliged to provide proof that all the aforementioned requirements are fulfilled every time it opts for the criminalisation of preparatory conduct in a respective legislative instrument.

[1851] Brockhaus, 'Die strafrechtliche Dogmatik von Vorbereitung, Versuch und Rücktritt im europäischen Vergleich' (2006), p. 426. See also: Art 4 of Framework Decision 2008/841 0f 24 October 2008 on the fight against organised crime, OJ 2008 L 300/42, which allows Member States to exempt an offender from punishment if he renounces his criminal activities.

[1852] Rogers, 'The codification of attempts and the case for preparation' Criminal Law Review (2008), pp. 937–954.

It has been submitted that these offences may only be justified if they are clearly designed to reduce a substantial risk. Imposing liability for an insubstantial risk would arguably violate the *nulla poena sine culpa* as well as the *ultima ratio* principle.[1853] Furthermore, the underlying protected legal interest must be substantial to warrant an expansion of liability. Moreover, liability may only be imposed when the offender's conduct can in some sense be considered wrongful. In other words, and this applies to preparatory as well as attempt liability, the notion of actus reus must remain an important component in the framework of inchoate liability to avoid an attitude-based criminal law.[1854] The offender's conduct ought to corroborate the offender's intentions. As already mentioned, such a retentive approach would also correspond to the view adopted by the Council of the European Union which made it clear that "conduct which only implies an abstract danger to the protected right or interest should be criminalised only if appropriate considering the particular importance of the right or interest which is the object of protection".[1855] Accordingly, it will be a crucial task for the European legislator to develop coherent criteria for criminalisation in order to guide the application and further development of European criminal law.

It is further considered crucial that the legislator should be obliged to adopt a stringent fault requirement in these offences. Liability for preparatory offences can arguably only be justified in case the person creating a risk of harm possesses a significant culpability for the ultimate harm. In other words, proof of a firm intent ought to be required. Thus, something more than *dolus eventualis,* i.e. direct or indirect intent, will be necessary to establish liability.

11.2. Criminal attempts

Attempt liability should be based on a combination of factors from the two competing theories. Thus, overall a mixed approach seems to be preferable. As a rationale, it has been submitted that the offender's conduct should amount to an endangerment of the legal order as well as his subjective criminal proclivities should be clearly expressed in it.[1856] The objective endangerment rationale will arguably account for most cases of attempt liability and will also ensure that the concept of actus reus continues to play an important role to assure that liability remains rooted in an act-based criminal law. It will further provide a valuable restraint against undue inflations of criminal liability. The subjective element of the offender's criminal proclivities on the other hand will account for the imposition of

[1853] See: Chapter IV. 6.4.

[1854] See also Article 10 of the Charter of fundamental rights of the European Union that enshrines freedom of thought.

[1855] Draft Council conclusions on model provisions, guiding the Council's criminal law deliberations, Brussels, 27 November 2009, 16542/2/09 REV 2.

[1856] See: Chapter IV. 7.2.4.

liability for impossible attempts and also gives expression to the fact that intentions often constitute the primal ingredient for criminal censure in regard to attempts.

The mixed rationale should also be reflected in the chosen formula to demarcate attempts from preparation. Objectively an imminence of the commission of the offence should be required which amounts to an endangerment of the legal order. This should however not be interpreted in a way that already some part of the actus reus must have been brought about. Partial fulfilment of the actus reus can be a sufficient condition for liability but should not be a necessary one, as this would arguably cast the scope of the law too narrowly. It has already been mentioned that attempt liability is generally in all investigated systems confined to intentional conduct. What however intention should in this area of the law exactly denote to is a subject which can only be solved with the broader discussion of fault requirements in European criminal law, which would exceed the scope of this book.[1857]

It has been mentioned above that a demarcation formula will necessarily be vague, as it will have to apply to almost all offences throughout the special part of criminal law. Yet, to provide the courts with some further guidance, one could opt for incorporating guideline examples into the code as is the case in the American Model Penal Code. Therefore additional criteria such as the requirement of an intrusion of the perpetrator's conduct into the sphere of the victim or the protected legal interest and a close temporal connection of the conduct to the commission of the actus reus could be taken into account. Accordingly, the following conduct could be seen to constitute an attempt:

- unlawful entry of a structure, vehicle or enclosure in which it is contemplated that the crime will be committed,
- approaching the scene of the crime or the victim if an interference with the sphere of the victim and a close temporal connection to the contemplated offence can be established,
- lying in wait, yet only if the victim has already come sufficiently proximate to the sphere of influence of the offender (i.e. can be said to have entered the 'danger zone').
- Concerning complete attempts: when the offender has relinquished control or dominion over the causal chain of events (e.g. when wrongly filled in or falsified documents which could trigger the granting of subsidies are submitted to the competent authority)

It seems further to be common ground that impossible attempts will generally give rise to criminal liability. Exempted from this general rule are however imaginary offences, superstitious or utterly daft attempts. To demarcate punishable impossible attempts from the latter, the distinction between mistakes of law and mistakes of

[1857] See however: Blomsma 'Mens rea and defences in European criminal law' (2012).

fact could be utilised.[1858] While reverse mistakes of law lead to imaginary offences, reverse mistakes of fact lead to impossible attempts. If however the offender gravely errs about the laws of nature or invokes powers that lie outside the ambit of human control no liability should ensue. Yet, if a future European criminal law were to rely on the opportunity principle for prosecution those categories would most likely become redundant, as the case would arguably be dropped by the Public Prosecutor beforehand.

Contrary to the prevalent approach in English law, it has been submitted that a defence of voluntary withdrawal should be included into the law of attempts. In case an offender voluntarily withdraws from the criminal enterprise, neither considerations of special nor of general prevention would warrant the imposition of punishment.[1859] Furthermore, although not entirely convincing, it can be argued that the promise of immunity can provide an incentive for an actor to desist from committing the offence and thereby prevent the occurrence of harm. From a systematic point of view, the defence should be seen as a personal exemption from punishment in order to make sure that in multiple-actor scenarios only the person that effectively abandoned the criminal attempt may profit from immunity.

Pertinent to this exemption, the distinction between complete and incomplete and incomplete and failed attempts will be crucial.[1860] Therefore, it has been demonstrated that the scope of application of the defence varies significantly depending on whether one relies on the subjective conception of the offender or invokes objective criteria for the demarcation. An objective approach generally leads to a narrow scope of the exemption while reliance on subjective criteria leads to a withdrawal-friendly conception, which ultimately benefits the offender. It is submitted that from a systematic point of view, the approach in regard to withdrawal should reflect the approach adopted in regard to attempt liability in general. Thus, if the perspective of the perpetrator is not particularly emphasised in establishing when the threshold to liability has been passed, it would be inconsistent to rely heavily on it in regard to withdrawal. The choices made in the realm of withdrawal may however also be influenced by considerations of penal policy and the question how sympathetic the law would like to be to its offenders.

Be that as it may, the distinction between complete and incomplete attempts is of importance in order to determine whether desistance will suffice for withdrawal (incomplete attempts) or whether an *actus contrarius* will be required (complete attempts). The *actus contrarius* has to be at least partially causal for the non-occurrence of harm. A principled solution seems difficult to achieve here but as a rough yardstick it can be said that the exact content of the *actus contrarius* will to a great deal depend on the severity and scope of the offender's previous conduct and how far to the completion of the offence he has already progressed. The further

1858 See: Chapter IV. 8.
1859 See: Chapter IV. 9.1.–9.2.
1860 See: Chapter IV. 9.4.1.

events have advanced, the more the offender will have to do to successfully withdraw from the attempt.

A further pivotal requirement in regard to withdrawal is that the withdrawal occurred voluntarily. To distinguish *bona fide* changes of heart from withdrawal prompted by other factors, a psychological theory seems to be preferred by the courts. As a yardstick it can therefore be stated that a withdrawal will be considered voluntary if the offender thinks 'I do not wish to carry on even if I could' while it will be considered involuntary if he thinks 'I cannot carry on even if I wanted to'.

Finally in regard to the amount of punishment to be warranted by a criminal attempt, it can be stated that the law should provide for a facultative mitigation of punishment. This would also correspond to the mixed objective/subjective approach advocated here. Mitigation to three-quarters of the maximum penalty of the underlying offence seems to be defensible here. In many instances the absence of (tangible) harm will warrant a mitigation of punishment in relation to the complete offence, yet as this need not always be the case, the courts should be granted some leeway in meting out punishment.

Chapter V
Criminal liability of legal entities

1. Introduction

It has already been argued in a previous chapter that legal entities can be seen to possess certain unique attributes which justifies regarding them as fit subjects of criminal law. Two different arguments may lead to that conclusion. On the one hand, corporations arguably constitute intelligent, rational agents, pursuing their own goals and policies which warrants holding them responsible for their choices. On the other hand, it can be argued that as being a fit subject of criminal law is by definition a legal construct, the concept of legal personhood is not necessarily confined to natural persons of flesh and blood. This would create room to also include other legal constructions such as legal entities into the framework of criminal law.[1861]

Also in the realm of European Union law it seems to be a well established fact that legal entities are fit subjects of (criminal) law and can be held accountable for their wrongful acts. The competition law rules for example, enshrined in Articles 101 and Articles 102 TFEU are exclusively addressed to legal entities and aim to sanction any restriction or distortion of competition within the internal market. Although Article 23 (5) of Regulation 1/2003 on competition law formally provides that decisions to impose a penalty shall not be of criminal law nature, the at times astronomically high sanctions imposed by the Commission warrant to regard competition law in the light of the pertinent case law of the European Court of Human Rights (ECtHR) as criminal law.[1862] The ECtHR has namely held that the (national) label attached to a law is irrelevant for the application of Article 6 of the Convention as the criminal nature of the penalty can be deduced from the general character of the rule and the purpose of the penalty which are deterrent and punitive.[1863]

Also the Corpus Juris would pursuant to Article 13 introduce the criminal liability of organisations. Besides the competition law rules and the Corpus Juris, there are other strong signs that the liability of legal entities constitutes an important priority of the Union legislator. Mutual recognition shall for instance not be hampered by the fact that one Member State does not provide for corporate criminal liability in its national penal system. Financial penalties, for example, imposed on a

[1861] Van Strien, 'De Rechtspersoon in het strafproces' (1996), p. 14.

[1862] See also: Klip, 'European Criminal Law' (2012), p. 2.

[1863] See: *Öztürk v Germany*, appl. no. 8544/79, 21 February 1984. See also: *Sergey Zolotukhin v Russia*, appl. no. 14939/03, 10 February 2009.

legal person have to be recognised and enforced even if the executing state does not recognise the principle of liability of legal persons.[1864] Furthermore, by now a multitude of legal instruments oblige Member States to ensure that legal persons can be held responsible for offences established by the respective instrument.[1865] Many of these legal instruments are concerned with particularly pressing problems that characteristically involve corporate activity such as environmental crimes, subsidy fraud, bribery and money laundering. Arguably, the strong economic focus of the Union's legislation and competences already from the very beginning contained the seeds for the acceptance of corporations as fit subjects of criminal law. It can even be argued that the need for corporate criminal liability is even more pressing at the European level. Given the missteps of some financial organisations in the context of the ongoing financial crisis for instance, corporate criminal liability may provide one useful tool to tackle corporate malpractice. Likewise the Union's policy goals to achieve an effective protection of the environment, respectively the financial interests of the Union, may only be fully achievable if European rules will be applied to corporations. Often corporations will for instance be part of a subsidy fraud scheme or will engage in activities which are potentially dangerous for the environment, as they are carried out with dangerous or hazardous substances, etc. If due to these activities harm is caused to the Union's financial interests or the environment and a sufficient degree of culpability can be proven the corporation should incur criminal liability.

Thus, it seems fair to conclude that the liability of legal entities is firmly established and accepted in European Union law and that holding corporations accountable for wrongful conduct is considered an important task by the Union legislator. However, it should also be pointed out here that the European Union in its legal instruments to this day, has merely obliged Member States to recognise corporate responsibility (i.e. leaving the choice of law to apply, such as administrative law to the states) but has not yet gone so far to also require the introduction of corporate criminal liability throughout the Union.

Yet, from a doctrinal point of view the inclusion of corporations in the realm of criminal law can generally be considered problematic as criminal law was traditionally not designed with corporate actors in mind. Therefore, the path to a full acceptance of corporate criminal liability is littered with obstacles stemming from the traditional approach of criminal law focused on individual human

---

1864 See: Article 9 (3) of Framework Decision 2005/214 of 24 February 2005 on the application of the principle of mutual recognition to financial penalties, OJ 2005 L 76/16.

1865 To name just a few see: Article 5, 6 Framework Decision 2005/667 of 12 July 2005 to strengthen the criminal law framework for the enforcement of the law against ship source pollution, OJ 2005 L 255/164, Articles 6, 7 Directive 2008/99 of 19 November 2008 on the protection of the environment through criminal law, OJ 2008 L 328/28, Articles 5, 6 Directive 2011/36 of 5 April 2011 on preventing and combating trafficking in human beings and protecting its victims, and replacing Council Framework Decision 2002/629/JHA, OJ 2011, L 101/06. See also: Draft Council conclusions on model provisions, guiding the Council's criminal law deliberations, Brussels, 27 November 2009, 16542/2/09 REV 2.

wrongdoing. Only humans can be subjects of criminal law, so it is often argued, as only they possess a will and can act intentionally.[1866] Furthermore, the imposition of punishment and censure according to this traditional conception of criminal law doctrines requires that the actor is morally blameworthy. As corporations cannot be bestowed with moral responsibility they cannot incur guilt as would be necessary for the imposition of criminal punishment. According to this conception, corporations are thus exempt from criminal law as only individuals can act and be morally blameworthy in a way necessary to justify criminal punishment.[1867] In other words, as the principles of *nulla poena sine culpa* and *nulla poena sine actione* are considered to apply only to human agents, corporations are excluded from the realm of criminal law. This conclusion is often the corollary of a psychological conception of guilt which is linked to exclusively human concepts such as will, mind, consciousness and atonement. These concepts are difficult to reconcile with corporate actors and therefore cause friction in the framework of criminal liability. The inclusion of legal entities into the criminal law seems to be easier to achieve when the concept of guilt is not interpreted psychologically but rather objectively or normatively. Guilt conceived in terms of a violation of a general duty of care resting on all citizens would for instance be much better suited to be applied to corporations than the aforementioned psychological conceptions.

In any case, penal systems adhering to this orthodox view of criminal law will most likely nevertheless feel the need to regulate corporate activities and to tackle corporate wrongdoing. This will often be done by subjecting legal entities to for instance administrative rules, regulatory offences, etc., and to apply criminal law only to individuals within the corporation who acted culpably and can be held responsible with regard to the occurred criminal harm. As a substitute corporate wrongdoing is attempted to be tackled by either focusing on individual wrongdoing which occurred within an organisational context or by subjecting corporations to other regulatory regimes in which the focus of the legal framework is not exclusively on human attributes such as moral responsibility and blameworthiness. As will subsequently become apparent, this is precisely the approach adopted by the German penal system where legal entities are considered to lack the capacity to act and be blamed.[1868] Such stern individualistic focus can however lead to an expansion and distortion of traditional criminal law doctrines. Arguably, the broad approach to omission liability and duties of care in the German penal system can partially be explained by the desire to hold individuals responsible for the wrongdoings of the corporation. Furthermore, the broad German concept of perpetration by means can also be explained by the lack of corporate criminal

---

[1866] Van Strien, 'De Rechtspersoon in het strafproces' (1996), p. 11.

[1867] See for instance: Judgment of the German Constitutional Court 26 February 1997 BVerfG NJW 1997, 1841.

[1868] Schönke and Schröder, 'Kommentar zum Strafgesetzbuch' (2006), Vorbem §25 Mn 119. They are therefore exempt from criminal liability but, as will subsequently become clear, can nevertheless be sanctioned under the Administrative Offences Act.

liability which has prompted courts to hold individuals responsible as perpetrators if they e.g. exploit organisational structures within a company, etc.[1869]

If one however accepts that corporations can act and be at fault in a manner similar to humans, the essential issue from a dogmatic point of view becomes whether one decides to take the individual or the collectivity as a starting point for the attribution of liability. It has already been mentioned that in regard to the nature of corporate personality two opposed approaches can be distinguished.[1870] The atomic (or nominalist) approach views corporations as nothing more than collectivities of individuals. Thus according to this view individual wrongdoing remains the focal point of criminal law from which the liability of the organisation is subsequently derived. Attributing individual states of mind or conduct to a corporation however implies a legal fiction which can give rise to doctrinal frictions. Such an approach namely implies an anthropomorphic view in regard to corporations. Corporations are deemed to be sufficiently similar to human beings, and accordingly criminal law concepts, originally developed for individual wrongdoing are with little or no adaptations, applied to legal entities as well. As no tailor-made criminal law concepts for legal entities are created, the individual wrongdoing remains in the focal point of the law. How else then through its employees should a legal entity act? A corporation, so the argument runs, necessarily acts through individuals. The conduct of these individuals (act or omission, respectively) must subsequently be attributed to the legal entity. Yet, applying traditional criminal law concepts, tailor-made for individual wrongdoing to collective forms of wrongdoing seems a bit like trying to squeeze a square peg into a round hole.[1871] Concepts like mens rea and actus reus which form the bedrock of individual criminal liability are not readily applicable to corporations. It seems almost obvious that corporations will not cause, for instance, murder in the conventional sense as human actors would. A human actor may be the most immediate cause of the occurred criminal harm but a corporate actor may nevertheless be a pivotal indirect cause and therefore bear substantial responsibility for this outcome, as it showed for instance a blatant disrespect for pertinent diligent standards. The traditional building blocks of criminal liability, i.e. actus reus and mens rea, with their stern individualistic focus have difficulties to tap into these intricate collective causes of wrongdoing. Traditionally, criminal law has therefore often attempted to sidestep these issues by *inter alia* applying objective standards to corporations.

In any case, it is submitted that corporations should be perceived to constitute something more and something different than a collectivity of individuals.[1872] An organic (or realist) approach which holds that a corporation has an existence independent of its individual members seems therefore preferable. Rather than

1869 See also: Chapter III. 7.3.3.
1870 See: Chapter II. 2.2.2.
1871 Gobert and Punch, 'Rethinking Corporate Crime' (2003), p. 10.
1872 Van Strien, 'De Rechtspersoon in het strafproces' (1996), p. 90.

viewing corporations as individuals it would correspond better to corporate reality to view them as "living creatures or systems" and to devise corporate analogues for human conduct and guilt.[1873] For example a corporation may not be at fault in the same way than an individual may be but an equivalent could for instance be found in the corporate culture or policy expressing a culpable attitude towards a certain criminal event.

Be that as it may, the fact however remains that even if one is willing to accept an organic approach to corporations, the tools at the disposal of criminal law to assign liability, the concepts of actus reus and mens rea in particular seem artificial and inapt to capture corporate wrongdoing. For instance, in practice it will hardly ever be possible to say that a corporation has physically committed the actus reus of a criminal offence, without relying on a legal fiction. Rather, conduct in the realm of corporate wrongdoing will arguably most likely be interpreted normatively and revolve around the company's failure to adhere to applicable duties of care or diligent standards respectively. Corresponding to the nature of actus reus and mens rea as communicating vessels, an increasing normative interpretation of the objective element of liability (i.e. a diminished relevance of physical wrongdoing) results in a shift of emphasis to the subjective constituent elements of liability. Thus, in regard to corporate wrongdoing, the classical dichotomy between actus reus and mens rea seems to break down. As this research will subsequently strive to explain, in an organic conception of organisations, the essential ingredient for establishing corporate criminal liability arguably becomes corporate blameworthiness. This, as has been attempted to demonstrate in previous chapters, constitutes a development which, albeit to a lesser extent is also discernible in regard to individual liability.

2. Alternative and complementary methods to tackle corporate wrongdoing

2.1. Introduction

Before setting out to discuss the modes of liability flowing from a nominalist, or realist conception of corporate personality, this research will devote some space to discuss other methods applied by national penal systems to tackle corporate wrongdoing. These methods can take a variety of forms and be either administrative, civil or criminal in nature. One option to avoid the pitfalls of a general theory on corporate liability would for instance be to devise specific offences, tailor made to control corporate conduct and activities.

[1873] See also: Clough, 'Bridging the theoretical Gap: The search for a realist model of corporate criminal liability' Criminal Law Forum (2007), p. 277.

2.2. Regulatory offences

In the English penal system so-called regulatory offences are often applied to corporations. Contrary to traditional common law, regulatory offences are exclusively statutory in nature. However, unlike traditional statutory offences, regulatory offences are enforced by separate agencies and not by the police. Each regulatory offence establishes its own specialist agency on which the enforcement of the respective legislation is incumbent.[1874] Usually regulatory offences are concerned with either one aspect of any corporate activity (e.g. Health and Safety regulation) or with particular industries (e.g. Food Safety).[1875] Thus in areas where the public is increasingly exposed to corporate activity, for instance in regard to public health and consumer protection issues, the English legislator has deemed it appropriate to enact legislation which regulates and holds corporations responsible for the way in which their business is operated.[1876] In other words, these statutes are usually drafted with companies specifically in mind.[1877] An illuminating example for such a regulatory framework can be seen in the 1974 Health and Safety at Work Act. This comprehensive Act imposes a multitude of duties on employers and corporations in order to ensure the safety and welfare at work of all employees. To enforce these duties the Act established in section 10 a Health and Safety Commission and a Health and Safety Executive. The most recent development in this respect can be found in the Regulatory Enforcement and Sanctions Act 2008 which in part 3 creates a set of administrative sanctions that a range of enforcement bodies will be able to impose. These include the Financial Service Authority which has as its goal the regulation of the financial market, the Health and Safety Executive, the Environment Agency and the Forestry Commissioners.

A further important difference between these regulatory offences and traditional criminal offences emerges if one focuses on the enforcement strategies applied by regulatory agencies on the one hand and the police force on the other. Regulatory agencies tend to put more emphasis on compliance than on deterrence. Regulatory offences generally create a system of inspection and negotiation. Conversely police practices tend to focus more on deterrence and automatic enforcement.[1878] These aforementioned differences between regulatory and traditional offences have led to the categorisation of regulatory offences as "quasi crimes". This despite the fact that regulatory offences have developed into the most important tool in the English penal system to regulate corporate behaviour. Nowadays, corporations are far more likely to be prosecuted for regulatory rather than ordinary criminal offences.[1879]

1874 Wells, 'Corporations and Criminal Responsibility' (2001), p. 4.

1875 Wells, 'Corporations and Criminal Responsibility' (2001), p. 3. See also: 'Criminal Liability in regulatory contexts', Consultation Paper, LAW COM. No 195 [2010].

1876 Pinto and Evans, 'Corporate Criminal Liability' (2003), p. 310.

1877 Gobert and Punch, 'Rethinking Corporate Crime' (2003), p. 53.

1878 Wells, 'Corporations and Criminal Responsibility' (2001), p. 4.

1879 Pinto and Evans, 'Corporate Criminal Liability' (2003), p. 310.

Due to their specific nature, English regulatory offences can probably best be compared to the German Administrative Offences Act (Ordnungswidrigkweiten). They are not perceived as criminal offences, neither by the public nor by the defendant, even when sanctions are imposed in a criminal court.[1880]

Notwithstanding the fact that regulatory and administrative offences are succinctly regarded as "quasi crimes", the rationale underlying such offences is important for the purpose of this research, as it *inter alia* provides a short glimpse into the merging doctrinal currents in the modern risk society. The Canadian Supreme Court summarised the purpose of a regulatory scheme as follows:

> The objective of regulatory legislation is to protect the public or broad segments of the public (such as employees, consumers and motorists to name but a few) from the potentially adverse affects of otherwise lawful activity. Regulatory legislation involves the shift of emphasis from the protection of individual interests and the deterrence and punishing of acts involving moral fault to the protection of public and societal interests. While criminal offences are usually designed to condemn and punish past, inherently wrongful conduct, regulatory measures are generally directed to the prevention of future harm through the enforcement of minimum standards of conduct and care.
>
> It follows that regulatory offences and crimes embody different concepts of fault. Since regulatory offences are directed primarily not to conduct itself but to the consequences of conduct, conviction of a regulatory offence may be thought to import a significant lesser degree of culpability than conviction of a true crime. The concept of fault in regulatory offences is based upon a reasonable care standard and, as such, does not imply moral blameworthiness in the same manner as criminal fault. Conviction for breach of a regulatory offences suggests nothing more than the fact that the defendant has failed to meet a prescribed standard of care.[1881]

To sum up, it can be said that (English) regulatory offences are tailor-made provision to regulate corporate conduct. They have a quasi-criminal character but differ from traditional crimes in their definitional elements (the actus reus consists in many cases in an omission and liability is 'quasi'- strict), in the sanctions following a conviction but most noticeably in the mechanisms through which they are enforced.[1882]

Similarly, in the Netherlands, the Economic Offences Act (*Wet op de economische delicten*) contains many provisions which were particularly drafted to apply to legal entities and to regulate the corporate world. It *inter alia* criminalises violations of the Distribution of Goods Act (*Distributiewet*), Agriculture Act

1880 Hefendehl, 'Corporate Criminal Liability – Model Penal Code Section 2.07 and the Development in Western Legal Systems' Buffalo Criminal Law Review (2001), p. 286.

1881 Thomson Newspapers Ltd v Director of Investigation and Research (1990) 54 CCC 417. Cited in: Pinto and Evans, 'Corporate Criminal Liability' (2003), p. 314.

1882 Gobert and Punch, 'Rethinking Corporate Crime' (2003), p. 53.

(Landbouwwet), Commodities Act (*Warenwet*), Groundwater Act (*Grondwaterwet*) and the Protection of Soil Act (*Wet bodembescherming*). All these economic offences are of course highly relevant for many day to day business operations of legal entities and therefore play an important role to regulate corporate conduct. The crucial difference between the Dutch Economic Offences Act, the German Administrative Offences Act and English regulatory offences however is that the latter two formally impose no criminal but quasi-criminal or administrative sanctions while the Dutch Economic Offences Act is a criminal law Act by nature.

As will subsequently be discussed in more detail, in the German system administrative offences (*Ordnungswidrigkeiten*) play a vital role in regulating the economic and business world (e.g. national competition law) as well as many other aspects of every day life such as road traffic, food safety and protection of the environment. The only possible sanction to be imposed according to the Act is a regulatory fine and administrative offences are considered to differ substantially from criminal offences. Imprisonment is for example not an alternative to the imposed fine. The Act is sought to deal with minor offences only which entail a lesser degree of wrongdoing and were therefore segregated from the traditional realm of criminal law.[1883] Criminal law, so it is argued protects the very foundations as well as essential rights and interests of the community. Administrative offences, just like regulatory offences in England are sought first and foremost to protect public order. They, so it is often argued, do not involve a degree of ethical unworthiness such as to merit for its perpetrator the moral value judgment of reproach that characterises criminal punishment.

§1 (1) of the Act defines an administrative offence as an unlawful and reprehensible act contravening a legal provision which makes the offender liable to a fine. Administrative Offences are to be dealt with by the administrative authorities designated by law, save in so far as the Act confers the power of prosecution of such offences on the public prosecutor and their judgment and sentencing on the courts (§§35 and 36 Administrative offences Act).

As already mentioned, the only available sanction is a fine, which arguably carries with it no moral reproach and less social stigma than traditional criminal law sanctions. The structure and functioning of the Administrative Offences Act is however identical to the one of German criminal law (i.e. tripartite structure of crime, etc.). Moreover, the related nature of administrative and criminal offences is revealed by §46 of the Act which holds that the provisions of the ordinary law governing criminal procedure, and in particular the Code of Criminal Procedure, the Judicature Act and the Juvenile Courts Act are applicable by analogy to the procedure in respect of administrative offences.

Due to its scope of application, there are however some noteworthy differences in comparison to criminal law. First, administrative offences are prosecuted according to the opportunity principle (§47), while in criminal law the principle of

[1883] Bohnert, 'Introduction', in Senge (ed), Karlsruher Kommentar zum Gesetz über Ordnungswidrigkeiten (2006), Mn 84.

legality is applied.[1884] Both areas of law adhere to the principle of guilt, but the Administrative Offences Act seems to apply a slightly different concept than criminal law as it utilises the term "reprehension" instead of guilt, which in turn also facilitates the inclusion of corporate wrongdoing into the scope of the Act. This is due to the fact that "reprehension" is sought not to contain a degree of ethical unworthiness. It is further worthwhile mentioning here that the German legislator has opted for a unitarian mode of participation due to practical considerations in the Administrative Offences Act.[1885] This arguably goes to show that in the regulatory context, considerations of efficiency and expediency play a much more important role as is the case in regard to conventional wrongdoing.

2.3. Strict liability offences

Another solution which bypasses the aforementioned problem of moral blameworthiness of corporations is to declare it irrelevant for corporate responsibility. Therefore another category of offences which are frequently applied to control corporate conduct are strict liability offences. These offences are often used in the business and economic sphere in the English and Dutch penal system, but are alien to German criminal and administrative law, where the principle of guilt is sought to prevent the introduction of such offences. In any case, as they do not require any proof of mens rea, they avoid the aforementioned daunting challenge to establish fault on the part of the corporation.[1886]

2.4. Personal liability of corporate directors

From the perspective of traditional criminal law probably the most obvious way to tackle corporate wrongdoing is to hold individuals within a corporation responsible for their personal wrongdoing.[1887] In this case, the general principles of criminal liability, as outlined in previous chapters, are applied to individual wrongdoing. A manager for instance, who commits fraud while on company business will incur the risk of personal prosecution. As already indicated, this is the prevalent and exclusive approach taken by German criminal law which due to its individualistic focus attempts to attribute liability to individuals for collective wrongdoing. Yet also in the Netherlands and England this path is open to the prosecution.

If one includes legal entities as fit subjects into the realm of criminal law further possibilities to hold individuals responsible arise. If a corporation has been found to

---

1884 Bohnert, 'Introduction', in Senge (ed), Karlsruher Kommentar zum Gesetz über Ordnungswidrigkeiten (2006), Mn 95.

1885 Jescheck and Weigend, 'Lehrbuch des Strafrechts: Allgemeiner Teil' (1996), p. 647, Smith, 'Strafbare Voorbereiding, Een rechtsverglijkend onderzoek' (2003), p. 58.

1886 Smith and Hogan, 'Criminal Law' (2008), p. 247.

1887 Smith and Hogan, 'Criminal Law' (2008), p. 247. See also Article 51(2) 2. DPC.

be criminally liable for a harm occurred, an individual employee or director can for instance be held responsible as a participant in the corporation's wrongdoing.[1888] It is for instance worthwhile recalling here that many statutes in English law impose secondary liability on directors, manager, etc. for an offence committed by a body corporate under some provision of the relevant Act.[1889]

Furthermore, also the converse situation is conceivable, i.e. that the corporation is held liable as a participant in the individual's wrongdoing.[1890] A big advantage of this approach is that it introduces an assessment of the corporation's fault, as accessorial liability requires intentional conduct by the participant. This could quite easily be established if one scrutinises a company's polices, practices or culture, which may encourage, facilitate and aid or abet, criminal conduct by individuals.[1891] It would then fall to the courts to determine what amounts to a sufficient contribution by a corporation, to an offence committed by a natural person to warrant a conviction as an accessory.[1892] An example of such an approach can be found in the English decision of *National Coal Board v Gamble*.[1893] In this case a weighbridge operator employed by the Coal board issued a ticket to a lorry driver that allowed him to drive his truck on the road, despite the fact that the fully loaded truck exceeded the maximum permissible weight. Although the operator insistently warned the truck driver and only reluctantly issued the ticket, the Coal Board was held liable as an accessory to the lorry driver's offence.

These possibilities draw attention to the intricate question as to the relationship of individual and collective responsibility. This is because of the fact that it might not always be easy to pinpoint within a corporation the individual responsible for the occurred harm. In an entity where responsibility can be diffused and the chain of command complex, traditional criminal law might struggle to attribute liability to a particular individual. Furthermore, in some cases, the committed individual offences could be the outcome of persistent corporate pressure to resort to illegal methods rather than the criminal proclivities of an individual. This is, however, not to say that individual responsibility is completely inapt to tackle corporate wrongdoing, but rather that it needs to be recognised that in most cases in addition to the prosecution of individuals, the company ought to shoulder a share of the responsibility and legal blame for the committed offence.[1894] In other words, individual and corporate criminal liability should not be viewed as mutually exclusive, but rather as complementary approaches to tackle corporate crime.[1895] An individual should not become the scapegoat for corporate wrongdoing but by

---

1888 Smith and Hogan, 'Criminal Law' (2008), p. 247.

1889 See: Chapter III. 5.2.

1890 See: De Hullu, 'Materieel Strafrecht' (2009), p. 164. See also: National Coal Board v Gamble [1959] 1 QB 11.

1891 Gobert and Punch, 'Rethinking Corporate Crime' (2003), p. 71.

1892 Gobert and Punch, 'Rethinking Corporate Crime' (2003), p. 71.

1893 [1959] 1 QB 11.

1894 Gobert and Punch, 'Rethinking Corporate Crime' (2003), p. 38.

1895 Gobert and Punch, 'Rethinking Corporate Crime' (2003), p. 50.

the same token, a corporation should not become the scapegoat for individual wrongdoing.[1896] Whether in a particular case, proceedings should be brought against an individual, the corporation, or both will of course depend on the facts and circumstances of each particular case. This also seems to be the view of the Union legislator who in many legal instruments has stated that the liability of legal persons shall not have the effect to exclude criminal proceedings against natural persons who have committed a criminal offence.[1897]

3. Models of Corporate criminal liability

3.1. Introduction

Generally speaking, when it needs to be evaluated whether or not a corporation can be seen as the perpetrator of a criminal act, two separate questions come to the fore. First, it needs to be determined which conduct can be objectively attributed to the corporation.[1898] Second, it needs to be determined when this conduct also subjectively needs to be attributed to the corporation.[1899] This dichotomy centres on the establishment of blameworthiness in regard to the corporation. Only conduct for which the corporation is responsible, i.e. blameworthy can be reasonably attributed to the corporation. It is namely conceivable that in a particular case, an individual is to blame for the occurred criminal conduct and not the corporation.[1900] Incorporating legal entities into the criminal law necessarily entails that bedrock principles of criminal law such as the principle of guilt ought to be applied to corporations as well in order to avoid a distortion of the framework of criminal liability. Yet, it has to be acknowledged that corporations may be at fault in a different manner than is generally accepted in regard to individual wrongdoing. Culpability and liability of corporate actors may well be premised on a different set of principles as applied to individuals, but this does not diminish the fact that the same fundamental principles should apply and protect individual and corporate actors alike.

It has already been pointed out that the different conceptions of corporate personality, i.e. the atomic or organic view lead to different models of corporate criminal liability. It is evident that, depending on one's point of view, different

[1896] Gobert and Punch, 'Rethinking Corporate Crime' (2003), p. 50.

[1897] See for instance Article 6 (3) of Directive 2008/99 of 19 November 2008 on the protection of the environment through criminal law, OJ 2008 L 328/28. See also: Klip, 'European Criminal Law' (2012), p. 210.

[1898] Roef, 'Strafbare overheden – Een rechtsvergelijkende studie naar de strafrechtelijke aansprakelijkheid van overheden voor milieuverstoring' (2001), p. 326.

[1899] Roef, 'Strafbare overheden – Een rechtsvergelijkende studie naar de strafrechtelijke aansprakelijkheid van overheden voor milieuverstoring' (2001), p. 326.

[1900] Roef, 'Strafbare overheden – Een rechtsvergelijkende studie naar de strafrechtelijke aansprakelijkheid van overheden voor milieuverstoring' (2001), p. 327.

solutions to the predicament when liability can reasonably be attributed to a corporation may be found. Accordingly, a multitude of different criteria have been developed and applied by the courts.

Generally speaking, in the quest for such criteria one can either strive to apply traditional criminal law concepts, designed for individual wrongdoing to corporations, or search for new, concepts, tailor-made for the needs of corporate wrongdoing.[1901] Proponents of the atomic view generally favour an anthropomorphic approach which looks to assign human characteristics to corporations. However, as already mentioned, applying the traditional actus reus and mens rea distinction to corporate wrongdoing is prone to lead to problems as in regard to legal entities it seems at times hardly possible to distinguish conduct from culpa, viz. blameworthiness, unless the legislator opts to apply a strict objective interpretation to these concepts. Nevertheless an anthropomorphic approach strives to apply the conventional tools of criminal law to corporate actors as well. Therefore the law can *inter alia* tap into the (individual) conduct and states of mind of corporate members (e.g. employees, managers, directors, etc.) and derive corporate liability from them (vicarious or identification liability) or sidestep the matter and create an objective link between the occurred harm and the corporation by focusing on the (financial) gain generated by the wrongful conduct under evaluation (benefit theory).

In any case, a nice example of an anthropomorphic approach can be found in the English penal system, but as will subsequently become evident, it also constitutes the prevalent approach to corporate liability in the German Administrative Offences Act and residues of it are also visible in the Dutch penal system. By and large, it can be said that the English penal system has adopted a nominalist approach regarding the nature of corporate personality. A corporation is regarded as a collectivity of individuals and the idea that a corporation itself can act and be at fault is regarded as a fiction. As Lord Reid nicely held in *Tesco Supermarkets Ltd v Nattrass*:

> I must start by considering the nature of the personality which by a fiction the law attributes to a corporation. A living person has a mind which can have knowledge or intention or be negligent and he has hands to carry out his intentions. A corporation has none of these: it must act through living persons, though not always one or the same persons.[1902]

The prevalent anthropomorphic approach is vividly illustrated by a statement of Lord Justice Denning in *HL Bolton (Engineering) Co v. T.J. Graham & Sons, Ltd*:

> A company may in many ways be linked to a human body. It has a brain and nerve centre which controls what it does. It also has hands which hold the tools and act in accordance with directions from the centre. Some of the people in the company are mere servants and agents who are nothing more than hands to do the work and

1901 De Hullu, 'Materieel Strafrecht' (2006), p. 160.
1902 [1972] AC 153.

> cannot be said to represent the mind or will. Others are directors and managers who represent the directing mind and will of the company, and control what it does. The state of mind of these managers is the state of mind of the company and is treated by the law as such.[1903]

It becomes apparent that according to this approach the responsibility of a corporation is necessarily derived from the responsibility of an individual actor.[1904] Only if in the case at hand individual responsibility can be established, does the question of corporate liability arise. Based on this view of a corporation as a fictional entity, one can roughly distinguish two different models of corporate liability: vicarious and identification liability.

On the one hand, the two models differ greatly in terms of their essence, structure and scope, but on the other they show the same desire to assimilate and adapt the orthodox imposition of criminal liability on human beings. By invoking these ideas of assimilation and adaptation, the law attempted to make legal norms designed to govern human conduct, i.e. requiring human characteristics, applicable to corporations as well.[1905] Accordingly, the two models have common points of departure. Both models initially look at the behaviour and mens rea of a human being who has brought about the underlying offence. The two models subsequently create auxiliary legal structures through which the liability, conduct or mens rea of this human being is imputed to the corporation thereby rendering it criminally liable.[1906]

However, the concept of vicarious liability, as will soon become clear is a much more objective one than the identification doctrine. It constitutes a mode of attribution rather than a model of liability as it attributes liability for the acts of another without considering the blameworthiness of the body corporate. This may explain why the doctrine in the English penal system is by and large only applied to establish corporate liability for strict liability offences. The vicarious liability doctrine again shares its objective approach with the benefit theory, which also formerly turns a blind eye to the issue of corporate culpability and proceeds to attribute liability on the grounds of the objective advantage generated by the wrongful conduct for the corporation. In the following section these two objective models of liability will briefly be discussed before the analysis turns to the identification doctrine.

1903 [1957] 1 QB 159.

1904 Colvin, 'Corporate Personality and Criminal Liability' Criminal Law Forum (1995), p. 2.

1905 Lederman, 'Models for Imposing Corporate Criminal Liability: From Adaptation and Imitation Toward Aggregation and the Search for Self-Identity' Buffalo Criminal Law Review (2000), p. 651.

1906 Lederman, 'Models for Imposing Corporate Criminal Liability: From Adaptation and Imitation Toward Aggregation and the Search for Self-Identity' Buffalo Criminal Law Review (2000), p. 651.

3.2. Objective models of liability: Vicarious liability and the benefit theory

The doctrine of vicarious liability has already been outlined and discussed in a previous chapter which is why the treatment of the notion can be brief here.[1907] The doctrine constitutes a peculiarity of common law which is not as such recognised in the civil law systems of Germany and the Netherlands. Based on the maxim "*qui facit per alium facit per se*" (he who acts through another acts through himself), the doctrine of vicarious liability holds that one can be held responsible for the acts of another person as if they were one's own acts.[1908] In other words, "vicarious liability is a mechanism by which the law attributes blame for the acts of another".[1909] Consequently, where a statute imposes vicarious liability, or where courts have found the doctrine to be applicable, a corporation can be held vicariously liable for the acts of its employees or agents, just like a natural person would be liable in these circumstances.[1910] The doctrine proceeds to the attribution of the act of the individual to the corporation in a two-step process. First, it needs to be established whether the conduct of the individual fulfils all the elements enshrined in the underlying offence. Once this has been established, the liability of the individual is imputed to the corporation, based on the legal relationship between the corporation and the individual, i.e. agency or employment. This imputation is based on the legal fiction that the actions and/or the state of mind of the individual are the actions or state of mind of the corporation.[1911] Thus, the doctrine embodies a strict objective approach to corporate conduct (how else than through its employees can a corporation be deemed to act?) and sidesteps the conundrum of corporate culpability by effectively declaring it irrelevant. The creation of a body corporate, which participates and carries out intrinsically dangerous processes is according to this approach deemed sufficient per se to attribute harmful and dangerous consequences to the corporation.[1912]

Arguably the doctrine's biggest drawback in regard to corporate liability is its link to individual liability. As the doctrine is only activated through the criminal liability of some individual, this means that a corporation cannot be held criminally liable if no individual liability can be established. Precisely this, however, can prove to be a daunting challenge in practice and presents problems of proof to prosecutors. In modern capitalistic society where the increasing division of labour leads to an increasing diffusion of responsibility, it may often be clear that a criminal wrong

---

1907 See: Chapter III. 7.2.3.

1908 Fletcher, 'Basic Concepts of Criminal Law' (1998), p. 190.

1909 Smith and Hogan, 'Criminal Law' (2008), p. 258.

1910 Smith and Hogan, 'Criminal Law' (2008), p. 248.

1911 Lederman, 'Models for Imposing Corporate Criminal Liability: From Adaptation and Imitation Toward Aggregation and the Search for Self-Identity' Buffalo Criminal Law Review (2000), p. 652.

1912 Heine, 'Rethinking Criminal Liability of Enterprises: International Developments, Basic Models, National Consequences', in Faure and Schwarz (eds), De Strafrechtelijke en civielrechtelijke aansprakelijkheid van de rechtspersoon en zijn bestuurders (1998), p. 171.

has occurred, it might, however, not always be equally clear who is to blame.[1913] Furthermore it can sometimes prove to be impossible to identify one single cause of a criminal harm, but rather different individuals within the corporation may bear varying degrees of responsibility. Arguably, it would be commendable in these cases to attribute the offence to the corporation as a whole rather than to attempt to unearth individual responsibility, as this might very well prove to be the proverbial search for the needle in the haystack.

Apart from these practical considerations it can further be argued that the doctrine of vicarious liability violates the fundamental criminal law principle *nulla poene sine culpa*. In short, this principle holds that only defendants whose blameworthiness has sufficiently been proven should be subject to criminal sanctions. The doctrine of vicarious liability, however, would make a corporation criminally liable regardless of the company's fault. As long as it can be proved that an individual has committed a criminal offence, the corporation will be held liable, even when it has not been at fault or behaved in a blameworthy manner.[1914] In other words, under the doctrine of vicarious liability, a company would be held responsible for the behaviour of a maverick employee even if it had set up an exemplary system of control and harm prevention. This may also conflict with the principle of legality as corporations may arguably not be expected to be aware of the conduct of all its employees which would in certain cases add an unwelcome element of surprise to the imposition of corporate liability. For the aforementioned reasons and due to the over-inclusiveness of the doctrine, English courts have viewed the doctrine with circumscription and a degree of antipathy.

An interesting variation of vicarious liability in the English penal system, which arguably avoids some of the frictions the doctrine causes in regard to the principle of *nulla poena sine culpa*, can however be found in the Bribery Act 2010. The Act creates four prime offences which are enshrined in sections 1, 2, 6 and 7. Section 1 criminalises the offering, promising or giving of a financial or other advantage (i.e. active bribery), while section 2 deals with requesting, agreeing to receive or accepting a financial or other advantage (i.e. passive bribery). Section 6 on the other hand creates a discrete offence of bribing a foreign public official.[1915] The most relevant provision for the discussion here is however to be found in section 7. This section imposes vicarious liability on corporations for failure to prevent bribery carried out on its behalf.[1916] Thus a commercial organisation will incur liability pursuant to section 7 of the Bribery Act 2010 if a person associated with the corporation bribes another person to obtain or retain business or a business

1913 Gobert and Punch, 'Rethinking Corporate Crime' (2003), pp. 78–81.

1914 Gobert and Punch, 'Rethinking Corporate Crime' (2003), p. 62.

1915 See: Sullivan, 'The Bribery Act 2010: Part 1: an overview' Criminal Law Review (2011), pp. 88–95, Yeoh, 'The UK Bribery Act 2010: contents and implications' Journal of Financial Crime (2012), p. 42.

1916 Gentle, 'The Bribery Act 2010: Part 2: the corporate offence' Criminal Law Review (2011), p. 102.

advantage for the corporation.[1917] The payment of the bribe by the person acting on behalf of the corporation must amount to an offence under section 1 or 6 of the Bribery Act 2010. The scope of people to be associated with the corporation is quite broad as according to section 8 any person who performs services for or on behalf of the corporation will qualify. If the person in question is an employee of the corporation, the act establishes a rebuttable presumption in section 8 (5) that the employee constitutes an "associated person".[1918]

This potentially creates a very wide basis for corporate criminal liability in the context of bribery. This broad scope is however circumscribed by section 7 (2) of the Bribery Act 2010 which introduces a statutory due diligence defence if the organisation on the balance of probabilities can prove that it had in place, adequate procedures designed to prevent bribery by those associated with it.[1919] From this provision it can arguably be deduced that the Act contains important regulatory aspects and aspires to change corporate governance and achieve commercial conduct-compliance.[1920] Moreover, by creating a serious criminal offence to which the applicable defence is proof of regulatory compliance also shows that criminal and regulatory categories increasingly merge in the context of corporate liability.

Leaving the Bribery Act aside, the discussion can now turn to a cognate theory to the doctrine of vicarious liability namely the so called benefit theory. Much like the doctrine of vicarious liability, it adopts an objective conception of corporate wrongdoing and bypasses the culpability conundrum by placing the emphasis on the question who benefited from the criminal conduct.[1921] In this case the objective link for attributing liability to a company is thus less the relationship between the individual and the corporation but rather the alleged profit the corporation reaped from the wrongful conduct. The Dutch Supreme Court applied this criterion in the *Vroom & Dreesman* judgment.[1922] In this case, a leading employee had, against the explicit instructions of the company, sold furniture for a price in excess of the relevant statutory maximum (a strict liability offence). The Supreme Court held that the conduct could nevertheless be attributed to the company, as it had benefited from it.

This criterion is also often applied in connection with other models of attribution such as the identification doctrine. The European version of the identification

---

1917 It is interesting to note here that the offence of section 7 will be committed irrespective of whether the acts or omissions which form part of the offence take place in the UK. In other words this is an offence of universal jurisdiction. See: section 12 (5) of the Bribery Act 2010.

1918 Sullivan, 'The Bribery Act 2010: Part 1: an overview' Criminal Law Review (2011), p. 95.

1919 Gentle, 'The Bribery Act 2010: Part 2: the corporate offence' Criminal Law Review (2011), p. 102.

1920 Gentle, 'The Bribery Act 2010: Part 2: the corporate offence' Criminal Law Review (2011), p. 107.

1921 Kelk, 'Studieboek materieel strafrecht' (2005), p. 385. Roef, 'Strafbare overheden – Een rechtsvergelijkende studie naar de strafrechtelijke aansprakelijkheid van overheden voor milieuverstoring' (2001), p. 337.

1922 HR 27 January 1948, *NJ* 1948, 197.

doctrine for instance, as well as the German Administrative Offences Act, allow for the attribution of conduct or rather fault of a representative to the company if the corporation benefited from it.

The benefit theory suffers from much the same shortcomings as the doctrine of vicarious liability and *in itself*, it is submitted, ought not to be sufficient to attribute a criminal conduct to a corporation. Admittedly, the theory can function as a strong indicator that the criminal conduct can be objectively attributed to the company, but it completely neglects issues of blameworthiness.[1923] Nevertheless, it will subsequently become clear that the objective vicarious liability and benefit theory are part and parcel of the Dutch approach towards corporate liability as conduct that benefited the company or respectively was carried out by an employee and the like may be attributed to the corporation.

3.3. The identification doctrine in English law

To remedy some of the perceived shortcomings of the vicarious liability doctrine, the English courts in the 1940's began to devise a new route to establish corporate liability – the identification doctrine. The term 'identification doctrine' generally refers to an English doctrine of corporate liability but it is also known in the Netherlands and applied in the German Administrative Offences Act. As all forms of derivative corporate liability this theory is based on a strict anthropomorphic view regarding corporations. The corporation is seen as a collectivity of individuals and is perceived as an analogous human being. The corporation is identified through its company organs or other natural persons.[1924] Accordingly, the theory holds that a company is deemed to have committed a crime if one of its organs has fulfilled the actus reus and mens rea of the respective crime while acting within his/her scope of employment.

Before the introduction of Article 51 into the Dutch Penal Code which holds that criminal acts can be committed by natural as well as legal persons, the doctrine was applied in the Netherlands as well, but the Supreme Court discarded this theory in the *A.T.O.* judgment.[1925] The court held that it is not required for a corporation to incur criminal liability that the criminal conduct has been brought about by a company organ. Despite this renunciation it will be demonstrated in subsequent sections that some residues of the anthropomorphic perception are still visible in Dutch jurisprudence. In English and German law the doctrine is still the prevalent approach to establish the liability of legal entities.

1923 Roef, 'Strafbare overheden – Een rechtsvergelijkende studie naar de strafrechtelijke aansprakelijkheid van overheden voor milieuverstoring' (2001), p. 337.

1924 De Hullu, 'Materieel Strafrecht' (2006), p. 328. Kelk, 'Studieboek materieel strafrecht' (2005), p. 384.

1925 HR 27 February 1951, *NJ* 1951, 474.

English judges were relatively slow to accept that corporations could also be liable for traditional penal offences. This can *inter alia* be explained by the fact that the prosecution of corporations within the orthodox model of criminal law creates difficulties. This is hardly surprising, if one takes into consideration that the criminal law was tailor-made to control human behaviour and was not developed with companies in mind.[1926] Primarily "human concepts" such as actus reus and mens rea cannot be applied easily to an inanimate fictional entity.[1927] The solution of English criminal law flowing from the nominalist conception that a corporation is a fiction and is not capable of performing an actus reus or forming a mens rea was to treat the minds and bodies of controlling officers as supplying the mental and physical faculties of a corporation.[1928] To put it more simply, the identification doctrine equates the corporation with certain key personnel who act on its behalf.[1929] The foundation for the notion that a corporation could be directly liable for a criminal offence was laid in three cases in 1944.[1930]

Within every company, so the argument goes there exists a class of persons who are the "directing mind and will" of the corporation. Accordingly, these persons, when acting in the company's business, are regarded as an embodiment of the company. In *Lennard's Carrying Co, Ltd v Asiatic Petroleum Co, Ltd*, Lord Viscount Haldane, delivering the speech for the House of Lords nicely summarised this line of thought:

> A corporation is an abstraction. It has no mind of its own any more than it has a body of its own; its active and directing will must consequently be sought in the person of somebody who for some purposes may be called an agent, but who is really the directing mind and will of the corporation, the very ego and centre of the personality of the corporation.[1931]

Thus, the acts and states of mind of these persons are regarded as the acts and state of mind of the corporation. Hence, the corporation is not held liable for the acts of others but for what are deemed to be its own acts.[1932]

It is interesting to note here that the identification doctrine, like the vicarious liability doctrine, follows a two dimensional structure. Similarly, under the identification doctrine the conduct of an individual is considered first. Subsequently it is considered whether or not under the given circumstances it is appropriate to

---

1926 Gobert and Punch, 'Rethinking Corporate Crime' (2003), p. 9.

1927 Gobert and Punch, 'Rethinking Corporate Crime' (2003), p. 10.

1928 Smith and Hogan, 'Criminal Law' (2008), p. 248.

1929 Colvin, 'Corporate Personality and Criminal Liability' Criminal Law Forum (1995), p. 8.

1930 Moore v Bresler [1994] 2 All E.R. 515; R v ICR Haulage [1944] 30 Cr App R 31; DPP v Kent and Sussex Contractors [1944] KB 146. See also: Pinto and Evans, 'Corporate Criminal Liability' (2003), pp. 39–46. See further: Wells, 'Corporations: Culture, Risk and Criminal Liability' The Criminal Law Review (1993), p. 559.

1931 [1914–1915] All ER 280.

1932 Smith and Hogan, 'Criminal Law' (2008), p. 248.

regard this individual conduct as representing the company. If that is deemed to be the case, the company is held criminally liable.[1933] According to the supporters of the theory this approach is closer to reality than vicarious liability. As a company is a fictional entity, so it is argued, it necessarily has to act through human representatives. It seems logical to restrict the scope of people who are deemed to represent the company to a relatively small group of persons. Moreover, it appears to be a more accurate depiction of reality to perceive only certain individuals due to their status, their authority and their behaviour to represent the company.[1934] To sum up, the identification doctrine circumscribes the scope of corporate liability by curtailing the scope of people that can make a corporation liable. This rectifies much of the over-inclusive effects of the vicarious liability doctrine.[1935]

3.3.1. The application of the identification doctrine

The landmark decision that established the doctrine in the English penal system was the case of *Tesco Supermarkets v Nattrass*.[1936] In this case the House of Lords established that a company could be held responsible for an offence requiring mens rea if the person who had brought about the actus reus could be identified with the company. The defendant, a large chain of supermarkets was charged with an offence under the Trade Description Act 1968. The offence occurred due to a local store manager's failure to supervise his employees properly. Tesco argued that the store manager was not sufficiently high up on the ladder of responsibility within the corporation to be identified with it. The House of Lords concurred. Lord Reid held, in regard to the circumscribed scope of people that may be identified with the company as follows:

> Normally the board of directors, the managing director and perhaps other superior officers of a company carry out the functions of management and speak and act as the company. Their subordinates do not. They carry out orders from above and it can make no difference that they are given some measure of discretion. But the board of directors may delegate some part of their functions of management giving to their delegate full discretion to act independently of instructions from them.

It becomes already apparent from this dictum that the pitfall of this doctrine lies in identifying the persons that may be identified with the corporation. The approach of the English penal system is especially restrictive, as only the board of directors, the

---

1933 Lederman, 'Models for Imposing Corporate Criminal Liability: From Adaptation and Imitation Toward Aggregation and the Search for Self-Identity' Buffalo Criminal Law Review (2000), p. 656.

1934 Lederman, 'Models for Imposing Corporate Criminal Liability: From Adaptation and Imitation Toward Aggregation and the Search for Self-Identity' Buffalo Criminal Law Review (2000), p. 656.

1935 Colvin, 'Corporate Personality and Criminal Liability' Criminal Law Forum (1995), p. 9.

1936 [1972] AC 153.

managing director and perhaps other superior officers of a company can be identified with the company. In other words, only senior managers will be deemed to represent the company. Thus, it can be said that the identification test gives rise to a multitude of questions, in particular regarding the difficult identification of those who warrant to be identified with the corporation. At the end of the day, metaphors referring to the directing mind and will of a company, etc. are not particularly illuminating in this respect.[1937]

Corporations have *inter alia* been held not to be criminally liable for the acts of a depot engineer or a weighbridge operator.[1938] The extremely narrow scope of the doctrine within the English criminal law, is nicely demonstrated by the judgment of the Court of Appeal in *R v Redfern and Dunlop Ltd (Aircraft Division)*.[1939] The company was accused of fraudulently evading export provisions of the Customs and Exercise Management Act 1979. The European Sales manager had sold tyres for combat aircrafts to a company located in Switzerland, allegedly aware of the fact that the Swiss company was in fact a sham company and the tyres destined for Iran. The Court of Appeal considered the manager, who was four steps down in the "chain of command" from the chief executive not to wield sufficient power within the company to be identified with it. Equally proceedings like *R v P & O European Ferries (Dover) Ltd* bear witness to the narrow scope of the doctrine.[1940] The P&O trial arose after the Herald of Free Enterprise disaster in which nearly 200 people lost their lives. The ferry had left the harbour with its bow doors open which lead to the capsising of the vessel. Despite the fact that independent reports had found severe shortcomings on part of the company the prosecution failed because the judge was not convinced that a sufficient senior company manager had acted reckless in regard to the occurred harm.[1941]

3.3.2. Acting within the scope of corporate duty

The person to be identified with the company must have been acting within the scope of his employment or authority, in the sense that at the time when he performed the required actus reus and mens rea of the offence, he acted within the assigned area of operation.[1942] Only then can his actions and state of mind be treated as the acts of the company. In other words, the controlling officer must act *intra vires*. Any *ultra vires* conduct cannot be imputed to the company.

1937 Gobert and Punch, 'Rethinking Corporate Crime' (2003), p. 64.

1938 John Henshall (Quarries) Ltd v Harvey [1965] 2 QB 233, Magna Plant Ltd v Mitchell [1966] Crim LR 394. See also: Smith and Hogan, 'Criminal Law' (2008), p. 249.

1939 [1993] Crim LR 43.

1940 [1990] 93 Cr App R 72.

1941 Wells, 'Corporate Manslaughter: A Culture and Legal Form' Criminal Law Forum (1995), p. 63.

1942 Smith and Hogan, 'Criminal Law' (2008), p. 251.

3.3.3. The Meridian Case: Towards a more flexible approach of identification?

In the case of *Meridian Global Funds Management Asia Ltd v Securities Commission*, the Privy Council, grappling with the narrow scope of the identification doctrine offered a more flexible approach to the problem of attributing mental states to a corporation.[1943] In this case Meridan was prosecuted for an alleged breach of security legislation and the crux of the case was whether the company had knowledge of the scheming of its investment managers. Lord Hoffman delivering the judgment interpreted the identification doctrine as a sub part of a broader rule of attribution and suggested that the directing mind model established in *Tesco Supermarkets v Nattrass* might not always be appropriate.[1944] He held that whether an act in breach of a statutory offence could be attributed to the company was a question of construction of the respective statute, examining the language of the particular statute, its content and policy.[1945] In essence, while the identification doctrine can constitute a valuable tool in some cases, it should not constitute the end of an investigation, but courts should rather consider all applicable rules of attribution.[1946] Thus a statute may impose corporate liability also in cases of knowledge situated outside the directing mind of the company.

This purposive construction came to be acclaimed by many as a welcome relaxation of the rigid identification doctrine.[1947] However, the prospect of an expanded scope of corporate liability in the English penal system was rejected by the Court of Appeal in *Attorney General's Reference (No 2 of 1999)* at least in respect to common law crimes.[1948] The proceedings arose in the aftermath of the 1997 Southall rail crash and the company was indicted on seven counts of manslaughter (a common law crime). The prosecution claimed that: "the ingredients of the offence of gross negligence manslaughter are the same in relation to a body corporate as to a human being, namely grossly negligent breach of a duty to a deceased causative of his death". It was, so the argument went, therefore "unnecessary and inappropriate to enquire whether there was an employee in the company who is guilty of the offence of manslaughter who can properly be said to have been acting as the embodiment of the company".

The Court of Appeal rejected the argument and held that the identification doctrine remained the only basis in common law for corporate liability for gross negligence manslaughter. The court thus distinguished Meridian as involving a statutory offence, while manslaughter was a common law crime. As it could not be

---

1943 [1995] 2 AC 500.

1944 Wells, 'Corporations and Criminal Responsibility' (2001), p. 103.

1945 Smith and Hogan, 'Criminal Law' (2008), p. 250, Wells, 'Corporations and Criminal Responsibility' (2001), p. 103.

1946 Gobert and Punch, 'Rethinking Corporate Crime' (2003), p. 68.

1947 See: Wells, 'Corporations and Criminal Responsibility' (2001), pp. 103–105. Gobert and Punch, 'Rethinking Corporate Crime' (2003), pp. 68–69.

1948 [2000] QB 796.

proven in this case that a member of the directing mind of the company had acted grossly negligent, the identification doctrine was inapplicable and the case was dismissed.

It remains to be seen which impact the Meridian ruling will have on subsequent cases, but it is submitted that the desirable relaxation of the identification doctrine has introduced a degree of uncertainty in the English law on corporate responsibility, which in turn may also diminish foreseeability and accordingly be at odds with the principle of legality.[1949] In any case, it will subsequently be shown that the English penal system in regard to manslaughter charges has recently created a new path through which corporate liability may arise.

3.3.4. The impact of the Corporate Manslaughter and Corporate Homicide Act 2007

Recently the English legislator has adopted a new Act in regard to corporate criminal liability. It departs from the narrow anthropomorphic approach of the identification doctrine and can be seen as step towards an organic view of legal entities. The Act will be discussed in more detail below, but it also contains some elements which may also prove influential for the interpretation of the identification doctrine in the future.

The Act imposes corporate liability for the breach of a duty as a result of management failure.[1950] Thus at least in the realm of manslaughter, the pitfalls of the identification doctrine have now to some extent been removed.[1951] However, pursuant to section 1 (3), an organisation is guilty of an offence only if the way in which its activities are managed or organised by its senior management is a substantial element in the breach referred to in subsection 1. The Act subsequently defines senior management as: persons who play significant roles in –

(i) the making of decisions about the whole or a substantial part of its activities are to be managed or organised, or
(ii) the actual managing or organising of the whole or a substantial part of those activities.

It becomes apparent that this definition goes beyond the limited amount of people who could be regarded as the directing mind under the traditional identification doctrine. It remains, however, to be seen if judges will be influenced by this broader definition when considering the scope of persons to be identified with the corporation in the application of the identification doctrine more generally.[1952]

1949 Smith and Hogan, 'Criminal Law' (2008), p. 250.
1950 See: Section 1 (3), (4).
1951 Smith and Hogan, 'Criminal Law' (2008), p. 253.
1952 Smith and Hogan, 'Criminal Law' (2008), p. 253.

3.4. The identification doctrine in the German Administrative Offences Act

In the German Administrative Offences Act the liability of legal entities is enshrined in §30. It reads as follows:

(1) If a person
   1. acting in the capacity of an agency authorised to represent a legal entity, or as a member of such an agency,
   2. as the board of an association not having legal capacity, or as a member of such a board,
   3. as a partner of a commercial partnership authorised to representation, or
   4. as the fully authorised representative or in a leading position as a procura holder, or as general agent of a legal entity or of an association as specified in Nos. 2 or 3 has committed a criminal or administrative offence by means of which duties incumbent upon the legal entity or the association have been violated, or the legal entity or the association has gained or was supposed to gain a profit, a fine may be imposed on the latter.

(2) The fine shall be
   1. up to one million Euro in cases of a wilfully committed offence;
   2. up to five hundred thousand Euro in cases of a negligently committed offence.

   In cases of an administrative offence the maximum amount of the fine shall be assessed in accordance with the maximum fine provided for the administrative offence in question. The second sentence shall also apply in cases of an offence, which at the same time is both a criminal and an administrative offence if the maximum fine imposable for the administrative offence is in excess of the maximum fine in accordance with the first sentence.
(3) Section 17 subsection 4 and section 18 shall apply mutatis mutandis.
(4) If criminal proceedings or administrative fine proceedings in respect of the criminal or administrative offence are not initiated, or if they are discontinued, or if no punishment is deemed appropriate, the fine may be assessed separately. It may be specified by means of a statute that the fine may also be assessed separately in further cases. Separate assessment of a fine on the legal entity or association shall however be ruled out if the criminal or administrative offence cannot be prosecuted for legal reasons; section 33 subsection 1 second sentence shall remain unaffected.
(5) The assessment of a fine against the legal entity or association shall preclude forfeiture pursuant to sections 73 and 73a of the Criminal Code or Section 29a being ordered against it for the same act.[1953]

[1953] Translation taken from: www.oecd.org/dataoecd/62/54/2377479.pdf.

§30 thus provides for the imposition of a fine on a legal entity or association if (i) its representatives have committed a criminal or administrative offence (ii) by means of which duties incumbent upon the legal entity or the association have been violated, (iii) or the legal entity or the association has gained or (iv) was supposed to gain a profit. In other words, according to the German Administrative Offences Act a legal entity can incur liability if it can be established that one of its organs has committed an offence, which benefited the company or violated a duty of care resting on the company. From this brief description it already becomes apparent that the mode of liability enshrined in the Act is the identification doctrine, as a natural person must have committed an offence from which the liability of the corporation is derived.[1954] It follows that before a fine may be imposed on a corporation, liability for an offence must first be attributable to a company representative.[1955] This means that a representative must have played an active role in the commission of the offence before liability of a legal person can arise as a side effect of the individual's wrongdoing. Thus, the general approach of the Administrative Offences Act is to conceive corporations as fictional entities, which can neither act nor be at fault themselves. Only through their representatives, i.e. natural persons, can they act and commit offences.[1956] As the liability of the corporation hinges on the liability of a natural person legal lacunas can arise, as it might not always be easy to trace down a person who committed the offence within the organisation's framework. Therefore §30 (4) provides the room in certain circumstances to impose a fine on a corporation even though no individual is prosecuted for the offence. A fine can even be imposed if the identity of the person having committed the offence cannot be established.[1957] Yet, it is only the identity that need not be established. It must nevertheless be proven that a person pursuant to §30 (1) has committed the offence. Thus §30 (4) only superficially mitigates some of the shortcomings of the identification doctrine, but fails to remove it completely.

Similar to the English penal system the scope of people who can be identified with the legal entity is confined to persons who take a leading position within the company. Thus, to use the English terminology, only conduct of directors or managers who represent the directing mind and will of the company and control its activities can be attributed to the corporation.

It has already been mentioned that such a narrow approach is undesirable as offences committed by personnel below the directing mind and will, could not give rise to liability of the legal entity. This doctrinal lacuna is however partially remedied by §130 of the Act. This provision proscribes the failure to take supervisory measures by the owner of the company. Accordingly if a person falling outside the scope of §30 commits an offence, the failure of the owner of the

[1954] See: 2 November 2005 OLG Jena NStZ 2006, 533, 16 November 1995 OLG Düsseldorf NStZ 1996, 193.

[1955] See: 20 March 1996 OLG Dresden OLG-NL 1996, 215.

[1956] See: 20 March 1997 OLG Dresden NStZ 1997, 348.

[1957] See: 8 February 1994 BGH NStZ 1994, 346.

company to take supervisory measures which would have prevented or made the contravention much more difficult can give rise to the liability of the corporation as well.[1958] In short, corporate liability can thus arise in case the owner of the company consciously omits to exercise supervision over persons placed under his control. The failure to supervise is assessed on a case by case basis. Factors that may play a role thereby are the internal structure and organisation of the company as well as the internal division of tasks and the nature and scope of the controlling and supervisory measures in place.[1959] Thus, it seems fair to conclude that §130 in conjunction with §30 also entails an important regulatory dimension by aiming to increase corporate compliance with prevalent diligent standards.

Next to the requirement that the offence in question must have been committed by a representative of the corporation a further important requirement is that the violation committed by the individual is of such a quality as to warrant the imposition of a fine to the corporation. In other words, the cardinal question here is when an occurred offence can be seen as corporate wrongdoing. One possibility hereby is that the representative(s) committed an offence by means of which duties incumbent upon the legal entity or the association have been violated. The subsequent question then becomes which duties exactly can be seen to be incumbent upon the legal person?

In practice the most important duty is the duty to take supervisory measures pursuant to §130 of the Administrative Offences Act.[1960] The failure to supervise constitutes a violation of a duty of care incumbent on the owner of the company. This provision makes it thus possible to hold a corporation liable if a representative of the corporation or the association as outlined in §30 has failed to fulfil his duty to

---

1958 §130 reads as follows:

(1) Whoever, as the owner of a firm or an enterprise, wilfully or negligently fails to take the supervisory measures required to prevent contravention of duties in the firm or the enterprise which concern the owner in this capacity, and the violation of which is punishable by a penalty or a fine, shall be deemed to have committed an administrative offence if such a contravention is committed which could have been prevented or made much more difficult by proper supervision. The required supervisory measures shall also comprise appointment, careful selection and surveillance of supervisory personnel.

(2) A firm or an enterprise in accordance with subsections 1 and 2 shall include a public enterprise.

(3) If the administrative offence is subject to punishment, it may be punished by a fine not exceeding one million Euro. If the violation of duty is punishable by a fine, the maximum amount of the fine for a violation of obligatory supervision shall be dependent on the maximum amount of the fine provided for the violation of duty. The second sentence shall also apply in the event of a breach of duty which at the same time is punishable by a penalty and a fine if the maximum amount of the fine is in excess of the maximum amount in accordance with the first sentence. (Translation taken from: www.oecd.org/dataoecd/62/54/2377479.pdf).

1959 2 November 2005 OLG Jena NStZ 2006, 533.

1960 See: Rettenmaier and Palm, 'Das Ordnungswidrigkeitenrecht und die Aufsichtspflicht von Unternehmensverantwortlichen' NJOZ (2010), pp. 1414–1419.

take appropriate supervisory measures.[1961] As already mentioned, this construction however contains the danger that a company can avoid liability for a violation of §130 if it has delegated the duty to supervise to people outside the scope of §30 which can give rise to legal loopholes.

Moreover, duties incumbent upon the legal person are duties which pursuant to administrative or criminal law are connected to the sphere of the corporation's activities. One can think here of duties flowing from the legal entity's position as an employer, manufacturer, tradesman, entrepreneur, owner of assets or vehicles, importer, exporter, distributor, etc.[1962]

Finally, also general offences can amount to a violation of a duty incumbent upon the legal entity if the commission of the general offence can be seen as a violation of a duty of care falling within the sphere of the company. Here general duties of care pursuant to §13 GPC play an important role. One can think for instance of duties flowing from health and safety regulations. If a corporation for instance sells certain goods it is under a duty to prevent the consumer from any danger caused by this product. Likewise it is a duty of the legal entity to protect its employees from work related dangers. Similarly, if the corporation runs for instance a department store it is under a duty to protect any customers from danger.[1963]

A further possibility to conclude that an occurred violation constitutes corporate wrongdoing enshrined in §30 is that through the violation, the legal entity or the association has gained or was supposed to gain a profit. Under gain of profit any increase of the corporation's assets is generally subsumed. Also indirect gain such as for instance an improved position on the relevant market achieved by bribery or corruption can fall in this category.[1964] It should be noted here that in case a gain of profit has occurred the individual committing the offence need not have acted purposefully in regard to the gain. Naturally, this is however necessary if the corporation was supposed to gain a profit which brings attempted offences against property within the scope of §30.

The effective gain in profit must be wrongful as otherwise the gained profits would not be eligible for confiscation orders. Furthermore a causal link between the gained profit and the committed offence is required.[1965] This criterion bear some

[1961] Rogall, '§30 OWiG', in Senge (ed), Karlsruher Kommentar zum Gesetz über Ordnungswidrigkeiten (2006), Mn 75.

[1962] Rogall, '§30 OWiG', in Senge (ed), Karlsruher Kommentar zum Gesetz über Ordnungswidrigkeiten (2006), Mn 75.

[1963] Rogall, '§30 OWiG', in Senge (ed), Karlsruher Kommentar zum Gesetz über Ordnungswidrigkeiten (2006), Mn 76. Compare thereto also the provisions of the Bribery Act 2010 outlined above in chapter: V. 3.2.

[1964] Rogall, '§30 OWiG', in Senge (ed), Karlsruher Kommentar zum Gesetz über Ordnungswidrigkeiten (2006), Mn 82.

[1965] Rogall, '§30 OWiG', in Senge (ed), Karlsruher Kommentar zum Gesetz über Ordnungswidrigkeiten (2006), Mn 84.

resemblance to the benefit theory, discussed above, which limits the scope of §30 as not every offence aims at or achieves a gain of profit.[1966]

3.5. The identification doctrine in European Union Law

Also the Union legislator seems to advocate a variation of the identification doctrine. In the Council's draft guidelines and model provisions for criminal law the following provision can be found which is *mutatis mutandis* enshrined in a variety of legal instruments[1967]:

> 1. Each Member State shall [take the necessary measures to] ensure that a legal person can be held liable for offences referred to in Articles [Article on Criminal Offence] where such offences have been committed for its benefits by any person, acting either individually or as part of an organ of the legal person, who has a leading position within the legal person based on
>
> a) a power of representation of the legal person,
> b) an authority to take decisions on behalf of the legal person, or
> c) an authority to exercise control within the legal person.
>
> 2. Each Member State shall also ensure that a legal person can be held liable where the lack of supervision or control, by a person referred to in paragraph 1, has made possible the commission of an offence referred to in Article [Article on Criminal Offences] for the benefit of that legal person by a person under its authority.
>
> 3. Liability of a legal person under paragraphs 1 and 2 shall not exclude criminal proceedings against natural persons who are perpetrators, inciters or accessories in the offences referred to in Articles [Article on Criminal Offences].
>
> [...]

The provision seemingly combines aspects of the English identification doctrine with aspects from the German Administrative Offences Act. It identifies certain leading persons within the company with the legal person. If those persons commit

---

1966 Roef, 'Strafbare overheden – Een rechtsvergelijkende studie naar de strafrechtelijke aansprakelijkheid van overheden voor milieuverstoring' (2001), p. 169.

1967 Draft Council conclusions on model provisions, guiding the Council's criminal law deliberations, Brussels, 27 November 2009, 16542/2/09 REV 2. See for instance: Framework Decision 2002/475 of 13 June 2002 on combating terrorism, OJ 2002 L 164/3, Framework Decision 2005/667 of 12 July 2005 to strengthen the criminal law framework for the enforcement of the law against ship-source pollution OJ 2005, L 255/164, Directive 2008/99 of 19 November 2008 on the protection of the environment through criminal law, OJ 2008 L 328/28, Directive 2011/36 of 5 April 2011 on preventing and combating trafficking in human beings and protecting its victims, and replacing Council Framework Decision 2002/629/JHA, OJ 2011, L 101/06.

an offence for the benefit of the company the corporation can incur liability as well. Thus, in line with the teachings of the identification doctrine the liability of the organisation is indirect. It is deduced from the behaviour of a natural person which in turn triggers the liability of the organisation. The scope of liability is however circumscribed as the offence committed by the representative ought to have been committed for the benefit of the legal person.

On the other hand, the scope of the offence is broadened as the failure to take supervisory measures can lead to liability of the organisation as well. Thus, it seems possible that in case a person falling outside the scope of paragraph 1 commits an offence, liability may still arise if the lack of supervision or control by one of the company's representatives has made the commission of the offence for the benefit of the legal person possible. This construction seems to largely resemble §130 of the German Administrative Offences Act and introduces a duty to properly supervise and control their personnel on high ranking employees. Such an expansion of liability is arguably to be welcomed as the scope of people to be identified with the corporation should not be cast too narrow, as this can lead to legal lacunas, which is sufficiently demonstrated by the experiences of the English penal system with the doctrine.

The exact scope of the European identification doctrine is however difficult to determine abstractly. An assessment must therefore remain tentative and admittedly borders speculation. The definition of persons in a leading position to be identified with the corporation outlined in the model provision is rather vague. It would at least in theory provide room to also identify persons on the level of lower or medium management with the company, but it remains to be seen how the ECJ will interpret the provision. Should the ECJ for instance draw inspiration from its case law in competition law then a broad interpretation of the doctrine is conceivable. There, an agreement or concerted practice can namely arise from the actions of any employee acting within the scope of his employment. The corporation will incur liability even despite the fact that the employees were not authorised or instructed to act in that way by senior management.[1968] The only way for a corporation to exonerate itself from an alleged infringement of competition law is thus to prove that the person who acted on behalf of the corporation acted *ultra vires*.[1969] Drawing inspiration from this approach might lead to a broad interpretation of 'power of representation', 'authority to take decisions' or 'authority to exercise control'.

3.6. The attribution of fault

It has already been mentioned that anthropomorphic theories of corporate wrongdoing such as the identification doctrine generally strive to attribute the fault

1968 Jones and Sufrin, 'EC Competition Law: Text, Cases, and Materials' (2004), p. 147.

1969 See: 7 June 1983, Joined Cases C-100–103/80, *SA Musique Diffusion française and others v Commission of the European Communities*, ECR 1983, 01825.

of natural person(s) to the corporation. Of utmost importance in this respect is the question if the mens rea of any of its employees can be attributed to the corporation or whether this is only the case for the mens rea of high ranking officials. It has been shown that the identification doctrine narrowly circumscribes the scope of people which can be identified with the corporation and therefore rejects the idea that the mens rea of low level corporate officials or employees can be attributed to the corporation. Conversely, the Dutch Supreme Court on the other hand seems to have accepted this possibility. In 1990 it held that criminal conduct of employees could be attributed to a corporation and that the knowledge of the employee could be regarded as the knowledge of the corporation.[1970] The Supreme Court corroborated this view in 1996 when it held that the mens rea of an employee could be attributed to a corporation under certain circumstance. Decisive, according to the courts view, was in this respect the way how responsibility had been delegated within the corporation and which task(s) the employee had been entrusted with.[1971] That the director of the company had not approved of the occurred conduct was in this case irrelevant.[1972]

3.7. The pitfalls of the identification doctrine

From the foregoing it can be deduced that apart from its apparent narrow scope the identification doctrine suffers another drawback, stemming from the derivative nature of the doctrine which is that the mens rea standard required by the underlying offence needs to be present in an individual in a high ranking position within the company. If no individual of the directing mind of the company possessed the required mens rea, or can be considered to have committed the offence in question, the corporation will not be found liable. In other words the objection focuses on the fact that corporate responsibility will hinge on conduct of corporate personnel rather than on the fault of the company.[1973] Thus, it becomes patent that the same concerns in regard to the *nulla poena sine culpa* principle, mentioned before in respect to the vicarious liability doctrine apply *mutatis mutandis* to the identification doctrine.[1974]

In addition it may not always be easy to identify one or several persons within a company whose actions and state of mind can be attributed to the company. Different individuals within the corporation may bear varying degrees of responsibility for an occurred criminal result and fault may be diffused throughout the company.[1975] The identification doctrine, thus gives rise to a multitude of

---

1970 HR 20 November 1990, *NJ* 1991, 238, para 5.1.

1971 HR 15 October 1996, *NJ* 1997, 109.

1972 HR 15 October 1996, *NJ* 1997, 109.

1973 Colvin, 'Corporate Personality and Criminal Liability' Criminal Law Forum (1995), p. 15, Wells, 'Corporations: Culture, Risk and Criminal Liability' The Criminal Law Review (1993), p. 560.

1974 Gobert and Punch, 'Rethinking Corporate Crime' (2003), p. 62.

1975 Gobert and Punch, 'Rethinking Corporate Crime' (2003), p. 61.

intricate questions not the least of which is how to identify and single out those individuals deserving of identification status. This is especially so as the 'realpolitik' of corporate decision making is often convoluted and not easily accessible by courts. "A pliant board of directors may be little more than a 'rubber stamp', and a CEO with a high profile may be a mere figurehead. Junior executives may wield far more power behind the scenes than their job title would imply".[1976] It seems therefore fair to conclude that it does not make much sense to confine corporate liability to the conduct of persons who are engaged in the formulation of the companies policies when it is often the people implementing it that wield control over the commission of the offence. Criminogenic corporate policies and practices may stem from any level of staff and may only have been rubber stamped by the board of directors. To link corporate criminal liability to the conduct of high ranking representatives such as the company board seems thus to be completely out of touch with corporate reality. It may for instance be evident that a company was involved in defrauding a European Agency by wrongfully claiming export refunds, but if the management of the company was actively involved in the scheme is an entirely different question.

Furthermore, the doctrine makes it considerably easier to hold small scale companies liable while it may encounter difficulties in regard to medium sized, let alone large corporations. In small corporations, the persons considered to constitute the directing mind of the company are likely to take a hands-on approach and be actively involved in the corporation's day to day business operations, including illegal activities. Conversely senior officers in large scale operations are unlikely to be involved in the company's daily business.[1977] Moreover, decisions in large corporations are often taken at the level of branches or units or, to complicate matters even further, at the level of middle management.[1978] In these cases a large scale company might be able to avoid responsibility for these decisions.

This is demonstrated by the fact that the rare cases where a company was held liable for manslaughter in England all involved small scale companies with uncomplicated corporate structures.[1979] This doctrinal defect might even provide an incentive for a company to diffuse its decision making structures to insulate itself from liability. Furthermore, in practice it might prove almost impossible for the prosecution in cases with large and complex structured companies to pierce the corporate veil and unravel which individual actually committed the crime.[1980] Thus, probably the biggest practical drawback of the identification doctrine is that it might encourage corporations to structure its internal lines of communication in such a manner that criminogenic aspects of the company's operations do not reach

1976 Gobert and Punch, 'Rethinking Corporate Crime' (2003), p. 65.
1977 Gobert and Punch, 'Rethinking Corporate Crime' (2003), p. 63.
1978 Colvin, 'Corporate Personality and Criminal Liability' Criminal Law Forum (1995), p. 15.
1979 Gobert and Punch, 'Rethinking Corporate Crime' (2003), p. 63.
1980 Clarkson, 'Corporate Culpability' Web Journal of Current Legal Issues (1998), p. 5.

the directing mind and will of the corporation which would absolve it from criminal liability.[1981]

This myriad of criticism has earned the doctrine the reputation in England that "it works best in cases where it is needed least and works worst in cases where it is needed most".[1982] Evil tongues even alleged that the English courts in attempting to remedy the weakness of vicarious liability by constructing the identification doctrine created "a cure that was worse than the disease".[1983]

Arguably, the smaller the company the better the infamous identification doctrine seems to function. In small scale organisations it seems easier to locate an individual who acted culpably and may be identified with the company. To remedy some of the shortcomings of this common law doctrine it may yet be advisable to expand the scope of persons who can be identified with the company in a way which reflects modern corporate structures.[1984] Therefore one should however avoid linking the scope of persons to rigid concepts such as the mind and will of the corporation and rather look at how responsibility has been delegated within the company and which tasks the employee in question has been entrusted with. It should certainly not be required that the directors, etc. of the company acted culpably or approved of the occurred conduct. Although such an approach would overcome some of the under-inclusiveness of the doctrine, the aforementioned frictions with the principle of guilt would linger on. In fact, the broader the scope of people to be identified with the company the closer the doctrine will resemble a vicarious liability of the company for the conduct of its employees.

Furthermore, at a theoretical level, the question remains if an atomic and anthropomorphic view of corporations can really capture the unique nature of legal entities and if concepts such as actus reus and mens rea, initially designed to tackle individual wrongdoing can and should be applied to corporations as well.

3.8. Alternative models of liability

In the course of time other models have been devised and applied to attribute liability to corporate actors. Thus, the cardinal question here once more is to conceive criteria by which it can be determined whether or not one can speak of corporate conduct or fault respectively. There is a wealth of literature attempting to overcome the shortcomings of the identification doctrine. Discussing all of them in detail would exceed the scope of this research. Therefore the discussion will be confined here to some examples which may be invoked to impose primary responsibility on a corporation.

1981 Gobert and Punch, 'Rethinking Corporate Crime' (2003), p. 69.

1982 Gobert and Punch, 'Rethinking Corporate Crime' (2003), p. 63.

1983 Gobert and Punch, 'Rethinking Corporate Crime' (2003), p. 70.

1984 Clough, 'Bridging the theoretical Gap: The search for a realist model of corporate criminal liability' Criminal Law Forum (2007), p. 299.

The aggregation theory

One theory tapping into the logic of systemic failures and collective knowledge is the so-called aggregation theory which strives to combine the acts, omissions and mental states of more than one individual within the body corporate in order to establish the actus reus and mens rea of the corporation.[1985] Thus, according to this theory the behaviour of a variety of individuals within the organisation may be combined to amount to the actus reus of a particular offence. Likewise, the theory would make it possible to aggregate the mental states of several persons so that in toto they will amount to the required fault element of the offence in question.[1986] For instance, if the conduct of person A, B and C cumulatively caused the prescribed harm and if their aggregated state of minds amount to the required mens rea element of the crime, the company could be held liable. The doctrine effectively broadens the scope of people to be identified with the corporation but perpetuates the dogma of a corporation as a fiction. In other words, the aggregation doctrine builds on the models of derivative liability but expands it in the direction of corporate fault. Instead of one person to be identified with the corporation, the doctrine of aggregation, finds several.[1987]

The aggregation theory adheres to the two-pronged approach of vicarious liability and the identification doctrine, whereby liability is located in the behaviour of an individual actor, and subsequently attributed to the company.[1988] Yet, the aggregation of various elements into one offence may turn innocent activities of individuals into corporate wrongdoing.[1989] It is submitted here that aggregation might prove to be a valuable tool to establish objective mens rea standards such as negligence but seems unwarranted in cases of subjective mens rea standards as intent or recklessness. A series of minor failures by company employees might certainly add up to a gross breach of a duty of care by the company.[1990] However, the same result seems unachievable in regard to subjective mens rea standards. Several semi-innocent minds cannot at the end of the equation amount to an intentional wrongdoing.[1991] The difficulty seems to stem from the dichotomy of knowing and wanting composing the mental element. The element of knowing is frequently conceived as a rational element, while wanting is traditionally conceived

1985 Gobert and Punch, 'Rethinking Corporate Crime' (2003), p. 83.

1986 See: Wells, 'Corporations and Criminal Responsibility' (2001), p. 156.

1987 Clarkson, 'Corporate Culpability' Web Journal of Current Legal Issues (1998), p. 6.

1988 Lederman, 'Models for Imposing Corporate Criminal Liability: From Adaptation and Imitation Toward Aggregation and the Search for Self-Identity' Buffalo Criminal Law Review (2000), p. 663.

1989 Lederman, 'Models for Imposing Corporate Criminal Liability: From Adaptation and Imitation Toward Aggregation and the Search for Self-Identity' Buffalo Criminal Law Review (2000), p. 663.

1990 Smith and Hogan, 'Criminal Law' (2008), p. 252.

1991 Smith and Hogan, 'Criminal Law' (2008), p. 252.

as an emotional element.[1992] The former element is concerned with cognition, i.e. the awareness and understanding of facts. The rational element is easily accessible to aggregation. It almost seems an issue of common sense to us that information can be accumulated or disseminated. Things are however a bit more complicated in regard to the latter limb of mens rea. First and foremost, the emotional element seems inextricably bound up with human beings. The emotional element is conceived to contain holistic concepts such as desire, aspiration, indifference or hope. These notions however defy any attempt of splitting off, let alone being aggregated. They are either present in the mind of the defendant or not, but cannot be divided or accumulated.[1993]

Furthermore, the doctrine too depends on the proof of human fault. The individuals whose acts and mental states can be cumulatively attributed to the company still need to be identified, and if that proves impossible, the prosecution is bound to fail. Finally, it is questionable whether a corporation should be regarded as an aggregation of individuals or rather as a "living" system.[1994] It arguably prevents the law to look deeper for a culpable corporate culture or ethos.

The doctrine can however also be attacked at a more fundamental level. Social science for instance has proven that group decisions are different from individual decisions. Thus the question arises whether the simplistic arithmetic concept of aggregation actually corresponds to organisational reality.[1995] Be that as it may, the doctrine, although frequently applied in the US, has been brought before English Courts several times to no avail. For instance in *R v HM Coroner for East Kent, ex parte Spooner* the Court rejected the aggregation argument and held:

> Whether the defendant is a company or a personal defendant, the ingredients of manslaughter must be established by proving the necessary mens rea and actus reus of manslaughter against it or him by evidence properly to be relied on against it or him. A case against a personal defendant cannot be fortified by evidence against another defendant. The case against a corporation can only be made by evidence properly addressed to showing guilt on part of the corporation. The case against a company can only be made by evidence properly addressed to showing guilt on part of the company as such.[1996]

[1992] Lederman, 'Models for Imposing Corporate Criminal Liability: From Adaptation and Imitation Toward Aggregation and the Search for Self-Identity' Buffalo Criminal Law Review (2000), p. 668.

[1993] Lederman, 'Models for Imposing Corporate Criminal Liability: From Adaptation and Imitation Toward Aggregation and the Search for Self-Identity' Buffalo Criminal Law Review (2000), p. 669.

[1994] Smith and Hogan, 'Criminal Law' (2008), p. 257.

[1995] Lederman, 'Models for Imposing Corporate Criminal Liability: From Adaptation and Imitation Toward Aggregation and the Search for Self-Identity' Buffalo Criminal Law Review (2000), p. 673.

[1996] [1989] 88 Cr App R 10.

And also in *Attorney General's Reference (No 2 of 1999)*, the Court of Appeal rejected the aggregation doctrine.[1997] However, it is worth noticing at this point that the new Corporate Manslaughter Act against all odds endorsed the aggregation doctrine. Thus the aggregation doctrine has finally gained some support in the English penal system which arguably constitutes an important step towards the creation of a concept of organisational fault. The endorsement of the aggregation doctrine by the Corporate Manslaughter Act is also in line with the prevalent Dutch approach, where it is generally accepted that the mens rea of a corporation for a specific crime can be aggregated from the guilty minds of several persons.[1998]

The theory of social perception

A further criterion to establish the perpetration of legal entities is derived from social and economic perception. Briefly stated, a conduct will be deemed to be committed by a corporation if the (criminal) conduct is seen by society as the conduct of the corporation.[1999] As such the theory has apparent ties to the social theory of conduct. In the Dutch penal system this criterion is derived from civil law, where the Dutch Supreme Court convicted a municipality to pay damages to a building contractor who had been wrongly accused by a representative of the municipality to be responsible for the collapse of a nursery school. The Supreme Court held that the conduct of the representative could be attributed to the municipality, because his conduct was perceived in society as the conduct of the municipality.[2000] By the same token could the theory be applied to establish fault on the side of the corporation.[2001]

The biggest drawback of this theory arguably is its indetermination. Social perceptions of when and how a corporation acts or is at fault can function as a rough yardstick to determine which conduct can be reasonably attributed to a corporation, but can arguably not provide the legal certainty required by criminal law.[2002] The social perception theory refers to situations where the conduct of an individual, according to common parlance, is deemed to be the conduct or fault of the corporation. The District Court of Rotterdam used the theory for instance to convict a foundation which ran a day nursery for the death of a six month old baby due to an inadequate bed. The court convicted the foundation for negligent killing and held

1997 [2000] QB 796.

1998 Kelk, 'Studieboek materieel strafrecht' (2005), p. 392. Roef, 'Strafbare overheden – Een rechtsvergelijkende studie naar de strafrechtelijke aansprakelijkheid van overheden voor milieuverstoring' (2001), p. 335. See also: HR 16 June 1981, *NJ* 1981, 586.

1999 Roef, 'Strafbare overheden – Een rechtsvergelijkende studie naar de strafrechtelijke aansprakelijkheid van overheden voor milieuverstoring' (2001), p. 334. Kelk, 'Studieboek materieel strafrecht' (2005), p. 385.

2000 HR 6 April 1975, *NJ* 1980, 34.

2001 Van Strien, 'De Rechtspersoon in het strafproces' (1996), p. 90.

2002 Roef, 'Strafbare overheden – Een rechtsvergelijkende studie naar de strafrechtelijke aansprakelijkheid van overheden voor milieuverstoring' (2001), p. 335.

that not only was the operational management pervaded with sloppiness, but also was the conduct of the day care staff regarded in society as the conduct of the foundation. Parents, so the court argued would not entrust a particular staff member with their children but rather the day nursery itself.[2003]

Especially in Dutch legal literature, some have strongly argued for the application of the social perception theory in criminal law.[2004] It has been proposed to apply the theory on a case by case basis and to determine by means of evaluation of different factors like the business activities of a corporation, whether or not a specific criminal conduct can be attributed to a corporation.[2005] Yet, the Dutch Supreme Court has until now not explicitly accepted the criteria to establish corporate wrongdoing.[2006] In any event, such an approach would arguably create a wide basis of corporate liability. The theory would however on the other hand also establish a minimum standard for corporate criminal liability as it is unlikely that the conduct of an individual would be attributed to a corporation if the criminal conduct is not regarded as the conduct of the corporation in society.[2007]

The duty of care approach

As already mentioned, in practice the conduct of a corporation causing harm will mostly amount to a violation of a duty of care or a (culpable) failure to adhere to applicable diligent standards. According to this approach a corporation may incur liability if it can be proven that it took insufficient measures to prevent the occurrence of harm. The business and economic world is a highly regulated one and a variety of laws impose duties on legal entities to conduct themselves in a particular way on pain of criminal sanction. In national law numerous provisions can be found that aim to regulate the way how businesses "dispose of waste, treat the environment, address health and safety concerns, produce and sell food and other products".[2008] Accordingly, a corporation can be held responsible if it has violated such an incumbent duty of care.[2009] Arguably this reliance on duties of care is also linked to the prevalent view in the risk society that corporations are in a better position to control and prevent the wrongdoing of others. From this it can be deduced that the duty of care approach constitutes a kindred theory to the aforementioned social perception theory as corporate wrongdoing in society will

---

2003 Rb Rotterdam 31 January 2005, *LJN* AS4414.

2004 Knigge, 'Doen en laten; enkele opmerkingen over daderschap' Delikt en Delinkwent (1992), pp. 128–154.

2005 De Valk, 'Aansprakelijkheid van leidinggevenden' (2009), p. 302.

2006 Kelk, 'Studieboek materieel strafrecht' (2005), p. 386.

2007 De Valk, 'Aansprakelijkheid van leidinggevenden' (2009), p. 303.

2008 See: 'Criminal Liability in regulatory contexts', Consultation Paper, LAW COM. No 195 [2010] p. 9, para 1.34.

2009 Kelk, 'Studieboek materieel strafrecht' (2005), p. 386. Roef, 'Strafbare overheden – Een rechtsvergelijkende studie naar de strafrechtelijke aansprakelijkheid van overheden voor milieuverstoring' (2001), pp. 335–337.

arguably often be perceived as a failure to prevent harm. Corporations in modern society operate under a general duty to prevent wrongdoing and are therefore obliged to adopt internal systems to achieve this goal.[2010]

Basing liability on duties of care essentially allows the adoption of an organic perception of corporate personality and makes the imposition of liability on a corporation possible even if in the case at hand no identifiable individual has committed the offence. Thus, the duty of care approach would not only cause less friction with traditional principles of criminal law as might for instance be the case with vicarious liability and the identification doctrine but it arguably also well reflects corporate reality. It is submitted that the duty of care approach is of considerable importance, especially as the legislator increasingly imposes duty of care provisions on corporate actors. Furthermore, as will be subsequently shown, the Dutch Supreme Court introduced a duty of care approach for the attribution of conduct to a corporation in 2003.[2011] Likewise the English Corporate Manslaughter Act underlines the importance and potential usefulness of duties of care in regard to corporate wrongdoing. Besides this, it is generally arguable that corporate liability should (objectively) be grounded in the culpable failure of a corporation to "assess and manage risk, and to monitor effectively and supervise those whom it has placed in a position to cause physical and economic harm, or commit crimes".[2012] From this it becomes apparent that as a corollary, this will shift the emphasis in terms of establishing liability to corporate culpability and blameworthiness.

Comparable to such an approach is the aforementioned category of English case law which revolves around circumstances where a person had *a right to control* the actions of another and (s)he deliberately refrains from exercising it.[2013] In these circumstances inactivity may be regarded as encouragement to another to perform an illegal act, and, therefore as aiding and abetting.[2014] It is apparent that this new line of case law can be of particular importance in regard to corporate responsibility, as a corporation in many cases can be regarded as having a right to control the activities of its employees. In addition, this line of case law underlines the particular importance of duties of care in regard to corporate wrongdoing, as a significant proportion of corporate offences are crimes of omission rather than commission.[2015] Furthermore, it has already been submitted that frequently, a corporation's fault will lie in its failure to adopt protective mechanisms that would have prevented the harm from occurring.[2016]

English Courts seem to have endorsed this judicial avenue and increasingly apply it. This was for instance the case in *R v Gaunt* where a manager failed to take

2010 See also: Gobert, 'The Corporate Manslaughter and Corporate Homicide Act 2007 – Thirteen years in the making but was it worth the wait?' The Modern Law Review (2008), p. 421.

2011 HR 21 October 2003, *NJ* 2006, 328.

2012 Gobert and Punch, 'Rethinking Corporate Crime' (2003), p. 97.

2013 See: Chapter II. 3.2.2. III. 5.2. and V. 2.4.

2014 Smith and Hogan, 'Criminal Law' (2005), p. 117.

2015 Gobert and Punch, 'Rethinking Corporate Crime' (2003), p. 39.

2016 Gobert and Punch, 'Rethinking Corporate Crime' (2003), p. 39.

steps to prevent his employees from racially harassing another (black) employee.[2017] The court held that "by reason of his inaction he accepted that those responsible for those incidents may have taken the inaction as an encouragement of the conduct". A similar kind of reasoning can be found in *JF Alford Transport LTD* where in the first instance a company was convicted for omitting to take steps to prevent its drivers from falsifying their tachograph records.[2018]

The attribution of liability in European competition law

The mode of attributing liability to corporations for collusive practices pursuant to Article 101 TFEU, preventing, restricting or distorting competition within the internal market has already been outlined in a previous chapter.[2019] In addition Article 102 TFEU prohibits the abuse of a dominant position by an undertaking, which may affect trade between Member States. An undertaking in a dominant position in the relevant market is thus according to Article 102 TFEU placed under a special duty to act fairly and may not attempt to gain additional advantages by using their market dominance.

It has already been stated that pursuant to Article 101 TFEU once a collusive conduct has been established, an infringement of this Article can be attributed to a company and give rise to liability, if a subjective and an objective condition can be established. The standards to establish both requirements are considerably broad. The objective limb will be fulfilled if it can be established that the undertaking intended through its conduct to contribute to the common objectives of the cartel and that it was aware of the planned or implemented conduct of the other participants in pursuance of the common objectives or that it could reasonably have foreseen that conduct and that it was ready to accept the attendant risk.[2020] The subjective limb on the other hand effectively holds that the attribution of an infringement of the competition rules depends on the manifestation of the undertaking's intentions. This subjective requirement is however easily inferred from the objective conduct of the undertaking concerned, especially if one takes into consideration that a sufficient manifestation of the undertaking's intentions can be inferred from its tacit approval of and its failure to publicly distance itself from the cartel.

Likewise the threshold of liability according to Article 102 TFEU seems not to be very stringent either. An undertaking which can be proven to possess a dominant position within the common market must have abused this position in such a way

---

2017 [2003] EWCA Crim 3925.

2018 R v JF Alford Transport LTD [1997] 2 Cr App R 326.

2019 See: Chapter III. 11.

2020 8 September 2010, Case T-29/05, *Deltafina SpA v European Commission*, [2010] not yet reported, para 59, 8 July 2008, Case T-99/04, *AC-Treuhand AG v Commission of the European Communities*, [2008] ECR II-01501, para 130.

that it may affect trade between Member States. The ECJ has interpreted the notion of abuse broadly. It has for instance held that abuse constitutes an objective concept.

> The concept of abuse is an objective concept relating to the behaviour of an undertaking in a dominant position which is such as to influence the structure of a market where, as a result of the very presence of the undertaking in question, the degree of competition is weakened and which, through recourse to methods different from those which condition normal competition in products or services on the basis of the transactions of commercial operators, has the effect of hindering the maintenance of the degree of competition still existing in the market or the growth of that competition.[2021]

From this it can be deduced that an undertaking may incur liability for abusing its dominant position even if the abuse was unintentional.

The broad offence definitions enshrined in Articles 101 and 102 TFEU and their objective interpretation seem to facilitate the attribution of liability in competition law. This should not come as a complete surprise as these Articles were tailor made to address corporate wrongdoing and to apply to a highly complicated and economically driven matter. In connection with the broad and abstract legal interest protected by competition law rules, i.e. the unfettered functioning of the internal market, this leads to a broad scope of corporate liability. It follows that the wording of the offence in question as well as the underlying protected legal interest can facilitate, or respectively hamper the imposition of corporate criminal liability. Thus, the legislator should in the drafting process be clear from the outset about the addressee of the offence in question as well as about the underlying protected interest.

The broad approach taken in regard to Articles 101 and 102 TFEU makes it even arguable that establishing corporate liability in the realm of competition law borders strict liability. The objective requirements seem to carry the most weight and matters of corporate culpability are often easily implied by the objective conduct of the undertaking. Thus, despite the fact that Article 23 (2) of Regulation 1/2003 requires an intentional or negligent infringement of the competition rules by an undertaking, it seems as if the model of liability applied there does not entirely give sufficient consideration to notions such as blameworthiness and culpability which are vital for a framework of corporate criminal liability. An example of an approach which arguably better manages to do justice to the aforementioned aspects is the Dutch doctrine of functional perpetration.

2021 13 February 1979, Case, C-85/76 *Hoffmann-La Roche & Co. AG v Commission of the European Communities*, [1979] ECR 461, para 91.

The *IJzerdraad* criteria – functional perpetration

Dutch courts have for some time now, applied a concept originally developed to determine the criminal liability of a natural person to corporations as well. This concept has already been outlined and discussed in the realm of multiple actor scenarios.[2022] This introduction can therefore be brief. The doctrine was first established in the famous *IJzerdraad* (iron wire) judgment and essentially revolves around two criteria, which, if fulfilled, make it possible to attribute criminal liability to the perpetrator behind the scenes who did not (physically) cause the criminal harm. In doctrinal terms this notion is called functional perpetration.

The criteria established in the *IJzerdraad* judgment are often dubbed the criteria of power and acceptance. In the context of the natural person, the notion of power revolves around the factual control of the suspect over the (non-) manifestation of the criminal conduct. This aspect constitutes the normative core of the concept of power. The perpetrator with control over the factual perpetrator is in a (hierarchic) position to prevent the criminal conduct from occurring.[2023] The notion of acceptance on the other hand is a much more subjective criterion which in essence requires an intentional involvement in the conduct factually committed by another actor.[2024]

The Dutch Supreme Court has adopted these criteria also to determine the perpetratorship of corporations. For instance, in the so-called *Kablejauw*-arrest (cod-judgment), the Supreme Court held a ship-owning firm responsible for a violation of fishing regulations, because it had the power to control the conduct of its fishers and accepted it.[2025] By the very same token a night club was held responsible for the conduct of its bouncers who discriminated against Turkish nationals by refusing them admittance to the club.[2026]

The *IJzerdraad* criteria applied to corporate wrongdoing put the emphasis on the institutional practices of a corporation. The concept of power in this context emphasises the idea of hierarchy in an organisation and the ability to influence the acts of individuals and groups through the operation of that hierarchy.[2027] The notion of acceptance on the other hand involves a judgment on corporate monitoring of risky or illegal business.[2028] In conjunction, these criteria also carry a normative weight, as they imply a judgment on the quality of corporate diligence in

---

2022 See: Chapter III. 7.2.2.

2023 Gritter, 'Functioneel plegen door een natuurlijke persoon', in van der Leij (ed), Plegen en Deelnemen (2007), p. 20.

2024 Gritter, 'Functioneel plegen door een natuurlijke persoon', in van der Leij (ed), Plegen en Deelnemen (2007), p. 28.

2025 HR 1 June 1981, *NJ* 1982, 80.

2026 HR 14 January 1992, *NJ* 1992, 413.

2027 Field and Jörg, 'Corporate Liability and Manslaughter: should we be going Dutch?' The Criminal Law Review (1991), pp. 166 et seq.

2028 Field and Jörg, 'Corporate Liability and Manslaughter: should we be going Dutch?' The Criminal Law Review (1991), pp. 166 et seq.

establishing, monitoring and enforcing appropriate standards.[2029] From this brief introduction it is already perceivable that the doctrine of functional perpetration applied to corporations would provide room for an organic perception of corporate wrongdoing and may also carry the seeds of an organisational model of corporate liability.

The application of the *IJzerdraad* criteria to corporations has been criticised in legal literature. The criteria, so the argument goes, have been developed to determine the liability of natural persons and should therefore not be applied to corporations as the application of one and the same concept to two diametrically opposed legal subjects could lead to unwanted spill-over effects between the two and result in an expansion of criminal liability. Furthermore it has been argued that the application of a concept developed for individual wrongdoing would not leave enough room to establish corporate criminal liability.[2030]

By applying the *IJzerdraad* criteria to corporations as well, the Dutch Supreme Court has established an equation of natural and legal persons. The underlying rationale of this is an anthropomorphic view in regard to corporations. The corporation is seen as equivalent to a human being and is deemed to posses specific human characteristics to conduct *inter alia* acts of power and volition.[2031] The assumption taken by the Dutch Supreme Court is that a corporation, just like a human being can control the conduct of other persons and accept it. While these criteria certainly are suitable tools to attribute a criminal conduct to a corporation, there are also some pitfalls inherent.

The notions of power and volition (i.e. acceptance) are definitely suitable cornerstones to determine corporate liability, but especially the requirement of acceptance can lead to problems, in particular in regard to large and complex organisations.[2032] When exactly can it be said that a corporation accepted a certain conduct? Is it necessary that a specific person accepted the conduct or can one also resort to the company policy and management?[2033] Some authors have argued that the notion of acceptance implies mens rea of the corporation. The corporation, so the argument goes must have been aware of the criminal conduct.[2034] Others have adopted a more objective approach and claim that it is sufficient if the occurred conduct corresponds to the normal company policy.[2035]

2029 Field and Jörg, 'Corporate Liability and Manslaughter: should we be going Dutch?' The Criminal Law Review (1991), pp. 166 et seq.

2030 De Valk, 'Aansprakelijkheid van leidinggevenden' (2009), p. 297.

2031 Roef, 'Strafbare overheden – Een rechtsvergelijkende studie naar de strafrechtelijke aansprakelijkheid van overheden voor milieuverstoring' (2001), p. 330.

2032 De Hullu, 'Materieel Strafrecht' (2006), p. 162.

2033 De Hullu, 'Materieel Strafrecht' (2006), pp. 162–163.

2034 See: Roef, 'Strafbare overheden – Een rechtsvergelijkende studie naar de strafrechtelijke aansprakelijkheid van overheden voor milieuverstoring' (2001), p. 333.

2035 Torringa, 'De rechtspersoon als dader; strafbaar leidinggeven aan rechtspersonen' (1984), p. 34.

The prevalent opinion in the Netherlands, however, interprets the acceptance criteria subjectively.[2036] Acceptance, so the argument goes, requires certain awareness and will or acceptance of the criminal conduct.[2037] This amounts in practice to the inclusion of a mens rea standard in the notion of acceptance.[2038] It was initially contentious which mens rea standard exactly would be enshrined by the notion of acceptance, but as will shortly be discussed, in a subsequent landmark decision, the Dutch Supreme Court further developed the concept and introduced a duty based negligent standard in this respect.

3.8.1. The Drijfmest (slurry) judgment

In 2003 the Dutch Supreme Court delivered a landmark decision regarding the actus reus of legal entities.[2039] In this case the suspected corporation (A) was charged with pollution of the ground as an unknown third party had deposited slurry in breach of the law on soil protection (*Wet Bodembescherming*) on a property which the defendant managed on behalf of the owners (B). The property was on behalf of the suspect (A) effectively managed by C who was employed by B. The lower court had convicted the suspected corporation (A) because it considered it a task of the management that the property was held in accordance with the law. The Supreme Court found this reasoning insufficient and held that the exact scope of the management should have been closely scrutinised before the conduct could be attributed to the corporation. The court summarised and elaborated on earlier jurisprudence on this matter. It dwelled on the legislative history of Art 51 of the Dutch Penal Code and concluded that the legislator had granted total freedom to the judiciary to determine when a specific conduct can be attributed to a corporation. As a starting point the court held that a corporation can be seen as the perpetrator of a crime if the respective criminal conduct can be reasonably attributed to the company.[2040] Thus the Court views the issue as an attribution of a conduct to the company.[2041]

The court outlined some general indications when a criminal conduct could be reasonably attributed to a corporation. This, so it was argued, is dependent on the facts of the particular case, *inter alia* including the nature of the conduct in question. A universally valid criterion could therefore not be established. However, according to the court an important point of reference could be seen in the fact that

---

2036 Gritter, 'Duidelijkheid omtrent corporatief daderschap' Tijdschrift voor Onderneming en Strafrecht (2004), p. 35.

2037 De Hullu, 'Materieel Strafrecht' (2006), p. 152.

2038 De Valk, 'Aansprakelijkheid van leidinggevenden' (2009), p. 297, Gritter, 'De strafbaarheid van de rechtspersoon', in van der Leij (ed), Plegen en Deelnemen (2007), p. 54.

2039 HR 21 October 2003 *LJN* AF7938 = *NJ* 2006, 328.

2040 De Hullu, 'Materieel Strafrecht' (2006), p. 160, Gritter, 'Duidelijkheid omtrent corporatief daderschap' Tijdschrift voor Onderneming en Strafrecht (2004), p. 32.

2041 Gritter, 'Duidelijkheid omtrent corporatief daderschap' Tijdschrift voor Onderneming en Strafrecht (2004), p. 33.

the conduct occurred within the domain of the company. If the conduct occurred within the domain of the corporation it can be attributed to it. A conduct is deemed to have occurred within the domain of the corporation if one or more of the following circumstances occurred:

- at stake are acts or omissions of the corporation by somebody who works for the corporation due to an employment contract or for other reasons
- The conduct corresponds with the normal corporate management (*bedrijfsvoering*)
- The conduct served (benefited) the corporation in its business
- The corporation could control whether the conduct could or could not take place and if comparable conduct was according to the course of events accepted. Acceptance, encompasses also situations in which a duty of care was violated by a corporation if the observance of the duty could be reasonably expected from the corporation.[2042]

The first circumstance (i.e. working for the corporation due to employment or for other reasons) is quite expansive. Consequently every act/omission of an employee could be attributed to the corporation. Seen from the perspective of the company this comes close to vicarious or risk liability for the acts/omissions of its personnel.[2043] The position of the employee within the company seems irrelevant in this respect. Under the heading of working for the company for other reasons, independent contractors and even other corporations can be subsumed. The circumstances of the case at hand in conjunction with the underlying offence will determine whether or not a particular conduct can be attributed to the corporation.[2044] This approach bears some resemblance with the Meridian judgment of the English Privy Council where the court adopted a more flexible approach regarding corporate perpetration in order to mitigate the shortcomings of the identification doctrine.[2045]

The second criterion (i.e. the conduct corresponds with the normal corporate management) centres on the question whether a conduct is not alien to conventional corporate management. Relevant evaluation points might therefore be the corporation's normal business activities and the way in which it conducts its day to day business operations.[2046] The court made it clear in that judgment that the *IJzerdraad* criteria, despite being developed for natural persons could also be

[2042] HR 21 October 2003 *LJN* AF7938 = *NJ* 2006, 328, para 3.4.

[2043] Gritter, 'De strafbaarheid van de rechtspersoon', in van der Leij (ed), Plegen en Deelnemen (2007), p. 48.

[2044] Gritter, 'De strafbaarheid van de rechtspersoon', in van der Leij (ed), Plegen en Deelnemen (2007), p. 48.

[2045] See: Chapter V. 3.3.3. See also: Gritter, 'De strafbaarheid van de rechtspersoon', in van der Leij (ed), Plegen en Deelnemen (2007), p. 48.

[2046] Gritter, 'De strafbaarheid van de rechtspersoon', in van der Leij (ed), Plegen en Deelnemen (2007), pp. 50–51.

applied for the attribution of human conduct to a corporation. Accordingly, conduct which falls outside the scope of normal corporate management cannot be attributed to the corporation.

The third criterion (i.e. that the conduct benefited the corporation) serves to exclude corporate liability in cases where the conduct benefited for instance solely the employee and not the corporation. An often cited example in legal literature here is the employee of a grocery store who under the counter sells heroin to customers.

It becomes apparent that the Dutch Supreme Court in this judgment has opted for an open, flexible and casuistic approach towards corporate liability.[2047] "Corporate reality" as well as the multitude of different offence definitions made the establishment of one universally applicable criterion to attribute conduct to a corporation unfeasible and undesirable.[2048]

The Dutch Supreme Court enshrined many of the aforementioned theories outlined above in this landmark decision. The criterion that the conduct should have occurred within the domain of the corporation bears resemblance to the social perception theory, while the third criterion resembles the benefit theory and the last criteria the *IJzerdraad* criteria.[2049] The first three criteria amount in essence to an objective standard, while the *IJzerdraad* criteria, as mentioned before, carry a more subjective connotation.[2050]

What is however more important here is that the court expanded the scope of the *IJzerdraad* criteria in regard to the actus reus of legal entities in this judgment. To be more precise, he expanded the scope of the acceptance criterion, by holding that "acceptance" could also be assumed if the corporation had breached a duty of care (which could be reasonably expected of it) to prevent the conduct from occurring.[2051] In other words, a corporation will be deemed to have accepted a particular criminal conduct, if this can be derived from the course of events, for instance if the company has neglected its duty to supervise. The fact that acceptance can be derived from the course of events, amounts furthermore to a more objective interpretation of the *IJzerdraad* criteria in regard to legal entities. The duty resting on a corporation in regard to a particular conduct in a case can *inter alia* be derived from the foresight of the corporation that the conduct might occur, but also from provisions containing duties of care.[2052] It is submitted that this expansion puts a high burden on corporations, as they are now bound, as far as can be reasonably expected, to prevent any criminal conduct from occurring. This in essence amounts to an objectification, i.e. a negligence standard for the acceptance criteria. In this

2047 De Valk, 'Aansprakelijkheid van leidinggevenden' (2009), p. 330.

2048 Gritter, 'De strafbaarheid van de rechtspersoon', in van der Leij (ed), Plegen en Deelnemen (2007), p. 57.

2049 Rense, 'Rechtspersonen in het strafrecht' Delikt en Delinkwent (2005), pp. 273–274.

2050 De Valk, 'Aansprakelijkheid van leidinggevenden' (2009), p. 316.

2051 Gritter, 'Duidelijkheid omtrent corporatief daderschap' Tijdschrift voor Onderneming en Strafrecht (2004), p. 35.

2052 De Valk, 'Aansprakelijkheid van leidinggevenden' (2009), p. 318.

context one could also raise the question whether the *IJzerdraad* criteria as fleshed out by the Supreme Court still respect the requirements flowing from the principle of guilt.[2053]

The choice of the Dutch Supreme Court to adopt a multi-tier approach to impute conduct to a corporation needs, given the complex and diffuse topic to be acclaimed. The court emphasised a case by case evaluation regarding corporate conduct and established guidelines for future decisions.

However, the judgment has not only earned acclaim in legal literature as it gives rise to some contradictions and uncertainties. Some issues need to be highlighted here. First, the point of reference for attribution that the conduct occurred in the domain of the company means that in theory also conduct that occurred outside the domain can be attributed to the corporation. Furthermore, also conduct that occurred in the domain need not necessarily be attributed to the corporation. This follows from the argumentation of the Supreme Court that conduct in the domain of the company is a mere point of reference.[2054] The one or the other will depend on the circumstances of the case at hand, taking into account the nature of the criminal conduct. Especially where the underlying offence (i.e. crime of omission, situational liability and duty of care provision) gives room for direct liability of the corporation, an attribution of the conduct to the corporation will not be necessary. In these situations, where the interpretation of the actus reus of the offence is decisive, the finding that the company had the power of disposition will suffice to establish corporate criminal liability.[2055] It is however questionable whether the courts will for the reasonable attribution of liability dare to "look outside the box" of the corporate domain.[2056]

More problematic however are the four criteria given by the court in which a conduct is deemed to have occurred within the domain of the corporation. As mentioned before, the four circumstances constitute fairly different criteria. The first circumstance refers to the factually acting person (employee), while the correspondence with the normal corporate management refers to the conduct and the *IJzerdraad* criteria refer to the corporation itself. The court left the question of the relationship and hierarchy of the criteria unanswered. This could prove problematic in practice as it is conceivable that the four criteria lead to contradicting results. Which criterion is then determent and which criterion has to be applied by the court in such a situation?[2057]

Furthermore, the open approach adopted by the Supreme Court gives considerable powers to the courts and raises questions of legal certainty and

2053 See: Roef, 'Strafbare overheden – Een rechtsvergelijkende studie naar de strafrechtelijke aansprakelijkheid van overheden voor milieuverstoring' (2001), p. 341.

2054 Mevis in HR 21 October 2003, *NJ* 2006, 328.

2055 De Valk, 'Aansprakelijkheid van leidinggevenden' (2009), p. 330.

2056 De Valk, 'Aansprakelijkheid van leidinggevenden' (2009), p. 330.

2057 See also: De Hullu, 'Enkele opmerkingen over het strafrechtelijk daderschap van rechtspersonen', in Harteveld, et al. (eds), Systeem in ontwikkeling: liber amicorum G. Knigge (2005), pp. 273–288.

legality. It is namely questionable that corporations can deduce from this judgment how they have to organise their business to avoid criminal liability.[2058]

In regard to the relationship and hierarchy between the four criteria, different views have emerged.

The *IJzerdraad criteria* are sometime applicable

As mentioned before, the *IJzerdraad* criteria, contrary to the other criteria enshrined in the judgment contain an element of blameworthiness. This raises the question of the relationship between this subjective and the other objective criteria. The author concurs with the view of some writers that the *IJzerdraad* criteria are only applicable in particular circumstances.[2059] Arguments for this stance can *inter alia* be deduced from the reasoning of the Supreme Court itself as it explicitly held that the *IJzerdraad* criteria can be used for the attribution of a conduct to a corporation *in particular circumstances*.[2060] A determining factor here can be the underlying offence, i.e. whether a traditional crime requiring mens rea, a strict liability or a regulatory offence is at stake. In the latter case it is unlikely that the courts would apply the *IJzerdraad* criteria as it would require them to infer a mens rea standard which is not enshrined in the law. In other words the nature of the offence could be a determining factor here. The reference of the Supreme Court to the aforementioned "discriminating night club" judgment where the *IJzerdraad* criteria were used in an offence requiring mens rea would also point in this direction. This approach would also correspond more closely to the requirements flowing from the principle of guilt.[2061]

Furthermore the conduct requirement enshrined in a respective offence can be of relevance here. If the offence imposes a duty of care which can be violated by the company itself, or does not require a physical conduct like situational liability offences the *IJzerdraad* criteria do not seem to be applicable.[2062] Thus the nature of the offence as well as the nature of the conduct can be determining factors here.

Acceptance is no longer required

Some scholars have deduced from the *Drijfmest* judgment that the objectification of the acceptance criterion has upgraded the criterion of power to the all-determining

---

2058 De Hullu, 'Enkele opmerkingen over het strafrechtelijk daderschap van rechtspersonen', in Harteveld, et al. (eds), Systeem in ontwikkeling: liber amicorum G. Knigge (2005), pp. 273–288.

2059 De Valk, 'Aansprakelijkheid van leidinggevenden' (2009), p. 318.

2060 HR 21 oktober 2003, *NJ* 2006, 328, para 3.4 [...] De ijzerdraadcriteria zijn weliswaar ontwikkeld met het oog op het functionele daderschap van een natuurlijke persoon [...], maar dat zij *in voorkomende gevallen* tevens kunnen fungeren als maatstaven voor de toerekening van een gedraging van een natuurlijk persoon aan een rechtspersoon. [emphasis added].

2061 De Valk, 'Aansprakelijkheid van leidinggevenden' (2009), p. 331.

2062 De Valk, 'Aansprakelijkheid van leidinggevenden' (2009), p. 320.

factor.[2063] It has for instance been claimed that in regard to corporate liability the power to control will be decisive and that the Supreme Court has equated "acceptance" with blameworthiness.[2064] This conclusion however seems too far reaching. While admittedly, the judgment brought an objectification to the notion of acceptance it seems too far fetched to conclude that the power to control is now the all-determining factor. This would cause an expansion of corporate criminal liability.

The *IJzerdraad* criteria ought to be conclusive

Finally, some authors have argued that the *IJzerdraad* criteria ought to be decisive. It has for instance been argued that the principle of guilt in criminal law would demand a subjective criterion in regard to corporate liability.[2065] Therefore the subjective principle of acceptance is endorsed. It is argued that the vagueness of the four criteria would demand an unambiguous choice for one criterion. However, it is submitted that a sole reliance on this criterion seems to be unwarranted, especially in regard to strict liability offences, where the legislator has explicitly refrained from imposing a fault element. It is not warranted to raise the threshold of liability for corporations beyond the one enshrined in the law. Furthermore, as the Supreme Court in the slurry judgment explicitly stated that the goal of this judgment was exclusively to discuss the attribution of conduct to the corporation, it seems a wrench of the court's words to deem only the *IJzerdraad* criteria decisive for establishing corporate liability.

3.8.2. Jurisprudence after the Drijfmest (slurry) judgment

The Dutch Supreme Court applied the *Drijfmest* doctrine in 2005. In this case a corporation (a ship owning firm) was charged with violating the Fishery Act (Visserijwet) in co-perpetration with the vessel and its crew which had lessened the scale of the net knitting in order to catch more fish.[2066]

It is striking here that the corporation was charged with co-perpetration, a possibility which was not explicitly mentioned in the slurry judgement. However, as the slurry judgement revolves around the question when a corporation can be regarded as the perpetrator of a crime and according to Dutch law the co-perpetrator, perpetrator by means and the instigator are regarded as perpetrators, it should not come as a complete surprise that the court applied the *Drijfmest* doctrine to co-perpetration as well. It is certainly arguable that if one takes into account the close connection between a perpetrator and a

2063 De Valk, 'Aansprakelijkheid van leidinggevenden' (2009), pp. 321–323.

2064 Rozemond, 'De methode van het materiele strafrecht' (2006), pp. 50–51.

2065 De Hullu, 'Materieel Strafrecht' (2006), p. 165.

2066 HR 29 March 2005, *LJN* AR7619.

co-perpetrator it is defendable that the doctrine should apply to co–perpetration as well.[2067]

The Supreme Court ruled in this decision that the conduct could be reasonably attributed to the corporation as a co-perpetrator. The court thereby relied on three criteria. It regarded the fact that the conduct (i.e. fishing) corresponded with the normal corporate management, the corporation profited from the conduct (benefit theory) and that the conduct was performed by persons who were employed by the corporation (first drijfmest criterion) as sufficient to hold the corporation criminally liable. It should be highlighted here that the Court of Appeal had also used the *IJzerdraad* criteria to ground the corporation's criminal liability. It had argued that the corporation had violated its duty of care to prevent fishing in breach of the Fishery Act from occurring. The court thought that the corporation was under a duty to inform its staff (by a written statement or by other means) that the fishing should be carried out in accordance with the law. This quite stringent duty of care construction was omitted by the Dutch Supreme Court and only the aforementioned objective, i.e. normative, criteria were applied. The omission of the more subjective *IJzerdraad* criteria in this case may be explained by the underlying offence which was an economic regulatory (de facto) strict liability offence. The application of the subjective *IJzerdraad* criteria (especially the acceptance criterion) would have thus resulted in a higher threshold for criminal liability than foreseen in the law itself.[2068]

The Court of Appeal s'Hertogenbosch in 2006, convicted a corporation for an *intentional* breach of the environmental protection law and in line with the considerations above applied the *IJzerdraad* criteria. The corporation had in the course of its day to day business burned waste such as power cables in breach of the Dutch environmental law. The court held that generally the burning of waste fell within the normal course of corporate conduct and that the employee who actually burned the waste was employed by the corporation and bestowed with great liberties how to carry out his work (i.e. criteria one and two of the *Drijfmest* judgment). The court then continued that by not properly supervising its employees and not issuing instructions how to proceed if the waste contained other material than wood, the corporation had violated the duty of care standard which could reasonably be expected by a corporation in this situation, especially as it was aware of the fact that the waste could contain other material besides wood as well.

The court thus imposed quite a far-reaching duty of care standard on corporations as it seems that they are not only under a duty to properly supervise their personnel, but also to give clear instruction that the work is carried out in accordance with the law. This approach which almost amounts to a form of risk liability for the conduct of employees, makes it clear that the diligence expected by a corporation is considerably higher than in regard to individual actors.

2067 Gritter, 'De strafbaarheid van de rechtspersoon', in van der Leij (ed), Plegen en Deelnemen (2007), p. 56.

2068 See also: De Valk, 'Aansprakelijkheid van leidinggevenden' (2009), p. 327.

One year later, in 2007 the Court of Appeal s'Hertogenbosch used *inter alia* the benefit theory and also the *IJzerdraad* criteria to hold a corporation responsible as a co-perpetrator in *intentionally* polluting water in the course of the construction work for a roundabout.[2069] The court held that the conduct corresponded to the normal corporate management, had benefited the corporation and that it was within the corporation's power to determine and control the conduct of the employees and that it had accepted the conduct (i.e. the pollution).

In 2009 the Court of First Instance, Roermond, convicted a corporation for negligent manslaughter (Article 307 DPC) applying the *IJzerdraad* criteria.[2070] The court held that the *IJzerdraad* criteria can be used to attribute the conduct of an executive employee who had instructed another employee to clean guttering on the roof of the business premises without sufficient safety measures in place to the corporation. In the course of this work the employee had slipped and fallen of the roof and subsequently died. As the underlying offence required mens rea to be present, the court applied the *IJzerdraad* criteria and held that the corporation had violated the duty to carry out work in accordance with Health and Safety regulations (*Arbeidsomstandighedenwet*) and held the corporation liable for the death of the worker.

To conclude, it can be stated that the Dutch courts have applied the *Drijfmest*-doctrine in a very flexible manner. In many of the aforementioned judgments the court based the attribution of criminal conduct to a corporation on a combination of criteria. A factor determining the choice of the courts to prefer one criterion over another seems to be the underlying offence with which the corporation is charged. If the underlying offence requires the proof of mens rea it is most likely that the subjective *IJzerdraad* criteria will be applied, while more objective criteria like the benefit theory will come into play when the underlying offence is a strict liability offence or an economic offence where the fault element is often filled in objectively.[2071] Furthermore, the post-drijfmest case law has also made it abundantly clear that the criteria outlined in this judgment will apply to all forms of perpetration (i.e. co-perpetration, perpetration by means and instigation) and not solely for direct perpetration of a corporation.

Finally, the normative interpretation of the *IJzerdraad* criteria in the *Drijfmest* judgment can be seen as a move towards a more organic or realist perception of corporate wrongdoing, as a duty of care provision does not necessarily require a connection to individual wrongdoing but rather paves the way for direct corporate liability. From the (ambiguous) case law discussed above, it is however not clearly deducible whether the often invoked duty of care is aimed at individuals or the corporation itself. Put differently, the scope and origins of these duty of care standards applied by the courts are somewhat elusive and furthermore the diligence required by corporate actors seems to be significantly higher than for

2069 Hof's-Hertogenbosch, 24, April 2007, *LJN* BA4471.

2070 Rb. Roermond 27 January 2009, *LJN* BH1649.

2071 De Valk, 'Aansprakelijkheid van leidinggevenden' (2009), p. 320.

individuals.[2072] In some cases the courts seem to assume that a respective duty rests on the corporation itself, while in other circumstances the duty seems to be addressed to an individual and the violation of that duty is subsequently attributed to the corporation.[2073] It can however be argued that a higher duty of care standard for corporate actors does seem to be warranted taking into account the pivotal position of corporations in modern society and the scale of potential criminal harm to be caused by corporate wrongdoing. As the distance between those effectively carrying out the criminal offence and those responsible increases the required standard of diligence required by the latter seems to increase as well.

3.8.3. The Corporate Manslaughter and Corporate Homicide Act 2007

Just like the normative interpretation of the *IJzerdraad* criteria in the *Drijfmest* judgment arguably constitutes a move towards a more organic or realist conception of corporate wrongdoing, a similar development is discernible in the English penal system. Despite or because of the fundamental flaws pervading the derivative models of corporate responsibility (i.e. vicarious liability, or identification doctrine) recent English legislation has heralded the idea that corporate responsibility should be examined and based on a framework conceptually different from the one used to determine individual, i.e. human responsibility. The new Corporate Manslaughter Act constitutes a step in this direction. The failing of the trials against a corporation following large scale disasters such as the Zeebrugge (Herald of Free Enterprise) shipping disaster or the Southall rail crash provoked a public outcry in England and increased the pressure on the legislature to incorporate a specific offence of corporate killing. Wells explains the increase in public disquiet regarding corporate manslaughter on the one hand in a general decline of confidence in business and other institutions. On the other hand she forcefully argues that the emerging risk society with its focus on risk prevention has led to the recognition of corporate manslaughter as a cultural response to omnipresent hazards and risks which jeopardise the citizens' life.[2074]

Be that as it may, the immediate roots of the 2007 Act can be found in the Law Commission Report from 1996 which proposed the creation of a corporate killing offence based on management failure.[2075] However, the proposal provoked much controversy and discussion and it was not until a decade later that the government finally created another bill which became the present act.[2076] The bulk of the Act

---

2072 See for instance the standard applied in: Hof's-Hertogenbosch, 5, December 2006, *LJN* AZ4771.

2073 See for instance the aforementioned case: Rb. Roermond 27 January 2009, *LJN* BH1649, where the Court seemingly assumed that the duty of care rested on the executive employee who had ordered the work to be carried out in contravention of the Health and Safety regulatons.

2074 Wells, 'Corporate Manslaughter: A Culture and Legal Form' Criminal Law Forum (1995), pp. 45–72.

2075 'Legislating the Criminal Code: Involuntary manslaughter', LAW COM No 237 [1996].

2076 Ormerod and Taylor, 'The Corporate Manslaughter and Corporate Homicide Act 2007' Criminal Law Review (2008), p. 591.

entered into force in April 2008.[2077] In short, the Act imposes criminal liability on an organisation if the way it organised its activities, including a substantial contribution by its senior management, causes the death of a human being in breach of a duty of care owed by the organisation to the victim.[2078] Accordingly, the Act exclusively focuses on corporate wrongdoing and excludes individuals from its scope.[2079] In other words, it attempts to impose a strict division between organisational and individual fault.[2080] It abolishes the common law offence of gross negligent manslaughter as applied to corporations and provides in section 18 that individuals cannot be complicit in an offence of corporate manslaughter.[2081] Thus, the Act is best depicted as a new form of homicide rather than a new principle of attribution.[2082] In practice, however, the creation of this new corporate offence will lead to a bifurcation of proceedings in cases where it is deemed appropriate to charge an individual alongside a company, as juries will have to apply two different tests to establish manslaughter liability.[2083]

In essence, the Act abolishes the identification doctrine for corporate manslaughter charges, which has proved in the past to constitute a major obstacle in achieving convictions in high profile cases, and substitutes it with what one might term a "qualified attribution principle".[2084] Therefore the Act takes a step beyond the corporate liability limitations at common law and towards an organisational approach to corporate liability.[2085] A closer look at this new corporate offence is now warranted.

The new offence

The gist of the offence is enshrined in section 1(1) and (3) of the Act, read in conjunction. It provides:

2077 Ormerod and Taylor, 'The Corporate Manslaughter and Corporate Homicide Act 2007' Criminal Law Review (2008), p. 589.

2078 Ormerod and Taylor, 'The Corporate Manslaughter and Corporate Homicide Act 2007' Criminal Law Review (2008), p. 589.

2079 Ormerod and Taylor, 'The Corporate Manslaughter and Corporate Homicide Act 2007' Criminal Law Review (2008), p. 591.

2080 Smith and Hogan, 'Criminal Law' (2008), p. 538.

2081 Horder, 'The Criminal Liability of Organisations for Manslaughter and other Serious Offences', in Hetherington (ed), Halsbury's Laws of England Centenary Essays (2007), p. 103, Ormerod and Taylor, 'The Corporate Manslaughter and Corporate Homicide Act 2007' Criminal Law Review (2008), p. 591.

2082 Ormerod and Taylor, 'The Corporate Manslaughter and Corporate Homicide Act 2007' Criminal Law Review (2008), p. 591.

2083 Ormerod and Taylor, 'The Corporate Manslaughter and Corporate Homicide Act 2007' Criminal Law Review (2008), p. 594.

2084 Ormerod and Taylor, 'The Corporate Manslaughter and Corporate Homicide Act 2007' Criminal Law Review (2008), p. 592.

2085 Horder, 'The Criminal Liability of Organisations for Manslaughter and other Serious Offences', in Hetherington (ed), Halsbury's Laws of England Centenary Essays (2007), p. 106.

(1) An organisation to which this section applies is guilty of an offence if the way in which its activities are managed or organised –
  a. causes a person's death, and
  b. amounts to a gross breach of a relevant duty of care owed by the organisation to the deceased.

(3) An organisation is guilty of an offence under this section, only if the way in which its activities are managed or organised by its senior management is a substantial element in the breach referred to in subsection (1).

It becomes apparent from the above that this new offence will to a vital extent focus on the aggregate responsibility of senior managers.[2086] It acknowledges that management failure may be seen as the cause of a person's death.[2087] Furthermore, one can deduce a five pronged evaluation scheme from section 1 of the Corporate Manslaughter Act 2007. In essence the prosecution will have to establish the following: (i) that a relevant duty was owed to the victim by the organisation; (ii) that the breach of the duty was a result of the way the organisation had organised and managed its activities; (iii) that a substantial element of the breach of the duty was due to the way the senior management staff had organised and managed activities; (iv) that the breach of the duty amounted to a gross one; and finally (v) that the victim's death was caused by the breach of the duty.[2088]

The actus reus of corporate manslaughter

According to the above cited section 1 (1) of the 2007 Act, liability revolves around the gross breach of a duty of care. Thus the actus reus of the offence consist of an (act or) omission causing the death of a human being. The reproach enshrined in a conviction is that the corporation's conduct fell far below of what is expected of such an organisation in these particular circumstances.

The relevant duty of care

The 2007 Act casts a wide net of criminal liability on organisations. Section 2 of the 2007 Act sets out the scope of the duty of care imposed on organisations:

(1) A relevant duty of care, in relation to an organisation, means any of the following duties owed by it under the law of negligence –
  (a) a duty owed to its employees or to other persons working for the organisation or performing services for it;

2086 Smith and Hogan, 'Criminal Law' (2008), p. 537.

2087 See: Wells in: 'Criminal Liability in regulatory contexts', Consultation Paper LAW COM No 195 [2010], p. 206.

2088 Smith and Hogan, 'Criminal Law' (2008), p. 539. Ormerod and Taylor, 'The Corporate Manslaughter and Corporate Homicide Act 2007' Criminal Law Review (2008), p. 598.

(b) a duty owed as occupier of premises;
(c) a duty owed in connection with –
  (i) the supply by the organisation of goods or services (whether for consideration or not),
  (ii) the carrying on by the organisation of any construction or maintenance operations,
  (iii) the carrying on by the organisation of any other activity on a commercial basis, or
  (iv) the use or keeping by the organisation of any plant, vehicle or other thing
(d) a duty owed to a person who, by reason of being a person within subsection (2) [a detained person], is someone for whose safety the organisation is responsible.

First and foremost it is important to stress here that the 2007 Act does not impose any new duties, but is based on duties which already exist in civil law, arising either by statute or by common law.[2089] The duties enshrined reflect the duties arising from the common law of negligence, or where applicable a statutory duty that replaced the common law duty. A point in case for the latter is for instance the Occupiers Liability Act 1957.[2090] Chances are that the duties most relevant in practice will stem from an employment relationship (section 1 lit. a), or the occupation of premises by the organisation (section 1 lit. b).[2091]

The duties of employers would *inter alia* include an obligation to provide safe places of work and extend beyond the traditional duties owed to employees to third persons "working for the organisation or performing services for it" (section 1 lit. a), including most notably subcontractors.[2092]

As occupiers of premises, corporations will in future be liable for e.g. dangerous staircases (for instance if they are dimly lit) or faulty electrical wiring.[2093] Pursuant to section 25 of the 2007 Act the term premises will include land, buildings and moveable structures. Furthermore, duties arising from the supply of goods by the organisation might arise from the provision of foodstuff, but will probably extend further to any case of traditional product liability. Duties arising from provision of services might, most notably cover rail travel and other transport, while duties arising from construction or maintenance operation would include building operations.[2094] Finally, duties arising from the use or keeping of any plant, vehicle

2089 Smith and Hogan, 'Criminal Law' (2008), p. 540.
2090 Smith and Hogan, 'Criminal Law' (2008), p. 540.
2091 Smith and Hogan, 'Criminal Law' (2008), p. 540.
2092 Ormerod and Taylor, 'The Corporate Manslaughter and Corporate Homicide Act 2007' Criminal Law Review (2008), p. 599.
2093 Ormerod and Taylor, 'The Corporate Manslaughter and Corporate Homicide Act 2007' Criminal Law Review (2008), p. 599.
2094 Ormerod and Taylor, 'The Corporate Manslaughter and Corporate Homicide Act 2007' Criminal Law Review (2008), p. 599.

or other thing might prove to be especially far-reaching and could even function as a catch-all clause.

The conclusion to be drawn from the foregoing is that the pivotal task of the courts in cases of corporate manslaughter will be to identify existing civil law duties. Given the potential breadth of the categories of duties and the width of the common law to be examined this could amount to a daunting challenge. It is therefore not surprising that the English legislator has decided to entrust this task to the judges pursuant to section 2 (5).[2095] This provision will make it possible to maintain consistency between civil and criminal law and will bar juries to intuitively infer a duty in the case of an occurred death.[2096] It should be stressed here that the fact that the judge must make any findings necessary to decide the duty issue is highly unusual for the adversarial trial system in England and is in stark contrast to the common law position on gross negligent manslaughter where the issue is left to the jury.[2097]

The fault element in the 2007 Act

In the search for criminal fault the Act, as already mentioned abolishes the deficient identification doctrine and focusses instead on management failure. The Act now appears to make it possible to aggregate the fault of a variety of individuals within the organisation to establish a failure of management by the organisation.[2098] This is because pursuant to section 1 of the Act the jury is entitled in a holistic manner to assess the way in which a corporation organises and manages itself. The aggregation of fault is however, restricted by the requirement that the role of senior management was a substantial element in the occurred breach of the duty of care.[2099] However, the fact that the role of senior management must be substantial for the breach of the underlying duty and not its sole cause may indicate that wrongful conduct of employees may be added to the wrongful acts of senior management in order to determine whether a management failure has occurred.[2100]

2095 Section 2 (5): For the purpose of this Act, whether a particular organization owes a duty of care to a particular person is a question of law. The judge must make any finding of act necessary to decide that question.

2096 Horder, 'The Criminal Liability of Organisations for Manslaughter and other Serious Offences', in Hetherington (ed), Halsbury's Laws of England Centenary Essays (2007), p. 112.

2097 Ormerod and Taylor, 'The Corporate Manslaughter and Corporate Homicide Act 2007' Criminal Law Review (2008), p. 600.

2098 Horder, 'The Criminal Liability of Organisations for Manslaughter and other Serious Offences', in Hetherington (ed), Halsbury's Laws of England Centenary Essays (2007), p. 109, Ormerod and Taylor, 'The Corporate Manslaughter and Corporate Homicide Act 2007' Criminal Law Review (2008), p. 602.

2099 See: Section 1 (1), (3).

2100 See: Horder, 'The Criminal Liability of Organisations for Manslaughter and other Serious Offences', in Hetherington (ed), Halsbury's Laws of England Centenary Essays (2007), p. 109. More skeptical as to this possibility is: Gobert, 'The Corporate Manslaughter and Corporate

Thus, the offence retains some of the shortcomings of the identification doctrine, due to the requirement that the senior manager(s) played a substantial role in the management failure. Accordingly some discrimination between small and large scale companies might prevail. Due to these peculiarities, the new mechanism imposing liability on corporations might be termed "qualified aggregation principle".[2101] Put differently, the Act, as already indicated, recognises the need for an organic, or organisational model of corporate liability based on management failure. However, at the same time it circumscribes this possibility by restricting it to 'senior management' and linking it to individual managers.[2102]

The concept of a gross breach clearly draws on the gross negligence offence at common law, and section 1 (4) (b) dwells on the concept and provides: "a breach of a duty of care by an organisation is a gross breach if the conduct alleged to amount to a breach of that duty falls far below what can reasonably be expected of the organisation in the circumstances."

It needs to be stressed here that the 2007 Act does not go so far as to allow the finding of guilt based on a corporate culture as for instance the Australian Model Criminal Code does.[2103] This is however not to say that the elusive term of corporate culture cannot play an important evidential role in practice. A particular corporate culture could for instance substantiate the claim that a corporation tolerated illegal behaviour by its employees or that senior managers individually consented or tolerated such behaviour.[2104]

Furthermore, section 8 (3) of the 2007 Act introduces a factor that strikingly resembles "corporate culture" into the evaluation whether a gross breach of a duty of care has taken place. It requires the jury to take into account whether and to what extent the organisation has failed to comply with health and safety legislation and, more importantly adds:

> "The jury *may* also –
> a. consider the extent to which the evidence shows that there were attitudes, policies, systems or accepted practices within the organisation that were likely to have encouraged any such failure […] or to have produced tolerance of it […]".

Homicide Act 2007 – Thirteen years in the making but was it worth the wait?' The Modern Law Review (2008), p. 427.

2101 Ormerod and Taylor, 'The Corporate Manslaughter and Corporate Homicide Act 2007' Criminal Law Review (2008), p. 592.

2102 See: Wells in: 'Criminal Liability in regulatory contexts', Consultation Paper, LAW COM No 195 [2010], p. 213.

2103 Horder, 'The Criminal Liability of Organisations for Manslaughter and other Serious Offences', in Hetherington (ed), Halsbury's Laws of England Centenary Essays (2007), p. 109.

2104 Horder, 'The Criminal Liability of Organisations for Manslaughter and other Serious Offences', in Hetherington (ed), Halsbury's Laws of England Centenary Essays (2007), p. 110.

Thus the provision effectively makes corporate culture a possible building block in the determination of fault on the company's side.[2105] The jury is at liberty to scrutinise a notion such as a corporation's overall objectives, published policy statements, monitoring and compliance policies. The sum of these notions might encapsulate what one might call a corporate culture.

Senior management

As has already been noticed, the Act places a significant restriction on the management failure test by requiring that a substantial element in the breach (of a relevant duty of care) was due to the ways the corporation's activities are managed and organised by its senior management. The Act subsequently defines senior management in section 1 (4) (c) as:

> (c) [...] the persons who play significant roles in –
> (i) the making of decisions about how the whole or a substantial part of its activities are to be managed or organised, or
> (ii) the actual managing or organising of the whole or a substantial part of those activities.

It has already been stated that despite the fact that this definition goes beyond the category of individuals constituting the "directing mind and will" pursuant to the identification doctrine, it can be seen as a regrettable limitation, especially as it, to a certain extent, brings back the inquiry onto the issue of identifiable subjects and their role within the organisation. Furthermore the limitation might prove to be a slippery slope for the courts, forcing them to engage in difficult line drawing exercises based on employment law.[2106]

Two important consequences flow from the fact that the contribution of the senior managers only needs to be a substantial element. Firstly it follows that the conduct of non-senior managers who are involved in the management and organisation of activities can also play an important role. Secondly, it follows that the contribution of non-senior managers can be substantial as well, as long as it does not render the contribution of the senior management less than substantial.[2107] In other words, it is conceivable that more than one substantial contribution to the breach occurred.[2108] This is even more so, as English courts traditionally have interpreted the term "substantial" simply to mean "not insignificant" or not wholly

[2105] Horder, 'The Criminal Liability of Organisations for Manslaughter and other Serious Offences', in Hetherington (ed), Halsbury's Laws of England Centenary Essays (2007), p. 110.

[2106] Ormerod and Taylor, 'The Corporate Manslaughter and Corporate Homicide Act 2007' Criminal Law Review (2008), pp. 589–611.

[2107] Ormerod and Taylor, 'The Corporate Manslaughter and Corporate Homicide Act 2007' Criminal Law Review (2008), p. 604.

[2108] Ormerod and Taylor, 'The Corporate Manslaughter and Corporate Homicide Act 2007' Criminal Law Review (2008), p. 604.

trivial.[2109] It remains to be seen how English courts will approach this section and accordingly how much of a restriction the 'senior management element" will prove to be in practice.

Causation

The occurred death must have been caused by the way in which the corporations activities are managed or organised. The causal link will be established according to the traditional principles outlined in a previous chapter.[2110] In other words, if it can be proven that the death would have occurred regardless of the management failure, the required causal link would be absent and no liability would attach to the company.[2111]

Preliminary conclusion

The 2007 Corporate Manslaughter Act constitutes a first step towards a liability of legal entities based on corporate fault in the English penal system. It arguably represents an improvement on the common law position, in which it was unlikely for a company to be convicted of manslaughter. However, academic opinion in English law remains firmly divided as to whether the Act effectively provides really any added value over and above the preceding common law.[2112] Nevertheless, it is submitted that due to the new Act it is now much more likely that cases as those arising from transport disasters such as the Herald of Free Enterprise would end in a conviction of the company.

In a pertinent case, a corporation was for instance found guilty of corporate manslaughter, after an employee died during the course of soil investigation work. The victim had entered a 3,5 metres deep trial pit to obtain soil samples to conduct shear vane tests within it. The company had no proper safety system of work in place as a result of which the trial pit was entirely unsupported. Unfortunately the pit collapsed causing the death of the victim. The prosecution had argued that a pit of this depth would have required shoring or support by any other means to make it safe and that the death was therefore the result of a gross breach of a duty of care owed by the company to the deceased as one of its employees. The court followed the prosecution's argument and held "that it was plainly foreseeable that the way in

2109 Horder, 'The Criminal Liability of Organisations for Manslaughter and other Serious Offences', in Hetherington (ed), Halsbury's Laws of England Centenary Essays (2007), p. 106, citing R v Cato [1976] 1 All ER 260.

2110 See: Chapter II. 4.6.1.

2111 Ormerod and Taylor, 'The Corporate Manslaughter and Corporate Homicide Act 2007' Criminal Law Review (2008), p. 605.

2112 For a more critical point of view see: Gobert, 'The Corporate Manslaughter and Corporate Homicide Act 2007 – Thirteen years in the making but was it worth the wait?' The Modern Law Review (2008), pp. 413–433.

which the company conducted its operations could produce not only serious injury but death. The standard by which it fell short of its duty of care was found by the jury to have been gross". Accordingly the company's conviction was upheld.[2113]

4. Corporate culture and ethos

4.1. Introduction

It has already been pointed out that a full incorporation of legal entities into criminal law entails that also bedrock principles such as the principle of guilt must apply to corporations. But how can the guilt of a corporation, for example for the death of a person, best be established? It has been shown that the atomic view of corporate personality strives to attribute the fault of a natural to a legal person. This however does not correspond to corporate reality and can lead to arbitrary results as exemplified by the doctrine of identification. To prove fault on part of one or even several representatives, arguably does not show that the corporation itself was at fault.[2114] An organic or organisational model of corporate liability seems therefore preferable. Corporations are best conceived as rational corporate agents which can act and be at fault in different ways than individuals, which should be reflected in the concept of fault applied to them by criminal law.

4.2. Organisational fault

Also in regard to the mens rea of corporations, one should keep in mind that there are several ways to approach the issue and accordingly different legal concepts are conceivable to establish the guilt of a corporation. Besides the possibility to attribute the mens rea of a natural person to a corporation one can also focus on the corporation itself and deduce mens rea for instance from a corporation's policy or culture, the normal course of events, the company management or the company's decision-making processes.[2115] A corporation's culture or policy is arguably a unique set of characteristics which can *inter alia* arise from the corporation's structure, goals, training provisions, compliance systems, reactions to past violations, the incentive system and remedial steps.[2116] All these aspects are also clearly under the control of the corporation which provides an additional argument

---

2113 R v Cotswold Geotechnical Holdings Limited, [2011] EWCA Crim 1337.

2114 See: Wells in 'Criminal Liability in regulatory contexts', Consultation Paper LAW COM No 195 [2010], p. 208. See also: Wells, 'Corporations and Criminal Responsibility' (2001), p. 157.

2115 Vellinga-Schootsstra, 'Het daderschap van de Rechtspersoon', in van der Neut (ed), Daderschap en Deelneming (1999), p. 51, Kelk, 'Studieboek materieel strafrecht' (2005), p. 391, De Hullu, 'Materieel Strafrecht' (2006), p. 259.

2116 See: 'Wells in Criminal Liability in regulatory contexts', Consultation Paper LAW COM. No 195 [2010], p. 203.

to link the establishment of liability and more particularly fault, to these concepts.[2117] By and large, only aspects over which the corporation exerted control, may arguably provide the basis of corporate liability.

Thus, rather than focusing on individual fault, a more organic model of corporate mens rea focuses on the corporation as a whole. According to this view a corporation is perceived as an independent organic entity with its own distinctive goals, its own distinctive culture and its own distinctive personality.[2118]

It has for instance been argued that:

> fault inheres when a company has organised its business in such a way that persons and property are exposed to criminal victimisation or the unreasonable risk of harm, when the company has failed to devise and put into place systems for avoiding criminological risk, when its monitoring and supervision of those whom it has put in a position to commit an offence or cause harm is inadequate, and when the corporate ethos or culture is such as to tolerate or encourage criminal offences.[2119]

It is submitted that such a realist concept of corporate fault is to be preferred over the attribution of individual fault to the corporation, especially in regard to large scale, multinational corporate actors. This would also nicely fit the needs of European criminal law, as in the European context it will arguably often be these organisations that will constitute the focal point of the law. Such an approach furthermore better reflects the nature of the corporation as an organic entity, essentially independent of their individual members. To equate corporate and individual fault as done by the derivative models outlined above, may convey a misleading and at times incomplete picture of why corporations become entangled in criminal wrongdoing. These models namely fail to account for the role of the company's internal structures, policies, practices, procedures, ethos and culture in the occurrence of harm.[2120] The occurred result may often be connected to the corporation's ways of doing business rather than the acts of one or several deviant individuals. Corporations, it has been suggested can be seen as profit driven, rational actors and the goals, culture or ethos of a company may be tolerant or even conducive to anything profitable. Thus in an environment where goals have to be achieved and profits generated "by hook or by crook" individuals may often feel that they have to achieve corporate goals whatever the costs.[2121] Consider for instance a company which sidesteps prevalent European safety standards in order to

---

2117 See also: Clough, 'Bridging the theoretical Gap: The search for a realist model of corporate criminal liability' Criminal Law Forum (2007), pp. 275 et seq.

2118 Gobert and Punch, 'Rethinking Corporate Crime' (2003), p. 38, Gómez-Jara Díez, 'Corporate Culpability as a limit to the overcriminalization of corporate criminal liability: The interplay between self-regulation, corporate compliance, and corporate citizenship' New Criminal Law Review (2011), p. 86.

2119 Gobert and Punch, 'Rethinking Corporate Crime' (2003), p. 81.

2120 Gobert and Punch, 'Rethinking Corporate Crime' (2003), p. 80.

2121 Gobert and Punch, 'Rethinking Corporate Crime' (2003), p. 18.

gain an advantage over its competitors. Such an approach would constitute a fundamental reconceptualisation of the nature of corporate criminality and better capture the collective nature of corporate wrongdoing in the realm of criminal law.

Once it has been accepted that corporate fault can be expressed in terms of corporate policy or culture, refinements such as compliance or reactive fault may be introduced.[2122] There is a wealth of organisational theories which all entail a specific take on corporate culpability, from which criminal law can draw inspiration from. The German author Günter Heine has for instance proposed to use a concept of guilt that is based on the way the legal entity manages itself. Corporations, so the argument goes, cause harm as a result of a flaw in the structure management, a fault in the particular way how the corporation has organised itself (*Betriebsführungsschuld*). Corporate guilt, he claims "should be understood as the substantial disposition of the company in such a way as would prevent it from making rational decisions about co-ordination and reorganisation, and would allow defective risk management leading to socially detrimental effects".[2123]

Others have propelled the view that in order to establish corporate blameworthiness one should focus on the company's reaction to having committed the actus reus of an offence.[2124] This has been termed 'reactive fault'. According to this view corporate fault is defined as "unreasonable corporate failure to devise and undertake satisfactory preventive or corrective measures in response to the commission of the actus reus of an offence by personnel acting on behalf of the organisation".[2125] This model would thus expand the time frame of the inquiry to cover also a company's reaction to the commission of an offence. The focus would accordingly rest less on the corporation's general policies but rather on what it specifically proposes to do to implement a programme of internal discipline, structural reform, or compensation.[2126]

In any case the penal systems of England and the Netherlands seem to have recognised that equating individual with corporate fault can sometimes give rise to unsatisfactory results. Both systems have therefore seemingly started to slowly move towards a model of organisational fault. However, in both systems the concepts have not yet been fully developed and still largely remain in a nascent stadium. First traces of such an approach can for instance be found in the

2122 Wells, 'Corporations and Criminal Responsibility' (2001), p. 158.

2123 Heine, 'Rethinking Criminal Liability of Enterprises: International Developments, Basic Models, National Consequences', in Faure and Schwarz (eds), De Strafrechtelijke en civielrechtelijke aansprakelijkheid van de rechtspersoon en zijn bestuurders (1998), p. 173.

2124 Fisse and Braithwaite, 'The allocation of responsibility for corporate crime: Individualism, Collectivisim and Accountability' Sydney Law Review (1988), p. 505.

2125 Fisse and Braithwaite, 'The allocation of responsibility for corporate crime: Individualism, Collectivisim and Accountability' Sydney Law Review (1988), p. 505.

2126 Fisse and Braithwaite, 'The allocation of responsibility for corporate crime: Individualism, Collectivisim and Accountability' Sydney Law Review (1988), p. 506.

aforementioned 2007 Corporate Manslaughter and Homicide Act where also a corporation's culture can play an important role in establishing fault.[2127]

An example of such an approach in the Dutch penal system can be seen in the case of a hospital that was convicted for negligent manslaughter after a patient had died due to an old, defect anaesthetic machine. The court established mens rea in this case by holding that the hospital had violated its duty to properly maintain the quality and reliability of its anaesthetic machine.[2128] It should however be noted here that the crime in question in this case was a crime of negligence. Crimes of negligence which carry an inherent duty of care are, arguably more easily susceptible to such a "corporate centred" approach than intentional crimes.[2129]

As has been mentioned above, also a combination of the "corporate-centred" and the "individual-centred" approach is conceivable.[2130] For instance, the mens rea of individuals in conjunction with specific aspects of the corporate policy can lead to the assumption of corporate mens rea.

In regard to crimes of negligence it is possible to deduce corporate fault directly from the violation of a duty of care. In 2006 the Dutch Supreme Court found a corporation which ran an indoor swimming pool, guilty of negligent manslaughter of two children who had drowned because the corporation had violated a duty of care by insufficiently supervising the pool.[2131]

In 2008 the Court of Appeal 's-Hertogenbosch convicted a corporation who organised outdoor activities for the negligent killing of a customer during an off-road driving lesson in the course of a company outing.[2132] The corporation's employees had not sufficiently instructed the customers to fasten the seatbelts during the ride in the "Rough Terrain Vehicle" (RTV) which led to the death of the victim. The court ruled that (corporate) guilt could be established if, taking into account the particular circumstances of the case at hand, the corporation had not applied the diligence which was generally expected of it. The court found that especially by not properly instructing its customers to wear a seatbelt at all times, the corporation had acted negligently and handed down a conviction.

However, Dutch jurisprudence has also assumed intention applying the very same reasoning. In 2004 the Court of Appeal 's-Hertogenbosch found conditional intent in regard to a corporation who had not investigated whether waste which was stored on behalf of another company on its premises was dangerous.[2133] Due to the fact that the corporation had neglected this obligation to inspect, it had, so the court ruled, exposed itself to the considerable risk that the waste was dangerous. In

---

2127 See: Chapter V. 3.8.3.

2128 Rb Leeuwarden 23 December 1987, *NJ* 1988, 981.

2129 Kelk, 'Studieboek materieel strafrecht' (2005), pp. 392–394, De Hullu, 'Materieel Strafrecht' (2006), p. 259.

2130 See: HR 15 October 1996, *NJ* 1997, 109, discussed above.

2131 HR 22 August 2006, *NJ* 2006, 484. For the conviction of a school in similar circumstances see: Rb. Utrecht, 9 October, 2000, *LJN* AA7372.

2132 Hof's-Hertogenbosch, 16 October 2008, *LJN* BF9498.

2133 Hof's-Hertogenbosch, 20 January 2004, *LJN* AO4003.

essence therefore, intention seems in many cases to be covered by the acceptance of a particular conduct.[2134]

It seems fair to state that also in regard to the mens rea of corporations the concept of "reasonable attribution" is central in Dutch law. A corporation will be deemed to possess mens rea, when, all things considered, it seems reasonable to blame the corporation for the occurred wrongdoing. It is clear that such an assessment can only be made on a case by case basis. In this assessment, the form of the corporation (small, medium or large scale), the type of offence in question and the position of the involved individuals within the company, etc. will have a role to play. Such flexibility needs to be welcomed, especially in a field of law, as diverse and complicated as corporate crime.

5. Conclusion

5.1. Introduction

The foregoing discussion has shown that there exists a variety of ways by which legal systems can tackle corporate wrongdoing. One obvious way therefore is to devise offences tailor-made for corporate actors. These offences can take a variety of forms and can be either concerned with one specific aspect of corporate activity or with particular industries. They can be of criminal, administrative or civil law nature. The use of alternative systems beside criminal law should arguably be continued. In the light of the *ultima ratio* principle, criminal law ought only be applied to severe forms of wrongdoing and other illicit behaviour which does not require treating the offender as criminal should be tackled by other regulatory regimes. The creation of specific offences seems also to be the approach often adopted by the European Union which in its legislative acts frequently regulates pressing problems that typically involve corporate activity (e.g. corruption, money laundering, tax evasion, subsidy fraud, insider dealing, etc.). These offences can for instance impose particular diligent standards on a corporation and aim to foster compliance and good practices.

One category of offences which are particularly well suited to be applied to corporations are offences establishing duties of care. Corporate criminality will often be based on a culpable failure of the company to organize its business and supervise its workforce in ways as to prevent the occurrence of harm. If a law introduces a duty of care a corporation can fail to adhere to the imposed standards and incur liability for an omission. The big advantage of duty of care offences in this respect arguably is that they allow to adopt an organic view of corporate personality and make the usage of legal fictions redundant. The importance of duties of care in the realm of corporate wrongdoing is *inter alia* demonstrated by the English 2007 Corporate Manslaughter Act and the German Administrative

2134 De Valk, 'Aansprakelijkheid van leidinggevenden' (2009), p. 336.

Offences Act. In those situations in which duties of care thus apply to corporations they provide a simple and effective way of establishing and reflecting corporate conduct and fault.

While arguably the majority of corporate prosecutions will continue to be brought under specific (corporate) offences, there remains a small but certainly not insignificant number of cases which will fall outside these special provisions. In these cases an additional doctrine is needed in order to hold a corporation criminally liable. It has been submitted that an organic theory of corporate liability should be preferred over an atomic one as it better corresponds to corporate reality and reflects the nature of the corporation as a living system. Despite the fact that the widely used identification doctrine does not fall into this category of doctrines and only crudely reflects corporate reality and nature, it arguably will continue to play a role in regard to corporate criminal liability. Its usage in European Union legislation as well as in the German and English system would suggest so. It has however also become evident that in some of the investigated countries strong tendencies towards an organic concept of liability are discernible. It therefore seems slightly peculiar that the European Union continues to rely on the identification doctrine when some national penal systems have already taken steps towards a more organisational model of corporate liability.

In any case, to remedy some of the shortcomings of the doctrine, discussed above, it is submitted that the scope of people to be identified with the company should be interpreted broadly. A strict linkage to high ranking representatives should certainly be avoided. Rather a flexible approach seems to be preferable where the scope of people to be identified with the company ought to be determined on a case by case basis, taking into account how responsibility has been delegated and with which tasks the employee in question has been entrusted. Accordingly, one important baseline in this assessment will be whether the employee acted within the scope of his employment or tasks that have been assigned to him. As a corporation must also be blameworthy in order to warrant the imposition of liability, the independent conduct of a maverick employee should arguably not lead to the liability of the company. One could therefore draw inspiration from the English *Meridian* judgment where it was held that in order to establish who can properly be identified with the company one ought to look at the relevant offence and by constructive interpretation determine whose conduct should be taken to be that of the company for the offence at hand. In addition, corporations may also be granted a due diligence defence if it can be proven that the corporation de facto and not merely formally had taken appropriate and reasonable steps to prevent the occurrence of the offence in question.[2135]

Yet, expanding the scope of people to be identified with the company will inevitably blur the distinction between vicarious and identification liability.[2136] The

2135 Gobert and Punch, 'Rethinking Corporate Crime' (2003), pp. 100–102.

2136 Clough, 'Bridging the theoretical Gap: The search for a realist model of corporate criminal liability' Criminal Law Forum (2007), p. 274.

further one expands liability to low-level employees the closer one gets to a vicarious liability of the company for the conduct of its employees. This would however cause frictions with the principle of guilt as a corporation might incur liability for conduct for which it is effectively not to blame.

In any case, despite the fact that the doctrine is arguably founded on a misconceived perception of corporate personality and wrongdoing, it seems well suited to be applied to small-scale organisations with simple organisational structures and hierarchies which facilitate the finding of individual wrongdoing to be attributed to the company.

From a pragmatic point of view the doctrine may also have the advantage that well-established concepts of criminal law, with which practitioners are familiar, without too much ado, can be applied to corporations as well. The doctrine is however bound to encounter difficulties in regard to large-scale let alone multinational corporations. As has been attempted to show, the connection of individual wrongdoing and corporate liability may confer a de facto immunity on larger corporations. Especially in the context of European Union Law which to a large extent focuses on transnational, serious crime, controlling, regulating and sanctioning of conduct by large-scale corporations will arguably be vital. Already a glimpse at competition law confirms that the severest of violations are often committed by large corporations with intricate internal structures and hierarchies, convoluted levels of management and supervision, where responsibility is diffused throughout the company. Therefore the European Union should, it is submitted, aim to supplement the identification doctrine and strive for an autonomous, organic conception of corporate criminal liability. In particular in these cases it seems preferable to attribute the occurred offence to the corporation as a whole rather than to attempt to unearth individual responsibility. This would also be in line with the position taken by the Council of Europe which holds the view that an enterprise should be liable, whether a natural person who committed the acts or omissions constituting the offence can be identified or not.[2137] European criminal law, it is submitted, should attempt to avoid the pitfalls of national criminal law theory and strive for a fresh start. Such an approach certainly requires a fundamental reconceptualisation of criminal liability taking into account the peculiarities of corporate reality and wrongdoing. This constitutes by no means an easy task and arguably much additional research will be needed to devise tailor made concepts for corporate wrongdoing. Yet, the foregoing comparative discussion has provided some insights which could be used as a first stepping-stone towards a corporate notion of criminal liability.

[2137] 20 October 1988, Council of Europe Recommendation No. R (88) 18.

5.2. Corporate liability

It has been attempted to show that particularly in the context of corporate wrongdoing the traditional dichotomy of actus reus and mens rea starts to collapse. This arguably is due to the fact that in practice the core of corporate liability will mostly rest on the failure to act or rather prevent. In comparison to the social act requirement advocated in this book, it is submitted that corporate conduct ought to be interpreted in the social context in which it occurs.[2138] Conduct acquires meaning in relation with a concrete society and as part of a particular social system or subsystem. In regard to legal entities the social context in which the conduct emerges is the corporate world as a subsystem of modern industrial society where corporations are perceived as responsible actors and active agents. The focus should accordingly rest on organisational conduct rather as opposed to individual conduct.

Given the diversity of corporate realities and the multitude of different offence definitions, the establishment of one universally applicable criterion to attribute liability to a corporation may be unattainable. Some general guidelines can nevertheless be distilled. One essential factor could arguably be the notion of control. If a certain conduct will give rise to the liability of the corporation will, it is submitted, depend to a large extent if the corporation had factual control over the manifestation of the criminal conduct. This may for instance be the case if the offence in question has been caused by the company's failure to properly assess and organise its business and supervise and monitor its workforce as may be reasonably expected by it. Thus, the company's operational management and policies may be of importance here. If the occurred conduct fits into the prevalent company management scheme and policies then the offence arguably ought to be attributed to the company.[2139]

It has been submitted that, corporations are under a general duty to prevent wrongdoing and are obliged to put in place precaution and safety mechanisms to achieve this goal. To determine whether a corporation has fallen short of what could reasonably be expected of it, the factually occurred conduct and the corresponding company policies could constitute the vantage point for the assessment of corporate criminal liability. These criteria presuppose that a corporation possesses a capacity for (self-)organisation.[2140] An important question in the establishment of corporate liability may therefore be whether or not the corporation in question has achieved a level of internal complexity that allows it to organise itself in a meaningful way. These criteria also carry a normative judgment in regard to a corporation's diligence

2138 See: Chapter II. 2.

2139 Roef, 'Strafbare overheden – Een rechtsvergelijkende studie naar de strafrechtelijke aansprakelijkheid van overheden voor milieuverstoring' (2001), pp. 338 et seq.

2140 Gómez-Jara Díez, 'Corporate Culpability as a limit to the overcriminalization of corporate criminal liability: The interplay between self-regulation, corporate compliance, and corporate citizenship' New Criminal Law Review (2011), p. 85.

in establishing, monitoring and enforcing appropriate standards to prevent the occurrence of harm

It should be pointed out here that if one wishes to subject corporations to the rule of criminal law, liability for individual as well as corporate wrongdoing should only be imposed if the corporation acts culpably. Vicarious or risk liability which militate against the principle of *nulla poena sine culpa* should accordingly be avoided. The cardinal question however then becomes how exactly corporate fault can be established. Corporations have evolved to agents of our modern society and agency naturally entails rights, including the right not to be punished unless proven guilty.

Despite the wealth of theoretical models on organisational fault it should arguably be acknowledged that there is no ideal model of corporate blame. Just as with individual fault, any model will have its flaws, and compromises will have to be made to arrive at an enforceable and practical solution in regard to corporate fault. What makes matters more complicated in regard to legal entities in comparison to individuals is that a legal entity can take a variety of forms, reaching from small, one man companies, to large globally active corporate groups with a multitude of subsidiaries, plants and branches.

As previously discussed, in small-scale organisation the allocation of guilt in one individual may be relatively straightforward. If one however leaves the sphere of small-scale organisations, the need for a general concept of organisational fault becomes more pressing. It is here where atomic concepts of corporate wrongdoing frequently fail to produce satisfactory results and the true nature of legal entities as independent entities or corporate citizens comes to the fore. To establish corporate fault one, it is submitted, should rather focus on the corporation itself and deduce mens rea for instance from a corporation's policy, the normal course of events, the company management or the companies decision-making processes.

It is submitted that there are certain features of the way in which corporations organise themselves which may reflect fault on part of the organisation. One could also in this respect assess the corporate culture or ethos which may be conducive or even encourage unlawful behaviour.[2141] A corporate culture that encourages employees to 'cut corners' and ruthlessly pursues profit-maximisation, may not only provide an incentive to act wrongfully but may also allow individuals to rationalise their illegal conduct.[2142] One may think here for instance of the malpractices *inter alia* prevalent in the banking sector, which surfaced at the start of the ongoing financial crisis. Applying the concept of corporate culture to these entities and their practices could help to establish fault and blameworthiness in this context.

Furthermore, the structure of the corporation can play a role as a high degree of decentralisation may point in the direction that the people responsible for

---

2141 Bucy, 'Corporate Ethos: A Standard for Imposing Corporate Criminal Liability' Minnesota Law Review (1991), pp. 1095–1184.

2142 Clough, 'Bridging the theoretical Gap: The search for a realist model of corporate criminal liability' Criminal Law Forum (2007), p. 276.

implementing and supervising the corporate polices or goals may not be found in the board which adopted them. Thus, the management structure may be such that certain formal representatives are insulated from responsibility.[2143] Moreover, the company's internal education system as well as its reactions to past violations can provide insights into a corporation's blameworthiness.

Additional factors that one could apply to determine corporate culpability could be corporate compliance as well as self-regulation. All these factors provide a relevant proxy to assess whether or not a corporation can be blamed for a certain occurred criminal harm. All these elements are under the control of the company and constitute an element of corporate choice which adds legitimacy to the notion of organisational fault as a basis of liability. The corporation is held liable for its choices and through its choices may avoid liability in the future. Thus, also in this respect the concept of control may play a pivotal role. If a corporation can prove beyond reasonable doubt that it has taken all reasonable care to prevent the occurrence of harm, it can arguably not be considered to be in control as to the manifestation of the harmful event and can therefore not be considered as having breached the pertinent duty of care. "If a company can show that it had taken appropriate and reasonable steps to avoid the harm that occurred, it should be able to avoid criminal sanctions".[2144] By combining the concept of corporate culture with the concept of control over the commission of the offence, the proof of due diligence may function as a rebuttal of primary responsibility. It provides an opportunity for the corporation to show that it has not been at fault in carrying out its responsibility, reflected in the approach based on corporate culture and control. This would introduce an across-the-board due diligence defence which prevents the establishment of corporate liability in case the corporation acted with due care, i.e. has made a *bona fide,* reasonable effort to identify and prevent the harm in question.

Accordingly, such a normative, organisational approach to corporate liability based on control in conjunction with corporate culture and ethos would arguably also introduce more safeguards for corporate actors as it provides an opportunity for the company to rebut liability by showing that it was not in control over the manifestation of harm and therefore not blameworthy by raising a due diligence defence. Such an approach would, it is submitted, even provide more safeguards and protection than traditional atomistic models of liability, such as the identification doctrine, which as has been demonstrated, can at times give rise to arbitrary results.

2143 Clough, 'Bridging the theoretical Gap: The search for a realist model of corporate criminal liability' Criminal Law Forum (2007), p. 275.

2144 Gobert and Punch, 'Rethinking Corporate Crime' (2003), p. 100.

CHAPTER VI
CONCLUSION – TOWARDS A GENERAL PART OF EUROPEAN CRIMINAL LAW

1. INTRODUCTION

After having finalised the comparative analysis, it is now time to assess the findings of this research in the broader context of the discussion on criminal liability in contemporary society. At the outset of this research some recent social developments have been outlined which continue to shape and influence criminal law.[2145] These social trends will arguably also influence the emerging European criminal law. The increased competences of the Union legislator in the context of criminal law pursuant to Art 83 TFEU as well as the possible creation of a European Public Prosecutor's office as foreseen by Art 86 TFEU is accompanied as well by the risk that European criminal law may be used extensively and as a result over-burden national administrations.[2146] However, due to the fact that criminal law is different from other legal domains as it by definition restricts certain human rights and fundamental freedoms and as an excessive use of criminal legislation may undermine its very effectiveness, efficiency and legitimacy, such an approach ought to be avoided.[2147] It has therefore been attempted throughout this book to carefully balance competing interests to prevent overcriminalisation from taking place. Current developments in national criminal law have been analysed and ongoing changes in the framework of criminal liability have been highlighted. This chapter will first briefly recap some current trends in criminal law which this research has brought to light and will subsequently devote some space to dwell on a set of principles, which it has been argued should guide the ongoing development of European criminal law.[2148] These should help to assure to keep European criminal law within reasonable boundaries as well as to respect and protect fundamental rights and liberties. This way it is hoped that European criminal law will contribute to the creation of a true Area of Freedom, Security and Justice.

After these general remarks the results of this thesis will be briefly summarized and there will be a description of what general principles of European criminal law as regards the objective attribution of liability could look like.

2145 See: Chapter I. 5.4.

2146 See also: European Parliament Report on harmonization of criminal law in the EU, 24.04.2012, no 2010/2310.

2147 See also: European Parliament Report on harmonization of criminal law in the EU, 24.04.2012, no 2010/2310.

2148 See also: Chapter I. 4.3.

1.1. The increasing normativity of criminal liability

One development which emerged during the comparative analysis is an increasing normative approach in the imposition of criminal liability. More and more doctrines are interpreted normatively which threatens to upset the balance between the safeguard and crime control function of criminal law. It seems as if in particular the objective elements of criminal liability are frequently released from their traditional objective, physical anchor. In its place a more duty centred approach to criminal liability seems to emerge. The increasing number and scope of risks perceived in the culture of control as well as the modern focus on crime prevention has put the emphasis in society and in criminal law on taking precautionary measures and acting prudently.[2149] Accordingly, the reproach inherent in the establishment of criminal liability nowadays often consists of a blameworthy contravention of prevalent diligent standards or duties of care respectively. In other words, accepted social behavioural patterns that formerly guided people in certain segments and areas of society have in many cases become the vantage point in the assessment of criminal liability.

However, as the weight of objective or physical wrongdoing diminishes, more strain on the subjective elements of criminal liability is exerted. If liability becomes more duty-based the most pivotal question next to "was there an applicable duty of care in the circumstances at hand and was it applicable to the defendant?" becomes "did the defendant deviate from the duty of care standard in a blameworthy manner?" From this it can arguably be deduced that in a framework where criminal liability increasingly rests on duties of care, the dichotomy of actus reus and mens rea starts to come under pressure and loses significance.

In any case, this increasing normativity deprives criminal law of an important safeguard function. If liability is no longer linked to physical wrongdoing, criminal liability potentially becomes boundless. To counteract these tendencies other general principles of criminal law may be able to provide some limits to the scope of liability and protect individual liberties.

1.2. The limits of criminal liability

As liability becomes more founded on violations of duties of care, one important safeguard and counteragent of criminal liability arguably becomes due diligence. If punishment is imposed for contraventions of diligent standards, the antidote to liability becomes due diligence. If the defendant can prove that when carrying out his conduct all reasonable care has been observed, his conduct is in line with the requirements imposed by law and no breach of legal norms can be attested.[2150]

2149 De Jong, 'Daad-Schuld' (2009), p. 69.

2150 Gritter, 'De antonimiteit van daderschap en zorgvuldig gedrag', in Keulen, et al. (eds), Pet af – Liber amicorum D. H. de Jong (2007), p. 64.

Conversely, the minimum threshold for primary liability then becomes the violation of prevalent diligent standards. If the defendant acted with due care and took reasonable measures to prevent the manifestation of harm, liability can arguably not arise. To hold otherwise would impose punishment on people who had no possibility to prevent the harm from occurring. Such an approach would come close to imposing punishment on people acting under *vis absoluta.*

Furthermore, the concept of control can take an important safeguard function in an increasing normative framework of liability.[2151] Criminal liability, it is submitted, seems only justifiable for criminal outcomes that are under control of the actor. This would also be in line with the aforementioned due diligence standard as an actor cannot arguably be considered to have exerted control over the manifestation of harm if he acted with due care. The notion of control aligns the central focus of criminal liability on the responsible, rational subject and therefore provides limits to the introduction of risk liability, status offences and thought crimes. The concept of control, it has been argued can play an important role in a variety of doctrines such as the conduct requirement[2152], participation in crime[2153] and corporate liability.[2154] Depending on the area of application, the notion will, it is submitted, take different contours. In the context of the conduct requirement for instance the cardinal issue will be whether or not the defendant can be considered to have been in control of his conduct, while in regard to participation in crime the question will more generally become whether control over the commission of the offence and the criminal harm can be established.

Another important restraint on the expansion of liability can be found in the harm principle. It becomes particularly important in regard to the question of how far removed from the occurrence of harm conduct may be in order to give rise to liability. Generally criminal liability should reside and be linked as closely as possible to the prohibited criminal harm. The effects of this linkage are particularly visible in the law of attempt where the scope of liability can be circumscribed by the requirement that the defendant's conduct amounted to an endangerment of the protected legal interest. The emphasis on criminal harm also entails, it is submitted that how farther conduct is removed from the occurrence of harm, i.e. the more innocuous it is, the more ought to be required in terms of culpability.[2155] This highlights the nature of actus reus and mens rea as communicating vessels and helps to assure that the normative core of the two notions is preserved in the culture of control. Such an approach however presupposes that the increasing normativity in criminal law will not also expand to the realm of mens rea. Were both concepts to be interpreted more objectively, or rather normatively, criminal liability may become boundless.

2151 See: Chapter I. 4.3.2. and I. 5.1.

2152 See: Chapter II. 2.2.

2153 See: Chapter III. 13.

2154 See: Chapter V. 5.2.

2155 See: Chapter I. 3.1.

In any event, the harm principle in the context of this research serves to assure that the subjects of criminal law are recognised as rational and responsible agents. It protects personal autonomy and emphasises the equal respect for persons by limiting claims of (remote) harm. Furthermore, the principle potentially increases consistency in the law and fosters the equal treatment of similar cases by forcing criminal law to make fundamental commitments with regard to general rules on the prevention of crime and the risk of harm.

The penultimate principle that has emerged in this analysis as a safeguard against expanding punitivity and the arbitrary imposition of punishment is the principle of guilt. It assures that only freely and deliberately chosen conduct will trigger liability. To enable citizens to make this choice the scope of criminal law and more particularly criminal doctrines must be sufficiently clear and unambiguous. Furthermore, it introduces the requirement that the assessment of criminal liability ought to be founded on individual wrongdoing and culpability. This, *inter alia*, precludes the development or interpretation of doctrines in such a way that they would give rise to guilt by association.[2156] This is arguably of utmost importance in the context of participation in crime. The stern individualistic focus of traditional criminal law has, as has been demonstrated, difficulties to deal with collective forms of wrongdoing. In this context the principle of guilt helps to ensure that when dealing with collective wrongdoing, the net of criminal liability is not cast too widely and that the mutual attribution of objective elements of criminal liability to participants is kept within reasonable limits.

Finally the principle of legality can help to mitigate some of the pitfalls created by the increasing normativity by stressing the notion of foreseeability. It needs to be duly foreseeable for the citizens whether or not a certain conduct will give rise to criminal liability. Furthermore, harm should by and large only be attributed to a defendant if it was within reasonable limits foreseeable that his conduct may cause this particular sort of harm. The scope of the concept of foreseeability in this context will to some extent be linked and be determined by (1) the content of the provision or doctrine at stake, (2) its envisaged scope of application, and (3) the number and status of those to whom it is addressed.[2157] From this it can be deduced that in terms of foreseeability a distinction will have to be made between foreseeability for regular citizens and foreseeability for professionals in the business world. Regarding the requirements of foreseeability arguably more can be expected in regard to people carrying out professional activities as they are used to having to proceed with a high degree of caution when pursuing their activities. Likewise they are expected to be acquainted with prevalent standards of diligence, etc. applicable to their business sector.[2158]

2156 See: Chapter III. and III. 8.1.2.

2157 See: *Kononov v Latvia*, appl. no. 36376/04, 17 May 2010. See also: Veegens, 'A disrupted balance? Prevention of terrorism and compliance with fundamental legal rights and principles of law – The Dutch anti-terrorism legislation' (2011), pp. 103 et seq.

2158 See also: *Van Anraat v the Netherlands*, appl. no. 65389/09, 6 July 2010, para 81.

Combined these principles may be able to assure that the individual generally remains the starting point of criminal liability and that in instances where a collective approach is necessary it remains within reasonable boundaries. Membership to a group, a joint criminal endeavour, etc. may in certain instances be considered as partial criminal wrongdoing, but this should not in itself be sufficient to give rise to liability. In addition, the defendant's contribution to the occurred harm as well as his culpability ought to also warrant the application of criminal sanctions. Furthermore the combined force of these principles may prevent modern criminal law and doctrine from drifting towards risk liability or an attitude based criminal law.

Such an approach would on the one hand respect the fundamental values outlined in Art 2 TEU on which the Union is founded and on the other fit nicely into the newly-emerging European criminal policy.[2159] In addition it would closely correspond to the approach taken by the criminal justice systems of the Member States. This, it is submitted, may decrease the probability that the emergency break procedure pursuant to Articles 82 (3) and 83 (3) will be triggered as a response to European legislation and increase the legitimacy and compatibility of European criminal law.

The main challenge for European criminal law will arguably lie in establishing a balance between the criminal law's safeguard and crime control function. While efficiency and expediency are certainly important factors especially in the context of serious (cross border) crime, individual rights should nevertheless not be taken lightly and need to be protected. After all, the ends hardly ever justify the means.

After these general remarks it is now time to recap how general principles of European criminal law regarding the objective attribution of liability could appear. In drafting these principles this investigation has however not only been guided by the normative criteria outlined above, but it has also been attempted to take into consideration the perceived needs of the European Union. Therefore special heed has been paid to the different policy areas in which European criminal law is expected to function as well as to the peculiarities of the forms of wrongdoing it will deal with. Presumably, European criminal law will primarily deal with serious crime, having a cross-border dimension, such as terrorism, trafficking in drugs, arms or human beings, money laundering, corruption, fraud, etc.[2160] It is to be expected that these forms of wrongdoing will often be carried out by organised crime groups, etc. and will frequently involve sophisticated criminal techniques and strategies. Likewise is it conceivable that in may instances also legal entities

---

2159 See: Commission Communication: Towards an EU Criminal Policy: Ensuring the effective implementation of EU policies through criminal law, 20.09.2011, COM (2011) 573 final, European Parliament Report on harmonisation of criminal law in the EU, 24.04.2012, no. 2010/2310, Draft Council conclusions on model provisions, guiding the Council's criminal law deliberations, Brussels, 27 November 2009, 16542/2/09 REV 2, The Stockholm Programme – an open and secure Europe serving and protecting citizens, 4 May 2010, OJ 2010 C 115/1.

2160 See also: Article 83 (1) TFEU.

and other organisational structures will play a role in these forms of wrongdoing. These structural peculiarities pose a challenge for criminal law in general and for European criminal law in particular and the general principles presented here, strive to take these needs of European criminal law into account.

2. A European concept of actus reus

2.1. The conduct requirement

The conduct requirement constitutes an important baseline for the fair and just attribution of criminal liability. It functions as a first filter to avoid punishment for unexternalised thoughts by requiring a minimum objective manifestation of the perpetrator's intention in the outside world. It serves to exclude conduct over which the actor had no control and can therefore not be seen as the work of a responsible agent.[2161] Thus, the notion of control may play a pivotal role on this fundamental level of the attribution of liability. Only conduct which reflects the person as a rational, responsible agent can constitute the foundation of criminal liability. Control helps to ensure that only conduct carried out by a person possessing 'rational agent capacities' can trigger criminal liability and that defendants are therefore treated as subjects rather than objects by criminal law.

To distinguish criminally relevant from irrelevant conduct ought to be evaluated in the light of the underlying offence, the circumstances of the case at hand, etc. In other words conduct should be assessed within the social context in which it occurs. Although traditionally the focus in all investigated penal systems lay on a physical conception of conduct, all systems show signs of a shift towards a more normative or social conception of conduct.

Given the complex environment in which European criminal law will primarily operate, it is submitted that this 'social theory of conduct' could achieve satisfactory results. Organised crime, terrorism, money laundering, etc. constitute sophisticated forms of wrongdoing, where conduct can take a variety of forms and where a focus on physical conduct can be misleading and lead to unsatisfactory results. In a modern technological and interlinked society, conduct can also take a less tangible and more virtual form. Social norms and reasonable expectations can therefore play an important role. We more and more frequently conceive particular harmful incidents as the conduct of someone who, through organisational structures or other means, from a social point of view controlled or should have controlled the situation. The social conduct requirement would be flexible enough to encompass also these more virtual forms of conduct. Consider for instance the example of an entrepreneur who condones the practice of his employees to pour large quantities of acid based materials (by-products of the production process) into the floor drain.

[2161] See: Chapter II. 2.

This theory thus gains an extra dimension once the focus shifts from the traditional individual direct perpetrator to the factual responsible perpetrators behind the screen or to legal entities.[2162] Especially, legal entities have become important actors in contemporary society and will also have an important role to play in European criminal law. However, their conduct can hardly be expressed in terms of physical conduct. For corporate conduct also a more normative theory of action might be recommendable in order to capture the peculiarities of this new form of wrongdoing. Thus, a mixed social/normative concept of action might correspond best to the needs of European criminal law in modernity.

Broadly stated, all penal systems agree that conduct which cannot be seen as an expression of human agency can neither constitute the basis for imposing criminal liability. This excludes conduct caused by spasms, reflex action or convulsion as well as conduct carried out while unconscious or induced by the irresistible force of natural events or a third person (*vis absoluta*). However, this basic rule can be watered down by the influence of normative criteria which becomes apparent in the realm of road traffic offences and self-induced loss of deliberate control. In the former cases the loss of control must be almost complete and in the latter cases concepts such as *culpa in causa* make the attribution of liability despite the loss of control possible.

2.2. Omission liability

The social theory of conduct also provides room for better incorporating omissions as a basis for liability in the framework of criminal law.[2163] Duties of care *inter alia* play an increasing role in regard to environmental and product liability and will continue to do so at the European level. In case the European Union establishes for instance diligent standards for certain activities, the failure to comply with these standards can have the same effects as active behaviour and should therefore give rise to criminal liability. Central to the concept of omission liability is the notion of duties of care. In order for liability to arise the existence of a duty of care has to be proven which the defendant violated. The establishment of a duty of care essentially constitutes a societal value judgment which makes it difficult to establish clearly the origins and scope of these duties. Nevertheless this research has attempted to provide legislators and courts with a rough yardstick.

One crucial aspect in regard to duties of care and a guiding principle should arguably be the notion of foreseeability flowing from the principle of legality. It ought to be foreseeable for the person involved that a certain conduct is expected of him by society. Foreseeability in this respect is probably best interpreted objectively, as duties of care express a general social value judgment. The law should therefore ask if it was foreseeable for a reasonable person in the shoes of the defendant that a

[2162] De Hullu, 'Materieel Strafrecht' (2009), p. 154.

[2163] See: Chapter II. 3.

duty of care was owed.[2164] Therefore a number of factors like his social role, individual capacities, the particular circumstances of the case at hand and prior conduct can play a role. The latter, in particular in situations where the defendant bears some responsibility for the fact that the victim is dependent on his performance of certain acts, i.e. when the victim has been induced to act to his detriment.[2165] Another important factor can be found in the degree of dependency prevalent between the offender and the victim. Finally, the establishment of a duty of care should adhere to general requirements of criminal justice and therefore be fair, just and reasonable. This would also provide room for considerations of legal, social and public policy to enter the equation. Due to policy reasons the creation of a duty of care may for instance be considered unfair or unreasonable if it may lead citizens to give up socially beneficial activities or would force them to take unnecessary and costly safety precautions.

Based on this line of thought, it is argued that mutual (social) expectation or reliance ought to give rise to a duty to act if (i) the expectation is or should have been anticipated by the potential carrier of the duty in its respective social role, (ii) the expectation is conceived binding by society (iii) the carrier of the duty himself recognises or should have recognised that a particular action will be expected of him and (iv) the expectation is of such gravity that a disobedience of the duty to act would significantly shake the foundation of trust on which society is built.[2166] Furthermore, it should be established that: (v) the required conduct could have reasonably been expected by the victim and (vi) the scope of harm warrants the imposition of a duty of care.

It is clear from Article 49 of the Charter of fundamental rights of the European Union that omissions are part and parcel of European criminal law. Yet the Union has until this point not explicitly legislated on the matter. The forgoing discussion has shown that the duties to act to be found in the three investigated penal systems are manifold and are categorised in different ways. Nevertheless, they can in substance be summarised to five categories of duties of care which may stem from: (i) a special relationship to the victim (ii) voluntary undertakings, and (iii) specific qualities of the offender as well as (iv) ownership or responsibility for a source of danger and (v) the creation of a dangerous situation.

The wealth of European Union legislation, regulating a particular work sector, product-, environmental standards, etc., can also give rise, or respectively determine the scope of duties of care. Furthermore, the Charter of fundamental human rights of the European Union itself could play a role in establishing duties of care.

2164 Herring and Palser, 'The duty of care in gross negligent manslaughter' Criminal Law Review (2007), pp. 24–40.

2165 See: Mead, 'Contracting into Crime: A Theory of Criminal Omissions' Oxford Journal of legal Studies (1991), p. 153.

2166 Otto, 'Die Grundlagen der Strafrechtlichen Haftung des Garanten wegen Unterlassens' Jura (1985), p. 537.

Amongst others, the right to life (Art. 2), integrity of the person (Art. 3) or respect for private and family life (Art. 7) might all play a role here.

Crucial in regard to omission liability will also be the taking into account of certain limiting factors that circumscribe the scope of duties of care. Therefore the principle of individual autonomy and the corresponding distinction between duties to act and duties of care may have an important role to play. Criminal law should for one, punish wrongdoing and not enforce morality. This principle in essence holds "that individuals should be respected and treated as agents capable of choosing their acts and omissions".[2167] The emphasis on individual choice entails that the imposition of liability on paternalistic grounds should be avoided. It should generally not be up to the state to determine what is in the individual's best interest. Respect for this principle will arguably prevent the imposition of far-reaching duties of care for collective goods and protected interests.

Furthermore the principle of reliance could act as a resistance to the expansion of duties to act. This concept holds that everybody should be able to rely on the conform conduct of third parties or the victim in regard to their legal obligations. In other words, citizens should be able to rely on the fact that conduct of their fellow citizens is in compliance with the law. This principle will be of particular importance in regard to duties of care enacted for reasons of crime control such as the responsibility for the acts of people over which one exercises control, like children, employees, etc.

Moreover, the concept of impossibility of the required conduct limits the scope of duties. This concept has its origin in the principle *lex non cogit ad impossibilia* or *ultra posse nemo tenetur*.[2168] Thus, liability can be avoided where it was impossible for the person to comply with the duty (e.g. because (s)he was paralysed). Just as with affirmative actions an omission needs to reflect human agency in order to constitute the basis for the imposition of criminal liability, but it must furthermore be established whether or not in the particular situation it could have reasonably been expected by the person to fulfil his/her duty. Therefore, the individual capacities of the person in question as well as the exact circumstances of the case at hand will have an important role to play.

Finally, it is submitted that in the context of omission liability the notion of due diligence may also fulfil an important safeguard role. If it can be proven that the offender acted with due care and took all reasonable measures to prevent the particular harm, then a breach of the obligation enshrined in the offence can arguably not be established and the imposition of liability seems unwarranted.

2167 Ashworth, 'Principles of criminal law' (2006), p. 26.

2168 De Jong and Knigge, 'Het materiele strafrecht' (2003), p. 69, Roxin, 'Strafrecht Allgemeiner Teil, Band II: Besondere Erscheinungsformen der Straftat' (2003), pp. 629–632, Vogel, 'Norm und Pflicht bei den unechten Unterlassungsdelikten' (1993), pp. 182–189, Wilson, 'Central Issues in Criminal Theory' (2002), pp. 121–125.

2.3. Causality

In order to attribute liability for a certain harmful result to an actor the doctrine of causation takes a central position.[2169] Generally speaking, the notion of causation is a multi-purpose tool which can have an explanatory as well as an attributive function. Accordingly, one can distinguish two levels of causation. At one level it needs to be assessed whether a particular conduct was in fact causally connected with the result, but there remains the further question whether or not the person will be held liable in law for having caused the occurrence of the harm.[2170] This raises the question whether the imposition of criminal liability requires a different conception of cause in law and in fact.

Penal systems have generally developed different answers to this question, but this investigation has shown that corresponding to the shift in the doctrine of conduct towards a more virtual concept of conduct, the doctrine of causation is increasingly seen as a legal concept detached from the traditional physical notions of causation. Also in regard to questions of causality the conduct of the individual is increasingly placed in the social context in which it occurs, which means that normative considerations become more and more important in establishing a causal link. It is therefore submitted that a European causation doctrine should best be based on a legal/normative conception, thereby taking into consideration the essential function of the doctrine, namely the reasonable attribution of a harmful result to the defendant's conduct. Such an approach would arguably also fit the needs of European criminal law. When looking at causation in the context of European Union law one should keep in mind that the Union operates in fields where the establishment of a causal link can constitute a difficult problem. Especially in the field of economic and commercial relations where often numerous factors operate simultaneously or successively and produce direct as well as indirect effects the establishment of a causal link can be a daunting challenge. The legal/normative approach advocated here would be flexible enough to produce satisfactory results in this context as well as provide sufficient safeguards for the defendant.

The very baseline of establishing a causal link should be the *conditio sine qua non* or 'but for' test. It provides a first yardstick for the establishment of causal responsibility, especially in paradigm cases. The proposed baseline principle is further shaped by the common rule that the conduct in question need not be the sole or main cause of the result. This rule is a recognition of the fact that in principle the 'but for' test produces an infinite amount of causes. Yet, other factors contributing to the occurrence of the result need not stand in the way of the assumption of a causal link. The rule might be seen as an expression of the aforementioned goal of the doctrine in criminal law i.e. the attribution of criminal liability for a particular

[2169] See: Chapter II. 4.

[2170] Norrie, 'Crime, Reason and History – A Critical Introduction to Criminal Law' (2001), p. 134.

result in the case at hand. As the law aims at achieving a single causal statement, it is necessary to realise that this is an oversimplification and that in reality most of the time, several causes will combine to bring about the harmful result.

Moreover, the establishment of a causal link should require a connection between the harm and the fault of the individual. This places the emphasis on the safeguard function of the law. A criminal law based on respect for human dignity and the rule of law ought to hold people responsible only for harm they caused which could have been prevented by observance of the standard of diligence required by law. Holding someone responsible for harm which would have occurred even though the person had acted in accordance with the law would ride roughshod over the fundamental principles such as individual autonomy and responsibility. Closely connected thereto is the requirement that liability should be confined to the type of harm proscribed by the offence in question. This can be deduced from the purpose of the violated rule in regard to the protected legal interest. The outer boundaries for the attribution of liability are always set by the purpose and scope of the offence in question. This follows *inter alia* from the principle of legality and the corresponding requirement of foreseeability. Here the notions of control and foreseeability thus resurface to provide a counterbalance to the attributive limb of the doctrine.

Subsequently it should be established whether other known factors might have broken the causal chain. For this to occur, the intervening cause must however be a potent one. As long as the initial cause remains a substantial and operating cause, the causal link will not be broken. The concept of foreseeability will again have an important role to play here. If it was (reasonably) to be expected that a certain event occurred as a background circumstance that worsened the original harm inflicted by the defendant the causal link will prima facie not be broken.

3. Multiple actor scenarios

In regard to participation in crime the Union faces several crossroads. First, there is the question whether European criminal law ought to adopt a unitarian or a differentiated concept of participation. This research has shown that a differentiated approach is adopted in the penal systems of Germany and the Netherlands, whereas the English system can be seen to take a middle ground between a strict unitarian and a strict differentiated conception. The crucial difference between the two approaches is their view on whether or not there is any necessary distinction between perpetrators and accomplices and more importantly perhaps, whether it must be taken into account at the level of attribution or rather later at the sentencing stage. This research has identified several different modes of liability but it has also been demonstrated that differentiated systems have difficulties to adhere to the strict separation of modes of liability in practice. Judges often reason inductively to squeeze facts into legal categories that they feel will allow them to impose an appropriate punishment. This leads to the blurring of boundaries between the different concepts. Instigation is upgraded to perpetration by means, aiding can become co-perpetration, etc. Thus, it seems that in unitarian as well as in differentiated systems judges enjoy considerable freedom in regard to the application of the different modes of liability. This in turn makes the claim of proponents of a differentiated system that the strict classification of different forms of conduct increases internal consistency, comprehensiveness and legal certainty, doubtful, to say the least. If however this approach is unable to live up to its own expectations and promises, one may pose the question whether such an approach can really fit the needs of European criminal law, given its high doctrinal complexity and at times cumbersome application.

The foregoing discussion has shown that differentiated systems in particular struggle to cope with contemporary forms of criminal wrongdoing which are characterised by an increasing division of labour, high degree of organisation as well as systematisation. Increasingly human beings use intermediaries (often due to an increase in the division of labour) to bring about a certain result and do not bring it about directly despite being in control and thus blameworthy for the criminal conduct.[2171] In such circumstances, the person carrying out the offence might seem less culpable than the mastermind organising the scheme. Likewise, the person who during the crime functions as a lookout or getaway driver, traditionally seen as forms of auxiliary participation might be the driving force behind the criminal enterprise, deserving more or just as much punishment as his partners actually committing the crime.

It has tentatively been demonstrated that the notion of perpetration is increasingly interpreted normatively in order to respond to contemporary challenges for the criminal law such as organised and white collar crime. Given the fact that the European Union's focus will be exactly on those areas of criminal behaviour, such as organised crime, trafficking in human beings, money laundering, corruption and computer crime, a normative approach arguably also seems to correspond nicely to the scope and requirements of a European criminal law. These are crimes which are rarely committed single-handedly and often involve large crime syndicates, operating on an international level, characterised by a high degree of structural complexity. Consider for instance a network specialised in trafficking in human beings where some forge visas for the immigrants, others prepare the cars and some function as drivers, while others coordinate the group's activities from the background. A hard and fast categorisation of the participants' role and liability can arguably be difficult to achieve in these situations. In order to capture the role of all participants as well as assign a correct label and proportionate punishment for their deeds to the members of the network, an overall assessment of the occurred criminal offence seems necessary.

Therefore the focus on the individual, physical perpetrator should be substituted by a holistic concept of perpetration in which not only the physical, or direct

[2171] Gritter, 'Functioneel plegen door een natuurlijke persoon', in van der Leij (ed), Plegen en Deelnemen (2007), p. 14.

perpetrator of the actus reus may be considered the primary responsible, but also other persons, if their conduct, contribution or role in the commission of the offence establishes that he bears a substantial responsibility for the wrong committed.[2172] "Substantial" in this context should mean something more than causation in fact here, as this would set the bar too low for liability as a perpetrator. There must at least be sufficient evidence that the person was a major participant and did not merely play a subsidiary role in the criminal enterprise.

Criminal law, it has been argued, generally comes into action when a legally protected interest has been harmed, or at least endangered. A legal interest may be harmed or endangered either directly or indirectly.[2173] Either the conduct of the perpetrator causes the violation of the norm directly, i.e. without the intervention of another, or the violation has been brought about indirectly by the conduct of another person (an intermediary) over which the primary responsible perpetrator exerted control and in addition possessed culpability regarding the commission of the offence. Thus the notions of legally protected interest and control in combination with the threshold of substantial responsibility will take a central role in the evaluation scheme proposed here.

If a person exerted control will to a large extent depend on the relationship between the primary responsible and the intermediary. This research has shown that generally one can distinguish horizontal from vertical forms of perpetration. This distinction is based on whether a relationship of subordination or one of equality underlies the commission of the offence. In relationships of subordination, as in business or economic relationships (e.g. employer–employee, etc.) control will often be easily established. Thus, if an employer orders his employees to falsify information on European grant papers in order to receive more subsidies he may be considered to carry primary responsibility for the fraud against the financial interests of the European Union. In other situations, special heed will have to be paid to the peculiarities of the case at hand.

Comparable thereto are cases where the primary responsible instigates or abets another to commit the offence. Consider for instance the case where Lucas induces Marc to declare the cheap slaughter by-products to be exported by his company to Russia as high value prime beef in order to receive more subsidies. However, a person can also possess a more complete form of control over the intermediary's conduct, namely in cases where the harm is caused by an "innocent agent" acting without mens rea, justified or excused. Under these circumstances the exerted control can be considered so complete that the person behind the "innocent agent" will be deemed directly responsible for the occurred criminal harm.

Moreover, several persons can bear responsibility for a criminal wrong if they acted according to a common purpose or plan (i.e. as equal partners in crime). They share responsibility for the occurrence of the criminal offence on the basis of their

2172 On „outcome responsibility" in general see: Honoré, 'Responsibility and fault' (1999), pp. 14–40.

2173 Rotsch, 'Einheitstäterschaft statt Tatherrschaft' (2009), p. 422 et seq.

common purpose or plan. One may think here of a group of people forging 50 Euro bills. One of the partners is in charge of the printing process, while another procures the necessary materials and yet another brings the money into circulation.

In this context one could then further raise the question if and to what extent such a common purpose or plan can generate responsibility for an unplanned, collateral offence committed in the course of carrying out the initial offence. How would it be for instance if one of the partners in the aforementioned example were to kill a police officer while procuring the paper for the banknotes? Naturally, the scope of the envisaged offence as well as the foreseeability of the occurrence of the collateral offence will play a role here.

Such a normative approach would thus lead to a broad concept of perpetration, capable of catering to the actuality of crime and all its manifold variations. Not only the person directly fulfilling the actus reus would be considered a perpetrator, but every participant who carries substantial responsibility for the criminal outcome will be deemed to have committed the offence himself. Furthermore such an approach could achieve satisfactory results in the context of systemic and organised wrongdoing.

This leaves a small category of cases unaccounted for, which can be termed forms of "trivial assistance". These cases could be covered by a separate offence of "trivial assistance". Under this category would fall cases of minor assistance, which fall below the substantial responsibility standard outlined above. Here traditional cases of aiding, such as lending a known burglar a screwdriver, or giving instructions on how to crack a safe, can be pigeon-holed. Thus, any kind of conduct that furthered or made the commission of the crime easier, swifter or "securer" can be subsumed here.

One further question that needs to be addressed here is if derivative liability principles should be applied or if liability should be inchoate. Applying derivative liability principles would circumscribe the scope of criminal liability, as depending on the link between the offence of the perpetrator and the aider required, attempted aid would not trigger criminal liability. If one however prefers to view the liability of the aider as free-standing and autonomous, the creation of an inchoate offence would seem more appropriate. Conduct aiding the commission of the criminal offence would then trigger liability regardless whether or not the perpetrator subsequently committed the criminal offence, thus criminalising attempted aid. From the perspective of fair labelling and the expressive function of criminal law it would arguably be preferable to view the facilitator's liability as derivative from the liability of the substantially responsible principal. This would not only circumscribe the scope of criminal liability in line with the *ultima ratio* principle but would also correctly express the social reproach in its label. For if liability is considered inchoate the defendant would be convicted of trivial assistance and no further reference to the crime he furthered would be made. As there is however arguably a difference between someone aiding a shoplifter and someone aiding murder derivative liability seems preferable as it maintains the connection to the underlying offence and the wrongdoing of the perpetrator.

Such a two-pronged approach consisting of a broad normative concept of perpetration and an auxiliary offence of assistance would possess several advantages for European criminal law. First it would dispense with the difficult problem of line drawing between the different concepts of participation and would shift the focus from the internal boundaries to the arguably more important outer limits of criminal liability. This would not only make the system of participation in crime simpler, more effective and easier to apply for the courts but would arguably also improve individual justice, as the exact degree of the participants wrongdoing and culpability can now easier be taken into consideration by the judge at the sentencing stage. Here courts could also obtain guidance by the adoption of sentencing guidelines.

Furthermore, a normative approach to perpetration would correspond to the actuality of crime in which often persons other than the direct perpetrator play an influential and determining role and thus bear (substantial) responsibility for the harmful outcome. To properly reflect their degree of responsibility a holistic conception of crime and not a strict focus on the individual perpetrator seems warranted. The auxiliary offence of assistance would cover all contributions falling below the substantial responsibility threshold outlined above. Here contributions which had an impact on the commission of the offence but were not crucial or indispensable for it could be subsumed. As these participants cannot be deemed to carry a substantial responsibility for the commission of the offence, but at best peripheral responsibility, a mitigation of punishment for these participants seems defensible. To adopt a separate offence for auxiliary assistance would appropriately reflect the role and culpability of this category of participants. Moreover, such a two-pronged approach would also be in line with the requirements of Article 6 ECHR as defendants would receive sufficient information concerning the nature and cause of the accusations against them, which would allow them to develop an effective defence against the charges. Additionally, it would increase legal certainty in line with the requirements of Article 7 ECHR, as it would be more foreseeable for an offender whether his conduct will give rise to primary or secondary responsibility.

4. Inchoate offences

It has been submitted here that a European criminal law based on respect for human dignity and the rule of law may generally only impose punishment for conduct that caused harm to a protected legal interest. However, due to the social change in attitude towards crime it has become a well-established fact that criminal law is more and more frequently applied to not only reduce harm but also to reduce the risk of harm. One possibility to expand the scope of liability to cover also the risk of harm can be found in inchoate offences. The focus in this respect lay on the expansion of liability *ratio temporis*. This research has focused in particular on the criminalisation of preparatory conduct and on the doctrine of attempts.[2174]

It has been shown that from the perspective of criminal policy the Union will have to face the challenge to strike a balance between the manifest pattern of criminality which emphasises the importance of the citizens' individual freedoms and the pattern of subjective criminality which focuses more on the dangerousness of the offender for society as a whole. The increased focus on crime prevention in the culture of control has also increased the popularity of the subjective pattern in national criminal law, which denotes a shift to an actor-based criminal law. This arguably underlines the increasing punitive tendencies and ongoing inflation of criminal law in contemporary society.

To countermand these tendencies and to keep the scope of criminal liability within reasonable boundaries, it is submitted that a set of constraints should be developed that guide the introduction of offences geared at crime prevention. It is here where several traditional principles of criminal law could be combined to achieve this goal. The principle of *ultima ratio* as well as the harm principle can function as a first yardstick in this respect. In the light of the former, it is submitted that conduct which only poses a remote danger to the protected legal interest and where the endangerment is still factually and temporally uncertain, should not be subjected to criminal sanctions.[2175] Furthermore, liability may only be imposed if the offender's conduct can in some sense be considered wrongful.[2176] This arguably follows from the *nulla poena sine actione* principle. The foundation of criminal liability ought to rest on a person's conduct and not on his evil thoughts, dangerousness or attitude.

The harm principle as defined in this thesis would entail that the underlying protected legal interest ought to be substantial in order to warrant an expansion of criminal liability. As trivial interests should not be protected by threat of criminal sanctions it follows that preparatory offences ought to only be accepted if they are designed to reduce a substantial risk. The aspect of risk creation can be seen as an endangerment of the protected substantial legal interest which may function as a link or substitute for harm. If a person carries out conduct which by its nature, quality and purpose is exclusively directed in bringing about a criminal offence, the criminalisation of such conduct may be legitimate. For instance, the procurement of certain dangerous substances necessary for the production of drugs or arms might be subsumed here. In these circumstances the protection of a legal interest, i.e. the crime control function of criminal law may prevail over its safeguard function.

2174 See: Chapter IV.

2175 Deckers and Heusel, 'Strafbarkeit terroristischer Vorbereitungshandlungen – rechtsstaatlich nicht tragbar' ZRP (2008), p. 171.

2176 Husak, 'Overcriminalization' (2008), pp. 73 et seq, Sieber, 'Legitimation und Grenzen von Gefährdungsdelikten im Vorfeld terroristischer Gewalt – Eine Analyse der Vorfeldtatbestände im "Entwurf eines Gesetzes zur Verfolgung der Vorbereitung von schweren staatsgefährdenden Gewalttaten"' NStZ (2009), p. 356.

Finally, flowing from the principle *nulla poena sine culpa*, liability for preparatory offences seems only justified in case the person creating a risk of harm, possesses a significant culpability for the ultimate harm.[2177] This requirement may in the case of criminalising risk of harm amount to a culpability standard of direct or indirect intention and exclude the application of *dolus eventualis*. Thus, the conception of actus reus and mens rea as communicating vessels becomes clearly visible in this respect.

However, these principles may only provide a rough yardstick for determining when the criminalisation of risks of harm will be legitimate in European criminal law but cannot provide absolute limitations to the scope of criminal liability. In addition the principles of necessity, suitability and proportionality should be observed. In regard to necessity and suitability this could *inter alia* be established by expert as well as evaluation reports. The former may assess *ex ante* whether the conduct in question is indeed dangerous enough to warrant criminalisation and also list and discuss other legislative, perhaps less intrusive alternatives. The suitability of the measure could be assessed *ex post* by evaluation reports or impact assessments which may determine whether or not the rule in question had the desired effect.

In regard to the criminalisation of preparatory conduct the European Union will also have to decide if a general part doctrine of preparation should be developed or if the question is better addressed on a case by case basis (e.g. by introducing endangerment or possession offences). While the former approach may have some advantages from a doctrinal and theoretical point of view, it is submitted that a case by case approach fits better into the prevalent common traditions of the European Union and the Member States. Furthermore, a case by case approach may also provide a better restraint to overcriminalisation, as the legislator would be obliged to provide proof that all the aforementioned requirements are fulfilled every time it opts for the criminalisation of preparatory conduct in a respective legislative instrument.

Turning from the preparatory phase to the attempt phase, the cardinal question for European criminal law will simply stated be whether a more safeguard-minded objective conception or a more crime control orientated subjective approach should be preferred. This research has shown that the scope of attempt liability is significantly shaped by the balancing of these two competing theories. In order to strike a fair balance between the law's safeguard and crime control function and in correspondence with the prevalent approach within the Member States it has been submitted that a mixed approach seems to be preferable. As a rationale for imposing attempt liability the offender's conduct should amount to an endangerment of the legal order as well as his subjective criminal proclivities should be clearly expressed in it. The objective endangerment rationale will arguably account for most cases of attempt liability and will also ensure that the concept of actus reus continues to play

[2177] Husak, 'Overcriminalization' (2008), pp. 174 et seq.

an important role to assure that liability remains rooted in an act-based criminal law. It will further provide a valuable restraint against unduly inflations of criminal liability. The subjective element of the offender's criminal proclivities on the other hand will account for the imposition of liability of impossible attempts and also gives expression to the fact that intentions often constitute the primal ingredient for criminal censure in regard to attempts.

The mixed rationale should also be reflected in the chosen formula to demarcate attempts from preparation. Objectively an imminence of the commission of the offence should be required which amounts to an endangerment of the legal order. Thus, next to a close temporal connection an intrusion of the offender's conduct into the sphere of the protected legal interest should be required. Such an approach implies a moderate, harm-centred conception of criminal liability, loosely corresponding to the pattern of manifest criminality. It would arguably help to assure that criminal liability retains strong ties to the harm proscribed by the criminal offence and prevent liability from invading the realm of thoughts and attitudes.

The requirement of 'imminence' should however not be interpreted in a way that already some part of the actus reus must have been brought about. Partial fulfilment of the actus reus can be a sufficient condition for liability but should not be a necessary one, as this would cast the scope of the law too narrowly. In a typical European fraud case this would arguably mean that the falsification of documents should not yet give rise to attempt liability. Only once the falsified documents have been submitted or sent to the competent authority can an endangerment of the protected legal interest be assumed and liability should arise.

However, in this context it seems almost a matter of course that the harm principle in conjunction with the underlying protected legal interest will be of importance as it influences and shapes the scope of attempt liability. The wider the scope of a protected legal interest, the earlier it will accordingly be possible to construe its endangerment and therewith some form of (remote or (in)tangible) harm. Thus, the greater the collective interests one allows to be protected by threat of criminal sanctions the further the scope of attempt liability might expand. For the European legislator caution as regards the protection of collective or universal interests seems therefore desirable.

It has already been mentioned that attempt liability is generally in all investigated systems confined to intentional conduct. This, it is submitted, ought also to be the approach adopted by European criminal law. The innocuous or ambiguous nature of the defendant's conduct should arguably be compensated by his firm criminal intention in order to substantiate the legitimate imposition of criminal liability. What however intention should in this area of the law exactly denote to is a subject which can only be solved within the broader discussion on fault requirements in European criminal law.[2178]

[2178] See: Blomsma 'Mens rea and defences in European criminal law' (2012).

A general part of European criminal law will also have to address the issue namely to what extent impossible attempts should give rise to criminal liability. In line with the approach common to the investigated Member States it has been argued that with the notable exception of imaginary offences and superstitious or utterly daft attempts, impossible attempts should generally lead to liability. To distinguish punishable impossible attempts from non-punishable, a demarcation formula will be needed. One possible solution, supported here, is to utilise the distinction between mistakes of law and mistakes of fact. While (reverse) mistakes of law lead to imaginary offences, reverse mistakes of fact lead to impossible attempts. If however the offender gravely errs about the laws of nature or invokes powers that lie outside the ambit of human control no liability should ensue. In these instances the occurred conduct is not only inept but furthermore inapt to bring about the envisaged criminal harm. Thus, no endangerment of the protected legal interest has objectively arisen. Accordingly, the link to the proscribed harm can be considered merely tenuous and the principle of harm would therefore bar the attribution of liability for these variations of impossibility.

Finally, it has been submitted that a defence of voluntary withdrawal should be included in the European law of attempts. If a person voluntarily withdraws from a criminal endeavour and prevents the occurrence of harm, neither considerations of special nor of general prevention seem any longer to warrant the imposition of punishment. An important choice in regard to the scope of the defence is the question whether the law should rely on the subjective conception of the offender or invoke objective criteria for demarcation. An objective approach will generally lead to a narrow scope of the exemption while subjective criteria, by and large, lead to a withdrawal-friendly conception, which ultimately benefits the offender. It is submitted that from a systematic point of view the approach in regard to withdrawal should reflect the approach adopted in regard to attempt liability in general. Thus, if the perspective of the perpetrator is not particularly emphasised in establishing when the threshold to liability has been passed, it would be inconsistent to rely heavily on it in regard to withdrawal.

A further important distinction concerning the scope of the defence is the distinction between complete and incomplete attempts. In case of the latter, mere desistance from the criminal enterprise will generally suffice for a withdrawal, whereas in case of complete attempts the law requires an *actus contratius*. Which conduct exactly will suffice for an *actus contrarius* is difficult to determine in abstraction, but the investigation of national penal law has shown that a great deal will depend on the severity and scope of the offender's previous conduct and how far towards the completion of the offence he has already progressed. The further events have advanced, the more the offender will have to do to successfully withdraw from the attempt.

To determine when a withdrawal was really voluntary the law can rely on a psychological or a normative evaluation scheme. The approach in national criminal law seems to favour the former which is why it can be stated as a rough yardstick that a withdrawal will be considered voluntary if the offender thinks 'I do not wish to carry on even if I could' while it will be considered involuntary if he thinks 'I cannot carry on even if I wanted to'.

Last but not least, European criminal law will have to decide how much punishment criminal attempts should warrant. In line with the mixed objective/subjective approach advocated here, it has been submitted that a facultative mitigation of punishment could be established for criminal attempts. Mitigation to three-quarters of the maximum penalty of the attempted offence could be an option. In many instances of criminal attempts it namely seems arguable that the absence of (tangible) harm will warrant a mitigation of punishment in relation to the complete offence, yet as this may need not always be the case the courts should be granted some leeway in meting out punishment.

5. Corporate criminal liability

Regarding the criminal liability of legal entities a variety of questions will have to be addressed by the Union legislator in order to develop a coherent approach to the matter.[2179] It has been argued that corporations in the context of European Union law are considered to be fit subjects of law. They are responsible agents who can act and be at fault and can accordingly be held responsible for their shortcomings. Especially in the context of environmental crime as well as in regard to offences against the financial interests of the Union legal entities will presumably often play an important role.

As to the nature of corporate personality, it has been submitted that an organic theory should be preferred over an atomic one as it better corresponds to corporate reality and reflects the nature of the corporation as a living system. A corporation is namely something more and something different than simply the sum of its parts.

However, the approach adopted in existing European legislation arguably shows traces of an atomistic conception, applying the so-called identification doctrine. Despite the fact that the doctrine is arguably founded on a misconceived perception of corporate personality and wrongdoing, it seems, admittedly well suited to be applied to small-scale organisations with simple organisational structures and hierarchies which facilitate the finding of individual wrongdoing to be attributed to the company. The doctrine is however bound to encounter difficulties in regard to large-scale let alone multinational corporations. One reason for that can be found in the fact that the identification doctrine always requires a link to individual wrongdoing in order to establish corporate liability. Especially in the context of European Union Law which to a large extent focusses on transnational serious crime, controlling, regulating and sanctioning of conduct by large scale corporations will be vital. Consider for instance the example of a large corporation emitting hazardous substances into a nearby river. It may be difficult in such situations to

[2179] See: Chapter V.

establish beyond reasonable doubt that the management or board of directors was aware of the offence and acted culpable, potentially insulating the corporation from liability.

Therefore, it has been proposed that the European Union should supplement the identification doctrine and strive for an autonomous, organic conception of corporate criminal liability. European criminal law can learn from the problems encountered by national law and strive for a fresh start. What will be needed is a fundamental reconceptualisation of criminal liability in the context of corporate wrongdoing, paying close heed to corporate reality and practice. Much more research will be needed to achieve this goal and the best that can probably be hoped for is that this research provides a first stepping stone for following discussions.

In reference to the social act requirement advocated in this book, it is submitted that corporate conduct ought to be interpreted in the social context in which it occurs. Conduct acquires meaning in relation with a concrete society and as part of a particular social system or subsystem. In regard to legal entities the social context in which the conduct emerges is the corporate world as a subsystem of modern industrial society where corporations are perceived as responsible actors and active agents. The focus should accordingly rest on organisational conduct rather than on individual conduct. Accordingly, it has been argued that corporate conduct will frequently take the form of a contravention of applicable diligent standards, or respectively duties of care.

One important factor in this evaluation, reflecting the core function of the conduct requirement identified here will be, whether or not a corporation can be seen as having had factual control over the manifestation of the criminal conduct. Therefore the company's operational management and policies may be of importance. If the occurred conduct fits into the prevalent company management scheme and policies then the offence prima facie ought to be attributed to the company. Corporations can be deemed to operate under a general duty to prevent wrongdoing and are therefore expected to implement effective precaution and safety mechanisms to achieve this goal. Such an approach presupposes that a corporation possesses a capacity for (self-) organisation. An important question in the establishment of corporate liability may therefore be whether or not the corporation in question has achieved a level of internal complexity that allows it to organise itself in a meaningful way.

After the conclusion has been reached that a certain conduct constitutes corporate conduct, the assessment will have to turn to the question whether or not the corporate defendant can also be blamed for it. It should not be overlooked that if one wishes to subject corporations to the rule of criminal law, liability for individual as well as corporate wrongdoing should only be imposed if the corporation acts culpably.

When this exactly will be the case arguably defies a simple answer. This research has argued that there are certain features of the way in which corporations organise themselves which may reflect fault on part of the organisation. One could for instance assess the corporate culture or ethos which may be conducive or may even encourage unlawful behaviour. A corporate culture that encourages employees to 'cut corners' and ruthlessly pursues profit maximisation, may not only provide an incentive to act wrongfully but may also allow individuals to rationalise their illegal conduct. The notion of corporate culture may for instance be particularly useful to tackle the malpractices of some organisations in the financial sector. A corporate culture that encourages high risk investments and speculations could certainly give rise to corporate fault.

Further, the structure of the corporation can play a role as a high degree of decentralisation may point in the direction that the people responsible for implementing and supervising the corporate polices or goals may not be found in the board which adopted them. Thus, the management structure may be such that certain formal representatives are insulated from responsibility. Moreover, the company's internal education system as well as its reactions to past violations can provide insights into a corporation's blameworthiness.

Additional factors that one could apply to determine corporate culpability could be corporate compliance as well as self-regulation. All these factors provide a relevant proxy to assess whether or not a corporation can be blamed for a certain occurred criminal harm. All these elements are under the control of the company and constitute an element of corporate choice which adds legitimacy to the notion of organisational fault as a basis of liability. The corporation is held liable for its choices and through its choices may avoid liability in the future. Accordingly, in this context as well the notion of control may play an important role. It follows that should it be proven beyond reasonable doubt that the corporation had taken all reasonable care to prevent the occurrence of a particular harm and acted diligently, control will be absent and a contravention of the pertinent duty of care cannot be assumed. This would thus introduce a due diligence defence for corporations and prevent corporations from being held liable for harm which lay outside their sphere of influence or control and hopefully strike a fair balance between the criminal law's safeguard and crime control function also in the context of corporate wrongdoing.

6. Concluding remarks

This research has attempted to reveal how rules regarding the objective attribution of liability for European criminal law could appear. By comparing the national rules on actus reus, participation, inchoate offences and corporate criminal liability in England, Germany and the Netherlands and merging them with pertinent fragments of European Union law, some general principles have been identified. The comparative analysis carried out in this book has also shed some light on current social developments which influence criminal law. In regard to the concepts under investigation here, an increasing normativity in the attribution of liability in order to successfully tackle contemporary forms of wrongdoing has emerged. As a result an expansion in the scope of criminal liability and an increased emphasis on the law's crime control function is discernible. These developments and trends in the realm of criminal liability will certainly also have an impact on European criminal law. Yet, a European criminal law ought to be based on considerations both of effective enforcement as well as a solid protection of fundamental rights and liberties. "It needs to be designed focusing on the needs of European Citizens and the requirements of an European Area of Freedom, Security and Justice, while fully respecting subsidiarity and the last-resort-character of criminal law".[2180]

In order to achieve that goal several principles have been identified which functioned as guiding criteria in the development of general concepts of European criminal law. These principles provide a counterbalance to the expansion of criminal liability and may help to keep European criminal law within reasonable boundaries. It should namely not be possible to take the benefits of criminal law without also submitting to burdens. If within the objective rules of attributing liability certain restraints are removed, the logic of actus reus and mens rea as communicating vessels dictates that the decrease on the objective part of liability, ought to be compensated by an increase in the subjective component. Otherwise criminal liability threatens to become boundless. In order not to fundamentally change the balance of criminal liability for the worse, removal of requirements from one vessel seems permissible only in the event that the other vessel is not leaking.

2180 Commission Communication: Towards an EU Criminal Policy: Ensuring the effective implementation of EU policies through criminal law, 20.09.2011, COM (2011) 573 final, p. 12.

Selected Bibliography

Alexander, 'Criminal Liability for Omissions: An Inventory of Issues' in *Criminal Law Theory: Doctrines of the General Part,* (Oxford University Press, 2002)

Alldridge, 'The doctrine of innocent agency' Criminal Law Forum (1990) pp. 45–83

Alldridge, 'Relocating Criminal Law' (Dartmouth Publishing Company Limited, 2000)

Ambos, 'Is the development of a common substantive criminal law for Europe possible? Some Preliminary Reflections' Maastricht Journal of European and Comparative Law (2005) pp. 173–191

Ambos, 'Toward a universal system of crime: Comments on George Fletcher's Grammar of Criminal Law' Cardozo Law Review (2007) pp. 2647–2673

Arenson, 'The Pitfalls in the Law of Attempt: A new Perspective' The Journal of Criminal Law (2005) pp. 146–167

Arzt, 'Zur Garantenstellung beim unechten Unterlassungsdelikt' JA (1980) pp. 533–654

Ashworth, 'Defining criminal offences without harm' in *Criminal law – Essays in honour of J C Smith,* (Butterworths, 1987)

Ashworth, 'Criminal Attempts and the role of resulting harm under the code and in the common law' Rutgers Law Journal (1988) pp. 725–772

Ashworth, 'The scope of criminal liability for omissions' The Law Quarterly Review (1989) pp. 424–459

Ashworth, 'Grunderfordernisse des Allgemeinen Teils für ein europäisches Sanktionsrecht: Landesbericht England' ZStW (1998) pp. 461–472

Ashworth, 'Is the Criminal Law a lost cause?' The Law Quarterly Review (2000) pp. 225–256

Ashworth, 'Principles of criminal law' (Oxford University Press, 2006)

Ashworth, 'Conceptions of Overcriminalization' Ohio State Journal of Criminal Law (2008) pp. 407–425

Ashworth, 'Principles of criminal law' (Oxford University Press, 2009)

Ashworth, 'The Unfairness of risk-based possession offences' Criminal Law and Philosophy (2011) pp. 237–257

Ashworth, 'United Kingdom' in *The Handbook of comparative criminal law,* (Stanford University Press, 2011)

Ashworth and Steiner, 'Criminal omissions and public duties: the French experience' Legal Studies (1990) pp. 153–164

Asp, 'The importance of the principles of Subsidiarity and Coherence in the development of EU Criminal Law' European Criminal Law Review (2011) pp. 44–55

Badar, 'Mens Rea – Mistake of Law & Mistake of Fact in German Criminal Law: A Survey for International Criminal Tribunals' International Criminal Law Review (2005) pp. 203–246

Beck, 'Risk Society – Towards a New Modernity' (SAGE Publications Ltd, 1992)

Blankenburg, 'Patterns of legal culture: The Netherlands compared to neighboring Germany' The American Journal of Comparative Law (1998) pp. 1–41

Blomsma, Mens rea and defences in European criminal law (Intersentia 2012)

Bohlander, 'Principles of German Criminal Law' (Hart Publishing, 2009)

Bohnert, 'Introduction' in *Karlsruher Kommentar zum Gesetz über Ordnungswidrigkeiten,* (Verlag C.H. Beck, 2006)

Bosch, 'Beginsel van Strafrecht' (Kluwer, 2008)

Böse, 'The principle of proportionality and the protection of legal interests' European Criminal Law Review (2011) pp. 35–43

Brammsen, 'Die Entstehungsvoraussetzungen der Garantenpflichten' (Duncker & Humbolt, 1986)

Brockhaus, 'Die strafrechtliche Dogmatik von Vorbereitung, Versuch und Rücktritt im europäischen Vergleich' (Verlang Dr. Kovac, 2006)

Bucy, 'Corporate Ethos: A Standard for Imposing Corporate Criminal Liability' Minnesota Law Review (1991) pp. 1095 et seq.

Buruma, 'Bestraft zonder iets gedaan te hebben' in *De gedraging in beweging,* (Wolf Legal Publishers, 2007)

Buxton, 'Joint Enterprise' Criminal Law Review (2009) pp. 233–243

Buxton, 'Being an accessory to one's own murder' Criminal Law Review (2012) pp. 275–281

Charalambakis, 'Zur Problematik der psychischen Beihilfe' in *Festschrift für Claus Roxin,* (Walter de Gruyter, 2001)

Chiao, 'Action and agency in the criminal law' Legal Theory (2009) pp. 1–23

Chiao, 'Intention and attempt' Criminal Law and Philosophy (2010) pp. 37–55

Child, 'The differences between attempted complicity and inchoate assisting and encouraging – a reply to Professor Bohlander' Criminal Law Review (2010) pp. 924–932

Christopher, 'Tripartite structures of criminal law in Germany and other civil law jurisdictions' Cardozo Law Review (2007) pp. 2675–2695

Claessen, 'Misdaad en straf' (Wolf Legal Publishers, 2010)

Claessen, 'Over hiv-jurisprudentie en Groningse seksfeesten' Strafbald (2010) pp. 150–157

Clarkson, 'Corporate Culpability' Web Journal of Current Legal Issues (1998) pp.

Clarkson, 'Attempt: The Conduct Requirement' Oxford Journal of legal Studies (2009) pp. 25–41

Clarkson and Keating, 'Criminal law: Text and Materials' (Sweet & Maxwell, 2003)

Clough, 'Bridging the theoretical Gap: The search for a realist model of corporate criminal liability' Criminal Law Forum (2007) pp. 267–300

Colvin, 'Corporate Personality and Criminal Liability' Criminal Law Forum (1995) pp. 1–44

Darbyshire, 'Eddey & Darbyshire on the English Legal System' (Sweet & Maxwell, 2001)

De Hullu, 'Zijn er grenzen aan de strafrechtelijke aansprakelijkheid?' (Gouda Quint bv, 1993)

De Hullu, 'Enkele opmerkingen over het strafrechtelijk daderschap van rechtspersonen' in *Systeem in ontwikkeling: liber amicorum G. Knigge,* (Wolf Legal Publisher, 2005)

De Hullu, 'Materieel Strafrecht' (Kluwer, 2006)

De Hullu, 'Materieel Strafrecht' (Kluwer, 2009)

De Jong, 'Tussen schuld en gedraging: normativering' in *De gedraging in beweging,* (Wolf Legal Publisher, 2007)

De Jong, 'Vormen van strafbare deelneming' in *Plegen en Deelnemen,* (Kluwer, 2007)

De Jong, 'Daad-Schuld' (Boom Juridische Uitgevers, 2009)

De Jong and Knigge, 'Het materiele strafrecht' (Kluwer, 2003)

De Valk, 'Aansprakelijkheid van leidinggevenden' (Kluwer – Deventer, 2009)

Deckers and Heusel, 'Strafbarkeit terroristischer Vorbereitungshandlungen – rechtsstaatlich nicht tragbar' ZRP (2008) pp. 169–173

Delmas-Marty and Vervaele, 'The implementation of the Corpus Juris in the Member States – Volume I', in (eds), (2000)

Dennis, 'The mental element for accessories' in *Criminal law – Essays in honour of J C Smith,* (Butterworths, 1987)

Dressler, 'Reassessing the Theoretical Underpinnings of Accomplice Liability: New Solutions to an Old Problem' Hastings Law Journal (1986) pp. 91–140

Dressler, 'Reforming Complicity Law: Trivial Assistance as a lesser offence?' Ohio State Journal of Criminal Law (2008) pp. 427 et seq.

Dubber, 'Policing possession: The war on crime and the end of criminal law' Journal of Criminal Law and Criminology (2001) pp. 829–996

Dubber, 'The Promise of German Criminal Law: A Science of Crime and Punishment' German Law Journal (2005) pp. 1049–1072

Dubber, 'Theories of Crime and punishment in German criminal law' The American Journal of Comparative Law (2005) pp. 679–707

Duff, '"Can I help you?" Accessorial liability and the intention to assist' Legal Studies (1990) pp. 165–181

Duff, 'Criminal Attempts' (Clarendon Press, 1996)

Duff, 'Theories of Criminal Law' The Stanford Encyclopedia of Philosophy (2002) pp.

Duff, 'Answering for Crime' (Hart Publishing, 2007)

Duttwiler, 'Liability for omission in International Criminal Law' International Criminal Law Review (2006) pp. 1–61

Elzinga, 'Medeplegen' in *Plegen en Deelnemen,* (Kluwer, 2007)

Engländer, 'Kausalitätsprobleme beim unechten Unterlassungsdelikt' JuS (2001) pp. 958 et seq.

Epstein, 'The harm principle and how it grew' University of Toronto Law Journal (1995) pp. 369–417

Eser, 'The Principle of Harm in the Concept of Crime: A Comparative Analysis of the Criminally Protected Legal Interests' Duquesne University Law Review (1966) pp. 345–417

Faure and Visser, 'How to punish environmental pollution? Some reflections on various models of criminalization of environmental harm' European Journal of Crime, Criminal Law and Criminal Justice (1995) pp. 316–368

Feely and Simon, 'The new penology: Notes on the emerging strategy of corrections and its implications' Criminology (1992) pp. 449–474

Feinberg, 'Doing & Deserving -Essays in the theory of responsibility' (Princeton University Press, 1970)

Field and Jörg, 'Corporate Liability and Manslaughter: should we be going Dutch?' The Criminal Law Review (1991) pp. 156–171

Finkelstein, 'Involuntaty Crimes, Voluntary Committed' in *Criminal Law Theory: Doctrines of the General Part,* (Oxford University Press, 2002)

Fischer and Rehm, 'Alcohol consumption and the liability of offenders in the German criminal system' Contemporary Drug Problems (1996) pp. 707–730

Fisse and Braithwaite, 'The allocation of responsibility for corporate crime: Individualism, Collectivisim and Accountability' Sydney Law Review (1988) pp. 469–513

Fletcher, 'Rethinking Criminal Law' (Little, Brown and Company, 1978)

Fletcher, 'Constructing a theory of impossible attempts' Criminal Justice Ethics (1986) pp. 53–69

Fletcher, 'On the moral irrelevance of Bodily movements' University of Pennsylvania Law Review (1994) pp. 1443–1453

Fletcher, 'Basic Concepts of Criminal Law' (Oxford University Press, 1998)

Fletcher, 'The Grammar of Criminal Law' (Oxford University Press, 2007)

Friedrichs, 'ENRON et al.: Paradigmatic white collar crime cases for the new century' Critical Criminology (2004) pp. 113–132

Garland, 'The culture of high crime societies' British Journal of Criminology (2000) pp. 347–375

Garland, 'The Culture of Control – Crime and Social Order in Contemporary Society' (Oxford University Press, 2006)

Garvey, 'Are attempts like treason?' The New Criminal Law Review (2011) pp. 173–212

Gentle, 'The Bribery Act 2010: Part 2: the corporate offence' Criminal Law Review (2011) pp. 101–110

Giddens, 'Risk and Responsibility' The Modern Law Review (1999) pp. 1–10

Glazebrook, 'Situational liability' in *Reshaping the criminal law – Essays in honour of Glanville Williams,* (Stevens & Sons, 1978)

Gobert, 'The Corporate Manslaughter and Corporate Homicide Act 2007 – Thirteen years in the making but was it worth the wait?' The Modern Law Review (2008) pp. 413–433

Gobert and Punch, 'Rethinking Corporate Crime' (Butterworths Lexis Nexis, 2003)

Gómez-Jara Díez, 'Corporate Culpability as a limit to the overcriminalization of corporate criminal liability: The interplay between self-regulation, corporate compliance, and corporate citizenship' New Criminal Law Review (2011) pp. 78–96

Gritter, 'Effectiviteit en aansprakelijkheid in het economisch ordeningsrecht' (Boom Juridische uitgevers, 2003)

Gritter, 'Duidelijkheid omtrent corporatief daderschap' Tijdschrift voor Onderneming en Strafrecht (2004) pp. 31–38

Gritter, 'De antonimiteit van daderschap en zorgvuldig gedrag' in *Pet af – Liber amicorum D. H. de Jong,* (Wolf Legal Publisher, 2007)

Gritter, 'De strafbaarheid van de rechtspersoon' in *Plegen en Deelnemen,* (Kluwer, 2007)

Gritter, 'Functioneel plegen door een natuurlijke persoon' in *Plegen en Deelnemen,* (Kluwer, 2007)

Gritter and Sikkema, 'Van kennelijke bestemming naar daadwerkelijke voorbereiding: subjectivering van het Nederlandse strafrecht?' Nederlands Juristenblad (2008) pp. 99–101

Gröning, 'A Criminal Justice System or a System Deficit? Notes on the System Structure of the EU Criminal Law' European Journal of Crime, Criminal Law and Criminal Justice (2010) pp. 115–137

Haidt and Baron, 'Social roles and the moral judgment of acts and omissions' European Journal of Social Psychology (1996) pp. 201–218

Hamdorf, 'Beteiligungsmodelle im Strafrecht' (Edition iuscrim, 2002)

Hamdorf, 'The concept of a Joint Criminal Enterprise and Domestic Modes of Liability for Parties to a crime: A Comparison of German and English Law' Journal of International Criminal Justice (2007) pp. 208–226

Hart, 'Punishment and Responsibility' (Oxford University Press, 2008)

Hart and Honoré, 'Causation in the Law' (Oxford University Press, 1985)

Harteveld, 'Doen plegen' in *Plegen en deelnemen,* (Kluwer, 2007)

Hartmann, 'Sonderregeln für die Beihilfe durch "neutrales" Verhalten?' ZStW (2004) pp. 585–617

Hassemer, 'Kennzeichen und Krisen des modernen Strafrechts' Zeitschrift für Rechtspolitik (1992) pp. 378–383.

Hassemer, 'Sicherheit durch Strafrecht' HRRS (2006) pp. 130–143

Hefendehl, 'Corporate Criminal Liability – Model Penal Code Section 2.07 and the Development in Western Legal Systems' Buffalo Criminal Law Review (2001) pp. 283–300

Heine, 'Rethinking Criminal Liability of Enterprises: International Developments, Basic Models, National Consequences' in *De Strafrechtelijke en civielrechtelijke aansprakelijkheid van de rechtspersoon en zijn bestuurders,* (Intersentia, 1998)

Heinrich, 'Die Grenzen des Strafrechts bei der Gefahrenprävention' ZStW (2009) pp. 94–130

Herring and Palser, 'The duty of care in gross negligent manslaughter' Criminal Law Review (2007) pp. 24 et seq.

Herzberg, 'Strafverzicht bei bedingt vorsätzlichem Versuch' NStZ (1990) pp. 311–318

Hirsch, 'Untauglicher Versuch und Tatstrafrecht' in *Festschrift für Claus Roxin,* (Walter de Gruyter, 2001)

Hogan, 'The Criminal Attempts Act and Attempting the Impossible' Criminal Law Review (1984) pp. 584–591

Hogan, 'Omissions and the duty myth' in *Criminal law – Essays in Honour of J C Smith,* (Buttersworth, 1987)

Hollingsworth, 'Responsibility and Rights: Children and their parents in the youth justice system' International Journal of Law, Policy and Family (2007) pp. 190–219

Honoré, 'Responsibility and fault' (Hart Publishing, 1999)

Horder, 'The Criminal Liability of Organisations for Manslaughter and other Serious Offences' in *Halsbury's Laws of England Centenary Essays (2007),* (Lexis-Nexis, 2007)

Horder, 'Reforming the auxiliary Part of the criminal law' Archbold News (2007) pp. 6–9

Houtepen and Ter Meulen, 'New Types of Solidarity in the European Welfare State' Health Care Analysis (2000) pp. 329–340

Huber, 'Corporate Criminal Liability: Requirements under International Conventions and Application in European Countries' in *European Cooperation In Penal Matters: Issues and Perspectives,* (Wolters Kluwer Italia Srl, 2008)

Husak, 'The nature and justifiability of nonconsummate offences' Arizona Law Review (1995) pp. 151–183

Husak, 'Overcriminalization' (Oxford University Press, 2008)

Ingelfinger, 'Zeitliche Grenzen ehelicher Garantenpflichten' NStZ (2004) pp. 409–413

Jakobs, 'Der strafrechtliche Handlungsbegriff' (C.H. Beck'sche Verlagsbuchhandlung, 1992)

Jakobs, 'Bürgerstrafrecht und Feindstrafrecht' Ritsumeikan Law Review (2004) pp. 93–107

Jescheck and Weigend, 'Lehrbuch des Strafrechts: Allgemeiner Teil' (Duncker & Humblot, 1996)

Jones and Sufrin, 'EC Competition Law: Text, Cases, and Materials' (Oxford University Press, 2004)

Kadish, 'Complicity, Cause and Blame: A Study in the Interpretation of Doctrine' California Law Review (1985) pp. 323–410

Kadish, 'Reckless Complicity' The Journal of Criminal Law & Criminology (1997) pp. 369–394

Kaiafa-Gbandi, 'The importance of core principles of substantive criminal law for a European criminal policy respecting fundamental rights and the rule of law' European Criminal Law Review (2011) pp. 7–34

Keijzer, 'Collective aansprakelijkheid in het strafrecht' in *Glijdende Schalen – Liber amicorum J. de Hullu,* (Wolf Legal Publisher, 2003)

Kelk, 'Studieboek materieel strafrecht' (Kluwer, 2005)

Kessler, 'Beschikkingsmacht centraal bij functioneel plegen' in *Pet af: liber amicorum D.H. de Jong,* (Wolf Legal Publisher, 2007)

Keupink, 'Enkele opmerkingen over niet-distantieren bij medeplegen' in *De gedraging in beweging,* (Wolf Legal Publisher, 2007)

Kienapfel and Höpfel, 'Grundriß des österreichischen Strafrechts' (Manz, 2003)

Klip, 'Criminal Law in the European Union' (Kluwer, 2005)

Klip, 'Slappe rechters' Delikt en Delinkwent (2010) pp. 1253–1263

Klip, 'European Criminal Law' (Intersentia, 2012)

Knigge, 'Doen en laten; enkele opmerkingen over daderschap' Delikt en Delinkwent (1992) pp. 128–154

Knigge, 'Het opzet van de deelnemer' in *Glijdende Schalen – Liber amicorum J. de Hullu,* (Wolf Legal Publisher, 2003)

Krabbe, 'Uitlokking' in *Plegen en Deelnemen,* (Kluwer, 2007)

Krebs, 'Joint Criminal Enterprise' The Modern Law Review (2010) pp. 578–604

Kugler, 'Two concepts of omission' Criminal Law Forum (2003) pp. 421–447

Kühl, 'Die strafrechtliche Garantenstellung – Eine Einführung mit Hinweisen zur Vertiefung' JuS (2007) pp.

Kuhli, 'Objektive Zurechnung bei eigenverantwortlicher Selbstgefährdung' HRRS (2008) pp. 385–388

Kwakman, 'De causaliteit in het strafrecht. Het vereiste van conditio sine qua non als enige bruikbare criterium' Nederlands Juristenblad (2007) pp. 992–999

Lacey, 'Responsibility and Modernity in Criminal Law' The Journal of Political Philosophy (2001) pp. 249–276

Lacey, 'Psychologising Jekyll, Demonising Hyde: The strange case of criminal responsibility' Criminal Law and Philosophy (2010) pp. 109–133

Lampe, 'Willensfreiheit und strafrechtliche Unrechtslehre' ZStW (2006) pp. 1–43

Lampe, 'Tätersysteme: Spuren und Strukturen' ZStW (2007) pp. 471–518

Lanham, 'Primary and derivative criminal liability: An Australian Perspective' Criminal Law Review (2000) pp. 707–718

Leavens, 'A Causation Approach to Criminal Omissions' California Law Review (1988) pp. 547–591

Lederman, 'Models for Imposing Corporate Criminal Liability: From Adaptation and Imitation Toward Aggregation and the Search for Self-Identity' Buffalo Criminal Law Review (2000) pp. 641–708

Loth, 'Zeven stellingen over de gedraging in het strafrecht' in *De Schets nader bekeken,* (Gouda Quint bv, 1992)

Lynch, 'The Mental Element in the actus reus' The Law Quarterly Review (1982) pp. 109–142

Machielse, 'Vrijwillig terugtreden in Nederland en Duitsland' in *Systeem in Ontwikkeling – Liber amicorum G. Knigge,* (Wolf Legal Publisher, 2005)

Machielse, 'De opmars van de uit uiterlijke verschijningsvorm' in *Constante waarden, Liber amicorum Prof. mr. Constantijn Kelk,* (Boom Juridische uitgevers, 2008)

Mackor, 'Strafrecht en neurowetenschappen. Hoop, huiver of hype?' Rechtsfilosofie & Rechtstheorie (2010) pp. 3–8

Mallens and Hornman, 'Vrijwillige terugtred bij poging' Delikt en Delinkwent (2010) pp. 1224–1251

Markesinis, 'Judicial style and reasoning in England and Germany' Cambridge Law Journal (2000) pp. 294–309

Mathis, 'Criminal Attempts and the Subjectivism/Objectivism Debate' Ratio Juris (2004) pp. 328–345

McCulloch and Pickering, 'Pre-Crime and Counter-Terrorism' British Journal of Criminology (2009) pp. 628–645

Mead, 'Contracting into Crime: A Theory of Criminal Omissions' Oxford Journal of legal Studies (1991) pp. 147–173

Michaels, 'The functional method of comparative law' in *The Oxford Handbook of Comparative Law,* (Oxford University Press, 2006)

Mols and Wöretshofer, 'Poging en voorbereidingshandelingen' (Ars Aequi Libri, 1994)

Montesa and Givaja, 'When Parents pay for their children's wrongs: Attribution of liability for Antitrust infringements in Parent-Subsidiary scenarios' World Competition (2006) pp. 555–574

Mooij, 'Handelingsvrijheid' Delikt en Delinkwent (1999) pp. 840–851

Mooij, 'Toerekeningsvatbaarheid' (Boom, 2004)

Moore, 'Act and Crime – The philosophy of action and its implications for Criminal law' (Clarendon Press, 1993)

Moore, 'The Metaphysics of Causal Intervention' California Law Review (2000) pp. 827–877

Moore, 'Causation and Responsibility' (Oxford University Press, 2009)

Morse, 'Criminal Responsibility And The Disappearing Person' Cardozo Law Review (2007) pp. 2545–2575

Neubacher, 'Der halbherzige Rücktritt in der Rechtsprechung des BGH' NStZ (2003) pp. 576–681

Nieboer, 'Schets materieel strafrecht' (Gouda Quint bv, 1991)

Norrie, 'Punishment, Responsibility and Justice' (Oxford University Press, 2000)

Norrie, 'Crime, Reason and History – A Critical Introduction to Criminal Law' (Cambridge University Press, 2001)

Noyon, Langemeijer, & Remmelink, (Eds.). Wetboek van Strafrecht – losbladig commentaar, (Deventer: Kluwer 2010)

O'Malley, 'Risk, Power and Crime Prevention' Economy and Society (1992) pp.

Ohana, 'Desert and Punishment for Acts preparatory to the commission of a crime' Canadian Journal of Law and Jurisprudence (2007) pp. 113–142

Ormerod and Fortson, 'Serious Crime Act 2007: The Part 2 Offences' Criminal Law Review (2009) pp. 389 et seq.

Ormerod and Taylor, 'The Corporate Manslaughter and Corporate Homicide Act 2007' Criminal Law Review (2008) pp. 589–611

Ormerod and Williams, 'Smith's law of theft' (Oxford University Press, 2007)

Otto, 'Die Grundlagen der Strafrechtlichen Haftung des Garanten wegen Unterlassens' Jura (1985) pp. 530–542, 592–602, 646–654

Otto, 'Grundkurs Strafrecht: Allgemeine Strafrechtslehre' (De Gruyter Recht, 2004)

Pace, 'Delegation – A doctrine in search of a definition' Criminal Law Review (1982) pp. 627 et seq.

Padfield, 'Clean water and muddy causation a question of law or fact, or just a way of allocating blame?' Criminal Law Review (1995) pp. 683–694

Parsons, 'Criminal Liability for the act of another: Accessorial Liability and the doctrine of joint enterprise' Journal of Criminal Law (1998) pp. 352–359

Pelser, 'Preparations to commit a crime – The Dutch approach to inchoate offences' Utrecht Law Review (2008) pp. 57–80

Peristeridou, The principle of legality in European criminal law (2013) Forthcoming

Pinto and Evans, 'Corporate Criminal Liability' (Sweet & Maxwell, 2003)

Punch, 'Suit violence: Why managers murder and corporations kill' Crime, Law & Social Change (2000) pp. 243–280

Puppe, 'Der halbherzige Rücktritt' NStZ (1984) pp. 488–491

Puppe, 'Der gemeinsame Tatplan der Mittäter' Zeitschrift für Internationale Strafrechtsdogmatik (2007) pp. 234–246

Puppe, 'Die Selbstgefährdung des Verletzten beim Fahrlässigkeitsdelikt' Zeitschrift für Internationale Strafrechtsdogmatik (2007) pp. 247–253

Puppe, 'Die Rechtsprechung des BGH zum Rücktrittshorizont' Zeitschrift für Internationale Strafrechtsdogmatik (2011) pp. 524–530

Reed, 'Joint Participation in Criminal Activity' Journal of Criminal Law (1996) pp. 310–324

Reed, 'Case Note: Joint Enterprise: Withdrawal' Journal of Criminal Law (2005) pp.

Reichman, 'Managing Crime Risks: Toward an Insurance Based Model of Social Control' Research in Law, Deviance and Social Control (1986) pp.

Remmelink, 'Inleiding tot de studie van het Nederlandse Strafrecht' (Gouda Quint bv, 1995)

Rense, 'Rechtspersonen in het strafrecht' Delikt en Delinkwent (2005) pp. 272–298

Rettenmaier and Palm, 'Das Ordnungswidrigkeitenrecht und die Aufsichtspflicht von Unternehmensverantwortlichen' NJOZ (2010) pp. 1014–1019

Riesenhuber, 'English common law versus German Systemdenken? Internal versus external approaches' Utrecht Law Review (2011) pp. 117–130

Robinson, 'Causing the conditions of one's own defence: A study in the limits of theory in criminal law doctrine' Virginia Law Review (1985) pp. 1–63

Robinson, 'Should the Criminal Law Abandon the Actus Reus – Mens Rea Distinction?' in *Action and Value in Criminal Law,* (Clarendon Press, 1993)

Robinson and Darley, 'Objectivist versus Subjectivist Views of Criminality: A Study in the Role of Social Science in Criminal Law Theory' Oxford Journal of legal Studies (1998) pp. 409–447

Röckrath, 'Kollegialentscheidungen und Kausalitätsdogmatik – Zurechnung überbestimmter Erfolge in Straf- und Haftungsrecht' NStZ (2003) pp. 641–646

Roef, 'Strafbare overheden – Een rechtsvergelijkende studie naar de strafrechtelijke aansprakelijkheid van overheden voor milieuverstoring' (Intersentia Uitgevers Antwerpen – Groningen, 2001)

Roef, 'Strafrechtelijke Verantwoordelijkheid in de Risicomaatschappij' in *Risico en voorzorg in de rechtsmaatschappij,* (Intersentia Uitgevers Antwerpen – Groningen, 2004)

Roef and Prakken, 'Strafbare Voorbereiding in Nederland: Juridische Overkill' in *Voorbereidingshandelingen in het Strafrecht,* (Wolf Legal Publisher, 2004)

Rogall, '§30 OWiG' in *Karlsruher Kommentar zum Gesetz über Ordnungswidrigkeiten,* (Verlag C.H. Beck, 2006)

Rogers, 'The codification of attempts and the case for preparation' Criminal Law Review (2008) pp. 937–954
Rogers, 'Shooting (and judging) in the dark?' Archbold Review (2012) pp. 8–9
Rotsch, 'Tatherrschaft kraft Organisationsherrschaft' ZStW (2000) pp. 518 et seq.
Rotsch, 'Einheitstäterschaft statt Tatherrschaft' (Mohr Siebeck, 2009)
Rousseau, 'Gesellschaftsvertrag' (Reclam, 1998)
Roxin, 'Strafrecht Allgemeiner Teil, Band II: Besondere Erscheinungsformen der Straftat' (Verlag C.H. Beck, 2003)
Roxin, 'Strafrecht Allgemeiner Teil, Band I Grundlagen: Der Aufbau der Verbrechenslehre' (Verlag C.H. Beck, 2006)
Roxin, 'Täterschaft und Tatherrschaft' (De Gruyter Recht, 2006)
Rozemond, 'De algemene strafbaarstelling van voorbereidingshandelingen in het licht van de pogingsjurisprudentie van de Hoge Raad' Delikt en Delinkwent (1994) pp. 651–675
Rozemond, 'De methode van het materiele strafrecht' (Ars Aequi Libri, 2006)
Rozemond, 'De Subjectivering van het Nederlands Strafrecht' Nederlands Juristenblad (2007) pp. 2301 – 2305
Rudolphi, 'Häusliche Gemeinschaft als Entstehungsgrund für Garantenstellungen?' NStZ (1984) pp. 149–154
Rudolphi in Systematischer Kommentar zum Strafgesetzbuch (Metzner, Frankfurt am Main, 2000) §13
Ryu, 'Causation in Criminal Law' University of Pennsylvania Law Review (1958) pp. 773–805
Sayre, 'Criminal Attempts' Harvard Law Review (1928) pp. 821–859
Sayre, 'Criminal Responsibility for the acts of another' Harvard Law Review (1930) pp. 689–723
Schatz, 'Der Pflichtwidrigkeitszusammenhang beim fahrlässigen Erfolgsdelikt und die Relevanz hypothetischer Kausalverläufe – Zum Einwand rechtmässigen Alternativverhaltens bei fehlgeschlagener Lockerungsgewährung' NStZ (2003) pp. 581 et seq.
Schmitz, '"Wilde" Müllablagerungen und strafrechtliche Garantenstellung des Grundstückseigentümers' Neue Juristische Wochenschrift (1993) pp. 1167–1171
Schöberl, 'Die Einheitstäterschaft als europäisches Modell' (Neuer Wissenschaftlicher Verlag, 2006)
Schönke and Schröder, 'Kommentar zum Strafgesetzbuch' (Verlag C.H. Beck, 2006)
Schuilenburg, 'Technologie en Misdaad – Over de opkomst van een protocollaire samenleving' Flexmens (2006) pp. 22–25
Schwitters, 'Risico's verzekerd, verantwoordelijkheden op drift' Justitiele verkenningen (1996) pp. 9–23
Searle, 'The future of philosophy' The Royal Society (1999) pp. 2069–2080
Shearing and Stenning, 'From the Panopticon to Disney World: The development of discipline' in *Criminological Perspectives: Essential Readings,* (Sage Publications, 2003)

Sieber, 'Legitimation und Grenzen von Gefährdungsdelikten im Vorfeld terroristischer Gewalt – Eine Analyse der Vorfeldtatbestände im "Entwurf eines Gesetzes zur Verfolgung der Vorbereitung von schweren staatsgefährdenden Gewalttaten"' NStZ (2009) pp. 353–364

Simester, 'On the so called Requirement for Voluntary Action' Buffalo Criminal Law Review (1998) pp. 403–430

Simester and Shute, 'On the General Part in Criminal Law' in *Criminal Law Theory: Doctrines of the General Part,* (Oxford University Press, 2002)

Simester and Sullivan, 'Criminal Law: Theory and Doctrine' (Hart Publishing, 2007)

Smith, 'Two Problems in Criminal Attempt' Harvard Law Review (1957) pp. 422–448

Smith, 'Liability for omissions in the criminal law' Legal Studies (1984) pp. 88–101

Smith, 'A Modern Treatise on the Law of Criminal Complicity' (Clarendon Press, 1991)

Smith, 'Proximity in attempt: Lord Lane's "midway course"' Criminal Law Review (1991) pp. 576–582

Smith, 'Criminal Liability of Accessories: Law and Law Reform' The Law Quarterly Review (1997) pp. 453–467

Smith, 'Withdrawal in Complicity: A Restatement of Principles' The Criminal Law Review (2001) pp. 769–785

Smith, 'Strafbare Voorbereiding, Een rechtsverglijkend onderzoek' (Boom Juridische uitgevers, 2003)

Smith and Hogan, 'Criminal Law' (Oxford University Press, 2005)

Smith and Hogan, 'Criminal Law' (Oxford University Press, 2008)

Sowada, 'Die Garantenstellung aus vorangegangenem Tun (Ingerenz)' Jura (2003) pp. 236–246

Spencer, 'Trying to help another person commit a crime' in *Criminal law – Essays in honour of J C Smith,* (Butterworths, 1987)

Spencer and Virgo, 'Encouraging and assisting crime: Legislate in haste, repent at leisure ' Archbold News (2008) pp. 7–9

Stannard, 'Making up for the missing element – a sideways look at attempts' Legal Studies (1987) pp. 194–204

Stewart, 'The End of "Modes of Liability" for international crimes' Leiden Journal of International Law (2012) pp. 1–74; Available at SSRN: http://ssrn.com/abstract=1953521

Strijards, 'Hoofdstukken van materieel Strafrecht' (Uitgeverij Lemma BV, 1992)

Strijards, 'Strafbare voorbereidingshandelingen' (W.E.J Tjeenk Willink Zwolle, 1995)

Strikwerda, 'Wie kan verantwoordelijkheid dragen voor de dood van Savanna?' Delikt en Delinkwent (2008) pp. 291–313

Sullivan, 'Intent, Purpose and Complicity' Criminal Law Review (1988) pp. 641–648

Sullivan, 'First degree murder and complicity – conditions for parity of culpability between principal and accomplice' Criminal Law and Philosophy (2007) pp. 271–288

Sullivan, 'The Bribery Act 2010: Part 1: an overview' Criminal Law Review (2011) pp. 87–100

Swoboda, 'Die Lehre vom Rechtsgut und ihre Alternativen' ZStW (2010) pp. 24–50

Tadros, 'Criminal Responsibility' (Oxford University Press, 2005)

Tak, 'The Dutch criminal justice system', (2003) WODC report Nr 205, available at: www.wodc.nl/onderzoeksdatabase/ov-200801-the-dutch-criminal-justice-system.aspx

Taylor, 'Procuring, Causation, Innocent Agency and the Law Commission' Criminal Law Review (2008) pp. 32–49

Tiedemann, 'Grunderfordernisse einer Regelung des Allgemeinen Teils' in *Wirtschaftsstrafrecht in der Europäischen Union,* (Carl Heymans Verlag KG, 2002)

Tjong Tjin Tai, 'Zorgplichten en zorgethiek' (Kluwer, 2006)

Torringa, 'De rechtspersoon als dader; strafbaar leidinggeven aan rechtspersonen' (Gouda Quint BV, 1984)

Van der Wilt, 'Genocide, Complicity in Genocide and International v. Domestic Jurisdictions' Journal of International Criminal Justice (2006) pp. 239–257

Van der Wilt, 'Ontwikkeling van nieuwe deelnemingsvormen' Delikt en Delinkwent (2007) pp. 138–183

Van Dijk, 'Strafrechtelijke Aansprakelijkheid heroverwogen – Over opzet, schuld, schulduitsluitingsgronden en straf' (Maklu, 2008)

Van Sliedregt, 'Ten to one – A contemporary reflection on the presumption of innocence' (Boom Legal Publishers, 2009)

Van Strien, 'De Rechtspersoon in het strafproces' (Sdu Uitgevers, 1996)

Van Swaaningen, 'Justitie als verzekeringsmaatschapij – Actuarial justice in Nederland' Justitiele verkenningen (1996) pp. 80–97

Van Toorenburg, 'Medeplegen' (Deventer, 1998)

Vedder, 'Convergerende technologieën, verschuivende verantwoordelijkheden' Justitiele verkenningen (2008) pp. 54 et seq.

Veegens, 'A disrupted balance? Prevention of terrorism and compliance with fundamental legal rights and principles of law – The Dutch anti-terrorism legislation' (Intersentia, 2011)

Vellinga-Schootsstra, 'Het daderschap van de natuurlijke persoon' in *Daderschap en Deelneming,* (Gouda Quint, 1999)

Vellinga-Schootsstra, 'Het daderschap van de Rechtspersoon' in *Daderschap en Deelneming,* (Gouda Quint, 1999)

Vellinga, 'Eenheid in Daderschap?' in *Systeem in ontwikkeling: liber amicorum G. Knigge,* (Wolf Legal Publisher, 2005)

Virgo, 'Joint enterprise liability is dead: long live accessorial liability' Criminal Law Review (2012) pp. 850–870

Visser, 'Zorgplichtbepalingen in het Strafrecht' (Gouda Quint, 2001)

Vogel, 'Norm und Pflicht bei den unechten Unterlassungsdelikten' (Duncker & Humbold, 1993)

Vogel, 'Criminal Responsibility – Parties to the offence' in *Enlarging the Fight against Fraud in the European Union: Penal and Administrative Sanctions, Settlement, Whistleblowing and Corpus Juris in Candidate Countries,* (Bundesanzeiger, 2003)

Wedzinga, 'Grondslagen van strafrechtelijke aanspraakelijkheid' Delikt en Delinkwent (1999) pp. 868–877

Weisser, 'Täterschaft in Europa' (Mohr Siebeck, 2011)
Wells, 'Corporations: Culture, Risk and Criminal Liability' The Criminal Law Review (1993) pp. 551–566
Wells, 'Corporate Manslaughter: A Culture and Legal Form' Criminal Law Forum (1995) pp. 45–72
Wells, 'Corporations and Criminal Responsibility' (Oxford University Press, 2001)
Wessels and Beulke, 'Strafrecht Allgemeiner Teil, Die Straftat und ihr Aufbau' (C.F. Müller Verlag, 2008)
Williams, 'Criminal Law: The General Part' (Stevens & Sons Limited, 1953)
Williams, 'The Lords and impossible attempts, or quis custodiet ipsos custodes?' Cambridge Law Journal (1986) pp. 33–83
Williams, 'Finis for novus actus?' Cambridge Law Journal (1989) pp. 391–416
Williams, 'Gross negligence manslaughter and duty of care in "Drugs" Cases: R v Evans' Criminal Law Review (2009) pp. p. 631 et seq.
Wilson, 'Central Issues in Criminal Theory' (Hart Publishing, 2002)
Wilson, 'Violence, Sleepwalking and the Criminal Law: Part 2: The legal aspects' Criminal Law Review (2005) pp. 614–623
Wilson, 'Dealing with drug induced homicide' in *Criminal liability for non-aggressive death,* (Ashgate, 2008)
Wilson, 'A rational scheme of liability for participating in crime' Criminal Law Review (2008) pp. 3–18
WODC report Nr 1919, 'Daderschap en deelneming doorgelicht', available at: www.wodc.nl/onderzoeksdatabase/ervaringen-van-de-rechtspraktijk-met-bestaande-deelnemingsfiguren-in-het-strafrecht.aspx
Wolswijk, 'Functioneel daderschap en IJzerdraadcriteria' Delikt en Delinkwent (2001) pp. 1088–1114
Wolswijk, 'Strafbaar nalaten: een zorgplicht minder' in *Systeem in Ontwikkeling. Liber amicorum G. Knigge,* (Wolf Legal Publisher, 2005)
Wolswijk, 'Medeplichtigheid' in *Plegen en Deelnemen,* (Kluwer, 2007)
Wolswijk, 'Inlichtingen versus aansporingen' in *Constante waarden – Liber amicorum Prof. mr. Constantijn Kelk,* (Boom Juridische uitgevers, 2008)
Yeoh, 'The UK Bribery Act 2010: contents and implications' Journal of Financial Crime (2012) pp. 37–53
Zedner, 'Pre-crime and post-criminology' Theoretical Criminology (2007) pp. 261–281
Zweigert and Kötz, 'Introduction to comparative law' (Clarendon Press, 1998)

Legislation

EU Legislation

Convention of 26 July 1995, on the protection of the European Communities' financial interests, OJ 1995 C 316/49;
Protocol of 27 September 1996, on the protection of the European Communities' financial interests, OJ 1996 C 313/02;

Second Protocol of 19 July 1997 to the Convention on the protection of the European Communities' financial interests, OJ 1997, C 221;

Joint Action 98/733 of 21 December 1998 on making it a criminal offence to participate in a criminal organisation in the Member States of the European Union, OJ 1998, L 351;

Regulation 466/2001 of 8 March 2001 setting maximum levels for certain contaminants in foodstuffs, OJ 2001 L 77/1;

Framework Decision 2001/413 of 28 May 2001 on combating fraud and counterfeiting of non-cash means payment, OJ L 149/1;

Framework Decision 2002/475 of 13 June 2002 on combating terrorism, OJ 2002 L 164/3;

Regulation 1/2003 of 16 December 2002 on the implementation of the rules on competition laid down in Articles 81 and 82 of the Treaties, OJ 2003 L 1/1;

Framework Decision 2004/68 of 22 December 2003 on combating the sexual exploitation of children and child pornography, OJ 2004 L 13/44;

Framework Decision 2004/757 of 25 October 2004 laying down minimum provisions on the constituent elements of criminal acts and penalties in the field of illicit drug trafficking, OJ 2004 L 335/8;

Directive 2004/35 of 21 April 2004 on environmental liability with regard to the prevention and remedying of environmental damage, OJ 2004, L 143;

Framework Decision 2005/667 of 12 July 2005 to strengthen the criminal law framework for the enforcement of the law against ship-source pollution OJ 2005, L 255/164;

Directive 2005/60 of 26 October 2005 on the prevention of the use of the financial system for the purpose of money laundering and terrorist financing, OJ 2005, L 309/15;

Framework Decision 2005/222 of 24 February 2005 on attacks against information systems, OJ 2005 L 69/67;

Framework Decision 2005/214 of 24 February 2005 on the application of the principle of mutual recognition to financial penalties, OJ 2005 L 76/16;

Framework Decision 2005/667 of 12 July 2005 to strengthen the criminal law framework for the enforcement of the law against ship source pollution, OJ 2005 L 255/164;

Regulation 396/2005 of 23 February 2005 on maximum residue levels of pesticides in or on food and feed of plant and animal origin and amending Council Directive 91/414/EEC, OJ 2005 L 70/1;

Regulation 561/2006 of 15 March 2006 on the harmonisation of certain social legislation relating to road transport and amending Regulations 3821/85 and 2135/98 and repealing Regulation 3820/85, OJ 2006 L 102/1;

Directive 2006/24 of 15 March 2006 on the retention of data generated or processed in connection with the provision of publicly available electronic communications services or of public communications networks and amending Directive 2002/58, OJ 2006 L 105/54;

Framework Decision 2008/841 Of 24 October 2008 on the fight against organised crime, OJ 2008 L 300/42

Directive 2008/99 of 19 November 2008 on the protection of the environment through criminal law, OJ 2008 L 328/28;

Regulation 1225/2009 of 30 November 2009 on protection against dumped imports from countries not members of the European Community, OJ 2009 L 343/51
Directive 2011/36 of 5 April 2011 on preventing and combating trafficking in human beings and protecting its victims, and replacing Council Framework Decision 2002/629/JHA, OJ 2011, L 101/06;

Dutch Legislation

Economic Offences Act (Wet op de economische delicten)
Law on health care tariff (Wet tarieven gezondheidszorg)
Narcotics Act (Opiumwet)
Law on prevention of money laundering and financing of terrorism (Wet ter voorkoming van witwassen en financieren van Terrorisme)
Law on weapons and ammunition (Wet Wapens en munitie)
Law on the prevention of the abuse of chemicals and strategical goods (Besluit strategisch goederen)
Law on soil protection (Wet Bodembescherming)
Terrorist Offences Act (Wet Terroristische Misdrijven)

German Legislation

Administrative Offences Act (OWiG: Ordnungswidrigkeitengesetz)
Weapons Act (WaffG: Waffengesetz)
Narcotics Act (BtMG: Betäubungsmittelgesetz)
Constitution/ Basic law (GG: Grundgesetz)

English Legislation

Treason Act 1351 and 1702
Metropolitan Police Act 1839
Children and Young Person Act 1933
Prevention of Crime Act 1953
Trade Description Act 1968
Licensing Act 1964
Law Commission Act 1965
Theft Act 1968
Firearms Act 1968
Health and Safety at Work Act 1974
Criminal law Act 1977
Magistrate Court Act 1980
Criminal Attempts Act 1981
Forgery and Counterfeiting Act 1981
Road Traffic Act 1988

Road Traffic Offenders Act 1988
Food and Safety Act 1990
Dangerous Dog Act 1991
Education Act 1996
Anti-Terrorism, Crime and Security Act 2001
Sexual Offences Act 2003
Domestic Violence and Victims Act 2004
Prevention of Terrorism Act 2005
Terrorism Act 2006
Fraud Act 2006
Serious Crime Act 2007
Corporate Manslaughter and Corporate Homicide Act 2007
Regulatory Enforcement and Sanctions Act 2008
Bribery Act 2010

Case law

ECtHR Case law

E.l., R.I. and J.O. –L. v Switzerland, appl. no. 20919/92, 29 August 1997;
Budayeva and others v *Russia*, appl. nos. 15339/02, 21166/02, 11673/02 and 15343/02, 20 March 2008;
S.W. v United Kingdom, appl. no. 20166/92, 22 November 1995;
Cantoni v France, appl. no. 17862/91, 11 November 1996;
Salabiaku v France, appl. no. 10519/83, 7 October 1998;
Osman v United Kingdom, appl. no. 23452/94, 28 October 1998;
Öneryildiz v Turkey, appl. no. 48939/99, 30 November 2004;
Goktepe v Belgium, appl. no. 50372/99, 2 June 2005;
Sergey Zolotukhin v Russia, appl. no. 14939/03, 10 February 2009;
Kononov v Latvia, appl. no. 36376/04, 17 May 2010;
Van Anraat v the Netherlands, appl. no. 65389/09, 6 July 2010;
Taxquet v Belgium, appl. no. 926/06, 16 November 2010;

ECJ Case law

13 July 1966, Joined Cases C-56 & 58/64 *Établissements Consten S.à.R.L. and Grundig-Verkaufs-GmbH v Commission of the European Economic Community*, [1966] ECR 00299;
14 July 1972, Case C-48/69, *Imperial Chemical Industries Ltd. v Commission of the European Communities*, [1972] ECR 00619;
21 February 1973, Case C-6/72, *Europemballage Corporation and Continental Can Company Inc. v Commission of the European Communities* [1973] ECR 00214;

16 December 1975, Joined Cases C-40–48, 50, 54–56, 111, 113 & 114/73, *Coöperatieve Vereniging "Suiker Unie" UA and others v Commission of the European Communities*, [1975] ECR 01663;

13 February 1979, Case, C-85/76 *Hoffmann-La Roche & Co. AG v Commission of the European Communities,* [1979] ECR 461;

7 June 1983, Joined Cases C-100–103/80, *SA Musique Diffusion française and others v Commission of the European Communities*, ECR 1983, 01825;

15 March 2000, Case T-25/95, *Cimenteries CBR and Others v Commission of the European Communities* [2002] ECR II-00491;

26 October 2000, Case T-41/96, *Bayer AG v Commission of the European Communities*, [2000] ECR II-03383;

16 November 2000, C-286/98 P, *Stora Kopparbergs Bergslags AB v Commission of the European Communities*, [2000] ECR I-9945;

6 January 2004, Joined Cases C-2/01 P and C-3/01 P, *Bundesverband der Arzneimittel-Importeure eV and Commission of the European Communities v Bayer AG*, [2004] ECR I-00023;

7 January 2004, Joined Cases C-2004 P, C-205/00 P, C-213/00 P, C-217/00 P and C-219/00 P, *Aaborg Portland and others v Commission of the European Communities*, [2004] ECR I-00123;

28 June 2005, Joined Cases C-189/02 P, C-202/02 P, C-205/02 to C-208/02 P and C-213/02 P, *Dansk Rørindustrie and others vs Commission of the European Communities*, [2005] ECR I-05425;

3 May 2007, Case C-303/05, *Advocaten voor de Wereld VZW v Leden van de Ministerraad* [2007] ECR I-3633;

8 July 2008, Case T-99/04, *AC-Treuhand AG v Commission of the European Communities*, [2008] ECR II-01501;

17 July 2008, Case C-66/08, *proceedings concerning the execution of a European arrest warrant issued against Szymon Kozlowski* [2008] ECR I-06041;

4 June 2009, Case C-8/08, *T-Mobile Netherlands BV, KPN Mobile NV, Orange Nederland NV and Vodafone Libertel NV v Raad van bestuur van de Nederlandse Mededingingsautoriteit* [2009] ECR I-04529;

3 September 2009, Case C-535/06 P, *Moser Baer India Ltd v Council of the European Union*, [2009] ECR I-07051;

6 October 2009, Case C-123/08, *criminal proceedings against Dominic Wolzenburg* [2009] ECR I-9621;

4 March 2010, Case T-401/06, *Brosmann Footwear (HK)Ltd and others v Council of the European Union*, [2010] ECR II-00671;

9 March.2010, Case C-378/08, *Raffinerie Mediterranee (ERG) SpA, Polimeri Europa SpA and Syndial SpA v Ministero dello Sviluppo economico and Others*, [2010] ECR I-01919;

8 September 2010, Case T-29/05, *Deltafina SpA v European Commission*, [2010] not yet reported;

16 November 2010, Case C-261/09, *proceedings concerning the execution of a European arrest warrant issued in respect of Gaetano Mantello* [2010] not yet reported;
2 February 2012, Case C-249/10 P, *Brosmann Footwear (HK)Ltd and others v Council of the European Union* [2012] not yet reported;

Dutch Case law

Rb. Alkmaar, 18 Oktober 2006, *LJN*, AZ0368;
HR 20 Februari 2007, *LJN* AZ0213;
HR 25 Augustus 1932, *NJ* 1932, 1255;
HR 21 Augustus 2007, *LJN* BA5019;
HR 28 December 1864, *W* 2663;
HR 7 May 1906, *W* 8372;
HR 19 December 1910, *W* 9122;
HR 19 June 1911, *W* 1911, 9203;
HR 21 April 1913, *NJ* 1913, 961;
HMG 18 February 1921, *NJ* 1921, 321;
HR 21 February 1921, *NJ* 1921, 465;
HR 25 August 1932, *NJ* 1932, 1255;
HR 13 March 1933, *NJ* 1933, 1385;
HR 19 March 1934, *NJ* 1934, 450;
HR 29 October 1934, *NJ* 1934, 1673;
Hof Amsterdam 14 June 1939, *NJ* 1940, 24;
HR 22 July 1947, *NJ* 1947, 469;
HR 27 January 1948, *NJ* 1948, 197;
HR 6 February 1951, *NJ* 1951, 475;
HR 27 February 1951, *NJ* 1951, 474;
HR 23 February 1954, *NJ* 1954, 378;
HR 18 October 1960, *NJ* 1961, 415;
HR 16 November 1965, *NJ* 1966, 404;
HR 25 June 1968, *NJ* 1969, 250;
HR 13 January 1970, *NJ* 1970, 144;
HR 27 March 1973, *NJ* 1973, 248;
HR 6 April 1975, *NJ* 1980, 34;
HR 22 February 1977, *NJ* 1978, 38;
HR 12 September 1978, *NJ* 1979, 60;
HR 12 September 1978, *NJ* 1979, 60;
HR 24 October 1978, *NJ* 1979, 52;
HR 15 January 1980, *NJ* 1980, 245;
HR 23 December 1980, *NJ* 1981, 534;
HR 23 December 1980, *NJ* 1981, 534;
HR 23 December 1980, *NJ* 1981, 534;
HR 1 June 1981, *NJ* 1982, 80;

HR 16 June 1981, *NJ* 1981, 586;
HR 17 November 1981, *NJ* 1983, 84;
HR 11 May 1982, *NJ* 1983, 3;
HR 19 April 1983, *NJ* 1983, 573;
HR 29 May 1984, *NJ* 1985, 6;
HR 26 February 1985, *NJ* 1985, 651;
HR 7 May 1985, *NJ* 1985, 821;
HR 07 May 1985, *NJ* 19985, 821;
HR 12 November 1985, *NJ* 1986, 782;
HR 26 November 1985, *NJ* 1986, 368;
HR 15 April 1986, *NJ* 1986, 740;
HR 15 April 1986, *NJ* 1986, 740;
HR 6 May 1986, *NJ* 1987, 77;
HR 27 May 1986, *NJ* 1987, 278;
HR 26 November 1986, *NJ* 1986, 368;
HR 17 March 1987, *NJ* 1987, 771;
HR 17 March 1987, *NJ* 1988, 166;
HR 31 March 1987, *NJ* 1988, 633;
Rb Leeuwarden 23 December 1987, *NJ* 1988, 981;
Hof 's-Gravenhage, 9 August 1988, *NJ* 1988, 979;
HR 25 October 1988, *NJ* 1989, 456;
HR 25 October 1988, *NJ* 1988, 456;
HR 29 May 1990, *NJ* 1991, 217;
HR 23 October 1990, *NJ* 1991, 328;
HR 20 November 1990, *NJ* 1991, 238;
HR 14 May 1991, *NJ* 1991, 769;
HR 29 October 1991, *NJ* 1992, 267;
HR 14 January 1992, *NJ* 1992, 413;
HR 2 June 1992, *NJ* 1992, 754;
HR 8 December 1992, *NJ* 1993, 321;
HR 15 December 1992, *NJ* 1993, 333;
HR 14. December 1993, *NJ* 1994, 293;
HR 25 June 1996, *NJ* 1997, 563;
HR 15 October 1996, *NJ* 1997, 109;
HR 29 April 1997, *NJ* 1997, 654;
HR 10 June 1997, *NJ* 1997, 585;
HR 10 June 1997, *NJ* 1997, 585;
HR 7 April 1998, *NJ* 1998, 558;
HR 22 June 1999, *NJ* 1999, 636;
Rb. Utrecht, 9 October, 2000, *LJN* AA7372;
HR 10 October 2000, *NJ* 2001, 4;
HR 21 November 2000, *NJ* 2001, 160;
HR 5 December 2000, *NJ* 2001, 139;

HR 12 December 2000, *NJ* 2002, 516;
HR 12 December 2000, *NJ* 2002, 516;
HR 27 February 2001, *NJ* 2001, 308;
HR 20 March 2001, *NJ* 2001, 340;
HR 8 May 2001, *NJ* 2001, 480;
Rb. Alkmaar 26 June 2001, *LJN* AB2375;
HR 13 November 2001, *NJ* 2002, 245;
HR 27 November 2001, *NJ* 2002, 517;
HR 11 December 2001, *NJ* 2002, 62;
HR 11 December 2001, *NJ* 2002, 62;
HR 17 September 2002, *LJN* AE6118;
HR 17 September 2002, *NJ* 2002, 626;
HR, 9 September 2003, *NJ* 2003, 637;
HR 7 October 2003, *NJ* 2004, 63;
HR 14 October 2003, *NJ* 2005, 183;
HR 14 October 2003, *NJ* 2004, 103;
HR 21 October 2003, *LJN* AF7938;
HR 21 October 2003, *LJN* AF7938;
HR 21 October 2003, *NJ* 2006, 328;
HR 21 October 2003 *LJN* AF7938 = *NJ* 2006, 328;
HR 18 November 2003, *LJN* AJ0517;
HR 18 November 2003, *LJN* AJ0535;
Hof's-Hertogenbosch, 20 January 2004, *LJN* AO4003;
HR 17 February 2004, *NJ* 2004, 400;
HR 30 March 2004, *LJN* AO3231;
Rb. Arnhem, 13 May 2004, *LJN* AO9471;
HR 18 May 2004, *NJ* 2004, 512;
HR 31 August 2004, *LJN* AO643;
HR 7 September 2004, *LJN* AP2570;
HR 26 October 2004, *NJ* 2004, 682;
Rb Rotterdam 31 January 2005, *LJN* AS4414;
HR 29 March 2005, *LJN* AR7619;
Rb. Rotterdam 6 April 2005, *LJN* AT3315;
HR 12 April 2005, *NJ* 2005, 577;
HR 12 April 2005, *LJN* AS6095;
HR 12 April 2005, *LJN* AS6095;
HR 24 May 2005, *NJ* 2005, 434;
HR 14 June 2005, *LJN* AT1801;
Rb. Amsterdam, 1 July 2005, parketnr. 13.529008.05;
Hof Den Haag, 20 November 2005, *LJN* AU6181;
HR 28 February 2006, *LJN* AU9096;
HR 13 June 2006, *NJ* 2007, 48;
HR 22 August 2006, *NJ* 2006, 484;

Rb. Groningen, 24 August 2006, *LJN* AY6882;
HR 20 September 2006, *NJ* 2006, 86;
Rb. Breda, 27 November 2006, *LJN* AZ4427;
Hof's-Hertogenbosch, 5, December 2006, *LJN* AZ4771;
HR 19 December 2006, *NJ* 2007, 29;
HR 23 January 2007, *LJN* AZ3587;
HR 20 February 2007, *LJN* AZ0213;
HR 13 March 2007, *NJ* 2007, 171;
HR 10 April 2007, *NJ* 2007, 224;
Rb. 's-Gravenhage, 24 April 2007, *LJN* BA4036;
Hof 's-Hertogenbosch, 24, April 2007, *LJN* BA4471;
Hof 's-Gravenhage, 9 May 2007, *LJN* BA4676;
HR 21 August 2007, *LJN* BA5019;
Rb Zutphen 9 November 2007, *LJN* BB7529;
Rb. Gravenhage, 11 November 2007, *LJN* BB8016;
Hof 's-Hertogenbosch 22 January 2008, *LJN* BC2604;
HR 4 March 2008, *NJ* 2008, 156;
HR 18 March 2008, *NJ* 2008, 209;
HR 29 April 2008, *NJ* 2008, 439;
Rb. Amsterdam 27, June 2008, *LJN* BF1083;
Rb. Breda 12 August 2008, *LJN* BD9861;
Hof 's-Hertogenbosch, 16 October 2008, *LJN* BF9498;
Rb. 's-Hertogenbosch 22 October 2008, *LJN* BG1023;
Hof Arnhem 22 December 2008, *LJN* BG8807;
Rb. Roermond 27 January 2009, *LJN* BH1649;
HR 3 March 2009, *NJ* 2009, 138;
HR 3 March 2009, *LJN* BF8844;
HR 3 March 2009, *NJ* 2009, 236;
HR 24 March 2009, *LJN* BG4831;
Rb. Haarelm, 22 April 2009, *LJN* BI3519;
Rb. Amsterdam 12 June 2009, *LJN* BI7422;
Rb. Amsterdam 12 June 2009, *LJN* BI7370;
Rb. Amsterdam, 12 June 2009, *LJN* BI7445;
HR 30 June 2009, *NJ* 2009, 481;
HR 7 July 2009, *LJN* BH9030;
Rb. Alkmaar, 10 September 2009, *LJN* BJ8580;
Hof Amsterdam, 16 December 2009, *LJN* BK6788;
HR 22 December 2009 *LJN* BJ9244;
Hof Leeuwarden 22 January 2010, *LJN* BL0315;
HR 9 March 2010, *NJ* 2010, 194;
Hof 's-Hertogenbosch 11 June 2010, *LJN* BM7414;
HR 5. October 2010, *LJN* BN2294;
Hof Arnhem, 21 October 2010, *LJN* BO1426;

HR 23 March 2011, *LJN* BO2629;
HR 12 April 2011, *NJ* 2011, 358;
HR 23 March 2012, *LJN* BT6362;

English and UK Case law

R v Tyler and Price [1838] 173 ER 643;
R v Michael [1840] 173 ER 876;
R v Dalloway [1847] 2 Cox CC 273;
R v Eagleton [1855] 6 Cox CC 559;
R v Handley [1874] Cox CC 79;
R v Coney [1882] 8 QBD 534;
R v Butt [1884] 15 Cox CC 564;
Coppen v Moore (No2) [1898] 2 QB 306;
R v. Pittwood [1902] 19 TLR 37;
Du Cros v Lambourne [1907] 1 KB 40;
Lennard's Carrying Co, Ltd v Asiatic Petroleum Co, Ltd [1914–1915] All ER 280;
Mousel Brother Ltd v London and North-Western Railway Co [1917] 2 KB 836;
R v Gibbins and Proctor [1919] 13 Cr App R 134;
Morris v Tolman [1923] 1 KB 166;
Allen v Whitehead [1930] 1 KB 211;
R v Larsonneur [1933] 24 Cr App R 74;
R v ICR Haulage [1944] 30 Cr App R 31;
DPP v Kent and Sussex Contractors [1944] KB 146;
R v Croft [1944] KB 295;
Kay v Butterworth [1945] 173 LT 191;
Johnson v Youden [1950] 1 KB 544;
Wilcox v Jeffry [1951] 1 All ER 464;
R v Whybrow [1951] 35 Cr App R 141;
R v Bourne [1952] 36 Cr App R 125;
Best v Samuel Fox & Co. Ltd [1952] AC 716;
R v Jordan [1956] 40 Cr App R 152;
HL Bolton (Engineering) Co. v. T.J. Graham & Sons, Ltd [1957] 1 QB 159;
National Coal Board v Gamble [1959] 1 QB 11;
R v Bainbridge [1960] 1 QB 129;
Bratty v A-G for Northern Ireland [1961] 3 All ER 523;
John Henshall (Quarries) Ltd v Harvey [1965] 2 QB 233;
Vane v Yiannopoulos [1965] AC 486;
R v Humphreys [1965] 3 All ER 689;
Sungarapulle Thambiah v The Queen [1966] AC 37;
Magna Plant Ltd v Mitchell [1966] Crim LR 394;
Fagan v Metropolitan Police Commissioner [1968] 3 All ER 442;
R v Winson [1969] 1 QB 371;

R v Lipman [1970] 1 QB 152;
Alphacell Ltd v Woodward [1972] AC 824;
Tesco Supermarkets Ltd v Nattrass [1972] AC 153;
R v Quick [1973] 2 All ER 347;
R v Richards [1973] QB 776;
R v Mackie [1973] 57 Cr App R 453;
R v Blaue [1975] 3 All ER 446;
Attorney-General's Reference (No 1 of 1975) [1975] EWCA Crim 1;
R v Cogan & Leak Leak [1975] 2 All ER 1059;
Haughton v Smith [1975] AC 476;
R v Cato and others [1976] 1 All ER 260;
R v Stone and Dobinson [1977] QB 354;
R v Grundy [1977] Crim LR 543;
R v Husseyn [1978] Crim LR 219;
DPP for Northern Ireland v Maxwell [1978] 3 All ER 1140;
R v Daley [1979] 69 Cr App R 39;
Attorney-General's Reference (No 1 and 2 of 1979) [1980] QB 180;
R v Sheppard and Another, [1981] AC 394;
R v Pagett [1983] 76 Cr App R 279;
R v Bailey [1983] 2 All ER 503;
R v Miller [1983] 1 All ER 978;
R v Dunnington [1984] QB 472;
R v Arthur Armour Mallie Whitefield [1984] 79 Cr App R 36;
R v Morris [1984] AC 320;
R v Taaffe [1984] 1 AC 539;
Attorney-General v Abel and Others [1984] QB 795;
R v Bell [1984] 3 All ER 842;
R v Shivpuri [1986] 2 All ER 334;
Gillick v West Norfolk and Wisbech Area Health Authority (House of Lords) [1986] AC 112;
R v Boyle [1987] 84 Cr App R 270;
R v Howe [1987] AC 417;
R v HM Coroner for East Kent, ex parte Spooner [1989] 88 Cr App R 10;
R v Watson [1989] 1 WLR 684;
R v Walker [1990] 90 Cr App R 226;
R v Kahn and others [1990] 2 All ER 783;
R v Clarke [1990] 91 Cr App R 69;
R v P & O European Ferries (Dover) Ltd [1990] 93 Cr App R 72;
R v Jones [1990] 1 WLR 1057;
R v Gullefer [1990] 3 All ER 882;
R v Campbell [1991] 93 Cr App R 350;
R v Stringer [1991] Crim LR 639;
R v Cheshire [1991] 3 All ER 670;

R v Williams and another [1992] 2 All ER 183;
R v Griffin, [1993] Crim LR 515;
Attorney-General's Reference (Nol of 1992) [1993] 96 Cr App R 298;
Attorney-General's Reference (No 2 of 1992) [1993] 4 All ER 683;
Attorney-General's Reference (No3 of 1992) [1993] 98 Cr App R 383;
R v Redfern and Dunlop Ltd (Aircraft Division) [1993] Crim LR 43;
Moore v Bresler [1994] 2 All E.R. 515;
R v Keith Neville Rackley [1994] 15 Cr App R (S) 794;
R v Rose [2004] EWCA Crim 764;
R v Millward [1994] Crim. LR 527;
R v Wheelhouse [1994] Crim. LR 756;
Gillick v West Norfolk and Wisbech Area Health Authority [1994] QB 581;
Meridian Global Funds Management Asia Ltd v Securities Commission [1995] 2 AC 500;
R v Adomako [1995] 1 AC 171;
R v Latif [1996] 2 Cr App R 92;
R v Geddes [1996] Crim LR 894;
R v JF Alford Transport LTD [1997] 2 Cr App R 326;
R v Marsh [1997] 1 Cr App R 67;
R v Giannetto [1997] 1 Cr App R 1;
R v Tosti & White [1997] Crim LR 746;
R v Ireland [1997] AC 147;
R v Wollin [1998] 4 All ER 103;
Empress Car Co Ltd v National Rivers Authority [1998] 1 All ER 481;
R v Powell and English [1999] AC 1;
Attorney General's Reference (No 2 of 1999) [2000] QB 796;
R v Mark John Leslie Mercer [2001] EWCA Crim 638;
R v Mihailis Litholetovs [2002] EWCA Crim 1154;
R v Wacker [2003] 1 Cr App R 22;
R v Hood [2003] EWCA Crim 2772;
R v Dagnall [2003] EWCA Crim 2441;
DPP v Santana Bermudez [2003] EWHC 2908 (Admin);
R v Gaunt [2003] EWCA Crim 3925;
Attorney-General's Reference (No 3 of 2003) [2004] EWCA Crim 868;
R v Bryce [2004] EWCA Crim 1231;
R v Dica [2004] QB 1257;
R v Lewis Bowles, Christine Bowles [2004] EWCA Crim 1608;
R v Stanley John Rodgers [2004] EWCA Crim 3115;
Attorney General's Reference (No 3 of 2004) [2005] EWCA Crim 1882;
R v Willoughby [2005] 1 Cr App R 29;
R v Webster [2006] EWCA Crim 415;
R v Carey [2006] EWCA Crim 17;
R v Fury [2006] EWCA Crim 1258;
DPP v Nedrik-Smith [2006] EWHC 3015 (Admin);

R v Kennedy [2007] UKHL 38;
R v Masters [2007] EWCA Crim 142;
R v Connolly [2007] EWCA Crim 790;
R v Rahman and others (Court of Appeal) [2007] EWCA Crim 342;
R v Rahman (House of Lords) [2008] UKHL 45;
R v Ellis [2008] EWCA Crim 886;
R v Luffman [2008] EWCA Crim 1739;
R v A [2008] EWCA Crim 2193;
R v David Paul Johnson [2008] EWCA Crim 2976;
R v Evans, [2009] 2 Cr App R 10;
R v Soloman [2009] EWCA Crim 48;
R v Starfield Badza [2009] EWCA Crim 1363;
R v Khan and others [2009] 1 WLR. 2036;
R v Gnango [2010] EWCA Crim 1691;
R v Cotswold Geotechnical Holdings Limited, [2011] EWCA Crim 1337;
R v Ian Bryan Stringer [2011] EWCA Crim 1396;
R v Carpenter [2011] EWCA Crim 2568;
R v Gnango [2012] Cr App R 18

German Case law

31 May 1920 RGSt 54, 349;
19 February 1940 RGHSt 74, 84;
11 January 1951 BGH NJW 1952, 430;
29 August 1952 BGHSt 3, 62;
20 November 1953 BGH NJW 1954, 567;
14 April 1955 BGH NJW 1955, 915;
26 May 1955 BGH = NJW 1955, 1078;
28 February 1956 BGH NJW 1956, 718;
25 September 1957 BGH NJW 1958, 149;
23 January 1958 BGH NJW 1958, 836;
29 April 1958 BGH NJW 1958, 1051;
16 September 1958 BGH NJW 1958, 1881;
21 April 1959, OLG Hamm NJW 1959, 1551;
3 July 1959 BGH GA 1960, 111;
27 July 1962 BGH NJW 1962, 2069;
18 November1969 BGH NJW 1970, 520;
30 September 1970 BGH NJW 1971, 152;
15 May 1972 BGH NJW 1972, 1207;
16 July 1974 OLG Hamm NJW 1975, 657;
16 September 1975 BGH NJW 1976, 58;
17 March 1977 BGH GA 77, 306;
25 August 1977 OLG Stuttgart NJW 1978, 900;

23 August 1979 BGH NJW 1980, 602;
30 April 1980 BGH NJW 1980, 1759;
20 May 1980 BGH NStZ 1981, 218;
30 July 1981 OLG Stuttgart NJW 1982, 295;
7 August 1981 OLG Stuttgart NJW 1981, 2369;
15 October 1981 BGH NJW 1982, 292;
26 January 1982 BGH NJW 1982, 1164;
27 April 1982 BGH NJW 1982, 2263;
7 May 1982 BayObLG NJW 1982, 1891;
2 February 1983 BGH NStZ 1983, 264;
5 July 1983 BGH NStZ 1984, 70;
20 December 1983 BGH NStZ 1984;
14 February 1984 BGH NJW 1984, 1469;
14 February1984 BGH NStZ, 1984, 410;
27 June 1984 BGH NStZ 1984, 452;
26 October 1984 BGH NJW 1985, 1035;
6 November 1984 BGH NJW 1985, 1350;
06 November 1984 BGH NJW 1985, 1350;
6 November 1984 BGH NStZ 1985, 165;
9 November 1984 BGH NStZ 1985, 319;
18 July 1985 BayObLG NJW 1986, 1504;
22 August 1985 BGH NStZ 1986, 25;
3 December 1985 BGH GA 86, 508;
7 February 1986 BGH NStZ 1986, 264;
21 April 1986 BGH NStZ 1986;
26 August 1986 BGH NStZ 1987, 20;
26 August 1988 OLG Düsseldorf NStZ 1989, 370;
15 September 1988 BGH NJW 1989, 912;
14 March 1989 BGH NJW 1989, 2479;
25 July 1989 BGH NStZ 1990, 227;
26 July 1989 BGH NStZ 1989, 473;
26 October 1989 BayObLG NJW 1990, 781;
28 November 1989 BGH NJW 1990, 1055;
6 July1990 BGH NStZ 1990, 587;
25 October 1990 BGH NStZ 1991, 123;
15 January 1991 BGH NStZ 1991, 280;
27 March 1991 BayObLG NJW 1991, 2582;
17 March 1992 BGH NJW 1992, 1708;
23 June 1992 BGH NStZ 1992, 498;
22 July 1992 BGH NStZ 1992, 545;
13 January 1993 BGH NStZ 1993, 233;
16 February 1993 BGH NJW 1993, 2125;
30 March 1993 BGH NStZ 1993, 386;

19 May 1993 BGH NStZ 1993, 433;
24 June 1993 BGH NJW 1993, 2188;
7 September 1993 BGH NStZ 1994, 29;
18 January 1994 BGH NStZ 1995, 122;
8 February 1994 BGH NStZ 1994, 346;
9 March 1994 BGH NStZ 1994, 394;
26 July 1994 BGH NStZ 1994, 537;
13 September 1994 BGH NStZ 1995, 80;
17 November 1994 BGH NJW 1995, 795;
15 February 1995 BGH NStZ 1995, 285;
17 March 1995 BGH NStZ 1995, 490;
7 April 1995 BGH NStZ 1996, 38;
2 August 1995 BGH NStZ 1995, 590;
8 August 1995 BGH NStZ 1996, 1;
8 August 1995 BGH NStZ-RR 1996, 1;
3 November 1995 BGH NStZ 1996, 227;
16 November 1995 OLG Düsseldorf NStZ 1996, 193;
20 March 1996 OLG Dresden OLG-NL 1996, 215;
18 April 1996 BGH NStZ 1997, 272;
13 August 1996 BGH NStZ 1997, 83;
12 September 1996 BGH NStZ 1997, 281;
17 October 1996 BGH NStZ 1997, 82;
20 March 1997 OLG Dresden NStZ 1997, 348;
15 May 1997 BGH NStZ 1997, 485;
6 June 1997 BGH NStZ 1997, 544;
12 August 1997 BGH NStZ 1998, 241;
7 October 1997 BGH NStZ 1998, 294;
11 December 1997 BGH NJW 1998, 767;
19 December1997 BGH NJW 1998, 1568;
21 January 1998 BGH NStZ-RR 1998,134;
6 September 1998 BGH NJW 1990, 654;
26 October 1998 BGH NStZ-RR 1999, 184;
12 November 1998 BGH NStZ-RR 2000, 42;
9 December 1998 BGH NStZ 1999, 128;
21 May 1999 BayObLG NStZ 1999, 627;
15 July 1999 BGH NStZ 1999, 609;
11 August 1999 OLG Rostock NStZ 2001, 199;
20 September 1999 BGH NStZ 2000, 34;
11 March 2000 BGH NStZ 2001, 205;
21 March 2000 OLG Naumburg NJW 2001, 2034;
11 April 2000 BGH NStZ 2001, 205;
19 April 2000 BGH NStZ 2001, 188;
15 June 2000 BGH NStZ-RR 2000, 327;

1 August 2000 BGH NJW 2000, 3010;
30 August 2000 BGH NStZ 2001, 29;
8 November 2000 BGH NJW 2001, 453;
14 November 2000 OLG Celle NJW 2001, 2816;
12 January 2001 BGH NJW 2010, 1087;
8 March 2001 BGH NJW 2001, 2409;
25 April 2001 BGH BeckRs 2001, 30176446;
24 October 2001 BGH NStZ 2002, 139;
7 November 2001 BGH NStZ 2002, 145;
14 November 2001 BGH NStZ 2002, 200;
31 January 2002 BGH NStZ 2002, 421;
26 June 2002 BGH NStZ 2003, 85;
9 July 2002 BGH NStZ 2002, 597;
14 August 2002 BGH NStZ 2003, 90;
28 August 2002 BGH NJW 2003, 371;
18 September 2002 OLG Nürnberg NJW 2003, 454;
26 September 2002 BGH NJW 2002, 3720;
9 October 2002 BGH NJW 2003, 150;
17 October 2002 BGH NStZ 2003, 253;
6 November 2002 BGH NStZ 2003, 141;
20 December 2002 BGH NJW 2003, 1058;
11 June 2003 BGH NStZ 2004, 38;
18 June 2003 BGH NStZ 2004, 41;
24 July 2003 BGH NStZ 2004, 30;
15 October 2003 BGH NStZ-RR 2004, 40
13 November 2003 BGH NStZ 2004, 151;
11 December 2003 BGH NStZ 2004, 204;
29 March 2004 BGH NJW 2005, 915;
29 July 2004 BGH NJW 2005, 915;
15 September 2004 BGH NStZ 2005, 261;
20 September 2004 BGH NStZ-RR 2004, 361;
2 December 2004 BGH NStZ-RR 2005, 71;
1 February 2005 BGH NJW 2005, 1205;
8 May 2005 BGH NStZ 2001, 475;
15 September 2005 AG Saalfeld NStZ 2006, 100;
2 November 2005 OLG Jena NStZ 2006, 533;
9 March 2006 BGH NStZ 2006, 331;
24 March 2006 OLG Jena BeckRS 2006, 06007;
26 September 2006 BGH NStZ 2007, 91;
24 October 2006 BGH NStZ 2007, 531;
14 November 2006 BGH NStZ-RR 2007, 37;
16 November 2006 BGH NJW 2007, 384;
8 February 2007 BGH NStZ 2007, 399;

11 February 2007 BGH NStZ 2008, 329;
13 July 2007 BGH NStZ 2007, 402;
29 November 2007 BGH NStZ 2008, 273;
11 December 2007 BGH NStZ 2008, 329;
13 March 2008 BGH NStZ 2008, 508;
2 July 2008 BGH NStZ 2009, 25;
8 July 2008 BGH NStZ 2009,92;
24 July 2008 BGH HRRS 2009 Nr 626;
20 November 2008 BGH NJW 2009, 1155;
12 February 2009 BGH NStZ 2009, 231;
29 April 2009 BGH NStZ 2009, 504;
9 June 2009 BGH HRRS 2009 Nr 796;
10 June 2009 BGH HRRS 2009 Nr 747;
17 July 2009 BGH NStZ 2009, 686;
18 August 2009 BGH NStZ-RR 2009, 366;
16 September 2009 BGH NStZ 2010, 81;
17 November 2009 BGH NStZ 2010, 224;
12 January 2010, BGH NJW 2010, 1087;
8 December 2010 BGH NStZ 2011, 209;
27 January 2011 BGH HRRS 2011 Nr 375;
3 March 2011 BGH HRRS 2011, Nr 714;
9 August 2011 BGH NStZ 2012, 85;
20 October 2011 BGH NStZ 2012, 142;
21 December 2011 BGH HRRS 2012, Nr 333
14 February 2012 BGH HRRS 2012 Nr 534;

Other case law

Robinson v State of California, 370 US 660;
Powell v State of Texas 392 US 514 (1968);
State v Tally [1894] 15 So 722;

Official documentation

EU documents

Explanatory Report on the Convention on the protection of the European Communities' financial interests, 23 June 1997, OJ 1997 C 191/1;

Green Paper on criminal-law protection of the financial interests of the Community and the establishment of a European Prosecutor, 11 December 2001, COM 2001/715;

Report from the Commission based on Article 11 of the Framework Decision 2002/475 of 13 June 2002 on combating terrorism, 8 June 2004, COM (2004) 409 and it's annex SEC (2004) 688;

Report of 30 April 2004 from the Commission of the Framework Decision of 28 May 2001 combating fraud and counterfeiting of non-cash means of payment, COM (2004) 346;

Report from the Commission based on Article 11 of the Framework Decision 2002/475 of 13 June 2002 on combating terrorism, 6 November 2007, COM (2007) 681 and its annex SEC (2007) 1463;

Second report from the Commission on the implementation of the Convention on the Protection of the European Communities' financial interests and its protocols, 14 February 2008, COM(2008) 77;

Draft Council conclusions on model provisions, guiding the Council's criminal law deliberations, Brussels, 27 November 2009, 16542/2/09 REV 2;

Communication from the Commission on the protection of the financial interests of the European Union by criminal law and by administrative investigations, 26 May 2011, COM (2011) 293;

The Stockholm Programme – an open and secure Europe serving and protecting citizens, 4 May 2010, OJ 2010 C 115/1;

Commission Communication: Towards an EU Criminal Policy: Ensuring the effective implementation of EU policies through criminal law, 20.09.2011, COM (2011) 573 final;

European Parliament Report on harmonisation of criminal law in the EU, 24.04.2012, no. 2010/2310;

Summary

Chapter I.

Ever since the entering into force of the Maastricht treaty the European Union has gained more and more competences in regard to criminal law. Therefore also the influence of European Union law on national criminal law has increased. The Treaty of Lisbon reinforces and expands the powers of the Union legislator with respect to criminal law. Taking these developments into account one can nowadays attest the emergence of a genuine European criminal law. Over the past years the Union has legislated extensively on a variety of criminal law topics such as terrorism, trafficking in human beings, weapons or drugs, organised crime, money laundering, subsidy fraud, etc. However, European criminal law has developed in an incoherent and fragmented manner. Most notably, European criminal law has thus far merely focused on specific offences (i.e. the special part of criminal law) and lacks explicit general principles dealing with criminal liability (i.e. the general part of criminal law). This lack of a general framework of criminal liability can create problems concerning the uniform application of Union law by national Member States as well as the equal treatment of EU citizens.

This dissertation aims to step into this lacuna and aspires to contribute to the development of a general part of criminal law for the European Union. In the realm of criminal law it is a general principle that the attribution of criminal liability requires an analysis of two aspects. Each crime can be split up into an actus reus, the material or objective element of crime, and mens rea, the mental, or subjective element of a crime.

This research focusses in particular on the former concept; the actus reus. The notion of actus reus is however not only a fundamental but also a diverse one and its investigation leads this research to a variety of different topics. The central question of this research can therefore only be broadly summarised as follows: What should the objective elements of attribution of a general part of European criminal law consist of? Or, in other words, how should the (objective) imposition of criminal liability in a general part of European Union law be evaluated and assessed?

Chapter I introduces and explains the central subject of this research. Furthermore, it explains the comparative methodology and briefly describes and introduces the three national criminal justice systems under investigation (i.e. England and Wales, Germany and the Netherlands).

The general research question is subsequently divided into several sub questions to map out the field of investigation more concretely and to familiarise the reader with the structure of this book. As already mentioned, the notion of actus reus namely plays a crucial role in many constructs of criminal liability which are discussed throughout this book. It not only constitutes one of the basic building blocks of criminal liability (chapter II) but is also essential in regard to participation in crime (chapter III), as well as in the context of inchoate liability (chapter IV). Finally the concept also plays an important role in the context of criminal offences committed by corporate actors (chapter V).

To achieve the goal of this thesis, i.e. creating a first blueprint of a general part for European criminal law, sole reliance on comparative research and comparative methodology will not suffice. Not only pertinent aspects of national criminal law as well as existing Union law need to be compared but to arrive at a general part of European criminal law these different aspects need to be merged. In order to be able to do so chapter I also outlines several formal and normative criteria which will guide the comparative synthesis throughout this book.

Chapter II. Perpetration – The elements of crime

Chapter II discusses the major building blocks of criminal liability which are commonly subsumed under the heading of actus reus. It commences by exploring the baseline of criminal liability which frequently finds expression in the doctrine of conduct. The rules of criminal law constitute a scheme, by which the imposition of criminal liability is guided. This scheme has as one of its goals to assure that the imposition of criminal liability is fair and just in every individual case. Underlying this scheme is a specific image of man which was traditionally firmly rooted in the Enlightenment tradition and which combines aspects of moral philosophy as well as cognitive and natural science revolving around the predicament of individual responsibility. This reveals that the issue has close ties and is influenced by the contentious philosophical question of what is it that makes us responsible. In other words, at the core of criminal law lies the notion of the "average person" who is held responsible for his/her conduct (i.e. act or omission). It is shown that the image of man underlying the criminal law, is fundamental to the ascription of criminal liability in every contemporary penal justice system. Therefore it is suggested that European criminal law should carefully pick its starting point for attributing liability, in order to assure that individual freedoms and liberties are protected as much as possible. This chapter sketches the general requirements conduct must fulfil in order to constitute the foundation of criminal liability and proceeds to argue that criminal liability ought not to be confined to human conduct but that corporate conduct may also constitute the basis of liability.

National criminal law doctrine has been shown to increasingly move away from a physical conception of conduct as "willed bodily movement" to a more normative or social theory of conduct. It is argued that to distinguish criminally relevant from irrelevant conduct ought to be evaluated in the light of the underlying offence, the circumstances of the case at hand, etc. In other words, conduct should be assessed within the social context in which it occurs. Although traditionally the focus in all investigated penal systems lay on a physical conception of conduct, all systems show signs of a shift towards a more normative or social conception of conduct.

Given the complex environment in which European criminal law will primarily operate, it is submitted that this 'social theory of conduct' could also achieve satisfactory results there.

After having discussed the theory of conduct in criminal law, the chapter subsequently turns to omission liability, i.e. criminal liability in the absence of action. In this context the different variations of omission liability are discussed and special heed is paid to the pivotal element of omission liability, namely duties of care. A variety of duties of care to be found within the investigated penal systems are discussed and potential predicaments as well as thresholds are highlighted. The chapter argues that one crucial aspect in regard to duties of care and a guiding principle in this context should be the notion of foreseeability flowing from the principle of legality. The law should ask if it was reasonably foreseeable for a person in the shoes of the defendant that a duty of care was owed. Thereby a number of factors like his social role, individual capacities, the particular circumstances of the case at hand as well as prior conduct can play a role. The latter is particularly relevant in cases where the defendant bears some responsibility for the fact that the victim is dependent on his performance of certain acts, i.e. when the victim has been induced to act to his detriment. Another important factor in this respect can be found in the degree of dependency prevalent between the offender and the victim. Furthermore it is submitted, that the establishment of a duty of care should adhere to general requirements of criminal justice and therefore be fair, just and reasonable.

Finally the discussion turns to the doctrine of causation which especially plays a fundamental role in the attribution of criminal liability in the context of result crimes. An analysis of national criminal law reveals that different conceptions of causation are prevalent in Germany, England & Wales and the Netherlands. Although the outcomes of causal inquiries in the three countries are largely similar, their theoretical approach to the topic differs significantly. This chapter reveals that the doctrine of causation in criminal law is increasingly conceived as a legal concept rather than a physical one, as was traditionally the case. Increasingly normative factors seem to influence the establishment of a causal link in national criminal law. Also in regard to questions of causality the conduct of the individual is more and more placed in the social context in which it occurs, which means that normative considerations become progressively important in establishing a causal link. It is therefore submitted that also a European causation doctrine should best be based on a legal/normative conception, thereby taking into consideration the essential function of the doctrine; the reasonable attribution of a harmful result to the defendant's conduct.

It is argued that the very baseline of establishing a causal link should be the *conditio sine qua non* or 'but for' test. It provides a first yardstick for the establishment of causal responsibility, especially in paradigm cases. The proposed baseline principle is further shaped by the common rule that the conduct in question need not be the sole or main cause of the result. This rule is recognition of the fact that in principle the 'but for' test produces an infinite amount of causes. Yet, other factors contributing to the occurrence of the result need not stand in the way of the assumption of a causal link.

Moreover, the establishment of a causal link should require a connection between the harm and the fault of the individual. This puts the emphasis on the safeguard function of the law. Arguably, a criminal law based on respect for human dignity and the rule of law ought to hold people responsible only for the harm they caused, which could have been prevented by observance of the standard of diligence required by law. Closely connected thereto is the requirement that liability should be confined to the type of harm proscribed by the offence in question. This can be deducted from the purpose of the violated rule in regard to the protected legal interest. The outer boundaries for the attribution of liability are always set by the purpose and scope of the offence in question. This follows *inter alia* from the principle of legality and the corresponding requirement of foreseeability.

Subsequently it should be established whether other known factors might have broken the causal chain. For this to occur, the intervening cause must however be significant. As long as the initial cause remains a substantial and operating cause, the causal link will not be broken. The concept of foreseeability will also have an important role to play here. If it were 'reasonably' to be expected that a certain event occurred as a background circumstance that worsened the original harm inflicted by the defendant, the causal link will prima facie not be broken.

Chapter III. Participation in crime – the multiple actor scenarios

Chapter III highlights several crossroads and pitfalls the European Union faces in devising coherent modes of criminal liability for participation in crime. This chapter demonstrates that national penal systems struggle to cope with contemporary forms of criminal wrongdoing, which are characterised by an increasing division of labour, high degree of organisation as well as systematisation. Intermediaries are used more and more (often due to an increase in the division of labour) to bring about a certain result and the perpetrator does not bring it about directly, despite being in control and thus blameworthy for the criminal conduct. After a careful evaluation of the different national modes of liability, it is submitted that the focus on the individual, physical perpetrator should be substituted by a holistic concept of perpetration. This concept articulates that while the physical, viz. direct perpetrator of the actus reus may be considered primarily responsible, equal culpability extends to other persons if their conduct, contribution or role in the commission of the offence establishes that they bear a substantial responsibility for the wrong committed. "Substantial" in this context should mean something more than causation here, as this would set the bar too low for liability as a perpetrator. There must at least be sufficient evidence that the person was a major participant and did not merely play a subsidiary role in the criminal enterprise.

Such an approach would give rise to a normative concept of participation in crime where the notion of the harmed or endangered underlying protected legal interest will take a central role. A legal interest may be harmed or endangered either directly or indirectly. Either the conduct of the perpetrator causes the violation of the norm directly, i.e. without the intervention of another, or the violation has been brought about indirectly by the conduct of another person (an intermediary), over which the primary responsible perpetrator exerted control and in addition possessed culpability regarding the commission of the offence. Thus the notions of legally protected interest and control in combination with the threshold of substantial responsibility will take a pivotal role in the evaluation scheme proposed here.

Such a normative approach would thus lead to a broad concept of perpetration, capable of catering to the actuality of crime and all its manifold variations. Not only the person directly fulfilling the actus reus would be considered a perpetrator, but every participant who carries substantial responsibility for the criminal outcome will be deemed to have committed the offence himself. Furthermore such an approach could achieve satisfactory results in the context of systemic and organised wrongdoing.

This would however leave a small category of cases unaccounted for, which can be termed forms of "trivial assistance". These cases could be covered by a separate offence of "trivial assistance". Under this category would fall cases of minor assistance, which fall below the substantial responsibility standard outlined above.

It is submitted that such a two-pronged approach consisting of a broad normative concept of perpetration and an auxiliary offence of assistance would possess several advantages for European criminal law. First it would dispense with the difficult problem of line drawing between the different concepts of participation and would shift the focus from the internal boundaries to the arguably more important outer limits of criminal liability. This would not only make the system of participation in crime simpler, more effective and easier to apply for the courts but would arguably also improve individual justice, as the exact degree of the participants wrongdoing and culpability can now easier be taken into consideration by the judge at the sentencing stage.

Furthermore, a normative approach to perpetration would correspond to the actuality of crime in which often other persons than the direct perpetrator play an influential and determining role and thus bear (substantial) responsibility for the harmful outcome. To properly reflect their degree of responsibility a holistic conception of crime and not a strict focus on the individual perpetrator seems warranted.

The auxiliary offence of assistance on the other hand would cover all contributions falling below the substantial responsibility threshold. Here contributions which had an impact on the commission of the offence but were not crucial or indispensable for it could be subsumed. As these participants cannot be deemed to carry a substantial responsibility for the commission of the offence, but at best peripheral responsibility, a mitigation of punishment for these participants seems defensible.

Finally, this chapter argues, that next to streamlining and simplifying the current state of affairs of accomplice liability such a two-pronged approach would also correspond to the requirements of Article 6 ECHR as defendants would receive sufficient information concerning the nature and cause of the accusations against them, which would allow them to develop an effective defence against the charges. Additionally, it would increase legal certainty in line with the requirements of Article 7 ECHR as it would be more foreseeable for an offender whether his conduct will give rise to primary or secondary responsibility.

Chapter IV. Inchoate offences

In this chapter on inchoate liability the emphasis rests on preparatory and attempt liability. These offences can be considered problematic as the actus reus in this situations, may when objectively viewed, often be innocuous and the emphasis therefore will often rest on the mens rea or culpability of the offender. Two patterns of criminality (i.e. the pattern of manifest criminality or subjective criminality respectively) which pervade the criminal law are discussed in this context and it is shown that the Union will have to face the challenge to strike a balance between the manifest pattern of criminality which emphasises the importance of the citizens' individual freedoms and the pattern of subjective criminality which focuses more on the dangerousness of the offender for society as a whole. It is revealed that in national criminal law the prevalent focus on crime prevention has resulted in an increased emphasis on the subjective pattern of criminality which also can be seen as a reflection of the increasing punitive tendencies and ongoing inflation of criminal law in contemporary society.

To countermand these tendencies and to keep the scope of criminal liability within reasonable boundaries, it is submitted that a set of constraints should be developed that guide the introduction of offences geared at crime prevention in European criminal law. It is here where several traditional principles of criminal law could be combined to achieve this goal. The principle of *ultima ratio* as well as the harm principle can function as a first yard stick in this respect. In short, in the light of these principles, only conduct which poses a concrete danger to a substantial rather than an auxiliary protected legal interest, may arguably be subjected to preparatory liability. For instance, the procurement of certain dangerous substances necessary for the production of drugs or arms might be subsumed here. In these circumstances the protection of a legal interest, i.e. the crime control function of criminal law may prevail over its safeguard function.

In addition, flowing from the principle *nulla poena sine culpa*, liability for preparatory offences seems only justified in case the person creating a risk of harm, possesses significant culpability for the ultimate harm. This requirement may in the case of criminalizing risk of harm amount to a culpability standard of direct or indirect intention and exclude the application of *dolus eventualis*.

In regard to the criminalization of preparatory conduct the European Union will also have to decide if a general part doctrine of preparation should be developed or if the question is better addressed on a case by case basis (e.g. by introducing endangerment or possession offences). Carefully weighing the pros and cons of the two approaches the chapter concludes that a case by case approach fits better into the prevalent common traditions of the European Union and the Member States. Furthermore, a case-by-case approach may also provide a better restraint to overcriminalisation, as the legislator would be obliged to provide proof that all the aforementioned requirements are fulfilled every time it opts for the criminalisation of preparatory conduct in a respective legislative instrument.

Subsequently the chapter turns from the preparatory to the adjacent attempt stage. Here again this research reveals that the cardinal question for European criminal law in this context will again become whether a more safeguard-minded objective conception or a more crime control orientated subjective approach should be preferred. The comparison of national penal law shows that the scope of attempt liability is significantly shaped by the balancing of these different views. In an overall assessment the Netherlands seem to adopt the most objective approach resulting in a narrow scope of attempt liability. English criminal law at times also contains traces of an objective approach but the approach reflected in jurisprudence arguably fluctuates between objective and subjective approaches. Germany on the other hand formally adopts a medium position, combining objective and subjective criteria alike but in practice often emphasises subjective elements in attempt cases.

In order to strike a fair balance between the law's safeguard and crime control function and in correspondence with the prevalent approach within the Member States it has been submitted that a mixed approach seems to be preferable for European criminal law. As a rationale for imposing attempt liability, the offender's conduct should amount to an endangerment of the legal order and should be a clear expression of his subjective criminal proclivities. The objective endangerment rationale will arguably account for most cases of attempt liability and will also ensure that the concept of actus reus continues to play an important role to assure that liability remains rooted in an act-based criminal law. It will further provide a valuable restraint against undue inflations of criminal liability. The subjective element of the offender's criminal proclivities on the other hand will account for the imposition of liability in regard to impossible attempts and also gives expression to the fact that intentions often constitute the primal ingredient for criminal censure in regard to attempts.

The mixed rationale should also be reflected in the chosen formula to demarcate attempts from preparation. Objectively an imminence of the commission of the offence should be required which amounts to an endangerment of the legal order. Thus, next to a close temporal connection an intrusion of the offender's conduct into the sphere of the protected legal interest should be required. Such an approach implies a moderate, harm-centred conception of criminal liability, loosely corresponding to the pattern of manifest criminality. It would arguably help to assure that criminal liability retains strong ties to the harm proscribed by the criminal offence and prevent liability from invading the realm of thoughts and attitudes.

The requirement of 'imminence' should however not be interpreted in a way that already some part of the actus reus must have been brought about. Partial fulfilment of the actus reus can be a sufficient condition for liability but should not be a necessary one, as this would cast the scope of the law too narrowly.

A general part of European criminal law will also have to address the issue in how far impossible attempts should give rise to criminal liability. In line with the approach common to the three investigated Member States it has been argued that with the notable exception of imaginary offences and superstitious or utterly daft attempts, impossible attempts should generally lead to liability. To distinguish punishable impossible attempts from non-punishable, a demarcation formula will however be needed. Several solutions to this problem emerging from national criminal law are presented and analysed. One possible solution, supported here, is to utilise the distinction between mistakes of law and mistakes of fact. Applying this distinction to the realm of attempt liability would mean that while 'reverse' mistakes of law lead to imaginary offences, 'reverse' mistakes of fact lead to impossible attempts.

If however the offender gravely errs about the laws of nature or invokes powers that lie outside the ambit of human control no liability should ensue. In these instances the occurred conduct is not only inept but furthermore inapt to bring about the envisaged criminal harm. Thus, no endangerment of the protected legal interest has objectively arisen. Accordingly the link to the proscribed harm can be considered merely tenuous and the principle of harm would therefore bar the attribution of liability for these variations of impossibility.

Finally, it is argued that a defence of voluntary withdrawal should be included in the European law of attempts. If a person voluntarily withdraws from a criminal endeavour and prevents the occurrence of harm, neither considerations of special nor of general prevention seem any longer to warrant the imposition of punishment.

However, to make the defence workable, some doctrinal distinctions need to be drawn. One important distinction concerning the scope of the defence is the distinction between complete and incomplete attempts. In case of the latter, mere desistance from the criminal enterprise will generally suffice for a withdrawal while in case of complete attempts the law requires an *actus contrarius*. Yet, which conduct exactly will qualify as an *actus contrarius* in the latter case is difficult to determine in abstraction, but this investigation of national penal law has shown that a great deal will depend on the severity and scope of the offender's previous conduct and how far to the completion of the offence he has already progressed. The further the advancement of events, the greater the effort required by the offender to successfully prove intention of withdrawing from the attempt.

Furthermore, to determine when a withdrawal was really voluntary, the law can rely on a psychological or a normative evaluation scheme. The approach in national criminal law seems to favour the former which is why it can be stated as a rough yardstick that a withdrawal will be considered voluntary if the offender thinks ‘I do not wish to carry on even if I could’ while it will be considered involuntary if he thinks ‘I cannot carry on even if I wanted to’.

Chapter V. Corporate Criminal liability

After an analysis of the different approaches concerning corporate criminal liability in the investigated national criminal justice systems, this dissertation has revealed a variety of questions to be addressed by the Union legislator in order to develop a coherent approach to the matter. Corporate wrongdoing causes friction within traditional criminal law as concepts such as actus reus and mens rea were initially not devised to be applied to inanimate corporate actors. The topic is nevertheless of high practical relevance and also provides a fertile ground for reassessing and critically appraising several traditional principles of criminal liability. In this chapter different models for tackling corporate wrongdoing are presented and analysed. These different models span from attributing criminal liability to individuals only, or devising tailor-made corporate offences to the creation of derivative and organisational models of liability. Traditionally derivative liability models seem to have been preferred by national criminal law but recent developments in England and the Netherlands clearly show a move towards more organisational models of liability.

Nevertheless, as already indicated in chapter II in the context of the conduct requirement the premises from which this research departs is that corporations are fit subjects of criminal law as they constitute responsible agents who can act and be at fault and can accordingly be held responsible for their shortcomings.

As to the nature of corporate personality, it is submitted that an organic theory should be preferred over an atomic one as it better corresponds to corporate reality and reflects the nature of the corporation as a living system. A corporation is namely something more and something different than simply the sum of its parts.

The comparative research conducted here has however brought to light that in national criminal as well as in European Union law traces of an atomistic approach are still discernible which is reflected in the so called identification doctrine. Although it is argued that this popular doctrine is based on a misconception of corporate personality and wrongdoing and its shortcomings and pitfalls are analysed and discussed, this thesis does not propose the abolishment of the doctrine but for practical reasons opts to maintain it to address simple cases of corporate wrongdoing.

However, it is subsequently argued that the European Union should supplement the identification doctrine and strive for an autonomous, organic conception of corporate criminal liability. European criminal law can learn from the problems encountered by national law and strive for a fresh start. What will be needed is a fundamental reconceptualisation of criminal liability in the context of corporate wrongdoing, paying close heed to corporate reality and practice. In correspondence with the social act requirement advocated in this book, it is submitted that corporate conduct ought to be interpreted in the social context in which it occurs. Accordingly, it has been argued, that corporate conduct will frequently take the form of a contravention of applicable diligent standards, or the respective duties of care.

One important factor in this evaluation, reflecting the core function of the conduct requirement identified here will be, whether or not a corporation can be seen as having had factual control over the manifestation of the criminal conduct. Thereby the company's operational management and policies may be of importance. If the occurred conduct fits into the prevalent company management scheme and policies then the offence *prima facie* ought to be attributed to the company.

After the conclusion has been reached that a certain conduct constitutes corporate conduct, the assessment will have to turn to the question whether or not the corporate defendant can also be blamed for it. It should not be overlooked, that if one wishes to subject corporations to the rule of criminal law, liability for individual as well as corporate wrongdoing should only be imposed if the corporation acts culpably.

When this exactly will be the case arguably defies a simple answer. This research has argued, that there are certain features of the way in which corporations organise themselves which may reflect fault on part of the organisation. One could for instance assess the corporate culture or ethos which may be conducive or may even encourage unlawful behaviour. Further, the structure of the corporation can play a role as a high degree of decentralisation may point in the direction that the people responsible for implementing and supervising the corporate polices or goals may not be found in the board which adopted them.

Additional factors that one could apply to determine corporate culpability could be corporate compliance as well as self-regulation. All these factors provide a relevant proxy to assess whether or not a corporation can be blamed for a certain occurred criminal harm. All these elements are under the control of the company and constitute an element of corporate choice which adds legitimacy to the notion of organisational fault as a basis of liability. The corporation is held liable for its choices and through its choices may avoid liability in the future. Accordingly, also in this context the notion of control may play an important role. It follows that should it be proven beyond reasonable doubt that the corporation had taken all reasonable care to prevent the occurrence of a particular harm and acted diligently, control will be absent and a contravention of the pertinent duty of care cannot be assumed. This would thus introduce a due diligence defence for corporations and prevent corporations from being held liable for harm which lay outside their sphere of influence or control and hopefully strike a fair balance between the criminal law's safeguard and crime control function also in the context of corporate wrongdoing.

Chapter VI. Conclusion:

In Chapter VI the results of this dissertation are summarised and the most problematic aspects are highlighted. Next to the draft blueprint of principles and doctrines for a general part of European criminal law the most important insight gained in this dissertation is that current social developments have led to a change in the traditional framework of criminal liability. The increasing focus on risk prevention as well as a general change in the contemporary conception of crime and criminal wrongdoing has led to an erosion or rethinking of traditional doctrines and differentiations which in turn led to a broadening of the scope of liability in many criminal justice systems. Crudely summarised, an increasing normativity in the imposition of criminal liability is discernible, shifting the emphasis on the crime control function of the law.

To counterbalance these tendencies and to reinforce the criminal law's safeguard function this dissertation has highlighted several principles that may be able to provide some limits to modern criminal law as well as protect individual liberties.

The first notion that arguably can take an important safeguard function in an increasing normative framework of liability is the concept of control. Criminal liability, it is argued, seems only justifiable for criminal outcomes that are under control of the actor. The notion of control aligns the central focus of criminal liability on the responsible, rational subject and thereby provides limits to the introduction of risk liability, status offences and thought crimes.

Another important restraint on the expansion of liability can be found in the harm principle. It becomes particularly important in regard to the question of how far removed from the occurrence of harm conduct may be in order to give rise to liability. It is argued that criminal liability should generally reside and be linked as closely as possible to the prohibited criminal harm.

The penultimate principle that has emerged in our analysis as a safeguard against expanding punitiveness and the arbitrary imposition of punishment is the principle of guilt. It assures that only freely and deliberately chosen conduct will trigger liability. To enable citizens to make this choice, the scope of criminal law and more particularly criminal doctrines must be sufficiently clear and unambiguous. Furthermore, it introduces the requirement that the assessment of criminal liability ought to be founded on individual wrongdoing and culpability. This, *inter alia,* precludes the development or interpretation of doctrines in such a way that they would give rise to guilt by association.

Finally the principle of legality can help to mitigate some of the pitfalls created by the increasing normativity by stressing the notion of foreseeability. It needs to be duly foreseeable for the citizens whether or not a certain conduct will give rise to criminal liability. Furthermore, harm should by and large only be attributed to a defendant if it was within reasonable limits foreseeable that his conduct may cause this particular sort of harm.

Combined these principles may be able to assure that the individual generally remains the starting point of criminal liability also in the modern culture of control as well as help to redress the balance between the safeguard and crime control function of criminal law.

Samenvatting

Hoofdstuk I

Sinds het in werking treden van het verdrag van Maastricht zijn de bevoegdheden van de Unie met betrekking tot het strafrecht alleen maar gegroeid. Daarmee is ook de invloed van Europa op het nationale Strafrecht toegenomen. Met het verdrag van Lissabon worden deze bevoegdheden opnieuw uitgebreid. Deze ontwikkelingen laten duidelijk zien dat er een Europees Strafrecht is ontstaan dat het nationale Strafrecht zal beïnvloeden en veranderen. De laatste jaren heeft de Unie een groot aantal rechtsinstrumenten aangenomen met betrekking tot verschillende onderwerpen zoals terrorisme, mensen-, wapen- en drugshandel, georganiseerde criminaliteit, witwassen, enzovoort. Dit Uniestrafrecht ontstaat echter op een onsamenhangende en fragmenteerde manier. In het bijzonder was het oogmerk van de Uniewetgever tot nu toe bijna uitsluitend gericht op specifieke delicten (d.w.z. op het bijzondere deel van het strafrecht) terwijl algemene beginselen van aansprakelijkheid (d.w.z. het algemeen deel) worden veronachtzaamd. Dit verschilt fundamenteel van de situatie in de meeste rechtsstelsels waar het strafrecht meestal wordt onderverdeeld in een algemeen en een bijzonder deel. Dit ontbreken van een algemeen deel kan echter tot problemen leiden voor wat betreft de uniforme aanwending van het Unierecht alsook met betrekking tot de gelijke behandeling van Unieburgers.

Dit proefschrift tracht deze lacune te vullen en heeft tot doel een bijdrage te leveren aan de ontwikkeling van een algemeen deel van Europees strafrecht. Een fundamenteel beginsel in het strafrecht of beter: een fundamenteel strafrechtelijk beginsel is dat het toerekenen van aansprakelijkheid doorgaans op twee grondslagen berust. Elk misdrijf kan worden onderverdeeld in een objectief of materieel element, de actus reus, en in een subjectief of mentaal element, de mens rea. Toch is deze tweedeling niet steeds hard te maken en een betere zienswijze zou daarom zijn om deze twee aspecten als communicerende vaten te benaderen.

Dit onderzoek belicht vooral het eerstgenoemde aspect van aansprakelijkheid, de actus reus. Dit concept is echter niet alleen fundamenteel maar ook heel divers en een analyse hiervan leidt onvermijdelijk naar een aantal gerelateerde onderwerpen. De centrale vraagstelling kan daarom alleen op een brede manier als volgt worden samengevat: *Hoe zouden de objectieve elementen voor stafrechtelijke aansprakelijkheid in een algemeen deel van Europees Strafrecht er moeten uitzien? Met andere woorden, hoe zou de objectieve toerekening in het Europese Strafrecht vorm moeten krijgen?*

In hoofdstuk I wordt eerst het onderwerp van het onderzoek nader toegelicht en wordt een plan van aanpak gepresenteerd. Voorts wordt de rechtsvergelijkende methodologie toegelicht en worden de drie onderzochte rechtsstelsels (Engeland en Wales, Duitsland en Nederland) geïntroduceerd.

De algemene onderzoeksvraag wordt volgens verder gedifferentieerd in meerdere deelvragen om het onderzoeksgebied beter te kunnen schetsen en om de lezer een degelijk overzicht van de structuur van het boek te kunnen bieden. Zoals reeds vermeld, speelt het concept van de actus reus een belangrijke rol in een groot aantal leerstukken van strafrechtelijke aansprakelijkheid die in dit boek aan de orde komen. De actus reus is namelijk niet alleen een fundamentele bouwsteen voor de individuele aansprakelijkheid (hoofdstuk II) maar blijkt ook essentieel in de context van strafbare deelneming (hoofdstuk III) en poging en voorbereiding (hoofdstuk IV). Tevens speelt het concept uiteraard een belangrijke rol voor wat betreft de aansprakelijkheid van de rechtspersoon (hoofdstuk V).

Voor een vruchtbaar onderzoek naar een mogelijk Europese 'actus reus' is het echter niet voldoende om alleen verschillende rechtsstelsels te vergelijken. Om een algemeen deel te creëren zullen de verschillende aspecten aan elkaar moeten worden gerelateerd. Om dit te kunnen bewerkstelligen worden in hoofdstuk I ook nog enkele formele en normatieve criteria gepresenteerd die tot een rechtsvergelijkende synthese kunnen leiden.

Hoofdstuk II. Daderschap – de fundamentele objectieve bestanddelen van het strafbaar feit

Hoofdstuk II bespreekt de fundamentele bestanddelen die in het algemeen onder het begrip actus reus worden begrepen. Om te beginnen staat in dit hoofdstuk een discussie van het strafrechtelijke gedragingbegrip centraal. Het strafrecht vormt een stelsel van toerekeningsregels waardoor het opleggen van strafrechtelijke aansprakelijkheid mogelijk wordt. Deze regels hebben tot doel ervoor te zorgen dat het toerekenen van strafrechtelijke aansprakelijkheid in elk individueel geval eerlijk en rechtvaardig is. Aan deze regels ligt traditioneel een specifieke kijk op de mens ten grondslag die van oudsher stevig is geworteld in de traditie van de Verlichting en die verschillende aspecten van zowel morele filosofie, cognitieve en natuurwetenschappen rond het thema van individuele verantwoordelijkheid in zich verenigt. Met andere woorden, aan de basis van strafrechtelijke aansprakelijkheid ligt de notie van de "gemiddelde autonome mens", die verantwoordelijk wordt gehouden voor zijn/haar gedrag (handelen of nalaten). Dit mensbeeld is essentieel voor aansprakelijkheid in alle moderne stafrechtsstelsels. Daarom wordt dan ook voorgesteld dat het Europese strafrecht zorgvuldig zijn uitgangspunt kiest voor de toerekening van aansprakelijkheid om ervoor te zorgen dat individuele vrijheden zo veel mogelijk worden beschermd. Daarna wordt een schets gegeven van de algemene eisen waaraan een gedraging zou moeten voldoen om als grondslag voor strafrechtelijke aansprakelijkheid te kunnen dienen en wordt beargumenteerd dat niet alleen menselijke maar ook gedragingen van rechtspersonen de grondslag voor aansprakelijkheid kunnen vormen.

Er wordt aangetoond dat de nationale strafrechtelijke doctrines in toenemende mate afstand hebben genomen van een zuiver fysieke opvatting van een gedraging als een "gewilde spierbeweging" en dat de aandacht is verschoven naar een meer normatieve of sociale handelingstheorie. Er wordt gesteld dat om de strafrechtelijk relevante van de irrelevante gedragingen te kunnen onderscheiden een gedraging beoordeeld moet worden in het licht van het onderliggende strafbare feit, de omstandigheden van het geval, en de persoon van de dader. Met andere woorden, een gedraging moet altijd worden beoordeeld binnen de sociale context waarin ze zich voordoet. Gezien de complexe omgeving waarin Europees strafrecht zal werken, wordt betoogd dat deze 'sociale handelingsleer' ook in deze context bevredigende resultaten zou kunnen bereiken.

Na de bespreking van de verschillende handelingsleren gaat dit hoofdstuk vervolgens in op het leerstuk van strafbaar nalaten. In dit verband worden de verschillende varianten van omissie- aansprakelijkheid besproken en wordt in het bijzonder aandacht besteed aan het centrale element van strafrechtelijk nalaten, namelijk de zorgplichten. Een aantal veel voorkomende zorgplichten, mogelijke valkuilen en drempels worden achtereenvolgens besproken. Er wordt gesteld dat een belangrijk leidend beginsel met betrekking tot de vormgeving en toepassing van zorgplichten het begrip voorzienbaarheid zou moeten zijn, dat uit het legaliteitsbeginsel voortvloeit. Bij aansprakelijkheid voor nalaten zou moeten worden gekeken of het voor een persoon, in de positie van de verdachte, redelijk voorzienbaar was dat er een strafrechtelijke handelingsplicht bestond. Daarbij zullen een aantal factoren, zoals de maatschappelijke rol, de individuele capaciteiten van de verdachte, de bijzondere omstandigheden van het geval maar ook voorafgaand gedrag een rol kunnen spelen. Het laatste aspect zal voornamelijk belangrijk zijn in situaties waar de verdacht gedeeltelijk verantwoordelijk is voor het feit dat het slachtoffer afhankelijk is van zijn handelen. Een ander belangrijk criterium in deze context kan worden gezien in de mate van afhankelijkheid tussen het slachtoffer en de verdachte. Verder wordt bepleit dat het vinden van een relevante zorgplicht moet beantwoorden aan algemene eisen van de strafrechtspleging en daarom eerlijk, rechtvaardig en redelijk moet zijn.

Tot slot geeft dit hoofdstuk ruim aandacht aan het leerstuk van de causaliteit dat in het bijzonder een belangrijke rol speelt in het kader van aansprakelijkheid voor gevolgdelicten. Uit de rechtsvergelijkende analyse van de nationale rechtsstelsels blijkt dat er in Duitsland, Engeland/Wales en Nederland verschillende causaliteitsopvattingen bestaan. Hoewel de uitkomsten met betrekking tot het vaststellen van een causaal verband in de drie landen grotendeels gelijk blijken te zijn, verschillen de theoretische grondslagen van deze causaliteitsopvattingen aanzienlijk. De verschillende benaderingen kunnen als volgt worden beschreven. De Engelse benadering kan als juridisch/principieel worden bestempeld, terwijl de Nederlandse aanpak juridisch/normatief kan worden genoemd en men in Duitsland de voorkeur lijkt te geven aan een uit twee-stappen bestaande metajuridische aanpak. Dit onderdeel van hoofdstuk II laat zien dat de leer van causaliteit in het strafrecht steeds meer wordt beschouwd als een zuiver formeel-juridisch begrip in plaats van als fysiek, zoals dat traditioneel het geval was. In toenemende mate spelen normatieve factoren een doorslaggevende rol bij het vaststellen van een causaal verband. Daarom wordt gesteld dat ook een Europese causaliteitsdoctrine moet worden gebaseerd op een juridische/normatieve opvatting. Daarbij zou moeten worden rekening gehouden met de wezenlijke functie van de leer, namelijk de redelijke toerekening van een schadelijk gevolg aan het gedrag van de verdachte.

In dit verband zou de leer van de conditio sine qua non als eerst houvast voor het vaststellen van een causaal verband kunnen dienen. Het biedt een eerste graadmeter voor de vaststelling van causale verantwoordelijkheid, vooral in paradigmatische gevallen. Dit algemeen uitgangspunt wordt dan vervolgens herijkt door de regel dat het gedrag in kwestie niet de enige of belangrijkste oorzaak van het resultaat hoeft te zijn. Deze regel is een erkenning van het feit dat in principe de conditio sine qua non test een oneindig aantal oorzaken produceert. Toch hoeven andere factoren die bijdragen aan het ontstaan van het resultaat niet in de weg te staan van de vaststelling van een oorzakelijk verband.

Bovendien blijkt uit de rechtsvergelijking dat voor het vaststellen van causaliteit een verband tussen de strafrechtelijke schade en de individuele schuld van verdachte moet worden vastgesteld. Dit legt de nadruk op de rechtsbeschermende functie van het strafrecht. Een rechtsstatelijk verantwoord strafrecht dat op waarden zoals rechtmatigheid, vertrouwen en respect voor de menselijke waardigheid is gebaseerd, kan namelijk alleen personen aansprakelijk stellen voor schade die redelijkerwijs had kunnen worden voorkomen door de naleving van door de wet geëiste zorgvuldigheidsnormen. Nauw daarmee verbonden is de eis dat aansprakelijkheid moet worden beperkt tot de aard van de door het concrete misdrijf verboden schade. Dit kan worden afgeleid van het doel van de geschonden rechtsregel met betrekking tot het beschermde rechtsgoed. De ondergrenzen voor de toerekening van aansprakelijkheid wordt namelijk altijd bepaald door het doel en de omvang van de misdrijf in kwestie. Dit volgt onder meer uit het legaliteitsbeginsel en de daarmee samenhangende eis van voorzienbaarheid.

Vervolgens moet worden vastgesteld of andere bekende factoren misschien de causale keten hebben doorbroken. Hiervoor moet de tussenkomende oorzaak echter wel causaal sterk genoeg zijn. Zolang de eerste oorzaak nog als aanzienlijk en operationeel kan worden beschouwd zal het causaal verband niet snel zijn doorbroken. Het vereiste van voorzienbaarheid zal daarom ook hier een belangrijke rol spelen. Als het bijvoorbeeld redelijk voorzienbaar was dat de toegevoegde schade door in de achtergrond liggende omstandigheden versterkt wordt, zou het causale verband *prima facie* niet zijn doorbroken.

Hoofdstuk III. Deelneming

Hoofdstuk III wijst op een aantal uitdagingen en mogelijke valkuilen waarmee de Europese Unie zou worden geconfronteerd bij het uitwerken van samenhangende deelnemingsregels. Dit hoofdstuk laat zien dat de nationale strafrechtstelsels in toenemende mate worstelen om met hedendaagse vormen van criminaliteit om te gaan, die immers worden gekenmerkt door een toenemende arbeidsverdeling en een hoge graad van organisatie en een afname van louter fysieke betrokkenheid bij het delict. Steeds vaker gebruiken criminelen 'tussenschakels' om een bepaald gevolg te verwezenlijken en zijn zij zelf niet direct betrokken bij het misdrijf ondanks het feit dat ze controle over de uitvoering van het delict hadden en daarom laakbaar handelden. Na een zorgvuldige evaluatie van de verschillende nationale deelnemingsregelingen wordt geconcludeerd dat de focus op de fysieke dader moet worden vervangen door een meer holistisch concept van plegen waarbij niet alleen de fysieke, directe dader van de actus reus kan worden beschouwd als de primaire verantwoordelijke, maar ook andere personen, indien uit hun gedrag, bijdrage of rol bij het plegen van het strafbare feit blijkt dat ze een 'substantiële verantwoordelijkheid' voor het strafbaar feit dragen. 'Substantiëel' betekent in deze context meer dan louter een causale verantwoordelijkheid omdat dit de lat te laag zou leggen voor het vaststellen van daderschap. Er moet tenminste altijd voldoende bewijs zijn dat de persoon een belangrijke schakel was en niet slechts een ondergeschikte rol speelde in het crimineel samenwerkingsverband.

Een dergelijke aanpak zou leiden tot een normatief concept van deelneming waar de notie van het gekrenkte of in gevaar gebracht beschermde rechtsbelang een centrale rol zal spelen. Een beschermd rechtsbelang kan óf direct óf indirect worden geschonden. Ofwel leidt het gedrag van de dader rechtstreeks tot de schending van de norm, dus zonder tussenkomst van een ander, ofwel wordt de schending onrechtstreeks veroorzaakt door het gedrag van een andere persoon (een tussenpersoon) die over de 'rechtstreekse' (meestal ook fysieke) dader controle uitoefende en die daarnaast zelf verwijtbaar handelde met betrekking tot het plegen van het strafbare feit. In die zin spelen de concepten 'wettelijk beschermde belang' en 'controle' in combinatie met de drempel van het vereiste van een substantiële verantwoordelijkheid een centrale rol in het in dit boek voorgestelde model van strafbare deelneming.

Een dergelijke normatieve benadering leidt tot een breder begrip van plegen, en is in staat om moderne vormen van criminaliteit in al zijn vele variaties aan te pakken. Niet alleen degene die rechtstreeks de actus reus volbrengt wordt dan beschouwd als dader, maar iedere deelnemer die geacht wordt een substantieel aandeel te hebben bij de totstandkoming van het gepleegde delict wordt geacht dit delict zelf te hebben begaan. Verder zou een dergelijke aanpak ook bevredigende resultaten kunnen opleveren in het kader van systematische en georganiseerde misdaad.

Dit model schept daarnaast conceptueel ruimte voor een klein aantal gevallen die men als vormen van 'triviale medeplichtigheid' zou kunnen beschouwen. Deze gevallen kunnen worden aangepakt via de aparte strafbaarstelling van 'triviale medeplichtigheid'. Onder deze categorie vallen gevallen van hulp die onder de hierboven geschetste grens van substantiële verantwoordelijkheid vallen.

Vervolgens wordt geconcludeerd dat een dergelijk tweevoudig deelnemingsconcept meerdere voordelen voor het Europese Strafrecht kan hebben. Ten eerste zou de focus op het mogelijke probleem van de afbakening tussen de verschillende concepten van deelneming verschuiven naar de misschien wel belangrijkere vraag naar de ondergrenzen van de strafrechtelijke aansprakelijkheid zelf. Dit zou niet alleen het systeem van deelneming eenvoudiger, effectiever en gemakkelijker toepasbaar maken, maar zou waarschijnlijk ook de rechtvaardigheid van het system verbeteren omdat nu de precieze mate van wederrechtelijkheid en verwijtbaarheid van de individuele deelnemer door de rechter eenvoudiger in aanmerking kan worden genomen bij het vastleggen van de strafmaat.

Bovendien zou zulk een normatief concept van deelneming beter sporen met de moderne vormen van strafbaar gedrag waar vaak andere personen dan de fysieke dader een belangrijke rol spelen en daarom verantwoordelijkheid dragen voor de ontstane schade. Om goed de juiste verdeling van verantwoordelijkheid te kunnen weergeven moet in dit soort situaties de focus op de fysieke dader worden vervangen door een meer holistische opvatting van daderschap.

Het aparte delict van triviale medeplichtigheid zou aan de andere kant van toepassing zijn op alle bijdragen aan een misdrijf die onder de drempel van de substantiële verantwoordelijkheid vallen. Hieronder kunnen bijdragen vallen die wel een impact hadden op het plegen van het strafbare feit, maar die niet cruciaal of onmisbaar waren. Aangezien deze deelnemers niet kunnen worden beschouwd als substantieel verantwoordelijk voor het plegen van het delict lijkt een vermindering van het strafmaat voor deze deelnemers verdedigbaar.

Ten slotte wordt gesteld dat de voorgestelde aanpak naast een stroomlijning en vereenvoudiging van de deelnemingsregels ook conform is met de waarborgen van artikel 6 EVRM omdat verdachten voldoende informatie over de aard en grond van de beschuldigingen tegen hen zouden ontvangen. Dit zou hen vervolgens in staat stellen een effectieve verdediging tegen de aanklacht te ontwikkelen. Daarnaast zou dit stelsel de rechtszekerheid conform de vereisten van artikel 7 EVRM verhogen omdat het zo voor verdachten makkelijker is te bepalen of hun gedrag aanleiding zal geven tot primaire of secundaire verantwoordelijkheid.

Hoofdstuk IV. Poging en voorbereiding

In dit hoofdstuk wordt aandacht besteed aan poging en voorbereiding. Twee benaderingen van criminaliteit (d.w.z. de objectieve benadering en de subjectieve benadering), die het strafrecht doordringen worden besproken en het wordt aangetoond dat de Unie de uitdaging moet aan gaan om een evenwicht te vinden tussen deze verschillende benaderingen. Een objectieve benadering van criminaliteit benadrukt namelijk het belang van de burger, zijn individuele vrijheden terwijl een subjectieve benadering van criminaliteit de nadruk legt op de gevaarlijkheid van de dader voor de samenleving als geheel. Uit het rechtsvergelijkend onderzoek blijkt dat de in het nationale strafrecht heersende aandacht voor preventie heeft geresulteerd in een subjectivering van het strafrecht. Dit kan worden gezien als een weerspiegeling van de toenemende repressieve tendensen en de voortdurende inflatie van het strafrecht in de risicomaatschappij.

Om deze tendensen tegen te gaan en de reikwijdte van strafrechtelijke aansprakelijkheid binnen redelijke grenzen te houden, wordt gesteld dat een aantal beperkingen ontwikkeld moeten worden als het gaat om de introductie in het Europese strafrecht van strafbare feiten gericht op de preventie van criminaliteit. Verschillende traditionele strafrechtsbeginselen kunnen worden gecombineerd om dit doel te bereiken. Het *ultima ratio* beginsel en de *harm principle* kunnen in dit opzicht als eerste maatstaf dienen. In het licht van deze beginselen zou alleen voorbereidend gedrag dat een concreet gevaar voor een belangrijk rechtsgoed oplevert mogen worden strafbaar gesteld. We kunnen hier bijvoorbeeld denken aan de aanschaf van bepaalde gevaarlijke stoffen die nodig zijn voor de productie van drugs of explosieven. In dit soort gevallen, zou de nadruk meer op de preventieve in plaats van de klassieke rechtsbeschermende functie van het strafrecht komen te liggen.

Daarnaast volgt uit het *nulla poena* beginsel dat aansprakelijkheid voor voorbereidingshandelingen alleen gerechtvaardigd lijkt in het geval dat de persoon die het risico voor het rechtbelang veroorzaakt heeft, ook opzet heeft op het ultieme kwade doel. Dit betekent dat met betrekking tot voorbereidingshandelingen alleen doel- en zekerheidsopzet volstaan voor strafrechtelijk aansprakelijkheid.

Met betrekking tot de strafbaarstelling van voorbereidingshandelingen zal de Europese Unie ook moeten beslissen of een algemeen leerstuk ontwikkeld moet worden, of dat de vraag beter van geval tot geval kan worden aangepakt. Na een zorgvuldige afweging van de argumenten voor en tegen deze twee benaderingen wordt geconcludeerd dat een benadering per geval beter past in de heersende gemeenschappelijke tradities van de Europese Unie en de lidstaten. Voorts zou een dergelijke aanpak ook beter een ‘overcriminalization’ kunnen voorkomen, omdat de wetgever elke keer dat hij kiest voor de strafbaarstelling van voorbereidingshandelingen verplicht zou zijn om aan te tonen dat aan alle hiervoor genoemde eisen in een respectievelijk wetgevingsinstrument wordt voldaan.

Vervolgens bespreekt dit hoofdstuk het leerstuk van de poging. Ook hier blijkt uit het rechtsvergelijkend onderzoek dat de hoofdvraag voor het Europees strafrecht opnieuw zal zijn of een meer objectieve, of subjectieve benadering de voorkeur verdient. Uit het onderzoek kan worden afgeleid dat de reikwijdte van de poging sterk wordt beïnvloed door de afweging van deze verschillende opvattingen. Nederland lijkt in vergelijking met de andere landen de meest objectieve benadering te hanteren wat leidt tot een relatief beperkte werkingssfeer van de poging. Het Engelse strafrecht bevat sporen van een objectieve benadering maar in de jurisprudentie zijn zowel objectieve als subjectieve benaderingen te vinden. In Duitsland is anderzijds door de wetgever formeel een middenpositie ingevoerd waarin objectieve en subjectieve criteria gecombineerd worden. Maar in de praktijk blijkt vaak de nadruk op subjectieve factoren te liggen.

Met het oog op een billijk evenwicht tussen de beschermende en preventieve functie van het strafrecht en in overeenstemming met de heersende aanpak binnen de lidstaten, wordt gesteld dat een middenpositie (d.w.z. een combinatie van objectieve en subjectieve factoren) het meest geschikt zou zijn voor het Europese strafrecht. Als basis voor het vaststellen van aansprakelijkheid voor poging is het daarom belangrijk dat de gedraging van een verdachte kan worden gezien als een bedreiging van de rechtsorde en bovendien moeten daarin duidelijk de criminele neigingen van verdachte tot uitdrukking komen. Op grond van een objectieve gevaarzetting zullen de meeste gevallen van de poging kunnen worden vormgegeven en daarmee kan ook worden gegarandeerd dat het strafrecht een daadstrafrecht blijft. Daarmee zou een onnodige uitbreiding van aansprakelijkheid kunnen worden voorkomen. Subjectieve factoren zullen vooral nodig zijn voor de strafbaarheid van de ondeugdelijke poging, en maken verder ook duidelijk dat de kwade intenties vaak de kern uitmaken van een poging.

Deze gemengd objectieve en subjectieve uitleg van de poging moet ook worden weerspiegeld in het onderscheid tussen poging en voorbereiding. Objectief gezien zal daarom voor poging een gevaarzetting van de rechtsorde door de gedraging aangetoond moeten worden. Dus naast een nauw chronologisch verband met het begin van uitvoering van het delict moet de gedraging van verdachte ook de sfeer van het beschermde belang hebben bereikt. Een dergelijke benadering impliceert een matige, objectieve benadering van strafrechtelijke aansprakelijkheid, waarbij de nadruk op de gevaarzetting van de rechtsorde komt te liggen. Dit kan ervoor zorgen dat aansprakelijkheid sterk verbonden blijft met de door het strafbare feit verboden schade en kan helpen voorkomen dat gedachten de grondslag voor aansprakelijkheid vormen.

Een gevaarzetting van de rechtsorde ligt echter niet pas voor als de delictsomschrijving al gedeeltelijk is voltooid maar kan ook vroeger worden aangenomen. Een gedeeltelijke voltooiing van het delict kan een indicatie voor een poging zijn maar is zeker niet altijd noodzakelijk.

Een algemeen deel van Europees Strafrecht zou vervolgens ook moeten bepalen in hoeverre ondeugdelijke pogingen strafbaar gesteld moeten worden. In overeenstemming met de praktijk in de onderzochte lidstaten wordt bepleit dat afgezien van putatieve delicten en absoluut ondeugdelijke pogingen in beginsel ondeugdelijke pogingen strafbaar moeten worden gesteld. Om strafbare ondeugdelijke pogingen van niet strafbare te kunnen onderscheiden is echter wel een criterium nodig. Daarom worden vervolgens verschillende uit de onderscheiden rechtsstelsels voortvloeiende oplossingen voor dit probleem geanalyseerd. Een mogelijke oplossing voor deze afbakening is het voor ogen houden van het onderscheid tussen feitelijke dwalingen en rechtsdwalingen. In de context van de poging zou dit betekenen dat in geval van rechtsdwaling sprake is van een niet strafbaar putatief delict en dat bij een feitelijke dwaling wel sprake is van een strafbare ondeugdelijke poging.

Indien echter de dader ernstig dwaalt over de wetten van de natuur of zich beroept op krachten die buiten de werkingssfeer van de menselijke controle liggen ligt geen aansprakelijkheid voor. In deze vrij hypothetische gevallen is namelijk het gedrag van de verdachte niet alleen onhandig, maar bovendien ongeschikt om het beoogde criminele doel te bereiken. Dus in deze situaties kan niet langer van een objectieve gevaarzetting van het beschermde rechtsbelang worden gesproken. Daaruit volgt dat de link met de verboden schade als uiterst zwak beschouwd kan worden en dat het schadebeginsel zich daarom tegen de toerekening van aansprakelijkheid verzet.

Ten slotte wordt in dit hoofdstuk geconcludeerd dat het leerstuk van de vrijwillige terugtred ook zijn plaats moet hebben in het Europees strafrecht. Indien een poger vrijwillig terugkomt op de reeds aangevangen handeling en het ontstaan van schade voorkomt dan lijken noch generaal preventieve overwegingen noch speciale preventieve overwegingen het opleggen vaneen straf te kunnen rechtvaardigen. Om het leerstuk van de vrijwillige terugtred in de praktijk praktisch hanteerbaar te maken dient wel nader te worden gedifferentieerd. Een belangrijk verschil met betrekking tot de omvang van het leerstuk is bijvoorbeeld het onderscheid tussen voltooide en onvoltooide pogingen. In het tweede geval zal reeds het afstand nemen/stopzetten van de criminele onderneming voldoende zijn voor de terugtred, terwijl in het geval van een voltooide poging een *actus contrarius* is vereist. Welke gedrag echter in een concreet geval precies voldoende is voor een *actus contrarius* is moeilijk abstract vast te stellen. Uit dit onderzoek blijkt echter dat veel zal afhangen van de ernst en omvang van het eerdere gedrag van de verdachte en hoe dit zich verhoudt tot de mogelijke voltooiing van het delict. Hoe meer de voor de poging relevante gedragingen en gebeurtenissen in een gevorderd stadium zijn, hoe meer de poger zal moeten doen om succesvol terug te treden.

Om bovendien te bepalen wanneer een terugtred echt vrijwillig is kan de wet teruggrijpen op psychologische of normatieve factoren. Uit de rechtsvergelijking blijkt een voorkeur voor de eerste oplossing en daarom kan worden gesteld dat een terugtred over het algemeen vrijwillig zal zijn als de dader zegt: "ik wil niet verder, al kan ik het wel", terwijl een onvrijwillige terugtred voorligt als hij denkt: "ik kan niet verder, hoe graag ik ook zou willen."

Hoofdstuk V. De strafrechtelijke aansprakelijkheid van de rechtspersoon

Na een analyse van de verschillende benaderingen van de strafrechtelijke aansprakelijkheid van rechtspersonen wordt besproken dat door de Uniewetgever een groot aantal vraagstukken moet worden aangepakt om een coherente aanpak van deze materie te ontwikkelen. Rechtspersonen passen moeilijk in het traditionele strafrecht omdat begrippen zoals actus reus en mens rea in eerste instantie niet zijn bedacht om toegepast te worden op kunstmatige, niet-menselijke actoren. Dit onderwerp is niettemin van grote praktische relevantie en biedt ook een vruchtbare voedingsbodem voor een herijking en het kritisch beoordelen van een aantal traditionele beginselen van strafrechtelijke aansprakelijkheid. In dit hoofdstuk worden daarom verschillende modellen voor de strafrechtelijke aanpak van rechtspersonen gepresenteerd en geanalyseerd. Het ene model richt zich meer op het aansprakelijk houden van individuen, het andere bepleit zelfstandige op bedrijven toegesneden delicten, en nog andere modellen kiezen voor een afgeleide of zelfs meer organisatorische benadering van corporatieve aansprakelijkheid. Traditioneel blijkt uit de nationale strafrechtsstelsels een voorkeur voor afgeleide modellen van aansprakelijkheid, maar recente ontwikkelingen in Engeland en Nederland laten duidelijk een verschuiving zien naar een meer organisatorische model.

Hoe dan ook, zoals reeds in hoofdstuk II in de context van het gedraging is toegelicht, is het standpunt van waaruit dit onderzoek vertrekt dat bedrijven voor het strafrecht relevante eigenstandige actoren zijn aangezien zij sociaal en functioneel gezien als verantwoordelijke agenten kunnen worden beschouwd die op hun eigen manier kunnen handelen en falen en derhalve daarvoor ook verantwoordelijk moeten kunnen worden gesteld.

Met betrekking tot de aard van een rechtspersoon wordt gesteld dat een organische theorie de voorkeur verdient boven een antropomorfe opvatting die de rechtspersoon onnodig vermenselijkt of deze slechts tot een collectiviteit van natuurlijke personen herleidt. Een rechtspersoon is namelijk meer en ook iets anders dan de som der delen.

Uit het rechtsvergelijkende onderzoek blijkt dat in de onderzochte stelsels nog vaak antropomorfe opvattingen domineren wat zich bijvoorbeeld uit in de vaak gebruikte “identification doctrine”. Hoewel kan worden vastgesteld dat deze populaire doctrine is gebaseerd op een misvatting van het concept ‘rechtspersoonlijkheid’, en er talrijke tekortkomingen en beperkingen aan deze traditionele leer kleven, wordt geconcludeerd deze niet volledig te verlaten maar wordt ervoor gepleit deze om praktische redenen te behouden voor de meest eenvoudige gevallen van ondernemingscriminaliteit.

Tegelijk wordt echter wel bepleit dat de Europese Unie de “identification doctrine” moet aanvullen met meer autonome, organische modellen van corporatieve aansprakelijkheid. Europees strafrecht kan veel leren van de problemen in de nationale rechtsstelsels die wellicht te veel vasthouden aan oudere modellen van aansprakelijkheid. Er is behoefte aan een fundamentele herijking en herformulering van de strafrechtelijke aansprakelijkheid van de rechtspersoon, waarbij de nadruk moet komen te liggen op de zakelijke realiteit en praktijk. In overeenstemming met de sociale handlingsleer die in dit boek wordt verdedigt, wordt bepleit dat gedragingen van een rechtspersoon ook altijd moeten worden uitgelegd in de maatschappelijke context waarin ze zich voordoen. Daarom wordt aangevoerd, dat het gedrag van bedrijven vaak in de vorm van nalaten of zorgplichtschendingen zal optreden.

Een belangrijke factor in dit voorgestelde model zou kunnen zijn of de rechtspersoon feitelijke controle uitoefende over de strafbare gedragingen. Daarbij is het gevoerde management en beleid van de rechtspersoon van groot belang. Als het gedrag past in de bedrijfsvoering en het beleid van de corporatie dan kan het strafbare feit in beginsel worden toegerekend.

Nadat is vastgesteld dat een gedraging van de rechtspersoon heeft plaatsgevonden moet vervolgens worden bekeken of de gedraging ook aan de rechtspersoon te wijten is. We mogen immers niet vergeten, dat als men bedrijven strafrechtelijk wil aanpakken, het schuldbeginsel moet worden gerespecteerd. Er moet dus antwoord worden gegeven op de vraag wanneer de rechtspersoon verwijtbaar heeft gehandeld.

Wanneer dit precies het geval zal zijn is niet makkelijk te beantwoorden. Dit onderzoek betoogt dat er bepaalde kenmerken zijn van de manier waarop bedrijven zich organiseren die schuld kunnen aantonen. De evaluatie van de bedrijfscultuur of het ethos van de corporatie zou bijvoorbeeld gebruikt kunnen worden om schuld vast te stellen. Verder zou de structuur van het bedrijf een rol kunnen spelen. Een hoge mate van decentralisatie kan namelijk erop wijzen dat de personen die voor de uitvoering en het toezicht van het beleid of de doelstellingen van de rechtspersoon verantwoordelijk zijn niet kunnen worden gevonden in het bestuur waar deze beslissingen zijn genomen.

Bijkomende factoren die een rol kunnen spelen bij het vaststellen van corporatieve schuld, kunnen "corporate compliance" en zelfregulering zijn. Al deze factoren vormen relevante aanknopingspunten om te beoordelen of een bedrijf met betrekking tot een strafbaar feit verwijtbaar heeft gehandeld. Zij maken in die zin deel uit van een expliciet organisatorisch aansprakelijkheidsmodel wat mogelijk meer legitimiteit geeft aan het schuldbegrip in het context van ondernemingscriminaliteit. Het bedrijf wordt aansprakelijk gesteld voor zijn (beleidsmatige) keuzes en kan derhalve ook trachten aansprakelijkheid in de toekomst te voorkomen door een aanpassing van die keuzes. Daaruit volgt dat ook in deze rechtspersoonlijke context het concept van controle een belangrijke rol speelt. Verder kan daaruit worden afgeleid dat als aannemelijk wordt gemaakt dat de rechtspersoon alles heeft gedaan om bepaalde schade te voorkomen (en dus zorgvuldig heeft gehandeld), dat dan ook kan worden vastgesteld dat er geen mogelijkheid tot controle bestond, en er dus ook geen aansprakelijkheid voorligt. Dit zou dan de invoering van een avas verweer voor bedrijven betekenen en kan voorkomen dat bedrijven aansprakelijk worden gesteld voor de schade die buiten hun invloedssfeer of controle ligt. Zo kan ook voor rechtspersonen een goed evenwicht tussen de rechtsbeschermende en de instrumentele functie van het strafrecht worden bewaakt.

Hoofdstuk VI. Conclusie

In hoofdstuk VI worden de resultaten van dit onderzoek samengevat, en worden eindconclusies geformuleerd alsook enkele aanbevelingen ter verbetering van de vastgestelde knelpunten. Naast het ontwerpblauwdruk van beginselen en leerstellingen voor een algemeen deel van het Europese strafrecht is het belangrijkste inzicht van dit proefschrift dat recente maatschappelijke ontwikkelingen hebben geleid tot een verandering in de traditionele kijk op de strafrechtelijke aansprakelijkheid. De toenemende aandacht voor risicopreventie en een algemene verandering in de hedendaagse opvatting van criminaliteit hebben geleid tot een erosie of heroverweging van de traditionele leerstukken die in veel strafrechtsstelsels tot een verbreding van de reikwijdte van de aansprakelijkheid hebben geleid. Kort samengevat kan een toenemende normativiteit in het opleggen van strafrechtelijke aansprakelijkheid worden vastgesteld, wat een versterkte nadruk op de controlefunctie van het strafrecht met zich meebrengt.

Als tegengewicht voor deze tendensen en om de rechtsbeschermende functie te vergroten heeft dit onderzoek een aantal beginselen geïdentificeerd die in staat worden geacht om bepaalde grenzen te stellen aan het moderne strafrecht zonder dat dit ten koste hoeft te gaan van de instrumentele inzetbaarheid.

Het eerste beginsel dat een belangrijke waarborgfunctie kan innemen in een toenemend normatieve invulling van aansprakelijkheid is het concept van controle. Er wordt geconcludeerd dat strafrechtelijke aansprakelijkheid alleen gerechtvaardigd lijkt voor criminele resultaten die onder de controle van de verdachte waren. Het concept van controle legt de centrale focus van strafrechtelijke aansprakelijkheid op het verantwoordelijke, in beginsel rationele rechtssubject en stelt daarmee grenzen aan de invoering van een risicoaansprakelijkheid, (denk aan de statusdelicten van een Gesinnungstrafrecht).

Een andere belangrijke begrenzing is te vinden in het schadebeginsel. Dit beginsel wordt vooral belangrijk met betrekking tot de vraag hoe ver verwijderd het gedrag moet zijn in relatie tot het mogelijk optreden van schade om aanleiding te geven tot aansprakelijkheid. Er wordt geconcludeerd dat strafrechtelijke aansprakelijkheid zo veel mogelijk geworteld moet blijven in en gekoppeld moet worden aan de verboden criminele schade.

Het derde beginsel dat in onze analyse naar voren is gekomen als een mogelijke waarborg tegen een grenzeloze uitbreiding van strafbaarheid is uiteraard het schuldbeginsel. Het verzekert dat alleen vrijwillig en bewust gekozen gedrag zal leiden tot aansprakelijkheid. Om burgers in staat te stellen deze keuze te maken moet de reikwijdte van het strafrecht en in het bijzonder de strafrechtelijke leerstukken voldoende duidelijk en ondubbelzinnig zijn. Bovendien zou daarmee gewaarborgd worden dat de beoordeling van de strafrechtelijke aansprakelijkheid gebaseerd blijft op individuele overtredingen en schuld. Dit zou, onder andere, kunnen voorkomen dat doctrines op een zodanige wijze worden geïnterpreteerd dat zij aanleiding geven tot schuld door associatie.

Tot slot is het legaliteitsbeginsel van belang om een aantal valkuilen die door de toenemende normativiteit zijn ontstaan, te vermijden door te wijzen op het concept van voorzienbaarheid. Het moet door burgers voorzien kunnen worden of bepaald gedrag aanleiding zal geven tot strafrechtelijke aansprakelijkheid. Bovendien zou schade over het algemeen alleen worden toegerekend aan een verdachte als het binnen redelijke grenzen te verwachten was dat zijn gedrag dit soort schade kan veroorzaken.

Gecombineerd zullen deze beginselen in staat moeten zijn om ervoor te zorgen dat het individuele rechtssubject over het algemeen het uitgangspunt van de strafrechtelijke aansprakelijkheid blijft, ook in de moderne risicomaatschappij, en kunnen ze bijdragen tot het bewaken van het evenwicht tussen de rechtsbeschermende en instrumentele functie van het Europese strafrecht in wording.

Curriculum Vitae Johannes Keiler

Johannes Keiler (born 1978 in Schwaz, Austria) studied law at the Leopold-Franzens-Universität Innsbruck and at University College Dublin. He specialised in criminal law and graduated in 2005. After working at the Regional Court in Innsbruck he successfully completed the Master of European Union and International Law at the University of Amsterdam in 2007.

In 2007 he joined Maastricht University as a PhD researcher and lecturer. He lectures in subjects including comparative criminal law, criminal procedure, and cooperation in criminal matters within the European Union.

School of Human Rights Research Series

The School of Human Rights Research is a joint effort by human rights researchers in the Netherlands. Its central research theme is the nature and meaning of international standards in the field of human rights, their application and promotion in the national legal order, their interplay with national standards, and the international supervision of such application. The School of Human Rights Research Series only includes English titles that contribute to a better understanding of the different aspects of human rights.

For previous volumes in the series, please visit http://shr.intersentia.com.

Published titles within the Series:

51. Marthe Lot Vermeulen, *Enforced Disappearance*
    ISBN 978-1-78068-065-1
52. Vera Vriezen, *Amnesty Justified?*
    ISBN 978-1-78068-075-1
53 Maite San Giorgi, *The Human Right to Equal Access to Heath Care*
    ISBN 978-1-78068-081-1
54. Jeroen Blomsma, *Mens rea and defences in European Criminal Law*
    ISBN 978-1-78068-104-7
55. Masha Fedorova, *The Principle of Equality of Arms in International Criminal Proceedings*
    ISBN 978-1-78068-111-5
56. Martine Boersma, *Corruption: A Violation of Human Rights and a Crime Under International Law?*
    ISBN 978-1-78068-105-4
57. Hendrik J. Lubbe, *Successive and Additional Measures to the TRC Amnesty Scheme in South Africa*
    ISBN 978-1-78068-116-0
58. Hana M.A.E. van Ooijen, *Religious Symbols in Public Functions: Unveiling State Neutrality*
    ISBN 978-1-78068-119-1
59. Sarah Haverkort-Speekenbrink, *European Non-Discrimination Law*
    ISBN 978-1-78068-126-9
60. Johannes Keiler, *Actus reus and participation in European criminal law*
    ISBN 978-1-78068-135-1